WRITING AND COLONIALISM IN NORTHERN GHANA

This book presents a new perspective on colonialism in Africa. Drawing on work from of a variety of subjects and disciplines — from the ancient Mediterranean to colonial Spain, and from anthropology to psychology — the author argues that colonialism in Africa needs to be understood through the medium of writing and the particular world it belonged to. Focusing on the LoDagaa of northern Ghana and their relationship with British colonialism, Hawkins describes colonialism as an encounter between a world of experience — a world of knowledge, practice, and speech — and "the world on paper" — a world of writing, rules, and a linear concept of history. The various ways in which "the world on paper" affected the LoDagaa are examined thematically. The first four chapters explore how writing imposed a form of historical consciousness on different aspects of LoDagaa culture — identity, politics, and religion — that was alien to them. The second half of the book examines how both the British colonial state and its postcolonial successor, the Ghanaian state, attempted to regulate indigenous forms of knowledge, gender relations, and social reckoning through courts. This ambitious and richly detailed book will appeal to both scholars and general readers interested in African history, British colonialism, and cultural and postcolonial studies.

SEAN HAWKINS is an associate professor in the Department of History at the University of Toronto.

Anthropological Horizons

Editor: Michael Lambek, University of Toronto

This series, begun in 1991, focuses on theoretically informed ethnographic works addressing issues of mind and body, knowledge and power, equality and inequality, the individual and the collective. Interdisciplinary in its perspective, the series makes a unique contribution in several other academic disciplines: women's studies, history, philosophy, psychology, political science, and sociology. For a list of the books published in this series see page 469.

Writing and Colonialism in Northern Ghana

The Encounter between the LoDagaa and "the World on Paper"

SEAN HAWKINS

UNIVERSITY OF TORONTO PRESS
Toronto Buffalo London

Reprinted in paperback 2014

ISBN 978-0-8020-4872-1 (cloth)
ISBN 978-1-4426-5768-7 (paper)

Printed on acid-free paper

National Library of Canada Cataloguing in Publication Data

Hawkins, Sean
Writing and colonialism in northern Ghana : the encounter between the LoDagaa and "The world on paper", 1892–1991

(Anthropological horizons)
Includes bibliographical references and index.
ISBN 978-0-8020-4872-1 (bound)
ISBN 978-1-4426-5768-7 (pbk.)

1. Dagaaba (African people) – Ghana – Social conditions.
2. Ghana – Colonial influence – History. I. Title. II. Series.

DT511.H39 2002 305.896′35 C2001-901787-1

This book has been published with the help of a grant from the Humanities and Social Sciences Federation of Canada, using funds provided by the Social Sciences and Humanities Research Council of Canada.

University of Toronto Press acknowledges the financial assistance to its publishing program of the Canada Council for the Arts and the Ontario Arts Council.

University of Toronto Press acknowledges the financial support for its publishing activities of the Government of Canada through the Book Publishing Industry Development Program (BPIDP).

To all my friends
but especially Phil, Pete, and Jim

Contents

Maps, Tables, and Figures

Maps

Tables

Figures

Preface

This book is not a history of the LoDagaa. Nor is it a history of colonialism. It is a history of the relationship between the LoDagaa and colonialism, as well as its aftermath, as understood through the medium of writing. As such this book falls at the intersection of many different areas of interest: African history, British colonialism, anthropological thought, and postcolonial studies. There are great advantages to looking at the past from this particular vantage point. In developing my central theme – the interconnectedness of writing and colonialism – I have built on the insights of scholars from all four disciplines who have noticed that writing was an indispensable instrument of colonialism: a means of making colonialism real and of creating, appropriating, and distancing colonial subjects. The result is the first full-length history of this kind for sub-Saharan Africa.

Although this is not a history of the LoDagaa, it is no less a work of African history for not being so. The twinned experiences of writing and colonialism are important elements of the LoDagaa past, and they contribute much to our understanding of the cultural and social aspects of colonialism in Africa. Because this book is not about colonial policy, its contribution to our understanding of colonial intentions is limited. However, it has a great deal to say about the dispositions that writing brought to colonial practices. Similarly, just as this book is not about colonialism per se, neither is it about writing; rather, it is situated at the intersection of the two. I have not attempted to add to theories of writing; instead I have borrowed from existing theory as it helped to illuminate the sources. Finally, I am not an anthropologist. This is worth bearing in mind, especially as this book appears in a series called "Anthropological Horizons." Although I am critical of certain forms of anthropological thinking that once dominated the discipline, I have nothing but admiration for the valuable work that the many anthropologists discussed in this book carried out in this particular part of West Africa – that is, the Voltaic region of northern Ghana, northern Togo, and much of Burkina Faso. My criticisms refer only to particular aspects of anthropological thought of the past, and are relevant not because they are particularly original, but because these ideas continue to affect how both local intellectuals and government agencies represent and understand the social practices of the LoDagaa. As for current anthropological thought, this book is very much informed by it and takes inspiration from its insights.

Throughout this book I have offered critical readings of ethnographic and autoethnographic writing about the LoDagaa. If taken out of context, there is a danger that my analysis of these texts may at times sound overly critical and even unappreciative. Although my interpretations differ at times with those of the authors of these texts, on most matters I agree with, and indeed rely on, their work. As will become apparent, this is especially true of the writing of LoDagaa intellectuals, whose texts are often at the center of my work. I have learned a great deal from their scholarship and would like to acknowledge from the start how much their work contributed to my understanding of the matters discussed in this book.

In the course of my education, my research, my professional career, and the writing of this book I have incurred a great number of debts to many people in England, Ghana, the United States, and Canada. I have thanked most of these people at earlier opportunities. Here I would like to thank those whose assistance was particularly relevant to this book. First, I owe a great deal to John Iliffe for his tutelage many years ago. Although he did not read this manuscript, he has read many earlier versions of things that appear here in their final form, and whatever strengths there are in what I have to say now are due in no small part to his patience and guidance in the past. Over a decade ago, Rodney Needham very kindly read and commented on a very rough version of an argument found in Part 4 of this book. Comments by John Lonsdale and John Peel on my earlier use of material that is also used here were also very helpful. Murray Last and Adrian Hastings made useful editorial suggestions for arguments found in Part 2 of this book when they appeared as articles, as did anonymous readers for an earlier version of the first half of Chapter 6, which also appeared as an article. In a contribution I wrote for a forthcoming book, Jean Allman, Susan Geiger, and Nakanyike Musisi gave me the opportunity to think out ideas that are formulated in Chapter 7 on the autonomy of women. Their comments were also very helpful. Bishop Gregory Kpiebaya kindly shared his views with me, and Father Eugene Suom-Dery was very helpful in providing me with research material.

Phil Morgan helped me shape this book and give it focus at a stage when it was particularly unwieldy and in need of direction. For this and many other things, I will always be grateful. An anonymous reader for the University of Toronto Press made some extremely useful suggestions at the end of the writing process. I learned a great deal from a course Allan Greer invited me to teach with him as I was revising this book for the last time. Franca Iacovetta, with assistance from Ian Radforth and Nakanyike Musisi, helped with the task of weeding out the awkward prose. Her assistance was invaluable and this book is much more fluent thanks to her efforts. Of course, as it is both right and standard to add, all the errors are mine. I am responsible for the translation of all quotations taken from those primary and secondary sources that appear in French in the endnotes and bibliography.

I would like to thank Michael Lambek for considering this book for his series and my editors at U of T Press for seeing the book through to completion. I am especially grateful to Anne Laughlin, not only for helping me sort out the problems that have arisen in seeing this book to press, but also in being so understanding of the concerns of a first-time author.

My greatest debts are owed to my friends, several of whom I have already mentioned. Over the years, they have encouraged me, given me support, revived my confidence when it was flagging, and, ultimately, made this book possible. I can mention only a few names here, even though many others have my thanks. Simon Szreter was very supportive in different ways during my years in England. Before, during, and after that sojourn, Paul Aterman has been an extraordinarily generous friend. I also owe many thanks to all the members of the "H.D.C.," particularly Pat Riordan. But most of all I want to thank Phil Morgan, Pete Ripley, and Jim Jones. At a difficult time in my life they rallied to my support without hesitation. Their commitment and selflessness taught me much about friendship and personal integrity. This book is dedicated to all my friends, but especially to them.

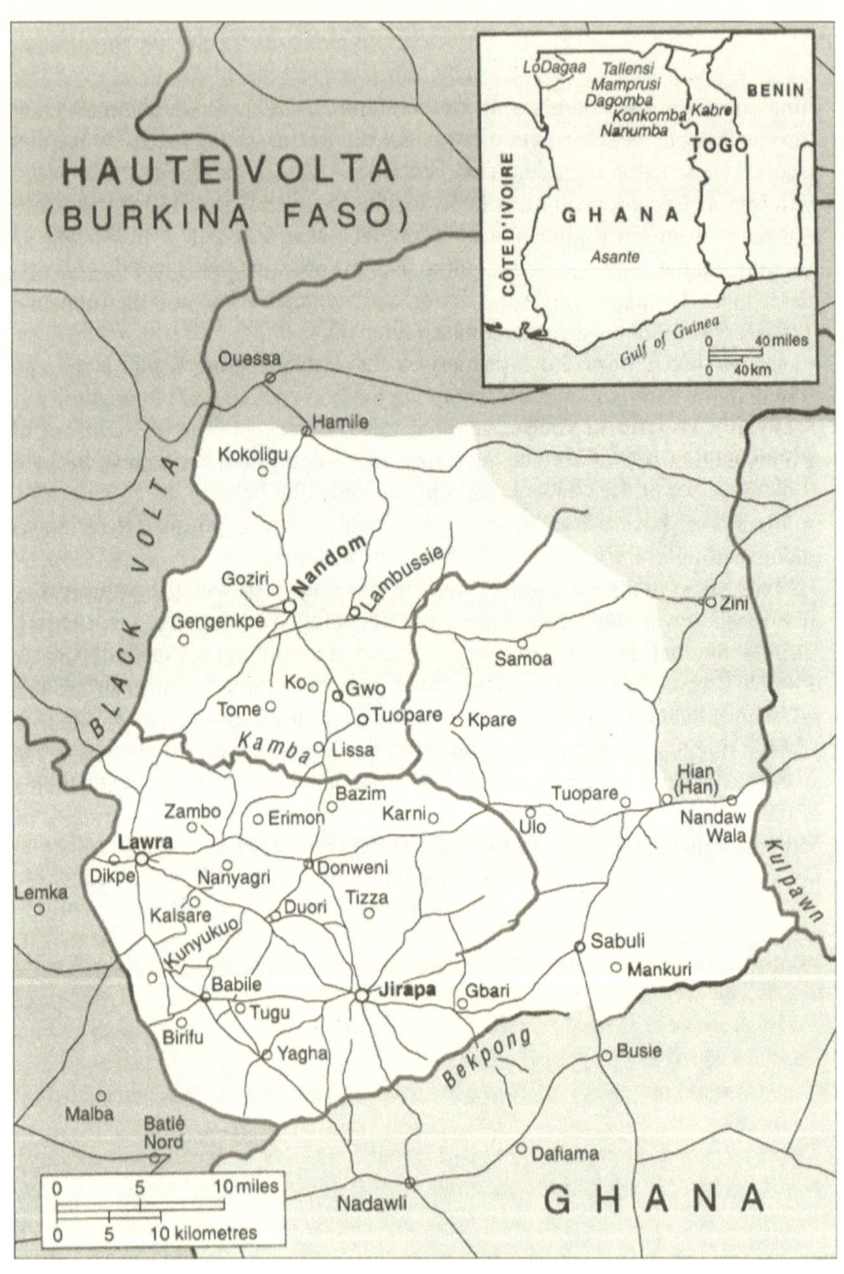

Map 1. Lawra District, Northern Ghana, *c.* 1960

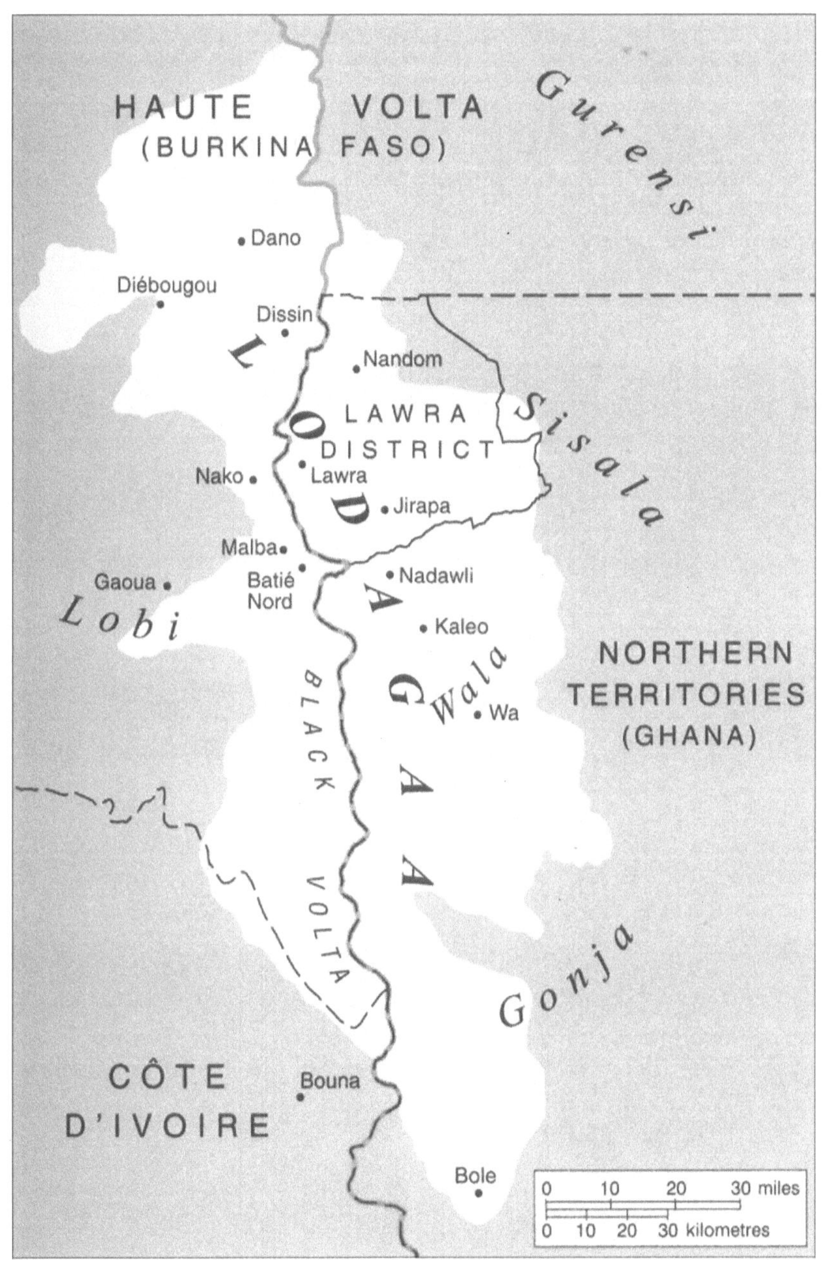

Map 2. Distribution of *Dagaare* Speakers, *c*. 1950

WRITING AND COLONIALISM IN NORTHERN GHANA

Introduction: Colonialism as an Encounter between "the World on Paper" and the World of Experience

What has made it impossible for us to live in time like fish in water, like birds in air, like children? It is the fault of Empire! Empire has created the time of history. Empire has located its existence not in the smooth recurrent spinning time of the cycle of the seasons but in the jagged time of rise and fall, of beginning and end, of catastrophe. Empire dooms itself to live in history and plot against history.

Coetzee, *Waiting for the Barbarians*

"Empire," to use Coetzee's singular archetype, attempted to appropriate people through the medium of writing, to colonize them through the power of writing, and to regulate their lives through the order of writing. That it did not entirely succeed in these aims in no way diminishes the central role that writing played in the imperial project. More than steamboats, quinine, breechloading rifles, machine guns, or any other material instruments commonly associated with conquest, writing made colonialism possible; yet the subject has been relatively neglected in studies of twentieth-century African history.[1] Belloc's offensive imperial conceit – "Whatever happens we have got / The Maxim-gun, and they have not" – might well have been true of the physical conquest of Africa by European powers, but it tells us little about how colonial rule was both effected and experienced. Writing, not the barrel of the gun, was more often than not the medium of colonialism. How writing and colonialism were interconnected is the central theme of this book.

This book is divided into four parts of two chapters each. In Part 1, I discuss how the British used naming to invent, appropriate, and rule the people (now known as the LoDagaa) who happened to live in the northwestern corner of the Northern Territories of the Gold Coast at the beginning of the twentieth century, and how, in turn, these names affected the sense of identity of these people. In these chapters I argue that putting the LoDagaa on paper was even more difficult than conquering them physically. I focus on the role that mapping, narrative history, migratory labor, and clothing, as well as naming, played in British efforts to make representations of the LoDagaa and turn them into colonial subjects. The conquest of the LoDagaa preceded their effective appropriation by the British, but without the latter the former would have been unworkable. The ability to represent the LoDagaa was as important as the power to conquer them. Later, writing also became an important medium through which indigenous writers made representations of the LoDagaa and communicated them to the external world. All of these actions belonged to "the world on paper," a world that existed beyond the immediate and local experiences of the LoDagaa but that had been encroaching on them since the end of the nineteenth century. By the end of the twentieth century "the world on paper" had become the official arbiter of legitimacy, a regulator of authenticity, and a source of power.

In Part 2, I discuss politics and religion, again examining large issues, in this case the invention of colonial chieftaincy and the postcolonial reimagination of god. History was indispensable in legitimating colonial political engineering and postcolonial theological arguments. In both of these instances writing bequeathed an excessive regard for the past, a pernicious form of historicism that made the past a source of legitimacy and, ultimately, power. As such, writing was both a means of robbing the LoDagaa of sovereignty not invested in the past and a way of denying them the autonomy and historicity necessary to legitimate changes in the present and future. For the LoDagaa – and indeed for many other cultures in sub-Saharan African – the "jagged time of rise and fall, of beginning and end" was an alien form of historical consciousness: something imposed from outside, and once created difficult to escape.

In Parts 3 and 4, I discuss the changes that occurred as a result of the colonization of LoDagaa knowledge and social relationships in colonial and postcolonial courts and show the ways in which many LoDagaa resisted these assaults on cultural and social sovereignty. When the British "pacified" this region, they not only suppressed those forms of behavior deemed threatening to colonial order, but also attempted to suppress forms of knowledge that posed, at least potentially, even more fundamental threats to their rule. These indigenous forms of knowledge were predicated on a belief that power emanated from the invisible world. For their part, the British were determined to make "the world on paper" the source of all power. The imposition of courts was a fundamental, albeit highly imperfect, part of that strategy; and because the LoDagaa resisted colonial assaults on their cultural beliefs and social practices outside the courts

TABLE 1
Synopsis of Thematic Comparisons between the World of Experience and the World on Paper

World of Experience	World on Paper	#	World of Experience	World on Paper	#
Speech	Writing	Intro.	Negotiations	Rules	Ch. 7
Path	Road	Ch. 1	Women	Wives	Ch. 7
Memory	Narrative	Ch. 1	Adultery	Seduction	Ch. 7
Work	Labor	Ch. 2	Husbands	Plaintiffs	Ch. 7
Scarification	Clothing	Ch. 2	Lovers	Defendants	Ch. 7
Tengaansob	Naa	Ch. 3	Conjugal union	Marriage	Ch. 8
Naangmin	Jehovah	Ch. 4	Descent	Biology	Ch. 8
Signs	Words	Ch. 5	Residence	Payments	Ch. 8
Knowledge	Political Authority	Ch. 5	Funerals	Litigation	Ch. 8
Bagre	Christianity	Ch. 6	Ambiguity	Power	Concl.
Cowries	Money	Ch. 6			

rather than from within them, there was a sharp dissonance between what was said in the courts and what was done outside them.

In the second half of the book I show how writing affected individuals on a personal, daily basis. Colonial courts applied a logic to social practices that does not exist in most oral cultures. It was a logic predicated on the understanding that social reality was the product of rules and clearly articulated norms, and not "the smooth recurrent spinning time of the cycle of the seasons." Writing was also a way of imposing a foreign geometry of representation onto LoDagaa culture and social practices and then justifying attempts to make reality accord with a reading of the resulting representations.

Clearly, I have organized this book around themes rather than a chronology. In each chapter I analyze (rather than simply narrate) the encounter between the LoDagaa and "the world on paper" over a period of roughly one hundred years – from the early 1890s to the beginning of the 1990s. Above all, this book is about a single, unifying theme: the role of writing in the invention of a people at the beginning of this century, in their appropriation by their conquerors during the colonial period, and in structuring relationships between them and the external world since then.

Situating the LoDagaa

The people on the other side of "the world on paper" discussed in this book are known today in anthropological literature as the LoDagaa, and have been variously identified in other discourses as the Dagarti, Dagara, and Dagaba or Dagaaba – to list but a few of the names that have been deployed to identify and define an ethnicity that still does not really exist beyond "the world on paper." The British conquered these people physically in the first few years of the last century, but their colonization through the power of writing occurred over a much longer period of time. Indeed, the invention, appropriation, and colonization of the LoDagaa were never accomplished. These acts were uneven, inconsistent, contested, and resisted.

It is relevant to ask who these people really were. They have been viewed in various ways: as insubordinate and recalcitrant subjects who infuriated many colonial administrators; as an important source of labor for the colonial and postcolonial economies to the south; as minor ethnographic celebrities made famous in the academic world by a British anthropologist; and as backward and primitive people in some Ghanaian stereotypes. The people referred to as LoDagaa were both more and less than a name, inhabitants of a particular place on a map, bearers of a specific set of cultural features, and speakers of an identifiable set of dialects. Efforts to define the LoDagaa are fraught with difficulty, especially because this particular ethnonym was an invention and is not used by the people themselves. Chapter 1 explains why this term has been used here and what meanings have been attached to other ethnonyms, some of which have enjoyed some local currency.

Complex patterns of migration over several centuries across open cultural and social frontiers complicated the history of the LoDagaa and militated against the emergence of any singular sense of identity. In circumstances such as these, the most reliable indicator of historical identity is probably language. The people referred to as the LoDagaa are speakers of one of several dialects of *Dagaare*, itself part of the Mole-Dagbane language group.[2] By the middle of this century a series of *Dagaare*-speaking congeries had come to occupy an area running along both banks of the Black Volta from Diébougou in the north to Bole in the south, and extending in some places up to forty miles to the east or the west. In 1950 approximately 159,686 *Dagaare* speakers were living to the east of the Black Volta,[3] and another 123,696 to the west.[4] It has been estimated that today there are a quarter of a million *Dagaare* speakers on either side of the Black Volta.[5] Another recent study has claimed that there are one million *Dagaare* speakers in Ghana and Burkina Faso, making it the "fourth largest indigenous language of Ghana after Akan, Ewe and Dagbane." This somewhat inflated number is accounted for by the inclusion of all western Mole-Dagbane dialects under the rubric of *Dagaare*.[6]

Although the LoDagaa are distributed over a wide area, along both banks of the Black Volta in Ghana and Burkina Faso (see Map 2), they are concentrated mainly in what was known until recently as Lawra District (see Map 1), which is the focus of this book.[7] An area of 1,088 square miles, it is today an administrative division of the Upper West Region of Ghana. In 1987 the district was split, along with others in the Upper West Region, and the eastern half became Jirapa-Lambussie District. I have retained the term Lawra District in its more inclusive sense to refer to the geopolitical division of the past. To the north and west of Lawra District was the state of Burkina Faso, the international boundaries being the eleventh degree of latitude and the Black Volta River, respectively. To the east and south were the Kulpawn and Bekpong rivers, roughly its respective borders with Tumu District and Wa District. These three districts constituted the region as a whole until 1987. The Upper West Region is among Ghana's most remote parts as measured from the south, which dominates the country's economy and politics just as it did when it was a British colony known as the Gold Coast.

The topography of Lawra District, like that of the surrounding area, consists of relatively flat, sometimes monotonous, savanna. Uncultivated areas of sparse bush are interspersed with trees. The domestic architecture, in contrast to government, missionary, and commercial buildings that employ concrete, corrugated metal sheeting, and lumber, is still constructed primarily of timbers and a mixture of mud and cow dung. From the outside, these household buildings, with their thick, windowless walls and flat roofs, have a forbidding aspect.[8] Settlements were highly dispersed in the past, although they tended to cluster on better-drained lands; poorly drained areas were left vacant. During the colonial period, small towns did grow up along the road network the British imposed on the landscape, but most LoDagaa still live away from these roads and towns. The distinction between cultivated and uncultivated land was marked. Most farming was done some distance from people's houses, sometimes two or three miles away. Access to farms and neighboring settlements was by means of a complex web of footpaths maintained by constant use.

In 1984 the population of Lawra District was 156,174,[9] though this number needs to be qualified because a significant number of the men were residing in southern Ghana, where they worked as migrant laborers. Although the LoDagaa constituted the vast majority, there were people of different linguistic and cultural backgrounds in the district, most notably Sisala to the very east. The population density, 144 per square mile, was high. For almost all the inhabitants, the principal means of livelihood was agriculture. Migrant labor was the principal source of money. For most LoDagaa, the only other available careers were as public servants in the district administration, employees of the Catholic Church, or petty traders in the markets.

This book contributes toward only a part of the history of the LoDagaa – a history that remains to be written. Such a history would need to recognize the two most prominent and enduring features of the LoDagaa past: their relationship with the land and their struggle with disease. It would also need to consider more fully the harsh effects of colonization and the false promises of decolonization, the integration of their homeland into the mineral and agricultural economies of the south, the dramatic conversion of one-quarter of the population to Christianity, and many other significant changes that occurred in the past century.

First and foremost, the LoDagaa were farmers. The vagaries of the rains, the quality of soils, and the availability of labor were to them what inflation, taxes, and the availability of work are to most inhabitants of the West today. There were two distinct seasons in their year. During the period of rains, from as early as April until as late as October, almost all of their available time and labor was given to hoeing, planting, weeding, and harvesting a variety of crops: guinea-corn, millet, groundnuts, yams, maize, and beans. Most of this food they ate; a little of it they sold. But this incomplete snapshot should not be viewed as some sort of timeless pastoral idyll. For one thing, not all LoDagaa were farmers. Many became migrant laborers during the past century, living for varying periods of time outside their natal societies, but almost always returning home. Furthermore, in sharp contrast to the farming season, life was relatively leisured in the dry season, at least until food resources began to be exhausted.

The land was not merely a source of sustenance, it was also a homeland invested with deep meanings and associations that only intensified during the last century. Before colonial conquest the LoDagaa had been highly mobile, taking their ancestor and personal shrines with them, but leaving their shrines to the land, Earth shrines (*tengaan*), behind. In the new lands they moved into they found the Earth shrines of the previous occupants or created new ones if these could not be found. Colonization slowed down this mobility by creating borders, but it also created new patterns of movement through long-distance labor migration. However, this new mobility was temporary and only partial. Ritually sustainable and socially complete communities could not be created outside the district; for this reason the land drew back those who moved away. What migrant workers kept returning to was not only the physical world of the land, but also an invisible world. Writing recently of the Kabre of northern Togo – a culture similar in many respects to the LoDagaa, not least in their experience of colonialism and labor migration – Charles Piot has noted that "it is the spirits who stay put while people come and go."[10] A history of the LoDagaa cannot confine itself solely to the visible world because their world, like that of the Kabre, is "a world in which half of life's co-habitants are invisible spirits and ancestors."[11] In the twentieth century the LoDagaa of the visible world continued to circulate within and beyond Lawra District, but the more they moved the more the land of their parents became the focus of their lives, the fixed points to which shifting households, perennially migrant women, and migrant male laborers returned to in order to access their ancestors and to consult with the spirits found there.

Farming and the relationship with the land dominated the everyday experience of most LoDagaa in both old and new ways in the twentieth century. But perhaps the most dramatic aspects of their culture, if not also their history, were concerned with illness. As suggested by the different recitations associated with the *Bagre*, a medical cult into which patients were initiated as part of their treatment, disease was central to LoDagaa culture. A version of a *Bagre* performance recorded in 1951 began with the following explanation of why the initiates and their guides had convened: "Gods, ancestors, guardians, beings of the wild, the leather bottles say we should perform, because of the scorpion's sting, because of suicide, aches in the belly, pains in the head."[12] Like many other areas of Africa, the LoDagaa homeland was strongly affected by disease. One district commissioner initially expressed relief at having escaped the confines of the Guinea forest, and enthused about the open spaces, the panoramas from the occasional hills, and the fresh air. A month later he was expressing despair about the frequency of disease: "It is a disturbing country and begins to get on one's nerves after a time."[13] Yaws, onchoceriasis, sleeping sickness, influenza, cerebo-spinal meningitis, malaria, and bilharzia posed greater challenges to the material resources of the LoDagaa than to those of colonial officers; at the same time, however, the LoDagaa had far stronger psychological resources for dealing with them than did their conquerors. A former British medical officer described conditions for most LoDagaa in the late 1940s in unusually sensitive terms, writing of villages at the end of the dry season as "retaining only a tenuous hold on existence":

> It is during the early rains, when humidity rises, that the bone pains of yaws come on, the guineaworms emerge (and guineaworm can paralyse a village), and the annual attack of clinical malaria comes on. It is a long time since the last harvest, and energy is short. Epidemics during the dry season may have left the remaining population exhausted and dispirited. ... The houses were windowless, and in the cold of the dry season they slept together in heaps, to retain warmth that they had not the food energy to replace if they lost.[14]

Although he exaggerated the precariousness of conditions somewhat, suggesting that most villages were on the brink of starvation, no other outsider's account of the LoDagaa has come so close to capturing the existential realities these people faced.

Just as this book is not about the LoDagaa, but rather about their encounter with "the world on paper," it is not a book about colonialism, but rather about an important yet neglected aspect of colonialism. In the sections that follow I explain the two concepts that are central to my analytical framework for understanding this encounter – "the world on paper" and the world of experience.

Writing and Colonialism

In setting out to explore the connections between writing and colonialism, I suggest reasons for rethinking colonialism as a particular type of cultural encounter. The world of the LoDagaa was one of experience – knowledge, practice, and speech – whereas the world that increasingly surrounded the LoDagaa from the beginning of the last century was a world of writing, a world that endeavored to invent, appropriate, and regulate its subjects. This latter world, which belonged to the British and those who succeeded them in the role of governing the LoDagaa, was part of what the cognitive psychologist David Olson has called "the world on paper," a world divorced from reality. Those who live in such a world, suggests Olson, are deeply conditioned by its assumptions: "Our understanding of the world, that is our science, and our understanding of ourselves, that is, our psychology, are by-products of our ways of interpreting and creating written texts, of living in a world on paper."[15]

The British lived in just such a world, one in which writing was not only an instrument of colonialism but also a way of making colonialism real. The basic cognitive activities of European travel and exploration, "such as naming (or eliciting names), distinguishing and lumping, and representing ordered arrangements," were also part of European colonialism. Regarding these activities, Johannes Fabian has noted that they "somehow acquire significance only when we put them in writing."[16] Similarly, Mary Louise Pratt has said of nineteenth-century travel writing that "discovery" had no meaning on its own: "It only gets 'made' real after the traveler (or other survivor) returns home, and brings it into being through texts: a name on a map, a report to the Royal Geographical Society, the Foreign Office, the London Mission Society, a diary, a lecture, a travel book." This observation, that there could not have been any discovery unless it had been mediated by texts, is also true of twentieth-century colonialism in Africa: colonial rule could not be made real until it had been documented on paper.[17]

The world on paper of the British was that of a capitalist culture with imperial pretensions eager to assert its dominance over large numbers of cultures in northern Ghana that did not possess a similar medium of communication. As Brian Street has argued, we must resist the temptation of believing that literacy has only one form, that it is both autonomous and deterministic, or that it is a neutral medium.[18] Written cultures also carry within themselves political and ideological assumptions. The dispositions of the British were determined not only by the cognitive effects of writing but also by what writing was used for and how it was used. At different times this world on paper intersected with a parallel world of writing created by the Society of Missionaries of Africa, whose evangelical work among the LoDagaa at the end of the 1920s receives some attention in this book. However, the term writing is used here to refer to the colonial use of literacy, where writing and colonialism existed in a reciprocal relationship – one in which writing provided the necessary psychological disposition as well as practical tools for colonial rule, and colonialism applied attitudes and practices of writing while imbuing them with political and ideological features.

The effects of writing were both instrumental and psychological. Writing obviously made the practical activities of colonial administration and governance much easier. As Jack Goody has noted, even though colonial bureaucracies were not highly developed, "knowability meant governability, and both entailed the extensive use of the written record."[19] That LoDagaa culture and society were predicated on oral communication gave the British an added sense of arrogance. It also led them more readily into believing that the world on paper really represented the world of experience – a mistake Olson has identified as a common feature of literate thought.[20] Here it is useful to recall Stephen Greenblatt's caution about not confusing the ability of writing to aid communication with claims made by the Europeans in the early modern period, during a much earlier series of encounters, that writing was better able to represent reality than speech. As he observed: "It may be that the Europeans' possession of writing (and their impression that the New World natives did not) increased the *conquistadores*' self-confidence, but neither confidence nor success is a reliable indicator of superior access to reality."[21]

That the British believed that writing had certain effects is as important to understanding colonialism and its aftermath as any effects it really had.[22] An otherwise unremarkable entry in the informal diary of the District Commissioner of Lawra illustrates how colonial officers saw writing not only as a means of appropriating reality, but also of controlling it. On 19 March 1917 a colonial appointee had complained that the elders under his authority had threatened to kill him. When the district commissioner interviewed the elders two days later, they feigned ignorance of the whole affair. Unable to discover a conspiracy, the officer issued the following warning: "I told them to be careful and that the matter had been written down."[23] The act of writing down of information was meant to instill fear and thereby gain obedience. That this act could have had little practical effect on the elders, who could not read, did not matter; what mattered to the district commissioner was that he had shown both that he ruled and how he ruled.

With regard to the confluence of writing and power in the ancient Mediterranean world, the editors of a recent collection of essays noted that rulers often used writing simply "to show that they were rulers." Such ritual uses of writing should not be underestimated in colonial Africa any more than in the Roman Empire, where, as Allan Bowman and Greg Woolf have observed, "often the fact that things were written down may have been as important as what it said."[24] In the same vein, the work of Michael Clanchy has done much to help us understand how important writing was in providing psychological support to the Norman Conquest of England. Although legend suggests that England was brought "under the rule of written law" with the arrival of the Normans, as symbolized in the creation of the Domesday Book, Clanchy has shown that "the bureaucracy's appetite for information exceeded its capacity to digest it." The effects of this famous document were "symbolic rather than practical." Nevertheless, it associated royal power with writing "in a novel and unforgettable way."[25] Similarly, we need to understand British colonial writing, which emerged from the culture and society that the Normans had conquered and effectively introduced writing to eight hundred years earlier, at both practical and symbolic levels.

Ever since paper first intruded upon their experiences, writing has been central to how the LoDagaa have attempted to cope with their conquest and the interference of external authorities, be they colonial administrators, postcolonial governments, or religious authorities. The history told in the following chapters is perhaps most immediately understood through a story recorded in 1921. The commandant of the administrative division (Gaoua) of the French colony (Haute-Volta) adjoining Lawra District had sent an envoy with a letter of summons to be read to a number of *Lobi* settlements, neighbors of the LoDagaa, which were resisting foreign rule. The inhabitants of one settlement, Malba, "solemnly took the letter, pretended to read it and handed to the Messenger a large leaf on which they had inscribed certain signs. The Messenger was told to tell the Commandant that the Lobis had received his letter, and had written one in answer (the leaf). That they meant no one to think that the French were the only people who could write and send letters."[26] Although anecdotal, the story was not apocryphal. These resisters clearly saw writing as a tool and a symbol of political power.

Elsewhere in Africa, several scholars have noted that people often made a similar connection between writing and colonialism and its aftermath, the postcolonial state. In the highlands of Kenya, writing, including its associated rituals and symbols, was even more important to Mau Mau insurgents. As James Smith has observed, it was "iconic of political potency in the colonial arena, being both the sine qua non for entry into the emergent African elite ... and an instrument of political violence immanent in the forms of bureaucratic representation and reification."[27] Writing was more than merely a symbol – it was also a weapon. Bogumil Jewsiewicki noted that in the "colonie belge" style of Zairian painting, "explicit references to writing allude to social control. The administrator or the judge is always accompanied by a table, enabling him to put people into writing, making them slaves of the state."[28] In eastern Zambia, where Mark Auslander's work tells us of rituals of witchfinding and antiwitchcraft medicine among the Ngoni in 1988, a Doctor Moses made full use of a wide repertoire of writing's symbols:

> In the course of the cleansing, he gave each person a magical version of the government-issued National Registration Card, which all Zambian citizens must present at security checkpoints. Just as the state photographs, interrogates, and classifies all Zambians for their cards, the diviner used his hand mirror (itself the size of an I.D.) to capture the image of each individual. Having "photographed" everyone, the diviner – like his official counterparts – then certified in writing whether they were "good" or "evil." Long numerical strings assigned to accused witches were also reminiscent of the long National Registration numbers assigned to each citizen. These were then inscribed in razored lines on the accused's skin, which itself became a kind of bureaucratic document upon which moral evaluations were imprinted. Furthermore, the potent antiwitchcraft medicines were impressed into these incisions with a large object modeled on the ubiquitous rubber stamp, which closes all transactions at state offices, banks, hospitals, clinics, and border crossings.[29]

And in the southern Sudan, where by the postcolonial era "movements of 'paper' now marked the conclusion of each new court case and the passing of each taxation season," non-literate Nuer saw that "paper" had made them vulnerable to "'political' forces beyond their control through the medium of writing." At the same time, as Sharon Hutchinson has shown, it was also "the principal medium through which contemporary Nuer men and women sought to tap the powers of the government."[30]

The use of writing and the production of written knowledge obviously had practical as well as symbolic implications. In a study of the relationship between "speaking, writing and authority" in the Kingdom of Taqali in the Nuba hills before European colonization, Janet Ewald noted: "Graphocentric thinkers and bureaucratic states seek to grasp knowledge or power by systemization. This effaces diversity. We render ourselves deaf to people who rejected literacy and centralizing paradigms of state formation." Only by examining issues of "authority, orality, and literacy," she argues, can these lost voices be recovered.[31] And only when these voices are heard does the dissonance between the claims of writing – structure, rigidity, control, stability, and authority – and the dispositions of speech – unsystematic, flexible, context-bound, and ambiguous – become apparent.

Because of the advantages of speech over writing, the Taqali did not use writing to communicate internally. Instead, it was used by the state to create a "false image of stability and authority that the kings wished to convey," and "to enhance their domain in the eyes of the [Ottoman state] and its agents."[32] Much the same statements can be made about the role of writing among the LoDagaa: although it did not succeed in displacing the world of experience, of which speech was an integral part, writing was used by the British colonial state to create an illusory sense of control. Also, it deeply affected the relationships between the LoDagaa and the external world. When and where the two intersected, the LoDagaa were forced to adapt, appeal, or defer to the assumptions and expectations of the world on paper.[33]

Histories written in the 1960s and 1970s of colonial Africa often overlooked the cultural aspects of colonialism, and more recent studies, even though they have certainly broadened our cultural understanding of colonialism in many very important ways, have largely neglected the connections between writing and colonialism. African historians have certainly not overlooked written documents as sources for studying colonialism, but they have generally ignored the implications of writing itself in the history of colonialism. It is only in the work of a few scholars, such as Ewald, Hutchinson, Auslander, Jewsiewicki, and Smith, as well as that of Timothy Mitchell, Robert Thornton, and Isabel Hofmeyr, that one finds an explicit analysis of these connections; the work you are now reading, which draws on their insights, is the first book-length study of the subject.[34] Historians of Africa have often thought of Christianity and Islam as religions of the book, in the singular, religious sense of that word, but they have not thought of colonialism as an equally literate phenomenon with its own books.[35] This oversight is all the more curious given that these same historians have sat for long periods of time poring over the very evidence of the bookishness of colonial culture.

Although documents have never been neglected, for some time now African historians have been more concerned with recovering the spoken word on the grounds that it provided the most direct evidence of the experiences of Africans living outside of the world on paper.[36] The appropriate and necessary emphasis on oral history has further marginalized the role of writing in the history of colonial and postcolonial Africa – a period during which few people in Africa were not affected by the world on paper. A historian of northern Ghana reflected in the 1970s: "After my reading of an infinite quantity of minutes and memoranda, the colonial encounter in Africa still seems to me to be a cultural mystery of the first order. ... The colonial encounter has not, on the whole, had the imaginative treatment it deserves."[37] A quarter of a century later, the mystery of these documents and of colonialism itself still has not received the attention it deserves. Some of this mystery lies in the medium of these documents and not simply in their content.

In his study of European designs on Egypt in the nineteenth century, Mitchell remarked: "Colonial power required the country to become readable, like a book."[38] In her recent study of oral culture in a Transvaal chiefdom, Hofmeyr argued that writing was "a, if not *the*, key cultural institution of colonialism."[39] Similarly, in her study of change among the Nuer across half a century, Hutchinson contended that writing, guns, and money were the most notable "new media emanating from outside their immediate social world."[40] As these and a few other studies suggest, the role of writing in the history of colonialism in Africa is a rich topic that deserves a great deal more attention.[41]

Despite the role of Islamic scholars and Christian missionaries in the dissemination of literacy, each with their own set of implications for this medium,[42] most people in sub-Saharan Africa encountered writing through colonial rule. The consequences of writing were neither abstract nor impersonal, as historians of the Spanish colonization of the Americas have shown over the past few decades. In a review of quincentenary reassessments of colonization, James Axtell observed that among the major themes to have emerged was the view that "the conquest of America was in part a victory of paper and print over memory and voice."[43] Only Thornton has made a similar argument for the other side of the Atlantic, calling the "discovery" of Africa also "a discovery on paper." He noted that most Victorians had access to Africa through the medium of narrative ethnography. "Its 'availability' to the experience of the scholar or the educated layman," he added, "depended on the existence of a text that described Africa, or some aspect of it." Indeed, the purpose of much exploration was to write literary adventures, which led Thornton to conclude: "Had the great Victorian travelers not written anything, it would not be said today that they had 'discovered' anything."[44] Much the same observation can be made about colonialism: without writing the British could not have said they had ruled anyone.

The work of scholars such as Walter Mignolo and Constance Classen has highlighted the importance of writing in the encounters between the Spanish and the peoples of Peru and Mexico. Mignolo has shown how the Spanish saw writing as a means of recording knowledge and of transmitting information, as a device for discerning between truth and falsehood, and as an instrument for imposing law over chaos. Both Mesoamerican and Andean cultures possessed elaborate semiotic systems, but they did not attach the same importance to them as the Spanish did to their alphabet.[45] In her study of the role of literacy as a form of "anticulture" in Andean colonial history, Classen noted that writing provided the Spanish with "the power to order reality and to conserve that order." The Incas became fascinated by writing, realizing that it was a source of "power and authority" under Spanish rule.[46]

Writing was a fundamental difference in both American and African colonial encounters; it authorized the colonizer to record and reorder the world of the colonized according to European cognitive schemes, and to make representations of the "Other." For the Spanish, writing was also an ideological device for denying the validity of indigenous memories and knowledge insofar as these did not subscribe to literary structures and take a written form: "Once it was concluded that the Amerindians did not have historiography, Spanish chroniclers appointed themselves to write and put into a coherent form the narratives that, according to their perception, Amerindians told in a thoroughly incoherent manner."[47] But there were also important differences between colonialism in the Americas and Africa. From the early modern period through to the Enlightenment, questions of language were much more in the forefront of European minds in their encounters with other cultures. "Language is the instrument of empire," wrote Antonio de Nebrija, the famous Spanish grammarian, to Queen Isabella in 1492.[48] We need only contrast these words with those of Belloc four hundred years later to appreciate the change in imperial attitudes. In Spanish encounters with the cultures of the Americas, both language and writing were at the center of the conceptualization of difference. There was a deliberate attempt to displace indigenous languages and replace them with Spanish. But much of this linguistic arrogance was linked back to writing – to the idea that a written language was far superior and, therefore, naturally hegemonic.[49]

By the time European colonization of Africa began, even though indigenous societies were often referred to as cultures "without writing" by colonial observers, more recent technological differences had come to take precedence in the minds of the colonizers. In addition, the language policies adopted by Europeans in Africa were much more ambivalent, oscillating between assimilative and adaptive models. Whereas European languages became the medium for secondary and postsecondary education, indigenous or "native" languages were preferred for primary and religious instruction. Overall the level of literacy was deliberately maintained at extremely low levels.[50] With some notable exceptions, such as the work of scholars like Ngugi wa Thiong'o and Fabian, the relationship between language and colonialism has been almost as neglected as the one between writing and colonialism.[51] Although my concern here is not with the role of language or literacy in colonial policy, but rather with the effects of writing, the two were obviously linked. In general, European governments in Africa guarded their privileged access to colonial writing through an effective monopoly. Even so, the issue of writing was never as prominent in their discourses as it was in the case of the Spanish in the New World. One reason they were less explicit about its importance was that they had the Maxim-gun and the Spanish had not, but we should not be misled by imperial jingoism into thinking that writing was less important simply because Europeans no longer boasted about it.

Until recently, most African historians had not given enough attention to the cultural dimensions of colonialism and the cognitive aspects of the encounters it created; but anthropologists – long decried by historians for the synchrony of their studies – proposed just such an approach over two generations ago. In the 1930s, at the behest of the Rockefeller Foundation and under the leadership of Bronislaw Malinowski, a number of anthropologists in Britain began looking at colonialism as a form of "culture contact."[52] For a brief time they studied both the changes that colonialism had unleashed and African reactions to them; but by the 1940s the initiative had waned and such a perspective on colonialism was again largely ignored. The neglect of "culture contact" as a paradigm for understanding colonialism in Africa has been unfortunate.[53] In the Americas, the cultural elements of encounters between colonizing and indigenous cultures have been explored in far greater detail.[54] To be fair, there are some extenuating reasons, beyond a failure of historical imagination, why such an important element of colonialism in Africa has been neglected. The conquest of the Americas is removed from the historian by as many centuries as that of Africa is by generations, and so in the African case there has been less room for perspective and less time for the growth of as large and mature a historiography. In addition, because it occurred at the beginning of the history of European expansion, the interaction between Europe and the Americas occasioned much more contemporary reflection on the dynamics and modalities of cultural encounters.

Through the 1960s and into the 1970s the study of colonial encounters in Africa was dominated by political and economic studies. These approaches were overshadowed by the ascendancy of social history in the 1980s, by which time colonialism had receded into the background. Only in the past decade have the cultural aspects of colonialism begun to attract the attention they deserve.[55]

Among others, Frederick Cooper and Ann Stoler have been instrumental in stimulating reappraisals of colonialism. Of particular relevance here is their call more than a decade ago for a more thorough examination of the production of knowledge by colonial regimes by "connecting what was written to what was said and to what was done." They advocated a sustained analysis of "how colonial regimes constructed their categories of authority" and "how these classifications were appropriated and reworked by colonized women and men themselves."[56]

As John Comaroff and Jean Comaroff have noted, these new views of colonialism should not displace older ones; rather, they should contribute toward our understanding of the broader picture. Colonialism in Africa was experienced in different ways, at different times, and in different places. For some colonial subjects colonialism was "about domination and violence, invasion and exploitation," or "about the material conditions of existence," while for others "it was equally an encounter with European knowledge and techniques and modes of representation."[57] In this book I argue that the LoDagaa encounter with the world on paper was an important feature of their experience of colonialism, and I examine that encounter by carefully scrutinizing the role and impact of writing. As the Comaroffs have observed, in the past decade scholarship on colonialism has witnessed several significant shifts in topics and approaches, including those from "dialectics" to "dialogics" and from "political economy to poetics."[58] In shifting the lens from "the violence of the gun to the violation of the text" – to use another of the Comaroffs' useful descriptions of recent changes – this book reflects some of these new perspectives on colonialism.

Much of the credit for these new perspectives goes to the work of contemporary anthropologists. The political critique of anthropology that began in the dying days of the last European empires in Africa had, by the 1980s, developed into a broader and more sustained examination of both cognitive and historical issues involved in the encounter between anthropologists and the peoples they studied. One of the most important observations to emerge from this discussion was the importance of writing in "the poetics and politics of ethnography," to borrow the subtitle from an important collection of essays on the subject.[59] In his introduction to the same book, James Clifford declared that writing was not "a marginal, or occulted, dimension" to what anthropologists did: it was actually more central to the whole enterprise of anthropology than even observation and participation. He argued that despite claims of "transparency of representation and immediacy of experience" the emphasis on "text making and rhetoric serves to highlight the constructed, artificial nature of cultural accounts."[60] Elsewhere, Fabian sharply criticized anthropology as a form of cognitive imperialism that, through its propensity to temporize differences and its emphasis on visualism, denied coevalness between the literate West and the oral cultures of the "Other."[61] Although other factors were involved, writing was a fundamental requirement for these ideological devices of distancing. More recently, Fabian has suggested that "the most valuable epistemological contribution made by anthropology's literary turn" was the recognition that writing, "often called writing-up," was an "essential element in the production of ethnographic knowledge."[62] And again in the 1980s, Pierre Bourdieu's argument (from a decade earlier) made a significant impact on how Africa was studied. He argued that writing and its concomitant "objectivism," which were so central to anthropological discourse, reduced the social world to "a totality intended for cognition alone." For him, writing was deeply opposed to the "logic of practice," the very phenomenon anthropologists struggled to capture in their study of cultures within which social practices were not generated by rules but by "habitus" – dispositions, improvisations, and strategic acts.[63] (Olson argued later and independently of these anthropologists that among the cognitive effects of writing is the blurring of representations and the things they represent, thereby making the distortions of writing invisible to those caught up in the world of literate perceptions.)[64]

Notwithstanding the unprecedented degree to which these works highlighted the cognitive effects of writing on anthropology and related discourses, we should acknowledge that some early anthropologists in Africa would have recognized the same problems, albeit in different terms. In his study of the Tallensi of northeast Ghana, with whom the LoDagaa shared a large degree of cultural and social affinity, Meyer Fortes acknowledged the importance that writing played in the production of anthropological knowledge:

> The hardest part of an anthropologist's work begins after he leaves the field. In the field he is engrossed in concrete human activities. ... he is carried by the living stream of social life. He hardly has to stop and think. Thus the crucial scientific task begins when he starts to write up his field material. It is not merely a question of putting his observations on record. ... It involves breaking up the vivid, kaleidoscopic reality of human action, thought, and emotion which lies in the anthropologist's note-books and memory, and creating out of the pieces a coherent representation of a society, in terms of the general principles of organization and motivation that regulate behaviour in it.[65]

Fortes, a contributor to Malinowski's "culture contact" project, knew well before it became fashionable to say so that writing was an integral part of what anthropologists did.

Given that the anthropology of this earlier period has come to be seen as a decidedly colonial discipline, collaborating implicitly with the colonial project, it is surprising that historians of colonialism in Africa have not taken sufficient note of the insights that historians and critics of anthropology have provided and applied them to the phenomenon of colonialism itself. If writing played such an important role in the production of anthropological knowledge, it would seem reasonable to suppose that it had a similar place in the production of colonial knowledge as well as in the practices of colonial rule. This neglect of the colonial culture of writing by African historians is ironic when one considers that historians of medieval and early modern Europe were alerted to the importance of writing in social and cultural history in no small part through the work of an anthropologist working in Africa, Jack Goody. The theme and geographic focus of this book have a special resonance, given that Goody had been responsible for making the LoDagaa minor ethnographic celebrities in the 1950s and 1960s, before going on to produce a series of provocative and influential studies on the effects of literacy in the 1970s and 1980s.[66]

Historicism and Dissimulation

In the 1970s anthropologists began calling into question the whole concept of tradition, arguing that it was little more than a means of objectifying and distancing African societies.[67] At the same time, historians of colonial Africa began to be aware that many traditions – that is, cultural, political, and social practices – had been invented and their novelty disguised. Consequently, any notion of tradition has involved considerable confusion. These historians noted that Europeans invented versions of the African past to suit the needs of colonial rule; at the same time Africans also invented traditions in order to benefit from the new colonial order.[68] As Terence Ranger pointed out: "The invented traditions of African societies – whether invented by the Europeans or by Africans themselves in response – distorted the past but became in themselves realities through which a good deal of colonial encounter was expressed."[69] In African cultures, the relationship between the present and the past became problematic during the colonial period, in ways it is difficult to imagine it ever could have been before this time. Colonial notions of tradition conferred an otherwise unobtainable (and hitherto unnecessary) degree of external legitimacy on institutions and practices.[70] The circumscription of legitimacy to the past was in part a result of the colonial culture of writing – part of the wider colonial ideology of denying historicity to African societies.[71]

Colonialism wrought changes of a scale and type hitherto unknown to most Africans. Discomfort with such transformations presupposed the growth of a particular form of historical consciousness; that is, one bounded by *logos* or discursive knowledge instead of *mythos* or practical consciousness.[72] Jean-François Bayart is correct in criticizing the notion that contact with the West gave Africa history; yet at the same time colonialism, as a particular type of relationship with the West, did represent a distinct type of historical experience, just as industrialization had for pre-industrial Western societies.[73] The notion of tradition, based on the awareness of a break between past and present, created new forms of historical consciousness.[74] However, oral representations of the past in precolonial Africa were generally the product neither of a narrative continuum nor of a rigid adherence to the task of preserving "the irreducible alterity of the past."[75] Indeed, in many cultures – including LoDagaa culture – representations of the past were not structured by a linear sense of time or based on concerns over veridical or forensic evidence. As Peter Naameh, a local historian and Catholic priest, noted of the LoDagaa, "the question of reaching objective certainty about what happened in the very distant past may be quite secondary in Dagara historical consciousness, to how knowledge about the past helps to iron out present difficulties and ensure peace in the society."[76]

In restoring historicity to African cultures through the writing of history, we must be aware of the differences in historical consciousness between the world on paper and the world of experience. Just as writing conditions our understanding of reality, so too does it distort the academic understanding of the past, because we are "unwittingly burdened," as Hofmeyr reminds us, by a "highly institutionalized, text-bound, linear and chronological understanding of history."[77] In colonial and postcolonial Africa, the features of written historical discourse have produced a problematic relationship between academic and non-academic forms of historical consciousness as well as between the past and present.[78] Due to both the internalization of colonial criteria for legitimacy and indigenous responses to external challenges, consciousness of the past suffered from historicism – "an excessive regard for the institutions and values of the past."[79] David Henige referred to these effects of writing on the historical consciousness of the Baganda and Banyoro in the early twentieth century as being like those of a "disease."[80]

The backward-looking character of rural African cultures during the colonial era was not an inherent cultural dynamic; rather, it was a result of the loss of former securities.[81] Stock has suggested a useful distinction between "traditional" and "traditionalistic" behavior. The former is merely a habitual action, while the latter is "the self-conscious affirmation of traditional norms." He has argued that some forms of modernity emerge only when the distance between these two forms of tradition becomes irreconcilable, and acknowledgment of a disjuncture with the past is unavoidable.[82] Similarly, cultures are not objective entities, but historical processes in a state of constant flux. Their constitutive elements are not coherent or cohesive, only a diverse array of shifting "symbols and meanings." With writing, cultures become "historicist and self-reflexive" through the processes of representation and explanation.[83] In the case of the LoDagaa these historicist and self-reflexive tendencies are at the heart of both the colonial and indigenous representations discussed in this book.

For the LoDagaa, colonialism meant, among other things, foreign rule, the need for new identities, the creation of chiefs, the imposition of taxes and a money economy, extensive labor migration, Christian evangelism, and the attempted regulation of their social lives by courts. By the end of the twentieth century many of the conditions under which they lived their lives were much different from those their ancestors faced at the end of the nineteenth century. But as the following chapters reveal, continuity has been a stronger historical trend, for all the apparent change; but this is not to say that the LoDagaa were in any sense "traditional."

Continuities and discontinuities in Africa have been understood in terms that are at once both temporal and essentialist; the former have been seen as "African," authentic, and traditional and the latter have been seen as "Western," foreign, and modern. As Susan Vogel has noted: "The widespread assumption that to be modern is to be Western insidiously denies the authenticity of contemporary African cultural expressions by regarding them a priori as imitations of the West."[84] The assumptions behind the traditional/modern continuum have merely disguised spatial relationships: as between "periphery" and "center," "small-scale" and "large-scale," or, preferably, "local society" and "wider world."[85] Continuity is not synonymous with tradition, nor is it an antonym of change. The idea that continuity in African societies was the result of a deterministic relationship between the past and the present is the result of a "mystification" of historical processes in Africa.[86] Continuity was the result of "regulated improvisations" executed by individuals, not "mechanical determinism" operating on a culture.[87] In colonial discourse tradition was an ideological construct used to deny historicity to conquered societies, as well as to assign them to a "different Time" by denying coevalence.[88] As Fabian has noted: "Tradition and modernity are not 'opposed' (except semiotically), nor are they in 'conflict.' All this is (bad) metaphorical talk. What are opposed, in conflict, locked in antagonistic struggle, are not the same societies at different stages of development, but different societies facing each other at the same time."[89] Temporal distinctions are really only masquerades for spatial distinctions. The local became the traditional, the external colonial world the modern. Just as continuity and change are not necessarily antonyms, neither are local perspectives necessarily contradictory with regional, national, or global ones.[90] According to Valentin Mudimbe, Western colonial discourse on Africa reduced spatial differences "into a Western historicity."[91] When discontinuities are seen in spatial terms, the traditional is set within its generative contexts and can be seen as local as opposed to traditional; similarly, the modern becomes little more than the intersection of internal and external realities. As I argue throughout this book, changes among the LoDagaa were primarily experienced in spatial rather than temporal terms; it has only been the world on paper that has sought to situate them in time.

Written Representations and Indigenous Knowledge

"Without documents, memory had stemmed from the living wisdom of the local community," explains Clanchy, "whereas the dead hand of writing ... defined and extended boundaries by its 'external marks' across both time and space."[92] In LoDagaa culture, one of the main effects of writing has been to redefine the nature of both time and space; something I became aware of while watching the Hollywood version of the Broadway musical *Brigadoon* with a crowd of LoDagaa children in the mission house of the Sisters of the Immaculate Conception.[93] The movie's storyline was based on a "foolishly improbable" premise: in the eighteenth century, Scottish villagers made a bargain with God that if the scourge of witchcraft were removed from their midst they would agree to reside in a realm of timeless suspension, coming back to life, and real time, for only one day every hundred years.[94] Two centuries, or two days, later, a couple of American tourists intrude upon this world of "nights that are one hundred years long."[95] Although they can interact with the visitors, the people of the village cannot leave without bringing about the village's destruction. Lerner, the musical's lyricist, was apparently very interested in the "occult" or "psychic" worlds, and in many of his musicals he endeavored to erase time or to disregard its boundaries. The effect in *Brigadoon* was nothing short of ethnographic, presenting an imagined village suspended in time.[96] A reviewer of a 1986 revival of the original Broadway production noted: "Almost forty years ago it was a work curiously out of touch with its times ... 'timeless.' It is simply the case that 'Brigadoon' is a fantasy and all successful fantasies are timeless, but I have to admit that timelessness has a tendency to make me nervous."[97] This is the same fantasy upon which much anthropology in Africa was once premised – that other cultures inhabit another world of timeless immobility. This observation has been made many times in recent decades; less obvious is the role that writing has played in creating these suspended worlds. When the LoDagaa encountered the world on paper they were fixed in time and robbed of crucial forms of historical autonomy. Later, in the postcolonial period, they were forced to try to regain some of this lost sovereignty by rewriting the past. Much of their relationship with the world on paper has taken place through discourses about the past.

Written representations of the LoDagaa were the product of the intersection of different worlds, and had effects similar to those of the plot of *Brigadoon*. Writing was indispensable to the West's project of appropriating and distancing Africa. As Jewsiewicki has noted, the rest of the world has not been of interest to the West "unless irreversible time sheltered us from its initiatives."[98] Thus, the question of where to situate the LoDagaa is problematic. As Steven Feierman has noted, the problem of locating "other" societies is inherent to the study of Africa in the West. If these societies are distanced, it suggests that they are "not subject to the same historical forces," but if they are seen as "coeval, living in the same era, subject to the same historical forces, struggling with the same issues, then we lose the picture of cultural variation which is the heart of anthropology."[99] Such questions are central to the discipline of anthropology, but they were also fundamental to the project of colonialism – indeed, it can be argued that anthropology would not have been possible without colonial empires, just as neither would have been possible without writing. However, colonialism was much more successful on paper than in practice. As Bayart observed, perhaps the salient feature of the last three centuries of African history has not been the integration of Africa within the global orbit of Western capitalism, but "the latter's inability to pull the continent into its magnetic field."[100] The same can also be said of the relationship of the LoDagaa to the world on paper. The failure of integration was not due to the incompleteness of historical forces; rather, it was the result of the bilateral relationship between external and internal forces. The intermediaries in this relationship were observers, in the guise of administrators, chiefs, missionaries, anthropologists, priests, and academics. Through their intercession, the LoDagaa came to occupy "the intermediate space between the so-called African tradition and the projected modernity of colonialism," a space that Mudimbe informs us is "the locus of paradoxes that called into question the modalities and implications of modernization in Africa."[101]

All observers, whether outsiders or insiders, had a common audience insofar as the people they hoped to reach with their writing lived beyond the LoDagaa in the world on paper. However, observations did not only involve the writings of a few individuals and their audiences, as each text also involved many other people. Administrators and judges, clerks and ethnographers, and anthropologists and priests "put people into writing," but they did so with the collusion of sundry subjects, litigants, informants, collaborators, and parishioners. These often silent and invisible participants were often aware of the purposes to which their information was to be put. Nowhere was this more elegantly articulated than in the testimony of one of the performers who took part in a recitation associated with initiation into the *Bagre*:

> It is the European who wants to know matters of the old country. They are collecting material everywhere. That is why we also want to show them how it is done. But [the ancestors] should give us permission, so that we can perform it for them to take home and [play back the recorder]. They will unravel everything that we give them. So that they will know the ways that we the people of Birifu have always followed. It is not only in this place that they are interested. They will go elsewhere to record and also learn the ways of those other people. So that is that. Now we want to begin.[102]

So said Nikara, one of several informants from the village of Birifu who collaborated with Goody in 1970 in recording the poetry associated with the cult of the *Bagre*. This book considers the wider transcription and decoding of LoDagaa culture and social practices. It shows how the desire for knowledge on the part of external observers both elicited articulations of extant knowledge and fostered the production of new knowledge. It also discusses how this knowledge was used to fashion representations of the LoDagaa by internal observers that were not dissimilar to the signs recorded on a large leaf by the inhabitants of Malba.

At the beginning of this century the LoDagaa were colonized, and the outside world intruded upon them to an unprecedented degree: or, to look at the encounter in a manner more felicitous to the themes of this book, the LoDagaa intruded upon the consciousness of the wider world. Writing was the medium through which the British invented and then appropriated the LoDagaa, denied them historical autonomy and initiative, and attempted to regulate their disputes. It was also the tool that missionaries used to fix indigenous beliefs in time, to make them inflexible and unchanging, and, ultimately, to deny legitimacy to religious syncretism. All manner of encounters – ethnological, administrative, judicial, and theological – engendered representations by external observers. Later, internal observers created representations to deal with the outside world that had come to impinge on their lives. In the texts of these internal observers we can discern what Pratt has called "autoethnographic expression," that is, representations that "engage with the colonizer's own terms."[103] But both types of observers made their representations in writing; or, as in the case of litigants, they had their representations recorded by others. It is true that the LoDagaa made oral representations of many aspects of their own world, but these were never intended to situate the LoDagaa in another, exterior world, or to be translated from one reality to another. Written representations had a very specific audience – the outside world.

This book draws on a wide range of documents: colonial record books and reports, administrative diaries and letters, ethnographic articles and monographs, anthropological theses and books, missionary periodicals and theological arguments, colonial and postcolonial court records, local histories, and sociological studies. These various presentations are all linked by the argument that they all distorted, to one degree or another, the reality they sought to depict. They might better be called misrepresentations, but that word implies that the purpose of knowledge is to reflect reality. Richard Rorty, in a position he has called "anti-representationalism," has said that knowledge is better understood as "a matter of acquiring habits of action for coping with reality."[104] In a similar context, Greenblatt has suggested that we look at the statements of Europeans about the "New World" during the early modern period less for their veridical value and more as examples of "representational practices." He does not advocate abandoning hermeneutical operations that seek to ascertain what really happened, but he warns us that "instances of brazen bad faith" are often not much different from "homely (and often equally misleading) attempts to tell the truth."[105]

In examining such distortions, my intention is not to engage in revisionist deconstruction or postmodernist resignation. Instead, it is to understand written representations as necessary strategies that different observers adopted to cope with particular realities. A problem all observers confronted was the difference in expectations, between cultures predicated on writing and those based on orality, in how knowledge and practices were categorized and ordered. These different expectations were, in turn, the product of different systems of cultural and social understanding. But the difference was not equal; expectations imposed from outside were privileged because of the power differentials that existed for most of the past century between the world of the LoDagaa and the world of their colonizers.

Colonial power and writing created a sense of ontological and epistemological arrogance – an arrogance arising in no small part from the fact that what the LoDagaa knew was not enshrined in writing. In rejecting simplistic political criticisms of anthropology, Archie Mafeje observed that "the intellectual effort was a service to colonialism not because of crude suppositions about direct conspiracy or collusion but mainly because of the ontology of its thought categories."[106] Piot, himself an anthropologist, made a similar connection between the work of anthropologists and the needs of colonial rulers, arguing that "anthropology's complicity with imperial culture" was more in its "colonizing theoretical gaze" than in any practical service. A case in point is a study written by the famous German ethnographer Leo Frobenius after he passed through northern Togo in 1909. According to Piot, he placed the Kabre within a "timeless past" and described their culture as a "textual museum in which customs are neatly boxed, catalogued, and displayed." As the first "post-pacification document," Piot says that Frobenius's text "provided a type of close-up witnessing – indeed, of surveillance – for colonial administrators anxious about the management of their subjects. ... In thus naming, describing, cataloguing, and inventorying all that it could, Frobenius's text rendered Kabre knowable and nonmysterious."[107] The point is that what made the text useful was not that it was an anthropological presentation of the Kabre, but simply that it was a written representation that had succeeded in "putting people into writing."

A few years earlier, Captain Read, a colonial military officer, carried out a similar service for the British by putting the LoDagaa "into writing" for the first time in a systematic way. Although he was an untrained observer, his text had many of the same effects as Frobenius's much more professional work.[108] The assumptions and expectations that other British officers brought with them, many of which they also left behind, were shrouded in a cloak of universality because they were written. According to Wyatt MacGaffey, attempts to impose external distinctions and categories that were unsustainable in terms of indigenous usage and practices became the source of an "epistemological ethnocentrism" within the early anthropology of Africa.[109] I would argue that it was the practice of writing that produced this form of ethnocentrism, which, though not the product of "brazen bad faith," was still pernicious in its unintentional effects. What was true of anthropology was true of all other forms of writing. However, this does not mean that all that was written was somehow untrue.

Writing as Documents

This book emphasizes the role of writing in the encounter between the LoDagaa and the world on paper, but it is important to recognize that sometimes writing was just writing, something more prosaic than poetic, not a practice but a thing. Still, writing simply as writing, as in the creation of documents, is far from transparent, as all historians would attest. Besides applying the normal scrutiny that historians give any document, I have endeavored here to expose the biases of writing within these documents. The five main types of documents produced by the intersection of the world on paper with that of the LoDagaa were administrative, anthropological, missionary, indigenous, and judicial. The first four types are unexceptional, but judicial records, which I use extensively in the second half of this book, are more problematic because they record speech. They have also been neglected as historical sources until recently.[110] Historians in general have failed to appreciate the wider significance of local and everyday disputes within African societies, partly because when individual disputes came before colonial courts they were often recorded in annoyingly summary fashion.[111] Read in isolation, the resulting records often appear trivial and inconsequential. There is no denying that such material is, initially at least, difficult to understand even when records are relatively full accounts of what litigants said.[112] But when the surviving twenty-eight volumes of records of LoDagaa disputes, constituting over ten thousand pages, are read together against relevant administrative and anthropological material, they help us develop a ground-level perspective on aspects of LoDagaa social practices.[113] By subjecting these sources to careful scrutiny, it is possible to uncover the effect that writing has had on some of the experiences of the LoDagaa. However, writing about court records is not the same as writing directly about those experiences; and since this study focuses on the former rather than the latter, it is an exercise in cultural rather than social history.

Courts documented the nature of social disputes among the LoDagaa as well as the interface between indigenous culture and colonial and postcolonial rule. The purpose of colonial administration in the Northern Territories, in the absence of any substantive policy, was the maintenance of "law and order." In 1931 the most senior officer in the Northern Territories administration was prompted to reflect: "We have been here for a generation. During that time we have provided internal security; we provide staff for a few schools which the people have built; we provide to some extent for the health of the people and of their cattle; we seem to have done little else."[114] (At times the colonial government was more worried about cattle – especially inoculating them – than it was about the health of people.) In 1942 the District Commissioner of Lawra remarked: "The salient feature of object lessons in this country, however, appears to be that they are never learnt, except bad ones such as English legal procedure, tin roof architecture, and Christian intolerance."[115] Courts were one of the most fundamental and intimate intrusions into the lives of the LoDagaa. The colonial obsession with "law and order" is strongly reflected in the available sources: by far the largest body of archival material consists of court record books. From 1907 until 1932 there are the record books of the District Commissioner's Court. In 1932 colonial chiefs officially took over the hearing of disputes until 1960. Some of the record books survive from the Native Authority Courts (Native Courts) created in 1935, as do most of the record books from the Local Authority Courts (Local Courts) established in 1954. After 1960, all the record books survive from the District Magistrate's Court (District Court).

In dealing with court cases it is important not to regard them as individual events and not to accept the apparent causes documented in the records. Cases should be treated collectively as a series of "events of articulation"; we need to look for the broader indigenous issues that gave rise to individual disputes.[116] "In normal social life, people do not make verbal statements just to inform others of the notions they hold," observed Ladislav Holy and Milan Stuchlik. "Verbal statements are not made in a vacuum, but in specific social encounters, in situations involving other people."[117] In oral cultures it is often in encounters with outsiders, or in a public arena within the same culture, that verbal statements about implicit knowledge are made. Among the LoDagaa no such arena existed before the colonial period; there had been no moots for the airing of grievances, much less any official agents who resolved disputes. Therefore, colonial courts not only resolved disputes among the LoDagaa, but also acted as agencies for both articulating and producing indigenous knowledge. Judicial procedure forced upon litigants the task of constructing representations of their own interests and actions in a public arena. In several respects the effect of courts on oral cultures is directly analogous to that of anthropologists as described by Bourdieu: "Quite apart from the form which the questioning must take so as to elicit an ordered sequence of answers, everything about the inquiry relationship itself betrays the interrogator's 'theoretical' (i.e., 'non-practical') disposition and invites the interrogatee to adopt a quasi-theoretical attitude."[118] Anthropological questions resemble judicial procedures: the theoretical disposition of the interrogator mirrors the jural attitude of the court, and the interrogatee becomes the litigant. Although the methods of articulation were similar, there was one highly significant difference: knowledge elicited during court proceedings had direct and practical implications and was very likely to be contested by the other litigants or witnesses, whereas ethnographic information was most often abstract and given in an uncontested setting. Furthermore, anthropological accounts were coherent distillations of information, whereas representations made in the courts often lacked this imposed coherence and consistency. This makes court records invaluable tools for assessing the uncontested representations of both external and internal observers.

Court records also provide us with insights into one of colonial rule's most important interventions in African social life. Nowhere was the colonial presence more obvious or more intrusive than in the courts. Here, antagonistic litigants transformed social knowledge from the context of everyday life into isolated and contradictory representations. A close reading of LoDagaa disputes recorded by the courts often invites uncomfortable feelings of voyeurism. Matters that had once been private suddenly entered the unmediated world of the colonial public sphere.[119] Similarly, matters that had once been public, such as divination into the causes of death at funerals, were suppressed by the colonial state and became private, clandestine matters. When LoDagaa litigants came before the courts and made representations of indigenous knowledge, they did so in terms of categories of experience that the courts recognized.

The intrusion of observers was analogous to that of the courts. One observer, working in the late 1980s not far from where Fortes conducted his research in the 1930s, noted that researchers and informants never meet as equals because researcher, who could always leave, remained inextricably linked to a world beyond that of their informants: "For many African peoples ... whether or not to impart information to an outsider is a volatile existential concern relating to issues of autonomy and control."[120] Researchers often asked about things that are unarticulated within a culture – part of "habitus" (i.e., implicit knowledge), and so did courts; but in the colonial courts there was far less protection, and the cost of silence was high. Martin Chanock noted that litigation relating to conjugal unions "was one of the colonial government's most important interventions into African life." When disputes were brought before the colonial courts, intimate sexual and social relations between people were suddenly exposed in the most public fashion. Colonial justice brought about significant changes in how social space was defined. It involved "the intrusion of legality into the space of kinship and family" in that it moved "family law" from the private to the public sphere: "So family 'quarrels,' which had previously been settled within a lineage, became public 'cases' to be settled outside. And 'cases' implied 'courts,' and 'courts' implied 'laws.'"[121] In both the colonial and postcolonial periods, courts defined the relationship between the private sphere of litigant's lives and the public sphere of government regulation.

Law and Marriage

In order to understand the court records, we must abandon the normative or jural expectations that are implicit in most written cultures. This means seriously considering the idea that the LoDagaa had no laws; that is to say, they held no consensus of normative expectations, and none of their conflicting norms were articulated as rules. What they had instead were social practices.[122] An underlying premise of my discussion of court cases is that laws cannot be separated from written modes of communication and perception, and that their discovery within LoDagaa practices was the result of administrative convenience and indigenous adaptation. When we stress the differences between written and oral means of conflict resolution, we are able to avoid the inevitable confusion that arises when the analytical concepts of one society are applied to another. In particular, it is possible to avoid the thorny problem of defining law. Whatever meaning or significance we attach to laws, in written cultures they are articulated rules intended for regulating society. Social practices in oral cultures that provide a form of regulation are ascriptively deemed to be jural approximations of laws, even though they are not based on rules. In Lawra District in the twentieth century, laws and rules were manifestations of a foreign, written culture.[123]

The construction by colonial administrators of rules from selective research into LoDagaa culture disguised the conflict between indigenous dispositions and the epistemological and categorical assumptions of literate thought. This is equally true of the anthropological and ethnographic accounts that I draw from throughout this book. The Voltaic region, including all of northern Ghana and parts of surrounding states, was studied by some of the world's most famous anthropologists.[124] These accounts, although indispensable, suffer from the limitations of their method of production. When they were written, it was an unassailable tenet of anthropology that oral cultures must be studied through observation: this was considered a patently objective method for appropriating knowledge. This is no longer so, but through its emphasis upon observation, anthropology once presupposed that "looking at" was also a means of "reading" cultures, a technique of literate perception.[125] Methods of research and the categories of description were not questioned.[126]

Despite administrative assumptions and ethnographic descriptions to the contrary, the LoDagaa did not possess laws. However, in responding to the judicial structures that were imposed upon them, they feigned jural interpretations of social practices. In their dealings with the courts the LoDagaa were forced to adapt to literate procedures; in so doing, they adopted foreign concepts from literate categories of social representation. If one substitutes legal phenomena and ideas of marriage for religion and magic, many of Goody's observations on the importance of "restricted literacy" in northern Ghana are applicable to our understanding of the effects of the colonial courts:

> It cannot be unimportant to the intellectual life of any society that some of its most highly valued members [chiefs] are absorbing religious [legal] ideas, practising divinatory systems [judicial procedures] and acquiring mental [political] skills that have emerged in quite another context, at quite another time. These ideas always undergo a process of reinterpretation at the local level, but they can never be wholly absorbed into the particular culture to which they have been transmitted without at the same time modifying that culture in certain major respects.[127]

Colonial writing was not widely disseminated, but its cultural products were. These products – the particular ideologies implicit in colonial writing – affected issues of identity, sovereignty, legitimacy, legality, and patriarchy. The analogy may be continued. Goody, who was interested in the interchange of religious ideas and methods of magic (particularly Islamic), identified universal religions with writing and the book, specialization of functions, and structures of power. All these elements are found equally in legal forms and judicial procedures.

Whereas the physical colonization of the LoDagaa was concerted and based on coercion, the legal colonization of their culture, because it was internal and hidden, was a more subtle process. Chanock, writing of law as a form of colonialism in southern Africa, noted that "this has been a most important transformation: one, it might be said, of the hidden effects of colonialism, and one which continues to develop in the post-colonial era. Yet the nature of this transformation tends to be hidden behind the ideological screen of continuity implied in the notion of a customary law."[128] I have deliberately set out to analyze colonial rule and its subsequent metamorphosis into postcolonial government from a cultural perspective: as an attempt to subjugate and regulate an oral culture and force it within the conceptual framework of a literate society.

Writing was also at the heart of efforts to defend African societies against charges of "lawlessness," which was once thought to be a self-evident condition in non-literate societies. As Chanock has also observed: "The disciplinary development of the anthropology of law came from its role as a defender of the cultures of the world against an evolutionary stereotype which identified law as an achievement of advanced civilisations and which saw lawlessness as the defining mark of savage societies."[129] Instead of attacking this stereotype, anthropology accepted its basic contention – that laws were prerequisites of social organization – and sought to identify laws in oral societies, regardless of whether these descriptions accorded with indigenous perceptions. Another difficulty with the work of much of this anthropology was its origins in, and dependence on, the conceptual framework of Western jurisprudence. Vansina made the point that applying this type of conceptual predilection was similar to attempting to approach African languages from the perspective of Latin grammar.[130] Courts are, of course, a feature of many non-literate societies, but they do not necessarily subscribe to the procedure or the rhetoric of literate decision-making bodies, and need not pretend to be above politics. Law, or the often illusory idea of it, is a distinct ideological preoccupation of literate, rule-bound societies.[131]

Only by stressing the differences between methods of dispute settlement in oral and literate societies can we begin to understand the effects of colonial administration in a particular historical instance. "Whether or not precolonial communities had or did not have 'law' is to some extent a dull definitional debate," argued Chanock, "but the direction of the answer one gives to this question and the results of research on the colonial period are inextricably connected."[132] The concept of law is specifically a literate phenomenon. When we reject its application to an oral culture, on either comparative or evolutionist grounds, it is not to suggest that other forms of dispute settlement do not exist in these cultures; rather, we are saying that the alternative forms do exist that are particular to those cultures and that their uniqueness should not be erased by analogy to laws. When we adopt the perspective of orthodox legal anthropology, we ignore the changes that occur when oral methods are subjected to the constraints and influences of the rule of writing. Conversely, as Chanock notes: "By adopting a 'no-law' approach we enable ourselves more clearly to pick out the processes of law creation, of the imposition of ways of defining problems and solutions and the forcible molding of institutions, and, consequently, of responses."[133]

The main organizing paradigm of colonial law, and its related notion of patriarchy, was the idea of marriage. At the beginning of the last century many European observers, who were still in the firm grip of Victorian attitudes toward marriage, the position of women, and the evolution of societies, questioned the morality and sometimes the existence of African marriage. These observations assumed that marriage was a fundamental bulwark of civilization. In the Victorian mind, sexuality, morality, and legality were inextricably linked. The question of whether marriage was a social institution indigenous to Africa directly parallels that of whether African societies possessed law; both questions arose in the context of cultural contact precipitated by colonial rule. Much of the recent criticism of the anthropological study of law can be applied to the study of marriage. In the 1950s the question of whether marriage existed in Africa was a legal and, by extension, a moral issue. Questions regarding the ontology of law and marriage were and still are inextricably linked: "the law related to the family is often regarded as being quintessentially the area in which customary African law survived. ... Indeed in terms of the time which officials claim to have spent on it [marriage] was one of the colonial government's most important interventions into African life."[134] The interconnectedness of law and marriage was further underlined by the conceptual derivation of anthropological analyses: "Whatever other differences may be expressed concerning its analysis, the conjugal bond is almost universally regarded as a jurally constituted and contractually defined relationship, a view grounded firmly in the concepts of western jurisprudence."[135] In fact, so prevalent has this perspective been that John Comaroff referred to it as an "established jural orthodoxy."[136]

The debate of the 1950s was significant enough in its day to involve some of the most prominent anthropologists, jurists, and missionaries working in Africa, which resulted in the appearance of two important studies: Radcliffe-Brown and Forde's *African Systems of Kinship and Marriage* and Phillip's *Survey of African Marriage and Family Life*. In response to ethnocentric judicial decisions handed down in the settler societies of eastern and southern Africa during the first half of the century, liberal-minded Africanists wanted to establish that marriage was a category of "customary law" in all African societies.[137] Their arguments were the outcome of a movement that had led to the "conceptual normalization of marriage in comparative anthropology" in the 1920s through the 1940s, whereby order and clarity were imposed on indigenous practices in order to eliminate ambiguity and diversity.[138]

Even though moral language was explicitly absent from the discourse of the 1950s, moral concerns were strongly implicit. Marriage was not a neutral term; it was laden with moral and legal assumptions that were legacies of the nineteenth century. The Victorian ideology of marriage perceived sexuality not as a condition coincidental with marriage, but rather one to be repressed within it; marriage did not make sexuality moral, only less immoral, and susceptible to control.[139] Of course practice in Britain, witnessed by declining family size, abortion, infanticide, prostitution, and divorce in the second half of the nineteenth century, diverged from ideology, but the latter was to have a far greater impact on the understanding of African societies in the first half of the twentieth century.[140] Indeed, the divergence only reinforced the urgent need for the ideal over the actual.

The most important pronouncement of nineteenth-century anthropology on the subject was McLennan's *Primitive Marriage*, a text that clearly reflected the anxieties of late Victorian males – anxieties predicated on the evolutionary theory of primitive promiscuity. As Stocking has noted, for Victorian men marriage existed to control female sexuality so as to assure "'certainty of male parentage.'"[141] Just as law is inextricably bound up in literate expectations and assumptions, the notion of marriage has been mired in Western preoccupation over blood. Even Radcliffe-Brown, a fierce critic of McLennan's theories, argued at the middle of the last century that the primary purpose of marriage was to determine the legitimacy of children.[142]

In this application of a failed moral ideal to Africa, it is especially significant that those doing the moralizing were colonial administrators and missionary priests. That they were men is an obvious point, even though historians have not yet fully explored this reality.[143] In the Northern Territories, as was usually the case elsewhere in Africa, administrators were not just men, but bachelors like their Catholic missionary colleagues.[144] This meant they had little first-hand experience of the complexities and subtleties of "connubial" life even in British society, let alone the African societies over which they presided.[145] It also allowed them the latitude to construct and enforce ideals that were not possible in their own societies, just as missionaries hoped to find forms of religiosity no longer attainable in the increasingly secular metropole.

Conjugal unions in Africa differed from conjugal unions in Eurasia, of which Victorian marriage was but one particular form. Drawing a broad comparison between conjugal unions in North India and sub-Saharan Africa, Stanley Tambiah has observed that in Africa there was a separation of rights *in uxorem* from rights *in genetricem* that often permitted women some degree of sexual and social autonomy, with prestations serving mainly "to secure all children born to a married woman to her husband." In North India, the Eurasian counterpart to Africa in Tambiah's survey, sexual control over a wife and the biological (as opposed to social) legitimacy of children were far more important: "If the wife's 'purity' through exclusive access to her husband was assured, then the children's status could be directly linked to their father's. ... the husband's right *in uxorem* and *in genetricem* were seen as indissolubly merged." These differences were accordingly manifest in "ideological valuations" attached to conjugal practices in Africa and North India. In contrast to the elaborate and explicit emphasis on the formation and dissolution of unions in North India, Tambiah noted that "such ideological and ritual elaborations are conspicuously weak, even absent, as far as I can see, in the African ethnography concerning the conjugal state."[146]

Why does such ambiguity characterize conjugal relationships across much of Africa? Is it based on the lack of fit between anthropological and administrative categories and the social practices of many African societies? As Jane Guyer has pointed out, in Africa much more emphasis is placed on "initiation, achievement of membership in ritual societies, steps in age-grades, and, above all, the achievement of ancestorhood at death. What Eurasian traditions refer to as conjugality is not a key institution in Africa either as the architecture within which people live their sexual and reproductive lives or a channel though which property is transmitted."[147] However, as the ideology of marriage has gradually been applied to African societies, representations of practices have tended imitate that ideology. These themes are discussed in the final two chapters of this book.

Marriage, as both an institution and status, was the product of different economic and social conditions than those that prevailed in most African societies. Its use by anthropologists and historians as a descriptive and analytical device was the result of a liberal defense of African societies against the prevailing European characterizations of them as licentious and anarchic. In the evolutionary schema of late nineteenth-century students of jurisprudence and early twentieth-century founders of anthropology, marriage was the beginning of civilization. By continuing to deploy this culturally specific and highly ideological term, contemporary anthropologists and historians run the risk of reinforcing its ethnocentric assumptions. When we perceive marriage as the source of sexual control, morality, and social order, we are distorting the history of conjugal unions in Africa.[148] The uniqueness of conjugal arrangements in Africa has been obscured by a comparative methodology that ignores differences in favor of similarities.

Conclusion

What is the relevance of the history of writing and colonialism to the history of the LoDagaa? Does the focus of this book not make it a history of what observers of the LoDagaa have thought instead of a history of the LoDagaa? The answer is that this is the history of an encounter, a neglected but far from marginal process. What I have endeavored to understand from representations of the LoDagaa is how different observers (both external and internal) coped with reality, and what effects these coping strategies had when read back into the reality they represented. These effects were the outcome of subtle and complicated interactions between the colonial world on paper and the indigenous world of LoDagaa experience. The concepts of law and marriage were central to this process, as were those of tribe, chief, and God. The world on paper attempted to impose a form of historical consciousness on different aspects of LoDagaa culture – identity, politics, and religion – that was peculiar to the world on paper. They then used their historicism to place the sovereignty they had stolen from the LoDagaa in the past. Their attempted colonization of LoDagaa culture through foreign categories of knowledge and experience affected indigenous knowledge, morality, gender relations, and social reckoning. A large part of this interaction occurred through the courts and was controlled by the LoDagaa, who resisted the direct intrusion of writing into the world of experience, which was still ordered by speech, practice, and memory rather than writing, rules, and history. However, in some of their other dealings with the outside world the LoDagaa did not have the same latitude, and here the pernicious effects of writing as the embodiment of relations between their local lives and wider political, religious, economic, and social sources of power were felt more directly. The remainder of this book explores these varied and complex interactions between the world of experience and the world on paper.

PART ONE

Ways of Appropriating the LoDagaa

Chapter One

Maps and Narratives

I went to West Africa looking for a "tribe" called the "Lobi." Previous writers had reported the existence of such a people in the border regions of the Gold Coast and Haute-Volta. In fact I never found a group of people who replied to my question "We are Lobi."

Jack Goody, *The Social Organisation of the LoWiili*, 1956

In order to rule the LoDagaa it was necessary to appropriate them. The British did this in at least five different ways. The first was to locate them in space as part of the wider European project of exploring Africa – a project that had been under way for most of the nineteenth century. The second was to situate the LoDagaa in time. Just as the British saw the creation of the Northern Territories as a matter of defining boundaries and filling in blank spaces on their maps, so too did they see the LoDagaa past as uncharted and in need of being written. According to the conventions of the world on paper, until mediated by texts the LoDagaa did not inhabit any definitive space or time. Third, the British appropriated the LoDagaa in a much more literal way, through the physical expropriation of their labor. But the system of forced labor they created, and the patterns of labor migration they encouraged, relied in turn on further acts of domination, including a fourth strategy of appropriation: the clothing of LoDagaa "nudity" through the registration and inscription of "naked" bodies and the creation of a consumer demand for cloth. The desire to be clothed, to hide one's body from the gazing prejudice of outsiders, eventually proved to be sufficiently powerful that the LoDagaa sold their labor voluntarily; this provided the bridge between forced labor and labor migration. The fifth way the British attempted to appropriate the LoDagaa was through naming them. Because the British did not seize the land of the LoDagaa, even though they had conquered it, but expropriated their labor instead, naming the LoDagaa became more important than mapping their land; it was ultimately people they wanted to rule, not territory.

The world on paper was deeply implicated in all of these efforts to appropriate the LoDagaa. It created new and unprecedented forms of identity in terms of social and political communications over a much wider area than before; the extension of identity across time; the awareness of group identity through labor migration; the association of clothing with external legitimacy; and the assimilation of invented ethnonyms. Yet from the start, the fundamental problem the British faced was the difficulty of knowing who exactly it was that lived in the northwest corner of their new colonial acquisition. Until they could say who the people were who had fallen under their rule, they could not really rule them, let alone possess them and convert them into proper colonial subjects.

The elusiveness of ethnic identity among the LoDagaa was an immediate source of consternation to colonial administrators at the very beginning of their rule, but later served as the opportunity for creating a series of stereotypes that endured well after their departure. The strategies adopted to capture the LoDagaa on paper resulted in a series of images that accurately reflected colonial attitudes and assumptions while grossly distorting the cultural reality of these people. In the colony of Haute-Volta the French developed even more elaborate images of a group of people they called the *Lobi*. Most of these people were speakers of a language called *Lobi*, but many along the banks of the Black Volta were *Dagaare* speakers – people who are today generally thought of as belonging to one of several LoDagaa congeries, but who were often confused with the *Lobi* throughout the past century. Because of the greater difficulties the French had in overcoming their resistance, representations of the *Lobi* were both more sophisticated in their iconography and more explicitly ideological than the ones the British developed for the LoDagaa. The French popularized "fantastic tales" about the *Lobi* to justify their brutal tactics of repression and to act as object lessons for surrounding populations. The name *Lobi* came to evoke fear and trepidation. In the postcolonial state of Burkina Faso, even a generation after the departure of the French, they were still seen as "the last savages."[1] Male *Lobi* informants interviewed by Madeleine Père in the 1970s noted that this reputation for savagery was still so strong that it precluded the possibility of marrying women from outside, who refused even to visit the region. One informant explained that if a man married a woman from outside and lived all his life away from the region, "one day he will return here in secret to die, but neither his wife nor his children will come."[2]

Even though rarely used in the northwest of Ghana today, the term Lobi is still used in southern Ghana as a pejorative name for the people from this area.[3]

The British shared many of the French views about the *Lobi* and applied them to some of the *Dagaare*-speaking people east of the Black Volta, but eventually they considered most of the LoDagaa to be "Dagarti" – a term with its own set of images and negative connotations. The British proved to be less effective than the French in fashioning negative images of the "Dagarti," partly because they had less need to succeed: resistance to the British occupation of the east bank of the Black Volta was less successful and more short-lived. Even so, in their efforts to appropriate the LoDagaa on paper they did encounter difficulties, which though less formidable were as profound as the problems the French faced in asserting physical dominance over the *Lobi* on the ground. This chapter explores the first two forms of appropriation: maps and narratives. Labor, bodies, and names are discussed in the next chapter.

Mapping the LoDagaa

Until the middle of the twentieth century there was considerable confusion in the appellations used by colonial administrators and ethnographers to refer to the inhabitants of both banks of the middle section of the Black Volta. The confusion had arisen because of the absence of any terms of self-designation among these people; this situation was compounded by the license it afforded to colonial observers to use different and often contradictory names.[4] At the beginning of colonial rule the British referred to the inhabitants of the northwest corner of the Northern Territories as the Lobi and the Dagarti. By 1905 it was reported that these two "tribes" were not as discrete as had been assumed, and a new designation was devised, Lobi-Dagarti, to refer to people of "mixed race."[5] Despite inconsistencies in usage over subsequent years, these names continued in use without question until 1913, when British officers were visited by their French counterparts from across the Black Volta, and, as the report below captures, "a general discussion ensued between the French and English as to the people of Lorha":

> The French held that they were not Lobis at all and the English held that they were. The French interpreter was called up who is a French Lobi and the English interpreter, an English Lobi, nephew of the chief [of Lawra]. They were told to speak to each other but were unable to do so, the language being not only a different dialect, but a totally different language, the interpreters simply shaking their hands at each other. The French call their people opposite Lorha BIRIFONS, these are the same people as our Lobis and have the same language. Our interpreter admitted that our people were BIRIFONS much to the delight of the French officer who said that we could now see how it was we tamed these people so

> easily, as he can never get his people to do anything but fight and murder each other. There is a large town here called BIRIFO and the people here now declare that they are Lobis, but of a different tribe. Whilst the French are called Lobi WULESSI, our people are termed Lobi BIRIFO.[6]

The exchange was extremely confusing for the British, in part because their administrative intelligence was so poor. The confusion was, however, understandable, considering the ethnographic situation, which was one of the most complicated and bewildering in all of ethnographic literature. Unraveling this confusion is a difficult task, but necessary to understanding the LoDagaa encounter with the world on paper, and their colonization.

The British continued using the terms Lobi and Dagarti for administrative purposes after this meeting, but a few exacting officers began employing the apparently more precise designations of the French. Henri Labouret, a French colonial officer, used the latter terms in his survey of the people of the adjoining French colony, which was published in 1931 and became the standard ethnographic account for the region.[7] However, R.S. Rattray, an anthropologist in the British colonial service, persisted in using the term Lobi in his 1932 survey of the peoples of Lawra District, even though he noted that the proper term was "Lober." These were *Dagaare*, not *Lobi*, speakers. Lobi was the Anglicized form of Loberu, the dialect of *Dagaare* spoken along the eastern bank of the Black Volta, as well as the term used to refer to speakers of *Lobi* to the west of the river.[8] (To avoid unnecessary confusion, I have italicized the term *Lobi* whenever it is used to refer to *Lobi*-speaking people or their language; Lobi, unitalicized, refers to speakers of a dialect of *Dagaare*. Similarly, I have italicized *Dagaare*, the language spoken by the LoDagaa, in order to avoid confusion with either Dagara or Dagarti.)

In a 1954 report to the Colonial Office, Goody devised a naming system to simplify the interminable complications to which this plurality of designations gave rise.[9] The names that Goody attempted to systematize in the 1950s were very similar to those identified by officers in the 1910s. However, the term LoDagaa, a neologism, emerged as an all-encompassing sobriquet. Figure 1 places this nomenclature within the context of earlier and later systems. It was predicated on two lexical referents – *Lo* generally indicating things west and *Dagaa* things east – used by those people designated as LoDagaa to refer to cultural and social similarities among, and differences between, themselves. According to Goody, this form of oppositional identification did not constitute consciousness of self or group identity, nor were the criteria for their indigenous manipulation merely directional. Depending on the context, these terms might have been used to designate a preferred rather than an actual location within

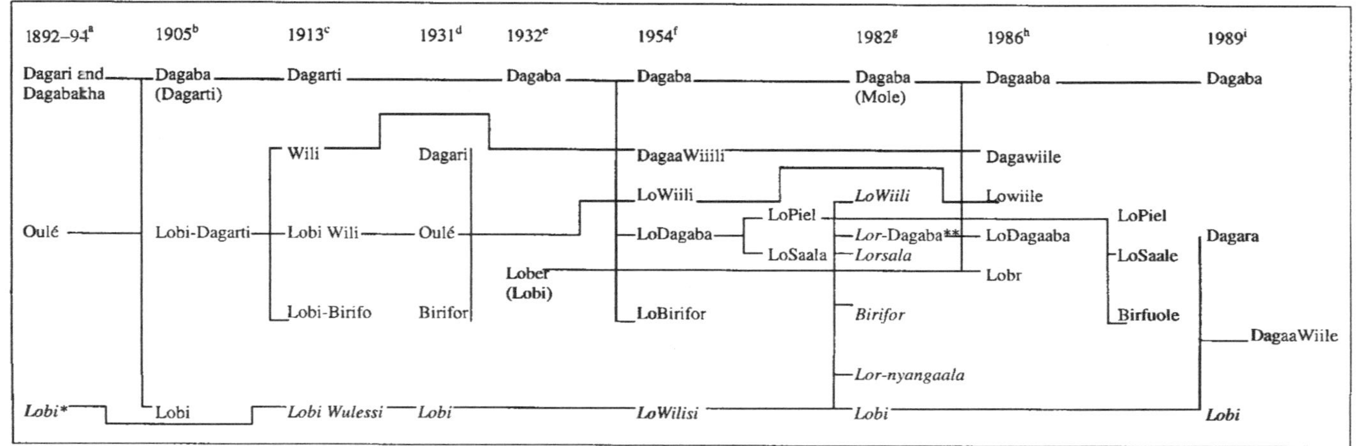

Sources:

[a] Binger 1892; George Ekem Ferguson (1894) in Arhin 1974.
[b] NAG ADM 56/1/50, Reports on Tours of Inspection North West Province, March–May 1905.
[c] NAG ADM 61/5/1, Lawra District Record Book, 6 (11 October 1913).
[d] Labouret 1931.
[e] Rattray 1932.
[f] Goody 1954.
[g] Tuurey 1982.
[h] Archbishop Peter Dery (1984) cited in Angsotinge 1986.
[i] Der 1989.
*Italics indicate that these were deemed to be people linguistically and culturally separate from the LoDagaa.
**Allegedly a linguistic and cultural hybrid of the *Lobi* and Dagaba.

Figure 1. Designations of LoDagaa Congeries, 1892–1989

different cultural and social spaces. The referents to which one or the other term might have been applied were many and varied: conjugal payments, xylophones, out-standing disputes, dancing, inheritance of movable wealth, labial adornments, and dialect.[10]

The constituent designations that Goody identified, although ethnographically sound and at times corresponding to indigenous criteria, lacked the contextual fluidity with which groups recognized differences or similarities.[11] Furthermore, Goody's system tended to ignore the complications that half a century of colonial rule had bequeathed. By this time, in their dealings with external agencies, the inhabitants of Lawra District had come to identify themselves with one or the other of the predominant administrative names, Lobi or Dagarti.[12] Collectively, the different cultural and social spheres that Goody identified were given the name LoDagaa in recognition of the broader cultural and social similarities between them, particularly the use of a common language, *Dagaare*. Map 2 shows the distribution of the people designated as being LoDagaa as of the middle of the twentieth century.

Goody's approach to this extremely complicated ethnographic situation had its critics, particularly Edmund Leach, a fellow anthropologist, who alleged somewhat unjustly that Goody's differentiation between various LoDagaa congeries was simply "the way that Dr. Goody has chosen to describe the fact that his field notes from two neighbouring communities show some curious discrepancies."[13] The term LoDagaa has been more of a problem for indigenous academics and religious leaders, who have taken particular exception to the ethnographic fragmentation that Goody identified and emphasized. At times Goody has actually been blamed for the complexity of the ethnographic picture; in one instance it was argued that the complexity Goody had observed was belied by a fundamental sense of unity between various congeries that was greater "than meets the eye of an outside observer."[14] Since the early 1980s members of the local Catholic elite have tried hard to define and fix a single ethnonym for all those whom Goody designated as LoDagaa. Two different names have emerged, Dagara and Dagaba (or Dagaaba), and with them different sets of associated meanings (a point to which we will return below).[15] Yet these names are no less arbitrary, and certainly far less inclusive, than the term LoDagaa, despite claims that they are more authentic; indeed, they are still not used as terms of reference by the people designated as Dagara or Dagaaba.[16] I have used the term LoDagaa for three reasons: to stress the invented nature of identity; to highlight the relationship between these people and the British, who ultimately were responsible for the term LoDagaa; and to avoid intruding upon local cultural disputes.[17]

The use of invented ethnonyms, whether colonial, ethnographic, or autoethnographic, might be excused as a necessary mnemonic device, given the absence of fixed indigenous alternatives, were it not that these terms have been far from neutral. Names were strategies for appropriating the LoDagaa and for reducing the three-dimensional complexity of their world to the two-dimensional reality of the world on paper. For that reason it is important to explain how the LoDagaa came to be an object of external consciousness and ascribed identities. To this end, we must relate how these people came to be located on paper. In this particular context the two tasks, naming and mapping, were closely related. "It is significant," wrote Bourdieu in his critique of objectivism, "that 'culture' is sometimes described as a *map*; it is the analogy which occurs to an outsider who has to find his way around in a foreign landscape and who compensates for his lack of practical mastery, the prerogative of the native, by use of a model of all possible routes."[18] It should hardly be surprising, then, that the intrusion of the external world upon the relatively isolated experiences of these people began with a cartographical inquiry.

In 1888 a French colonial officer, Louis Gustave Binger, conducted a voyage of exploration into an area of the West African savanna that had not yet been appropriated by European consciousness. The project was under the direction of the French undersecretary for the colonies, so the intelligence it was to provide had practical implications for the rivalry between competing colonial powers. But Binger admitted to a more personal motivation for making such a lengthy, arduous, and solitary journey. He began the account of his travels as follows:

> Little by little, I played with the dream of filling in one of the large blank spaces on the map of Africa. To appease a public that abhors empty spaces, and based on traditional legends and indigenous testimony that are often difficult to understand or interpret, cartographers had randomly scattered several indeterminate waterways, hypothetical mountains, and names of states and peoples between the two arms of the Niger and the Gulf of Guinea that are as imprecise as memories of antiquity. It is that unexplored land, at the heart of this unknown, that I wanted to penetrate.[19]

This was the same "blank space of delightful mystery" that Conrad's Marlow had meditated upon as a child.[20] However, as Simon Ryan has argued with regard to antipodean cartography, such spaces should not be seen as innocent reflections of "gaps in European knowledge," but rather the result of acts of erasure that wiped away indigenous knowledge "in preparation for the projec-

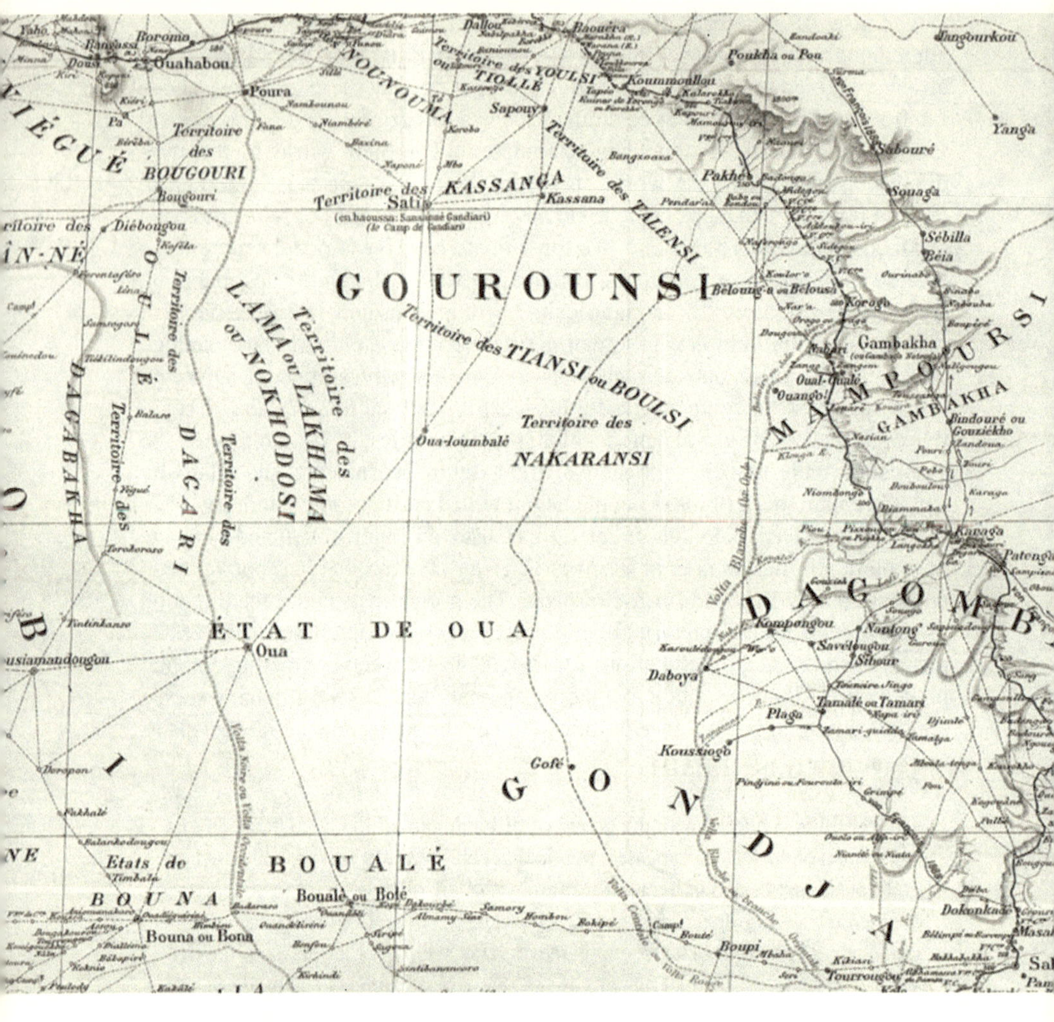

Map 3. Detail of “Carte de Haut-Niger au golfe de Guinée par les pays de Kong et le Mossi.” From Binger, *Du Niger au golfe de Guinée* (1892).

tion and subsequent emplacement of a new order." Geography became a text; the blank page "intimate[d] that there has been no previous history," and offered space for those in the world on paper to impose one.[21]

Binger's route is as notable for the areas it left uncharted as for the details it supplied. His journey from Kong through Mossi, Mamprusi, Dagomba, and Gonja, and back to Kong, circumscribed the area of the Voltaic region that was least amenable to being reduced to writing (see Map 3). Binger designated the area as "Gourounsi." The fact that he gave any names at all to the area enclosed by his route seems to have been the product of his own *horror vacui*, as these designations proceeded from neither direct experience nor even primary informants. At Oual-Oualé he obtained his intelligence of the "blank space" from two Dagomba informants. They told him of a heterogeneous mix of people called the Gourounsi (Gurensi), who lived in the area between the Mamprusi, the Dagomba, the Gonja, and the Wala. Because they did not live in hierarchical states like their neighbors, Binger assumed that they had been forced into the bush by "the more advanced people surrounding them."[22] The paucity of information on this area's inhabitants suggested that they were peripheral to the surrounding societies. Binger attributed their apparent lack of political development to the constraining effects of neighboring states. He also observed, following his own difficulties crossing the northeastern corner of this region, that "The blacks themselves, both traders and others, speak only with fear of Gourounsi and its inhabitants."[23] For subsequent observers, the lack of political authority among these politically decentralized societies would be less threatening but also more problematic. States provided boundaries and structures both within societies, through political hierarchy, and between societies, through territorial sovereignty. Stateless societies were difficult to rule simply because of their amorphousness.

In this area farthest removed from his direct experience and that of his informants, Binger's information became extremely sketchy. To the very west of the Gourounsi area, he identified three smaller subgroupings between the Black Volta and the *Lobi*: "Oulé," "Dagari," and "Dagabakha." He speculated that the last two were the same people.[24]

It was not until 1894 that a representative of European interests actually came into contact with the LoDagaa. The British had dispatched George Ekem Ferguson, the renowned Fante from the Gold Coast who had already built a distinguished career as an officer in the colonial service, to conclude treaties with, among other states, Bole, Bouna, and Wa. The mission was a response to concerns over possible French claims following the publication of Binger's account of the neighboring territories and people in 1892. By dint of being the first European representative to visit Bouna and Wa, which were believed to exercise sovereignty over the *Lobi* and Dagarti respectively, Ferguson's intelligence secured and reinforced the impression that the region had been successfully appropriated and apprehended.[25] However, it was not until 1905 that a colonial officer, Captain Read, conducted the first thorough reconnaissance of Lawra District. He distinguished a series of "English" Lobi settlements along the eastern bank of the Black Volta extending no more than twenty miles back from the river. Although they had refused to obey chiefs where the administration had appointed them, he claimed that he found the Lobi more "truthful" than any other "natives" with whom he had dealt – an indirect reference to the other ethnic groupings he thought he had identified. His descriptions of these other groups revealed an essentialist understanding of presumed cultural distinctions and ostensible pyschological differences:

> Along the Lobi or Western boundary the Dagarba, or Dagarti as he is generally mis-called, are intermixed with the Lobis and the same description applies equally to both. At Tizza, Duri and Irimon [Eremon] the inhabitants are Lobi-Dagarti, but at Bazim they are pure Dagarti, this intermixing is also noticeable in other places to the south. They are uncivilised and turbulent in the extreme on the west, but an improvement is made towards the centre and east where there are many Mahomedan settlements. Except in the latter places the men are generally naked and invariably armed with bows and arrows.[26]

This highly colonial account of differences between Lobi and Dagarti articulated the district spatially in the absence of any other readily observable criteria. It served not only as a device for appropriating the subject people, but also as a means of exercising control by creating rivalries between settlements. For example, while visiting the settlement of Nandaw Wala in 1906, the district commissioner lectured the people on the need to accept colonial rule, threatening that unless they cooperated the Dagarti would "disappear from the map," as the country would be handed over to chiefs from other "tribes." He added, by way of taunt more than threat, that "whereas the Fra-Fras and Lobis had been our trouble in the N.T.'s they had now become sensible and were going ahead, whilst, they, the Dagartis, made no progress and were as foolish as ever, that soon amongst the people the term Wa Wa (fool) and Dagarti would be synonymous. This insulting method of address seems to touch their pride, and is, I am sure, beneficial."[27]

In 1918 another officer noted that the Lobi were more "manly" than the Dagarti, and that they worked harder and produced more powerful and respected chiefs. The following year the chief of Lawra told a delegation of Dagarti chiefs touring his area that even though he knew they regarded the Lobi as "bush meat," "they [the Dagarti] had no roads or RH's [resthouses] like those in his country, nor had their chiefs any power."[28] By the early 1920s, active resistance to colonial rule had been suppressed for some time, and the Lobi were favorably reappraised, in terms of their record as workers and subjects rather than as warriors and rebels.[29] In part this was due to the proximity of the Lobi to Lawra, and the greater familiarity the administration had with them as a result.[30] But it was also due to the British strategy of using ethnic rivalries to bring the Dagarti, who were seen as representing the "local Bolshevist element against the Government and law and order," into closer step with colonial rule.[31] Nevertheless, the colonial administration had an interest in perpetuating the image of the Lobi as violent and primitive, even after they had been "pacified," as a means of justifying colonial conquest and of demonstrating one of its successes.

The chief of Lawra's words to his Dagarti guests make it clear that these negative ideas about the name Lobi had already been internalized by the inhabitants of the district by the late 1910s, when military recruits from the First World War were returning home with perceptions they had acquired while in the south. One recruit told the chief of Gengenkpe, a nominally Lobi settlement, "that he smelt like a cow and that he was a bush meat who had never been out of his own country."[32] Although the word Dagarti had negative connotations outside the district, the word Lobi was even more prejudicial and remained a term of derision, implying primitiveness and savagery.

To a great extent, colonial administrators differentiated the people of the district according to their reactions to colonial rule rather than actual cultural differences. Colonial administrators obviously preferred to see reactions to their rule as the product of ethnicity rather than experiences of that rule; otherwise, they might have had to question the legitimacy (or at least the appropriateness) of their colonial project. For them, crude and rough characterizations were more satisfactory explanations for their uneven success at asserting authority. It meant they did not have to look harder for the real reasons their authority was being resisted.

Administrators were also driven to use differentiating characterizations of people out of frustration at their inability to gather more concrete knowledge of the district. The spatial arrangements of the district were gradually ordered on paper, with the construction of roads and the naming of settlements, but this administrative ordering did not correspond with the spatial realities of human habitation and movement. There was a rather consistent complaint that the physical space of the district was difficult to articulate. In 1905 Read noted that there were over three hundred Dagarti "towns" (or areas of settlement), but countless Lobi "villages," which were "intermixed," making it "very difficult to ascertain the boundaries of villages and the names of them."[33]

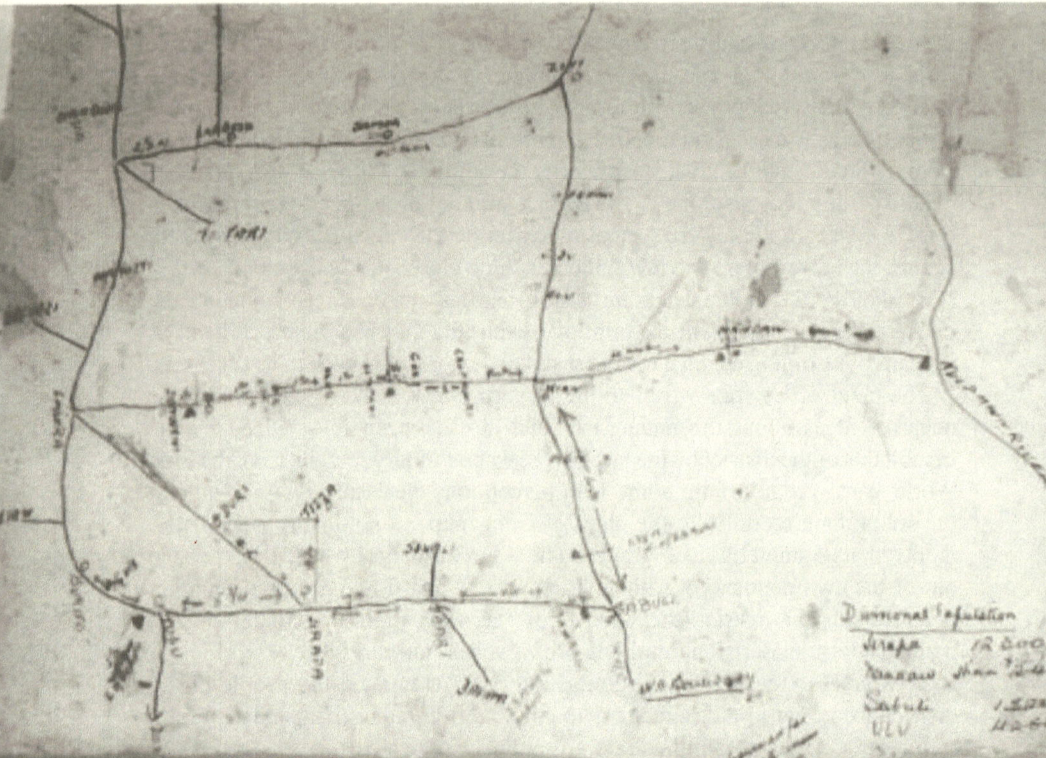

Map 4. Lawra District, *c.* 1911 (NAG ADM 61/5/1, Lawra District Record Book, insert). Note the absence of any recorded information away from the grid network of the roads. The only deviations are the diagonal road from Lawra to Jirapa, the triangulation of Duri-Tizza-Jirapa, and a few branch roads.

The so-called Lobi villages were even less amenable to demarcation because they were smaller and more dispersed, which inspired another administrator to remark two years later that "it is practically impossible to find out the name of a village as they all run into one another." Colonial roads passed through "nothing but farms and compounds scattered everywhere."[34] Forty years later, Goody noted that there were few "marked discontinuities," and that compounds were "scattered unevenly across the landscape in such a way that it is difficult to tell where one settlement ends and the next begins."[35] Certainly, early descriptions of this area stressed how specific or particular the human geography was. Writing of the difficult administrative conditions encountered among "the tribes of the *Lobi* family" in the adjoining French colony, Labouret stated: "The number of so-called villages, being simply named and inhabited spaces, is 1,252. They are made up of ... some isolated farms built at random on fertile earth. ... [All of this] shows how fragmented society is in this land and why the French administration, which found nothing more than a confusion of individual interests when it first arrived, had great difficulty in asserting its authority for some time."[36]

The first map of the Lawra District (Map 4), dating from around 1911, was exclusively a record of the embryonic road network that the administration had constructed using requisitioned labor. The second district map (Map 5), from around 1927, was seemingly more complete; the main additions were crayoned tribal names and the locations of resthouses, which were eagerly constructed by colonial chiefs for the district commissioner. At one time there were at least twenty-eight resthouses in Lawra District, not counting those which had been overrun by termites and decay. As Martin Staniland has remarked, "there was a universal passion for resthouse building" among all administrators in the Northern Territories: "If independence had been delayed for another ten or fifteen years, the entire surface of the N.T. would have been covered with resthouses, chicken-runs, and half-finished bridges."[37] Map 5, though an improvement over Map 4, is remarkably amateurish, but what is most significant to note here is that detail and exactitude were far less important than creating the illusion that the district had been physically registered on paper, with ethnonyms filling in the blank spaces between the roads.

The additions and corrections on Map 5 reflected the growing accumulation of knowledge as well as attempts to appropriate the entire space of the district. What is *not* apparent is that this more complicated grid in no way reflected the pattern of indigenous footpaths. There was still a strong divergence between the spatial ordering that administrators thought they had created and the indigenous definition and use of space. Away from the grid of roads constructed during the colonial period (see Map 1) was a complex web of indigenous footpaths radiating from dozens upon dozens of settlements located far from any roads. Human habitation remained dispersed or scattered. The hundreds of intersecting footpaths represented spatial arrangements independent of those shown on earlier and later official maps.

History and Identity

The LoDagaa did not possess a concept of history in any literal, discursive sense, just as they did not have roads. In the absence of a single historical

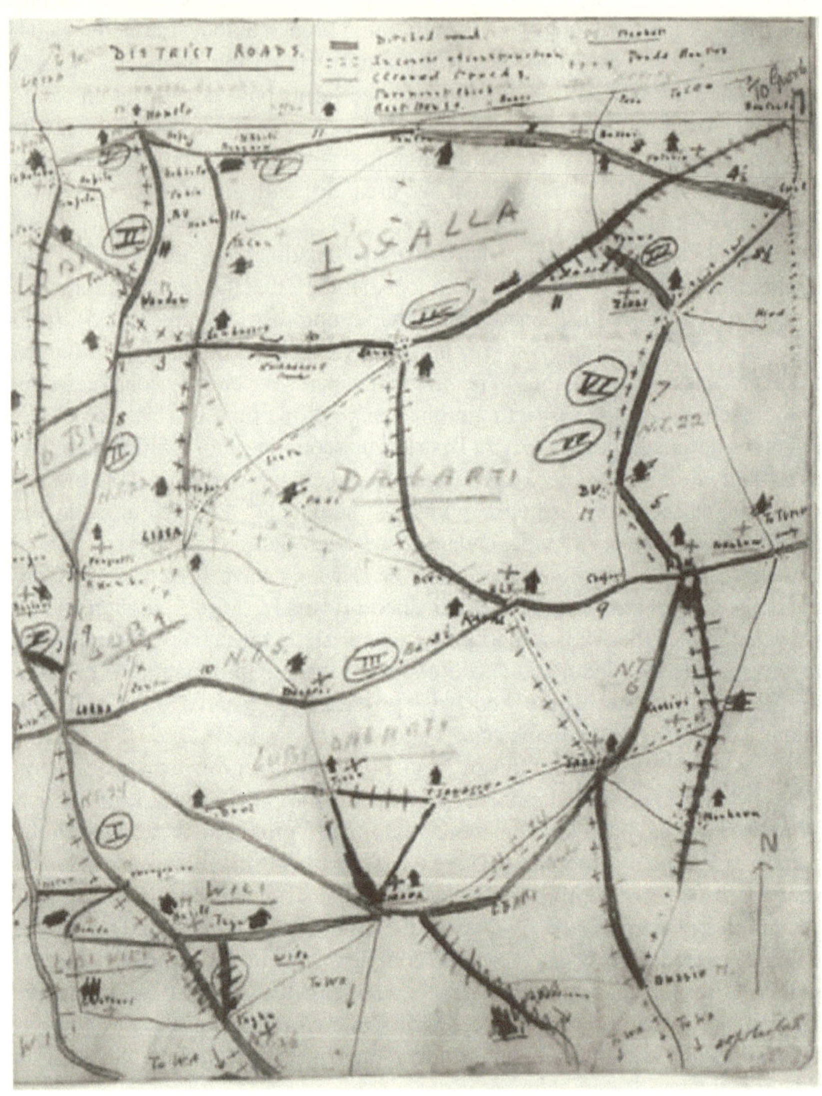

Map 5. Lawra District, *c.* 1927 (NAG ADM 61/5/11, Lawra District Record Book, 428).

narrative, or even any definite historical traditions, observers in the colonial period made several false assumptions about the precolonial experience of the LoDagaa; especially, they exaggerated the separation between decentralized and hierarchical political formations.[38] The LoDagaa were considered to be savages, and to be isolated both from surrounding states and from time itself – perceptions that ignored the network of paths that had long connected the LoDagaa with one another and surrounding societies. The rigid divide between states and "stateless" people ignores interactions between such groups and refuses to acknowledge other forms of authority, and so is historically untenable and conceptually confused.[39] The histories of these groups were interrelated. The boundaries of the states of the middle Volta basin were imprecise and shifting, just as were the intervening settlements of politically decentralized peoples. Although clear evidence of interaction between these different groups does not often survive, fragmentary evidence suggests that the conceptual dichotomy between political forms distorts the precolonial patterns of history in this region. The LoDagaa belonged to a wider cultural and historical sphere, most immediately that of the middle Volta basin.

The lack of fixed identities among the LoDagaa congeries was a direct result of the patterns of their precolonial history. There was a strong degree of cultural and linguistic affinity between congeries, which recognized their common kinship through the distribution of patriclans over an even wider region; however, effective political formations were limited to localized households.[40] The distribution of settlements at the end of the nineteenth century was the result of isolated and sporadic migrations that were already under way in the second half of the seventeenth century. Evidence of these migrations is extremely fragmentary, and the various authors who have grappled with this distant past have only agreed on the broadest chronology.[41] The migrations were uncoordinated and relatively local, and often involved either the assimilation of the indigenous inhabitants of the area entered or the adoption of the prevailing culture, both of which obscured cultural boundaries. Another factor militating against any clear historical understanding of these migrations was their many causes. External threats or pressures precipitated some; others were the result of internal social tensions associated with the breakup of households. Less dramatically, but perhaps even more commonly, migrations were piecemeal, and had the goal of finding better land for farming. All of these factors make historical reconstruction especially difficult.

It was on quite another level that the world on paper attempted to make sense of the LoDagaa past, through efforts to establish a single narrative that would merge these many small and incremental events into a coherent whole. This project involved treating the LoDagaa culture as a single historical entity.

Language, oral traditions, and cowry shells all yielded clues in this search for origins, a search that reflected the forensic and teleological urge of the literate narrative. But this evidence is extremely misleading because of what is left out.

The language spoken by the LoDagaa came from east of the White Volta, and traditions suggest there were one or two migrations at some point in the seventeenth century, and cowry shells tell us that the LoDagaa economies were not isolated from neighboring societies; but none of these things mean that a single historical narrative exists for us to retrieve. The origins of the language spoken by the LoDagaa do not tell us about the physical origins of its speakers, which must have been different because of the effects of intermarriage and assimilation.[42] A single migratory jump from the vicinity of the White Volta to that of the Black Volta by a small number of people, as suggested by traditions, is plausible; however, the spread of language over a similar distance could only have occurred as the result of a much more significant demographic shift, and the movement of so many people would have undoubtedly left a lasting tradition unless it had taken place over an extended time through incremental forays to the west.[43] Finally, the existence of cowry shells as a currency among the LoDagaa raises more questions than it answers. Nevertheless, several researchers one after the next have tried to delineate a single narrative of LoDagaa origins.

We do know that well before the second half of the last millennium, in the middle of the West African savanna, there was a zone of remarkable cultural homogeneity that ethnographers have identified as the Voltaic region.[44] It is unlikely that the agriculturists of this region experienced any major foreign intrusions before the fifteenth century, but thereafter various conquerors established states among these decentralized or acephalous societies. Some autochthones were incorporated within these new structures; others congregated in the areas between states. Over succeeding centuries more and more territory was occupied by centralized polities, yet a substantial number of people remained free of foreign domination until the Voltaic zone was partitioned between rival colonial interests at the end of the nineteenth century.

The arbitrary boundaries of colonial administration served to obscure cultural contiguity and historical continuity across this wider region. The clearest marker of this was language. The dialects spoken by the constituent LoDagaa congeries – dialects that made up *Dagaare* – did not constitute an autonomous language; rather, they were a dislocated cluster of dialects belonging to a wider language group, Mole-Dagbane. The languages and dialects of this group were spoken mainly to the east of the White Volta. By the beginning of this century the western Mole-Dagbane speakers, the largest group of which were the LoDagaa, had become separated from their vastly more numerous eastern neighbors by Grusi-speaking people, most notably the Sisala.[45] Languages very similar to *Dagaare* were spoken by the Tallensi, Builsa, Kusasi, Nankanni, and Kassena, whose social order was not dominated by states, as well as by the Mamprusi, Dagomba, and Nanumba, all of whom lived in states.

The traditions of the Mamprusi and Dagomba relate that a founding horsemen first arrived among the Kusasi around the beginning of the fifteenth century; after conquering the autochthones, this interloper and his followers adopted their language through intermarriage.[46] It is most likely that some of the distant ancestors of the LoDagaa were displaced by the creation of Dagbon, and that this set in motion a period of westerly migration by groups of Mole-Dagbane speakers from the vicinity of the White Volta to that of the Black Volta.[47] It is also possible that some LoDagaa were the descendants of a westerly movement of Dagomba separatists.[48] Dagomba and Wala traditions refer to two waves of migration, the first leading to settlement and incorporation rather than conquest and dynastic rule, and the second to the founding of a state claiming a limited form of sovereignty over the earlier migrants.[49] At best, these traditions of origin derived from external sources trace the precolonial history of the LoDagaa back to the period of the Dagomba migration that resulted in the formation of Wa, around 1650.[50] Around the time that immigrant households from Dagbon were establishing themselves at Wa, an equally significant drama was unfolding in the region – the formation of the Gonja state. The Gonja state was not fully established until the middle of the seventeenth century, at which time people called "Lubi" and "Daghati" were reported to be traveling to the trading center of Daboya in order to purchase salt.[51]

By the end of the seventeenth century all of the major historical entities that were to come under British colonial rule two hundred years later, as parts of the Northern Territories, were roughly in place in the middle Volta basin. From this time onward the region was increasingly influenced by the northward expansion of the Asante – a development that gravely threatened the savanna states and adversely affected the politically decentralized peoples outside their sovereignty. This geopolitical shift was the result of the increasing importance of coastal trade. In 1732 Gonja was seriously compromised by a sustained campaign of expansion launched by the Asante; in the dry season of 1744–45, Asante musketeers attacked Dagbon and brought about its voluntary submission.[52] We do not know whether these events had a direct bearing on the LoDagaa, as they predate any definite, indigenous traditions of migration. Labouret, who collected fragments of the history of these migrations in the early part of this century, stated that the *Lobi*-speaking inhabitants of what was to become Lawra District had crossed the Black Volta in search of new lands to the west sometime around 1770; of their movement prior to this, nothing was recollected.[53]

If little is known about the political and social history of the LoDagaa before the twentieth century, even less is known about their economy, although their use of cowry shells as a medium of exchange at the end of the nineteenth century permits some limited speculation. How and when these shells entered the LoDagaa economy remains a singular mystery.[54] In the absence of any gold (as among the *Lobi* to the west), salt (which was controlled by Gonja from Daboya), or other material resources of sufficient value to generate substantial reserves of cowries, the strongest hypothesis would appear to be that at some point in the past, people had been sold in order to acquire cowries. This accords with Françoise Héretier's study of cowries among the Samo of Burkina Faso and Charles Piot's study of wealth among the Kabre of northern Togo (both falling within the wider Voltaic region);[55] however, there is no direct evidence to support such a theory among the LoDagaa. Slavery certainly existed among the LoDagaa at the end of the nineteenth century, but not on a scale to suggest it had ever been prevalent enough to account for the large number of cowries in circulation at the start of the twentieth century. It is reasonable to assume that cowries had long been a feature of the economy of the LoDagaa, since the disruptive events of the nineteenth century would not have been conducive to protracted trade with external communities. Furthermore, the cowry was so thoroughly integrated into LoDagaa culture by the turn of the last century that it must have been used for a considerable time before this.[56]

It is known that the cowry had for a long time been a unit of exchange throughout Sudanic trade networks, particularly within the Niger Bend, to the north of the Voltaic region. By the sixteenth century, cowries, which entered the Sudan across the Sahara, had permeated the Sudanic states.[57] By the beginning of the nineteenth century the Sudanic cowry economy had integrated large areas of the savanna.[58] Cowries had for many years been a feature of trade along the Guinea coast, but it was not until the late eighteenth century that the use of cowries as a medium of exchange spread significantly inland, reaching the Volta basin in the second half of the nineteenth century.[59] Cowries that spread from the Sudan differed from those of the coast; the former originated in the Maldives and were lighter and somewhat smaller than the latter, which were imported from Zanzibar. In 1908 a colonial officer observed that in Lawra District loads of twenty thousand cowries could be carried comfortably, suggesting that they were still predominantly of the Maldives variety, which had emanated from the north.[60] Since that time, cowries of the coastal variety have entered the LoDagaa economy, thereby obscuring precolonial concentrations.[61] What we can suggest from our current knowledge of cowries in the region is that sometime between the seventeenth and eighteenth centuries, somewhere between the White and Black Volta rivers, the LoDagaa acquired a large number of cowries. Establishing how, when, and where the cowries were acquired is important to our understanding of the economic history of the Voltaic region, but perhaps not as important as what the existence of these shells tells us about the wider political history of the region.

Though their point of entry is obscure, the existence of cowries constitutes irrefutable evidence of interaction – largely before the nineteenth century – between the LoDagaa and the trading networks of the region. The LoDagaa were not isolated communities incapable of relations with outsiders, as was commonly asserted in colonial descriptions of LoDagaa politics (as Chapter 3 details). Rather, their economic interaction with trading networks and physical proximity to states suggest that LoDagaa "statelessness" had to have been the result of deliberate acts intended to maintain radical forms of political autonomy. No doubt the states of the middle Volta basin were more powerful in some respects than the politically decentralized societies to their periphery; but the persistence of "stateless" groups indicates that surrounding states had only a limited ability to conquer and incorporate them. Decentralized societies were historical forces in themselves, capable of exerting a powerful influence on their larger, politically centralized neighbors. States were themselves susceptible to fissionary tendencies and vulnerable to demographic pressures. According to Yves Person, the *Lobi*, after they began crossing the Black Volta at the beginning of the eighteenth century, were responsible for "an extraordinary upheaval" over the next century that forced the rulers of Bouna to concede territory to them. Later claims by rulers of Bouna to the French that they held sovereignty over the *Lobi* were illusory.[62]

Similarly, the LoDagaa who settled near Wa were never entirely integrated into that state, despite claims made to Ferguson. Although a significant number of LoDagaa had left the area of Wa by the middle of the nineteenth century, a sizeable proportion remained. The relations between the LoDagaa who inhabited the limited areas of Wala sovereignty had with that state have never been very clear, but a 1934 colonial memorandum dealing with the commutation of tribute stated that the "traditional" sovereignty of the Wa Naa had actually been extended through colonial rule: "Prior to their inclusion in the Wala kingdom, neither the Dagarti, the Issalla nor the Lobi recognised any authority other than that of the head of the family, or Tindana to whom they paid religious dues. But the position of the chief is now well established among them."[63] According to Person, Wa had never been a powerful state, simply because it was surrounded by "ungovernable masses."[64]

There is no direct evidence to suggest that from the mid-eighteenth to the mid-nineteenth century the region inhabited by the LoDagaa was subject to marauders in search of captives and cattle to satisfy Asante demands. But the absence of evidence is not itself conclusive.[65] Presumably, evidence suggesting that the LoDagaa were the object of attacks would come from the sequence of their migrations. The *Lobi* abandoned the east bank of the Black Volta for reasons that are not apparent. Labouret suggested that their migration had been "progressive, recent, fragmentary and peaceful"; this does not point to any external threat.[66] The reasons given for later migrations almost always related to the search for better land, and these migrations were also described as gradual and peaceful. Similarly, in a 1932 account of later, related migrations, the District Commissioner of Lawra, J.C. Guinness, stated that the histories of particular households of Lawra District indicated that their ancestors had migrated into a largely uninhabited area through "peaceful penetration."[67] When Goody investigated these traditions in the early 1950s, he received the same information as both Labouret and Guinness.[68] Thus most of the inhabitants of Lawra District probably entered the area somewhere between the end of the eighteenth century and the middle of the nineteenth, mainly to take advantage of lands recently vacated.

The most immediate effect of these migrations was to render elusory any sense of common identity. The mobility of settlements, their ever-shifting configurations, and the uncertainty of relations between settlements meant that the ethnographic situation within this area of shared culture verged on kaleidoscopic. Perhaps the most peculiar feature of these migrations was that despite the continuity of culture and language maintained over several centuries, individual household histories among the LoDagaa did not stretch back more than two or three generations. Histories recorded at several junctures during the first half of the twentieth century all shared this common feature: the relative shallowness of both household reckoning and memory.[69] Households traced their histories back for several generations through common lines of patrilineal descent that constituted networks of shared histories; they also belonged to much wider patriclans whose lines of connection were no longer remembered except as they were reflected in common names and similar totemic avoidances. Unlike the Gonja to the south, whose history was chronicled by Islamic scholars, and the Dagomba to the east, who recorded their history in the music of their drums, the LoDagaa did not devote any particular aspect of their culture to preserving their history.[70] One concept of historical knowledge, *tenkouri yil*, literally "speech of the old country," relied on the events of the past and memory of particular ancestors being imparted orally from one generation to the next. Such knowledge often concerned outstanding debts between households as well as information relating to the tenure of borrowed lands. A second, less literal concept of historical knowledge, noted by Goody, was *tenkouri sor*, "way of the past," which referred to the routes of migration that household ancestors had followed: "This is both a concrete and metaphorical expression.

The road exists. It is the path leading to the 'old country,' the place from which the particular clan section has come in the past, the route of migration. The path is recognised not only in speech but in sacrifice too, and it is there that one sacrifices, for example during the recitation of the Bagre, on the side of the path leading to the 'old country.' But path also means 'way' in the metaphorical sense."[71]

Although the pathway to the past was both practical and figurative, such information was not structured within a narrative or ordered in terms of a linear concept of time. Knowledge of the past was most often imparted in stories that were not intended to satisfy a temporal sensibility, but rather to answer questions about the order of things: "In other words, how did the present order come about?" As Tuobataabaaro Angsontinge noted in his study of these oral narratives: "Above all, the tales offer explanation for why the members of the group do the things the way they do." The ways of the past were part of the present, and therefore not only didactic but also etiological.[72] Like the physical footpaths of the district observable from aerial photographs, historical knowledge was meandering and fragmentary, forming a larger, weblike structure that no one could see from the ground.

Elders were the natural repositories of such knowledge, but there was no special or deliberate discursive exercise through which either type of information, about memories or about routes, was transmitted.[73] It seems likely that such knowledge was often lost through the sudden death of elders. In the early 1930s a colonial officer made inquiries into the history of an area of Lawra District. "All our grandfathers who used to tell the stories are dead," he was told, "and many died without telling their sons of the family histories, and so now no one remembers them any more."[74] Because the history of each household was unique, knowledge of the past was not duplicated in other households. Furthermore, neither type of knowledge was cumulative. In part this was due to the nature of the LoDagaa past, which, in contrast to the shared, narrative traditions of neighboring centralized polities, was constantly fragmented: socially by the segmentary nature of social organization, and physically through successive dislocations wrought by migration. Patriclans were widely dispersed as a result of "the gradual way in which the Dagara came to be constituted"; but despite the separation from a common ancestor, "who remains unknown due to the duration of time separating him from the present," patriclans continued to be recognized on the basis of a nonveridical knowledge of the past. One of the most sensitive of local historians, Father Peter Naameh, has argued that what was important was "how knowledge about the past helps to iron out present difficulties and ensure peace in the society."[75]

The LoDagaa were aware of their past, but in ways less explicit than oral traditions. A sense of the past, represented by the theme of migration, was implicitly enshrined in LoDagaa wisdom. As Constantin Dabiré has noted, "Dagara wisdom defined humankind as being like the Traveler, forever in transit on this earth."[76] But awareness of the past was even more concrete than this. According to one colonial officer, St John Eyre-Smith, throughout Lawra District there were "ancient slag heaps, middens, and broken pottery," and these "traces of former occupation and cultivation" were still used by the inhabitants of the 1930s to map out "every inch of the land."[77] However, because these features were not written down, they were not acknowledged as histories by the colonial administration.[78] LoDagaa consciousness of the past was not recorded and extended in a narrative chronology; rather, it was embodied and compressed in a mentality and topography.[79]

In the District Magistrate's Court during the postcolonial period, litigants often used topographic features as mnemonic devices to resolve land disputes, or more commonly to substantiate alternative readings of the landscape. In a dispute heard in 1974, the magistrate, having been shown the significant features of a piece of land by witnesses during a walking tour, described the land in question in the following terms: "Besides a few baobab trees and other numerous trees and shrubs of assorted types, the whole area described above laid fallow and flat, being well demarcated by piles of stones and mounds that figure prominently round the described area."[80] Success in claiming land in court was directly related to the ability to explain these human imprints on the landscape. The failure of the British to read the landscape, to acknowledge these imprints as meaningful symbols, resulted in the misconception that the LoDagaa did not possess an inscribed past. In fact they did; it was literally written on the land.

The refusal of the colonizers to read the landscape for signs of the past – a refusal made that much easier by the construction of roads and resthouses as signs of occupation – was coupled with an unwillingness on their part to recognize those who could read these signs. Among the LoDagaa, as throughout the Voltaic region, land was not owned but held or borrowed.[81] Earth shrines were established wherever people settled. The shrines the LoDagaa observed after migrating to the area east of the Black Volta were the same as those that the *Lobi*, and the settlers before them, had acknowledged. "Every stretch of the country has its appropriate altar," Goody reported in the 1950s, "which was either shown to the first settler by the previous inhabitants or discovered by the founding ancestor himself."[82] It is significant that the British, albeit unintentionally, created their own parallel system of shrines in the form of government resthouses. As Map 5 makes clear, the construction of these buildings was an attempt to establish a physical presence on both land and paper. That this map was dotted with resthouses and does not indicate a single shrine (*tengaan*) suggests the use to which it was put; it was not drawn to reflect indigenous spatial organization, but rather to reflect structures imposed by the British.

The area defined by a *tengaan* was represented topographically by means of particular rocks, trees, or gullies, or by ridges constructed to divide one ritual area from the next. The *tengaan* itself usually consisted of an existing outcrop of rocks, or stones placed near a tree. The first settlers in an area were responsible for locating the shrine of the previous inhabitants, or creating one if one could not be found, and for appointing a custodian or Earth priest (*tengaansob*, pl. *tengaandem*) to ensure that the Earth was propitiated and its sanctions observed. As throughout the Voltaic region, subsequent immigrants were offered use of parcels of land, but not ownership, which ultimately resided in the *tengaan*.[83] The distribution of land in any one *tengaan* mirrored the pattern of migration into that area, with later migrants borrowing land from earlier settlers or from the *tengaansob*. Land allocated by the *tengaansob* could not be alienated, but as an area became more densely populated through successive migrations and natural population growth, parcels of land within a field already allocated were often transferred to incoming lineages.[84] As this process continued, land became more fragmented and the history of its distribution more complicated.

Given the apparent frequency of migration among the LoDagaa during the precolonial period, it is reasonable to suppose that when an area became too heavily settled, immigration ceased and any social tensions were reduced by emigration. Yet according to disputes brought before the District Court in the 1970s, tensions had emerged after three generations of relatively stable settlement and continuous population growth. Although the LoDagaa system of land tenure was not altered directly by colonial rule, increasing population pressure and the tendency of colonial rule to halt further regional migration all increased the pressures on this system. By the 1970s a clear sign of both the declining authority of the *tengaandem* and the rising shortage of land was the number of times that violence was threatened before disputes were brought before the District Court.[85]

In several of these cases, the dispute arose after the death of an elder with extensive knowledge of the complicated titles to particular farms.[86] The passing of the elder seems to have contracted the genealogical depth to which his descendants could trace their claims.[87] As there was no ownership of land, present use or possession did not necessarily indicate title. In the 1980s, as tenure became more complicated and the possibility that magistrates would be able to disentangle rival claims became more remote, the District Court attempted to apply a statute of limitations to these matters.[88] Although a household's interests were grounded in its particular history, during litigation this history was subject to comparison with accounts of rival households, and the court often found it impossible to assess competing sets of traditions without access to a collective memory. The *tengaandem* were the traditional sources of authority on such matters, but they were seldom present before the courts. In a 1982 case, the magistrate actually remonstrated the *tengaansob*, accusing him of being more ignorant of the history of the particular parcel of land than the defendant, whose witness he was. In deciding the case in the plaintiff's favor, the magistrate said he was impressed with the plaintiff's knowledge of "historical events," even though his own brother had appeared as a witness for the defendant and disputed the plaintiff's title to the land through their father.[89] The *tengaandem* were almost completely marginalized by this time, due to the refusal of the British to recognize them as political entities, and the refusal of the *tengaandem* to be co-opted into the colonial system.[90]

The court showed a decided preference for narratives that, even if contrived, had the coherence of a road rather than the complexity of intersecting footpaths. This pattern of footpaths reflected the fluidity of the precolonial history of the LoDagaa; the relative immobility of their colonial and postcolonial history led to unprecedented pressures. These were partially alleviated by the substitution of a generational cycle of labor migration for the periodic migration of settlements, as the LoDagaa went from being heroic travelers to exploited migrant laborers.[91] Despite such exploitation, within LoDagaa culture labor migration was seen as a rite of passage for the young men, displacing the *Bagre* as the primary form of initiation. Those who did not participate in this form of adventure tourism came to be seen as unenlightened.[92]

Chapter Two

Labor, Bodies, and Names

Shades of Babatu, I don't know how we should get on without him.

District Commissioner, Lawra District, 1918

To appropriate the LoDagaa, the British situated them in versions of space and time that belonged to the world on paper. However, situating them was not the same as using, controlling, or knowing them. This chapter looks at how the British attempted to use, control, and know the LoDagaa, focusing in particular on British efforts to expropriate their labor, dress their bodies in colonial attire, and name them according to the terms of ethnographic science. Labor migration became a central feature of LoDagaa male culture during the twentieth century. The bow and arrow had been the symbols of male courage at the start of the century; by the end, it was the bicycle that represented virility.[1] Similarly, clothing, which was often worn by migrant laborers, and ethnonyms, which were first used by migrant laborers outside Lawra District, became important parts of, as well as issues in, LoDagaa culture.

Seizing Labor

There is little evidence that LoDagaa congeries were forced by an external pressure – demographic, environmental, political – to migrate into Lawra District in the nineteenth century. However, having established themselves there by the middle of the century, they were threatened by the marauding Sofa forces of Samori Ture's son and by Babatu's Zabarima slavers in the last decades of the century. Both groups also ravaged other areas of the middle Volta basin that fell between states. Although the region had been attacked periodically since the time of the Asante subjugation of Dagbon and Gonja, these new slavers were wholly unprecedented in their ruthlessness and in the scale of their operations. The weakness of Wa also contributed to these events; because of threats to their sovereignty, the Wala enlisted Zabarima and Sofa assistance, in effect recruiting them into the region as mercenaries.[2] The LoDagaa congeries living north of Wa were raided by both forces, but they did not suffer the wider devastation experienced by some other communities in the region. Both groups of slavers were well known and still feared by the LoDagaa at the turn of the twentieth century; but there was only sketchy evidence of incursions by either force, partly because whenever the inhabitants faced an external threat, they fled if possible instead of actively resisting.[3]

These two groups did relatively little physical damage, but that does not mean that the threat of such damage did not have deep psychological effects.[4] French and British intervention had curtailed the activities of both Samori and Babatu by 1897, but these same European powers soon began a program of occupation on a far greater scale than that of their slave-raiding predecessors. The inhabitants of Lawra District had little time to recover from the raids before they found themselves under colonial rule. Indeed, the arrival of the British occupying forces in Lawra District in 1903 must have struck the LoDagaa as a disturbing continuation of the insecurities of the recent past. Certainly, it heralded a return to aspects of their longer-term past, namely, those related to migration. However, the local movement of households for social and agricultural reasons would give way to the migration of individual men for economic and personal reasons, as long-distance labor migration replaced local migrations.[5]

Soon after the Northern Territories were created, as an afterthought to the incorporation of Asante within the Gold Coast Colony, the colonial government realized that they offered little economic potential; it was even feared that the region might become an economic liability.[6] This attitude changed in 1906, however, when the chief commissioner received a request for northern laborers from the managers of the Tarkwa gold mines. He initiated what came to be known as the "labor crusade."[7] Before an effective administration had even been established in Lawra District, officers were requesting workers for the far-off mines of the south. The initial reaction was negative, especially among elders, whom officers immediately identified as "old obstructionists" and "fetishists" because of their strong desire to keep their young men at home to assist in farming.[8] Even the newly created chief of Lawra was reported to be extremely suspicious; because of his fears, he refused to provide representatives to join a party from the northwest that toured the mines at the end of 1906. "It was evident in spite of all my assurances," wrote the district commissioner, "that he thought it was a device to obtain slaves."[9]

From modest beginnings, the number of recruits increased dramatically in subsequent years.[10] Initial fears that LoDagaa men would be enslaved were soon allayed, but resentment soon arose from several other quarters. The workers resented the deplorable conditions in the mines and the brutal treatment to which they were subjected,[11] and the journey to the south and back was difficult.[12] At the same time, antipathy grew among those elders persecuted by the chiefs, who were eager to satisfy increasingly demanding officers. The chiefs were offered incentives to participate in the recruitment drives, receiving 5s for each recruit, and this only exacerbated the negative features of the labor migration, by encouraging them to use coercion in meeting informal government quotas.[13] Nevertheless, officers continued to demand recruits from the chiefs. So long as it was the chiefs who procured "volunteers," the officers could maintain the illusion that government coercion was not involved.

Abuses and complaints led to a temporary suspension of recruiting activity under administrative auspices in February 1910, but a steady flow of informal or voluntary recruits continued to reach the south until the beginning of the First World War.[14] At the outset of the war, during a new wave of official recruiting, the chiefs of Lawra and Nandom complained that more and more young men were migrating informally to the south, at the same time as they were expected to recruit soldiers and manganese miners. By this time work was available on cocoa plantations as well as in the mines. Agricultural work was preferred by migrant laborers because it was more familiar and because by taking plantation work they could avoid being conscripted for mine work.[15] Both chiefs voiced concern that with this double-exodus (i.e., formal and informal), the district would soon lose all its young men. On the same day the district commissioner met three men from Gengenkpe on their way to Kumase to search for fourteen of their kinsmen, who had left in 1913 and not yet returned five years later.[16]

Although production at the gold mines was reduced in 1914 because of the war effort, new official labor demands were imposed on the Northern Territories. During the war, officers asked the chiefs for military recruits, and for workers for the strategically important manganese mines. After the war, laborers were needed to build the southern railways. In meeting these requests, the chiefs resorted to extortion when simple coercion failed. In 1915 the headman of Tugu, Kayani, was accused of demanding money from two of his subjects in lieu of recruits: fifty thousand cowries from one man and the same again plus £4 in silver from another.[17] But such complaints were rare. For example, in 1917 the district commissioner learned privately through his interpreter that a rumor was circulating in the district that compounds unable to supply recruits were required to pay their headmen and chiefs.[18] The following year the chief of Samoa was accused of demanding £5 from seven different compounds before he would excuse them from contributing recruits.[19] Just how onerous these demands for labor actually were for individual settlements is difficult to assess owing to the lack of any proper statistical compilations. We have only glimpses of how stressful such demands must have been on households. In 1918, the chief commissioner spoke to an assembly of 106 chiefs and headmen at Lawra, urging them to supply military recruits. At a result, 625 men were enlisted in less than two months, "without the help or presence of military authorities." To put this in perspective, this single drive resulted in the procurement of roughly one-third of the annual tribute the Asante had demanded from the larger states of the Volta basin a century earlier![20]

Officers generally ignored the possibility that this double-migration might damage the district's subsistence economy. In 1917 the chiefs of Jirapa and Nandom asked that arrangements be made so that the workers recruited for the manganese mines could return in time for the farming season, or, alternatively, that their dependants be given allowances. These suggestions fell on deaf ears; administrators actually encouraged migrant laborers to stay away longer. As one officer explained, "all are unwilling to go as they say they cannot get back for the farming season, [but] I have pointed out that there is no need why they should get back."[21] In August 1918 the chief of Zini reminded the district commissioner of an earlier proposal he had made that something be done to restrict the informal migration of young men to the south following the harvest, otherwise it would be useless for the administration to ask for any more recruits.[22] Nothing was done in anticipation of that year's exodus, and by the end of October it was noted that "all the chiefs are groaning about the emigration of the young men."[23]

The administration maintained the fiction that as long as the chiefs were willingly supplying recruits, recruitment was not forced.[24] They regarded workers nominated and recruited in this manner as volunteers who merely required their chiefs' encouragement. Officers responsible for carrying out such directives were less convinced. In 1917 one district commissioner remarked on the difficulty of obtaining military recruits: "Genuine volunteers do not require to be asked or persuaded."[25] A year later, while carrying out a recruiting campaign at Sabule, another officer virtually admitted that many people confused the British with the Zabarima slavers of Babatu.[26]

Many workers migrated informally because by doing so they avoided the constraints imposed on formal workers through contracts.[27] Even the chiefs apparently did not understand this point. In 1918 the chief of Lawra told the district commissioner: "I am grieved. If these boys want work why don't they enlist as soldiers as we have ordered them. I am getting tired of this. The country will soon lose all its young men."[28] Obviously, informal migration was already popular by this time, and could only have exaggerated the effects of formal recruitment. During 1917 and 1918 Lawra District was affected more than usual by disease and pestilence: locusts, rinderpest, anthrax, smallpox, influenza, and cerebro-spinal meningitis were all reported within a period of seventeen months.[29] This coincided with a period of heavy-handed military recruitment. Although there are no figures for the number of recruits by district, between 1914 and 1918, 567 Dagarti and 318 Lobi were recruited from the northwest, 92 percent of these in the last two years of the war.[30] Most of these recruits must have come from Lawra District.

After the war, government recruiting continued, for workers to build the transportation infrastructure of the south. When the district commissioner visited the settlement of Yagha in 1919 to ask for recruits, the headmen produced only six young men from over thirty compounds. Further investigation revealed that there were fifty-one potential recruits in the village but that the headmen had hidden them in an attempt to avoid further losses of able-bodied men.[31] That year, 966 workers were sent from Lawra and Tumu Districts for railway construction alone.[32] The following year's campaign was no less intense, and equally unpopular with everyone but the chiefs. Again, little attention was paid to either the reluctance of the "volunteers" or the concerns of their elders about farming. Indeed, recruiting activity reached its height in the middle of the farming season. By July, seven hundred recruits had been gathered from Lawra District, despite an outbreak of cerebro-spinal meningitis and the fact that it coincided with the height of agricultural activity.[33] There were reports of recalcitrant settlements, including Yagha, which officers attributed to "the old men with their foolish talk and stories of the wild days when there were no chiefs in the country. In every palaver here, the cause can generally be traced to some disgruntled old man."[34] A month later, after recruiting had ceased and the farming season was coming to an end, the chiefs again began to complain again about informal migration, which the district commissioner referred to as "leakage." In response, he condoned the chiefs' practice of requiring migrant laborers to obtain their consent before making the annual trip to Kumase.[35]

By 1924 the administration could no longer pretend that recruitment through the chiefs was voluntary, and it stopped participating directly in procuring labor for the south.[36] However, informal migration continued, although it is difficult to know at what rate owing to the lack of statistics. Until the 1930s the journey to the south was difficult and arduous; the three hundred miles to Kumase had to be walked. Many young men went to work in the mines because they offered the highest pay; most, however, were dissuaded by the poor conditions and concomitant health dangers, and migrants gravitated toward the cocoa farms, where the pay was less but the work was familiar. The appearance of motorized transport in the late 1920s radically altered migration patterns by allowing workers to depart at the end of one farming season and return before the next began, leaving enough time in the south to make the journey worthwhile. The journey now took less time, and was less expensive as migrants no longer had to pay for food en route. Between 1934 and 1939 the number of trucks passing through Lawra heading south increased from 105 to 611.[37]

In 1948, 9 percent of all Dagarti and Lobi enumerated in the census were living in the south.[38] Very few of these were actual immigrants; almost all returned north within a year, to be replaced the following year by further waves of young migrant laborers. An important factor in this pattern was the shortage of free land in the south, which made permanent settlement virtually impossible. By 1948 several migrant laborers had chosen to settle in Bole District, to the south but still within the Northern Territories, on account of the increasing population density in Lawra District and the availability of land in this sparsely populated area.[39] It is not clear what effect increasing migration had on the local economy in Lawra District between 1924 and 1954; however, it seems that LoDagaa migrants, who contributed significantly to the mining and cocoa farming sectors, never earned enough to make a significant contribution to the domestic economy.[40] In 1943 the district commissioner said of the seasonal exodus, which had begun that year before the harvest: "As far as I can see we are powerless to stop it, though it has a damaging effect on agriculture and hence on the subsistence level of the country."[41]

Throughout the colonial and postcolonial periods, the population of Lawra District increased steadily. The seasonal out-migration compensated for the decline of local migration that had been so prominent in the LoDagaa past. It may also have alleviated temporarily the demographic pressure on land and food resources.[42] But it also meant overexploitation of land, greater demands on the labor of those who remained behind, and, ultimately, a decline in production. Had there not been some alternative type of migration, further migration along precolonial patterns would have been necessary, even though similar population densities elsewhere, and geopolitical boundaries, would not have allowed it. By 1960, 31 percent of Dagarti males were migrant laborers; of these, 13 percent were miners, 46 percent were farm laborers, and 28 percent were general laborers.[43] These figures indicate that after 1948 the pattern of seasonal migration continued unabated; only those involved with the mining industry would have had to be absent for any protracted period of time.

In the early 1950s Goody repeated the mantra of many administrators: "Annual migration has had comparatively little effect as yet on the organized social life of the community, for the average age of these labourers cannot

TABLE 2
Lawra District Censuses, 1911–84

1911	1921	1931	1948	1960	1970	1984
56,442	58,718	67,615	89,187	114,193	123,514	156,174

Sources: RAT ADM 217, Northern Territories Annual General Report, "Lawra-Tumu Census Report 1931"; Gold Coast 1950; Ghana 1964, 1972, 1987.

greatly exceed twenty."[44] Yet well before the 1950s it had already affected social life by both weakening and strengthening household ties. With independence, more and more LoDagaa began to stay in the south for longer and longer periods – many, especially those born there in the 1960s and after, for most of their lives. But most, even those who had achieved a relative degree of economic independence, relied on their natal communities for social and ritual security, and ultimately returned.[45] By the mid-1970s, the court records reveal, households in Lawra District were finding it more and more difficult to maintain relations with their absent members and to reabsorb returning workers. This coincided with rapid economic decline in the south. It follows that the problem was probably the result of a significant number of migrants returning at the same time, combined with a decline in the number of youths leaving for the south. Up till that time the LoDagaa had been fortunate in being able to export a part of their large population increase. This convenient outlet for youthful aspirations and overcrowding was now temporarily obstructed. However, the need for a population safety valve remained.

By the 1970s the safety valve that labor migration had provided against demographic pressures and generational conflict was beginning to fail. Disputes over land tenure became more common because of attempts by returning migrant laborers to claim land on which to farm.[46] The growing shortage of land affected returnees in particular; many of them had difficulty establishing access to household lands after a period of absence. Given the increasing complexity of patterns of tenure after several generations of continuous settlement, and given that memories were fading regarding who had lent whom which piece of land, returnees increasingly faced the danger that their claims to parcels of household land might have been conveniently forgotten (i.e., given away) during their absence. Also, their participation in the cash economy made them easy to marginalize vis-à-vis the cowry economy.[47] As chances of prospering in the south declined for potential migrants in the 1970s, young men who now left for the south did so as much out of necessity as for reasons of adventure as labor migration began to become a strategy for survival rather than an opportunity for money making.

In the early 1990s "increasing land shortage, declining soil fertility, and lack of local income opportunities" led to many local households retaining only one "able-bodied man" to farm while the others went south.[48] By this time the external economy had also improved markedly over previous decades.

What were the overall effects of labor migration on Lawra District? Unfortunately, little systematic analysis has been done on labor migration in northwestern Ghana. However, David Cleveland's study of the same phenomenon in northeastern Ghana in the 1970s provides scope for comparisons. Working from data from the Kusasi village of Zorse, he found that labor migration taken to alleviate demographic pressures may actually have acerbated the problem by increasing fertility rates.[49] The immediate effects of predominantly male labor migration on gender balances are obvious. In northern Ghana as a whole, the ratio of men to women fell from 95:100 in 1931 to 75:100 in 1960, resulting in a substantial "social deficit."[50] Working from the 1970 census figures for the whole of the Upper Region, Cleveland calculated that without labor migration each adult member of the population (i.e., those between 15 and 64 years of age) would have had to produce a surplus equivalent to 75 percent of personal needs. The required surplus rose to 100 percent once labor migration was factored in, with much of the burden falling on women. Measured in real terms, the extra surplus that each remaining farmer had to produce in order to keep sustaining children and elders was equivalent to a 50 kilogram bag of grain – a burden that could not be met by those at home or by migrant laborers through remittances.[51] Besides suffering from the loss of their labor, as Cleveland noted, "the migrants' home communities in the savanna continue to bear the costs of sickness, injury, and old age."[52] According to Nsiah-Gyabaah's survey of households in the Upper West Region in the late 1980s, overpopulation (in terms of the carrying capacity of the land) had produced a "cycle of grim poverty and stress" and made it difficult for many households "to meet their basic needs." These pressures in turn led to overgrazing, overexploitation of soils, deforestation, and more out-migration.[53]

Labor migration certainly was a subtler phenomenon than slave raids; however, we must not be fooled by the sleight of hand that turned forced labor into a structural necessity for survival.[54] As Père has noted, labor migration among the LoDagaa and the *Lobi* created a vicious circle: the very economic conditions that forced people to leave the region were perpetuated by the loss of their labor, "leaving behind elders and children on ancestral land that they are too weak to cultivate and exploit."[55] In order to compel LoDagaa men to migrate without actually forcing them to do so, the British needed to create conditions under which they had no choice but to leave their district. Taxation, introduced in the 1930s, disguised the less subtle mechanisms of early colonial rule, but it was not sufficient to make labor migration a central feature of LoDagaa life. The most important factor in making labor migration so necessary was the assimilation of colonial attitudes toward the body.

Bodies and Clothing

Although it was difficult for the British to locate the inhabitants of this district spatially, the task of differentiating them culturally, begun by Read, proved even more problematic. The inherent confusion of external designations, based on the presumed cultural differences between Lobi and Dagarti, became obvious during the 1913 visit by French colonial officers described above. Nevertheless, British officials preferred to keep thinking in terms of "two tribes" and continued to presume that the administrative boundaries of the district represented a logical cultural field. The 1913 meeting also illustrated the relatively sophisticated knowledge of French officials; British officers were amateurs in comparison. No district commissioners had even a rudimentary knowledge of *Dagaare* at this time, whereas their French counterparts were already aware of the importance of such linguistic competence.[56] British officers were satisfied to rely on translators, sometimes as many as three at a time. Interpreters often worked from *Dagaare* to a neighboring language, then to Hausa, and finally to English. This made communications cumbersome and inexact. It also made it difficult for administrators to hear the differences among the LoDagaa.

Using the metaphor of language to describe the cultural heterogeneity of the LoDagaa, Goody noted that differences "take place imperceptibly like dialects merging into one another."[57] Because they were unable to listen to the LoDagaa, administrators turned instead to what they could see. This predilection for dealing with images rather than language meant that confusion over the identity of the inhabitants of the district was unavoidable. Just as looking was substituted for hearing, apprehension replaced comprehension. In the absence of any appreciation of linguistic or cultural subtleties, officers of the first generation of British rule satisfied themselves with creating visual stereotypes meant to validate the "two tribes" theory of the district.

Other forms of misunderstanding were based more on prejudice than ignorance. Commenting on orders he received in 1918 to prevent French subjects from migrating into Lawra to avoid military service, the district commissioner reported in his diary:

> M. Marsan [the French officer in charge Diébougou, one of the two administrative districts opposite Lawra District] says that he does not anticipate any trouble from his people, as they are mostly Lobi Burifons and Dagartis. He added that it

> was in the Gaoua district where there might be trouble because of the extraordinary turbulence of the Lobi Wulegesis and Lobi Wilos whom it was impossible to tame on account of their uncompromising attitude. This bears out what I have said with regard to the Wilos [inhabitants of Yagha and its vicinity]. M. Marsan also agreed that their turbulence might be due to the very much stronger brand of "peto" [millet beer] to which they are addicted.[58]

This attempt to connect continued resistance to colonial authority with alcoholism shows us, again, that distinctions were not based on criteria of material culture, social structure, or language, but on the association of deviance with imaginary cultural pathologies. What Fabian has noted of late nineteenth-century travel writing in Equatorial Africa applies equally to early twentieth-century colonial ethnography: "The lack of valid criteria involved all the travelers in confused and corrupt practices of shoring up uncertain ethnic ... distinctions with racial classification." As a result, "tentative and fragmentary information" led to "judgmental stereotypes of people" that masqueraded as classification.[59]

Sometime after 1918 in the District Record Book, differences were recorded respecting "the four [*sic*] tribes, or perhaps it would be correct to say races of the District." These were taken to be the Lobi (64 percent), Dagarti (17 percent), and Sisala (19 percent). The Lobi were seen to comprise three constituent groups: Lobi Burifon, Lobi Dagarti, and Lobi Wili. The former were reported to be "Lobi proper," but a later gloss placed a question mark next to this statement. The Lobi Dagarti were merely the product of intermarriage, whereas the Lobi Wili were "in reality not Lobis at all but a branch of the Dagartis." "I would have classed them under the heading Dagarti," one district commissioner added, "but for the fact that they have become known as Lobi Wili and to change would now only lead to confusion." Despite the ethnographic indeterminacy, the following characterizations were made:

- *Lobi Burifons*: "are bluff manly jovial people, very friendly and hospitable and extremely hard working ... they are easy to manage when taken the right way, and enjoy a joke even against themselves."
- *Lobi Dagarti*: "perhaps are not quite so wild and show a tendency to cloth themselves."
- *Lobi Wili*: "are still rather wild, in-tractable, and intolerant of any authority and have the reputation of being extremely ready to settle affairs with bows and arrows."[60]

The Dagarti were described as "a curiously reserved and some what sullen people, very hard to know," and as "artists in passive resistance."[61] Character, not culture, social organization, or language, remained the means by which colonial administrators apprehended the LoDagaa and differentiated between their various congeries. In one sense this was quite appropriate: the LoDagaa were not objects of intellectual speculation, but subjects of colonial rule, and their reactions to that repression were all that immediately concerned most district commissioners.

After these caricatures based on political reactions to colonial rule, the second most preferred way of apprehending the LoDagaa was through seeing. The images Rattray used to illustrate his chapters on the Dagaba and Lobi in *The Tribes of the Ashanti Hinterland* (Figures 2–5) translated verbal caricatures into visual form. In the photographs of the three Dagaba young men (Figures 2 and 3), the rigid posture of the subjects – their knees locked together, their heels together, and their hands close to their sides – is palpable. Each wears a costume across his chest and over his back, probably of goatskin, decorated with tassels weighted with cowry shells.

In marked contrast, the two Lobi men in Figures 4 and 5 have struck much more relaxed poses, with their legs apart and hands dangling. But much more significant is the outsider's preoccupation with nudity. Whereas the Dagaba youths were photographed wearing cotton drawers, the Lobi youths were being used to illustrate the "method of tying the penis."[62] The Dagaba men look tense, as if at attention, as would indeed have been the case if they were employed by the administration. In the second set of photographs the young Lobi men seem bemused, with slight smiles creeping across their faces. Conversely, the Dagaba men have been posed with military discipline, and photographed from both front and back, and this underscores the photographer's power over the subjects and lends ethnographic authority to the images.

The images of the Lobi men are voyeuristic, not only because of the prying focus on their genitals but also because of the evident lack of authority the photographer held over the subjects. This implicitly reinforced the administrative stereotype of Lobi aggressiveness and insolence. These images bolstered the distinction between the Dagaba and Lobi that Rattray made in his work in a way that mere words could not convey. Indeed, presented this way the images suggest two distinct ethnicities rather than two groups of young men with different hairstyles and costumes who shared many invisible cultural and social features and lived in close proximity to each other.[63]

Efforts to use visual information to identify who was who in this complicated ethnographic situation eventually foundered; even so, the history of these attempts tells us much about how the LoDagaa were recorded on paper. A 1912 letter from the Chief Commissioner of the Northern Territories to district

Figure 2. "Dagaba." From R.S. Rattray, *The Tribes of the Ashanti Hinterland* (1932), fig. 105. Note the rigid, military-like posture and somber faces of the subjects. Their dress exhibits an interesting contrast between LoDagaa and European clothing. Across their chests they are wearing a local costume, probably of goastskin. Below that they are dressed in imported cotton underwear.

commissioners outlined recent research in Nigeria that indicated that marks on faces and/or bodies could be used to read an individual's tribe. In the hope of yielding similar results, "sketches of a negro head, in full-face, profile and back, and of a mouth showing teeth" were circulated.[64] Administrators were to map the bodies of their subjects, treating them as "bodyscapes."[65] Earlier, Read had observed that markings were applied to the body through scarification for the following purposes: to denote the individual's "tribe"; to indicate slave status; to adorn the body; to avert illness; and to signify royalty. Of these five interpretations, the first was the product of a literate reading of these signs. Indigenous informants never offered such a reading. But because the origins of these "tribal markings" were deemed to have been "in the dim past," and therefore not known to their bearers, the purpose and meaning of these inscriptions were open to such speculation. Read asserted that they were "undoubtedly" signs of identification that were used to distinguish "friend from foe" in the tribal, sectional, and familial warfare of the past.[66] However, closer examination a decade later revealed that LoDagaa bearers of these markings did not see them as signs of ethnic identification.[67] They were marks of individual adornment meant only "for pleasure."[68]

Although officers eventually realized that these marks could not be read,

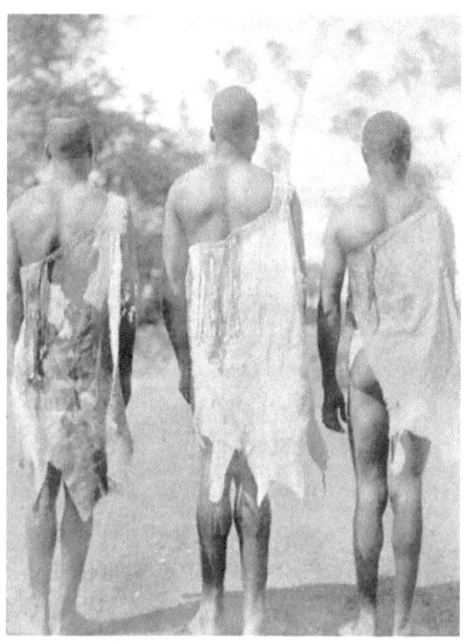

Figure 3. "Dagaba." From R.S. Rattray, *The Tribes of the Ashanti Hinterland* (1932), fig. 106. Note the effect of this rear-view image when combined with the frontal image of these three subjects in Figure 2. Unable to reciprocate the camera's gaze, they become objectified, as if on display. (The use of this image on the cover of this book is meant to have the opposite effect; that is, to ask the reader to look *with*, instead of *at*, the LoDagaa and their encounter with the world on paper.)

eleven pages in the District Record Book were devoted to "tribal marks" – more than for any other single topic. The drawings appeared at the beginning of the book and would have been seen by all subsequent officers assigned to the district. A variety of markings were recorded in crudely drawn cartoons, showing several different aspects of faces and bodies.[69] Notwithstanding attempts to associate different styles with certain areas, as in the descriptive title "Nandom man," these drawings had no ethnographic validity. Nevertheless, their psychological utility is apparent. The feature common to all of them is the fascination the officers who made them had with the unclothed bodies of their subjects. Scarification patterns with no apparent meaning were meticulously recorded (Figures 6–15). When these were reprinted in 1924, the images (Figure 16) looked very similar to police photographs or mug-shots, familiarizing colonial administrators with imaginary archetypes of colonial subjects as suspects.[70] The physical exaggerations found in the amateur images in the District Record Book, such as the incredibly broad shoulders, reveal the administrators' interest in these people as workers. Even though the patterns did not have the meaning officers wanted to attribute to them, the drawings gave visual immediacy to colonial names – names that had even less connection with the world of experience than colonial drawings.

Figure 4. "Showing the method of tying the penis." From R.S. Rattray, *The Tribes of Ashanti Hinterland* (1932), fig. 115. Note the relaxed poses of the subjects here compared with the "Dagaba" in Figures 2–3. Interestingly, this image tells the viewer nothing different than its companion (Figure 5) does. However, the repetition of virtually identical images served to reinforce the idea of "Lobi" nudity compared with the image of "Dagaba" propriety.

The careful attention paid to body adornments in the District Record Book suggests that the intention was to appropriate the LoDagaa physically, just as maps had been created to appropriate the district territorially. The images in the District Record Book (now found in the National Archives of Ghana) are striking in how they illustrate the highly visual nature of administrative experience. Officers posted to Lawra District would have found in these images a reassurance that the natives were already known and identified, even though in all other respects they were extremely elusive. In this sense, the purpose of the drawings, as with the crudely drawn sketch maps of the district from this period, was not practical but psychological. As Jan Nederveen Pieterse has argued: "*Knowing* the colonized is one of the fundamental forms of control and possession. One application of this knowledge is that subject peoples are turned into visual objects."[71]

In the absence of even a rudimentary understanding of the human geography of the district – an absence that extended even to the ethnic identities of the inhabitants – administrative maps and body diagrams served as substitutes for actual knowledge of the complicated ethnographic situation. Between 1907 and 1957 almost fifty different officers performed seventy-nine tours of service in Lawra District.[72] Such frequent rotation of personnel meant that most officers

Figure 5. "Showing the method of tying the penis." From R.S. Rattray, *The Tribes of the Ashanti Hinterland* (1932), fig. 116. Note the slightly upward turn of the mouths of both subjects. This contrasts markedly with the somber faces of the "Dagaba" in Figures 2–3.

were never in the district long enough to realize how little they actually knew about the area they were charged with administering. They instead relied on visual devices – these few maps and diagrams – to assuage their fears of the unknown. The *horror vacui* of information that Binger experienced had been filled with writing. The fact that many officers were content to use what they knew to be incorrect ethnic names indicates that they were more concerned with order than reality. This attachment to the order they created on paper should not be underestimated.

The British persisted in using names they knew did not fit; in a similar fashion, they created chiefs among the LoDagaa (see Chapter 3) and then pretended they had always existed. In 1928, one officer provided the following *apologia* for imposing these chiefs on indigenous society: "To anyone who has viewed the hopeless tangle of sectional migrations and settlements ... it will scarcely be necessary to say that before the white-man came there was in this

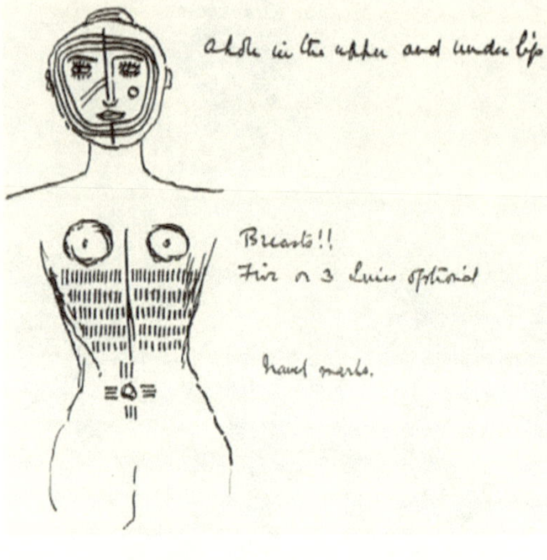

Figure 6. "Tribal Marks." From NAG ADM 61/5/1, Lawra District Record Book, 10. Showing marks thought to be those of a "Lobi" woman. Text reads: "A hole in the upper and under lip / Breasts!! / Five or 3 lines optional / Navel marks." Compare this image with Rattray's photographic study "A Lobi woman." See Figure 18 below.

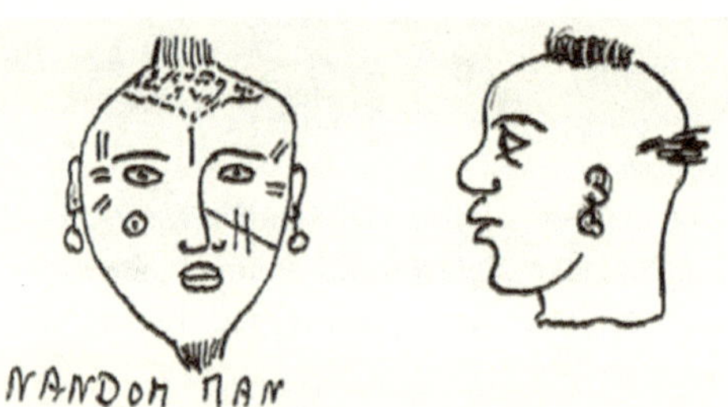

Figure 7. "Tribal Marks." From NAG ADM 61/5/1, Lawra District Record Book, 11. "Nandom Man." Note the side-perspective, which is reminiscent of a police mug-shot. See Figures 16a–16b.

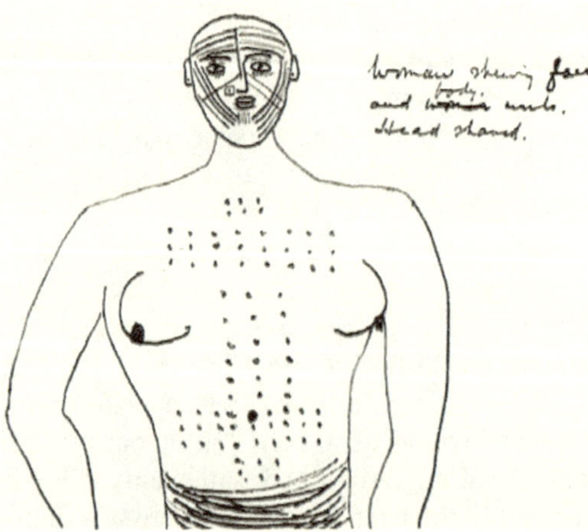

Figure 8. "Tribal Marks." From NAG ADM 61/5/1, Lawra District Record Book, 11. "Woman showing face and body marks. Head shaved." The marks were believed to be typical of women from Nandom.

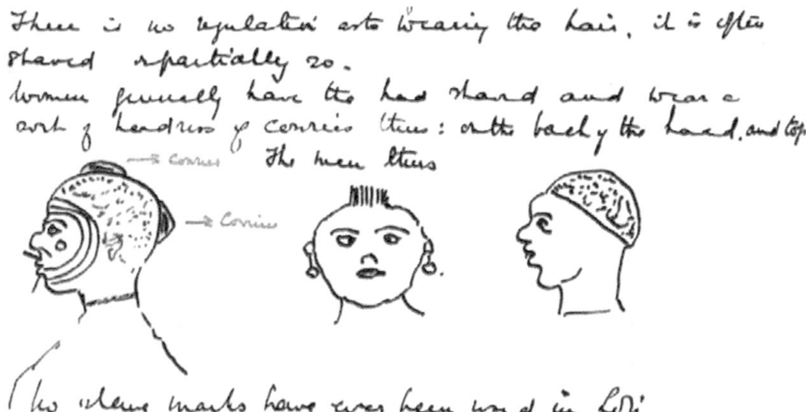

Figure 9. "Tribal Marks." From NAG ADM 61/5/1, Lawra District Record Book, 10. Text reads: "There is no regulation as to wearing the hair, it is often shaved partially so. Women generally have the head shaved and wear a sort of headdress of cowries thus: on the back of the head and top. The men thus / No slave marks have ever been used in Lobi."

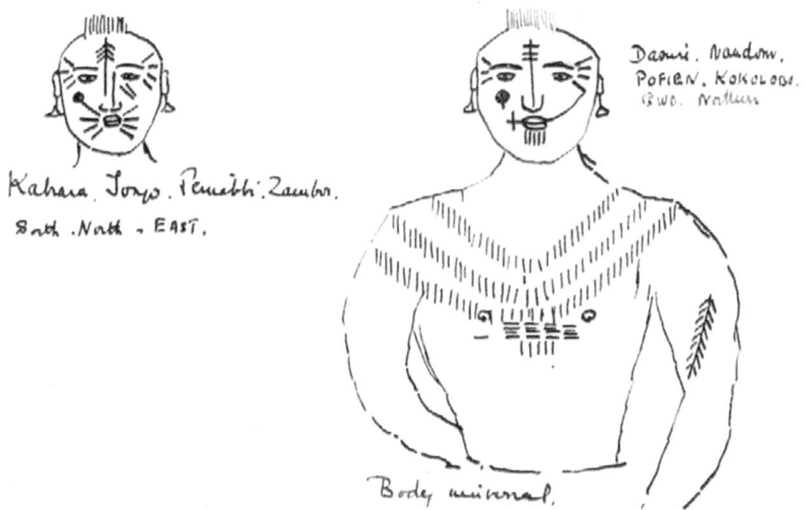

Figure 10. "Tribal Marks." From NAG ADM 61/5/1, Lawra District Record Book, 8. Right: markings found in the area around Lawra. Left: markings found in the vicinity of Nandom.

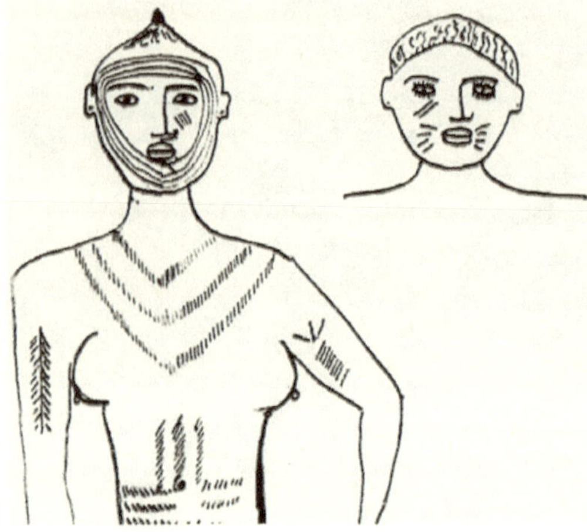

Figure 11. "Tribal Marks." From NAG ADM 61/5/1. Lawra District Record Book, 29. "Lobi Dagarti" women from Jirapa. The British officers who drew these figures classified the men and women depicted in figures 6–10 "Lobi," whereas those in figures 12–15 were called "Dagarti." Jirapa was thought to be one of the transitional settlements between these two ostensible "tribes" or "races."

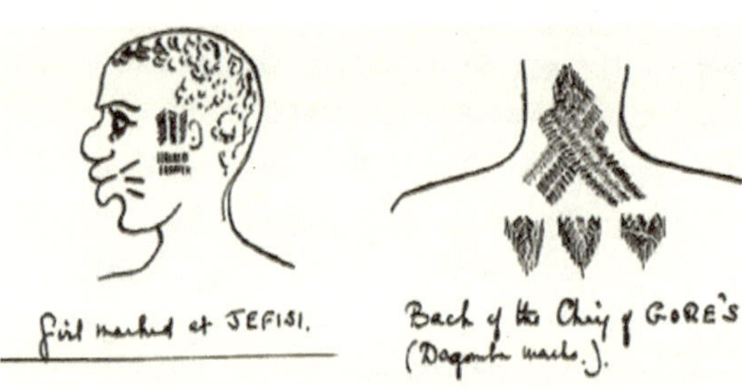

Figure 12. "Tribal Marks." From NAG ADM 61/5/1. Lawra District Record Book, 16. Text reads: "Girl marked at Jefisi / Back of the Chief of Gore's neck (Dagomba mark)."

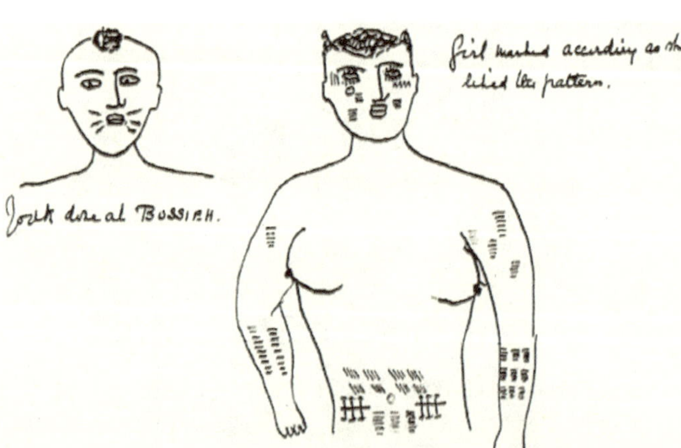

Figure 13. "Tribal Marks." From NAG ADM 61/5/1. Lawra District Record Book, 16. Text reads: "Look done at Bussieh / Girl marked according as she liked the pattern."

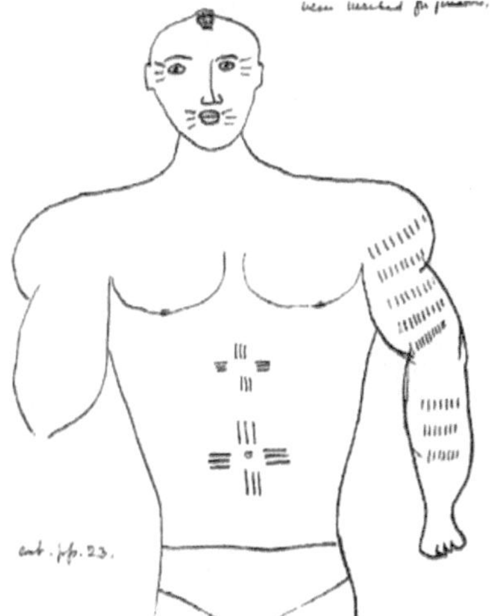

Figure 14. "Tribal Marks." From NAG ADM 61/5/1. Lawra District Record Book, 17. A "Dagarti" man from Ulo. The text at the top right of the image indicates that he has "been marked for pleasure." Despite the attempt to read scarification patterns as signs of ethnicity, it was quite clear that these markings were individual adornments, not tribal markings. See also Figure 13 above.

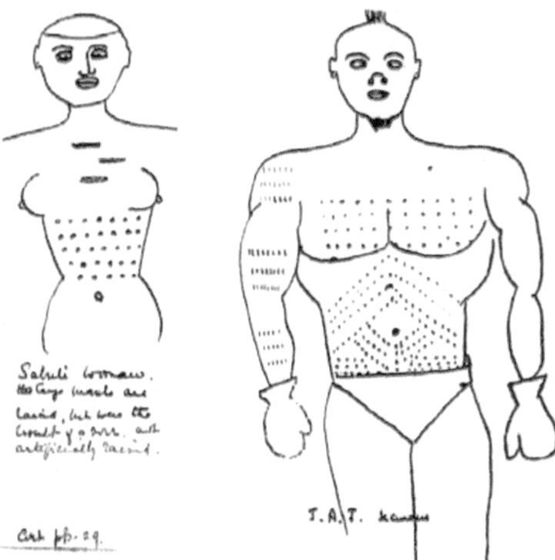

Figure 15. "Tribal Marks." From NAG ADM 61/5/1. Lawra District Record Book, 23. Text reads: "Sabuli woman. The large marks are raised, but were the result of a sore, not artificially raised." Here, as through this series, the exaggerated shoulders reflected colonial views of the LoDagaa as workers.

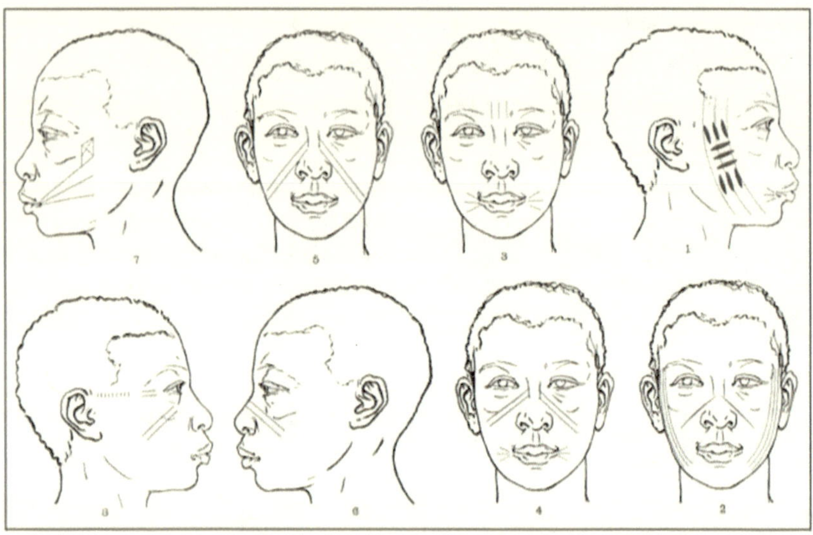

Figure 16a. "1, Wala; 2–8, Dagarba." From C.H. Armitage, *The Tribal Adornments of the Natives of the Northern Territories of the Gold Coast Colony* (1924), 15.

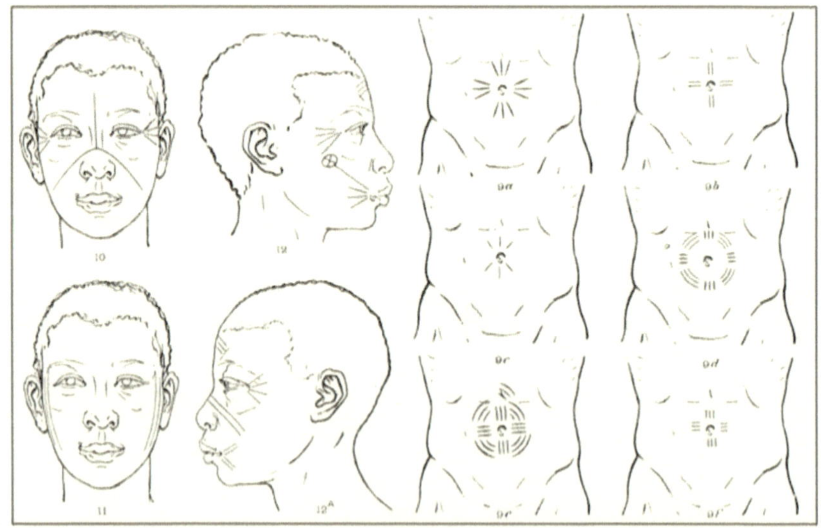

Figure 16b. "9, Dagarba; 10–12a, Lobi." From C.H. Armitage, *The Tribal Adornments of the Natives of the Northern Territories of the Gold Coast Colony* (1924), 17.

part of the country no political authority whatsoever. Some kind of order had to be made, and thus it was that Chiefs were imposed on the people."[73] This same sense of hopelessness informed efforts to define and appropriate the LoDagaa. The crudely drawn representations of LoDagaa bodies were the product of the same search for order and control. Just as the maps in the District Record Books bore little relationship to the reality they were meant to depict, the drawings of LoDagaa scarification patterns bore no relationship to ethnicity. Yet, as with ethnographic photographs, they created the illusion of power and control in the face of an overwhelming lack of knowledge. These images were part of the attempt to appropriate and control reality by cataloguing it and reducing it to paper. Maps discipline and normalize the world for those who construct and read them; the mapping of LoDagaa bodies served a similar purpose.[74] It was in effect an act of erasure. Scarification patterns were not understood as clothing the body, but as transparent signs on the body. Similar misreadings occurred elsewhere in Africa. As John and Jean Comaroff have put it: "In their outward 'nakedness,' the Africans went about fully clothed."[75]

The observations of officers and, later, missionaries reveal a persistent fascination with the aesthetics of LoDagaa bodies that bordered on "a preoccupation with the erotic."[76] In justifying his description of the LoDagaa as "savage," Ferguson had written: "These people ... move about in perfect nudity, their lips, noses, and ears are pierced, into which straws and beads are inserted as ornaments."[77] An early intelligence report on Lawra District described an area "extremely well stocked" with "a very big and strongly built race."[78] The lack of clothing was often remarked on, and always in connection with political unrest, wild tempers, physical disputes, or some other form of "primitive" behavior.

During the colonial era, the LoDagaa quickly developed an interest in clothing; having cloth and being well dressed became a matter of great importance to them. Soon after the British arrived, increased trade and labor migration made cloth more available, even though it was still relatively expensive. The LoDagaa did not produce their own cloth, and while a trade in cloth woven within the region existed before the colonial era, the wearing of clothes made of such fabric would have been extremely rare. Goody noted in his observation of mortuary practices in the 1950s that at some unspecified time in the past the LoDagaa had shifted from burying the dead in animal skins to using hand-woven cloth. To symbolize their new status the dead were literally "dressed up" in smocks, pants, and red fezes or some other form of head covering. After neophytes had completed their initiation into the cult of the *Bagre*, they too dressed up, and were led around in a public procession to indicate their new status.[79]

Appointed chiefs quickly took to wearing smocks made of cloth woven on the narrow hand looms of the region. The costumes appealed to the vanity of the chiefs and they also satisfied the expectations of colonial officers, who actively encouraged chiefs to differentiate themselves from the rest of the population and assume attire befitting their new status. Other colonial employees, such as soldiers, police, translators, and clerks, likewise set themselves apart by wearing clothes intended to convey their sense of being different, privileged, and associated with colonial power. Binney, the district commissioner's translator and later chief of Lawra, was noted for his sartorial boldness in the 1910s. On one occasion he was described as "dazzingly resplendent" in a white turban, sky blue "dzibbu" with a scarlet sash, red and yellow sword belt and sword, white trousers, and red leather boots.[80] Early migrant laborers were also able to wear clothes, which they either purchased in the south or had made locally from imported broadcloth or hand-woven material. For them, clothes were symbols of pride at their success in traveling south and acquiring cash. Retired servicemen from both world wars wore their uniforms as costumes of prestige.

These people all wore clothing as a symbol of status; in contrast, the dead and initiates to the cult of the *Bagre* wore it for ritual display. For the rest of the population, precolonial ways of adorning the body did not change significantly during the first half of the twentieth century.[81] In the past men had either tucked the penis under a string band tied around the waist or concealed it under a skin from a similar string. However, the wearing of shorts had become quite common by the middle of the century.[82] Women, who had little opportunity to earn money of their own sufficient to purchase clothing, still hung coverings made of leaves from a string band around their waists.[83]

After independence, cloth became a prominent issue in conjugal litigation. No doubt it had been an issue for women some time before that. Many wives came to expect that their husbands would supply them with cloth, either as part of efforts to secure their consent, or as a means of ensuring conjugal stability. When some LoDagaa, who had begun to cross the Black Volta in the 1930s, were interviewed by the District Commissioner of Bole, they complained that they had problems attracting and keeping wives in their new area because of cloth. It was now more available, but they considered it both costly and dangerous: "If we dressed our women it would not only be expensive, but the ladies would at once have an eye for the man who could give them the most clothes. They would get restive, commence to travel and abandon the duck-bill lips [labial adornments] which we like. We want them to sit at home, cook our food and produce children."[84] To what extent the district commissioner put words in the mouths of these men is difficult to judge, but concern over cloth definitely became a preoccupation among the LoDagaa.

At first government officials encouraged the wearing of cloth, to encourage trade and labor migration and also to satisfy their sense of propriety. In 1920 Binney reported that women would gradually begin to clothe themselves following a recent trend among "headwomen" to wear cloth. The district commissioner replied: "It is about time that they became a little more civilized."[85] But colonial attitudes eventually changed, and the wearing of clothes came to be associated with detribalization. Some administrators became alarmed by the spread of interest in clothing beyond migrant laborers. In 1944 an officer complained that the Lawra Naa, following examples in the south, had decided unilaterally that girls in the Native Authority School should wear skirts. The officer was annoyed by the chief's initiative and declared his decision to be medically and psychologically "unsound." In a gloss, the chief commissioner added: "I agree. But clothes will come eventually."[86] And come they did. At first strips of Mossi cloth were tailored into smocks, but by the 1940s printed cotton cloth predominated.[87]

It was the missionaries who actively encouraged the wearing of clothes in the 1930s; by this time colonial administrators were already worrying about the effects. Photographs taken by the missionaries suggest that in the early 1930s most converts did not wear cloth. Christian converts began going south during the decade in order to obtain the cloth they needed to conform to the notions of respectability that the missionaries were successfully inculcating in them,[88] and by the end of the decade missionaries were advising male converts to clothe their wives and even distributing cloth to female converts themselves; this attracted yet more women eager to give up the indigenous costume of leaves in favor of cloth.

By the 1950s, initiations into the *Bagre* cult, which required neophytes to appear in public with their bodies painted with whitewash in distinctive stripes, had declined in number due to an increasing sense of "modesty" among the LoDagaa as well as a more general desire to appear "decently dressed in public."[89] These new attitudes to the body were apparent among Christian converts and followers of indigenous beliefs alike.

Throughout the history of colonial labor migration, cloth was the most important acquisition of laborers. When Carola Lentz and Veit Erlmann interviewed a worker in the 1980s who had spent almost thirty years in the south as a miner, he could still remember what first attracted him to the life of a migrant laborer. The shorts and trousers of returning migrants had caused much excitement among young men in the 1950s, prompting them to go off in search of clothing: "When you worked up to five months or four months you have stayed long, then you stopped. ... When you have got enough clothing for you to go home and make *life* [i.e., to show off], oh you are gone! You go and farm and once the farming is done you're back South again."[90] For the generation that grew up in the time of relative prosperity after the Second World War, to dress well was a mark not only of style, but of modernity itself; it was a repudiation of external stereotypes of them as anything less than civilized.[91] The life of labor migration had many other attractions, such as the chance to escape the authority of elders and to circumvent conjugal obligations. But in the recollections of those lured south in the second half of the twentieth century, it was cloth and clothing that counted most.

By the 1980s the difficulty men had in obtaining cloth in the inflationary external economy was cited as the main hindrance to forming conjugal unions.[92] Père observed that among the *Lobi* and LoDagaa in Burkina Faso, the desire for clothes was still the main reason migrant laborers gave for why they needed money. And being dressed wasn't good enough – they had to be *well* dressed. Clothes had become a necessary counterargument to external representations: "These are clearly a proud people who will not tolerate being put in an inferior position, even in matters that many Westerners might regard as trivial, such as clothing."[93]

The Disappearance of the Lobi

The LoDagaa clothed their bodies in reaction to external stereotypes and also for personal adornment. The substitution of clothes for scarification represented the assimilation of new standards of deportment and personal style. As access to clothing increased in the second half of the twentieth century, the meaning of clothing became more diffuse. Rather than connoting a specific status in colonial or postcolonial society, clothing now indicated a wider identity, that of "civilization" and "modernity." It was no longer a question of whether people wore clothing, but of how well dressed they were. Nevertheless, even when they wrapped their bodies in the attire of this hegemonic identity, the LoDagaa still carried names that excluded them from full membership. One of Lentz's informants, who was living in Europe in the 1980s, identified most eloquently the problems that the LoDagaa faced: "The Asante people from the south have certain pejorative terms for us. ... We have to find some way of preventing them ... [but] we have not been able to identify ourselves and tell them what to say. We have not been able to tell them: this is what we are. So anybody calls us by any name, some of them pejorative, some not, but we accept them. So the problem is to define who we are."[94]

With the growth of a literate class of LoDagaa from Lawra District in the postcolonial period, a series of individuals and organizations attempted to address these problems. However, the search for an identity, which was largely a male project,[95] proved to be problematic.

Important vehicles for defining who the LoDagaa were in the 1980s and 1990s were youth associations in Lawra (the Lawra Paramountcy Youth Association), Jirapa (the Jirapa Area Youth and Development Association), and Nandom (the Nandom Youth and Development Association).[96] The main problem these associations encountered was a lack of cohesion between the literate leaders of these quests, "the people who know the book," and the general population of migrant laborers and peasant farmers. There were also tensions between the older and younger generations of literates. In addition, the questions these groups raised had far more relevance for ordinary LoDagaa when they were in the south – where conflicting and disparate loyalties and concerns absorbed their time and interests – than when they were home.[97] Despite the problems these associations had in creating a sense of ethnic community within their various areas, they had some success in presenting a front of political unity to external authorities (who ranged from regional politicians to the national media) at annual general meetings, which were accompanied by festivals of local dancing and song, where members wore T-shirts as "association uniforms."[98] The ideological attachment of these associations to "progressive development" and "modernisation" was not matched by sufficient resources or mobilization to affect any real change. "The upliftment of our people from the socio-economic woes of hunger, poverty, ignorance, disease, etc. which is the lot for most communities in third world countries," as one member saw his association's goal, was replaced by efforts at cultural reform and preservation.[99]

Beyond the level of local organizations and practical discourse, literate LoDagaa also attempted to create a wider sense of unity in the world on paper.[100] There, consensus eluded them again, for reasons that have as much to do with the evolutionary ideas the British introduced as they do with problems of communications and mobilization. As Lentz has shown, self-appointed intellectual leaders among the LoDagaa – mostly members of the local Catholic elite – were attracted to the notion of a tribal history as a means of creating a sense of common identity and redressing the notion that they did not have a past analogous or equivalent to those of the precolonial states that are now part of contemporary Ghana. Just as the colonial authorities sought to disentangle and override the seemingly endless series of migration histories of households by searching for the origins of the LoDagaa as a series of "races" or "tribes," LoDagaa intellectuals in the 1970s and 1980s embraced a similarly alien and privileged perspective on the past, but for different purposes. No longer was the objective to situate the LoDagaa in time; instead, the goals were to "restore the Dagara to historical initiative" and to "urge a general Ghanaian public to abandon its prejudices about the remote 'primitive' north."[101] The most immediate way of accomplishing these goals was to find connections with the history of the precolonial states of the region. These links could not be made through oral memory. The task required recourse to the world on paper, where this macro-narrative had already been inscribed, first by administrators and then by priests.[102] The colonial narrative of conquest and flight was replaced by a postcolonial story of rebellion and exodus. But the Dagomba association was central to both narratives, and both favored a plot of unilineal diffusion, which ignored the multilateral convergences so central to the diverse migration histories and as a result bore little or no relationship to the oral traditions of migration and origin that most LoDagaa knew.[103] The conventions of written history were foreign to the sensibilities of a historical consciousness based on speech rather than text. As Lentz has argued:

> Written histories attempt to establish an overall temporal framework, an emphasis alien to oral traditions, which are concerned to link the past with the present but not to establish an absolute chronology. ... the very idea of reconstructing an historical text of the Dagara as a collectivity within the wider world of the West African savanna is an essentially literate notion, very different from the multifarious patriclan stories which aim at justifying local boundaries and hierarchies.[104]

Writing became the metaphoric equivalent of cloth.[105] Just as cloth was used to make LoDagaa bodies respectable in terms of external perceptions, writing lent an alien sense of dignity to the LoDagaa past by associating it with the traditions of respected states. In the 1980s and 1990s, history became a counterideology to external stereotypes for the literate LoDagaa elite. History also became the medium through which various intellectuals attempted to fashion a sense of common ethnicity. Only by constructing a single narrative of origin could such an ethnicity be created; but as detailed below, this could only be accomplished by simplifying the many different paths of the ancestors (*tenkouri sor*).

Even though different conclusions have been drawn from it, there was a consensus on the idea of a Dagomba origin for the LoDagaa. This was because it worked so well to remedy their reputation for primitiveness, which was based on the apparent absence of a single historical narrative and the notion that they were stateless. It also provided the blueprint for a unified sense of ethnic consciousness.[106] The major stumbling block on paper (ignoring the problems that have arisen with disseminating this history) was the Lobi/Dagarti divide inherited from the British. As we have seen, during the first generation of colonial rule the Lobi came to be seen in a more positive light than the Dagarti, despite the greater prejudice of initial descriptions, because of their seemingly more positive reaction to colonial rule. A reputation for hard work and honesty replaced their earlier reputation for treachery and violence; meanwhile, the Dagarti came to acquire a reputation for resistance and sullenness. The rehabilitation of the Lobi in administrative eyes might have continued had it not been for the discovery of evidence at the end of the 1920s suggesting they were more primitive than their Dagarti neighbors to the east. This time their primitiveness was measured in terms of social evolution rather than cultural pathology.

In 1927 the district commissioner, Eyre-Smith, began investigating charges of political oppression by one of the colonial chiefs whom the British had appointed. In his report he noted:

> The people in the Tugu Sub-Division [that included the village of Yagha referred to in a previous quotation], erroneously called Lobi-Wili, are Dagatis, they are not wild, but very primitive, the same clans or families that occupy these villages are to be found in different villages in the Jirapa, Lawra, Nandom, Ulu and Han divisions. The state of affairs in Lawra and Nandom divisions is different to that in the Jirapa division, for the reason that the majority of the clans in these two divisions inherit through their mother and in consequence there are several very large families, whereas among the Dagatis inheritance is father to son so that a family may quickly become extinct.[107]

Social primitiveness now replaced earlier discourses on Lobi political wildness. In 1932, Rattray concluded from his own fieldwork in settlements southeast of Lawra that the people he called the Lobi, "perhaps the most primitive of any of the tribes in the Northern Territories," had reached a transitional stage in an evolution from matrilineal to patrilineal descent:

> As we have seen, in one respect the transition is complete – the son belongs to the clan – that is totemic group – of his father, not of his mother. ... In spite of this important breakaway from the older traditions ... inheritance of property is still through the sister's son, though here again we find that time and changes are causing the full practice to become irksome, and it will not be long, I believe, before the Lobi also follow the system now in force among their near neighbours.[108]

Thirty years after Rattray's fieldwork, George Murdock wrote in his ethnographic survey of Africa that the Lobi represented "the first step" in "the probable evolution of social organization" in the Voltaic region, a stage through which their co-linguists had passed and, therefore, through which they too would at some point pass.[109] Predictions of this kind infest observations on the

TABLE 3
Lobi and Dagarti Population of Lawra District, 1921–31

	1921 Lawra Census	1931 Lawra Census (1)
Lobis	39,952	40,031
Dagartis	8,304	16,940

Source: RAT ADM 217, Annual General Report, Northern Territories, Lawra-Tumu Census Report 1931

differences between people of this area and were based mainly on nineteenth-century social evolutionary ideas.[110] However, some administrators seem to have been unaware of the evolutionary assumptions behind theories of matrilineal inheritance. For example, one officer noted in the district annual report for 1937–38 that a shift from patrilineal to matrilineal inheritance was taking place due to the influence of Akan customs on migrant laborers. A year later this caused another officer to comment: "One's immediate reaction to such a statement is one of astonishment." He argued that if any shift had occurred, it was in the other direction, as Rattray had indicated, and added that "even where inheritance of property is through the mother, the children of a marriage remain in the clan (i.e., the father's family). Originally, amongst the Lobis, this cannot have been so; but the transition has reached the stage where, for personal relationships, the clan is becoming more important than the blood group."[111] Whereas matrilineal inheritance was equated with unsophisticated biological reckoning, patrilineal descent was seen as the result of social development.

The shift in classificatory emphasis from colonial caricatures to social evolution is the most likely explanation for the astounding anomaly between the census statistics of 1921 and 1931 for Lawra District, during which time the Dagarti population doubled while the Lobi population remained static. This phenomenon – the relative stasis (or even decrease) of one group and the increase of another despite identical demographic conditions – also occurred between the censuses of 1948 and 1960. Yet when the "tribal" statistics of the 1948 census are compared with those of 1960, it is clear that other factors besides new criteria for classification must have been involved in these anomalies.

The Lobi population in 1931 for Lawra District alone was greater than the total Lobi population of the whole of the Northern Territories in 1948, apparently indicating that the Lobi had experienced another demographic decline. But there is no evidence of a real (as opposed to nominal) decline among the peoples designated as Lobi; indeed, between 1931 and 1960 a large number of

TABLE 4
Lobi and Dagarti (Dagaba) Population of Northern Territories, 1948–60

	1948	1960
Lobi	38,031	32,250
Dagarti	107,436	166,250

Source: Gold Coast 1950, Table 23; Ghana 1964, Table 1

people who came to be designated as Lobi immigrated to Wa and Gonja Districts from the French colony of Côte d'Ivoire.[112]

The use of inheritance patterns as a criterion for ethnic ascription can account only in part for this second set of disparities. Shifting self-definition in terms of the Lobi/Dagarti dichotomy must also have been an important influence. As early as 1918 one district commissioner, commenting on the names under which military recruits registered, noted: "It is curious that so many Lobis have changed their names on enlisting and enlisted as Dagartis as if ashamed of the name Lobi. But I think it is now a thing of the past. One recruit however who left Lorha in the spring of this year as Mora Lobi comes back with his discharge certificate as Mora Dagarti."[113] Yet, as the 1913 encounter with French officers revealed, the Lobi/Dagarti divide had no real cultural, linguistic, or social meaning in Lawra District – it was an administrative invention. (Nevertheless, the dichotomy persisted into the postcolonial era.) The discovery of differences in patterns of the devolution of moveable property suddenly promised to make sense of decades of ethnographic confusion and to situate the people of the district in history – even if it was a purely conjectural narrative.

The perceived differences between the Lobi and Dagarti and the explanations offered for them were largely imaginary. As Eyre-Smith observed, all the people of the district had associated patriclans. The distinctions that Rattray observed mainly pertained to the devolution of property, and were explained by the existence of additional matriclans in some congeries, and the relative emphasis accorded to these by the different subgroups within those areas of both uterine and agnatic reckoning. The word "matrilineal" was highly misleading. The allegedly matrilineal Lobi of Lawra District inherited only movable wealth through the uterine line; land passed patrilineally, just as residence everywhere was virilocal. This social system has been more appropriately described as one of dual descent.[114] Furthermore, the Lobi of Lawra spoke *Dagaare* along with their Dagarti neighbors. Although the Lobi of Lawra District shared named matriclans (*belo*) with the *Lobi*-speaking inhabitants west of the Black Volta, their main cultural links were with their co-linguists to the southeast, the

Dagarti, with whom they also shared the same patriclans, making the LoDagaa as a whole more of a frontier community than a bounded society.[115]

Two further points need to be made about these distinctions based on inheritance. First, they were not alternative and opposed social ideologies; rather, inheritance patterns were the result of marriage patterns. In the case of conjugal unions between men of unilineal groupings and women of dual descent, the male offspring of those unions were able to choose between agnatic and uterine inheritance. This latitude or capacity for self-definition must obviously qualify any notion of socially exclusive or deterministic rules. Differences in patterns of descent did preclude unions in the opposite direction – that is, a husband of dual descent and a wife of unilineal reckoning – as the male offspring of such a union would not have been entitled to inherit from either household. The boundary as such was between men of dual descent and women of unilineal descent, but not necessarily the other way around. This would suggest that dual descent was not the last vestige of an antecedent stage in the evolution from matriliny to patriliny, but, far less dramatically, a social practice acquired by a patrilineal group through protracted unions along the interface with a neighboring group with matriclans.[116]

Second, a similar qualification regarding the rigidity of the devolution of property must be made. There was nothing determinant about these patterns that could constrain deviation. Where the inheritance of movable wealth was matrilineal, this was only one aspect of the implications of descent. As Goody discovered in research conducted between 1950 and 1952 in Lawra District, it was necessary to examine the wider devolution of property outside the narrower considerations of *post mortem* inheritance. There were, he reported, several significant strategies employed in areas of dual descent for circumventing *post mortem* succession through the uterine line: *inter vivos* transmission; cross-cousin marriages (father's sister's daughter); deliberate retention and affiliation of a daughter's child (*yiribe*); and, finally, in the more distant precolonial past, the purchase and adoption of male slaves.[117] These social possibilities illustrate the negotiability of social relations.

The Lobi/Dagarti dichotomy was employed as a means to dissect the people who inhabited Lawra District – to create external distinctions in the absence of clearly articulated indigenous identities. In a report written for the Colonial Office in 1954, Goody reinforced these distinctions, declaring that "most of this monograph is concerned with the establishment of ethnographic facts." These facts, however, did not coincide neatly with the fluidity of reality.[118] Elsewhere, while explaining the motivation for his research in terms reminiscent of Binger's quest, Goody noted how allusive this reality was: "When I first came to Lawra, and asked about a 'Lobi' community outside of the administrative centre itself,

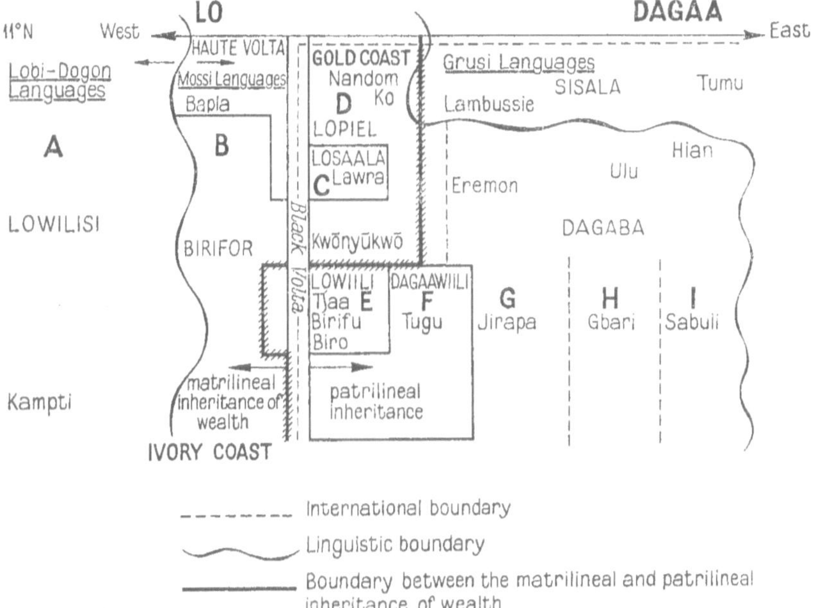

Map 6. "Diagram to Illustrate the Use of Directional Names, *Lo* and *Dagaa*, for External Reference" From J. Goody, *The Social Organisation of the LoWiili* (1956).

the LoWiili [of Birifu] were mentioned; it was some time later that I realised I had been directed to what for my purposes was the wrong community – as they did not inherit wealth matrilineally – but only towards the end of my field work did I understand why."[119]

Nevertheless, for Goody the fundamental and unchanging criterion for ethnic classification was the presence or absence of matrilineal inheritance. This brings us to his system of naming, which he based on two indigenous directional terms: *Lo* (west) and *Dagaa* (east). These were used in varying contexts by one group to refer to another. Goody mapped out this "system" according to patterns of inheritance, but he noted several other criteria an indigenous respondent might have chosen to identify with either *Lo* or *Dagaa*: conjugal payments, xylophones, *casus belli*, dancing, inheritance of movable wealth, dialect, and labial adornments (see Map 6). In any of these contexts, identity was defined in opposition to another group, and so did not constitute a form of ethnic consciousness.[120]

Just how contextual these referents were is captured well in the debate between Goody and his assistant Timbume. The anthropologist had classified Timbume as *Lo* on account of the uterine inheritance of movable wealth in his settlement, but Timbume insisted that he was *Dagaa.* Goody attributed Timbume's disposition to his having worked for some time in the south, where "language is the main referent of the two names because the important fact among migrant labourers and their employers is what they speak and not how they inherit." Although inheritance was obviously important, its use as the main criterion of identity was the result of anthropological fascination rather than indigenous concern. Goody's objections to Timbume's argument also attempted to erase the effects that colonization and labor migration had had on identities by the 1950s, even though Goody admitted that the term *Lo* was by that time limited to the *Lobi*-speaking inhabitants west of the Black Volta on account of its pejorative connotations. When Timbume countered that there were people who had *Lo* features in their culture but did not inherit matrilineally, Goody concluded that these people were "out of cultural alignment" with the underlying logic to their ethnographic situation. Matrilineal inheritance became the "central referent," and all other factors were relegated to the status of "subsidiary criteria."[121]

The practice of directional naming could only be reduced to the world on paper after other simultaneous possibilities, such as language, xylophones, and dances, had been precluded. The observer, Goody, had appropriated the authority of definition from Timbume, the practitioner. To borrow Bourdieu's metaphor, Goody's cultural alignment was that of the road, whereas Timbume's objections were several paths. This adherence to the straight line might be surprising, were it not for the fact that Goody was bound by the conventions of anthropology in its most restricted form – the ethnographic monograph. As Fabian has observed, such anthropological accounts are inherently concerned with "boundaries" and "liminal concerns."[122] Goody's idea that there was some form of underlying cultural alignment that could be unraveled through study, as if ethnographic complexity were merely a puzzle or conundrum, and not the residue of historical layering, can be traced back to the attempts by the first administrators to understand the people of Lawra District. Goody replaced the colonial logic of caricature with the ethnographic logic of classification, yet both approaches were misleading.

The amorphousness of the ethnographic situation in Lawra District was largely due to the inability of observers to recognize and respect the historical forces that had produced such complexity. Instead, they wished to reduce everything to two dimensions. For administrators, these dimensions were Lobi and Dagarti, and for Rattray and Goody they were matrilineal and patrilineal. Reality was multidimensional, and therefore militated against the LoDagaa developing ethnonyms that could be used to appropriate them and their history. Although administrators did not understand why ethnic identity in Lawra District was so complicated, Goody had been able to explain to them, just as their rule was coming to an end, that "the group, unable to visualise its unity from within, defines itself in opposition to the surrounding peoples."[123] Different congeries were simply unable to see themselves in a self-reflexive and self-conscious way, and when they gave names to other congeries they did so in terms of contextual criteria. In contrast, the "visualism" employed by observers was biased, according to Fabian, toward a particular kind of knowledge based on "convictions deeply ingrained in an empirical scientific tradition. Ultimately they rest on a corpuscular, atomic theory of knowledge and information. Such a theory in turn encourages quantification [censuses] and diagrammatic representations [drawings and maps] so that the ability to 'visualize' a culture or society almost becomes synonymous for understanding it."[124]

As with the clumsy attempts by British officers to draw their colonial subjects, giving names to the LoDagaa was a way of visualizing and therefore appropriating them. Censuses quantified those names and images. Early names were confusing and inconsistent, but with the use of inheritance as the determinant of identity, names could be fixed with seeming scientific exactitude. However, indigenous knowledge followed a different logic. Observers were interested in discursive or objective knowledge, whereas social actors possessed only practical knowledge – the unsystematized result of countless experiences and encounters with neighboring settlements and congeries. Any representation of the LoDagaa as a unity or collectivity of ethnographic facts cannot be other than a compromise. The knowledge that external naming created at different times was illusory. Prior to the twentieth century there had been no self-identities; they were unnecessary until the external world intruded on the experiences of the various LoDagaa congeries in ways that thrust them outside the confines of their former experiences.

Local Politics and Identity

External writing on LoDagaa identity came to an end with Goody. He had conducted most of his fieldwork in the last years of the colonial era, when there were still only a few literate LoDagaa, and even fewer LoDagaa who had traveled outside the Northern Territories for anything but labor migration. That situation changed after independence, when the LoDagaa gained access to postsecondary secular education, and with the development of an indigenous Catholic clergy, who often went abroad to study. By the 1980s the term Lobi had almost entirely disappeared in northwest Ghana as a term of self-designation. Even so, among indigenous writers on identity – most of them Western-educated teachers and priests – matrilineal inheritance of wealth became an important factor in how ethnic identities were articulated.[125] After two generations and more of external rule, many local intellectuals were interested in constructing a wider sense of ethnic identity, as a means of acquiring greater political recognition and more economic resources for the people of the region. In this project they did not rely on observations of current conditions, but turned to the history of the LoDagaa in the hope of discovering a hidden unity that had been denied by colonialism and anthropology. In particular, they took umbrage at Goody's argument that cultural, linguistic, and social fragmentation had resulted in distinct congeries. Yet for most LoDagaa, these postcolonial discourses were as removed from their everyday lives and concerns as were earlier colonial discourses on identity. Despite the keen interest in fostering a strong sense of local identity, neither colonial nor postcolonial discourses did so. Instead, these texts have produced contradictory and rival ethnonyms on paper.[126]

In 1982, Gabriel Tuurey, a graduate of the University of Ghana, schoolteacher, and local historian, wrote a short monograph on the origins of the people of the region in which he defined an overall ethnic identity that he referred to as Dagaba. Significantly, Tuurey was seeking to come to terms with his "roots" – namely, the suggestion that members of his clan were "descendants of Mossi ancestors." This path of historical investigation led him to appreciate the greatness of the Mossi and to ignore the stories he had been told in his youth that portrayed them as "dirty, lousy and despicable." Tuurey set out to make the "noble and courageous" Mossi, "who delight in displaying masculinity, martial adour and the love of justice," an integral part of the formation of the people he called the Dagaba.[127] To do this, he took several approaches. First, he referred to their language group as Mole instead of Mole-Dagbane, in an effort to stress Mossi contributions to the creation of the Dagaba, and he substituted Mole again for *Dagaare* to emphasize these links and suggest a common culture. Second, he stressed that the Mossi had been absorbed and assimilated much as the Normans had been in England.[128] According to Tuurey's account, "the first of its kind ever written by a Mole [*Dagaare*] speaker,"[129] the Dagaba were descendants of Mole speakers who left Dagbon (where Dagbane was spoken) during a period of civil strife and migrated to what, several centuries later, became the northwest corner of Ghana, a land called Dagao by its new inhabitants. After the migration these people coined the term Dagaba to distinguish themselves from their Dagomba ancestors.[130] His own ancestors fled Yatenga under similar circumstances several generations later.[131] In an attempt to deny historical priority to any of the different migrations that peopled the region, he argued that "no matter the ethnic origin of their ancestors," all descendants of these immigrants "must be Dagaba first and any other thing second."[132]

A third way of demonstrating the unity of the Dagaba and the influence of the Mossi focused on kinship. Tuurey stated emphatically that the Dagaba were patrilineal, "and would not accept the dominance of uterine kinship in their society"; this differentiated them from the Lobi, who had "strong matrilineal tendencies."[133] Echoing a line of evolutionary reasoning going back to McLennan's *Primitive Marriage* over a hundred years before, Tuurey argued that matrilineal inheritance arose from biological uncertainty over parentage – a problem that had never afflicted the Dagaba, "who were sure of the chastity and faithfulness of their wives."[134] The clear implication was that "matriclan tendencies" were the consequence of a relative absence of sexual morality. In addition, because strong patriclans created a sense of cohesiveness, social conditions had been more chaotic among the Lobi than among the Dagaba. If the Mossi were victims of negative stereotypes, the Lobi deserved their reputation, according to Tuurey: "Each individual was a law unto himself. As a result the Lobi were a wily and treacherous people capable of ... stealthily shooting with bow and poisoned arrows an opponent in an ambush and escaping the scene of assault. By such actions the Lobi were considered cowardly."[135]

Tuurey suggested that only the Dagaba were true Mole [*Dagaare*] speakers, whereas the Lobi spoke a language called Lor. This was the dialect of *Dagaare* that Rattray had identified as Loberu; it so closely resembled the parent language, Dagbane, that he had been able to make himself understood speaking the latter among the Lobi after only a short stay.[136] Tuurey contended that only one of the languages of the Lobi subgroups, that of the Lor-Dagaba of the Nandom area, was intelligible to Mole speakers, because it was a hybrid of Lor and Mole.[137] Tuurey, who was born south of Lawra District in Kaleo, presumed that the dialect of *Dagaare* spoken by his Dagaba was pure, whereas the dialect spoken by the inhabitants of Nandom was at best a corruption of the original resulting from a mixing with the earlier inhabitants. There was no explanation as to how this alleged linguistic miscegenation had occurred. Ignoring the effects of colonial rule, he merely stated that the present inhabitants of the Nandom area referred to themselves as either "Lobi or Dagara."[138] He argued that the Lobi had resided in the area long before the Dagaba arrived, and that except for those in Nandom and Lawra, most had left the region.[139]

The people of Nandom were indeed the product of intermixing, but so too were the Dagaba of Kaleo.[140] However, ignoring clear evidence of cultural intermingling, Tuurey assumed that the Dagaba were authentic. As an indication of this, he pointed to their apparent lack of social deviations, that is, their patrilineal descent. Nevertheless, the Dagaba were not, according to Tuurey, "one people," even though they had "a common culture, language, traditional religion, history, tribe and territorial area," because they had lacked any cohesive political force. He compared the various LoDagaa congeries with Germany before unification, referring to them as "a nation without a polity," and even sympathizing with the problems the British had faced in making sense of this complicated situation: "This was not political freedom, it was something worse than that. At best, it could be virtually described as political anarchy. ... This heavily segmented political situation in Dagao [the land inhabited by the Dagaba] must have greatly confounded the British."[141]

For Tuurey, history and tribe were synonymous, but the lack of clear identities threatened the idea of a single, coherent narrative. Writing of the period before the arrival of the British, he considered it "a pity" that a secular form of political authority based on physical rather than "spiritual" sanctions had not emerged, because it meant that "as individual and disunited clan groups" the Dagaba remained "weak."[142] His lament at the lack of precolonial political cohesion was very much in tune with the remarks of one district commissioner, A.C. Duncan-Johnstone, who in 1921 declared: "Had they been united under strong Chiefs with their splendid physique and warlike qualities, they might have caused an entirely different page of local History to be written."[143] Although he did not attempt to rewrite the political past of the LoDagaa, Tuurey was certainly interested in rewriting their cultural and social past.

The patrilineal character of the Dagaba provided Tuurey with a coherent perspective – a straight line or road – that gave his theory a trajectory. Although conceding that the Dagaba were the product of several migrations by different people, he refused to consider matrilineal inheritance of wealth as part of the same cultural and linguistic zone. Other *Lo* elements were not considered integral to Dagaba identity, even though the Dagaba had acquired many cultural traits from *Lobi*-speaking peoples to the west of the Black Volta: xylophones, filing of teeth, piercing of ears, wearing of discs in the perforated lips of women, and domestic architecture.[144] He was forced to concede these borrowings because these were not traits that existed among the Mole-Dagbane-speakers to the east. In his historical explanation, migrants from these areas had brought only their language and strict patriliny. That the same named patriclans were found among the people of both Nandom and Kaleo indicates, however, that Tuurey's *Dagaare*-speaking Lobi, or Lor-Dagaba, were also part of the migrations from the east that had brought the first Mole-Dagbane speakers to the region.[145]

Tuurey's analysis embraced the "facts" that Eyre-Smith, Rattray, and Goody had established and combined them with the distinctions that had been applied by early administrators. In order to make the idea of Dagaba identity consistent and linear, Tuurey needed to create a core culture with exclusively eastern origins. Although all other things *Lo* could be excised from the pure culture of the archetypical Dagaba, matrilineal inheritance of wealth could not be discounted: any people carrying this trait had to be excised from the group.

Goody's focus on inheritance led him to write about the LoDagaa in terms of an east/west axis, which corresponded with his map of cultural alignment. But in a 1997 study of *Dagaare*, Adams Bodomo has argued that its dialects fall more along a north/south axis, even though he too was careful to note that "they shade gradually into each other and it is almost impossible to draw a line of demarcation between the different dialects."[146] Nevertheless, he did identify four dialect groups: "Northern" (in the northwest of Lawra District, centered around Nandom and Lawra, and across the border into Burkina Faso); "Central" (in the southeast of Lawra District, away from the Black Volta, around Jirapa, Ulo, Dafiama, and Han, and south as far as Nadawli); "Southern" (centered on Kaleo and Wa); and "Western" (straddling the Black Volta in both Côte d'Ivoire and Ghana, and running south from Wa as far as Bole).[147] This north/south axis corresponds more closely with the distribution of *Dagaare*-speaking people (Map 2). Along this axis, the people to the south tend to regard the dialect of those further north as *Lo* (as in Loberu, Lobr, or Lor). Kojo Yelpaala noted: "The Dagaaba around Wa called those around Jirapa north of Wa, Lobi and the people of Jirapa call others around Lawra, west of Jirapa, Lobi." Accordingly, he argued that the term Lobi had "virtually no specific meaning."[148] Tuurey tried to give it meaning in the instance of Nandom, not because of any real grounds for linguistic differentiation, but because of his disdain for the matrilineal inheritance of wealth.

Gaspard Dery, another graduate of the University of Ghana, published an alternative survey of the LoDagaa in 1987 subtitled "Second Opinions on Existing Theories." Complaining about the generalizations in Goody's work, and its esoteric nature, he set out to produce "a simple and comprehensive" monograph on the Dagaaba.[149] Dery's work, like Tuurey's, was based on the work of previous researchers, but the questions it sought to answer arose from the public debate in the pages of the local Catholic newspaper, *The Diocese, Wa*, following the publication of Tuurey's pamphlet. The most significant concerned whether the Dagaaba were patrilineal or matrilineal by descent and inheritance. Dery argued that the devolution of movable property through the uterine line among a few congeries was tantamount not to matriliny but rather to dual descent, or more precisely dual inheritance.[150] Therefore, he argued, "allegations ... that the Dagaaba are matrilineal by inheritance are unfounded and must be dismissed."[151] By focusing on the continuities of kinship patterns, such as patrilineal descent, shared patriclans, and virilocal residence, instead of what he regarded as mere anomalies in inheritance patterns, Dery brought all LoDagaa congeries under the same classificatory umbrella, that is, Dagaaba. Unlike Tuurey, who argued that the people in the vicinity of Nandom were matrilineal, Dery argued that all Dagaaba were patrilineal. Against Tuurey's contention that inheritance of movable wealth along the uterine line was the result of sexual promiscuity, Dery, drawing from oral traditions, argued that where this practice had arisen it had been the result of generational tensions between fathers and sons. In the stories he cited, a man was given assistance by his sister's children when his own refused to help him with farming. After the work was finished the father declared that in future his maternal relatives should have a claim on his property.[152]

The next major attempt at sorting out this complex ethnic situation came in 1989 with an article by Benedict Der, a professor of history at the University of Cape Coast, in the inaugural issue of a journal dedicated to the study of the LoDagaa – a joint Ghanaian-Burkinabe endeavor written in English and French and published in Berlin. Der took Tuurey to task for labeling the people of Nandom and Lawra as Lobi and thus excluding them from "the real Mole-Dagbane speakers." He claimed that "oral traditions" indicated a common migration from Dagbon.[153] These same "oral traditions" had informed Tuurey's account. Both authors reiterated the theme of Dagomba origins and rebellion against political domination. However, the traditions were relatively new and were not orally based. Tuurey's account was drawn almost entirely from written sources, from which he derived his evidence and narrative of a Dagomba connection. Also, the medium of his history was self-consciously literate. Addressing himself to "the reading public," he countered any criticism that his work was "academically fictitious" simply because it dealt with the past of a people who had "neither developed nor acquired writing."[154] However, he presented a literate narrative derived from secondary sources instead of oral traditions.

Der's narrative of Dagomba origins was drawn from French (Binger, Tauxier, Labouret) as well as English (Eyre-Smith, Rattray, Goody) sources. More importantly, he drew heavily on the work of Père Jean Hébert, a missionary from Burkina Faso who was the principal researcher for a collaborative history of the LoDagaa of the Diébougou region. Aided by a team of indigenous researchers drawn from the Catholic community, he conducted extensive interviews in both Ghana and Burkina Faso (then Haute-Volta) during the 1960s and 1970s.[155] In the narrative of Dagomba origins with which he prefaced his history of the migrations of individual clans, Hébert relied on "a medley of disparate evidence."[156] As Lentz has noted, even though Hébert drew from oral testimony as well as the work of colonial ethnographers, his emphasis on "origins" clearly departed from the themes of "arrival and settlement" featured in the histories of different clans.[157] Der then grafted similarly disparate elements from the migration histories of patriclans, from places such as Nandom, Tom, Gengenkpe, Tuopare, Guo, and Ko, to emphasize that these patricians came generally from the south, from areas such as Nadawli. But he also claimed that these clan histories all spoke of a more remote origin in the east, among the Dagomba.[158] During her fieldwork Lentz found that such a narrative was "virtually unknown" among migrant laborers and village farmers, and that those who had heard of it "distinguished clearly between the migration stories as guaranteed by their forefathers and the Dagomba story usually heard from priests or catechists or other educated [literate] Dagara."[159]

Der associated the people of Nandom with this positive narrative from the world on paper in order to avoid associating them with other negative narratives from the world on paper (i.e., the ones that referred to Lobi primitiveness and the matrilineal inheritance of wealth). He also repudiated any *Lo* connections. He tried to undermine the allegation that the people around Nandom were Lobi by noting that in southern settlements, such as Kaleo, all co-linguists north of Nadawli were called Loor or Lobr, as distinct from *Lobi*, regardless of their pattern of inheritance. Indeed, Der suggested that the dialects spoken farther north were not hybrids, but actually closer to the original dialects spoken by the first immigrants from Dagbon. Southern dialects had deviated more strongly because of the influence of the Yarse (Mande traders) and the Mossi.[160] Thus the inhabitants of Nandom and Lawra were actually Dagara, whereas those living farther south were Dagaba, the product of intermarriage between the original immigrants from Dagbon and later immigrants from Yatenga, Bouna, and Ouagadougou.[161] He did not consider the influence of any autochthones on the emergence of the Dagara; indeed, he stated that *Dagaare* and *Lobi* speakers had not intermarried in Nandom, but only along the Black Volta farther south, around Lawra. This had resulted in the hybrid culture referred to as DagaWiile.[162] (If the inhabitants of the Nandom area had not intermixed with the matrilineal *Lobi* speakers to the west, then how had the Dagara acquired matrilineal features, and why were the DagaaWiile, who had intermarried, still patrilineal?)

Der introduced a temporal distinction between Dagara and Dagaba, even though all previous sources had considered the two words synonymous; yet he did not suggest how this distinction had arisen historically.[163] As the following excerpt suggests, he never fully resolved what to call the present inhabitants of northwest Ghana who shared the same language and culture and a similar social structure (including common clans): "If a common ethnological term has to be found to describe them as a people, one would suggest Dagara as that classificatory term since it is historically basic to the Dagara and Dagaba alike. Failing that, the compound name Dagara-Dagaba can be used to refer to them. The early Dagaba were, in effect, the grandchildren, the nephews, nieces and cousins of the Dagara."[164]

According to Der, the only true Dagara in Lawra District were the inhabitants of the Nandom area – the very people Tuurey rejected as Lobi. These rival claims reflect the politics of regionalism and ethnicity: Tuurey came from Kaleo in Wa District, whereas Der was from Bo, near Nandom, in Lawra District. Tuurey was using unilineal descent as the basis for his Dagaba classification in order to strengthen Mossi integration with the wider culture. What Mossi immigrants to Kaleo lacked in historical depth and demographic importance was more than compensated for by their social affinity. Der's isolation of the residents of Nandom as the true Dagara was a form of nativism, and seems to have been calculated to overcome any suggestion that the matrilineal inheritance of movable wealth was the result of contamination from another culture. It should be noted that as a matter of convention, by the 1980s the common term used by Ghanaian observers of the LoDagaa was Dagaaba, whereas the term preferred by Burkinabe observers was Dagara.[165]

The terms Dagari and Dagabakha, which Binger, who first reported them, speculated were synonymous, had diverged a century later. Clearly, no perfectly acceptable ethnonym has yet emerged among the literate leaders of the *Dagaare*-speaking peoples of the northwest corner of Ghana.[166] The attendant controversies over recent attempts at naming preclude the use of either term. As a purely mnemonic device, the term LoDagaa, however contrived, is actually the most suitable. It has the double advantage of implying no real sense of collective ethnicity and of not being rooted in time. It also acknowledges the obvious contiguity with the culture of the *Lobi*-speaking people to the west. Local writers dealing with identity have inherited colonial distinctions made on maps and in writing. But just as the roads the British imposed on the landscape were not based on the pattern of indigenous footpaths, the Lobi/Dagarti divide was a foreign invention. The substitution of "tribal" narratives for the fragmentary histories of individual patriclans meant that the contextual and multidimensional patterns of physical migration and cultural contiguity had to be suppressed in order to sustain a linear narrative going back in space and time to Dagbon. The physical and temporal extension of LoDagaa history contained in this narrative came at a cost.

The search for a discursive sense of identity begun by outside observers, and continued by local observers, was the product of the discontinuities that colonial conquest and incorporation in a wider world brought to the LoDagaa. But it is important to note that these discursive exercises in definition and classification have not been informed by, nor have they influenced, identities at a practical level: these identities remained amorphous, contingent, and local. This is due in no small part to the fact that the various LoDagaa congeries did not need names to know who they were and to understand themselves. For most LoDagaa, identities have only been necessary for dealing with external authorities and situations on an individual basis. Unfortunately, this lack of consciousness of ethnic identity has not proved as unproblematic for observers of the LoDagaa. External observers needed fixed and definite identities for purposes of appropriating the LoDagaa; internal observers needed identities for purposes of representing the LoDagaa to the outside world as a single collectivity. Unfortunately, this need for a single identity generated competing versions. All local writers were Catholics who had been brought into contact with members of different congeries as a result of their religious affiliation. Although Christianity provided a commonality of experience and belief, it did not transcend local rivalries and differences.[167] Tuurey's definition of Dagaba identity was the most obvious example of this; thus it is highly ironic that he concluded his pamphlet with an admonishment against ethnic fragmentation.[168]

Conclusion to Part 1

In the world of experience, the LoDagaa had neither a strong sense of narrative history nor a clear sense of ethnic identity. Because of their psychological need to possess the LoDagaa, the British set about situating them on paper in terms of both time and space. Local intellectuals furthered their project for different reasons. But interest in both history and identity was the preserve of observers – both external and internal – who belonged to the world on paper. In their efforts to imagine a history and ethnic identity for the LoDagaa, these observers assumed perspectives belonging to the world on paper. What observers did not see was that the experiential concerns of the LoDagaa were with land and cloth rather than history and ethnicity.

PART TWO

Political and Religious Ambiguities

Chapter Three

Rewriting the Past

Since we came under the white man's King our people have prospered, our children do not know what hunger is, we do not get our cattle stolen, sickness does not kill so many of our people, we are not raided for slaves.

Greetings of Nanweni, Chief of Lawra, to King George V, 1925

By making one type of history, that of stasis, authentic, and another type of history, that of change, illegitimate, the world on paper bequeathed forms of historicism that were debilitating to the exercise of LoDagaa historicity. Indigenous intellectuals attempted to regain sovereignty lost through colonial conquest and missionary evangelism by rewriting the past. They appealed to the conventions of a static, authentic history which held that legitimacy resided in the past; in doing so, they succumbed to the historicism of the world on paper. However, real sovereignty resided in history of the second type, which belonged to the world of experience. In the end, these efforts to wrestle power away from the world on paper simply reinforced the authority of writing by accepting its criteria of legitimacy. As Marshall Sahlins noted in another context: "There is a kind of academic defense of the cultural integrity of indigenous peoples that, although well-intentioned, winds up delivering them intellectually to the imperialism that has been afflicting them."[1]

One of the most enduring British stereotypes of the LoDagaa concerned their apparent lack of political organization. This stereotype grew to become part of an important discourse designed to legitimate colonial rule. Initially the British saw the absence of identifiable political structures through which to rule the LoDagaa as a tremendous inconvenience, but eventually they turned this situation to their advantage. In the first two decades of colonial rule, administrators created a network of chiefs who had no indigenous legitimacy. Because they relied entirely on administrative recognition, the chiefs were not constrained by the cultural beliefs and values of the people they ruled. But in the late 1920s this colonial regime was suddenly threatened by the advent of "indirect rule" – a doctrine of administration predicated on historical continuity. Suddenly the idea of chiefs had to be depoliticized by being historicized. This shift in discourse from politics to history created an enduring legacy among the LoDagaa in their dealings with the world on paper. The once reviled chiefs of colonial rule were later rehabilitated in the postcolonial period. As they lost much of their official status and were increasingly marginalized from government power, they acquired a legitimacy among their subjects proportional to the insecurities created by the political instability of national governments. However, the tyranny of historicism was such that discourse over chieftaincy – particularly as it related to issues of succession – was still trapped in arguments about history rather than politics.

In the following chapter I examine how, roughly three generations after indirect rule was first considered, the idea of inculturation produced similar discourses about the past. In the 1980s the Catholic diocese within which Lawra District fell entered into a period of debate about the nature of indigenous beliefs that challenged earlier missionary observations. This second phenomenon was also concerned with using a reimagined past to disguise and hence legitimate change. However, the changes that colonial administrators charged with implementing indirect rule attempted to historicize in the late 1920s and early 1930s were very different from those that indigenous priests empowered by inculturation were trying to legitimate in the late 1980s and early 1990s; they are as different as colonization and decolonization.

Part Two of this book focuses on these two parallel debates about chieftaincy and theology. In this chapter and the next I discuss how the world on paper became the arbiter for external recognition of LoDagaa political and cultural authenticity, and why observers have used the past as a source of legitimacy.

Writing Chaos into Colonial Order

Betraying an obvious preference for centralized states already well enshrined in nineteenth-century European evolutionary schema, Binger had contended that the LoDagaa and other Voltaic societies had been marginalized by "more advanced" people.[2] After Binger's very sketchy intelligence about these politically decentralized societies, Ferguson referred to them as "savage" and "barbarous tribes," describing the Lobi and Dagarti in particularly stark terms: "They live mostly in family communities, and resist intercourse, even among their own selves, with showers of arrows. ... As a tribe or district, none of them is capable of negotiating with a European Power, and can only be civilised by force of arms."[3] The first definite reports about the people of Lawra District did not appear until 1905, beginning with Read's reconnaissance of the district. He described the LoDagaa much as Ferguson had: "The Lobi native is of an extremely independent nature and will own no other authority beyond the head of his own family. ... They are of a very quick tempered disposition and always ready to resort to poisoned arrows. ... Fighting between compounds have been frequent occurrences, they are generally confined to compounds only, though sometimes the whole village will join in attacking another village."[4]

Prior to the arrival of the British, the inhabitants of Lawra District had experienced two generations of insecurity due to external threats; yet the colonial authorities, at least initially, paid little attention to this history or to the negative effects of their own presence on people's sense of security. Between 1903 and 1905, officers had made periodic and haphazard forays into Lawra District, appointing chiefs in the settlements they came across. The selection criteria were minimal – it was often enough that the candidate chief had not fled at the approach of a British officer with his Hausa troops, and that he had persuaded the other inhabitants to return.[5]

These stereotypes of LoDagaa society as anarchic and violent endured. Moreover, they acted as a justification after the fact for the colonial policy adopted between 1907 and 1932, under which "sergeant-major" chiefs were imposed on the LoDagaa.[6] In 1928 one senior administrator, A.W. Cardinall, maintained that even though abuses had occurred, the era of rule through the chiefs had been a necessary response to the "chaos" the British had encountered in much of the Northern Territories: "Conditions in the North were even worse and the present districts along the Northern frontier were in so anarchic a state that the astute Mr. Ferguson found himself forced to ignore them in his great treaty-making expedition of 1894, for therein he could place his finger on no single king." Although Cardinall did refer to the effect of slavers on security at the end of the nineteenth century, he saw them as merely contributing to this disorder and not the cause of it; for him, this disorder justified the "peace" that the British imposed on the LoDagaa and other cultures through the creation of "'sergeant-major' chieftains."[7] Similarly, in 1932 the District Commissioner of Lawra attempted to apologize for the effects of colonial rule by explaining "that before the white-man came there was in this part of the country no political authority whatsoever. Some kind of order had to be made, and thus it was that Chiefs were imposed."[8]

By 1907 the pragmatic strategy of administering the area through colonial appointees from within LoDagaa society had resulted in the creation of ten divisional chiefs in the following areas: Lawra, Nandom, Jirapa, Lambussie,

Samoa, Zini, Ulo, Nandaw, Lissa, and Sabuli.[9] Within each of these divisions, areas of settlement were subject to head chiefs, subchiefs, and headmen, depending on their size and order of recognition. As more settlements were discovered in subsequent years, the number of appointees in lesser categories expanded greatly. In some cases settlements came under chiefs even before a district commissioner had visited them.[10] By 1919 there were approximately 130 chiefs and headmen for a population of roughly 56,000 – that is, one colonial appointee to every 446 inhabitants. Lawra, Nandom, and Jirapa were the largest divisions, accounting for 38,241 of all inhabitants of Lawra District. In these divisions there were 36, 39, and 40 chiefs, subchiefs, and headmen respectively, giving a ratio of one appointee to every 333 persons.[11]

Initially chiefs had been created merely to serve as channels of communication between officers and inhabitants. But once civil administration began, they supplied labor for the administration. Between 1907 and 1917, besides supplying migrant laborers, the chiefs also procured forced labor. Such demands were unprecedented. The LoDagaa used a special term, *nasaal tumo* or "white man's work," to refer to these procurements.[12] Almost as soon as the chiefs began making such demands, they met resistance. When resisters were brought to the attention of the district commissioner, he invariably fined or imprisoned them without considering whether their reasons were justified, the chiefs' demands reasonable, or the distribution of forced labor among the subject population equitable. Throughout the early years, district commissioners meted out draconian punishments, often for insignificant infractions. One elder disobeyed the orders of the local subchief by refusing to work for the "whiteman" and was sentenced to three months with hard labor, fined twenty-five cattle and seventeen sheep, and ordered to have "his" people bring three hundred roofing sticks to Lawra for the administration.[13] Later the chiefs themselves imposed such penalties, with the approval of administrators. For example, when the district commissioner was informed in 1920 that a subchief had given six lashes to a man who refused to repair a resthouse, he simply wrote in his diary, "I agreed."[14]

During the first decade-and-a-half of colonial rule the administration demanded large amounts of labor to create and maintain a road network, to build an extensive system of resthouses, and to construct and expand administrative buildings in Lawra itself. Chiefs complained constantly about the recalcitrance of their subjects when it came to government work. Although this unpaid employment was never popular, the unofficial and heavier demands that some chiefs imposed upon their subjects created even greater antipathy toward the government. Until the mid-1920s officers were largely ignorant of the extortionate amount of labor demanded by chiefs, who put this labor to work on lands they had expropriated from their subjects. The most infamous of these

TABLE 5
Census of Tugu Subdivision, 1921–27

	1921	1927	Increase	Decrease
Males	1,362	1,242		120
Females	1,373	1,387	14	
Compounds	255	233		22
Cattle	637	413		224
Sheep	3,623	1,956		1,197

Source: RAT ADM 142, Political Prisoners, CNP to CCNT, 16 September 1927.

sergeant-major chiefs was Kayani of Tugu.[15] Kayani had been a mere headman, but in 1918 the district commissioner made him a subchief, under Jirapa, and eleven settlements were placed under his control. Immediately after receiving his chief's medallion, the highly prized insignia of colonial office, Kayani built a courthouse "better than that of Jirapa," comprising four chambers and a hall. Three of the rooms were waiting rooms for "witnesses" and the last a "retiring room" where "people could consult him privately."[16] Kayani's rise in the colonial hierarchy provoked rivalry with the chief of Jirapa, who was jealous that Kayani also had a government medal. However, the district commissioner defended Kayani as a "loyalist,"[17] and a year later another administrator praised Kayani for being "intelligent and progressive."[18]

The true state of affairs in Tugu subdivision did not emerge until 1927, when the district commissioner, St John Eyre-Smith, arrived unannounced in the area and encountered representatives of Kayani, who attempted "on false pretexts" to lead him along a route that avoided any of Kayani's farms. Undeterred, he came across "two compounds situated as two islands in a vast lake, Kayani's farms being the lake, with a tiny miserable farm around each."[19] Further investigation revealed similar conditions in other settlements under Kayani. Eyre-Smith wrote that in one "the state of affairs beggars description." Eleven men had had their lands seized by Kayani, with the result that half the population had left in 1920, along with the *tengaansob*. Most of the men in these settlements were being forced to work on Kayani's farms for six out of every nine or ten days. If they did not return when called, their hoes and axes were confiscated. The reason for the "great timidity [that] was observed in every village as regards making a complaint," Eyre-Smith explained, was intimidation by the chief: "On being asked why they made no complaints they explained, 'Kayani would not leave them' if they complained, meaning to imply life would be a worse hell. People were kept at his compound for more than a month, some days they would get food and other days they would not unless they had money to buy it."[20] Eyre-Smith equated the effects of such abuses with slavery, and attributed the marked decrease in population to "hunger hindering the production of children and death" as well as out-migration.[21]

The situation in Tugu was by no means exceptional. As early as 1921 a district commissioner had referred to the chiefs of Duori, Jirapa, Nandom, and Gengenkpe, as well as Tugu, as "Robber barons," adding that "all of these men in their castles live a distinctly medieval lifestyle."[22] Following Eyre-Smith's detailed investigation into the situation in Tugu, the Commissioner of the Northern Province commented: "Similar, although it is hoped less serious things, exist owing to flaws in administration based on native custom."[23] In response, Eyre-Smith wrote: "I regret to state that Lawra district must be in a deplorable state, if, as I am informed, similar practices have been going on throughout the district."[24] Indeed, many colonial chiefs had been abusing their power throughout Lawra District and beyond.

The new generation of officers that arrived in the Northern Territories at the end of the 1920s, which included Eyre-Smith, hoped that a shift to indirect rule would rectify the maladministration of the first generation of British rule.[25] The period of direct rule, justified in hindsight as having brought "peace," had merely established order – an order based on a silent violence of colonial tyranny carried out by chiefs in the name of British rule. The external threat of slavers who had periodically menaced from without was replaced by the persistent menace of the chiefs from within. There had been little attempt at any form of administration except the creation and maintenance of chiefs, which led one dissatisfied officer to comment in 1920 that "pages might have been written 'on what might be.' Why is it that it is necessary to write 'on what might be'? Lack of Policy. Lack of any preconceived Policy by the head of administration and lack of continuity of any sort of Policy by all officials."[26] This allusion to the role of writing in colonial rule is revealing. The complaint was that writing was being misused – that it was reacting to reality rather than changing it. Although writing had not yielded the British policy that reflected their ideological claims, it had provided them with the general illusion, broken only temporarily here, that they were in control of reality.

But there was a policy – one of expediency rather than transformation. Almost every measure adopted by officers in Lawra District until the arrival of Eyre-Smith had been designed to re-enforce the system whereby the inhabitants were ruled through colonial appointees. A section in the District Record Book titled "Policy," added in 1917, described administrative intentions as follows: "To endeavour to make the Paramount Chiefs as strong as possible and to rule through them."[27] So successful was this policy that it would not be an exaggeration to suggest that the chiefs, not the British, were the effective rulers of Lawra

District. Despite Eyre-Smith's revelations concerning the tyranny of many colonial appointees, rule through the chiefs continued without significant change until independence. The British blamed the chiefs' abuses of power in Lawra District in the late 1920s on social conditions rather than deficiencies in policy. The Commissioner of the Northern Province traced the problem to the native tribunals, which had begun to operate in a semiofficial capacity in 1917. "An excellent system amongst sophisticated people," he wrote, "but shown wanting when dealing with a very primitive people."[28] The Chief Commissioner of the Northern Territories replied that among politically decentralized populations, there was no adequate alternative to the prevailing form of administration: "It is regrettable, but nevertheless true about this country, that the more power a Chief is given, the more he will abuse it, and the difficulty comes in when it is a question of having Chiefs whose people obey and fear them, or Chiefs who have no power at all, and whose people neither obey nor fear them."[29]

Administrative expediency also explains how Kayani came to be rehabilitated after Eyre-Smith's departure. After six months of political detention, he was allowed to return to Tugu to live "quietly." Two years later, in 1930, the district commissioner expressed dissatisfaction with Kayani's successor, who only commanded the nominal respect of the people, and wrote to the provincial commissioner requesting permission to restore Kayani as chief.[30]

The British blamed the failures of direct rule on the LoDagaa and their forms of social and political organization, even though they had little idea of what these actually were. The lack of any rudimentary understanding of LoDagaa culture was symptomatic of how thoroughly inadequate British intelligence was during these early years regarding the effects of colonial rule. Without such intelligence there was no means of knowing to what degree colonial rule abrogated indigenous cultural beliefs and social norms. The political organization of the LoDagaa was virtually invisible to early colonial observers, whose ethnographic expertise did not extend beyond the ability to recognize and describe political hierarchies. Because they could not grasp the ethnographic situation that confronted them, they mistook complexity for confusion. LoDagaa culture was described as anarchic because the world on paper could not make sense of the indigenous political order, in much the same way as colonial maps could not make sense of the complicated networks of footpaths. In fact, there was more disorder – as measured by the abrogation of indigenous norms rather than external expectations – under colonialism than there had been before. Much of what the British (as well as the French on the other side of the Black Volta) described in writing as anarchy was actually very ordered.

The basic unit of social organization was the *yir*, or household. This was a unit of agricultural production and consumption as well as the residence of an individual descent group. Various descent groups formed patriclan "sectors" (*dooro*), which were part of larger patriclans. Because of household fission and shifting agriculture, the patriclans were widely dispersed and so did not form territorial groups, even though they possessed tutelary shrines belonging to the "old country" or *tenkouri*. In terms of economic cooperation and political action, the distinction between household and patriclan sector was imprecise. The relationship between related sectors varied with their physical proximity and ritual interdependence.[31] Sectors of the same clan often divided formally through a differentiation in nomenclature, in order to permit intermarriage, even though they still recognized common descent.[32] Rattray counted over thirty-two different patriclans among the LoDagaa, and Goody estimated there were more than forty.[33] With each patriclan dispersed over hundreds of square miles, the effective area of cooperation was "the distance which the sound of the war or funeral xylophone carries, for this [was] the call to action."[34]

Besides residential and descent groups, there were territorial patterns of ritual cooperation and obligation centered on *tengaan* and *tengaanble*, major and minor Earth shrines. These shrines were so inconspicuous that on the whole, officers were oblivious to their existence and importance. The Earth, as the source of all sustenance and the object of all labor, had a special hold on the LoDagaa. Participation in sacrifices to these Earth shrines, either in thanks or expiation, created areas of ritual interdependence or "parishes." Within such areas, theft and the shedding of blood were prohibited; any transgression of the edicts of the Earth, as interpreted by the custodian of the shrine (sing. *tengaansob*, pl. *tengaandem*) and various diviners, required sacrificial expiation. As Goody observed: "A premium was thus placed upon the peaceful intercourse between the members of a particular congregation."[35] The boundaries of these forms of indigenous social representation (residential, tutelary, territorial) were not rigidly defined. Such elasticity was partly the result of the various patterns of migration that had brought the different LoDagaa congeries into Lawra District, but it also seems to have been deliberately maintained to allow for future social fluidity and autonomy.

The common feature of all LoDagaa social formations was their radical political autonomy. All colonial descriptions of the LoDagaa perceived this autonomy as anarchy, and equated the relative absence of overt political authority or hierarchy with primitiveness. The difficulty with LoDagaa social formations was that they did not cohere around any explicit ideology or language of representation. Labouret highlighted this descriptive predicament in his study of the *Lobi*: "The society under study here is held together by very loose bonds, such that one might be tempted to believe that complete anarchy reigned in this land without chiefs and even villages. Closer scrutiny dispels this impression and soon reveals that individualism in the proper sense of the term does not exist among the Lobi."[36] Two generations later an indigenous scholar, Roger Somé, encountered similar difficulties describing power among the LoDagaa. Eventually he evaded the problem: "it is about a power that is difficult, if not impossible, for any outsider to perceive."[37]

One of the few British officers who recognized these multiple levels of social and political organization was Eyre-Smith. After investigating the abrogation of indigenous power and abuse of colonial power, he sought to alter the colonial system so that it might better meet the needs of the people, rather than the chiefs (and by implication the administration). At first he tried to obtain recognition for the elders. On this score, his "principal line of argument" was that "throughout the Dagati speaking villages in this district the village is the unit of administration and no chief can satisfactorily deal with a case unless he has the help of the elders in the village concerned."[38] After this modest proposal was rejected, he made increasingly radical proposals over the next five years. These recommendations also fell on deaf ears. His efforts culminated in a report he submitted to the colonial government in 1933, in which he bitterly attacked those who regarded the imposition of chiefs as having been an excusable necessity. He argued that "being unaware of their existing organisation, we substituted an autocracy irrespective of the very democratic land and religious organisation vested in the TENGANSOBE and the council of Elders [an overformalized description] which had existed for centuries."[39] Referring to what he believed other officers regarded as his "inconvenient discovery" of the *tengaan*, he suggested that at the very least, the political jurisdictions of the chiefs should be redrawn to correspond with indigenous areas of noumenal jurisdiction. Without such a readjustment, he argued, the chiefs would remain free to exploit subjects who fell within their political jurisdiction but inhabited lands belonging to a different *tengaan*.[40] In the longer term, he envisaged the incremental abolition of chieftaincies in Lawra District, by allowing positions to lapse following an incumbent's death. Finally, he articulated the central contradiction between colonial rule as practice and as ideology: "The question is, are we to consider the interests of the chiefs we have set up or are we to consider the welfare of the people?"[41] Needless to say, nothing changed.

Only two years after Eyre-Smith's last set of proposals to the administration, the chiefs he had envisaged abolishing were gazetted and granted exclusive exercise of judicial powers through Native Authority Courts. However, one of Eyre-Smith's recommendations, for a system of direct taxation, was implemented in order that the people might be clearer as to what demands their chiefs had a right to make on them.[42] When direct taxation was introduced, it was as a commutation of "tribute." In Lawra District, according to government assessments, each compound owed their chief five days' labor or a 50 lb basket of grains (millet or guinea-corn) per annum. This was not a traditional requirement; rather, it was a legacy from the period of direct rule that had come to an end in 1932.[43] The period of indirect rule that followed was little different from the period of direct rule that preceded it. If anything changed, it was that the position of colonial chief became more entrenched. Chiefs were given even greater official powers, while continuing to act as intermediaries between the administration, which became even less interventionist, and the people.[44] The main organizational difference was that three paramount chiefs, Lawra, Nandom, and Jirapa, were now selected from the ten divisional leaders created during direct rule.[45]

Inventing Chiefs

From 1932 until the end of the Second World War, the position of the chiefs, although modified, remained unassailed. They assumed more administrative responsibilities, and more of the prerogatives of the colonial government. Although they extorted their subjects less severely, they maintained their unprecedented positions of wealth as a complement to their official powers.[46] Complaints against the chiefs became even rarer than during the period of direct rule. It was not that abuses of power had ceased. The chiefs had simply become less flagrant and more ingenious. For example, in 1938 it was discovered that the Jirapa Naa had been disguising a series of illegal farms, in Tugu, Ulo, Karni, and Tizza, by claiming that they were Native Authority School farms.[47] The district commissioners' diaries for this period are full of incidents where it had been necessary to explain to the people the difference between a legitimate and an illegitimate order from a chief. Colonial subjects would have understood an illegitimate order, as the chiefs had no legitimacy, but only the power the colonial government had given them; the difficulty would have been in their recognizing a legitimate order. The phrase *nassal tumo ba e ya*, "this is not the white man's work," was used to refer to the chiefs' "tyrannical and power-loving tendencies."[48] The British as well as the chiefs did not understand that there was no actual difference – in the people's view, all orders were illegitimate, only some more so than others.[49]

Nevertheless, indirect rule did change how the British thought about legitimacy in important ways, on paper if not in practice. In ideological terms, indirect rule was intended to make administration more efficient and to confer legitimacy through association with "native authority." More importantly, the transformative and universal claims of imperialism, which had justified colonial conquest, were replaced by the stultifying ambition of "preservation" that now informed indirect rule.[50] Suddenly historical continuity with the immediate precolonial past had become the ideological basis of British authority. The colonial government passed various ordinances intended to regularize the chiefs' powers in the hope that they would rule through law (indigenous authority) rather than force (colonial rule). But for this to happen, laws had to be discovered that could be invested in the past. At the beginning of colonial rule, recognizable laws, in the form of articulated rules of social practice, were thought to have been marginal, if not virtually absent. Read had written: "The natives themselves are extremely reticent and suspicious of giving any information about their customs, but own that they have no laws beyond those of the fetish."[51] Difficulties of language and limited acquaintance influenced this view, but these remained perennial problems for almost all administrators.

By the late 1920s several officers had come to realize that the political structures and administrative methods of direct rule were unsatisfactory. Major criticism was made of the wholesale reliance on chiefs as delegates of colonial authority. In 1928, Cardinall, who had extensive administrative experience among the politically decentralized societies of the Northern Territories, offered a discouraging assessment of "native administration." Colonial rule through the chiefs had "entailed a complete disregard of native institutions," while "sovereignty over the people was given to chiefs, not in any way entitled to it." On the quality of judicial organization, he stated: "These tribunals keep no records and actually have no power of enforcing their decrees, even in the smallest and most trivial matters."[52] It should be noted that Cardinall was referring here to official power; unofficially, chiefs in areas such as Lawra District had seized a large amount of power. Although codification would have overcome these problems, administrators had virtually no knowledge of LoDagaa social practices. Indeed, prior to end of the 1920s the most comprehensive document on LoDagaa "laws and customs" had been Read's report of 1908. Cardinall broke this silent indifference when he complained that during the period of direct rule none of the intelligence necessary to embark on a transfer of greater powers to the chiefs had been gathered. His report amounted to an indictment of direct rule. He favored the introduction of indirect rule in principle, but his reservations led him to insist that adequate preparations be made for such a shift.[53] He referred to conditions in the Northern Province at the time of Ferguson's reconnaissance as anarchic and chaotic, and contended that the situation had changed little over a quarter of a century. Among his proposals was one for a "competent survey" to be undertaken by someone like Captain R.S. Rattray, the Gold Coast government's anthropological officer.[54] This resulted in the publication in 1932, on the eve of indirect rule, of a comprehensive two-volume ethnographic survey, *The Tribes of the Ashanti Hinterland*.[55]

Cardinall's picture of the conditions under direct rule was challenged even before Rattray's work became available.[56] In 1931 the recently appointed acting chief commissioner declared: "It is impossible to imagine any independent African unit whose jurisdiction before the arrival of the European was so limited as Mr Cardinall suggests."[57] Against Cardinall's specific contention that judicial organization had never existed among the politically decentralized peoples of the Northern Province, the chief commissioner insisted that it must have existed in the past and somehow fallen into abeyance. The chief commissioner's views were not based on any knowledge, presumed or real, of the precolonial past; rather, they reflected his inability and unwillingness to imagine that such lack of political organization could have been anything but a historical anomaly. Views such as his were not unique to the administration of the Northern Territories. Although colonial penetration in southern Sudan had been a more gradual process, a similar form of historicism was evident in colonial attitudes toward the Nuer of that region as officials contemplated the same shift from direct to indirect rule. As Douglas Johnson has observed:

> The contradictions inherent in policy which purported to be both traditional and evolutionary at the same time were never fully resolved in Nuer administration. The decision to rule through the chiefs' courts meant that the administration must first find chiefs. There was a belief that the Nuer must have once had powerful institutionalized judicial and executive authorities, but that these men had all been swept away by the events of the nineteenth century.[58]

Similarly, John Iliffe has noted the "short memories" of British officers in Tanganyika, which created opportune circumstances for fabricating history. "Since establishment of native administrations was as much a historical as a political exercise," adds Iliffe, "its outcome depended heavily on the historical views current among administrators or plausibly advocated by interested Africans."[59]

At the beginning of the century the LoDagaa were believed to lack clear identities, figures of authority, and any rules beyond religious observances. But by 1932, when indirect rule was established in the Northern Territories, a shift had occurred in the views of administrators in Lawra and other districts that was more significant than any substantive change in policy. Suddenly they had discovered ethnic identities, political organization, and customary law among the LoDagaa, which could provide the necessary basis for the ideological changes happening in the world on paper. These were to become the justification for granting official autonomy to colonial chiefs and for sanctioning their courts. Earlier perceptions of the LoDagaa were rewritten, not from any new understanding, but to meet administrative requirements.

The possibility of establishing an administration founded on indigenous institutions had been greatly strengthened by Rattray's work, but colonial authorities deliberately disregarded his professional competence in favor of the amateur misapprehensions of administrators. In 1932, before Rattray's two volumes appeared, the Governor of the Gold Coast wrote to the British Secretary of State for the Colonies claiming that after local officers began collecting ethnographic material in the late 1920s, "it soon became evident that the obstacles to the establishment of a system of native administration in certain, if not all, of the Divisions would not prove so difficult to surmount as had been asserted."[60] Colonial officers' reports were written with administrative convenience, not ethnographic subtlety, in mind. Rattray's work demonstrated that among groups such as the LoDagaa identity was weak, laws were few (and mostly religious in nature), and identifiable political authority was virtually nonexistent. However, unlike Read, he had found indigenous alternatives to these things, and so he did not describe these societies as either chaotic or unstructured. Like Eyre-Smith, he was particularly concerned that the powers exercised by "petty unconstituional European-made-chiefs" be constrained by recognizing the indigenous custodians of the Earth. Rattray insisted that only by understanding the layered history of political authority in the Northern Territories could a successful form of colonial government be created.[61]

Rattray's findings did not satisfy administrative expectations even though they might have allayed some of the administrations' fears of politically decentralized societies. Succession disputes in the states of the north, such as Wa, Gonja, Dagbon, and Mamprugu, were in fact more threatening to the colonial order, yet colonial rulers preferred the many-headed hydra to the headless variety of monster that the LoDagaa represented. In order to demystify the latter, the British required some understanding of the forms of political authority that at this point were still largely invisible to them. But administrators ignored Rattray's pioneering ethnographic insights, just as they had Eyre-Smith's proposals. They preferred historical fiction to ethnographic facts, and so the chiefs rather than the *tengaandem* became the basis for native authority in Lawra District. Throughout the British colonies of Africa, administrators shared a common disdain for the "scientific" knowledge produced by anthropologists and a preference for practical experience and political expediency.[62] When professional knowledge contradicted the ideology of indirect rule, it had to be ignored. As Henrietta Kuklick has noted of British colonial officers throughout Africa at this time, "they preferred not to confront evidence that their actions violated tradition, since to do so was to accept that the official doctrine of Indirect Rule was impracticable – and thus to undermine the very justification for the British presence in Africa."[63] The primary concern of officers in Lawra District was not with discovering the actual "customs" of the people, but with imbuing the political engineering of direct rule with an aura of legitimacy.

Nevertheless, custom was important in a generic sense. Besides being a synonym for legitimacy, in the minds of the British custom was the hidden dynamic of LoDagaa society, the invisible presence of all that at first acquaintance was absent: customary law, political organization, and ethnic identity. Even though chiefs had been created to administer this category of colonial knowledge, the relationship between colonial structures and indigenous society was (and remains) unresolved. The obvious way to resolve this relationship would have been to codify this elusive custom. This had not been possible during the period of direct rule owing to lack of ethnographic intelligence; yet even after this information became available at the outset of indirect rule, codification was still avoided as a dangerous interference.[64] Codification of custom might have interfered with an important administrative advantage: the ambiguity gave administrators the power to change custom as well as to have the final word on what was or was not customary.

In 1931 the chief commissioner had recommended the keeping of "tribal books" by men of the "tribe" as part of a campaign "to re-invest the native rulers with their pristine authority" and "to provide them with the wherewithal to maintain it."[65] This was four years after Eyre-Smith had begun reporting copiously on the chiefs' abuses. Among the problems he had blamed on the administration's overreliance on appointed chiefs was the chiefs' ability to make demands and enforce decisions that "they would not have done prior to our advent ... for what may be termed offences created as a result of European occupation ... in disputes that would not have arisen prior to our advent."[66] He had also noted the chiefs' lack of legitimacy among the people, and their ability to manipulate "native custom." Although the *tengaandem* had been marginalized by the creation of chiefs, Eyre-Smith insisted on greeting the *tengaansob* after greeting the chief when he visited settlements, and asking him about "native custom," because a chief "gives you a version that suits himself and his section, often quite contrary to custom."[67] Colonial authority had been largely relinquished to the chiefs through administrative neglect during the first generation of colonial rule. Despite their undefined legal status, chiefs had been levying fines and imposing punishments well before indirect rule was implemented with no regard to what might or might not be possible on paper. The keeping of "tribal books" would have been a distinct disadvantage to them. The chiefs had been unintentionally assisted in this gradual accumulation of prerogatives by district commissioners who had little understanding of what was really happening, and only ambiguous and discretionary guidelines as to the intention of administrative policy.[68]

More problematic than the status or content of "native customary law" was the relationship between the chiefs (and their courts) and the indigenous social structure. The colonial administration could create chiefs and invest them with unspecified, though substantial, powers, but it could not provide them with indigenous authority or legitimacy. In urging a reassessment of the political structures that the administration had created and come to rely on so exclusively, Eyre-Smith had argued that the administration must recognize the knowledge and authority of the elders and *tengaandem* if it was to keep the chiefs in check.[69] This argument implicitly raised two important questions. Who, in an economically undifferentiated and politically unarticulated (as opposed to inarticulate) society, were the custodians, repositories, and transmitters of "native custom"? And what was "native custom"? The LoDagaa had to perceive Native Courts as something more than repositories of the colonial government's authority. Otherwise, how could they be expected to regard them as legitimate? When indirect rule was implemented, the government conveniently forgot that it had invented chiefs. Partly this was a result of its desire to ignore the history of direct rule, and partly it was from enthusiasm over the administrative convenience promised by the shift to indirect rule.

Even if social practices had been codified, the court assessors were illiterate and would therefore not have been able to avail themselves of the possible advantages of such records. Twenty years after indirect rule had begun, and when preparations were being made for the transition from Native Authority to Local Council Courts, the Acting Chief Justice of the Gold Coast suggested that codification would be necessary before traditional authorities could be replaced, "as the sole repository of native customary law lies in the memories of linguists and certain Chiefs."[70] The chief regional officer (formerly chief commissioner) replied: "I do not share the Acting Chief Justice's view. ... In my opinion customary law is widely known and rarely disputed."[71] This begs the question of what disputants were arguing over in the courts. There may very well have been a consensus on "customary law" among colonial chiefs, but such equanimity obviously did not exist between litigants. Litigation before the courts was characterized by strong disagreement over what in fact constituted "customary law," that is, which particular social practice deserved such privileged status.[72]

Administrators had another reason for not wanting to put this authority into writing: they wished to maintain the fiction that it came from the past rather than the world on paper. Among the LoDagaa there were no models on which to base courts, except for the tribunals created under direct rule. Everything about the courts, from the chiefs who operated them, to the very idea of them, was a foreign imposition. Over time the problems of devolving management of the courts to the chiefs became more apparent, especially as external demands on the administration changed with the postwar momentum toward independence. In 1947 the District Commissioner of Lawra reported of the Native Authority Courts that "procedure is their greatest weakness ... initiation of suits is haphazard ... hearing of evidence is inadequate and no record of it is ever made." For the moment he noted that these problems did not matter as "the Courts have the good fortune of sitting in judgement on a docile population, which invariably does what it is told: however, this happy state of affairs is not going to last, for litigants will question their decisions more often and more vehemently as time goes on."[73] This was strikingly similar to criticisms made by Cardinall almost thirty years before.[74] LoDagaa litigants realized that when it came to settling disputes in practice, the chiefs' justice was based on political fact, not historical legitimacy.

The authority of the courts depended not on the correctness of their procedure nor on their status as repositories of custom, but on the sanctions that the administration allowed them to use. The LoDagaa differentiated their own norms and practices from those of colonial authority, which they referred to as a system of *ordir* maintained *bai forsi*.[75] The use of loan words indicated that there were no indigenous equivalents in the lexicon of the LoDagaa. The chiefs were neither the custodians nor the indigenous arbiters of social practices. Nevertheless they became the authorized translators of those practices from the private social domain of everyday life to the political arena of the colonial courts. The chiefs imitated the regalia of chiefs from states such as Wa, Gonja, and Dagbon, with robes, fezes for messengers, and wealth appropriate to their offices, but the symbols that conferred authority and had political meaning remained their government medallions. In the 1980s the villagers of Tugu still recalled that Kayani had "shed tears" when the British took away his medal.[76] A convenient historical fiction had been created by the new generation of administrators beginning in the late 1920s. They looked back on the period of direct rule as stagnant and unenlightening, and therefore tended to minimize its effects. Any changes that had taken place during that time were conveniently subsumed into the wider past for which they were not responsible, and assumed the status of custom.

Political Education and Representation

The world on paper created descriptions of anarchy that justified the imposition of chiefs under direct rule; it then created the historical ruse that justified them again under indirect rule. Although the authority of the chiefs was not written, it was eventually strengthened by the near-monopoly of knowledge of writing that they enjoyed by the end of the colonial period. This monopoly enabled them to solidify their positions as intermediaries between the world on paper and that of farmers and migrant laborers. Before civil administration had begun in Lawra District, one officer had suggested that the only solution for the "appalling state of savagery in Dagarti" was compulsory education for the children of appointed chiefs and headmen.[77] The reasons behind this suggestion were obviously prejudiced, but given the unimaginative expediency of subsequent policies, the implications were quite radical. With no government funds available, any initiative for providing colonial education relied on the resourcefulness of district officers. Not until 1917 was a school built in Lawra District, and it was established only as a means of developing a "governing class" of chiefs.[78]

In 1917 the district commissioner required that every chief keep a messenger or representative at Lawra in order to facilitate communication between the administration and the chiefs. Before this, any summons for the chiefs to meet at Lawra had required the circulation of a message stick, which often as not went missing. Chiefs, and even some subchiefs who were not required to do so, responded enthusiastically, sending either sons, nephews, or brothers to represent them. The messengers were given medallions inscribed with their division and office, made out of old cartridge shells by a local blacksmith, and were dressed in a uniform of "blue shirt or tunic, red sash, blue cap" that was "very smart." Soon after, their powers were extended "to act as chiefs' police or to use the Hausa word 'dogari.'" They were deemed to be more successful than constables in "political work," so the latter were suspended from labor recruitment, delivering summonses, and making civil arrests. "Being of the people, and unarmed, they were able to go every where amongst the people without exciting fear or suspicion."[79] The granting of greater autonomy came at the same time that the chiefs themselves were claiming that they no longer required constables to help them execute orders, and could now manage their own affairs without direct supervision.[80] While staying in Lawra the messengers received instruction from a Hausa employee of the government. Instruction, not surprisingly, was in Hausa, a language that officers used then instead of *Dagaare*.[81] By January 1918 the school already had twelve regular pupils, all of whom were reported to be making rapid progress. Furthermore, all of them were from chiefs' households, which was a requirement for being admitted to the corps, and eleven were actually heirs apparent.[82] When in 1919 an official government school was established, the same admission policy was followed, with all forty-eight pupils being messengers.[83]

Administrative attitudes toward education always betrayed an edge of paranoia. Standards of education were of little concern. Indeed, it can be said that the point of the whole enterprise was merely to provide evidence of some administrative initiative, while taking pains not to produce an indigenous intelligentsia that might cause political dissent. At most the aim was to create "Government servants," students educated to clerical standards but not beyond.[84] Although the language of instruction in the government school, English, was more politically relevant than Hausa, the standard of instruction was extremely low. One officer complained about "parrot" repetition of "high falutin sentences." Only one pupil, the brother of the district commissioner's interpreter, was entered in Standard II in 1920, at which point he was appointed "scribe" to the District Tribunal. The principle that "the chiefs must be taught to rule before their people can be allowed to take a hand also" ensured that just as the chiefs were the sole recipients of colonial authority, their families were also the exclusive beneficiaries of formal education.[85] In 1933, in the immediate aftermath of the much hailed but largely empty initiative of indirect rule, the colonial government suggested that all Native Authorities should establish segregated schools for the sons of chiefs. To encourage this policy, officials thought the chiefs should be told "at some future date" that only literate successors would be recognized as chiefs.[86]

In 1936 a Native Authority School offering instruction in *Dagaare* and providing the opportunity for further, albeit restricted, education was established. Of the sixty-seven pupils enrolled two years later, three were girls and all came from the households of chiefs, subchiefs, or headmen. The chiefs showed great enthusiasm for the school because the children were instilled with pride in their "Lobi and Dagarti blood, and taught to reverence the traditions of their fathers." The behavior of the students was of concern to the chiefs because children who had been educated at Wa, where a school had been opened four years earlier, had returned on their holidays as "conceited and detribalized imps."[87] The expansion in enrollment at Lawra was modest and gradual. By 1948 there were still only 140 pupils at Lawra, although village schools, with thirty-six pupils each, had been established at Eremon, Birifu, Duori, and Nandom.[88] The administration was intent that this education not foster any disruptive behavior among students. Students farmed their own food on lands provided by the chiefs and were encouraged to learn their own customs.

In 1945 the District Commissioner of Lawra recommended to the chief commissioner a "back to the land" course for all Standard VII students "to orient the minds of the literate young away from the 'coat-and-collar' outlook." He even suggested that it be modeled on German labor camps before the Second World War! He also proposed that such students be barred from entering the civil service until they had completed clerical duty with a Native Authority, as such employment had proved so unpopular owing to the want of opportunities for advancement.[89] The administration wanted it both ways: it did not wish to see newly educated young men leave the Northern Territories (although it had been happy to promote a more substantial exodus of uneducated labor); yet at the same time it was not prepared to make available suitable and rewarding opportunities closer to home. Successive attempts, reflecting a self-justifying paternalism, to protect the Northern Territories from "contamination" from the coast were to have a deleterious effect on local democracy a decade later, when without local consultation, the protectorate was amalgamated with the more cosmopolitan colony to the south in preparation for independence.[90]

After the end of the Second World War, there were only three literate chiefs in Lawra District – those of Lawra, Duori, and Tizza – and only eighteen literate chiefs in the rest of the Northern Territories.[91] It is not surprising, then, that both the Lawra Naa and Duori Naa came to play significant roles in the burgeoning politics of the protectorate after 1945.[92] Even though Lawra District remained economically marginal, the LoDagaa chiefly class played a disproportionate role in northern politics immediately before and after independence.[93] To take advantage of the new political opportunities required reading and writing, over which the chiefly families had a near-monopoly. When the first democratic elections were held in 1951, it was not the chiefs who stood as candidates (with the exception of the Duori Naa), but their literate sons.[94] The opening up of politics in the postwar era created intense rivalries between chiefs, with each of the major players attempting to construct a political fiefdom by virtue of his uncontested representation of his subjects.

The tension that developed between Birifu and Lawra was a prime example of these local rivalries. In 1948 the Lawra Naa was appointed one of three northern chiefs on the forty-member Committee on Constitutional Reform, which had been mandated to hold hearings on self-government for the Gold Coast. Worrying that the Lawra Naa was developing valuable political links, one of the chief of Birifu's sons, B. Gandaa, joined the southern-based United Gold Coast Convention Party the following year. After the death of the Birifu Naa in 1949, his successor and other sons began to agitate for their own self-government in the form of a local council separate from Lawra. They contended that the inhabitants of Birifu were "an entirely different tribe" (LoWiili as opposed to LoDagaba, according to Goody's schema) with separate "customs," and complained that ever since they had come under the authority of Lawra the "Burifoman" had been discriminated against. In response to the contention that this oppression had led to the emigration of people from Birifu, the district commissioner noted: "It is indeed due to oppression, but to the oppression of Birifors by the Gandaa family [the petitioners]." He also observed that the petitioners represented the seven literate persons in the Birifu area, all of whom belonged to the chief's household.[95]

The first steps toward democracy and independence created some anxiety among the chiefs. The local council elections of 1952 were a potential threat to the colonial status quo, even though these elective offices were administrative rather than political. At the same time as the chiefs or their proxies were contesting these elections, news of a powerful shrine, called *Naangminle* or "the little god," reached Lawra District from the neighboring French colony. It was reputed to purge supplicants and to afford them protection against their opponents, and several chiefs hired trucks to take themselves and their followers to be imbued with its powers. The two events – the elections, and the news of the shrine – were more than coincidental. The chiefs were in no greater need of mystical protection at this time; rather, their monopoly of political power was "threatened by the ballot, which could be seen as a possible instrument of retaliation in the hand of the aggrieved." Goody was in the midst of his fieldwork when news of the shrine passed through Lawra District. "In many villages I visited at that time," he wrote, "people knew of it, joked about it, and told grave tales of what it caused to happen. ... Down to earth comments were frequently heard about the chiefs who were rushing off to get absolution and protection."[96] These political anxieties proved to be premature and misplaced: ultimately the politics of history was to become more important than electoral politics when it came to the legitimacy of chieftaincy. In the elections of 1954, 1956, and 1960, all but one of the prominent candidates in both constituencies in Lawra District were the relatives of chiefs. The one exception had already succeeded his father to become a chief himself.[97]

So powerful had the leading chiefs in Lawra District become that they were to assume political roles at regional and national levels totally out of proportion to the size of the district.[98] Well into the postcolonial period, control of a major chieftaincy brought with it important opportunities on the national stage. For example, the Nandom Naa, Polkuu Konkuu Chiri, who died 1984, served on the board of directors of the State Gold Mining Company (a logical appointment, given that so many miners were from his area), and later as a member of the ruling Provisional National Defence Committee under Jerry Rawlings. Similarly, before retiring to Lawra and becoming resident chief in the 1980s, Abeifaa Karbo served as a member of Parliament under Kwame Nkrumah, and later as chairman of the Public Service Commission in Accra.[99]

Although the leaders of Ghanaian independence had intended to displace traditional rulers through the process of democratization, in Lawra District, where education had been a preserve for the elite, it only strengthened the political monopoly of the chiefs. More significantly perhaps, the opportunity to build political structures that better reflected the local culture's radical political autonomy was lost. By 1954, the year of local elections in preparation for independence, the colonial project of creating a "governing class" in Lawra

District had come to fruition. However, the politics of the postwar years sabotaged the ultimate goal of colonial education, which had been the creation of literate chiefs. The literate sons of chiefs, initially bereft of opportunities, did not immediately succeed their fathers, but acted as their political proxies after elected offices were created. In addition, since commoners tended to mistrust literate chiefs, those chiefs relied on illiterate subchiefs and headmen to act as intermediaries between themselves and the people.[100] Although too much education was seen as a liability in terms of winning local trust, it was a distinct advantage when it came to creating a local power base and acting as intermediaries with the external power structures. These included regional and national administrations, agency bureaucracies, political parties, and military regimes, all of which belonged to the world on paper. The ability of the major chiefs to communicate with this world was the source of much of their authority in the postcolonial period.

The first generation of independence was a contradictory and confused era. Many of the inconsistencies in colonial policy were perpetuated by national government. If anything, developments tended to mirror the first few decades of colonial rule, thereby undoing the tentative moves toward local government in the Northern Territories during the colonial withdrawal. Authority became more centralized, and personnel more remote, and at times the legitimacy of external, albeit national, governments became almost as questionable as it had been under direct colonial rule. The period began with the sudden incorporation of the Northern Territories into a wider nation-state in 1957 – a prospect that alarmed many of the north's nascent political leaders.[101] Continuity with the colonial past created contradictions, and the instability of national politics, with its checkered history of aborted governments, created confusion.

The opportunities that emerged at independence offered little to the common people of Lawra District: they were excluded from direct participation by the near-monopoly on literate education enjoyed by the ruling families. Political rivalries developed between chiefs as each attempted to ally his fiefdom with wider political interests outside the district.[102] National politics created party divisions along the lines of local competition between chiefs. In all three national elections, the two successful local candidates in Lawra District were both members of the Northern People's Party. Their closest rivals were, by default as much as by political persuasion, supporters of the Convention People's Party.[103] Until 1960 the authority of chiefs continued virtually untouched; even though they had lost some administrative prerogatives, their judicial and political powers survived almost intact.[104] That year, however, for political reasons, the CPP replaced the chiefs as court members with a single magistrate, which in effect took away their offical judicial powers. Although magistrates were not explicitly answerable to the government, they were government appointed.[105] As Nkrumah and the CPP asserted greater control over local politics, their measures to curtail "traditional" authority actually created political opportunities in areas such as Lawra District for the chiefly families who had become party faithful.[106] Because Lawra District was an NPP stronghold, the CPP was eager to interfere in local politics in the hope of overcoming one of the few remaining areas of opposition within an increasingly one-party state.

However, chieftaincy as a whole suffered a sharp decline in both power and prestige at the local level in the early 1960s. Once their official responsibilities had been taken away, chiefs were reduced to titular and ceremonial roles. Having lost their power, their illegitimacy was exposed.[107] Two generations of chiefly autocracy had created very negative memories in the minds of their subjects. When young LoDagaa men who had experienced or learned about French colonial rule from their parents were asked about the benefits of independence in the mid-1960s, "they all mentioned the fact that today there are no longer chiefs who abuse their wives, who forcibly requisition young people to work in Diébougou, who seize the products of their farms, who, in a word, control them."[108]

The status of chiefs in Lawra District oscillated somewhat under different regimes, but it was never reinvested with its former prerogatives. It is ironic, then, that as they were progressively stripped of their official status and made vulnerable by the shifting criteria of external recognition, they came to acquire some degree of indigenous legitimacy. For example, chiefs continued to hear disputes in an unofficial capacity, as litigants often preferred to bring their cases to the chiefs in order to avoid offending them, and in order to avoid the greater publicity and formality of the District Magistrate's Court. The magistrates in Lawra District were literate, were generally outsiders, and were representatives of the postcolonial state, and so were not to be trusted.[109] Successive magistrates tolerated the chiefs as arbitrators and ignored the fact that they heard the vast majority of disputes as agencies of first instance.[110] The chiefs were slowly able to create new roles for themselves because of the instability of postcolonial politics beginning in the mid-1960s, which prevented the emergence of popular democracy as a rival form of legitimacy, and because of the economic decline evident by the mid-1970s, which cost the state much of its remaining relevance.[111] Also, the near-collapse of channels of communication between citizens and the state by the mid-1980s meant that there was a need for representation of local interests at the national level. Finally, given the wider political context to which the LoDagaa were inextricably bound, it was impossible to go back to the conditions that existed before the creation of chieftaincy.[112]

As one of Lentz's informants from the Nandom area explained in the early 1990s, whatever its origins and history, "chieftaincy has come to stay."[113]

The Historical Ambiguities of Postcolonial Chieftaincy

Despite the growing acceptance of chieftaincy in the postcolonial era, the institution created a number of historical ambiguities among the LoDagaa. The most important of these concerned which criteria should be used to select or elect a chief. In September 1984 a candidate vying for the position of Lawra Naa – a vacancy that some people argued had been created by the long absence of Karbo – shot an elephant in Burkina Faso, on the other side of the Black Volta. Over several days the candidate and his supporters transported the dismembered carcass to Lawra piece by piece with a variety of conveyances, mainly bicycles. Hunks of flesh arrived wrapped in blood-sodden sacking, usually burlap, and were reconstructed in the courtyard of the candidate's compound. The skin was laid out, the feet and other prominent features placed in their appropriate positions, and the putrefying meat heaped in the middle. A few years earlier, when the position of Tizza Naa had become vacant, the successful candidate in that succession dispute had also killed an elephant and used this display of hunting skills as a claim to leadership.[114]

Elephants had once existed in areas settled by the LoDagaa, but none had been seen on the eastern bank of the Black Volta in over a generation. Nevertheless, the elephant still had a place in the symbolic language of the LoDagaa. Animals such as the elephant were regarded as "*dun soola*, literally, black animals" – that is, dangerous animals whose death at the hands of a hunter could invite "mystical dangers." The meat, a culinary rarity even in the precolonial past, was then distributed to the residents of Lawra. The gesture was meant to create continuity with the past, when communities had honored great hunters. Goody noted that the word *naa*, a cognate of the word for chief among the surrounding hierarchical societies, had once only been used to refer to men who had become rich and powerful by virtue of hunting or farming.[115] The attempt to create a succession crisis was ultimately unsuccessful, as was this symbolic claim to legitimacy. Political connections and administrative experience had become the new criteria for community honor.

However, the ambiguity of chieftaincy was political, not cultural. During a dispute over succession to a subdivisional chieftaincy in Zambo in 1977, the candidates did not resort to neotraditional practices to establish claims on the office of local chief. Instead the witnesses addressed the political machinations of the last two generations (see Figure 17). In an official hearing the plaintiff, Kyila Kpeng, alleged that the new incumbent, Babatuoronaa Kuorikuo, had no "traditional" right to the office. The defendant's father, Kuorikuo, had been appointed chief by the district commissioner in 1938, after the plaintiff's paternal "uncle," Tandor, had been removed for embezzling Native Authority taxes. Kuorikuo had continued as chief until the early 1960s, when he was removed from office by the CPP. Referring to interference in local politics by the CPP in the early 1960s, Zame Karbo, the Lawra Regent, explained: "At that time there was party politics and the place was full of troubles. At that time if you were not in support of the ruling party you had trouble always."[116] Various other witnesses explained that Kuorikuo had been removed after agitation in Zambo by propaganda secretaries of the CPP, who attempted to turn the people against him because of his support for the NPP. With governmental approval, the local administration installed Kpeng as Zambo Naa. Kpeng remained in office until 1966, when the National Liberation Council restored the defendant's father, who ruled until his death in 1969.[117] The defendant had taken over as chief in 1970, but was not installed until 1974, by which time the NLC had been superseded by the Second Republic, which would later be overthrown by the National Redemption Council.

The question at the heart of the dispute was this: By what authority did a chief rule? Was it colonial history, or national politics, or the people? Kpeng and his supporters had argued that Kyila had been the first chief of Zambo, and therefore any successor had to descend from the same clan. In cross-examination of one of Kpeng's witnesses, however, the defendant managed to establish that Kyila had been forced on the people: "How come it [was] that Kyila was appointed by a non-inhabitant and the people accepted? A: This was because in the past nobody could challenge the word of the whiteman. Q: In this [way] it was due to fear that Zambo people accepted Kyila as Zambo Naa? A: Yes it was due to fear of the whiteman."[118]

Conversely, Babatuoronaa and his supporters had relied on the restoration of Kuorikuo by the NLC as the basis of former's right to succession. However, Kpeng demonstrated the limitations of this reasoning by pointing out that just as he had been appointed chief by one regime, and another regime had restored the defendant's father, they were now under yet another regime and thus obliged to revisit the matter. Kpeng was recognizing the unavoidable reality that legitimacy ultimately depended on external recognition.[119] The authority of individual chiefs was repeatedly brought into question by the vagaries of national politics. Colonial authority had never been seriously challenged in Lawra District; national authority was repeatedly demonstrated to be vulnerable and reversible.[120]

Following the death of the Nandom Naa in 1984, a very similar dispute emerged. In a probing analysis of those events, Lentz summarized the issues in

External Agency	Plaintiff	Colonial Power*	Defendant
DC under direct rule	Kyila *c.* 1905–?	⇔	
DC under indirect rule	Tandor ? –1938	⑥	Kuorikuo1938– [until early 1960s]
Convention People's Party	Kyila Kpeng [until 1966]	⇔	
National Liberation Council		⑥	Kuorikuo 1966–9
Second Republic			Babatuoronaa Kuorikuo [*c.* 1974]
National Redemption Council		**?**	

*The arrows indicate the directions in which colonial power traveled between these two households.

Figure 17. Rival Claims to the Position of Zambo Naa, 1977

very similar terms: "Vehement debate ensued not only from the question who would be a legitimate and suitable successor for the late chief, but also from opposite views as to which procedure of decision making was to be considered the correct one, warranted by 'tradition.'"[121] Here again, all sides had to go back to the arrival of the British and the creation of colonial chiefs. One narrative claimed that the first recorded chief, or *naa*, was Kyiir, a wealthy trader and recognized leader of the village of Nandom. In this narrative the British did not create Kyiir's authority; they merely acknowledged it by making him chief. Accordingly, any successor was to be chosen by the incumbent, who was the source of his own power. In another narrative it was the *tengaansob* who was given the position of chief by the British, but he delegated it to Kyiir; accordingly, any successor needed the approval of the *tengaansob*. Both narratives were undermined by the fact that succession had always been contested and problematic.

What these two rival narratives had in common was an attempt to legitimate lines of succession by reading them back into the past, even though it was the colonial, and later postcolonial, state that actually determined who ruled.[122] Candidates needed to win the political favor of the national government, but also needed to disguise this interference by grounding their arguments in "the language of history."[123] Lentz concluded that despite conflicting appeals to the past, "there is not one single, straightforward tradition and for that matter history to which the disputants could turn to for arbitration." Even so, disputants had to pretend that there was "an undebatable, self-evident, mandatory truth derived from an unambiguous past."[124]

Many LoDagaa perceived chieftaincy as having been founded on little more than "fear of the whiteman," and individual chiefs as supported by little more than the shifting vagaries of national government. In the Zambo dispute each party had its own version of the past, each different in terms of its depth rather than its substantive detail. Issues of precedent were clearly important in legitimating rival claims. But as Kyila Kpeng's witness demonstrated, if one went far enough back in time, precedents vanished. Yet this has not created a movement against chieftaincy. Chieftaincy has been preserved among the LoDagaa not by acceptance of its historical legitimacy, but by the recognition that such a form of political organization is relevant in situations where alternative political structures have failed to meet local expectations.

In the 1990s, to mark their status, the chiefs of Lawra District used the same symbols their predecessors had borrowed from neighboring societies. There was a readily observable set of chiefly "traditions." This may seem like a historical charade, but it is far less contradictory when looked at from a spatial rather than a temporal perspective. In their analysis of change in colonial Africa, Godfrey and Monica Wilson postulated that the most important factor was the expansion in the scale of all forms of life. Although many of their arguments now seem outdated, they did point out how important changes in social and political scales are to historical consciousness: "Expansion in historical scale does not imply cutting adrift from the past ... but it does imply a relative freedom from the immediate and parochial past."[125] This freedom was veridical rather than rhetorical, as we can see in the Zambo dispute and as Lentz argued in her examination of the Nandom dispute. The important point is that disputants had been forced to make representations of the past because history had become the main language of politics. The use of the past to legitimate the present was a legacy of the British, as the administrative debate over chieftaincy during the late 1920s and early 1930s demonstrated. This invented history enabled the British to ignore the fact that there was nothing legitimate about the power of chiefs among the LoDagaa, and by implication nothing legitimate about their own power that was exercised through the chiefs.

Postcolonial chieftaincy disputes exposed the loss of sovereignty the LoDagaa suffered after the British conquered them and imposed chiefs. Because chieftaincy was a colonial creation, sovereignty has resided with external sources of power ever since conquest. An implicit understanding of this motivated suggestions first made in the 1980s that chieftaincy was an indigenous institution. In his 1982 monograph, Tuurey both regretted and deplored the lack of chiefs among the LoDagaa: "This was not political freedom, it was something worse than that. At best, it could be virtually described as political anarchy."[126] These words are strongly reminiscent of those of Ferguson and Read over three-quarters of a century before. What observers such as Eyre-Smith romanticized as a radical form of decentralized democracy was now seen as an embarrassment. For many indigenous intellectuals interested in creating ethnic consciousness and pride, the idea of a Dagomba origin for the LoDagaa offered redemption from colonial images of primitiveness, by associating them with a culture of hierarchical power. The LoDagaa were depicted as a heroic people who before colonial rule rebelled against chiefly authority rather than as backward primitives who had not evolved sufficiently to create hierarchical institutions (which is how external observers often saw them).[127] But ethnic pride did not address the question of how to recover political sovereignty lost as a result of colonial conquest.

The most immediate obstacle for those attempting to recover power from the world on paper was the argument that before colonialism, the LoDagaa never had chiefs and therefore never possessed political sovereignty. In an attempt to recover political sovereignty lost to the colonial state and still controlled by the postcolonial state, Tuurey set out to document as many instances of precolonial chiefly or royal authority as possible. In all, he identified only three possible centers of chiefly authority, all south of Nadawli in Wa District, and none established by the LoDagaa. Mossi migrants had established the first two of these in Kaleo and Wecheau, and the third was established in Dorimon by Dagomba princes from Bouna.[128] Implicit in Tuurey's argument was the suggestion that these chiefdoms were proto-states in the territorial and secular sense, representing the germs of statehood; in this way he was attempting to mitigate the sense of embarrassment that came with accusations of statelessness. He argued that "each village or clan was a state in itself," and compared this system with that of Germany before nineteenth-century unification. However, he also argued that the LoDagaa were "acephalous" and "a stateless nation"; this LoDagaa "nation" lacked "rulers on a territorial basis whose sanctions were physical rather than spiritual."[129]

The specter of a chiefly precolonial past was raised a year later by another indigenous scholar, not to legitimate existing political arrangements but rather to defend the cultural past of the LoDagaa against the negative implications of statelessness. Kojo Yelpaala, a LoDagaa law professor teaching in the United States, argued that the reported statelessness of the LoDagaa ignored the internal potential for political hierarchy. After rejecting the evolutionary assumptions of political typologies, criticizing the ethnocentrism of definitions of the state, and questioning the basis for the dichotomy between political formations, he suggested that only one form of political authority, namely "the highly centralized hierarchical state," had been absent from LoDagaa society at the turn of the century, and not all forms or possibilities of a state.[130] For Yelpaala, the concept of "statelessness" was instrumental rather than empirical, in that it had worked as the ideological justification for "subjugation and exploitation."[131]

Given that the LoDagaa were colonized along with the Dagomba, Mamprusi, and Gonja, the relationship between statelessness and conquest was undoubtedly more complex. It can equally be argued that acephalous societies were problematic and inconvenient to the British.[132] There is no doubt that the perceived absence of a state was the basis of much prejudice toward the LoDagaa. As Roger Somé has argued, it was the absence of a state that allowed colonial administrators to describe LoDagaa culture as acephalous or anarchistic, and caused them to overlook other forms of political authority.[133] This myopia allowed the colonial state to treat LoDagaa culture as a blank page on which they were free to impose their own political order. More importantly, the inability or refusal of the colonizers to see indigenous forms of political authority served to deny the existence of indigenous sovereignty. In order to recover this lost sovereignty, it was necessary to describe LoDagaa political authority as it existed before conquest. Indigenous scholars have found this a difficult task. Somé claimed that political authority in LoDagaa was too difficult to describe to outsiders because it was "not at all explicit." For his part, Yelpaala complained that statelessness did not describe "the nature or quality of the political organization of society but rather a problem with the skills of the researcher in observing and conceptualizing phenomena."[134] There had been political authority among the LoDagaa before conquest, but the conventions of the world on paper did not make it amenable to description. Where Somé sought out specific manifestations of it in the plastic arts of the *Lobi* and LoDagaa, Yelpaala appealed to the conventions of the world on paper.

Having defined stateless societies as "actually species of states with various degrees of decentralization or concentration of power," Yelpaala suggested that a cyclical model of political structure was more appropriate than evolutionary paradigms for examining the origins and vicissitudes of states within the Voltaic region.[135] Accordingly, any political formation had the potential to become a state. Echoing earlier colonial arguments made on the eve of indirect rule which insisted that political authority must have existed among the decentralized societies of the Northern Territories, Yelpaala contended: "It is *not unlikely* that most of the non-centralized societies beneath the Niger bend *must* have experienced at least centralized rule of *some sort* either as part of the empires or under *some* other *unrecorded ruler*."[136] Later in the same article he argued that on the basis of this model, as well as "*limited* publicized oral tradition," there was "sufficient information to come to the conclusion that *some time* before the arrival of the white man [the LoDagaa] *must* have experienced *some* centralization of political power."[137] The conditional, evasive, and imperative language of these statements reflects a lack of hard corroborative evidence, even though Yelpaala did suggest revisionist interpretations of existing material.

Yelpaala pointed to the existence of the word *naa*, meaning chief or rich person, as possible evidence that the LoDagaa were familiar with the concept of central authority. Arguing that the notion of *naa* was prevalent in certain stories of the LoDagaa, where he played the role of "lawgiver," Yelpaala claimed that there was no similar role for the *tengansob*, "suggesting that the institution of *tendaana may* be relatively new in the history of the Dagaaba."[138] There is absolutely no reason to doubt the antiquity or the ubiquity of Earth priests throughout the Voltaic region.[139] One of Rattray's informants told him at the end of the 1920s: "Formerly we did not know anything about Chiefs, we did not use the word *Na*. ... In olden times any man who had many sons commanded respect. ... When the Europeans came, these were the men who came forward to meet them with a white fowl, while the *Tengsob* ran away. They (i.e., the former) became the white man's Chiefs."[140] What Yelpaala ignored here was the secularization of political authority that British rule wrought; he was trying to square the past with the present rather than the present with the past, as Eyre-Smith had vainly attempted. Yet the reason for making the seemingly absurd suggestion that the position of *tengaansob* was more recent than that of chief is understandable, given the need to recover lost sovereignty by appealing to the conventions of the world on paper.

Reviewing examples of political centralization in the late nineteenth century in villages that had unified themselves when faced with threats from slavers (such as Busie, Ulo, and Han, all in Lawra District), Yelpaala stated: "It is plausible to suggest, then, that both internal and external conditions were such that the transformation of the Dabaaba state from a non-centralized system to a centralized one was a real, even an imminent possibility."[141] How then does one explain the fact that there is no extant evidence of any institutionalization of political offices among the LoDagaa? According to Yelpaala, political centralization had been possible at the end of the nineteenth century because of internal tendencies (clientage) and external pressures (insecurity), but the process of transformation (from a noncentralized to a centralized state) was undone by colonization and the imposition of colonial chiefs.

Yelpaala argued that because Western anthropology equated political authority and social order with the state, and because there was political authority and social order among the LoDagaa before colonial rule, then there must have been a state among the LoDagaa. Had he been able to situate sovereignty outside the state, he would not have had to invent a hypothetical political past for the LoDagaa and to define the concept of state in such amorphous terms (i.e., as requiring neither hierarchy nor centralization). Since he did define the state in this way, his quest to attribute signs of centralization and hierarchy to the decentralized and nonhierarchical political formations of the LoDagaa reveals other agendas beyond those of critiquing Western anthropology and recovering lost sovereignty: he was also attempting to deny the alterity of LoDagaa political formations and to deconstruct the concept of historical time.

Unwilling to recognize the different nature of political authority in LoDagaa society, Yelpaala was also unwilling to accept the validity of historical time, even though he accepted the historicist conventions of the world on paper. He did not rewrite the past, but instead reduced it to a speculative morass by arguing that "African time" was not linear but circular, and therefore indeterminate.[142] Although there are differences in forms of historical consciousness in different cultures, historical consciousness does not reflect different realities of time – time is neither straight nor round. It was not time that was different, but the nature of political authority. In his analysis of power among the *Lobi* and LoDagaa, Somé contended that authority could not be restored by arguing that these societies were not acephalous. What was required was a recognition that the nature of this authority was unfamiliar to most external observers. Accordingly, he did not look for it in history, but in artistic expressions that made this noumenal authority less remote and more concrete.[143]

Tuurey and Yelpaala were inspired to construct these arguments by the difficult situation of LoDagaa culture in the wider world of the late twentieth century. Colonialism had created chieftaincy and postcolonial conditions made chieftaincy necessary. Increased communications and integration within an emerging nation invited comparison with the histories of the dominant cultures of Ghana, all of which had traditions of political hierarchy and territorial states. In the late 1970s and early 1980s, Peter Skalnik noted a similar fascination with statehood and chieftaincy among the Konkomba, a society that had also enjoyed radical forms of political autonomy in the precolonial period. Although some sectors of society recognized that there had been no chiefs before British rule, those interested in "the emancipation of the Konkomba" from the stereotypes of outsiders were engaged "in a quest for recognition within the wider Ghanaian society in which chieftaincy is an important cultural feature."[144] Tuurey and Yelpaala were also responding to discourses that continued to marginalize the LoDagaa within Ghana as a stateless society. Implicit in their counterdiscourses was an attempt to recover lost sovereignty through appeal to historicist sensibilities. For Tuurey this took the form of expressing regret at the absence of a LoDagaa state. For Yelpaala, the "imminent possibility" of a centralized state among the LoDagaa was an abstract substitute for a form of historicity that would have allowed him to argue simply that "chieftaincy has come to stay," and that it was now an integral part of LoDagaa society, whatever it origins. However, that historicity (i.e., the ability to create rather than merely rewrite history) had been part of the very sovereignty that the British had stolen from the LoDagaa when they subjected them to the power of the world on paper.

Chapter Four

Reimagining God

Naamwin *and the elephant (*wob*) are the only realities that Dagara tradition does not "show" or teach, as the proverb says: Has anyone ever shown an elephant to a child? The elephant (whose name is used as a euphemism for God) is so enormous and unique an animal that it is sufficient to encounter it in order to know what it is. The proverb is used when one wants to spare oneself the trouble of giving advice, which will go unheeded, to someone who, sooner or later, will experience what he presently ignores; questioning* Naamwin *reveals in some ways the vanity of sophisticated theology:* de Deo non disputatur. *The reality of* Naamwin *is too self-evident for one to call it into question.*

Father Constantin Dabiré, 1983

Shortly after the Society of Missionaries of Africa began their evangelical work among the LoDagaa in 1929 they claimed that the indigenous god was remote and inaccessible whereas their own God was more immediate and approachable, and therefore unique.[1] Indeed, because of this alleged theological incommensurability, the missionaries rejected all forms of indigenous religious beliefs and practices save for the name of the indigenous god, *Naangmin*, which they adopted to refer to their God. As the missionaries understood that *Naangmin* was neither prayed to nor propitiated according to what they could see, this gesture of accommodation did not threaten their argument that the LoDagaa had not received God's revelation before their arrival. After three decades of missionary control, the Catholic Church in Lawra District began its own decolonization in the 1960s with a shift in personnel from foreign missionaries to indigenous priests. In the 1970s, by which time most priests were indigenous, modest gestures toward redeeming indigenous culture were made through the doctrine of inculturation (described below). In the 1980s these relatively cosmetic accommodations were overtaken by a more radical African theology which argued first, that God had always been revealed to the LoDagaa, second, that they had invoked the assistance of *Naangmin* before the arrival of the missionaries, and third, that much of their culture was therefore part of divine revelation. In making these revisionist arguments, members of the local Catholic elite did not have access to what their non-Christian ancestors had once believed, but they did have evidence that what they were arguing was true for what their non-Christian contemporaries believed. However, the cult of authenticity inherited from the world on paper via the Catholic Church made this evidence irrelevant. Instead, it was necessary to rewrite missionary accounts of what people had once believed. In trying to disguise evidence of changes in religious thinking and practices, especially syncretism, these members of the local church denied historicity to LoDagaa culture.

In Lawra District, the doctrine of inculturation, which was articulated in the aftermath of the Second Vatican Council, created pressures on indigenous priests to reimagine the past that were very similar to those which colonial officers experienced when indirect rule was introduced, as well as to those which some local observers later confronted in their rewriting of the political past.[2] The sentiment behind inculturation had been expressed many years before by Pope Pius XII, who declared in 1939: "Whatever there is in native customs that is not inseparably bound up with superstition and error will always receive kindly consideration and, when possible, will be preserved intact."[3] After 1960, when missionaries handed over religious leadership to an indigenous clergy, Catholic leaders among the LoDagaa were attracted to the idea of inculturation. The movement was given its earliest and strongest voice by Peter Dery, who in 1951 became the first LoDagaa ordained as a priest, and who was eventually elevated to the position of archbishop in 1977, presiding over all of northern Ghana. After becoming Bishop of Wa in 1960, he began to seek ways of making Catholicism responsive to the "deepest religious aspirations of the Dagara."[4] Most of the changes initiated in the first two decades – for example, the use of *Dagaare*, indigenous color symbolism, xylophones, drums, lamentations, and songs – were liturgical in nature rather than theological.[5]

Pressure gradually built throughout Africa to make more fundamental accommodations with indigenous beliefs and practices. This was reflected in the attitudes of LoDagaa clergy. To some priests, such as Father Edward Kuukure, inculturation had far more radical implications. He argued that it had "sounded the end of cultural imperialism and opened to Africans the era of their spiritual decolonization."[6] Significantly, Kuukure and other members of the local clergy attempted to carry out this decolonization on paper, through theological treatises. This was because the spiritual colonization of the LoDagaa had been carried out largely in missionary writings. What the missionaries wrote had never determined what the LoDagaa believed, but, unless repudiated, these writings would continue to determine what could be "preserved intact." The early missionaries argued that much of LoDagaa culture was "inseparably bound up with superstition and error." For example, in the late 1980s Father Regimius McCoy, the leader of the first missionaries among the LoDagaa in the 1920s, was still maintaining that "belief in the power of the ancestors and evil spirits led to a deformation in the understanding of what constituted a sinful act." For the founder of the Catholic Church in Lawra District, Christianity had occasioned an "authentic revolution in values" among converts – a position difficult to square with a radical program of inculturation.[7]

For the potential of inculturation to be fulfilled, "serious research into the customs and religious values of the Dagara people" would be required, in much the same way as the shift to indirect rule had required a period of ethnographic inquiry.[8] Knowledge of indigenous cultures was suddently important. Echoing a similar colonial distrust of "scientific" knowledge, in 1974 the Bishops of Africa and Madagascar called for research that they wished "not to be merely theoretical, nor to fall into 'antiquarianism,' but to contribute African solutions to problems of development and evangelization."[9] Accordingly, priests began to reinterpret the nature of god among the LoDagaa during the 1980s in order to narrow the distance between LoDagaa culture and Catholicism, and thereby redeem indigenous religious beliefs and practices from the condemnation of their missionary predecessors. Just as a new generation of officers in the Northern Territories had been called on to discover the nature of precolonial LoDagaa politics over a generation after those structures and ideas had been superseded by colonial designs, the first generation of indigenous Catholic priests were being called on to investigate the religious nature of their own culture's past after almost half a century of missionary evangelism.

Inculturation and the Character of God

The missionaries had argued strongly against commensurability between belief in *Naangmin* and belief in God. Given that those missionaries had provided the only written sources on what the LoDagaa had once believed, the indigenous clergy's project of retrieving evidence of what people once believed faced difficulties. They had to show that commensurability had been the product of divine revelation rather than historical changes. At stake was the nature of pre-Christian LoDagaa beliefs and practices; it was those, and not the beliefs and practices of contemporary non-Christians, that were deemed to have legitimacy. Discovering "traditional" religious culture was both a historical and a theological undertaking.

In order to gain access to their own culture, indigenous priests first had to confront the negative legacy of the missionaries' views and writings, which had long mediated their relationship with indigenous culture. For example, Peter Dery was only twelve years old in the early 1930s, when he first encountered the missionaries. Soon afterwards his father, one of the earliest converts, sent him to become a catechist. The missionaries instructed Dery to reject his own culture. Much of the indigenous clergy's familiarity with the culture of non-Christians was limited to childhood memories. As catechists, they had been distanced further from that culture by intensive alphabetization and religious training. In 1959 there were only six indigenous priests among the LoDagaa, and most of them had been born just before or shortly after the arrival of the missionaries. Twenty years later there were more than forty-five indigenous priests, and all of them were even further removed from indigenous culture, having been raised from birth in relatively strict Christian households. Seminarians first received instruction in indigenous culture in 1965, but it was not until the mid-1970s that several priests, who had completed degrees in Europe, began to study the relationship between Catholicism and the culture of the LoDagaa.[10]

An early missionary account of local "customs and religion" had described almost all features of indigenous culture as *bu-wiir*, "useless things" and referred to those who adhered to that culture as *bu-wiir puorobe*, "those-who-pray-to-the-useless-things." LoDagaa Catholics, following the missionaries' example, eventually began using the latter term to refer to non-Christians.[11] The missionaries' rejection of LoDagaa culture had been so wholesale because of their understanding of *Naangmin*. In the 1980s, priests and other members of the local Catholic elite began to criticize missionary characterizations of *Naangmin* as offensive. Three key critics were Paul Bekye and Edward Kuukure, Catholic priests who had studied abroad, and Benedict Der, an academic historian who had graduated from the University of Ghana.[12] Rejecting both early missionaries' writings and the ethnography of Goody, Der argued that the LoDagaa had always approached God "indirectly" and "implicitly." Kuukure wrote of the "rightful dismay and indignation of non-Christian Dagaaba when they hear themselves referred to as *Ngmin-be-puorbe* (non-worshippers of God)." Bekye felt that the missionaries had so exaggerated the deficiencies of indigenous beliefs that they completely misrepresented the character of *Naangmin*. Thus, he took it upon himself "to establish the status of traditional religion, such as the Dagaaba's, as a legitimate means of God's self-revelation."[13] For all three men it was crucial to prove that recognition of God's uniqueness had come before, not after, the arrival of the missionaries.

So when had God been revealed to the LoDagaa? One event that both foreign missionaries and local clergy were agreed upon was the rain that fell on 5 June 1932 after prayers to God in the midst of a regional drought. It has been described variously, by both missionaries and clergy, as "proof of God's special grace," "God's invitation of love," "the mystery of God's grace," and "God's way of manifesting or revealing Himself to the Dagartis."[14] Only three years after establishing their mission at Jirapa, the White Fathers witnessed one of the most sudden and wholesale waves of conversion in the history of their order.[15] They had come to Lawra District in 1929 after Eyre-Smith and Cardinall, both Catholic officers, encouraged them to extend their work to the west from their station at Navrongo, where they had enjoyed only modest success since 1906.[16] Here too their initial success was relatively modest; but after almost three years of intensive work, most of it medical, the mission claimed five hundred followers.[17] What turned this relatively small number of followers into a mass movement was, according to many devout Catholic observers, a major miracle. Late May and early June marked the beginning of the intensive and crucial period of farming. In 1932 the region was threatened with drought. The rains had failed. People made sacrifices to the local *tengaan* and to other shrines; when those failed, they resorted to a variety of other remedies, but without success. Several recent converts from the settlement of Daffiama led a delegation of nonconverts to the missionaries to ask for assistance. The superior of the mission, Father McCoy, responded by conducting prayers after winning concessions from the group. By remarkable coincidence, almost immediately after the service, as the participants began to disperse, there was a heavy rainfall. It was reported that the rain fell only around Daffiama and nowhere else. Neighboring settlements began to come to the mission, and after a few months the political and cultural landscape of the area had been reconfigured. Thousands of LoDagaa visited the mission, creating a temporary settlement of itinerant followers much larger than Jirapa itself. Some delegations came from as far away as the neighboring French colony. McCoy informed them that none of them could expect rain if they continued to make sacrifices to indigenous shrines.[18]

By the end of 1932 the missionaries were claiming several thousand converts in the region, almost all of them gained in the last six months of that year. Fifteen years later, in 1947, the Jirapa mission, with twenty-six outstations, was said to be attending to seven thousand converts, among whom there were twenty-six catechists. At the same time the neighboring mission at Nandom, opened in 1933, had thirteen thousand converts, thirty-eight outstations, and forty-one catechists.[19] If we accept these figures, then within fifteen years of the rain incident at Jirapa the White Fathers had laid claim to almost one-quarter of all LoDagaa "souls" in Lawra District.[20] By 1959 there were 36,432 baptized Catholics in the Diocese of Wa, which included Lawra District, and which was where most converts resided. By the mid-1980s there were three times as many, 94 percent of whom were LoDagaa.[21] Christianity came to be known among the LoDagaa as *Ngwinsore*, "the way of God," and anyone who entered the new cult was known as *mwinpuorobo* or *puor-puorbe*, "one who prays," as well as *baptizandi*.[22]

Why were so many LoDagaa attracted to the missionaries, to Christianity, and ultimately to conversion? Political and existential concerns – namely, the desire to escape forced labor, disease, death, and drought – are the best explanation (see Chapter 6). However, the mainstream explanations of this phenomenon have been theological. Missionary sources would have us understand that the reason for the sudden breakthrough was that after the rain incident the LoDagaa suddenly understood the nature of God; instead of a remote, inaccessible, and uncaring god, they encountered an accessible and caring God. Later interpretations by LoDagaa clergy have contended that this was not the first time that God had been revealed to the LoDagaa. They argued that the movement which followed the rain incident was due not to an "authentic revolution in values," but rather to a fundamental identification the followers made between their own god, *Naangmin*, and the God of the missionaries.

It is true that the White Fathers had urged those who congregated around the mission after the rain incident to abandon their shrines and attendant sacrifices not in the name of a new God, but in that of their own god, *Naangmin*. But according to the missionaries, *Naangmin* was an otiose deity with whom the LoDagaa did not attempt to communicate.[23] They told those beseeching rain that it was *Naangmin* who wished them to repudiate beliefs and practices surrounding their ancestors (*kpime*), lesser deities (*ngmini* or *weni*), and other noumenal agencies. In the White Fathers' annual report for 1931–32, McCoy explained that his strategy had been to demonstrate to those asking for prayers for rain "the futility of their superstitions and fetishes, that God is the sole master of people as well as the elements."[24]

The missionaries saw their work as a power struggle between, on the one hand, their God, and on the other, the ancestors, various lesser deities, and spirits of the LoDagaa. They attributed the absence of rain to a more powerful and immediate, not to mention jealous, noumenal agency. Writing over fifty years later in his memoirs, McCoy described his encounter with the delegation from Daffiama in stark terms. The elders with whom he had spoken had been willing to admit to the existence of an absolute god, but they considered attempts to solicit its aid futile. One member of the delegation was reported to have said: "He is too big to be concerned with us." To this McCoy claimed to have responded: "That is where you are wrong and where witch doctors and fetishists have led you astray. God knows each and every one of you and loves you." When they asked why this beneficent deity had postponed the rain, he told them it was because they had not asked God: "If God had intervened, you would have thought it was the spirits who were answering you and you would have continued to believe in their power and to live in slavery to them."[25] Curiously, many of the LoDagaa clergy shared McCoy's intense distrust of spirits and ancestors. Even Bekye accepted his argument that the LoDagaa lived in "constant fear" of these agencies. However, he argued that an "apparently transparent belief in God co-existed with an almost morbid fear and pre-occupation with spiritual agencies and the occult mystical powers."[26]

According to the missionaries, the *Dagaare* term for god was the compound of two words, which they rendered in various ways: *Naangmin*, *Naangmen*, *Naamwin*, or *Naawen*. The meaning of the first part of the term, *naa*, is problematic. It was taken to mean chief, and indeed, that was its meaning in neighboring hierarchical societies and, since the imposition of chiefs, the primary sense that the word acquired among the LoDagaa. The second part, in different dialects *ngmin*, *ngmen*, *mwin*, or *wen*, referred to any deity with a shrine on earth toward which ritual actions could be directed. Yet *Naangmin* had no shrine or altar; no sacrifices were offered to it, nor was any liturgy associated with it.[27] Most translations have rendered *Naangmin* as "chief-god," or God in the singular, absolute sense of the word. However, this translation is misleading. To begin with, the term *naa* did not mean chief before the arrival of the British. In addition, the antipathy the LoDagaa had displayed toward political authority "[made] it most unlikely that the original understanding of the term *naa* would have immediate chieftaincy overtones." Bekye argued that "wealthy-deity" would be a more accurate translation. If a *Dagaare* speaker wished to express the idea of a "chief-god," then the word *naa* would follow *ngmin*.[28] Goody noted that "the term *Naangmin*, 'head *ngmin*,' is itself an index of his lack of uniqueness."[29]

In 1991, Roger Somé, an academic philosopher and art critic, actually called into question the very existence of a supreme god, remote or immediate, among the LoDagaa. He argued that *Naangmin* was not an indigenous term but rather a neologism that emerged only after LoDagaa thought was Christianized by the missionaries.[30] Certainly the early missionaries were responsible for creating "new words out of the native language to replace some traditional religious names." The terms for heaven and hell used by contemporary LoDagaa Christians, *teng-velaa* ("good-land") and *teng-faa* ("bad land"), had been invented by the missionaries to replace terms from indigenous eschatology that they deemed superstitious, namely *dapar* ("land of the dead"), *kpimeteng* ("land of the ancestors"), and *dazuge-vuu* ("fire of wood").[31] Several authors have pointed out that theophoric names predated missionary conquest, but have failed to demonstrate that the name *Naangmin*, as opposed to *ngmin*, had not become more current in response to association and rivalry with the God of the missionaries.[32] Given that the term *Naangmin* appeared relatively often in contemporary speech, but not as often as *ngmin* even in aphorisms, proverbs, and theophoric names, and rarely in "cultic language," suggests at the very least that missionary evangelism was in part responsible for making references to *Naangmin* more prevalent throughout LoDagaa culture.[33] Somé's argument is compelling for these reasons, but it is not possible to prove his specific etymological contention about the origins of *Naangmin*; nor is it the strongest part of his wider argument, which is that there was a large degree of interchange between the beliefs of Christians and non-Christians (see below).

The conceptual integrity of *Naangmin* was further complicated by the claim that the word *ngmin* was sometimes used as an abbreviation, making it difficult to distinguish between god in the singular, absolute sense of the word and a particular god among several others.[34] Kuukure noted that in their efforts to construct a "hierarchically structured pantheon," many students of LoDagaa beliefs "ignore or confuse and confound the different levels of meaning in the usage of *ngmin* and *Naangmin*."[35] A case in point is Victor Hien and Father Hébert's study of theophoric names, published in the late 1960s. They claimed that "God is called *Namwin*, 'God the King,'" but that in daily speech "they almost always say *Mwin*."[36] But as Father Naameh has argued, those interested in seeing *Naangmin* as ubiquitous often elide *ngmin* with *Naangmin*, even though the former was most often used to refer to a specific deity rather than god.[37] Bekye also noted that "it is not always immediately clear whether the *ngmen* in a particular name refers to *Naangmen* or to another of the several spiritual agencies to which individual Dagaaba give private cult."[38] This ambiguity is not surprising, as the word was not part of any specialized religious language or liturgy, but most commonly invoked in everyday circumstances.

The apparent ubiquity of references to *Naangmin* in aphorisms, proverbs, and theophoric names is paradoxical, given the absence of any specifically religious forms of behavior toward this absolute deity.[39] Der attributed this to the deference that informed attitudes toward *Naangmin*. Kuukure described it as the result of a "'liturgical polytheism'" obscuring "ontological monotheism." Bekye argued that it was because "an eloquent liturgical silence seems to them the most appropriate attitude towards *Naangmen*."[40] None of these authors explored the possibility that the ambiguity surrounding *Naangmin* might have been the result of religious change, whereby the ideas propounded by catechists, missionaries, and priests affected non-Christians' religious concepts.[41] Another possible explanation for the ambiguity surrounding *Naangmin* was that it was not a deity, but a more abstract cosmological principle that the missionaries distorted by deifying.

Missionaries had conducted very limited research among the LoDagaa. They did not have time for proper inquiries in their first few years, when they focused intensively on medical work. Later, after the rain incident, such understanding was not necessary because they had succeeded in attracting a large following without it.[42] Their remarkable success also made it easier to dismiss LoDagaa religious thought as irrelevant and "useless." However, Cardinall, who spent many years among similar cultures, produced a subtle analysis of god among the Nankanni, Kassena, and Builsa. He noted that owing to the absence of "priests to inculcate doctrine" there was "much individuality of thought." But he added that in all three cultures belief in a supreme being was ubiquitous, as was the understanding that this entity was not approachable, which resulted in a strong sense of fatalism.[43] According to Rattray, the Nankanni believed in a form of predestination.[44] In Fortes's analysis of Tallensi religious thought the concept of fate was paramount. Among the Tallensi the linguistic equivalent of *Naangmin* was *Naawun*; however, Fortes translated this as heaven rather than god and considered it to be more abstract than a deity. He claimed that it was "the Final Cause by which the Tallensi rationalize chance and which they invoke when empirical and less recondite mystical explanations fail."[45] Invocations of *Naangmin* among the LoDagaa in the form of aphorisms, names, and proverbs could be explained by a similar sense of fatalism rather than as a manifestation of theocentric thought or God's revelation. In the 1970s S.W.D.K. Gandah, a local scholar and one of Goody's collaborators, observed that invocations of *Naangmin* were not intended as supplication or propitiation, but as expressions of desperation.[46] Goody was told in the 1950s: "One can swear by God with impunity, for nothing one can say or do can alter his disposition of things."[47] From this perspective *Naangmin* was not a remote god because it was not a god at all, but something more abstract – a cosmological principle rather than a theological entity.

The most interesting evidence for what the LoDagaa believed before the coming of the missionaries would have been found in the myth of the *Bagre*, which was recounted as part of the initiation into this healing cult. However, the earliest recordings of the long oral performances accompanying the main rituals of initiation date from 1951 and 1969, well after the missionaries' arrival. Goody recorded these near the village of Birifu. If measured simply in terms of frequency of references to *Naangmin*, the *Bagre* was the most theocentric of all LoDagaa cultural expressions. Yet *Naangmin* was not "intrinsic" to these two different versions of the myth recorded almost two decades apart.[48] This should hardly be surprising given that the myth sought to explain the origins of illness and affliction and therefore addressed the effective agencies of such intervention in peoples' lives – namely, the spirits, medical shrines, and god of the *Bagre* (*Bagr-ngmin*). Goody was told during his fieldwork in the early 1950s that *Naangmin* was unknowable, as opposed to unknown: "People 'call his name but do not know him.'"[49] This refrain ran throughout the White *Bagre* and Black *Bagre*, both recorded in 1951. Here the existence but remoteness of *Naangmin* was very clear:

> Well, about God, we hear his name without knowing him.
> God doesn't want us to see him. He is near yet far.
> We hear his name but know nothing of him.
> About the ways of God, we hear his name but we have ruined it.[50]

By 1969 the emphasis had shifted from the impossibility of knowing *Naagnmin* to the difficulty of acquiring such knowledge:

> God's affairs are so complex and so many! No one person can know them all.
> Its God's matter that no one can know.
> The affairs of God are too many for me alone.
> I know little, for the affairs of God, they are so many and I know them little.[51]

Both versions contained frequent references to *Naangmin*, but a belief in *Naangmin* was quite distinct from knowledge of *Naangmin*. Many of the theophoric names that Constantin Dabiré recorded in the early 1980s when he did fieldwork among the LoDagaa to the west of the Black Volta, such as *Mwin-zaa* ("distant-God"), *Mwin-pile* ("hidden-God"), and *Mwin-be-bagne* ("unknowable-God"), still stressed this remoteness. A member of the local clergy, Dabiré suggested that attitudes toward *Naangmin* were best illustrated by the proverb that one does not need to show an elephant to a child because it is so large, obvious, and unique.[52]

Divine Revelation or Cultural Syncretism?

The different versions of the myth of the *Bagre* that Goody recorded bore several remarkable similarities to the content of the Bible. "So striking," wrote Bekye, "that they cannot be over-looked." With this point Kuukure readily agreed. He noted "a startling parallel" between initiation into the *Bagre* and

Christian initiation.[53] Indeed, the Bible came to be known among the LoDagaa as "the white man's *Bagre*."[54] In Catholicism, converts discovered the story of Christ's death and resurrection. This theme would have had deep cultural resonance for any LoDagaa familiar with the ritual death and resurrection of *Bagre* initiates, although Kuukure, who made this comparison, cautioned that "the results" were "beyond compare" because the *Bagre* "does not really 'free from death.'"[55]

Goody admitted there might be some Christian influences in the *Bagre* due to "culture contact," but argued against such an interpretation even "though we can hardly rule this out as a possibility."[56] Perhaps the most striking similarities between the *Bagre* and the Bible were the explanation for how *Naangmin* came to be separated from the affairs of the living (viz, it was due to deception by the *kontome*, "beings of the wild") and the description of the fall of man as found in Genesis.[57] By rejecting the words of *Naangmin* and following the *kontome*, the LoDagaa severed their communications with *Naangmin*.[58] Bekye, whose knowledge of the *Bagre* came from Goody's work, noted that the two stories bore "striking similarities" with each other, so much so that the Christian myth would have been "very familiar to those catechumens who were initiates."[59] For Bekye this was proof not of "culture contact" but of "divine revelation." If one ignores the suggestions of divine revelation in Kuukure's and Bekye's comparisons, it is possible that these aspects of the *Bagre* were added or reworked in the wake of the rain incident. But without more research it is impossible to distinguish between diffusion and convergence.

Der, Kuukure, and Bekye sought to narrow the distance between Christian and non-Christian cultures, and thereby legitimate indigenous culture in the eyes of external religious authorities and make Christianity more relevant and immediate to the culture of non-Christians. In contrast, Somé attacked the very notion of commensurability between LoDagaa culture and Christianity. He insisted that indigenous religious concepts were historically conditioned rather than static, arguing that "The notion of a single god among the Dagara derives from a general acculturation brought about by Christianity and aggravated by a kind of imitation of the 'modern' world that has had a flattening effect."[60] Accordingly, any connection between the LoDagaa god and Christian God was the result of missionary convenience and indigenous mimesis, rather than genuine theological similarities or cultural affinities. Der, Kuukure, and Bekye – and even Goody, albeit for much different reasons, explained below – saw similarities in the content and/or structure of the two religious cultures as the best way of explaining why so many LoDagaa embraced Christianity so quickly. To Somé, however, these similarities were historical rather than original. He argued that the influence of Christianity began with the first contact between the missionaries and the LoDagaa, and was strengthened after "the missionaries assimilated Dagara beliefs into Christianity by making out that they all worshipped the same God." The only difference, he argued, was that Christians had destroyed their shrines because the missionaries considered them "satanic idols," whereas non-Christians had not. The process continued with the indigenization of the Catholic Church in the 1960s, further obscuring the lines of distinction between Christian and indigenous religious thought. "Of course," Somé added, "not all Dagara today have become Christians, but this has not stopped non-Christians from acquiring Christian ways of thinking, as they do not live apart but always with those who have converted."[61]

The use of *Naangmin* by missionaries as a term of evangelization, and later by indigenous priests as a term of equivalence, does raise important questions. However, there are profound difficulties in assessing the degree to which Catholicism altered indigenous cultural perceptions, not the least of which is the absence of direct evidence of what the LoDagaa believed before the arrival of the missionaries. Even so, Somé's argument is supported by evidence of a high degree of syncretism among converts. Conversion was not an unequivocal process, but rather one full of ambiguities. Renouncing indigenous practices and destroying shrines did not mean discarding beliefs.[62] Nor was the process permanent or unilateral. Converts replaced their "fetishes," which the missionaries had condemned, with crosses, medals of baptism, and statues of saints. But they continued to believe in their ancestors, even though they did not maintain shrines to them.[63] Similarly, non-Christians believed in the power of the medal of the Blessed Virgin Mary – known colloquially as the *mel* – even though they did not destroy their shrines. Significantly, those Christians who did destroy their shrines did so reportedly only after they had received the *mel*. Initially, for Christians and non-Christians alike, the *mel* was a more powerful "fetish" (or physical representation of noumenal power) than any indigenous shrine or religious object, and the missionaries were fully aware of it.[64] "It is highly likely, if not certain," one missionary conceded in 1937, "that among the throngs at the outset, many saw the medal only as a new fetish, more powerful than those they already possessed."[65]

When Christianity did not provide satisfactory answers, many recent converts returned to their former shrines and practices.[66] By the late 1930s and early 1940s, many converts were beginning to realize that the missionaries could not always provide rain, cure the ill, or revive the dying. Disillusioned, they turned back to the culture of their non-Christian neighbors.[67] But even those who remained faithful to their new religion (admittedly the majority) did not abandon the beliefs of their own culture. In a study of divination on the other side of the Black Volta in the early 1970s, a local Catholic priest observed that neither an adherence to Christianity nor a familiarity with "modernity" interfered with the survival of indigenous beliefs.[68] According to Naameh, the only dissenting voice among LoDagaa Catholic intellectuals, the early conversion process was not very theocentric. Converts were "focused on the missionaries who demonstrated greater powers than the fetish priests and divinities, and not God." Because *Naangmin* was considered by them to be "neither in space or time," they did not see god as the cause of drought or other afflictions.[69] When the missionaries spoke of their God as *Naangmin* and claimed to perform miracles in the name of this God, what their followers saw were the extraordinary or inhuman powers of the White Fathers. Their white robes were understood in terms of the whiteness of the *kontome*; their secretive defecations gave rise to the rumor that they did not have anuses; and their consumption of eggs and practice of siestas were seen as signs of extravagant and mysterious behavior.[70] Furthermore, the White Fathers were themselves aware of these miscommunications.[71]

The cult of *Naangminle* or "little god," which spread on either side of the Black Volta in 1952, suggests that Christianity had affected non-Christian culture. According to Goody, who witnessed the cult's sudden rise and success, even though his informants said "you cannot kill a fowl to God," "... in the *Naanmingle* cult, they did kill fowl and make material objects (e.g., bangles) associated with the shrine."[72] That the movement came twenty years after the rain incident, not to mention half a century after political and economic changes precipitated by colonization, suggests that "syncretic tendencies" had led to a re-evaluation by non-Christians of the character of *Naangmin*. But Goody rejected such an interpretation, as it implied that LoDagaa religion was "a static phenomenon and attributed the dynamic elements in the religious system to contact with the outside." Instead, he saw the cult of "the little god" as evidence of the return of *Naangmin* to the affairs of the living, and situated this moment within an internal cycle of responses to the problem of evil that oscillated between otiose and active understandings of *Naangmin*. In Goody's view, people's dissatisfaction with lesser agencies eventually led them to attempt to communicate with *Naangmin*, thereby making it an active noumenal agent. But when appeals to it failed to avert evil and misfortune, *Naangmin* was restored to a remote position well beyond the affairs of humans.[73]

Among the LoDagaa, the remoteness of *Naangmin* was an important theological device for accounting for evil. Many West African religions, including that of the LoDagaa, explained evil in terms of the remoteness of god, which makes the idea of an active god potentially offensive. Justin Ukpong has argued: "To say that such sacrifices are ultimately intended for God would mean saying that God is the cause of the epidemic or famine, and this is repugnant to these peoples' conception of God."[74] Significantly, Gandah did not see *Naangminle* as a refraction of *Naangmin*, but as a separate and subordinate deity.[75]

Goody not only rejected the idea that *Naangminle* emerged as a result of external influences, but also suggested that the wave of conversions that followed the rain incident was the result of "identification" rather than conversion. The facility with which the LoDagaa embraced Christianity, he suggested, was "indicative of the possibility that such a shift can take place not only between religions, as in conversion, but also within religions."[76] Writing in the 1970s, when the concept of "native agency" had recently gained ascendancy in academic studies of Africa, he was overly concerned with maintaining the integrity of indigenous thought in the face of major changes.[77] Goody's model of internal religious change is strongly reminiscent of Yelpaala's argument (which of course it preceded), wherein hypothesis masquerades as history. It is difficult to accept the argument for the former existence of an active form of god among the LoDagaa when there is no evidence of rituals, liturgy, shrines, cults, or priests once dedicated to *Naangmin*. Extant versions of the myth of the *Bagre* mentioned no means of reactivating *Naangmin*. Finally, if LoDagaa beliefs and practices were not "static," as Goody quite rightly argued, how then could they have been impervious to the changes taking place around them?

The colonial state's "pacification" and exploitation of the LoDagaa had greatly expanded communications within the region and with areas beyond. For example, the marginalization of independent *tengaan* and their displacement by a hierarchical and secular system of political office, as well as increasing labor migration, dramatically affected people's notions of space. All of these changes, along with the impact of the movement that followed the rain incident, make it difficult to isolate the *Naangminle* movement from external influences. However, it is difficult to see conversion primarily as the product of missionary influences. Robin Horton has suggested: "The beliefs and practices of the so-called worldly religions are only accepted where they happen to coincide with responses of the traditional cosmology to other, non-missionary, factors of the modern situation."[78] Even if the opportunity for the mass conversion had come from outside, the LoDagaa were the movement's agents and organizers. Over a few months during the farming season of 1932, the Jirapa mission station became the largest congregation of LoDagaa ever recorded. One missionary wrote: "From then on the mission was literally invaded, taken by storm. Monsignor told me that one Sunday he himself had seen 15,000 people at the mission."[79]

In the immediate aftermath of the rain incident, twenty thousand people were visiting the Jirapa mission every month.[80] By 1937 crowds of five to six thousand were a regular occurrence at the Nandom mission.[81] They came from over a wide area and included speakers of various dialects of *Dagaare*. In these circumstances, indigenous concepts would have been susceptible to rearticulation and elaboration. Many of those who converted were motivated by fear of chiefs rather than of spirits, by new ways of cheating death rather than a rejection of ancestors. Others converted out of a desire to acquire a wider identity and become part of a larger social network. In these cases, God was crucial. It provided the means of uniting all LoDagaa converts into a single group. Ancestors, spirits, and Earth shrines were all local and particularistic. The idea of God created a sense of unity between all converts. "There is no Dagao ... nor *gbangbaa* (slave), nor male nor female," wrote Kuukure, "all are one in Christ."[82] It was a symbol for an alternative social and political order to that of the colonial state and a source of ethnic consciousness. No doubt, the idea of *Naangmin* also became more important to non-Christians for similar reasons, whether or not Somé's claim that the term is a missionary neologism can be supported.

If not causally linked, the missionary reconceptualization of *Naangmin* and the spread of the cult of *Naangminle* two decades later were at least part of the same process of expansion in scale of communications and in levels of cosmological explanation. In 1956 Goody had argued that although colonial occupation had obviously influenced the ethnographic situation, the effects were so obvious that they were readily identifiable. "It is still possible to disentangle the one from the other," so he had "deliberately chosen to consider the political organisation as it existed at the beginning of the century."[83] In the 1970s, when Goody first admitted that change had occurred, he situated it within a hypothesized cycle of indigenous religious speculation. This preserved the idea of cultural authenticity and the primacy of native agency, but effectively denied the historicity of LoDagaa culture. Subsequent studies of the nature of *Naangmin* similarly bracketed LoDagaa religious concepts outside of history.

George Marcus and Michael Fischer have noted that anthropologists used the "ethnographic present" for two related reasons: to facilitate "the structural analysis of systems of symbols and social relations" by "bracketing the flow of time and the influence of events," and to act as conservationists. "Situating one's ethnography either before or after the 'deluge,'" they added, "serves the classic salvage justification for ethnography as a recorder of cultural diversity that was disappearing or being irrevocably altered."[84] These strategies are evident in Goody's work, and also in the arguments of Kuukure and Bekye, albeit in different ways. A quarter-century after Goody suggested that external influences on LoDagaa culture were largely irrelevant, Bekye argued that "Christian and Islamic influences on the Dagaaba are so recent that their traditional beliefs can still be studied in their relative integrity." Even so, Bekye and other clergy avoided testimony from contemporary non-Christians in favor of arguments based on religious parallels. For his part, Kuukure also insisted that beliefs had not changed. Conflating the past with the present denied historicity to LoDagaa beliefs.[85]

In the face of an interpretative paradigm that perceived LoDagaa beliefs as signs of divine revelation, historicity was irrelevant; yet the assurance of historical immutability was still considered important. Significantly, as a historian Der could not use divine revelation as an argument; however, he did argue that the LoDagaa had been communicating with *Naangmin* before the White Fathers arrived, and that Christianity had therefore not appreciably altered indigenous beliefs and practices. Instead of relying on the early missionaries in the northwest, Der preferred the testimony of the missionaries from the northeast, at Navrongo; although equally prejudiced, these men had developed a mediumistic interpretation of indigenous beliefs and practices.[86] Der also invoked authors – such as Binger, the colonial ethnographer Louis Tauxier, and Louis Girault, a missionary on the other side of Black Volta during the last years of the colonial era – whose texts conferred authority even though their evidence was tenuous at best.[87] But he avoided the reports by missionaries in the northwest, and in particular McCoy, on what the LoDagaa had believed at the time of their arrival in Jirapa.

The debate over the character of *Naangmin* revolved around what missionary observers of the 1930s said the LoDagaa believed and what, a half-century later, the indigenous clergy and other members of the Catholic elite understood those beliefs to be from the perspective of the 1980s. The major difficulty with assessing the various representations of what the LoDagaa believed before the coming of the missionaries – and, accordingly, the different interpretations of how they understood conversion – is that, as Gaanath Obeyesekere noted in another context, "there is no way one could become an ethnographer of a past that barely exists today."[88] Nevertheless, one of the curious features of the theological arguments of most clergy is their disregard for the voices of contemporary Christians and non-Christians.

When Der referred to his own experiences, he made the same mistakes his sources did. He recalled that during his youth his grandfather and other "non-Christian uncles" made sacrifices to *Naangmin* on the roof of the household compound, and then compared this to a similar sacrifice to "the cult of *Wen*" that Girault had observed among the LoDagaa around Diébougou in the 1950s.[89] What Der did not acknowledge about this corroborating evidence was that the site in question was called *mwinbagr*, found only in households whose members had been initiated into the *Bagre*. As Bekye later pointed out, Girault incorrectly attributed this shrine to *Wen* (or *Naangmin*) when it was clearly dedicated to "the spirit-patron of the *Bagre* initiation."[90] Kuukure was also critical of Girault's identification, although he conceded: "There is possibly some confusion and fusion of thought here in the minds of the people themselves."[91] Similarly, it is also possible that in the area where Der grew up, and at the time he witnessed the sacrifice, *Naangmin* was indeed included among the intended recipients of such a sacrifice. If so, it would have been the result of cultural change in what had become a predominantly Christian area. In the 1980s Kuukure and Dabiré (the latter speaking of the other side of the Black Volta) both reported that there were still no shrines, no priests, no cults, and no rituals directly associated with *Naangmin* in any of the areas they investigated.[92] Ironically, Der had argued that Goody's account of *Naangmin* as a distant and remote god with whom the people of Birifu did not attempt to communicate was "particular to that locality" and "cannot to be taken as representative of the whole Dagari area."[93] What made Birifu unrepresentative when Goody worked there in the 1950s and 1960s was that of all settlements in the district, it was perhaps the one least affected by Christianity.

It is very difficult to maintain that the distance between LoDagaa culture and the missionaries' religion did not shrink over time. Yet the indigenous clergy and other members of the local Catholic elite have insisted almost unanimously that indigenous ideas were always entirely commensurable with Christianity. The unfortunate effect has been to deny legitimacy to LoDagaa historicity. Even Somé, who admitted to the mutability of indigenous thought under "modern" conditions, denied the authenticity of these changes, arguing that only premissionary beliefs and practices were genuine: "If the Dagara want to preserve what remains of their culture, they have to rid themselves of Christianity, which, in the long term, will swallow them up."[94] If many LoDagaa were Christians, why was Christianity not part of LoDagaa culture? Somé's view of LoDagaa culture was implicitly essentialist, privileging culture over society. Here he agreed with the views of his Catholic adversaries, who had their own essentialist understanding of LoDagaa culture – one that privileged the past over the present.[95]

Had Der, Kuukure, and Bekye been able to take the 1980s as their starting point, they might well have been able to demonstrate the commensurability between the religious thinking of Christian and non-Christian LoDagaa, because conversion had not involved a wholesale change in the attitudes of converts, and because the unconverted did not remain uninfluenced by the ideas of their neighbors. But since these authors were not free to acknowledge these historical developments, they did not seek out indigenous testimony – an ethnography of the present rather than the past. In the past, missionaries could have "'looked the other way,'" as one contemporary missionary has put it, "when it came to certain traditional practices that native Christians felt constrained to perform."[96] For these authors the purpose of their arguments was to liberate Christian converts and clergy from the need for collusive subterfuge. Regrettably, it prevented any recognition of the synthesis or dialogue that had obviously occurred between "traditional" and Catholic beliefs and practices.[97] There is evidence to support the idea that in the 1980s LoDagaa Christians saw these "traditional practices" in a mediumistic perspective, and evidence to suggest that the concept of *Naangmin* had changed among non-Christians.[98] Which raises this question: Why should what the LoDagaa believed before the arrival of the missionaries be so much more important than what they might believe today, especially when the present is so much more accessible than the past?

The Past as a Source of Legitimacy

It seems clear that the conflicting accounts of *Naangmin* reflect attitudes toward the past as opposed to a fundamental theological ambiguity in "traditional" LoDagaa thought. For the missionaries, what the LoDagaa believed at the time of their arrival was essential and immutable. For the indigenous clergy, what Christian and non-Christian LoDagaa believed in the 1970s and 1980s was what was important; but they had to project these beliefs back in time, to a period before the missionaries, and argue that LoDagaa attitudes had not changed. The project of inculturation imposed a form of historicism on efforts to salvage indigenous culture from missionary condemnation. What mattered to the Catholic Church was evidence of the revelation of God before, not after, the arrival of the White Fathers. Robin Horton and David Westerlund have argued independently that the mediumistic approach to African religions found in much of contemporary African theology, which has affected Christian interpretations of LoDagaa religious concepts and thought, was the product of adherence to the conceptual framework of Western religious discourse. In the face of the "recalcitrant reality" of indigenous practices, contemporary African theology has often reinvented the past in order to demonstrate commensurability.[99]

Horton has pointed out that one of the main difficulties in the debate over the nature of non-Christian or indigenous religious thought in African cultures is that the concept is essentialist and ahistorical. He warns us that "much of our knowledge of these patterns [of thought] is derived from areas long under the twin influences of Christian missionary enterprise and the accelerated social change of modern times." It would be unreasonable to assume that local cultures did not change. According to Horton, the process of conversion on the part of some members of a culture was often mirrored by a less obvious movement on the part of those who did not convert, but who "found certain elements of the missionary message concerning the supreme being particularly congenial to their purposes, and used them freely to create new though still unmistakably indigenous syntheses."[100] However, these changes were seen as illegitimate – as the result of "cultural hybridism, schizophrenia, and other metaphoric diseases"[101] – and therefore unacceptable for the purpose of demonstrating a transcendental and fundamental commensurability between indigenous African and Christian deities. Only by always having had a God could African cultures be seen as respectable and acceptable.

Christian theologians in postcolonial Africa developed what Westerlund has called a "theology of continuity" in order to overthrow the "radical theology of discontinuity" that missionaries once practiced. According to this approach, God was known to all African cultures before the coming of missionaries and knowledge of revelation in the Bible.[102] The trends that Horton and Westerlund observed in religious discourses throughout Africa in the 1970s and 1980s – trends that were reflected in the arguments of the LoDagaa Catholic elite – accepted that the past was a source of legitimacy. Establishing the grounds for inculturation depended as much on historical arguments as on theological ones.

Instead of relying on secular history, the indigenous clergy appealed to a transcendental level of historical analysis and used divine revelation in order to argue for historical commensurability between local culture and Christian doctrine. The first attempt to posit an indigenous belief in and communication with God before the arrival of the White Fathers was actually made by a missionary. Writing in the late 1950s on the nature of non-Christian beliefs, Girault exploited the ambiguity surrounding *Naangmin* in order to suggest that the LoDagaa had once worshipped God but that because of their frequent migrations they had forgotten the meaning of their own religious practices: "These travelers have often lost the original meaning of the rituals that they continue to practice in an almost mechanical fashion; thus we often have reason to pity them."[103] (This argument is similar to the argument that the LoDagaa must once have had chiefs, who disappeared during the political chaos that preceded the arrival of the British.) Three decades later, Kuukure similarly claimed that God was the ultimate recipient of all LoDagaa communications with the noumenal world "although the reality of the intermediaries is often so heavy as to obscure this fact and make God appear only as an indirect beneficiary."[104] The problem with arguments like these, as well as other mediumistic interpretations of supreme beings in African theology, is that they claim access to a transcendent reality beyond the consciousness or even memories of believers. C.N. Ubah has argued that the observer should "learn from, and not teach, worshippers what they are doing."[105] In all that indigenous intellectuals have written on what the LoDagaa believed before the coming of the missionaries, there has been little or no room for indigenous testimony.

Instead of relying on indigenous testimony, writers have resorted to reconstructing "traditional beliefs" in order to support their "theology of continuity." Here, Bekye anticipated the criticism of Westerlund; he denied that such beliefs were the result of projection and insisted that LoDagaa religion was relatively immutable: "The image of God that emerges from a tradition, such as the Dagaaba's, cannot legitimately be said to be the creation either of Christian theology, or of nationalistic interests, both of which are recent experiences."[106] By arguing that LoDagaa culture was the product of "the long distant past," Bekye denied historicity to LoDagaa thought. He isolated "living tradition," received by way of generational transmission from a fount of "ancestral heritage," from the possibility of change.[107] Earlier missionaries would have agreed with this position insofar as they renounced "traditional" beliefs and thereby rejected the possibility that they could be modified or Christianized. According to Bekye, a premissionary belief in God existed beyond the level of appearances – as well as outside of secular history:

> Though the immediate destination of the people's offerings and sacrifices *appears* to be the *Tibe*, yet it is recognized that these offerings are in fact *Naangmen*'s prerogatives. But as these spirit-patrons – the *Tibe* – *seem* to act on *Naangmen*'s behalf, and in return for the survival services believed to be rendered by them to the people, *Naangmen seems* to concede to them the prerogatives of the material sacrifices that the people offer in shrines and at altars erected in their honour.[108]

Bekye's conditional language is similar to that used by Yelpaala. The passage is also contradictory: if the spirits rendered the services for which sacrifices were offered, then why was it recognized that these sacrifices belonged to god? And by whom were they recognized? This problem is common to all mediumistic interpretations of indigenous religions in Africa. As Ukpong has noted: "Either these gods [or lesser spirits] are recognized as *free beings* capable of initiating actions and carrying them through, and *responsible* for such actions and therefore meriting praise or blame, or they are mere instruments or channels without *free will* and *responsibility*. To say that the gods are both *free beings* and *instruments* does not make sense."[109] However, the purpose of mediumistic arguments was not theological consistency but cultural legitimacy.

Although these revisionists did not have any direct evidence of indigenous beliefs before the arrival of the missionaries, they argued that the way the LoDagaa responded to the White Fathers' message indicated that the beliefs of the missionaries and those of their followers were very similar. According to

Bekye, the commensurability between LoDagaa beliefs and Christianity was demonstrated by the relative ease of conversion: "This fact of the people being able to identify themselves, through a correspondence of parallel religious themes and concepts, in the drama of salvation history that involved humanity as a whole, was a factor of enormous importance that quickened their grasp of, and their ready response to the message of salvation that was being addressed to them."[110] Another member of the local Catholic elite, although admitting to the notion of a remote god among the LoDagaa, denied that this was "synonymous with a disavowal of a supreme God by the Dagara." Instead, he argued that an implicit appreciation of this God lay behind the conversion process. "The firm recognition of an absolute God proved an important foundation for the flowering of faith and brought about the conversion of this people to Catholicism."[111] However, these interpretations were predicated on the erroneous assumption that God was central to the early conversion process (see Chapter 6).

Arguments grounded in interpretations of the mass movement toward Christianity in the 1930s were invoked as tenuous props for arguments that denied any fundamental changes in indigenous religious thought. For the most part, the studies under review treated LoDagaa beliefs and practices as if they existed outside of history; yet the idea of the past, and of continuity with it, was a crucial element of their arguments. Der, Kuukure, and Bekye conflated the present with the past by either compressing or denying time. Kuukure and Bekye adhered to an ahistorical setting where indigenous beliefs did not change.[112] Although Der did use a more diachronic perspective, his use of historical evidence was contrived.[113] Even Goody, albeit for different reasons, saw the conversion process as belonging to a cycle of internal religious speculation and denied the possibility that colonialism and evangelism had wrought changes in LoDagaa thought.

These arguments over LoDagaa "tradition" raise the question of tradition versus practice that is at the heart of the disagreement between Vansina and Ranger. Vansina has argued that the term "tradition," although often greatly misused as "a flag of convenience to legitimate a position held on other grounds," is still valid. For him, tradition represents "fundamental continuities" that "shape" history: "They are 'out there.' They are phenomena with their own characteristics."[114] This approach has the advantage of defining tradition so as to exclude the "invented" or "imagined";[115] however, it also lends itself to notions of cultural determinism and even essentialism. Such problems are very evident in mediumistic representations of LoDagaa beliefs that speak of realities beyond either the intention or the consciousness of the believers themselves. Although admitting to the possibilities of change, Vansina's concept of tradition does not accept certain types of change. He argues that tradition needs autonomy and "is maimed when autonomy is lost."[116] It was when autonomy was lost that many African cultures were forced to imagine traditions in order to disguise change. Vansina's narrow definition implies, as Ranger has observed, that African experiences of colonialism were historically illegitimate, just as it exaggerates the degree of "stultification" that resulted from foreign rule.[117]

What, then, differentiates legitimate from illegitimate change? Vansina suggests that there are static principles inherent in traditions, "such as the existence of a single God," which do not change once they are formulated, and that these act as the criteria against which possible changes are tested within a tradition.[118] If it is accepted that the LoDagaa had not worshipped god before the arrival of the missionaries, and that this was a basic principle, then LoDagaa Christians cannot claim to be part of LoDagaa tradition. But what of Somé's argument that non-Christian concepts of god were modified by the spread of Christianity? Can the notion of an essential tradition be maintained? Does it mean that syncretism represents an abandonment of cultural autonomy? Or is such change not an exercise of cultural autonomy? In his study of Yoruba religion, Peel has argued that the dilemma posed by the paradigm of "tradition" is whether Yoruba religion is defined by whatever practices the Yoruba perform, or by practices that are uniquely Yoruba: "In the former case the defining unit of analysis is Yoruba society, in the latter it is certain given forms of Yoruba culture. ... An anthropology which thus privileges culture over society runs a serious risk of ignoring the implications of religious choices being made in the world today."[119]

LoDagaa practices and beliefs include Catholicism if we are to understand that designation socially, and to avoid falling prey to notions of cultural essentialism. If observers such as Der, Kuukure, and Bekye had been able to admit to the possibility, let alone the legitimacy, of indigenous cultural change, their arguments concerning the commensurability of Christian and non-Christian beliefs would have been situated in the present rather than in the past. But they represented ideas about *Naangmin* as static principles in order to establish their legitimacy. Attempts at proving the existence of a premissionary worship of god were highly contrived. Yet what was really being represented – a variety of contemporary LoDagaa religious beliefs and practices – was legitimate, just not in terms that would satisfy external religious authorities.

The indigenous clergy found it necessary to go back in time to establish the legitimacy of their representations of LoDagaa beliefs. However, given the available historical evidence, what they represented was not what the LoDagaa once thought – the only direct evidence they had for this was the very missionaries whose views they were trying to contradict – but the synthesis of Christian and non-Christian thinking that had already occurred. In this sense what does it mean to talk of non-Christian beliefs? Does this mean beliefs held before the arrival of missionaries, or beliefs held by contemporary non-Christians? Because of the tyranny of historicism, Catholic intellectuals have argued that the two are the same, and thereby have denied both moments historicity. Why not simply argue that non-Christian culture had already been Christianized as a result of cultural fusion? Mainly because inculturation was based on the idea of a unique and unchanging non-Christian culture that could trace its ancestry back to a time before the missionaries, it was necessary to disguise syncretism and reject the representations of their missionary predecessors that had documented a different version of non-Christian beliefs.

There was an irony here. Der, Kuukrue, and Bekye were all concerned with making indigenous beliefs seem more universal or macrocosmic. Their efforts to resolve the local with the universal parallel recent debates in the theory of conversion. Several authors have criticized Horton's argument that expansion in space, which usually coincided with conversion, created a more immediate and unique sense of god.[120] Ranger has suggested that missionary Christianity was not as macrocosmic as has been assumed.[121] That the White Fathers immediately called their God *Naangmin* is indicative of the degree to which they thought microcosmically. LoDagaa understanding of Christianity occurred in the context of local existential and political concerns: many converts sought ways of escaping drought, disease, and death; others worried far less about questions of eternal damnation or salvation than about colonial rule and the tyranny of the chiefs. But politics and religion were linked in other ways besides this. As Kuukure noted, the pyramid that structures most representations of *Naangmin* is historically untenable, as it relies on a colonial etymology: "*Naangmin* becomes head, chief *ngmin*, chief god, even though *naa* – chief in the colonial, administrative, hierarchical, pyramidal sense – would be surprising, since some have insisted that there were no such chiefs before the arrival of the Europeans."[122] And so we come full circle. Without the invention of chiefs, *ngmin* might not have been imaginable as *Naangmin* or God.

Conclusion to Part 2

In the 1930s, colonial political engineering created a fiction to legitimate and maintain the chiefs the British had invented. As a result, it was necessary for the LoDagaa to perpetuate a politics of continuity similar to the "theology of continuity" that Westerlund has observed in African theology. In applying indirect rule, administrators needed to rewrite the past to legitimate the changes they themselves had wrought. To avail themselves of the advantages of inculturation, priests needed to dehistoricize religious syncretism and create a world of timeless commensurability. In defining legitimacy in terms of the past, both British colonialism and Catholic evangelism created neotraditionalism. Sovereignty shifted from the present to the past, just as it shifted from indigenous societies to external authorities.[123]

The reinvention of the past that had been precipitated by indirect rule was really about disguising and perpetuating a colonial tyranny. Indirect rule did not preserve but rather marginalized and distorted indigenous politics. Accordingly, arguments over the authenticity of claims to the chieftaincy of Zambo in 1977 were not about tensions between the traditional and the modern, but about tensions between local and national sources of authority, and between noumenal and phenomenal forms of power. Christopher Steiner's study of the art markets of Côte d'Ivoire graphically illustrates the predicament of neotraditionalism. In the art markets it is Western dealers and collectors who determine and control value. Historicism – or, as defined above, an "excessive regard for the institutions and values of the past" – deeply influenced external aesthetic values. To sell in this market, artists and artisans had to produce fakes or reproductions, and this denied them the power to produce in terms of contemporary values. The fetish of the "authentic" or the "antique," not merely bequeathed but constantly reiterated by Western markets, imposed limitations on aesthetic expression by rejecting the contemporary as inauthentic or illegitimate. Although traders, and in turn artists and artisans, reacted to these values, they understood the Western focus on age as actually a preoccupation with an imaginary place – a timeless continent.[124]

LoDagaa traditions were produced within the same matrix as this trade in African art. It became necessary in the postcolonial period to invest the convergence of colonial and LoDagaa political practices with a traditional aura, like the fake patinas of freshly carved sculptures, in order to lend them legitimacy. Appeals to external values, whether by shooting an elephant (both precolonial and neotraditional) or by claiming office through descent from the first colonial appointee (thereby creating proto-tradition), were ultimately oriented not in time but in space. In many African societies during the colonial and postcolonial eras, the quest for legitimacy involved reducing the physical distance between local culture and district, regional, and national political structures, where stolen sovereignty resided, by assimilating historicist values that came from the world on paper. As Henige noted, whenever societies have lost sovereignty through foreign domination they have sought to recover some degree of legitimacy through "the discovery of hitherto unsuspected antiquity." "Some of the greatest historical works of antiquity," he observed, "were written during periods of foreign domination and with the expressed purpose of portraying the historians' peoples in a way palliative to their lost sovereignty and impressive to their new rulers."[125] David Schoenbrun has made a similar observation about the "scramble for legitimacy" in the Great Lakes region of East Africa, adding that "struggles for control of discourse about the African past are still shackled in an essentially European-derived conceptual framework."[126]

Historicism became an instrument of power and control among the LoDagaa and other African societies in the twentieth century by removing struggles over sovereignty, be they cultural, economic, or religious, from a political to a historical arena.[127] Notwithstanding their temporal language, the discourses over authenticity and legitimacy discussed in these chapters were actually grounded in spatial realities. They were not about regaining power from the past, but about reinventing the past in order to gain power from the outside world. But reinventing history did not resolve the tensions in twentieth-century LoDagaa culture. That required the recovery of lost sovereignty – the ability to invent "new structures to cope with a new situation."[128] The reimagining of tradition in African cultures should be seen as a substitute for the exercise of real power or sovereignty, that is, the autonomy to practice history; it is merely the freedom to invent the past rather than change the present. Conversely, the imposition of invented traditions should be seen as part of an exercise in disguising political power and forcing African societies to produce history rather than engage in politics. The remedy to neotraditionalism is the same as Marx's solution to the problems of philosophical idealism: "The philosophers have only *interpreted* the world, in various ways; the point is to *change* it."[129] The legacy of historicism in the writing of Western-educated LoDagaa leaders, as elsewhere in Africa, has been a preoccupation with interpretation and the paralysis of practice.

PART THREE

The Colonization of Space

Chapter Five

Suppressing Knowledge

At Gwoli on my way to Topari I had the amusing experience of unwittingly interrupting the fetish priest and his satellites whilst occupied in making fetish to prevent my entering the village, this they had been manufacturing for three days. ... After holding up the fetish priest to ridicule, I told the people he could no longer be allowed to act as chief, and told them to appoint another man.

District Commissioner, Black Volta District, 1906

During the twentieth century the LoDagaa experienced a series of changes that affected their sense of space. The world on paper reconfigured their relationship with important aspects of their own culture and their social relationships with each other by suppressing the cultural knowledge that had once informed how social tensions were expressed and resolved, and by eliminating practices that had once mediated social interaction outside areas of shared ritual jurisdiction. The suppression of knowledge used to define and resolve disputes within areas of ritual interdependence changed the relationship between the world of experience and the noumenal world. Similarly, the elimination of a military culture of self-defense and youthful exuberance affected relationships between settlements that fell in separate ritual areas. The British imposed new forms of dispute resolution. Although these were in some ways analogous to LoDagaa rituals, they were based on a foreign logic that belonged to the world on paper. These changes altered some of the ways in which the LoDagaa experienced cultural and social space. Earlier chapters have shown how labor migration and colonial authority affected notions of space. Equally important were the effects of colonial ways of settling disputes; the religious movement that rose partly as a response to the tyranny of the chiefs; the reception of missionary medicine; and reactions to colonial money.

These topics – the suppression of indigenous knowledge, the elimination of armed conflict, the imposition of alien forms of dispute resolution, the creation of a missionary counterculture to colonialism, the reception of missionary medicine, and the introduction and attempted regulation of colonial money – are the subjects of this part of the book. Understanding how these changes affected how the LoDagaa experienced space is pivotal to recovering forms of historical consciousness that are not about relationships with the past but about relationships between different spaces. The tyranny of historicism, or the cult of historical authenticity, was central to the world on paper, but it was quite foreign to how the LoDagaa understood legitimacy and power. We have already seen that the fragmentation of historical experience through incremental and multidirectional migrations, the resulting lack of a collective sense of identity, and the absence of an overriding political structure to act as a narrative vehicle all militated against a discursive sense of the past. We have also seen that the sense of history (or the past) that did exist was conceived of spatially rather than temporally. Similarly, I will argue that the historical changes discussed below were experienced spatially rather than temporally.

Noumenal Knowledge and Colonial Justice

In the first ethnographic account of the LoDagaa, Read observed: "There is no tribal organisation and no ceremonies of initiation to the tribe. ... As members of a tribe there are no rights and duties with respect to mutual defence, payment of fines, surrender of offenders and blood vengeance."[1] Nevertheless, he labeled the several congeries that he had already identified as tribes because no other concept was available to him with which to describe the social organization of the LoDagaa. These contradictory assumptions – that the LoDagaa constituted one or more tribes, and that they manifested none of the characteristics thought to pertain to this putative form of social organization – were part of a wider descriptive dilemma that confronted early observers.[2] The search for coherence led observers to deploy descriptive and analytical categories, most especially marriage, that had little or no relevance to LoDagaa culture. The use of external categories led to descriptions of what was lacking in LoDagaa culture and to critiques of these apparent deficiencies because of the expectations entailed in these categories; it was always the fault of the LoDagaa that they did not fit observers' categories. It was never considered that the language available to colonial officers might in any way be deficient.[3] Thus, colonial discourses were not amended; instead the LoDagaa were made to fit into the world on paper. As we have seen in the colonial reactions to the lack of identifiable political leaders in LoDagaa culture, gaps were often filled at a later stage through the invention of what was seen as lacking or inadequate.

The LoDagaa clearly possessed a distinct culture before the colonial period, yet it is not possible to speak of LoDagaa society as a discrete entity. However, it is possible to determine the scale and nature of social relations within this area of cultural contiguity at the beginning of the twentieth century. Even Read conceded that the "family" or, more precisely, household (*yir*), was a cohesive and regulated social entity: "The Lobi native is of an extremely independent nature and will own no authority beyond the head of his own family."[4] Writing of the LoDagaba some fifty years later, Goody remarked: "There is little delegation of authority outside the father-child relationship."[5] Between "tribe" and "family," or society and household, there existed networks of social relations created by parochial patterns of ritual cooperation and jurisdiction, principles of exogamous marriage, frequent migration, and household fission. In other words, social relations among the LoDagaa were conditioned and structured by physical proximity within an area of relatively dense habitation; we must recognize this social fluidity and not speak of any unitary, circumscribable entity. Social relations were influenced by three sets of considerations: descent (*yir*), locality (*tengaan*), and totemic identification (*belo* or *dooro*).[6] These were intersecting and contextual spheres of social action. The main area of relations between households was the negotiation, formation, and dissolution of conjugal unions. With regard to territorial groupings, relations were concerned mainly with ritual cooperation. Finally, in the area of clanship, the main medium of intercourse was retaliatory action between wider descent groups made up of allied households.

A central theme in the study of social relations is that of disputes. The only early account of this aspect of LoDagaa social life was Read's report, which was written in 1908, after the LoDagaa had been conquered but before colonial rule was fully established. The only other administrative officer to consider indigenous dispute settlement processes was Eyre-Smith, in a report written in 1931. These sources, along with the ethnographic works of Labouret and Rattray, and Goody's reconstructions nearly half a century after colonial conquest, constitute the only written evidence of LoDagaa methods of defining and resolving disputes. When Read declared that "there are no criminal laws among these pagans,"[7] he seems to have expected to find a corpus of explicit rules in this oral culture, as existed in his own literate culture. In later remarks prefacing the same report, he noted: "There are at the present time no Dagartis who are conversant with, and authorities on their own customs and fetish laws who can speak either English or fair Hausa, the only two languages that can be used for obtaining information. ... Many Dagartis have been enlisted as soldiers and I have interrogated many on the subject, but they never can give any information beyond that of their own families and others profess total ignorance, saying that they have been out of their country so long that they have forgotten them. The natives themselves are extremely reticent and suspicious of giving any information about their customs, but own that they have no laws beyond those of the fetish."[8]

The idea that "customs" could exist outside the knowledge or memory of the people to whom they belonged is revealing. It suggests a mechanical understanding and essentialist definition of culture. Relations between LoDagaa households were not rule-based; for them, knowledge was not a set of rules; rather, it involved different means of communicating with the noumenal world and various strategies for negotiating social relationships. Early colonial records suggest that this cultural and social knowledge was flexible, often circumvented, and to varying degrees discretionary.[9]

In the absence of identifiable structures of authority, Read grappled with this question: How were social relations regulated and disputes settled?[10] He reported that "in any case of an offence being committed the fetish is consulted or force of arms resorted to."[11] Read and other colonial observers assumed that law was the only means of ordering social intercourse. They concluded that the LoDagaa lacked regular means of resolving disputes, because of the absence of any clearly articulated rules or recognizable authority structures, and also the apparent violence of LoDagaa culture. The British had heard reports of this violence before their arrival, but they also observed it first-hand while conquering the region. Thereafter, colonial observers assumed that violence was the only means the LoDagaa had for expressing and resolving disputes. No distinction was made between violence used to settle disputes between LoDagaa settlements and violence used to prevent or resist outside intervention by slavers and colonizers; the two purposes were subsumed within the same stereotype, and as a result the British greatly exaggerated the aggressiveness of this culture. As we have seen, this was ideologically convenient for them. The LoDagaa did use violence to resolve disputes, but not as often as Read suggested, and not exclusively. Nevertheless, it was an important part of the LoDagaa practices, which the British dismissed because they did not seem to be controlled by clearly articulated rules. This lack of rules made these practices mysterious and somewhat frightening, as well as threatening to colonial rule. The world on paper demanded practices that had the seeming regularity and precision of writing.

Just as the British thought the LoDagaa were prone to violence, they also believed they were susceptible to superstitions. According to Read: "Belief in the fetish is absolute throughout the country and for any cause of disputes whether relating to property, in every degree, family quarrels, sickness, connubial relations, failure of crops and in fact everything that is not in the ordinary smooth course of events, fetish is made."[12] He noted that oaths were sworn by the parties to disputes, with the party who gave false testimony being poisoned by the "fetish" upon which the oath had been sworn. Although Read noted that this practice was very prevalent, he dismissed it as unsatisfactory because one of the parties was left "to await the sudden death of their opponents, in which case they were not infrequently disappointed."[13] In a world where life was relatively uncertain and death a constant threat, the swearing of oaths was a serious matter. From the perspective of believers, the guilty always died in the long term, and before they did they might be visited by several misfortunes, from crop failure to disease.

What the British referred to as "fetishes" were shrines dedicated to particular ancestors, deities, or elements of nature, such as the *tengaan*, which were perceived to have the capacity for intervention from the noumenal world into the world of phenomenal experience. These shrines provided the physical point of access to the noumenal world for the purposes of consultation, divination, and propitiation. To Read, these mundane and often inconspicuous embodiments of indigenous knowledge were the paraphernalia of irrational thought. Their unfamiliar form particularly troubled him. He spoke dismissively of "swish mounds, stones" and "forked sticks and a collection of hard wood branches with some sign of a fowl or a goat on them." Concerning amulets and medicines, he wrote disparagingly: "Charms against all kinds of evil and charms to produce evil are common everywhere and are as varied as fetishes. Ones most commonly seen are made of horns of goats or small buck, containing various articles which can only be described as rubbish."[14] He never considered the possibility that these ordinary objects represented deep cultural knowledge that imbued them with rational meaning. The visualism of Read's report – that is, its emphasis on seeing – was a result of his not being able to derive information through any other of his senses. Everything that could not be seen and written down, such as speech and the knowledge it conveyed, was invisible and therefore did not exist.

Shrines were not consulted to settle disputes but to determine the causes of particular afflictions, misfortunes, or problems. Oaths were most often used to determine whether accusations emanating from divinatory revelations were true or not. Goody reported in the 1950s that when a person was accused of some transgression against the *tengaan*, "he or she would go to the Earth shrine and call upon the congregation to attend. The accused would then publicly drink a calabash of water in which the earth had been sprinkled. ... drinking the mixture of water and earth is equivalent to swearing, 'if I have done what I am accused of, may the Earth kill me.'"[15] Oaths were also sworn in less formal circumstances by members of the same *tengaan* against members of different clans when one member was in dispute with another over an alleged violation of the sanctions operative within the *tengaan*. Here, though, the oath was not administered but merely sworn. Rattray observed: "The Lobi swear an oath by the land to bear witness to what they say is true. ... 'Let the soil kill me or him,' and at the same time throwing earth on the offending party."[16] The purpose of oaths was to invite noumenal intervention, thereby removing issues from the subjective level of social relations, which were fraught with conflicting interests and were not subject to any overriding political or social authority.

Read saw the use of both shrines and oaths as superstitious means of resolving differences in the absence of "customs." Subsequent administrators dismissed these practices just as casually, while remaining ignorant of the knowledge that informed them. In 1929 the annual report for the district stated that disputes were only "quarrels and squabbles," even though "revenge, vendettas, poison ordeals, witchcraft, the whole gamut of early man's superstitions are the causes [of conflicts and disputes] and these cannot for many years be eradicated."[17] For the most part these practices were regarded as belonging to a grotesque world of superstition, which was an area of indigenous experience few colonial officers were prepared or equipped to understand, let alone consider a legitimate form of cultural knowledge. Rather than being recognized as a means of defining and resolving disputes, this cultural knowledge was pathologized and blamed for generating conflict.

Colonial Suspicions

The administration's dislike of native oaths and medicines was in large part politically motivated: the chiefs did not control them. It was the elders and *tengaandem* who did, and during the period of direct rule they generally refused to cooperate with colonial authority and often passively resisted it by sowing dissension.[18] The colonial administration ignored age and access to the noumenal world as forms of authority and knowledge. The early chiefs often resented the elders and *tengaandem* as the male custodians of indigenous authority; the same men were discredited in Read's eyes for "being old, decrepit and quite incapable of enforcing law and order, besides being a stranger to water or any form of cleanliness."[19]

Officers also had contempt for oaths in litigation, which from an early date became a common practice in colonial-inspired courts. They felt that oaths, being based on no more apparent or reliable authority than superstition, contaminated the process. During an investigation in 1917 of complaints by several inhabitants of Bazim against the subchief of the area, the district commissioner conducted an arrogant "experiment" in order to prove the unreliability of oaths.[20] The two main parties were reported to have sworn on the "Bambor

Fetish." The district commissioner did not find this satisfactory assurance, and "a simple experiment was therefore tried":

> The Court interpreter mumbled an incantation over a bowl of water finishing up by sprinkling into it some permanganate of potash [potassium] concealed in his hand. Whereupon the water turned red to the great astonishment of those present. The witnesses again swore separately by Bambor, plunged their right hands into the calabash and held them above their heads. Binney, the Court interpreter then said, "Lo, the hand of the liar is turning white."[21]

The complainant became uncomfortable, whereas the respondent, a colonial headman, remained steady. The district commissioner felt that the complaint had been shown to be unsubstantiated. Significantly, he was prepared to accept the outcome of this contrived test simply because he, as its author, was in control of it. No attention was paid to the fact that the respondent would obviously have been prepared to trust in the "whiteman," as the whole matter revolved around disaffection caused by his close collaboration with the administration.[22]

Trust, not truth, produced the reactions that the district commissioner took to establish the veracity of the witnesses. In their indigenous context, the swearing of oaths and the consultation of shrines did not rely on the manipulation of such effects. Instead, belief was validated by the *post facto* attribution of noumenal causes to real, unstaged phenomena, such as lightning, disease, pestilence, bad weather, individual misfortunes, or merely the direction in which a sacrificial fowl expired on the ground during divination.[23] These forms of knowledge were not based on superstition, nor were they validated by magic. Instead, they were constructed around – for lack of a better comparative term – an etiology of affliction, misfortune, and deviance.[24]

To appreciate more fully the divergence between LoDagaa notions of causality and the judicial procedures employed by administrators (and later by chiefs), let us compare the incident above with an inquest held at Lawra in 1922 into the death of Bassalla, a member of the Lawra Naa's household. The deceased had complained of a pain in his hip. He had applied some medicine obtained from a medicine shrine, but the pain only grew more severe, moving to his stomach and head. He then consulted a diviner, who deduced that the affliction was the result of trouble with his tutelary shrine. A fowl was sacrificed at the shrine and accepted by the spirit, but the ailment did not improve. Finally he went to a neighboring settlement in search of further medicine to alleviate his complaint and died on the way back to Lawra. When the preinterment sacrifices were made to the household shrines, the spirits refused them. The

Lawra Naa explained to the inquest: "It is our fashion that if the fetish does not agree to take the fowls we must bury the body and make no funeral custom." At this point, witnesses attributed the cause of death to an unexpiated offense committed by the deceased against the *tengaan*. Awaiting further evidence, the hearing was adjourned. When it reconvened the chief explained that in the intervening period a wife of a member of the deceased's patriclan had revealed that he had slept with her, and it was now thought that this had led to his death. The woman had made the disclosure only after falling ill herself. However, the district commissioner concluded: "The circumstances are very peculiar, but it is possible that [the deceased] died from natural causes, probably heart failure."[25]

Although the LoDagaa did believe in death by natural causes, the attribution of natural causes in an instance such as Bassalla's death would have been seen as merely preliminary. Goody noted that in the LoDagaa world view, the causes of death had three levels: immediate, efficient, and final – in other words, apparent cause, agent, and force. "In the end this resolves itself into an inquiry as to who or what had grounds for hostility against the dead man, and so the cause of death is seen as a function of the individual's network of spiritual and human relationships. Death is treated as a social phenomenon and attributed to some conflict in the social system, either with living persons (witches, workers of curses, and sorcerers), or with past members of the society (ancestors), or with non-human agencies (shrines)."[26] Bassalla's death was finally attributed to a violation of sanctions against certain degrees of sexual relations.[27] It was not the transgression itself that led to the demise of the deceased, but the unexpiated nature of the offense. The attribution of causes to instances of transgression operated in a *post facto* manner. Expiation was most often delayed until the offended agency manifested its displeasure by visiting some kind of affliction on the offending person; a diviner was then consulted to discover the source of the affliction.[28] Sanctions connected with noumenal forces or agents were neither immediate nor prohibitory; instead they followed a slow course of manifestation (affliction), identification (divinatory disclosure), and remedy (sacrificial expiation).

The next officer to address the issue of LoDagaa etiology, nearly a generation after Read's observations, was Eyre-Smith. Not until his arrival in Lawra District did officers become even vaguely aware of the social importance of indigenous knowledge and practices in defining and resolving disputes. In 1931 he described for the first time in the administrative records the significance of what had previously been regarded as mere superstitions. He wrote of "religious laws," instead of superstitions, "enforced by sanctions that were involved in the beliefs and practices of the community." These beliefs and practices mediated relationships between men and women, affected the behavior of women during pregnancy and childbirth, influenced the rearing of children, and ensured the propitiation of noumenal spirits. Eyre-Smith admitted that "there was no penalty in the sense that we understand the word in relation to laws," but noted that "the violation of any of these laws or sanctions not only brought ill-fortune to the individual but to the family or clan." The jurisdiction of this indigenous system of knowledge was also reported to cover cases of assault and theft.[29]

What was especially significant about this report was that its author was willing to compare these practices to laws and to argue that they had greater legitimacy than the colonial procedures applied in the chiefs' courts. The comparison between LoDagaa knowledge and British laws was somewhat tenuous and inexact. Noumenal agencies did not act like jural authorities punishing wrongdoers.[30] Practices such as swearing, divination, and sacrifice were problem-solving and remedy-seeking, not punitive and decision-making. Any decision-making rested outside of LoDagaa control, in the hands of noumenal agencies. The purpose of Eyre-Smith's comparison was to suggest an alternative to the colonial courts of the direct rule period, which had been shown by this time to be extremely unsatisfactory. Not surprisingly, his suggestion was rejected, as the colonial administration was in the process of implementing indirect rule, a central feature of which was to be native courts modeled on legal principles of formalized procedure and judicial punishment. However, it is difficult not to suspect that the proposal was also rejected in no small part because of jealousy on the part of most administrators toward any alternative sources of authority.

When confronted with noumenal agencies, many early administrators ridiculed them and tried to convince the LoDagaa of their inefficacy; in this, they anticipated the tactics of some of the White Fathers.[31] Partly, they were acting out of fear that the noumenal world might offer a means of resisting colonial rule and inciting disobedience. To them, "fetishes" were not dangerous, but actions based on a belief in their efficacy were. From an early date, colonial authorities treated indigenous knowledge and the use of shrines as a political rather than a cultural or religious matter. An administrative ordinance of 1908 empowered district commissioners to "suppress" any native practice – "fetish," "custom," "rite," "ceremony," or "worship" – that might assist in the "commission of crime" or lead to a "breach of the peace."[32]

Several district commissioners complained about the presence of "wandering marabouts or mallams," whose written messages, prayers, amulets, and curses they perceived as especially threatening, not least because their meaning was readily available, even if it had to be translated. This concern over written charms was also a result of the administration's offensively patronizing attitude toward the LoDagaa, who were considered easily susceptible to agitation by literate Muslims. As one officer explained in 1919: "There are always some wild and discontented spirits amongst this savage people ready to listen to them. ... A man who professes to sell medicines which he guarantees as rendering the wrong doer immune from the consequences of his evil acts is in this uncivilized and superstitious country a person whose presence is most undesirable."[33] To the contrary, the danger posed by these itinerant Muslims was rooted in the widespread but as yet unarticulated resentment among the LoDagaa toward British occupation of their land and interference in their lives. According to colonial intelligence, the LoDagaa did not purchase Muslim charms and incantations in order to seek immunity from the effects of their own noumenal agencies: Muslim articles existed in conjunction with indigenous knowledge but did not supersede it. Where foreign knowledge proved more effective was in the phenomenal realm of colonial politics. To commoners, it promised immunity from the persecution of chiefs; to chiefs, it promised escape from the wrath and opprobrium of the district commissioner.

Partly because it was orally based, colonial officials did not regard LoDagaa knowledge as a serious source of resistance to colonial rule, even though they thought that belief in noumenal agencies diminished the power of the chiefs. The resistance of LoDagaa commoners usually took nonspecific forms, such as the refusal to obey orders, which unfortunately did not articulate the deeper attitudes behind such actions. Officers saw such resistance as simply further evidence that the LoDagaa were recalcitrant and ungovernable, not as an indication of underlying disaffection and resentment. Also, LoDagaa shrines were local, particular, and inaccessible to outsiders.[34] Consultation, divination, and propitiation were largely carried out through actions rather than through words. What Piot has noted of Kabre culture was also true of LoDagaa culture: "It is largely through the visual and nonverbal, through actions and display of mimesis ... that Kabre coax their spirits and magically affect the world in which they live. In so doing, they employ a symbolic code that 'speaks' not so much through words as through objects and actions."[35] Oaths among the LoDagaa, although spoken, left little evidence except when reported to the district commissioner, and even then the oath's intentions were still open to interpretation. As Goody has commented: "The written charm is considered to be so effective because it gives speech a concrete embodiment. ... Because they materialise speech, it is easier to extract the full power, the full meaning, from the written formulae than from oral incantations."[36] That Muslim charms were written affected the administration's assessment and appreciation of their dangers.

As the case of Malam Ali well illustrates, the meaning of Muslim charms was easy to discern. A Hausa Muslim from Sey on the Niger Bend, Ali had been expelled by the French administration in Gaoua after establishing a considerable reputation as a "wizard."[37] In 1919 he was arrested in Lawra – where he was already under surveillance, his reputation having preceded him – for allegedly burying packets in the government cemetery. These were found to contain written incantations and curses against the administration and its chiefs. On a hyena skin the following instructions had been inscribed, according to a translation provided by a local trader: "The method of using this hyena skin is to put it out in the sun by day and in the fire by night so the people mentioned in the writing, the chief and all his people, that is to say the Commissioner, may be taken sick, so that their skins might be hot like fever." The document was also full of Muslim praises interspersed with requests for power, respect, love, and immunity from the chiefs.[38]

Administrators took these written charms seriously, not only because they clearly articulated the resentment of many LoDagaa against colonial rule, but also because they offered a power – the magic of writing – to buttress that resentment. When officers encountered evidence that people were using indigenous shrines or oaths to resist the chiefs and their authority, they did not think it necessary to institute judicial proceedings. In part this was because the same cultural knowledge was being employed by colonial appointees to enforce colonial rule. But it was also because these efforts to combat the powers of the world on paper always failed. Eyre-Smith regarded the failure of indigenous knowledge to protect people from colonial rule as one of the main reasons for the success enjoyed by the White Fathers.[39]

In the first Court Record Book for Lawra District a number of incidents were recorded that mentioned resistance to chiefs by means of "fetish," but few of these were officially heard, and none directly implicated any *tengaansob*.[40] Featured more prominently in the records was the use of medicines and oaths in the political intrigues created by colonial rule. For example, Dakura, the paramount chief of Nandaw division, complained to the district commissioner in 1922 that Tanpor, the chief of Han, had used medicine to make his people swear allegiance to him. Dakura alleged that Tanpor had incited several settlements to disobey his, Dakura's, orders for government work. He claimed to have learned of the matter from those who had refused Tanpor's medicine, which allegedly had been forcibly administered to others with a cow's tail. Tanpor denied the allegations, maintaining that he had only made his people drink medicine against the infestation of crops by insects. However, he admitted to having used medicine on an earlier occasion in Han to ensure that the people performed government work. Significantly, this occurred when Tobia, the local *tengaansob*, was incarcerated in Lawra. In his testimony Tobia stated:

"Tanpor called all the people to make medicine on account of the flies. This medicine would kill any bad man. ... All these old men sitting here have to call me to make any fetish. I am not fit to say anything to the chief." Whether Tanpor had conspired against Dakura is less important than Tanpor's use of medicine for colonial purposes, which he justified in the following way: "If the Commissioner comes to Han he is not fit to get carriers, and if constables come they won't get any one for work. I got the people to drink medicine that would kill them if they did not agree to government work. ... Since I gave medicine, people have agreed [to] bring grass."[41] The Complaint Books for the first two decades of colonial rule are littered with reports by chiefs that their subjects refused to obey them, usually over the issue of forced labor. It is not known how often indigenous oaths or shrines were used to provide cohesion for these forms of passive resistance, or to enforce colonial orders and chiefly prerogatives.

The link between traditionalist elements and the use or manipulation of indigenous oaths and medicines was eventually broken as the chiefs assumed more initiative. In July 1920 the chief of Tugu reported to the district commissioner that he had "publicly sworn the lightning oath on the people of Punya and that already three of the elders had come to him to say that if he would take it back they would return their people."[42] In 1923 a neighboring settlement, Guorpuo, was prompted to attack Kayani after repeated demands to do government work. Before shooting arrows at the chief, they allegedly told him: "You are not now in the Commissioner's Court so do not talk to us as if you were there."[43] Kayani was able to defeat these recalcitrants by seeking the help of the Northern Territories Constabulary. Although chiefs attempted to access other forms of authority, they still relied on the coercive powers of the colonial state.

This reference to the world of the District Commissioner's Court was implicitly a reference to the world on paper. At a very early date the LoDagaa were aware of the power of paper as a symbol of colonial power and as an instrument or practice used to exercise that power. The order that colonial administrators attempted to create in the place of indigenous means of defining and resolving disputes was tied directly to the power of the world on paper and its symbols. Abuses of colonial authority were common throughout the period of direct rule, with colonial appointees and employees often copying government rituals for their own benefit. In 1910 the chief of Birifu complained that a man in the neighboring area of Kunyukuo was falsely claiming that the district commissioner had authorized him to hear disputes. As a result, people from Birifu had been taking their "cattle and women" cases to him for settlement.[44] In 1915, Polli, the district commissioner's messenger, told Saulieri of Zambo that the district commissioner had sent orders that she was to return to her previous husband and that, to reconcile their differences, the couple had to sleep together with the official government message stick. The woman obeyed these instructions, and only began to doubt their authenticity after Polli brought her to Lawra and tried to take her to the chief's house. "I refused," she explained, "because he told me at first I was called by the District Commissioner."[45]

Early on, most LoDagaa saw all written documents as official orders, with the result that even the most mundane pieces of paper were used for fraudulent purposes. For example, at Eremon in 1919 Ali Dagarti produced papers that he claimed were an order from the District Commissioner of Wa that a woman in the settlement be surrendered to him. It transpired that the documents had been nothing more than two sheets of foolscap with "schoolboy figures scribbled on them." The woman's husband felt that Ali had "brought that paper to make us fear," and took the matter to the chief, who referred it in turn to the District Commissioner of Lawra.[46]

Not until 1917 were regular Native Tribunals established in Lawra District. It was noted in the District Record Book that "formerly the people and even the chiefs themselves were continually coming in for every petty complaint."[47] Officers in Lawra assumed that they were hearing almost all disputes, but this was far from the case: well before this, on their own initiative, chiefs (and chiefly impostors) were hearing cases on their own. Their ability to do this, by carefully reproducing the rituals of the district commissioner's court, in some cases even down to fake summonses, highlighted how vulnerable most LoDagaa were to abuses of the power of the world on paper, and how arbitrary this world must have seemed to most people, who had no idea what these pieces of paper said. In the 1980s Hutchinson made these very points about the relationship between the Nuer and "paper." Even one of her literate informants complained: "You could be presenting your case before the district commissioner when all of a sudden he reaches into his breast pocket and pulls out a piece of paper and announces: 'It says here you are lying!' What can you do? You didn't see the paper written. How can you argue with a piece of paper? Your case is finished!"[48]

Similarly, although much earlier, when Dagga of Nandom brought a dispute before the district commissioner in 1909, he explained that the chief of Nandom had told him that "he [the chief] would try the case because the whiteman did not like trouble in the town [Lawra]. The King did not try the case so I took out a summons." When Dagga brought the summons back from Lawra, he pretended it ordered the man named in the summons to pay seven cows – three for the plaintiff and four for the chief.[49] The legacy of such practices is still reflected in LoDagaa attitudes today, as Alexis Tengan explains:

Writing on paper first entered into Dagara society during periods of domination,

> exploitation, slavery and colonial rule. In the past, the paper record was often used on various occasions, either as testimony against people in the colonial courts, or as a legitimate means to force people to pay more taxes and to participate in forced labor. In the past, chiefs appointed by the colonial administration and their clerks took down on paper, information about people, and whatever they wrote was always taken to be totally and objectively true.

Even to this day, he adds, the ironic pidgin expression "book no lie" is still used.[50]

Although paper was a powerful symbol, it was not as effective as indigenous knowledge, so it is not surprising that the chiefs used such knowledge more than paper to squash resistance and lend legitimacy to themselves, particularly in their role as agents for settling disputes. In 1918, during an inspection of the chief of Jirapa's court, the district commissioner recorded the following method employed to settle a case: "Both witnesses swore the lightning fetish so the chief has adjourned the case for a fortnight to see who has lied – as the perjurer will get frightened and confess according to the chief."[51] This practice apparently caused him little concern, as it was confined to a colonial court. Indeed, the same district commissioner was able to write only six weeks later that cases in the Native Tribunals were being conducted in "a most orderly manner and the procedure is modelled on that in my court."[52] But a decade later Eyre-Smith complained of the abuses caused by this assimilation of indigenous practices, claiming that the chiefs had manipulated the system of oaths to demand private court fees in the form of "presents." As we have seen, he also argued (unsuccessfully) that the administration should not allow the chiefs to displace the *tengaandem* from their role as administrators of oaths and arbiters with the noumenal world.[53]

In 1938, in response to an administrative questionnaire on the subject of "witchcraft," an officer reported: "I am afraid that a form of trial by ordeal, before the fetish, is very common in this [Lawra] District. ... But it is not in any way connected with the Native Courts."[54] However, Eyre-Smith's observations, and those of later officers, undermine this assurance: aspects of indigenous etiology did impinge on the procedures and decisions of the Native Authority Courts. True, there was no evidence to suggest that after 1935 the chiefs used oaths as a means of generating illicit revenue, but this was only because they were officially permitted to impose fines and collect fees.[55] The courts continued to administer oaths, or at least to use the swearing of oaths as assurance against perjury, but they did so in a context totally detached from LoDagaa culture, which conceived of disputes settled by oaths as cosmological rather than political. The chiefs retained oaths in their courts, not least to lend greater legitimacy to the imposed procedures and their own decisions. When later district commissioners learned that such practices influenced the decisions of the chiefs' courts, they made no secret of their exasperation that the chiefs were unable to operate without them. For example, in 1942, on a visit to Nandom, the district commissioner wrote in his diary: "Discussed a court case in which the Court reversed its decision after being struck by lightning, alleged at the instance of a litigant. Explained that if that was to happen the Native Authority might as well close down and we go back to the Tingansobs."[56] This was in essence what Eyre-Smith had seriously suggested a decade earlier. What the officer failed to recognize was that if the chiefs had failed to integrate indigenous etiology, they would have lost any semblance of authority among their subjects.

A different awareness of the importance of indigenous knowledge was prompted by the arrival of the White Fathers. Almost immediately after the rain incident, their influence led to rioting by recent converts. The disruptive influence of Christian evangelism on colonial political engineering convinced officers of the importance of LoDagaa knowledge. It also permitted the chiefs to assume the role of protectors of indigenous beliefs against the excesses of militant converts. Although administrators were not sympathetic to practices predicated on indigenous knowledge, they were determined to protect the LoDagaa from what they saw as the fanatical evangelism of particular White Fathers. Their desire to protect the LoDagaa, seen as naive and unsuspecting natives, from the powerful effects of Christianity had the same source as their deep suspicion of Islam. When Father McCoy, the leading missionary, complained about the influence that the elders and "Tindana" had over the chief of Karni three years after the rain incident, the district commissioner was prompted to write: "The fetishes have a great – and in the majority – a beneficial influence on the community."[57] In 1946 another officer, troubled by the disruptive influences of Christianity, wrote an essay defending the role of the *tengaansob* in LoDagaa society against the criticisms of the missionaries, who wanted it to be restricted even further.[58]

The chiefs derived their power from the colonial administration. Authority and legitimacy were less easily obtained from within LoDagaa society; indeed, indigenous authority was so bound up in noumenal knowledge and practices that it is possible to argue that it never belonged to the phenomenal world. As one anthropologist observed in the early 1980s of the LoBirifor living near Bole: "Authority is not invested in particular individuals, office holders, or any class in society enjoying a monopoly of its use. Such authority is located, in a sense, outside of society, and is vested in and exercised by a spectrum of mystical agencies."[59] Without due regard and attention to this etiology, there could be no access to indigenous forms of authority and legitimacy in LoDagaa culture. But no matter how they attempted to mask it, their power came from outside of LoDagaa culture, from the world on paper. The chiefs clearly represented the advent of unprecedented forms of phenomenal authority.

Spatial and Judicial Definitions of Disputes

Besides "fetish," the other means of resolving disputes mentioned in Read's report was the use of "arms," or retaliatory action. Again, as with much of what Read said in this report, the rough accuracy of the observation was vitiated by the conclusions he drew from it. He saw the use of force as diametrically opposed to law, and did not consider the possibility that it was an equally viable means of resolving disputes. In order to understand the use of violence in settling disputes, it is necessary to place the use of force in its cultural and social context. No mention of the nature, conditions, or reasons for this violence was made in any of the early reports, except to attribute "a lot" of fighting in the past to the "unfaithfulness" of wives[60] – a moral criticism more than an empirical observation. This comment, like several other of Read's, partially identifies a feature of LoDagaa culture that professional observers would discuss in depth only much later: it was not women's infidelity, but rather male competition for women, that led to most conflicts.[61]

Unfortunately, it is impossible to document the actual extent of violence between households at the beginning of the century. Some of the violence perceived by administrators was actually directed against foreign occupation through localized and sporadic resistance. Also, administrators exaggerated the level of indigenous violence to the point of caricature as an ideological justification for the violence of colonial rule. Nor is it possible to specify more satisfactorily the nature and causes of violence.[62] Reports did not consider force an adequate or recognizable means of settling disputes.[63] But administrators also misunderstood the role of violence among the LoDagaa simply because they had no real understanding of the social boundaries of the people who fell under their jurisdiction. It was precisely the fragmented and dispersed social structure of LoDagaa congeries that made violence a potential instrument for expressing and resolving some disputes, as this violence did not threaten any wider societal organization.[64] In addition, officers had little grasp of the demands of farming and hence the rhythm of violent disputes. As intensive agriculturalists, the LoDagaa had little time during the farming season, which ran from April through October, for anything but cultivation. Conflicts were usually expressed during the dry season, when social intercourse was at its height and people were free to prosecute perceived wrongs.

The British campaign of "pacification" carried out in Lawra District in the early years of the twentieth century sought to eliminate both conflict within the area and active resistance to foreign occupation. The French pursued the same policy of "pacification" on the other side of the Black Volta, but with far less success.[65] The French attributed the difficulties they encountered to the more rebellious character of the *Lobi* and western LoDagaa. The British, for their part, saw their relative success as the outcome of more enlightened administration. In 1921, following a series of "disturbances" on the French side of the river, the District Commissioner of Lawra attributed the relative calm of his own district to the administration's judicious use of force. Critical of the often desperate and severe measures to which the French resorted, he also claimed that the secret of British success was the attention they paid to settling indigenous disputes. "There are very few palavers up here," he quipped, "which cannot be settled very easily if taken in time, but if left are like sparks that start a bush fire."[66]

Tensions on the French side of the Black Volta had escalated to serious proportions by 1920. Armed conflict was breaking out directly opposite Lawra.[67] The British feared that if the violence spread to their side of the river, they would not have the military resources to control it. To gauge the situation, the administration relied heavily on intelligence supplied by chiefs in the villages along the river and by native employees, particularly Binney, the district commissioner's interpreter: "Binney asked a young man at Dappola the reason for this sudden outbreak and he said that all the troops and Whitemen had left Gaoua and were far away in the south (they are not due back for a month or two) so the people had decided to settle a few differences. He also volunteered the information that if it were not for the open country, our people would be at it too."[68] The explanation offered here is noteworthy: district commissioners commonly attributed fighting primarily to the "turbulent nature" of the LoDagaa, choosing to overlook the causes and purposes of conflict. The protracted efforts of French officers to suppress armed conflict actually aggravated the situation. French suppression of conflict did not eliminate social disputes, but instead led to perceived wrongs accumulating and festering. The LoDagaa eagerly turned to the District Commissioner's Court once retaliatory action had been eliminated, and later, the chiefs efficiently channelled disputes into their own courts, but none of this prevented or eliminated tensions; instead, the ways in which disputes were defined and resolved were reconfigured.

In 1917 the chief of Jirapa told the district commissioner "about the old days before the white man's rule." From this, the district commissioner "gathered how very local everything must have been. He spoke of expeditions against Tizza and Tugu and about Lorha fighting with Gberi [all within a few miles of each other], never further afield."[69] In July 1919 a number of young men from Gbetuor, situated between Birifu and Yagha, crossed the river into French territory to fight at Bache in a dispute between that village and Lemka: "For two years they say they have had no chance to fight and they are tired of sitting like women, while their French brothers fight whenever they like."[70] Although it was not noted at the time, their action seems to have been in retaliation for an incident in 1915 when settlements across the river raided their cattle.[71] But this was one of the last times any inhabitants of Lawra District participated in armed conflict. By the early 1920s the role of armed conflict among the LoDagaa had, for the most part, been greatly reduced. Fighting was remembered with nostalgia by elders who disapproved of the collaboration of the chiefs, and by young men who yearned to acquire respect through feats of bravery. Colonial rule had eliminated an important medium for social relations among the LoDagaa. Fighting had been displaced by judicial structures; colonial courts had replaced the use of arms.

To understand the connection between the causes of violence and the causes of litigation, we must examine the strategies the LoDagaa used for resolving disputes – strategies that were gradually displaced by colonial "pacification." According to Goody's report in the 1950s, armed force had "centered mainly around women," and had been resorted to because of theft or abduction of wives, and was quite distinct from the strategies used to negotiate conjugal unions: "Armed conflict was indeed merely the most extreme form of retaliatory procedure, itself the counterpart of reciprocal exchanges of goods and services."[72] Labouret also had concluded that economic considerations and not legal sanctions had mediated social intercourse among the *Lobi*.[73] Where groups fell outside these amorphous networks of economic interdependence, the use of force was not only permitted but necessary. The use of force survived much longer under French colonial rule, and this has enabled historians to reconstruct the complex criteria involved in defining disputes spatially. Regarding the shifting perceptions of conflicts, one group of observers noted:

> Men steal the wives of the men of opposed subclans or of other clans. All these events and their consequences unfold within defined limits, although it is important to understand that these frontiers are not discontinuous, but relative, progressive and, at times, imperceptible. It is not that they have no validity, but that they could be different for two neighboring men under various conditions.[74]

Boundaries had to be defined in every instance. Through such decisions the nature of disputes and their appropriate remedies were also defined.

To understand how private disputes involving male competition for wives came to be redefined in the public milieu of the colonial courts, we must examine the origins of the courts in the early years of direct rule. In 1906 at Ulo, a settlement that had been concentrated and fortified to resist Zabarima raids, we find the earliest description of a district commissioner operating as an agency for resolving disputes:

> The natives, the ice once broken, flocked in with complaints and summons; they evidently appreciate a judge who can enforce his decisions, the majority of the cases were demands for the restitution of Head-Money from parents. ... I had the King of Ulu and the Liman of Nandaw with me as advisers in native law and custom; the Court was never attended by less than a hundred interested spectators, and where a cause célèbre was on by many more.[75]

Most of these cases concerned the restitution of conjugal payments, which confirms that conjugal unions, or more specifically, the negotiation of such relationships, were sources of dispute at this date. A year later, another officer commented, albeit incorrectly: "It seems a very common thing amongst the Dagartis to take Head-Money two or three times over for their daughters, the lady staying for a short time with number one, returns to her parental roof and soon departs with number two who also pays Head-Money for her; in no case was restitution made to the first husband by the Father."[76] These disputes centered on timing rather than fraud. The dissolution of any union and the formation of another resulted in an intermediary period when the woman's status (i.e., whose wife she was) was in question. Such cases were not between rival households but between former affines. Former husbands needed to bring their ex-wives' households before the district commissioner because in cases of conjugal dissolution it was the woman's household that conducted all negotiations for the return of conjugal payments. There was no broader political structure through which to prosecute a rival household that had taken another household's wife. But it was not the responsibility of the woman's household to return payments; they too had no direct means of ensuring that the new husband would present payments within a reasonable period.[77]

A decade after a colonial officer first reported hearing such cases, the District Complaint Book still contained examples of the precolonial pattern of competition over women. Dassa of Ulo came to Lawra in 1916 to complain that Borko of Sabuli had taken his wife Banturi ten years before, and so Dassa had taken Borko's wife Porpila in retaliation. More recently, men of Borko's household had come to Dassa's compound with guns and bowstrings to seize their former wife, Porpila. When Borko was called before the district commissioner, he explained that two years earlier he had presented the conjugal payments for

Banturi to her father, who had returned them to Dassa, but since then Dassa had not paid anything for Porpila.[78] Cases of this type, illustrating retaliatory action, were common throughout the period of direct rule. They highlight the uncertain social context in which conjugal payments were negotiated, presented and, sooner or later, returned.

Retaliatory action became increasingly difficult, not just because the use of force was severely restricted, but more especially because of the danger that a rival would take a dispute to court and have the case heard in isolation. A case that came before the Jirapa Local Authority Court nearly forty years later, in 1954, demonstrated the dangers involved. Mwintuo had taken Buntariba's sister as a wife by presenting the required conjugal payments to her household, but after five years her brother encouraged her to run away from Mwintuo and be taken as a wife elsewhere. Mwintuo then came to court to have the conjugal payments returned to him. Buntariba explained in court that he had deliberately encouraged his sister to leave Mwintuo because of an outstanding debt between the two households. Buntariba's father had once taken a woman of Mwintuo's household as a wife, but she later left him and became the wife of another man. Since then, Mwintuo's household had not returned the conjugal payments that Buntariba's father had made. Buntariba's action was retaliatory, having been an effort to have the conjugal payments returned. Here the court, constituted by three divisional chiefs, argued that "according to the native customary law the defendant has to go to the right person to get his money and not from the plaintiff."[79] When an aggrieved rival came to court, specific causes were isolated from preceding disputes, and collective (household) liability was superseded by individual responsibility. The courts enabled Mwintuo to preempt Buntariba's action, which had been intended to pressure Mwintuo's household for the return of the earlier conjugal payments. Almost certainly, complicated circumstances such as these had caused officers at Ulo almost half a century before to mistake the nature of these types of disputes.

The settlements imposed by district commissioners provided the means for redefining conjugal unions. The role of colonial officers was not dissimilar to that of the chiefs in other areas of the Northern Territories. In the 1920s the LoBirifor migrated across the Black Volta to the margins of Gonja. Although these immigrants resisted the jurisdiction of Gonja chiefs in most respects, they were eager to avail themselves of their services in order to settle conflicts resulting from the competition for wives. In the absence of wider political structures, it was difficult for LoBirifor husbands – just as it was for all LoDagaa men – to exercise coercive authority over women:

> One of the few benefits which the Gonja system offered, and one which they [the

> LoBirifor] were quick to appreciate, was that the chiefs were willing, and to some extent able, to provide them with just this sanction. The Gonja chiefs not only took strong measures to return women to their husbands, but also punished the abductors with fines and ... [sometimes] took it upon themselves to chastise the women. A man who took such a case to the Gonja chief not only stood a reasonable chance of getting his wife back, but also had the satisfaction of seeing his rival punished, and his wife's resolve to abscond again somewhat weakened.[80]

In the period of direct rule, colonial officers in Lawra District, and their network of colonial chiefs, fulfilled the same function by providing coercive sanctions for increased control over women.

In cases involving migrant laborers recruited by the administration through its "labour crusade," district commissioners were particularly eager to protect conjugal unions against the interference of rivals. In terms of indigenous social practices, this was unprecedented. In two cases from 1908 the purpose of such decisions was very clear. In the first, Kompailah *vs.* Naiver, the plaintiff left his wife and went south to work in the mines. When he returned he learned that the defendant had taken his wife. Kompailah did not try to secure the return of his wife by any indigenous strategy, but instead immediately approached the court to issue a summons against Naiver. Before capitulating, the defendant explained his actions in the following terms: "I have got no wife so when I saw this woman I took her. I knew she was the Plaintiff's wife but she said her husband had gone away. I am willing to give up the woman if the District Commissioner says so." The woman, Kompo, was returned to her husband, Kompailah, even though she said: " I don't want to go back to either man. I want to go home, my husband's brother flogged me for going after other men when my husband went away."[81]

Similarly, the case of Depang *vs.* Quiniari underscores the willingness of district commissioners to protect the interests of husbands, especially when they were migrant laborers. Depang, a miner, returned home to find that his wife, Anwosa, had been driven away from his compound by his elder brother and been taken as a wife by the defendant – from her household compound and with her parents' consent. Furthermore, Quiniari had already presented the conjugal payments to the woman's parents to be returned to Depang. Quiniari explained his actions as follows: "I have no wife. ... I knew the woman was Depang's wife. I knew he paid head money." Anwosa corroborated this evidence but still insisted that "I won't go back to Depang," even though she liked him, because "his elder brother drove me from my house so I went and lived with my people and my mother gave me to defendant." Nevertheless, the district commissioner restored her to the plaintiff.[82]

These two cases were somewhat unusual, in that both involved migrant laborers, whom officers were bound to favor so as not to discourage other candidates from "volunteering." Nevertheless, they were indicative of other settlements imposed by district commissioners during the period of direct rule, in which litigants manipulated the expectations of the courts in order to exert control over women and to frustrate rivals.

Officers' cultural and moral ideas about conjugal unions quickly meshed with those of the chiefs. In 1906 the Liman of Nandaw, a LoDagaa settlement with a Muslim *zongo*, or strangers' quarter, attached to it, remarked after observing a session of the district commissioner's traveling court that, "the Whiteman's law was the law of the Koran."[83] In the first decade of direct rule, Muslim traders from Kunyukuo were sufficiently satisfied with the District Commissioner's Court at Lawra that they brought a succession of "marriage" cases before it. By 1919 non-Hausa Muslim residents of Kunyukuo were complaining of exorbitant court fees and the *zongo* headman's biases against them, and were bringing their cases to the chief of Lawra.[84] If the chief of Lawra was satisfying the litigation demands of Muslim traders in matrimonial disputes, he must have been following the district commissioner's example and applying attractive definitions of husbands' rights in "marriage" – definitions that did not hold indigenously.

In 1923 the chief of Jirapa complained to the district commissioner that a woman, Ponyuo, had run away from her husband's brother, who was looking after her while her husband was working in Kumase, to a man at Dakpa, outside the chief's jurisdiction:

> The chief of Jirapa sends in to say that the husband was taken by him as a labourer and if he does not look after the woman and lets her take another husband some time when he wants labourers for the Government he will have trouble. ... "My daughters have married Dakpa men and I want to take them back. I do not want my people to marry Dakpa people in consequence of this." ... The chief of Jirapa to come in and see me. On no account he is to interfere with Jirapa women married to Dakpa men.[85]

Here we see how chiefs took coercive action in cases that fell outside their jurisdiction. Because the chief of Jirapa did not have jurisdiction over both parties, and so was unable to impose his definition of the union, he was forced to threaten to withdraw women from households he did control who lived with men at Dakpa. His reasons for doing so had as much to do with pleasing the government as they did with protecting the interests of his recruit; but obviously the two were intimately connected. Men were absent as a result of labor migration, and women were unwilling to await their return. As a result of the protection that chiefs extended to conjugal unions, such relationships were redefined. Migrant workers' unions were given a hitherto unavailable degree of security and stability. By his action, the district commissioner was seeking to avoid any conflict between the two settlements that might have resulted from retaliatory action instigated by the chief.

Although the approach to conjugal disputes – redefining disputes over women into marriage rules – was unprecedented in terms of LoDagaa social practices, the actual procedure in the courts was perhaps not so culturally novel. No descriptions are available of how matters were conducted in the chiefs' courts, save for assurances by officers that these proceedings were modeled on those in their own courts. It is not difficult to imagine how both administrators and chiefs deported themselves, but it is difficult to know how these proceedings appeared to litigants. To most LoDagaa, the district commissioner was a remote personage. The chiefs, though less remote, were more immediate sources of fear. It should be noted that the only analogous gatherings in LoDagaa culture were markets and funerals. But the boisterous activity of buyers and sellers and the expressive behavior of mourners differed significantly from the deportment of litigants in the formal and constrained setting of the courts.[86] Fortunately, Cardinall's 1920 book *The Natives of the Northern Territories of the Gold Coast* sheds some light on the atmosphere in the court and the behavior of the participants:

> Living more or less closely together ... everyone knew the facts of the dispute. ... This mode of life ... explains also the inability of the people to understand and answer questions. In Court a man merely makes a statement, "So-and-so has stolen my cows," or some such allegation, and relapses into silence, and only with great difficulty can one learn any details. In fact, one cannot offhand even learn the complainant's name. ... This inability to answer questions arises, I fancy, from the impatience of the people. Everyone knows his name and everyone knows who stole, or probably detained, the cows. In fact everyone knows all about it. The Chiefs, who are being encouraged to hear the troubles of their own people, are equally cognisant of the facts.[87]

Several officers observed a similar reticence among the LoDagaa, for whom the interrogative procedures used in the courts must have seemed contrived. Yet, as artificial as judicial rituals were, there were precedents for them in LoDagaa culture. Divinatory processes followed this same question-and-answer format, the main difference being that such proceedings culminated not in a judgment or decision, but in a revelation.

One of the few descriptions of divinatory processes, recorded in 1938, illustrates their inquisitorial nature:

> The supposed offender is led before the "tingnasob" or "baybore" [diviner], and the cowries are thrown to discover whether he has offended or not [i.e., whether the shrine being consulted was the appropriate noumenal agency for the "offender" to seek remedy from]. If the answer is, Yes, he will be compelled to slaughter a fowl, after confession. If the fowl falls with its feet underneath its body, it is said that the whole truth has not been told. Further confession will be made, and another fowl slaughtered. This will continue until a fowl falls on its back, when his confession is said to have been accepted. The president will either be the "tingansob" (unassisted), or the head of the family assisted by the "baybore" according to whether it is a local nature deity, or the ancestral fetish, who is consulted. No fine is paid, no medicine drunk.[88]

As is clear in the above description, such matters were private. More significantly, it was not the supplicant who was interrogated but a noumenal agency. The role of intermediaries was restricted to mediation between the individual and the relevant shrine and to the interpretation of signs. Judicial procedures differed from this in three important respects. First, it was the litigant who was questioned. Second, it was the officer or chief who made the decision. Third, words were interpreted rather than signs. As procedure moved from the interpretation of signs to that of words, diviners were replaced by court clerks and assessors, and divination was replaced by writing.

There was a procedure in LoDagaa mortuary practices that resembled judicial procedures more closely, but it seems to have been far less prevalent during the colonial period than in the immediate precolonial past.[89] Formerly, the symbolic practice of "carrying the corpse" was conducted before interment, if it was thought that the death had been caused by witchcraft, to determine who might have been responsible.[90] Goody reported that the dead person's clothing was wrapped in a sleeping mat and balanced precariously on the heads of two men, who carried the bundle before the mourners. The person before whom the bundle fell was deemed to have been responsible for the death.[91] Labouret stated that among the *Lobi*, where the practice still existed in the 1930s, the corpse itself was interrogated, the questions being answered by the direction in which the bundle moved while being balanced in this manner. Goody discovered no evidence of this method among the LoDagaa in the area of his fieldwork in the 1950s.[92] But George Savonnet observed this type of verbal inquisition among LoDagaa congeries north of Lawra District in the mid-1960s, which suggests that this too may once have been a feature of the practice in Lawra District.[93]

In contrast, another funeral ceremony known as "diviners beer" or "finding the mystical trouble" was still performed in the 1950s several weeks after interment of the deceased in order to determine the agency that had brought about death. As Goody described it, a diviner carried out the investigation in the presence of representatives of the deceased's relatives, with one of them acting as the client:

> The L-shaped stick, which the diviner and client both grasp, the one at the top, the other at the base, is supposedly guided by the diviner as agent of his daimon. It selects one or more objects among the divinatory materials that lie scattered between them, and those chosen represent agencies responsible for the death; for most of the motley contents of the bag – sheep's tooth, fragment of cloth, oyster shell, river pebble – signify a possible cause. ... Then, still holding the stick, the diviner takes the small gourd containing his divining cowries and confirms his diagnosis by shaking the shells on the ground each time the questioner calls out the name of a possible agency. At the right name the cowries fall correctly, one up, one down.[94]

Again, the differences between indigenous forms of cultural articulation and judicial procedure are apparent.

Although court proceedings were not unprecedented in form, they were very different from indigenous rituals in their context and content. Indigenous rituals were conducted largely in connection with crises or deaths; thus the subjects of investigation differed, as did their timing. Indigenous practices were revelatory in intention, whereas judicial procedures were exercises in labeling (i.e., guilty or innocent, liable or not liable). Finally, processes of cultural articulation among the LoDagaa dealt with causation rather than blame, liability, and responsibility. Decision making by officers and chiefs was wholly unprecedented in terms of LoDagaa culture and social practices, under which such attributes had once been the exclusive preserve of noumenal agencies.[95] The suppression of indigenous knowledge and the imposition of courts fundamentally altered spatial concepts concerning the source of authority as well as the spatial context in which disputes were expressed, defined, and resolved. But before we can explore how the courts changed the nature of disputes, we need to understand some of the other important ways in which colonialism altered experiences. We have already seen how the introduction of labor migration, the growth of ethnic consciousness, the reconfiguration of political authority, and the reimaging of God all changed notions of space in different ways. In the next chapter we look at how colonial money and missionary medicine both reflected and influenced similar changes.

Chapter Six

Missionary Medicine and Colonial Money

At the time the missionaries arrived our people were passing through a very difficult time. There was a lot of human misery. The groups were poor due to lack of rain, the children were dying in great numbers and on top of this the chiefs and the D.C. were imposing forced labour on everybody. Then, when the missionaries arrived and the people heard about the miracles that were performed in Jirapa, they became interested in the white people and the new God. People were also attracted by the kindness and love shown to them especially when compared with the colonials and the chiefs. They believed and hoped that the white men of God would not make them suffer and would free them from their slavery and misery. I think that these are some of the reasons why people embraced the new religion. Nevertheless, it was a fact that many drew back when they realised that despite the religion of the white men children were still dying, the rain didn't always come and the D.C.'s forced labour was still on.

Robert Bongvlaa, early catechist, interviewed in 1979

The arrival of missionaries had been preceded by a generation of British political engineering, during which an autocracy of indigenous colonial appointees (i.e., chiefs) exercised unprecedented powers. However, colonial power was not hegemonic, and at the end of the 1920s many LoDagaa still strongly resented this new order. A few years later they created their own alternative order, one that promised, among other things, refuge from the rule of the chiefs. This parallel world mirrored the colonial world it sought to displace, but the source of its power was not summonses, court records, and other bureaucratic practices; rather, it was medicine. The counterculture of LoDagaa Christians emerged as a response to the colonial order. The evangelical strategies of the missionaries were based on indigenous beliefs, fears, and knowledge. Far from eradicating fear, the missionaries replaced one form of hope with another and one set of rituals with another. Rather than attacking indigenous knowledge as the British had, Catholic missionaries actually confirmed that knowledge through their use of medicine. Indeed, the missionaries used medicine as a medium of conversion with much greater success than the British used money to achieve similar ends. It is significant that medicine, not money, was commensurable with LoDagaa culture.

British efforts to replace cowry shells with colonial currency led to a decidedly different type of conversion – of work into wage labor, of needs into wants, of cultural practices into economic calculations, of quality into quantity. In this chapter I discuss the contrasts between missionary medicine and colonial money. Medicine was the basis of a remarkable and sudden wave of conversions exceptional in the history of missionary activity in Africa; money created prolonged resistance unprecedented in the economic history of colonial Africa. The failure of the British to succeed in their project of conversion illustrates not only their lack of hegemony, but also their lack of dominance when it came to altering the social and cultural values of the LoDagaa.

Missionaries, Catechists, and Politics

An insightful local historian and devout Catholic priest, Father Naameh, has argued that the British did not "pacify" the land because their methods consisted of the "forceful subjugation of a people and the imposition on them of the European rule and way of organising society." Rather, it was the missionaries who should be seen as having done so.[1] The missionaries set out to accomplish the "mystical" or "supernatural" pacification of the land by substituting belief in God for fear of agencies such as the *tengaan*.[2] This campaign began with attempts to eradicate the tyranny of anxiety through which, so the missionaries believed, indigenous spirits and deities ruled the LoDagaa. Yet this struggle against the beliefs and practices of the LoDagaa was far less successful than another struggle the missionaries undertook – namely, their battle with the chiefs who menaced the LoDagaa in much more obvious ways. This political struggle was more successful, not because the missionaries were able to reign in the powers of the chiefs, but because it attracted large number of converts. Most converts sought refuge from colonialism, not from their own culture.

Following their arrival at Jirapa in 1929, the White Fathers and their followers sought to create an alternative society to the colonial order. In doing so, they had to contend with chiefs, on the one hand, and indigenous beliefs on the other. The missionaries spent the first days after their arrival on a hill known to be the residence of local spirits. It was also the site of one of the district commissioner's resthouses. They were then given an "uninhabited plateau of land, believed to be the arena for the nocturnal activities of witches and other evil spirits."[3] This location, chosen by the Jirapa Naa, was intended to isolate the missionaries without rejecting them. The chief had good reason to be suspicious of the missionaries, but his attempt to use spirits to isolate them backfired. Soon after taking up residence in Jirapa, the missionaries learned how to use, if not exploit, indigenous beliefs. Regarding these beliefs, the missionaries objected not to their content – that power over life was controlled by the noumenal world – but to their specific direction – that the LoDagaa invoked and called upon the ancestors and various spirits and not God. As the missionaries began to attract followers, they came into conflict with the Jirapa Naa, not over indigenous beliefs but over political power.

The overtly political ramifications of the positive reaction to the missionary presence emerged soon after the rain incident in June of 1932. In several outlying settlements, a series of confrontations took place between zealous Christians, who took seriously the missionaries' inflammatory warning that God was withholding rain because the LoDagaa continued to believe in spirits and ancestors, and less credulous neighbors. When rain still did not come to other settlements shortly after the rain in Daffiama, recent converts held their neighbors responsible for the continuing drought. In an effort to abide by the missionaries' injunctions and to impose those injunctions on non-Christians, gangs of Catholic supporters from several settlements reportedly destroyed their own shrines and those of people in other settlements.[4] By July, after the iconoclasm of the previous month, several followers of the missionaries were openly repudiating the legitimacy of the colonial chiefs and defying their orders. One convert, Dapila of Bazim, was reported to have publicly declared that "there are no more chiefs now and no white men any longer but the White Fathers," and "they should not obey their headman any more." Following these remarks, a gang allegedly walked through the settlements around Bazim carrying a red cloth on a stick and "giving out that the authority of the chiefs was at an end."[5]

Many followers discovered in the missionaries an alternative source of external authority. In the early stages of the wide-scale movement toward Christianity, it was not God but the missionaries who were identified as having noumenal powers. Also, the missionaries were not perceived as remote authority figures like the district commissioner, whose powers were phenomenal. As Archbishop Dery, the son of one of their first converts, later reflected: "The missionaries were indeed a puzzle to the people. The people did not know where they came from and what to make of them. The missionaries, unlike the

British Colonial Officers, went among the people, visited them even in their homes, dispensed medicine to cure their diseases."[6] At this time there was usually only one colonial officer at Lawra, but already there were three missionaries at Jirapa, and several more after the rain incident.

Once converts discovered this alternative source of authority, they found ways of articulating long-suppressed grievances. For example, the administration and the missionaries clashed over the question of forced (by then known as Native Authority) labor, which the chiefs demanded of both pagans and Christians on Sundays.[7] The missionaries' opposition to the government on this and other related issues challenged the authority of the chiefs; it also meant that converts could defy the chiefs with some hope of success. Eyre-Smith had left the district for a posting in the Gold Coast Colony before the missionaries arrived, but he was kept apprised of conditions in his former district by migrant LoDagaa passing through his station on their way to the mines. In 1933 he suggested that the "religious revolution" had been the result of "the revulsion of the people against the tyranny of the chiefs," who were "no longer bound by the former sanctions of the community." In these circumstances, he added, commoners quite naturally sought "outside spiritual power" as a means of securing protection not available through the colonial administration.[8] Meanwhile, officers back in Lawra misunderstood the motives of converts. Thus, when chiefs complained that their once silent and largely passive opponents were defying work orders, officers sided with the chiefs. However, the officers' strong antipathy against anything that threatened their political engineering had limits. Aware that the White Fathers enjoyed some support outside the Northern Territories, administrators were careful not to offend the missionaries too much.[9]

Following the rain incident, the district commissioner and the missionaries became direct rivals – leaders of rival constituencies. However, successive district commissioners did not understand whose side they were really on. They chose to defend what they saw as the vulnerable pagan against the zealous Christian, yet in doing so, more often than not they were actually protecting the interests of the chiefs. Commenting on Father McCoy's conversion methods, one district commissioner noted: "With true respect to the Catholic Faith ... some of the good Father's actions have been a trifle injudicious. Well aware that historically, the coming of any new religion inevitably tends to undermine the old civil authority, by division of obediences, I yet feel that the undermining must be carefully done, in view of the fact that it is the Government's policy to reconstitute and strengthen this very authority."[10] In his memoirs, written over fifty years after the rain incident, McCoy noted that the administration's contention that the chiefs were "the recognized native authority" was a convenient distortion of the facts: "In many ways the chiefs held less power than the tendaana. But the British administration did not recognize the latter and governed exclusively through the former."[11] This argument was somewhat disingenuous, since the missionaries were even less willing to recognize the authority of the *tengaan* and its priests.

In the 1930s McCoy protested to the administration that catechists did recognize and respect the chiefs, but in his memoirs he admitted that one reason for the success of the mission had been the people's "remarkably unservile attitude toward their chiefs."[12] The destruction of shrines had not undermined "the old civil authority," since that authority had been ignored for nearly thirty years. Furthermore, despite their protestations, the chiefs were not mainly concerned with the threat this religious movement posed to indigenous culture. They defended indigenous beliefs and practices largely because many of the converts who carried out attacks on shrines were also the agitators who were announcing that the era of the chiefs had come to an end. Indeed, although the behavior of converts was dramatic, their attacks on indigenous shrines were motivated more by desperation than by deep religious opposition.

The missionaries and subsequent co-religionists strongly denied that conversions had political connotations. Father Barsalon, a colleague of McCoy's at Jirapa, reported that the district commissioner was worried about the prospects of a revolt, but attributed this fear to misinformation emanating from the chiefs. Yet he admitted that the movement was not exclusively religious and that stories of insubordination were not always fabricated. "It is clear that a fair number of people were swept up in the movement without knowing either why or what they wanted; there were even those who, in the hope of becoming 'children of the Fathers,' evaded the exactions of the chiefs and the levies and forced labor of the administration. Thus there were in fact some isolated incidents of insubordination toward the chiefs."[13] That the White Fathers offered many early converts a means of evading forced labor and other exactions is confirmed by other sources.[14] Having denied a religious motivation for these isolated incidents, Barsalon went on to suggest that administrative complaints were the result of jealousy: many people were flocking to the missionaries, whereas whenever the district commissioner visited a village the people disappeared except for the chief, a few elders, and their followers.[15] This observation belies the contention that the missionaries' greatest adversaries were witches or polygamists, and reveals that the missionaries were implicitly in competition with the colonial administration and the chiefs, with each side attempting to build its own society, one colonial and the other religious.[16] As Der has noted of this period: "It was not only a matter of the Christian faith and conduct being opposed to traditional religion and accepted customs, the more basic question of the authority of the chiefs vis-a-vis the Christians was brought into sharp focus."[17]

For three reasons, it was quite predictable that the missionaries would deny that their success among the LoDagaa had political causes or implications. First, they obviously preferred to stress the religious over the political dimensions of the process. Second, although they were aware that the colonial chiefs were generally resented, they sought to cast their confrontations with the administration as issues of religious conscience rather than political conflict. Third, they did not actually control events as they unfolded after the rain incident: it was the catechists who were in charge of the early converts in the various villages. After the rain incident, the pattern of evangelization became highly decentralized, with catechists in the dispersed settlements of the region working from their homes, which became centers of religious and social activity. "It was now the catechist," Der reminds us, "and not the missionary, who made direct contact with the people. The catechist played the leading role in the initial stages of conversions with the missionary remaining largely in the background."[18] The catechists endeavored to settle disputes between Catholic followers, advised converts to disobey orders from the chiefs to work on Sundays – as had been the practice before the arrival of the missionaries – and urged allegiance to a different source of authority. Catechists became to the missionaries what colonial headmen, subchiefs, and chiefs were to the district commissioner.

Most Catholic historians have, like Der, admitted that "a few over-zealous converts did think that in becoming Christians they were absolved from obedience to the chiefs"; but they have also insisted that at no time did Christians attempt to "usurp the power of chiefs."[19] Whether or not the chiefs were directly challenged, however, the revolutionary implications of the converts' behavior cannot be minimized. Because most of their energy was directed not against the colonial order but into the construction of an alternative order, the intensity of the latter was not as apparent as it might have been. As Magloire Somé has written of the effects of this Christian movement, which crossed to the other side of the Black Volta almost immediately, it was from the start "an usettling force on the socio-cultural structures, a sort of counterculture."[20] Converts did not have to attempt to overthrow the colonial order; they needed only to join the alternative one that the early catechumens and catechists were establishing. The missionaries might not have intended for their followers to become politically involved, but they were hardly in a position to control their many converts' motives and actions. The sheer number of followers indicates that the process must have been largely indigenous in organization: there was far too little time for the missionaries on their own to have affected a significant change in LoDagaa culture, as they themselves were only too aware. One missionary asked almost in desperation, "what could 3 or 4 missionaries do to catechize 50,000 to 60,000 people?"[21] Within two years of the rain incident there was a decline in the number of catechumens, but this was not seen as an entirely negative development; as some missionaries admitted, there had not been sufficient time to inculcate serious enough religious convictions.[22]

Even if the authority of the chiefs was not explicitly rejected, the creation and deployment of an alternative authority could not but have had political consequences. Over time, both the colonial administration and the missionaries convinced themselves that although their structures of control over the LoDagaa were predicated on and realized through native agents, it was they – the administrators and missionaries – who were in charge of events. The role of catechists in the church structure was very similar to that of chiefs in the colonial structure. Indeed, colonial and evangelical structures were analogous in many respects. The British had created an extensive network of chiefs, subchiefs, and headmen, just as the missionaries relied on their networks of catechists. The chiefs and subchiefs had been rewarded with medals bearing the likeness of the British monarch, which they jealously guarded as representations of the authority that had been granted to them. Similarly, the allegiance of converts was gained by distributing medals of the Blessed Virgin to postulants after six month of catechism, and these too were seen as important symbols of allegiance. The *mel*, as it came to be known, was so important that in 1932 administrators in the adjoining French colony attempted to prohibit catechumens from wearing it because of the political turmoil caused by the return of people who had traveled to Jirapa for conversion.[23] Both chiefs and catechists received remuneration from outside sources. And finally, although catechists did not directly attempt to usurp the chiefs, they did impinge on their prerogatives in settling marital disputes between converts, and so represented an alternative, external source of authority in settlements.

Because the conversion movement rose so suddenly, the first catechumens and early catechists must have had only a sketchy understanding of Christianity even if their zeal was unquestionable. Given that these early Christians carried out most of the evangelical work in Lawra District, we must question how well they understood what the missionaries were doing and saying, for it would have directly influenced what most LoDagaa heard and were told to do. Contemporary priests, most of whom see the arrival of the missionaries as only a sign of God's longer-term revelation to the LoDagaa, have argued that Catholic ideas were understood in indigenous terms.[24] Indeed, even Naameh has said that the "reality of conceiving many aspects of the new religion in continuity with the pre-Christian religious experience, was the fact which facilitated more than anything else the Dagara acceptance of the Christian message."[25] Although practices did change suddenly and abruptly, the effect on beliefs was more gradual and modest as new ideas were understood in the context of extant religious thinking. According to Naameh, in the early decades of religious change the missionaries were often identified as noumenal powers in their own right, albeit more efficacious than ancestors and spirits and other noumenal agencies. Any concept of a Christian God was as remote to most of the early converts as any indigenous high-god had been in pre-Christian religious thought and practice. The catechists communicated between the missionaries and their followers, translating the ideas of this foreign religion into local concepts.[26] This was inevitable, given that at the end of the first decade of missionary activity the ratio of missionaries to followers was 1:1,038, that of missionaries to catechists was 1:8, and that of catechists to followers was 1:134.[27] In 1919 the ratio of colonial appointees to subjects had been approximately 1:333.[28]

When leadership in the Catholic community was formalized with the program of Catholic Action in the late 1930s, the political tendencies of catechists again surfaced. It was noted that contrary to the program's intentions, "the members of these select groups quite naturally assume that because they have been chosen before others by the mission superior and assigned this work, this bestows on them a real superiority, which leads them to act like they are chiefs."[29] The movement began in the outstations of Kaleo, a village south of Lawra District, where the Christian community was perceived to be laxer than most. By 1944 it had spread to outstations in Nandom and Jirapa parishes. Male and female chiefs and subchiefs were appointed in each settlement, and by 1951 there were 280 members in seventy villages in Nandom parish alone.[30] Members took over from the catechists as leaders of their communities, and the latter focused their attention on evangelization. They were instructed in how to lead exemplary lives, administer baptisms *in periculo mortis*, reconcile conjugal disputes, encourage as well as enforce Christian practices, repress any practices that were contrary to the new faith, and "denounce every maker of false cures and warn every Christian who uses these cures."[31] Their work was a combination of adjudication, surveillance, and policing – very much the same tasks assigned to colonial chiefs.[32]

Clearly, the conversion process had political aspects, but the indigenous priesthood was reluctant to acknowledge as much. In a speech in 1983, Peter Dery, the Archbishop of Tamale, contended that allegations that the early converts had been politically motivated came from those determined to discredit converts. Claims that converts wanted to usurp the chiefs and replace them with the missionaries, or that they told their followers to stop farming on the chiefs' farms, were "fabrications" designed "to make Christianity unpopular."[33] However, given the political climate in Lawra District at the time, these "fabrications," if that was what they were, could only have made Christianity more popular. Men such as Poreku, the archbishop's father and one of the first converts, might very well have been filled with evangelical zeal, but the effects of their actions were unquestionably political. Soon after the rain incident, Poreku commanded a following of several thousand in the area of Zemopare. Whether he had political motives or not, many others, such as Robert Bongvlaa, did see conversion as a means of avoiding the authority of the colonial chiefs.[34]

Medicine and Conversion

Although the missionaries denied being in a political struggle against the authority of the chiefs, they in no way attempted to disguise their struggle against LoDagaa religious culture. Yet, there are definite grounds for questioning the degree to which their success was the result of confronting these beliefs and practices. One could argue instead that they succeeded by accommodating and integrating indigenous culture. Despite missionary rhetoric about liberating the LoDagaa from fear and insecurity, the missionaries succeeded precisely by harnessing these existential worries, not by extinguishing them. Accommodation, rather than confrontation, better describes missionary religious activity.

The religious iconoclasm during the drought of 1932 was relatively short-lived. Both before and after the rain incident, the missionaries attracted followers through medicine. Missionary sources stress how important medicine was as a conduit for potential converts. McCoy noted that he and the other missionaries established an initial following mainly by offering injections of emetine to treat dysentery, and sobita solution to treat yaws. Providentially for the missionaries, the founding of the mission coincided with an outbreak of dysentery.[35] The annual report for 1930–31 noted that the dispensary was the main means of attracting followers, but the following year, just after the rain incident, the increasing popularity of the mission was attributed as something else: "What draws them? At the outset they came looking for physical health, relief from their ills, but now they come looking for the light of the Faith."[36] However, illness continued to play a very important part in the conversion process well after the rain incident.

When we examine the activities of the missionaries over their first decade, we find that medical work far outweighed pastoral work at all the mission stations. Indeed, the reaction to medical services had "some of the dimensions of a mass pilgrimage," that Ranger noted in his study of the effects of medical work by missionaries in southeast Tanganyika.[37] Among the LoDagaa the movement sustained itself sufficiently to grow into a mass conversion. The White Fathers had more success than their Protestant colleagues in Tanganyika because they were working in a more propitious political climate, their efforts were more concentrated, and they spoke much more directly to the eschatological concerns of their patients turned converts.[38] From the beginning, the missionaries tried to represent Catholicism, and especially their medical successes, in indigenous terms.

As different recitations associated with the *Bagre* demonstrate, disease had been an important issue among the LoDagaa well before the missionaries arrived. Afflictions and their avoidance were central to the *Bagre*. After naming the various noumenal agencies that might intervene, the recitation listed possible reasons why a person might seek out a diviner. Then, using "the leather bottles," the diviner determined whether that person needed to be initiated within the *Bagre* in order to find protection from disease. Goody noted that the process of consultation and divination leading to initiation was also described as being "caught" by the *Bagre*. Some illnesses, such as guinea worm, were very closely associated with having been seized by the god of the *Bagre* (*Bagr ngmin*).[39]

Only recently has attention been paid to how missionary medicine affected both the dynamics of evangelization and the well-being of rural Africans.[40] The provision of medical care by the colonial governments was wholly inadequate.[41] Until the 1940s public health measures in the Northern Territories had been limited to ensuring that disease did not disrupt the colonial economy. During this time the region was severely affected by disease, and the colonial administration had done very little to improve the health of the LoDagaa. There was little awareness of the level of privation experienced in the district toward the end of the dry season. In the 1930s the first nutritional survey of the region revealed that at that point in the year, calorific intake often fell as low as five hundred to one thousand per day.[42] If anything, the colonial administration exacerbated health problems up until the 1940s, when the first real, albeit weak, measures were taken to improve the health of northerners generally.[43] The increased movement of people during colonial rule had facilitated the vectors for many diseases.[44] When they were dealt with at all, major illnesses such as cerebrospinal meningitis, influenza, trypanosomiasis, and onchocerciasis were treated almost exclusively as issues of public health (i.e., of the economic health and social stability of the Northern Territories). Public health measures focused on limiting the spread of outbreaks of infectious diseases by isolating the sick. Little or no effort was made to protect the LoDagaa from illness, even though, as noted above, their cattle were inoculated. A report written in 1931 on the condition of northern workers (many of whom would have been LoDagaa) seeking employment on the cocoa farms of the south described them as "dirty, lousy, and of very poor physique. They are veritable museums of helminths of all descriptions, yaws, and guinea-worms."[45] Although a traveling dispensary did begin visiting Lawra in 1928, treating eleven thousand patients in one year, the program was suspended in 1933 as a result of the Great Depression.[46] Any effective provision of medical treatment was, by default, left to the missionaries.

The White Fathers had begun treating patient for yaws, conjunctivitis, malaria, dysentery, and trypanosomiasis as early as 1929, and would continue to do so until 1939, when the dispensary was expanded and taken over by Franciscan Sisters. If we ignore the time that the missionaries spent soliciting rain and defending their followers against the criticism of the chiefs, almost all of their time during the first decade among the LoDagaa was taken up with attending to the ill. McCoy recounted in his memoirs the long hours the Fathers spent in the dispensary, and the effect this had on their work:

> The daily routine of the clinic would begin with a prayer aimed at reminding our patients that the curative power of medicines and the care dispensed was a result of God's great love for them as His children. We were conscious of our primary role as ambassadors of Jesus Christ to the people of the Northwest. And so there was a constant effort on our part not only to make them aware of it but also to keep ourselves from forgetting it as a natural consequence of the long hours spent treating the sick each day at the clinic or in their homes.[47]

Given their meager resources, the scale of the missionaries' medical work was genuinely impressive. Table 6 illustrates the time this work must have commanded, as well as the scale of the response that it elicited. Between 1929 and 1939 well over a quarter of a million dispensary visits were recorded; on average, more than one hundred patients were being seen every day.

We know from various sources that early medical interventions by the missionaries often had extremely dramatic effects. The missionaries attributed their very first medical successes directly to God. Weekly injections of sobita solution resulted in "spectacular success" in the treatment of yaws. Equally effective were the use of hot compresses to deal with conjunctivitis and quinine to relieve symptoms of malaria. Epsom salts, bismuth, and emetine were administered to deal with intestinal complaints; epidermal injections of turpentine were used to treat pneumonia. Much less effective were treatments for leprosy and sleeping sickness.[48]

In 1930 McCoy was credited with bringing people back from the verge of death on three separate occasions with a variety of remedies – brandy, emetine, and caffeine.[49] In one instance the missionaries were called to attend to a man who had fainted but was presumed to be dying. Smelling salts were administered but without effect. While brandy was sought, McCoy baptized the man, as he was one of those who "occasionally" came to church. "The crowd was attentive to my every word and gesture," the missionary recalled over fifty

TABLE 6
Analysis of Missionary Work among the LoDagaa, 1929–39

Year	A *Pères*	B *Frères*	C Communions	D Confessions	E Dispensary visits	F Ratio of D to E
1929–30	2	1	830	46	3,700	1:80
1930–31	2	1	831	68	16,425	1:242
1931–32	3	1	1,100	49	36,500	1:745
1932–33	6	1	3,109	178	50,449	1:283
1933–34	9	2	12,215	1,065	25,530	1:24
1934–35	10	1	14,283	2,407	33,685	1:14
1935–36	11	1	115,552	11,884	30,800	1:3
1936–37	11	1	135,840	31,105	59,630	1:2
1937–38	11	1	281,406	55,573	55,440	1:1
1938–39	11	1	298,360	77,735	62,887	1:1
Total	–	–	863,526	180,110	375,046	1:2

Source: Rapports Annuels, 1929–39

years later. When a small amount of brandy was fed to the patient, his breathing returned to normal and he opened his eyes. Soon others came to the mission in search of remedies for a wide variety of complaints.[50] An elder was brought to the mission in a "moribund" state and was similarly revived with an injection of caffeine. Before being revived, he was baptized and given the *mel*.[51] In another case, the missionaries were asked to call on a man named Nameri, who was diagnosed as dying of dysentery. Emetine was administered. After Nameri recovered, McCoy informed the "witnesses" to this "miracle" that "God was the real master of life and death, not any mere mortal, and that the life that comes from Him is stronger than death."[52]

In the absence of any clear communication between the missionaries and their patients, many LoDagaa at this early date would have understood these cures in ritual terms, making little distinction between religious rites and the administration of medicines. Notions of salvation among the LoDagaa were concrete rather than abstract. They dealt with the immediate existential threats of everyday life, such as "sickness, drought, poverty, shame, hunger and barrenness." According to Naameh, *Dagaare* concepts of salvation focused on threats that, in the absence of knowledge of "the law of scientific causality," imposed a "greater reliance on the invisible world for the solution of all problems."[53] In offering solutions to noumenal threats, the missionaries were providing those LoDagaa who attended the mission dispensary, or who called a priest when very ill, with salvation of an unintended variety.

It was not the effectiveness of specific medicines that excited the most attention, but what was taken to be evidence of cheating death. We find strong parallels between these "miracles" and the *Bagre*. Individuals underwent initiation into the *Bagre* in order to restore their health or to ward off the threat of illness. Divination revealed to individuals whether they had been or were in danger of being caught by the *Bagre*.[54] Initiation took place over many months, but the main performances were held in December, during the dry season and after the harvest had ended. The central ceremony was a dance held over four days. On the evening of the second day the neophytes were secluded in a room and told to lie down in order to ingest a liquid, which was nothing more dangerous than millet beer, but which they had been told contained the highly toxic powder of ground strophanus seeds. According to Goody's eye witness account of a performance of this ritual in 1951, the atmosphere was tense and foreboding, with the neophytes in a state somewhere between belief and disbelief. The poison resulted in the ritual death of the neophytes so the senior initiates could revive them. From the perspective of the Catholic ritual of deathbed baptisms, what was most interesting about this *Bagre* ritual was the offer of "a means of conquering death, which is later revealed as a sham."[55] The promises made in the long oral recitation that accompanied the *Bagre* dance, such as "Death kills, the *Bagre* god saves us, so death can't kill," were renounced during the second of these oral recitations, known as the Black *Bagre*, by which time the futility of attempting to evade death was conceded: "These things we do, though they can't banish death."[56] The difference between the ritual killing and revival of neophytes by the initiates and the baptism of patients in danger of death by priests is that the latter ritual often had even more dramatic and immediate consequences. Aspects of the *Bagre* were incorporated into regular rituals of baptism. Baptisms took place at Christmas, which coincided with the *Bagre*. The heads of catechumens were shaved before being anointed, as were the heads of initiates. And new Christians wore their finery to their baptism, just as successful *Bagre* initiates did at the end of the ceremonies when they re-entered society.[57]

McCoy and other missionaries did not hesitate to claim that whatever efficacy their remedies, prayers, or medicine had was a direct result of the will of God. They made no attempt in the early years to explain their culture's understanding of either meteorology or biochemistry. Instead, McCoy explained that those who had sought out and accepted the message of the missionaries were spared, whereas those who ignored his warnings and continued to believe in "witchdoctors and fetishists" were denied rain, stricken with cerebrospinal meningitis, or visited by swarms of locusts! The missionaries certainly brought new hopes, but they also tried to introduce new fears. They made every effort to tie their medical work to the wider eschatological concerns of the LoDagaa.[58] This willingness to adapt their message to indigenous concerns explains much of the success that the mission enjoyed. Missionaries such as McCoy were so zealous in their faith that they found it easy to understand how the LoDagaa attributed causation to noumenal agencies – the disagreement was merely over which agencies were responsible for the healing.

If drought and disease brought many LoDagaa to the missionaries, it was death that caused many to convert. Funerals were the central cultural performance among the LoDagaa. As one district commissioner noted: "The funeral custom seems to be what the market is to the Hausa, the court to an Ashanti and a football match to the British workman."[59] Given the centrality of death to LoDagaa culture – a feature that Goody himself highlighted in a lengthy monograph on "mortuary customs"[60] – it is not surprising that it played an important role in attracting converts. Richard Gray has correctly pointed out that in Africa as a whole "the relevance of eschatology to the debate on conversion has been overlooked."[61]

Baptism *in periculo mortis* was a very common conversion technique (Table 7). Indeed, up until 25 December 1932, all baptisms had been of people on their

TABLE 7
Baptism Rates among the LoDagaa, 1929–39

Year	Catechumens	Catechists	Baptized	Adults	Children	*In periculo mortis*	Total
1929–30	–	–	7	–	1	8	9
1930–31	432	–	68	1	1	142	144
1931–32	5,090	10	97	–	–	119	119
1932–33	20,962	44	425	42	44	897	983
1933–34	10,062	63	574	18	26	970	1,014
1934–35	7,186	51	1,215	168	17	1,031	1,216
1935–36	8,183	64	3,132	1,454	430	1,585	3,469
1936–37	7,391	70	6,937	2,812	845	1,773	5,430
1937–38	6,484	81	9,696	2,272	898	1,329	4,499
1938–39	6,209	93	12,458	1,885	1,058	1,114	4,057
Total	[6,209]	[93]	[12,458]	8,652	3,320	8,968	20,940

Source: Rapports Annuels, 1929–39.

"deathbeds."[62] Considering how often these rites were performed, it must be asked whether patients saw these baptisms as just another component in a wider set of rituals that included compresses and injections.[63] Most patients probably drew no distinction between being attended to by a diviner and being attended to by a missionary; just as missionaries resembled diviners, diviners resembled doctors.[64] In their early years, the missionaries functioned mainly as medical practitioners, rather than as priests. Although not officially a medical mission, the White Fathers in Jirapa competed with diviners and herbalists, not just spirits and gods; and not to save souls but to cure illnesses.[65] Holy water came to be known as *ngmenkuo*, or "spirits' water,"[66] and came to be associated with the other medicines administered to the dying.[67] By the end of 1931 the missionaries were training the first catechists to perform baptisms *in periculo mortis* as such events were a "regular occurrence."[68]

By 1939 the White Fathers had performed 20,940 baptisms, yet there were only 12,458 baptized LoDagaa. This enormous discrepancy alerts us to the fact that 43 percent of those baptisms were performed on those in danger of death. At first it might seem reasonable to assume that most of those baptized under these circumstances died. However, when we look at the first six years of baptisms in isolation, we find that of 1,215 people baptized by 1935, the majority, or 897, had been baptized *in periculo mortis* but had survived. Assuming that there were no deaths among baptized adults and children, this meant a survival rate of at least 28 percent for those who had been baptized in danger of death. Accordingly, over two thousand or roughly one-fifth of the converts made by 1939 would have been baptized *in periculo mortis* (Table 8).

Baptisms performed *in periculo mortis* underscore another aspect of the conversion process. With the exception of peaks in baptisms in the years 1936–37 and 1937–38, the majority of baptisms were performed on the very ill. Whether they were catechumens, relatives of Christians, or spontaneous converts we do not know; but presumably most of these people had first come for medical attention. That so many dying people sought out the missionaries is revealing. Indeed, a disproportionate number of those adults who underwent baptism were elders.[69] Given that the missionaries consciously manipulated their rudimentary medical knowledge, it is necessary to ask what these particular converts might have expected and how they would have understood these last rites. We cannot know, but evidence suggests that many expected to cheat death.

Many non-Christians felt that the missionaries were using last rites to steal souls. In 1939 the Tantuo Naa and Nandom Naa complained that "the Fathers have a habit of rushing to the deathbeds of Christians and pagans and try to snatch their souls from perdition."[70] A formula had been worked out the previous year between chiefs and missionaries by which souls could be shared.

TABLE 8
Analysis of Baptisms in periculo mortis, 1929–39*

	A	B	C	D	E	F	G	H
Years	Baptisms *in periculo mortis*	Baptisms of adults	Baptisms of children	Total baptisms	A as % of D	Number of baptized at end of year*	Survivors from A (F/yr – (B+C))	G as % of A
1929–30	8	–	1	9	89	7	6	75
1930–31	142	1	1	144	99	68 (61)	59	42
1931–32	119	–	–	119	100	97 (23)	29	24
1932–33	897	42	44	983	91	425 (328)	242	27
1933–34	970	18	26	1,014	96	574 (149)	105	11
1934–35	1,031	168	17	1,216	85	1,215 (641)	456	44
1935–36	1,585	1,454	430	3,469	46	3,132 (1,917)	33	–
1936–37	1,773	2,812	845	5,430	33	6,937 (3,805)	148	–
1937–38	1,329	2,272	898	4,499	30	9,696 (2,759)	–411	–
1938–39	1,114	1,885	1,058	4,057	27	12,458 (2,762)	–592	–
Total	8,968	8,652	3,320	20,940	43	12,458		28

Source: Rapports Annuels, 1929–39.

*Over the first six years, those in danger of death accounted for the vast majority of those who received baptism (see column "E"). The dominance of baptisms in periculo mortis was due in part to the four-year period that catechumens had to undergo before baptism, which also accounts for the delay between the remarkable events of 1932 and the sudden increase in baptisms of adults in 1935–36. However, even as late as 1939 they accounted for over a quarter of all baptisms. Due to their preponderance, it is possible to calculate an approximate survival rate for those who received baptism in danger of death during the six-year period 1929–35. By 1934–35, 897 of the 3,167 people who had been baptized in danger of death had survived long enough to appear in the annual statistics as among the living community of baptized Christians. This indicates a survival rate of at least 28 percent (column "H"). The actual rate might have been higher. We must also assume that there was a death rate among baptized adults and children, as the figures in column "F" for 1937–39 clearly indicate when compared to the combined figures for columns "B" and "C." Of course the infant mortality rate would have been very high. Although there are not precise figures, those which do exist for the Northern Territories in 1939 suggest an infant mortality rate of 240 per 1,000 births. But if infant mortality was high, we cannot also discount adult mortality. On the difficulty of assessing death rates in Ghana at this time, see Patterson, 1981, 85–95.

Note: Figures in parentheses are not cumulative and indicate increase over previous year.

Those who died *in periculo mortis* were to be buried as pagans, but only after the Christians had been allowed to pray over the body. Similarly, when a "fully developed Christian" died, the pagans were permitted "to perform the ceremonies which they believed necessary, but the Christians were to take possession of the body, and bury it in consecrated ground."[71] For pagans the fear was that if the proper sacrifices were not performed, the deceased would not be able to cross over into the world of the ancestors. For their part, the Christians feared that if they rejected the missionaries' advice and broke the prohibition against pagan sacrifices, they might deprive the deceased entry into heaven.[72] So pressing was this concern among relatives of Christians that the missionaries soon compromised on their prohibition against sacrifices at Christian funerals "to allay some of the opposition to the baptism of catechumens."[73] This was a major departure from Canon Law, which continued to be applied to Christian marriages even though it was even more unpopular.[74] That Christian funerals followed an indigenous rhythm was significant. Indeed, Dabiré has explained that one reason Islam had such limited success among the LoDagaa was that its funeral practices were considered too expeditious. A large part of the missionaries' success was due to their willingness to compromise on this extremely important aspect of LoDagaa culture.[75]

Although the missionaries did not admit it, LoDagaa and Catholic eschatology were not very far removed from each other. Despite missionary prohibitions, by the 1940s many converts found nothing incompatible between their adopted religion and their own culture.[76] For the LoDagaa "the communion with, and cult of the ancestors and other spirits [found] a perfect echo in the Christian communion of saints and cult of saints and angels."[77] Goody noted that many people in a settlement near Nandom in the 1950s had Christian names, "but possession of such a name did not always indicate a reluctance to participate in sacrifices to the ancestors."[78] In the early 1970s a study of divination was conducted among the LoDagaa of Burkina Faso in an effort to work out ways of Christianizing these means of communication. It found that although Christians themselves rarely sought out diviners, they often consulted with spirits and ancestors indirectly through their non-Christian relatives.[79] Both Der and Kuukure noted in the 1980s that the pagan practice of presenting an offering of twenty cowries to pay the ferryman to take the deceased across the river to the land of the ancestors had been transposed by Christians into "offerings for prayers and suffrages for the dead" in order to make sure that the dead went to heaven.[80]

In the short term at least, God does not appear to have been central to the conversion process. Death and the afterlife preoccupied Christians and non-Christians alike. It is possible that what the missionaries felt was evangelical adaptation, and what later observers described as identification, actually slowed down the conversion process by reducing the distance between Catholic faith and LoDagaa culture over time, thus making conversion less necessary. Certainly the conversion movement was over by the 1940s, having begun its decline not long after the rain incident. Somé has argued that because the missionaries believed that their success was the result of divine revelation, they failed to develop a coherent strategy for expanding the mission after the rain incident.[81] Der has argued that already by 1934 the rate of conversion at Jirapa had slowed down due to chiefly opposition and requirements for baptism. He claims that many of the early converts gained in the aftermath of the rain incident deserted once they discovered the long-term implications of Catholicism, such as monogamy and prohibition against sacrifices (except for those in funerary rites). After the mid-1940s the growth of the mission was due mostly to "self-augmentation" or natural increase.[82] As Robert Bongvlaa, an early convert, noted, many of the initial converts in Lawra District reverted back to their former beliefs and practices "when they realised that despite the religion of the white man children were still dying, the rain didn't always come and the DC's forced labour was still on."[83]

Cowries and Markets

Colonial attempts to suppress LoDagaa knowledge did not replace it but drove it underground; while it was increasingly ignored at the intersection of the world of experience and the world on paper, especially in the courts, it continued to influence practices and beliefs that were beyond the reach of the colonial state. (Nevertheless, the courts did have a profound effect on how the LoDagaa defined and resolved their disputes.) Any assessment of the missionaries' attempts to replace LoDagaa knowledge must distinguish between success as measured by the number of converts and actual changes in followers' beliefs and behavior. Converts often did not change their beliefs because the missionaries relied on co-option rather than the coercion that the British employed, which had the effect of minimizing the differences between Catholicism and LoDagaa beliefs. Whereas the worlds of the missionaries and their followers converged,[84] the world on paper of the British and the world of LoDagaa experience intersected. In addition, the primary ambitions of the British and the White Fathers, suppression and conversion respectively, were very different. Where the colonial state did adopt a strategy of conversion – of cowries into cash – it was unsuccessful.

The British had little difficulty establishing political control over the LoDagaa, but integrating them into the colonial economy was much more troublesome.

Even though individual young men willingly participated in the cyclical pattern of labor migration established by the British, most LoDagaa saw the external economy more as a threat than an opportunity. It robbed households of their labor on a scale far greater than any precolonial slavers had, and it disrupted the balance of power between generations. Despite the impact of labor migration, those at home worked to maintain the values and integrity of the internal economy. Nothing is more indicative of the resistance of the LoDagaa to the colonial economy than the fact that they continued to use cowry shells as a medium of economic interaction, ritual action, and social communication. The retention of cowries for three-quarters of the twentieth century can be read as a diagnostic symbol of the resistance of the local economy against the power and values of the external economy. However, the long survival and then partial demise of cowries was also an indication of an internal struggle between migrant laborers, who created pockets of experience hundreds of miles from Lawra District, and the leaders of their households back home. Money affected the relationship between generations of men: young men used access to cash to wrestle some authority away from elders, while elders used cowries in an attempt to preserve some of their authority.

Well before the British first attempted to integrate the LoDagaa into their imperial network of economic relations, the local economy had been connected to an external, trading economy, as demonstrated by the huge number of cowries in circulation at the beginning of the twentieth century. At that time there was a well-developed network of local markets throughout Lawra District and beyond. Most *tengaan* had markets, to which people from the surrounding area traveled to exchange goods on a limited scale once every six days. Outside of funerals, markets were the most significant areas of social intercourse. Each market fell under the jurisdiction of the local *tengaansob* and had its own shrine, which acted as a restraint against violence between people of different territorial groups. The social importance of these markets far outweighed their economic importance.[85] There is little evidence that external traders attended these markets, even though significant trade routes passed through Lawra District.[86] Before the arrival of the British there were foreign traders resident in Kunyukuo along a route running north parallel to the Black Volta, and in Ulo and Han to the west. However, this trade – the exchange of salt, iron, and cattle from the north for kola from the south – involved items the LoDagaa either produced themselves or did not consume, and so probably had little impact on their economy.[87]

The cowry shells used as currency had entered these markets long ago from the external economy; however, almost nothing is known about how they originally did so. We do know that by the end of the nineteenth century the local economy was quite autonomous. It continued to remain distinct from the colonial economy for much of the twentieth century despite British efforts to replace it with a cash economy dependent on wage labor. The persistence of two economies into the postcolonial period explains why cowries continued to be used in Lawra District even though they disappeared as a currency from neighboring areas in the first half of the twentieth century.[88] How and why the LoDagaa retained the cowry as a local currency tells us a great deal about how the world on paper and the world of experience intersected and interacted.

Having opened up the district to wider communication, the colonial administration tried to suppress the cowry economy in order to force the LoDagaa to enter the colonial economy. Constables supervised local markets in an effort to ensure that colonial currency was accepted at an arbitrarily pegged rate of one thousand shells to the shilling. Petty cases of refusing to accept colonial currency were common throughout the colonial period. Administrators paid special attention to the cowry economy during both world wars, when the supply of metal coinage was restricted and officers were eager that the currency in circulation keep circulating. During both these periods of concentrated assault on the internal economy, officers were not satisfied with merely ensuring that colonial currency was accepted; they also made attempts – all of which ultimately failed – to displace the cowry as the predominant medium of exchange.

During the First World War, officers attributed the persistence of the cowry to the refusal of petty traders, almost exclusively LoDagaa women, to accept coins. Officers also contended that external traders were racketeering – that is, systematically manipulating and exploiting rates of exchange between cowries and coins. There is no doubt that the unofficial exchange rate fluctuated. It was not unusual for the exchange rate to fall by as much as 25 percent in a single month, as happened in May 1917 when the rate fell from eight hundred to six hundred cowries to the shilling. Those most immediately affected by these fluctuations were government employees. The administration was often forced to pay them in local currency. As the district commissioner explained, they "naturally do not care to receive 600 cowries in exchange for 1/- and if they do not receive cowries it is difficult to purchase proper value in the market, on the other hand if the government wishes to do away with them [cowries] it is best not to support the exchange."[89] Extra attempts were made to ensure that shillings were accepted, for example, by temporarily changing the exchange rate in May of 1917 to eight hundred cowries to the shilling, the official rate having been temporarily abandoned as impracticable.[90] Despite vigilant efforts to enforce the new rate, only eleven months after that the rate had returned to six hundred cowries, and four months later it had been "forced down" to as low as five hundred cowries to the shilling.[91]

Blame for the low value of the shilling, and for the strong preference for the cowry, was ultimately placed on the heads of the Hausa, Bambara, Dioula, Zabarima, and Mossi traders residing in Kunyukuo *zongo*.[92] They were found to have been demanding payment for goods at the official rate of one thousand cowries to the shilling, and then, after amassing a large quantity of cowries, selling them back for coins at a rate of six hundred to the shilling.[93] By 1919 the administration was being forced to buy large numbers of cowries from the chiefs in order to maintain the exchange rate of one thousand cowries to the shilling for their employees. Within two months 2,101,000 cowries had been exchanged for £105.5s. in silver coin.[94] The officer who devised this scheme confidently predicted that it would "gradually get more silver among the people. I think a little compulsion to change their cowries into silver will do no harm as it will do them good in the long run and is part of their education. ... It is the traders who are at the bottom of the trouble, really, I think."[95] Yet within two years, the Lawra market was unable to meet local demand even though there was no shortage of foodstuffs in the district. Local traders merely avoided regulated markets such as Lawra, preferring indigenous markets where the cowry was the exclusive medium of exchange and where, as there was no need to refuse colonial currency, there were no fines.

What the administration ignored was that the LoDagaa greatly preferred cowries and had little use for colonial coinage. This preference meant they were vulnerable to traders, who until the 1950s could buy cowries cheaply in neighboring economies (where they had already fallen into disuse) and sell them locally at considerable profit. It also meant that in the postcolonial period, when the local economy was more successfully subjected to the rule of money, the LoDagaa were undercapitalized.[96] However, fluctuations in the value of the shilling had less to do with profiteering by external traders than with the dynamics of the internal cowry economy.

The LoDagaa only really needed colonial currency to buy imported hoes and, after 1935, to pay taxes. Both these requirements were marginal compared with the scale of conjugal payments. In 1938 the district commissioner observed that "the currency problem continues to be troublesome," and offered the following account:

> Cowries are much preferred by the people, and market prices are lowered if payment is made in them. The payment of bride-price is expected to be made in cowries. If offered in money, the rate allowed is six hundred cowries to the

> shilling, instead of the previously accepted rate of one thousand to a shilling. Probably, with the increase in market trade outside of the district, the use of cowries will gradually lapse, as it has done elsewhere.[97]

It was the erratic demand for coinage that made the rate of exchange fluctuate continually, thereby making coins unstable currency.[98] The cost of hoes and taxes was easily met from the reserves of colonial currency that entered the economy indirectly through remittances from migrant laborers. During the counting of tax revenue in 1937, the district commissioner was "surprised to see that most of the takings were ... practically all old coins, and a large proportion showing signs of having been buried." As the most common date on the coins was 1920, he wondered if this was the "result of soldiers coming home from the War? I trust this does not mean that tax is being paid out of the local equivalent of [savings]."[99]

Both the introduction of taxation and the regulation of the exchange rate were attempts to stimulate trade and economic development. However, the absence of cash crops and the emphasis in the local economy on production for consumption meant that money was neither prevalent nor necessary. Items such as imported hoes had to be of high quality in order to compete with those made locally. By the 1940s adventure and cloth, not hoes and taxes, were already the primary motivations for labor migration.[100]

The administration was constantly attempting to stimulate demand for other goods from the external economy. By 1918 imported items sold in local markets included cloth, beads, ornamental swords, and umbrellas.[101] A decade later the list had expanded to include "bicycles, umbrellas, tin trunks, hats, handkerchiefs, rubber shoes, clocks and matches." Some officers questioned the quality of the merchandise; the annual report for 1928–29 called it "cheap, shoddy stuff and of gaudy striking colour or pattern."[102] Because these items were purchased mainly by migrant laborers with currency earned in the south, this trade did not have an immediate impact on the role of the cowry in the local economy.

Ironically, one of the most popular imports was cowry shells. In order to meet shortfalls resulting from breakage, loss, and increased demand due to population growth, cowries had to be imported from other areas of the Northern Territories, from neighboring French territory, or from Asante. According to French colonial police reports, in only one month in 1946 ten metric tons of cowries were introduced into the region of Gaoua, opposite Lawra District.[103] In 1947 cowries were still being imported across the Volta despite rates varying from one hundred to four hundred to the shilling.[104] Polly Hill noted that in the mid-1960s cowries were still a "genuine medium of exchange" in northwestern Ghana, and were still being imported from Kumase.[105]

Although administrators in the 1940s blamed the shunning of colonial currency on the fact that local production still met indigenous needs, they expressed confidence that this "primitive economy" would soon be displaced as the demand for colonial money increased.[106] How that would happen (other than spontaneously) was not explained. Administrators in Lawra assumed that the cowry would pass away there as it had elsewhere, even though they had no idea why the process was taking so long.

It has generally been accepted that the decline of the cowry in West Africa was due to hyperinflation at the end of the nineteenth century, which made the metal money of colonial governments more attractive as well as more practical. Chris Gregory has recently proposed a "subalternate quality theory" for the disappearance of the cowry that makes particular sense for the LoDagaa of Lawra District, where there is no evidence of a period of cowry hyperinflation at the end of the nineteenth century. According to Gregory, more important than supply was the effect that coercive measures taken by the British, such as monetary taxation, had on the demand for the cowry. Gregory rejects explanations for the disappearance of cowries that are based on a "quantity theory of money," and suggests that we look at money in much the same way that Street has suggested we look at literacy – not as a neutral medium, but as a potential "instrument of power."[107] For Gregory, the past focus on late nineteenth-century hyperinflation in the cowry economies of West Africa has disguised the later, crucial role of the colonial state in imposing metal and paper money by force. (Accordingly, the inability of the British to displace the cowry among the LoDagaa speaks both to the lack of power at their disposal to support colonial money and the ability of the LoDagaa to resist that limited power.) We must also consider the "iconic, indexical, and symbolic meaning" of money. The disappearance of the cowry, Gregory suggests, was not "natural"; rather it was the result of new cultural values being imposed, along with measures to reduce the demand for shells (and hence the economic value of them).[108] Conversely, where the cowry survived it was because its value was preserved, both economically and culturally.

From an economic perspective, an important factor favoring the retention of the cowry was inflation – that is, the erosion of the value of money with respect to cowries. In a perceptive article published in the *West African Review* in 1947 on the use of cowries in Lawra District, it was noted that in 1940 one shilling had been worth from 650 to 720 cowries, but by 1946 the rate of exchange had fallen to 250 cowries. The exchange rate is more meaningful when seen against the prices of commodities. In 1940, the article tells us, an unspecified quantity of guinea corn cost 12s.6d.; six years later the same quantity cost £1.10s. – an increase of 140 percent. During the same period 1,200 cowries went from 2s. to

5s. – an increase of 150 percent. Thus cowries maintained their purchasing power and more.[109]

From a cultural perspective, the retention of the cowry by the LoDagaa throughout the period of colonial rule is an important diagnostic tool for assessing the degree to which their culture successfully resisted integration into the colonial economy. In a discussion of "currencies of conversion" among the Tswana, the Comaroffs noted: "Quantification was iconic of the kind of standardization and incorporation, the erasure of differences in kind, at the core of cultural colonization." The core of the difference between indigenous and colonial currencies was located in how indigenous forms of wealth, particularly cattle, "inhered in relations."[110] Piot has noted much the same of the Kabre, among whom cowries, the main expression of value, were used to create relationships with other people more than "to gain access to things."[111] As among both the Tswana and the Kabre, among the LoDagaa local currency mediated extremely important social relationships both between households and between generations within households. As a medium of ritual and social interaction, cowries were implicated in the most intimate aspects of LoDagaa life. Just as writing did not displace speech, and colonial roads did not supersede footpaths, colonial currency did not replace cowries because it did not have the same qualities. That cowries were not accepted in colonial markets, just as noumenal knowledge was not accepted in colonial courts, did not mean they just disappeared.[112]

In 1942, during yet another period of intense colonial pressure on the cowry economy, the district commissioner complained: "The trouble about cowries is due to the double standard and the refusal to accept coin, which undoubtedly bears hardly on wage earners as well as allottees and returned miners etc." He added: "The recalcitrants are the women and the origin of the problem lies in dowry and funeral dues. Only time can cure this in my opinion."[113] Most of the colonial currency entering the internal economy was indeed used for conjugal payments, as the district commissioner suggested in his diary eight months later:

> The institution of Separation Allowances has been interesting. Numbers of small girls have been brought up as nominated wives of soldiers. I am sure this was not in the minds of the authors of this great reform, but I am paying them as the promised husbands would, if not in the army, have been paying various brideprice instalments. The allowance takes the place of this, and is perfectly good native custom, though probably encouraging one of the less desirable manifestations of it, i.e. child betrothal. Another comment, at any rate on the local application, is that it puts still more currency, brought at great risk from England, out of

> circulation. At least I have been quite unable to trace any outlet for the sudden influx of money [soldiers' allotments] to the District since the war. There still is little to buy in the shops or from itinerant pedlars, and the markets seem no brisker than they were. A certain amount of mutual washing is done, chiefly in laying up cattle for the soldier on his return. But where does all the rest go?[114]

The underlying reason why the LoDagaa preferred the cowry had been explained to another district commissioner twenty years earlier by his interpreter, Binney: "They want cowries to marry women with."[115] The dynamics of the cowry economy were antithetical to those of a cash-based economy: cowries were a store of wealth whose value was derived directly from the fact that they were used to make conjugal payments, whereas cash had only a purchase value and its value was derived mainly from the loss of labor to the external economy. In the early 1980s Evans reported that among the LoBirifor of Kalba, "shells are scarce and difficult to get hold of unless one is part of the social and ritual networks through which they circulate."[116] Cowries functioned as a mechanism for maintaining social boundaries, between insiders and outsiders as well as between generations.

Because of the large amount of wealth involved, conjugal payments affected relationships both between and within households. It is difficult to state typical amounts for these payments because of variations between congeries as well as between households. Rattray mentioned a cowry payment of ten to fifteen thousand cowries among the Lobi, and a second payment of three cows.[117] Goody's figures for LoWiili payments were similar, although the average cowry payment was five thousand more.[118] Payments among the neighboring LoBirifor were higher: thirty thousand cowries and five to six cows.[119] Rattray noted that among the Dagaba, the initial cowry payment was larger than in areas of dual descent, ranging from thirty to fifty thousand cowries, but there was no uniform pattern for secondary payments, which could be made either in animals other than cattle or again in cowries – sometimes as many as another twenty thousand.[120] Notwithstanding these variations, all conjugal payments were extremely high. The value of payments cannot be measured against external indices, but must instead be measured against the relative scarcity of the goods (cowries and animals) involved. For example, at the end of nineteenth century a hoe had cost five thousand cowries, which was considered to be equal to the average value of a cow. Goody was told: "Poor men could not always afford to buy a hoe for each of their sons and these might have [had] to take turns at using their father's."[121] The LoDagaa had smelted iron (blacksmiths being the only economically specialized workers in the precolonial economy), but the scale of this production never satisfied local demand.[122] Iron was still "a scarce and valuable commodity" in the early twentieth century, and remained a material with "considerable ritual as well as economic value."[123] Given the reliance of the LoDagaa on labor-intensive agriculture, the importance of hoes to both their culture and their economy cannot be overestimated: they were the essential and irreplaceable tools of production. But if hoes, the means of agricultural production, were expensive, then conjugal payments, the resources necessary for household reproduction, were even more so.[124] Before new forms of wealth were introduced in this century, late nineteenth-century households had had to rely entirely on incoming payments received for female members to be able to make payments for wives of male members; this made both cowries and cows circulating forms of wealth.[125] The cowries used in conjugal payments were thus usually only acquired through the shift in residence of a female member of a household.

These forms of wealth were held not individually but as corporate property. Inheritance established custodianship over property, but it also involved a set of horizontal and vertical obligations. According to Rattray, among the Dagaba a father was responsible for providing the wealth necessary for a son to obtain a first wife.[126] So long as he continued to farm for his father, or his father's successor, a son was also entitled, subject to availability, to a further share of corporate wealth with which to obtain further wives. If he began to farm on his own, such entitlement ceased.[127] As Goody observed, a man farming separately from his lineage would not have been able to accumulate sufficient surplus or wealth to acquire a wife on his own.[128] In contrast, among the LoDagaba, Goody noted that a father was responsible only for the conjugal payments for his son's first wife; thereafter, even if he continued to farm for his father, the son relied on assistance from his mother's brother. Accordingly, such assistance was offered so long as the nephew farmed for his uncle.[129] Among all congeries, conjugal payments ensured the integrity of corporate farming and property-holding groups, and also created relationships of dependence between younger and older generations.[130]

Within the internal economy, cowries affected other forms of storable wealth, particularly cattle. Cows were often treated as an intermediary and self-reproducing form of wealth that could be realized for cowries when necessary.[131] The administration perceived the retention of cowries as directly related to attitudes toward cattle. In 1918 one officer noted a general disinterest in the cattle trade, but added: "Once the people begin to feel the need of money and discover that there is money in their cattle, they will begin to take greater interest."[132] A year later another officer complained: "At present many of them neither milk, eat or sell their cattle, which were and are to them but so many tokens."[133] Not until after 1945 did the administration shift its attention from regulating the cowry economy to promoting trade with southern Ghana (particularly the cattle market at Kumase). Colonial officers still considered indigenous attitudes to be the main obstacle to the commercialization or commodification of cattle. Such attitudes had been a source of frustration to earlier administrators keen to encourage commercial activity among the LoDagaa. Assumptions about LoDagaa attitudes toward cattle totally ignored the social and cultural uses of animals. As Goody reported in the 1950s: "The keeping of cattle and other domestic animals is regarded by the inhabitants as essentially peripheral to farming; their possession creates a reserve of wealth to be used for marriage payments and for sacrifices to shrines."[134]

In the immediate postwar period, cowries became increasingly scarce, through attrition from loss and breakage, as well as dispersion due to population growth. Also, traders were now finding it so time-consuming to acquire cowries from neighboring areas that the trade was hardly profitable.[135] Meanwhile, cattle became more plentiful, largely because of the successful vaccination program begun in 1930 against rinderpest. In the past, disease had decimated herds from time to time, keeping populations down. Hill has demonstrated that the expansion in cattle herds following the introduction of immunization led to a corresponding expansion in the cattle trade with the south. The cattle trade of the Northern Territories as a whole expanded threefold between 1954 and 1960, after the same increase in stocks between 1931 and 1952.[136] The increase in the cattle trade stabilized the size of holdings. In 1948 the ratio of cattle to the human population was 1:2.5, while in 1964 it was 1:2.9.[137] Cattle thus retained their value in the internal economy, in which exchange value was determined by availability or relative scarcity. Whether the expansion in trade was directly related to commercialization or was merely the result of the expansion of stock and the limited carrying capacity of land in areas like Lawra District, it is clear that cattle were being sold rather than just exchanged and sacrificed. By the late 1980s the commercialization of cattle and an accompanying economic crisis had made it difficult to obtain cattle in the region.[138]

During most of the colonial period, cowries maintained boundaries between the internal sphere of social relations, where they acted as a medium of circulation and an index of participation, and the external domain of economic relations, where cash acted as a medium of exchange and means of exclusion. Social practices and cultural values that directly affected the internal economy made it somewhat difficult for migrant laborers to act independently of their households during the colonial period. Even after they had earned the cash equivalent of the payments necessary to procure a wife, they still relied on their lineages for those forms of wealth peculiar to the internal economy. This situation began to change in the 1960s, when the cowry economy came under increasing pressure from the cash economy due to the shortage of cowries and the rising wages of migrant laborers. Cash began to be substituted. In the late 1970s a series of court cases over the appropriate medium of payments suggested that the increasing scarcity of cowries had begun to adversely affect those LoDagaa who participated in the external cash economy. Labor migration had long alleviated many of the tensions that had formerly led to internal migration; now, the return of migrants combined with growth in the population permanently resident in the district was creating land shortages. Also, migrant laborers were often discriminated against through the insistence that cowries be used to make conjugal payments. As it became increasingly difficult to exchange cash for cowries, these laborers were prevented from reintegrating themselves with the internal economy. Since the beginning of labor migration, tensions had been emerging between elders and young men over the appropriate age at which the latter should be given economic independence from their natal households. The retention of cowries as a medium of exchange was one way that the former could maintain some of their authority as recipients, custodians, and distributors of conjugal payments.[139]

Even when they could not assert their authority through control of cowries, elders were able to maintain their leadership because their main sources of authority were not material but noumenal. Age conferred on elders exclusive access to a series of noumenal agencies that were crucial in affording protection against misfortune, and in ensuring good health and prosperity within the household. The most important shrines were those controlled by household elders, such as the tutelary shrine of the household clan, the medicine shrine of the lineage, and the shrines of individual ancestors.[140] As Goody observed in the 1950s, "the power of the father is buttressed by his position as custodian of the ancestor shrines."[141] In the 1990s, Lentz found that migrant workers were most dependent on their households when it came to funerals, social security, and finding wives. Funerals in particular were considered crucial for "human dignity." For all LoDagaa, whether literate or illiterate, whether migrant workers or local farmers, whether Christians or non-Christians, the household and its ancestors were still a dominant presence because of the continuing relevance of the noumenal world, through which the world of experience derived its most significant meanings.[142]

Cowries continued to be used as a medium for conjugal payments into the 1980s, but their increasing scarcity made it necessary to supplement them more and more often with cash. Because there was no means of augmenting the declining number of shells in circulation, the encroachment of the national currency was irresistible. Only here does a "quantity theory of money" help explain the disappearance of the cowry, but the problem was one of scarcity rather than oversupply. Even as the cowry disappeared as a literal unit of value, it still retained its figurative value. In much the same way that Hutchinson has described how the Nuer "'cattle-ified'" cash instead of commodifying cattle, the LoDagaa "cowry-ified" cash rather than commercializing cowries.[143] The available sources make pinpointing the demise of the cowry difficult. The Court Record Books of the direct-rule period always quoted conjugal payments in currency even though they were most certainly made in cowries; and the courts of the postcolonial period cited payments in cowries even when the actual payment was in cash. Evans reported in 1981 that among the LoBirifor of Kalba, cash was used for such payments more often than cowries, but that informants continued to quote amounts in cowries. In other words, cowries continued to be used as the unit of account even when they were not the actual medium of payment.[144] As late as the early 1990s demands for conjugal payments in cowries were still not uncommon in Lawra District, even by Christian parents. This prompted the Bishop of Wa and other prominent Catholic leaders to call for measures to alleviate the problems associated with the shortage of cowries.[145]

However, tensions had begun to grow much earlier. In the late 1970s cases involving the substitution of cash for cowries began to reach the District Court – a possible indication that the scarcity of cowries was becoming acute. This was also a period of considerable inflation in the external cash economy, when the advantages of the cowry would have been especially clear, and the substitution of cash for cowries far less acceptable, even dangerous, as its value quickly eroded. By the 1970s certain sectors in LoDagaa society were calling for the replacement of cowries. This culminated in 1980 with the Lawra Confederacy Traditional Council advocating changes in "customary marriage procedures": "As regards to the high demand of bride-price and the continuous acceptance of white cowries as a means of dowry, the Traditional Council is fighting all odds and ends to reduce bride-prices and also to abolish white cowries as a means of dowry. The Council is also advocating strongly for the total abolition of the present animal and cowries system and the introduction of a nominal fee system."[146] In the 1980s and early 1990s there were successive calls for a reduction in conjugal payments because the cost of payments was increasing in terms of cash equivalents.[147]

These calls for reform were due to problems in the external economy, which became increasingly erratic and undependable in the 1970s and 1980s, rather than in the internal economy. For example, in 1979 Kuufam Bewaa claimed the remaining conjugal payments from Kpibagr, who had eloped with his daughter more than eight years earlier. Kuufam had initially refused to consent to the union because Kpibagr intended to take the woman with him to the gold mines of Prestea, where he worked as a miner. The woman had been returned to Kuufam after he persistently refused to accept the conjugal payments, but she eventually "escaped" from her father's house back to Kpibagr. At this point, sometime around 1972, Kuufam summoned Kpibagr's parents before the subchief to demand full presentation of all conjugal payments. The subchief was alleged to have mentioned that the "traditional rulers" had convened recently at Lawra, where they had decided that all payments should be reduced to a cash payment of 140 cedis. The plaintiff agreed to settle for two hundred cedis, "since cowries were difficult to come by," as well as one thousand cowries in lieu of farming services, five hundred cowries for mediation, three hundred sixty cowries as the "greeting," and three guinea fowl and a fowl. Later, however, Kuufam insisted that the cash payment had not included payment for the outstanding cattle. In 1976 the chief of Lambussie had settled this matter in Kuufam's favour; he interpreted the cedis as only representing the cowries, leaving the cattle outstanding. Three years later, Kpibagr had still not presented the cattle to Kuufam.

During the hearing before the District Court, the following exchange took place between Kuufam and Kpibagr, as inquisitor and respondent respectively: "How are dowries paid according to the custom of our area? A: With Christians all dowries are paid but with pagans the first is paid and then one farms for the in-laws for sometime before paying the second part. Q: Did you marry my daughter in the Christian or the pagan way? A: She was eloped in the pagan way and because you said we did not farm for you, you demanded full payment."[148]

Kuufam was trying to specify payments in terms of their timing. This was now necessary because cash had no specific social or cultural meaning, and so was open to reinterpretation when it was converted back into cowries. Within the internal economy, this confusion could not have arisen, as cowries represented distinct elements in the series of payments, whereas cash was culturally nonspecific.

The basis of the dispute seems to have been economic rather than cultural, even though the amount (two hundred cedis) was not disputed – only what it represented. In the intervening seven years between the cash payment having been made and the case coming to court, the value of the cowry was far more stable than that of the cedi. The subchief who first heard the case in 1972 told the court that ten thousand cowries had been equal to twenty cedis; by 1979 the same quantity of cowries was equivalent to two hundred cedis. It appears that Kuufam was attempting to reinterpret the original cash payment, which had no cultural meaning and therefore was open to such reinterpretation, in order to make up for the loss he had suffered during the intervening period due to spiraling inflation. Finally, although the subchief denied having forced Kuufam to accept cash or having stated that the Traditional Council had made such a ruling, the court ruled that he had. The court suggested that the chief had only denied making the statement because the council's ruling was "absurd," arguing that "custom must be permitted to prevail and if there are any amendments to it the entire people to be affected would be informed accordingly."[149] The plaintiff was awarded "payments of last dowries" assessed in the following manner: one bull at six hundred cedis, one cow at seven hundred cedis, and a final cow or ten thousand cowries at two hundred cedis. The difference between this and the first settlement is startling, and explains Kuufam's need to reinterpret the original cash settlement.

The disadvantages of cash as a medium for conjugal payments are equally well illustrated by the case of Nua Dagarti *vs.* Jattoe Dagarti. Sometime before 1974, Jattoe had taken Nua's daughter, Ayor, as a wife although she had a husband at the time. When Jattoe presented the payments, he explained to Nua that he could not "afford" cowries; but the former husband, Lolloh, demanded cowries as he had presented Nua with them and wanted the same in return. So Nua was forced to reject payments in cash. Jattoe later reported to Nua that there had been a Traditional Council meeting where it had been decided that payments should be made in cash and not cowries, so he was taking the matter before the Nadawli Naa, who had allegedly been party to this ruling, so they could reach a compromise. Lolloh again refused to accept the substitution of cash for cowries, saying that his senior brother, then in Kumase, would have to decide the matter.

In 1981, seven years later, the senior brother, Tamasu, returned and instructed Lolloh to receive cash instead of cowries. The Nadawli Naa asked Tamasu to calculate the cash equivalent of the cowries at the present rate, and a figure of ten thousand cedis was arrived at. This figure was later substantiated in court. The underlying issue of the dispute had been the exchange rate, which was claimed to have gone from approximately eighty cowries to ¢1 in 1974, to five cowries to ¢1 in 1981. (To place these figures in a wider context, in 1977 the daily wage for miners was ¢6.27 for surface workers and ¢6.29 for underground workers, but by 1981 the minimum daily wage of any worker in Ghana was, at least officially, ¢12.)[150] Jattoe strenuously objected to this calculation, stating that he had already given six hundred cedis to the chief in 1974 to be given to Lolloh as payment. This money had been rejected and had remained with the chief. The chief, however, claimed that he had received the cash as a fee for pleading Jattoe's case with Lolloh's household, and that it did not represent conjugal payments – a somewhat plausible interpretation at 1981 exchange rates, but not at those of 1974. The magistrate accepted Jattoe's rhetorical argument that the cash he paid to the chief must have represented the conjugal payments: "Which man would marry another man's wife for seven years without performing or returning the dowries? ... No man will give birth to children with a woman when he has not dowried her." It was decided that although the cash had not been accepted, Jattoe had fulfilled the necessary payments when presenting the cash to the chief; but, as we will see in Chapter 8, this decision had much more to do with issues of blood than money.[151]

The collision between cowries and cash in the 1970s and after did not produce the expected result. There is no evidence that the size of conjugal payments increased in this century.[152] But for those who came to rely on the money economy, these payments did become increasingly expensive. Money displaced cowries as the medium of exchange, but it did not dissolve the logic or values associated with the formation and maintenance of conjugal unions. Père's informants from the other side of the Black Volta told her in the 1980s that "Money has replaced cowries, which have gone away, as two kings cannot live together." However, as we have already seen, becoming a chief was one thing, gaining legitimacy or hegemony was another.[153] The integrity of the internal economy was maintained by the use of the cowry as the unit of account – virtual cowries if you will – even as actual cowries became scarcer and therefore less and less practical as a currency.[154] The disappearance of actual cowries toward the end of the twentieth century was due not to devaluation but to their increasing scarcity, which made them increasingly expensive in terms of cash. Their increasing scarcity not only maintained boundaries between the internal circulation of wealth and the external cash economy,[155] but also marginalized individuals participating in the external economy. During some years of the 1980s, when annual inflation rates soared well in excess of 100 percent, the cowry's attraction as an index of value was obvious. However, the attractions of the cowry were not only economic, but also aesthetic and cultural.

Ranajit Guha has pointed out the parallels between the transformation of living labor into money, or "dead labor," through the commodification of time by nineteenth-century capitalism, and the transformation of a living past by the British in India into an appropriated history through the objectification of time.[156] In a similar vein, Ewald has suggested that there is a connection between writing and commodity exchange. "Market exchange reifies goods or labor into commodities," she wrote, "standardized taxation ... likewise turns goods into commodities," and documents transform "sounds carried on living breath into objects that live independently of their human creators."[157] In these respects pinpointed by Guha and Ewald, money belongs to the world on paper and its various projects of conversion. The encounter between colonial currency and cowries did not redefine the relationship between the LoDagaa and their past, as in "the jagged time of rise and fall, of beginning and end," but it did affect relationships in the present between different spaces – namely, between the internal and external economies. These two worlds of values intersected but remained distinct. Colonial money represented dead labor; cowries represented, both literally and metaphorically, living and future labor. The lure of cash was for the things that it could buy, not the relationships it could create; whereas cowries built, maintained, and transformed relationships. Finally, colonial and postcolonial currency was vulnerable to the vagaries of time, but cowries maintained their value over time. The contrasts between these two media encapsulate some of the fundamental differences between the world on paper and the world of experience.

Unlike colonial money, missionary medicine did not embody values that clashed with those of the world of experience. On the contrary, it was popular precisely because it meshed so closely with indigenous concerns, rituals, and knowledge. Contrary to missionaries in other parts of Africa who placed more emphasis on the Bible – that is, on the written word – as a medium for their message, the White Fathers in Lawra District adopted local existential concerns and addressed them through a currency whose value was proven by experience rather than by annunciation or reading.[158] Missionary medicine, like cowries, was easily translated into *experience*; colonial money could only be translated into *things*, that is, experience commodified.

Conclusion to Part 3

All the encounters discussed in this part of the book are best described as spatial. The forms of LoDagaa knowledge that intersected with the logic and rituals of the colonial courts concerned the relationship between the phenomenal and noumenal worlds, as well as the relationships between settlements and between different ritual areas. The new currency of the courts, writing (in the form of a variety of bureaucratic practices), clearly belonged to the world on paper, just as the knowledge and practices it displaced belonged to the world of experience. The political disaffection that fueled the mass movement toward Catholicism led to the establishment of a parallel space, a counterculture, to the colonial world. The encounter between missionary medicine and LoDagaa beliefs, also predicated on knowledge of the relationship between the visible and invisible, resulted in a convergence of ideas and practices. Finally, where colonial money and cowries met the relationship was layered, producing independent spheres of value and exchange. All these encounters were different, but they were all about the meeting of different spaces. Accordingly, these encounters did not objectify time and create a history that can be conceived of temporally, as in a narrative; instead, they objectified space and so must be seen in terms of a series of new and changing spatial relationships.

Some practices from the world on paper became more dominant than analogous practices belonging to the world of experience. For example, how words fell on paper during the rituals of writing performed in the courts displaced the importance of the direction in which a mat fell on the ground during a ceremony at a funeral. However, knowledge from the world on paper did not replace knowledge of the noumenal world; the latter was only excluded from colonial rituals, which were designed to assert control over the world of experience. The courts did not represent a break with the past, but rather the emergence of a parallel world that was the source of new powers based on written words rather than actions and physical rather than noumenal force. The courts symbolized the world of external power that conquered the world of experience at the beginning of the twentieth century and that has attempted to regulate it ever since. But the world on paper did not succeed in regulating the world of experience, any more than it managed to replace knowledge of the noumenal world.

One might assume that because the LoDagaa embraced the courts, the values of those courts came to dominate their lives in ways that colonial money, which they resisted more successfully, did not. But the retention of the cowry also signified that the social practices surrounding conjugal unions resisted the logic of the world on paper. This is not surprising when one considers that the most important use of cowries was to make conjugal payments, and that conjugal unions were the main source of disputes brought before the courts. The preservation of the cowry indicates the degree of autonomy that social practices had in relation to the colonial courts. The LoDagaa went to court and made rhetorical representations of their world that fit the expectations of the world on paper (see Chapters 7 and 8), but they did not change the logic of practices that mediated social relationships in the world of experience.

PART FOUR

From Social Practice to Rhetoric

Chapter Seven

Women, Marriage, and Adultery

Dagaaba claim that "the woman is like a wild guinea fowl that we bring home (in marriage) to tame." Like the guinea fowl, she is gullible and "slippery" – difficult to get hold of. Men therefore have to use all sorts of tricks and persuasive words (during the process of courting) to win her hand.

Father Tengan, "The Institution of Marriage among the Dagaaba," 1990

The suppression of indigenous means of defining and resolving disputes made the courts inescapable. By the beginning of the 1930s the rule of the chiefs had become firmly entrenched in practice as well as on paper, although this by no means indicated the total conquest and displacement of LoDagaa knowledge and social practice by colonial ideas and methods. The chiefs dominated the LoDagaa politically in the name of different British monarchs; the cash economy transformed the meaning of work; and the courts intruded on experiences. Still, by decade's end many LoDagaa had succeeded in creating an alternative political order that mirrored the colonial regime. The persistent use of the cowry shell as a medium of exchange was another significant means of holding out against colonial domination. Although neither form of resistance was entirely successful in warding off the major political and economic transformations that colonialism imposed on the LoDagaa, successful resistance to the influence of the courts on practices enabled the LoDagaa to maintain a considerable degree of social sovereignty. A careful reading of court records, found in this and the next chapter, reveals forms of social rather than political or economic resistance.

During the 1930s, with the creation of Native Authorities, courts became an official and undeniable presence among the LoDagaa, a further step in the shift that Fortes called "the substitution of courts for bows and arrows." Fortes used the phrase in 1937 to describe the effects of colonialism on Tallensi culture, observing that "traditional attitudes about marrying another man's wife still maintain a strong hold, so that cases of seduction of e.g. a clansman's wife seldom or never reach a Chief's court. But with the substitution of courts for bows and arrows, it is now possible for a man to bring an action against someone in a distant settlement who in former times could have married his wife with impunity."[1] Notwithstanding its evolutionary assumptions and overtones of primitiveness, the phrase is apposite, as it highlights a real shift from social practice to rhetorical representations, or actions to words, in approaches to resolving disputes. LoDagaa litigants made increasing use of the courts from the early 1930s into the 1990s. Over this same period, these courts demanded that litigants frame their claims and arguments in terms of foreign categories of understanding. Nevertheless, social practices were not themselves directly affected by rhetorical representations made in the courts by either judges or litigants. Where particular practices came under the direct surveillance and control of the courts, such as those associated with adultery,[2] elopement, and child custody, the effect of court decisions on practices outside the courts was minimal. The dissonance between what was said in the courts and what continued to be done outside them is one of the main subjects of the rest of this book.

There were two main reasons for this dissonance. The first has to do with the unilateral direction of translation, from the world of experience to the world on paper but not back again. Even though litigants deferred to the rhetorical demands of the courts, social actors resisted changing their practices to make them accord with the world on paper. Although the means of defining and resolving disputes changed, social practices remained relatively unscathed by the paradigms of administrators and the judicial strictures of the courts. Early decisions by the courts produced outcomes that were neither probable nor, most often, even possible within the repertoire of available social practices. These decisions created unprecedented expectations that in turn brought more people to court as litigants. However, these expectations did not become normative; they could only be realized by coming to court. That new social practices were not created outside the courts to realize these new expectations suggests that for some people going to court became itself a social practice.

The second source of dissonance resulted from the false hegemony of words over actions, or of things said over things done but most often left unsaid.[3] The courts, and those who came to use them as a new form of social practice – namely, older, powerful, or wealthy men – believed that their decisions would be effective because of the power of words over actions. In contrast, women in general and young men without power or wealth did not ask the courts to intervene. This part of the book explores how these latter groups were either silenced or ignored in the court records where words reigned, but not outside the courts where actions were what mattered. The attention accorded to the voices of chiefs and old husbands in the court records disguised their lack of hegemony outside the courts. Similarly, the lack of attention given to the voices of women and young men in the court records ignored the agency they enjoyed outside the courts.

Of those marginalized by the courts, women were most conspicuous by their almost complete absence as litigants. However, they were by no means peripheral to the courts. Women spoke as witnesses to disputes about their own lives, and men, as litigants, told stories about women. Although colonial courts almost always denied the aspirations and interests of women, their work highlighted how important control over women was to the colonial project. This project was distinctly patriarchal, and shaped by the conjuncture of male interests – those of British officers and LoDagaa chiefs, elders, and other prominent men. The greatest challenge the LoDagaa posed to British control, even greater than their highly contextual, elusive, and local sense of identity, resulted from the autonomy that women enjoyed outside the courts. As the Northern Territories Annual Report of 1907 complained, referring specifically to the LoDagaa, "the constancy with which a woman changes her husband would be humorous if it were not for the trouble it gives."[4] Denied an active voice in the courts, women continued to exercise their agency outside them, speaking, again, through actions rather than words.

The courts attempted to shape the identities of LoDagaa women as wives, to define their relationships with men as marriage, and to use the concept of adultery to punish younger and less powerful men and so prevent them from eloping with the wives of older men and chiefs. However, the courts' use of concepts such as wife, marriage, and adultery was highly problematic because of the lack of commensurability between indigenous practices and these categories of colonial control.

The first ethnographic account of the LoDagaa was written in 1908 by Read, an unmarried military officer, who only a few years earlier had been using force to "pacify" the very people who now fell under his civilian administration. Now required to provide ethnographic data rather than military intelligence, he ended his report by expressing the hope "that the present family system will break down as soon as possible for the sake of the future welfare and prosperity of the country." He based his conclusions on the following observations: there was no marriage ceremony; "the head money system" was similar to purchase; LoDagaa women did not make good wives; the unfaithfulness of wives had led to a considerable amount of armed conflict before colonial intervention; and disputes over the custody of children were so common between rival males that, quoting a line from Homer's *Odyssey*, "'it is a wise child that knows his father.'"[5] The quotation, meant to convey the idea of social and moral anarchy, was also undoubtedly a reference to the theory of primitive promiscuity that dominated British anthropological thinking at that time.[6]

At the beginning of the twentieth century, LoDagaa women exercised a large degree of autonomy, so much so that one might say it was a wise husband who knew who his wife was. For the LoDagaa at this time, certainty of paternity was not a matter of concern. Indeed, Goody reported almost half a century later that it was said of children whose physiological and social paternity diverged that "they know their father," where father referred to *genitor* rather than *pater*.[7] But certainty of paternity was of considerable concern to Read and his successors, and this concern would affect LoDagaa attitudes by the end of the century.

For many early administrators, the absence of the same "ideological valuations" and "ritual elaborations" (to use Tambiah's terms) concerning relationships between men and women was as inconvenient and irksome as the absence of identifiable leaders and recognizable patterns of authority. The annual report of 1907 attributed the inconstancy of LoDagaa women to "the absence of any strict laws or even customs over matrimony."[8] In 1938, a generation later, after an intensive period of direct rule, the district commissioner of the same area was still able to write that "the ever-recurring problem of the district is the marriage problem."[9] These administrators did not define marriage, or attempt to ascertain whether it was a category of indigenous experience, or investigate its nature, or place it in the context of other indigenous social practices. Instead, they merely identified it and conveniently ascribed to it all possible social conflicts, thereby ignoring the complex and separate issues that informed disputes, which were often dismissed as "mammy palavers."[10] This identification of marriage as a social problem was highly significant for the colonial and postcolonial history of the LoDagaa. Not only were indigenous means of resolving disputes suppressed and displaced by the imposition of foreign judicial structures, but litigants before these courts were forced to define most disputes in terms of marriage, their ascribed cause.

In different written accounts of LoDagaa society – administrative, ethnographic, and autoethnographic – there are a number of discrete and integral descriptions of various social practices as marriage.[11] Despite this, the courts never arrived at a satisfactory definition of marriage. The lack of fit between administrative assumptions and LoDagaa experiences is not surprising, given that administrators were motivated mainly by expediency and were eager to impose their own conceptual order on LoDagaa practices. Autoethnographies written in the postcolonial period by LoDagaa Christians were equally distorted. Eager to narrow the distance between the idea of Christian marriage and indigenous conjugal practices, these accounts assimilated a standardized anthropological understanding of marriage and mimicked a logic derived from external sources rather than from indigenous practices.[12]

Although ethnographers were by no means oblivious to the problems of translation, they often ignored critical historical contexts as well as the methodological distortions that writing imposed on their observations.[13] Two significant exceptions were Labouret and Fortes. Writing of "the rules of marriage" of the neighboring *Lobi*, Labouret noted that because there were no fixed rules, the effect of the courts was to systemize local practices, with the result that elucidated rules constituted only "a type of compromise that is not based on indigenous institutions."[14] Similarly, writing of the "marriage laws" of the Tallensi, Fortes pointed out that it was necessary to distinguish "the more strictly legal from the less strictly legal customs" for the purposes of administration. Yet this was problematic, because "even the most innocuous and ostensibly non-legal custom sometimes has great legal importance." Furthermore, some of these practices had already changed a great deal since the advent of "the white man."[15] Even so, the Tallensi still did not make any distinction between "experimental" and stable or legal unions, which made any perceived rights quite uncertain: "Observance of the jural properties gives a husband a weapon with which he can assert his rights to and over his wife. It does not give him an absolute guarantee of these rights nor does it ensure the stability of the marriage."[16] In the absence of a means to exercise them, rights were only coincidental, and then only occasionally, with interests and practices.

The Tallensi spoke a language quite similar to that of the LoDagaa, and their social practices were also very similar. When Goody did his work among the LoDagaa in the early 1950s, colonial courts had been in existence for almost two generations, and yet he made no mention of them, just as Rattray had failed to mention their existence when he conducted his fieldwork in the same area in the late 1920s. Both anthropologists isolated and analyzed rights that were not assured in practice and never had been and never would be. A close reading of a number of ethnographic accounts, including the work of Rattray and Goody, reveals that conjugal unions were the result of complicated and uncertain negotiations that in turn produced ambiguities and contradictions in LoDagaa social practices. We cannot make sense of the court records until we recognize these social realities in the world of experience. A reliance on ethnographic and autoethnographic representations would lead to the ridiculous conclusion that practices in the world outside the courts did not make sense.

Negotiations, Complications, and Ambiguities

Despite the assumptions of Labouret and Fortes that *Lobi* and Tallensi social practices would in time come to accord with written distillations of them, this did not occur among the LoDagaa. The courts succeeded in conditioning the rhetoric and expectations as well as the normative statements of potential informants, but not the social practices surrounding the formation, maintenance, and dissolution of conjugal unions. Although affected by colonialism, these practices were not readily susceptible to change because of the inherent ambiguity of conjugal unions. The social practices that Read observed (albeit without understanding them) did not change significantly between the beginning of the century and the early 1990s.[17] This claim can be made without prejudice for several reasons. First, the retention of the cowry as a medium of exchange for so long, and as a unit of account for even longer, was a manifestation of the degree to which conjugal and affinal relations were conducted in a sphere separate from the colonial economy. Second, the causes of litigation before the District Commissioner's Court in the 1900s were the same as those recorded in the District Magistrate's Court in the 1980s. Finally, successive accounts by observers in every decade of the twentieth century show very little variation in practices, and those which do exist can be accounted for by variations between different congeries, not by historical change.[18] Such accounts can be corroborated by evidence gleaned from a careful reading of numerous court cases from 1907 onward.[19]

What did change, and often greatly, was the historical context of these practices and how they were interpreted in colonial and postcolonial milieus. The most obvious change was that external observers categorized a series of social practices as marriage at the beginning of the last century. What was repeatedly categorized by observers of LoDagaa social relations was in fact a series of practices not generically classified as marriage by the LoDagaa themselves. Such a taxonomic device simply did not exist among the LoDagaa at the beginning of the twentieth century. A series of social practices were interpreted as marriage, even though such a concept was not generative of those practices. Most subsequent observers viewed the various social practices involved in forming, maintaining, and dissolving conjugal unions as constitutive of marriage when in fact there still was no indigenous word for this external category of social representation. It is thus not surprising that even though he drew the wrong conclusions from it, Read could have doubted the existence of marriage among the LoDagaa. One of the most striking aspects of conjugal unions was that they were not the result of any marked ceremony. This observation was made by both Read and Goody, half a century apart, with the latter noting that in the wider Voltaic region, people placed "little emphasis on marriage ceremonies, that is, upon the transfer of bridewealth and change of residence of the woman."[20] Yet the transfer of conjugal payments from one group to another, and the corresponding shift in residence of women in the opposite direction, constituted one of the most significant areas of social relations. This was true whether measured in terms of the amount of time spent in negotiating these relationships, both conjugal and affinal, or in terms of the amounts of wealth alienated.

Although LoDagaa, practices remained remarkably consistent, innovative interpretations of those practices emerged in the courts. This meant that matters formerly contested through actions were transmuted into issues disputed through words. Although the term marriage was used as a means of access to colonial patriarchy and postcolonial legitimacy, this alien concept never achieved sufficient influence outside the courts to actually lead to an alteration or adaptation of practices. Language referring to conjugal unions remained highly contextual; it had to be to accommodate both the autonomy that women had enjoyed before the colonial period, which made unions uncertain, and the rivalry between men, which made them unstable. Among the LoDagaa the terms most commonly translated as marriage were the gender-specific and locational terms *de pog*, "take a wife," and *kul sir*, "go to a man." There were no terms referring to a conjugal institution; there was only the agreement of man and woman to live with each other. Similarly, terms for the dissolution of unions were equally locational, with the man sending the woman away or the woman leaving the man.[21]

Strategies leading to the formation of conjugal unions were diverse. Colonial accounts did not identify these different strategies. In written distillations of conjugal practices made by literate LoDagaa where these diverse practices were identified, one finds an insistence that all of these practices were equivalent to marriage. Yet at the same time, the diversity of practices, many of which contradicted each other, militated against such a convenient categorization. Dery named three different procedures for acquiring a wife, Bishop Kpiebaya four, Father Bekye eight, and Father Tengan nine. Although each procedure had a specific term attached to it, there was no word that referred to all of these methods generically.[22] Although Dery claimed that "marriage as a social institution is universal," Father Kuukure conceded that in terms of *Dagaare* terminology the term marriage was an "abstraction."[23]

Men followed three distinct types of strategies for obtaining wives, although all came under the same rubric of taking a wife: betrothal, courtship, and abduction or elopement. For women, betrothal and courtship were the most common forms of first unions. Rattray provided the first comprehensive description of these formal procedures, and Goody, following Fortes's lead, extended anthropological knowledge with a jural interpretation of the same practices.[24] But although these accounts are all internally coherent and persuasive, they do not mention that unions resulting from these two sets of strategies were the least stable. The integrity and consistency apparent in representations of these formal strategies were threatened by the third type of strategy, which Fortes described in a report to the colonial administration as the practice of "marrying another man's wife"[25] either by eloping with a woman from her household without prior negotiations, or by abducting another man's wife. In either event, success relied foremost on the woman's complicity, and payments were made retrospectively. Given how unstable more formal arrangements were, most unions were the result of these informal strategies. Yet most administrative and ethnographic sources were silent about them. This silence created an artificial distinction between, on the one hand, strategies that were recognized and so imbued with legitimacy in the writing of observers and court decisions, and, on the other hand, strategies that were largely unacknowledged because they were considered to be unorthodox even though they were employed at least as often as formal ones. The unorthodox strategies were most often reported in the court records as "stealing," "abducting," or "eloping" a woman.[26]

In a discussion of the forms of matrimonial alliance among the *Lobi* of Burkina Faso in the 1970s, Michèle Fiéloux referred to two procedures for acquiring wives: "marriage by negotiations" and "marriage by abduction." In the latter, the "theft" of a wife usually occurred with the woman's consent but without the knowledge of her husband or parents, unless such action was taken as a reprisal against another household, when force or even violence might have been involved. Of the 120 marriages she recorded in the village of Iridaka (across the river from Lawra) in 1972, 54 percent were the result of the seizure of a woman "from the social group to which she belongs (her father's or her husband's)," while only 37.5 percent were the result of prior negotiations.[27] Similarly, Hagaman observed in 1975 that among the LoBirifor of Kalba, near Bole, the longest-lasting unions were those involving "stolen" as opposed to "arranged" wives.[28] Comparable figures do not exist for the LoDagaa congeries of Lawra District, but the court records and the consistent patterns of conjugal instability they reflect suggest similar rates.

Writing in the 1930s, Fortes observed that although abduction was still common among the Tallensi, it was now possible for a party to bring an action against a rival "who in former times could have married his wife with impunity."[29] Fiéloux, writing of the practice among the *Lobi* forty years later, argued that colonial pacification had probably led to a certain devalorization of this practice by removing the threat of violence.[30] Despite colonial and postcolonial attempts to repress such practices, in the late 1970s the acquisition of a wife by "theft," though less common, was still a source of prestige (albeit somewhat diminished). As Fiéloux observed: "As a social act, abduction is valorized and linked to the status of men. The man who, through ill fortune, does not succeed in gaining a wife other than through the usual dealings between kin groups is the subject of mockery."[31] Abduction had been one of the main causes of armed conflict prior to the colonial conquest of the LoDagaa. Thus, the impunity that Fortes suggested for the precolonial period was jural, not physical. The point is that where unions of this pattern might have formerly been successfully executed, recourse to the courts on the part of former husbands created new kinds of uncertainty.

The conjugal history of Pornu of Tugu, recorded in 1913, illustrates the typical pattern of a woman's marital career.[32] Before the turn of the century she entered a union with a man named Chafo, with whom she had three children. This union dissolved (unacrimoniously it would seem, as the children, while still attached to Chafo's household, remained with Pornu) and was displaced by her relationship with a man named Nabile, with whom she stayed long enough to have two more children. She was repudiated by Nabile, an uncommon cause of conjugal dissolution, but shortly after entered a union with Muyah, by whom she had another child. Given that the minimum spacing between children was on average three years, these events probably took place over at least eighteen years. Once women had reached the age of childbearing they became residents of other households throughout their lives, "perennial migrants" in their own societies.[33] Even though they could not become full members of their husband's households and remained members of their natal households, they could not return home for any extended period of time unless they were very old.[34] Writing of LoBirifor women in the 1970s, Barbara Hagaman noted: "Once a woman is embarked on marriage, she remains married for the rest of her life." Although women often changed husbands, there was no time at which conjugal payments were not presented by one man or another after she embarked on such a life. As Hagaman put it: "A woman is never fully integrated into the residence of her husband and remains all her life as mobile as everything in the house which is not dug into the earth."[35] The fact that many unions were short-lived, and that most dissolved before a woman's fertility declined, meant that such careers were usually complicated.

As this brief discussion of conjugal unions suggests, strategies other than negotiations predominated. Even where conjugal unions were formed through negotiation, the procedures were not rule-bound, but complicated and uncertain. Such complexity and uncertainty runs contrary to the impression given by almost all the relevant written sources. All administrators, ethnographers, and indigenous observers have presented formal practices in a jural language of apparent regularity and precision. This exactitude is belied by the practical contexts in which such relationships were formed and maintained. In his relatively brief description of conjugal unions among the LoWiili, Goody presented the various practices he observed as part of an ordered and systematic transfer of five sets of discrete but connected "rights" from one group to another.[36] In a later work he identified yet a further right, that of a man to bury his wife.[37]

However, as can be seen in Tables 9 and 10, there was little correspondence between these ascribed rights and "marriage," even as a descriptive category. Conjugal payments "A" and "F" were uxorial rather than specifically marital; they defined not the status of unions but the status of women as wives. "A" was necessary only if one wanted to present "B, C, D, and E," but these did not define either the status of the union or the uxorial status of the woman. Rather, they defined the custody of children. "A" was not important unless accompanied by a corresponding change in the residence of the woman, and "F" was only possible if a woman had remained with her husband. Conjugal payments "B, C, D, and E" transferred rights over a woman's children (2), but these payments did not establish rights 3, 4, and 5. Indeed, these rights were not "transferred" but instead were carried by women wherever they went, and so were conferred by women through their choice of residence. Rights 3, 4, and 5 might be characterized as marital, but not as rights; they could be taken away as easily as a woman conferred them. Finally, although "B, C, D, and E" appear as a set in terms of their implications, subsequent payments were made more to preserve the relationship between a man and a woman's households than to create new rights. For example, writing of the second substantial payment, "D," Goody reported that in the 1950s "the balance of rights between spouses and between affines is not altered in any major respect."[38]

In his much more extensive analysis of inheritance among different LoDagaa congeries, Goody observed that considerable ambiguity and discretion surrounded the attainment of these household rights.[39] Among those congeries in which movable wealth was inherited matrilineally, he noted a number of circumventing strategies. Outside of the narrow considerations of *post mortem* inheritance, there were several important strategies permitting agnatic devolution of movable property in areas of uterine inheritance: *inter vivos* transmission; cross-cousin marriages; deliberate retention of a daughter's "illegitimate" children; and, in the precolonial past, the purchase of male slaves.[40] Given that such latitude was possible for circumventing normative statements about inheritance, it should hardly be surprising that conjugal unions were also negotiable. Moore made this same point in her study of

TABLE 9
Sequence and Names of Conjugal Payments

	Rattray 1932		Goody 1956a, 1962	Dery 1987	Tengan 1990d	Kpiebaya 1990
	Dagaba	Lober	LoWiili	Dagaaba	"North"	Nandom area
A)	"preliminary courting expenses" 1–2,000 cowries	*berefo* "earnest money" 100–500 cowries	*libie tuo* "bitter money" 360 cowries	*saadani* (south) peace offering or "greeting" (north) 360 cowries	*libi-kpee, libi-zu* "big money," "head money" 360 cowries	*libi tuo, libi-kpee* "bitter money," "principal money" 360 cowries
B)	*po-kyerebo* "something for marrying a woman," 30–50,000 cowries	*kyerefo* "bride-price" 10–15,000 cowries	*poo libie* "wife" "money" 20,000 (aprox.) cowries (+ 1 cock, 1 fowl)	*kyaro* 7–10,00 cowries	*kyaro* 10–20,000 cowries	*kyaru* "tax," 1 cock, 1 fowl, 10–15,000 cowries
C)			*ko pir* 1 "hoeing sheep" end of hoeing services	*kob tur* 1000 cowries end of farming	1,000 cowries	
D)	*kyerebo-pere* ram or cow, given after childbirth	*doe* cows	*doe* 1 cow and calves (+ *bidoo naab* "child-bearing bull" or *pooyaa naab* "daughter's bull")	*dee* 2 calves	*dee* 1 cow, 1 bull	*dee* 1 heifer, 1 bull
E)			*naab baara* final cow	*nabaara* "last cow," in the form of 7,000 cowries	*nabaara* "final cow"	*nabaara* "the final cow"
F)			*poo tshera libie* 20 cowries			

Table 10
Correspondence between Conjugal Payments and "Rights Transferred at Marriage"

Conjugal payments*	Rights in uxorem transferred at marriage	Action or payments conferring right
A) libie tuo	1) rights over sexual services	A
B) poo libie	2) rights over a woman's procreative powers**	B, C, D, E
C) ko pir	3) rights over domestic services	Residence
D) doe	4) rights over economic services	Residence
E) naab baara	5) rights of co-residence	Residence
F) poo tshera libie	6) right to bury a woman as a wife	F

Source: Goody 1956a, 1962
*See Table 9.
**Described as rights in genetricem.

Chagga "law," where the discrepancy between the exactitude of statements and the negotiability of practices was most apparent in terms of conjugal payments and inheritance.[41]

The most obvious reasons why conjugal unions were negotiable related to the timing and medium of payments. Payments were not made all at once but were deferred over the history of the relationship. The lack of specificity surrounding the meaning and timing of payments was a major source of negotiability. Another was the complicated conventions and expectations surrounding the presentation of conjugal payments. The agency for these negotiations was always a mediator or go-between, who was generally a non-kin associate of the man's household who was related to the woman's household.[42] In 1930 the chief of Han told the District Commissioner's Court that the services of a go-between were necessary in the negotiation of conjugal payments: "If the husband goes himself he will be vexed with the parents and probably fight, whereas if a representative goes for him there can be no quarrel."[43] The services of such an intermediary were required at several points in the history of a union.

After an initial payment was made that regularized the residence of a woman with a man, a series of other payments were required to maintain the union and establish specific interests. Added to this were a wide variety of payments over the life of the union so that it might endure.[44] The first substantial payment ("B") was presented privately. As Goody observed: "The transactions, while not secret, receive little publicity; negotiations with in-laws entail a certain amount of shame and on the first two occasions that the *poo libie* (cowry payment) is offered, the groom's agnatic kin (the bride-receivers) are told that what they have brought is insufficient and are ignominiously sent home."[45] Although the amount of this payment was not negotiable, the amount received was often disputed at the time it was presented.[46] Labouret provided a useful description of negotiations at this point among the Dagari and Oulé: "The amount of the dowry, normally 10,000 cowries, is never announced. After several days the father of the groom painstakingly musters 7,000 cowries, insisting that this is all he has. After talks that are as long as they are tortuous, the remainder is eventually handed over."[47] Labouret, Rattray, and Goody all reported that the payment was not accepted until the third occasion on which the mediator presented it.

Payments were not simply made or fulfilled, but socially negotiated, even though their amount was ultimately non-negotiable.[48] In the case of first unions, one practical advantage of dragging out negotiations may have been to prolong the benefits a woman's household derived from labor payments offered by a man's household. These took the form of farming and building services.[49] These services declined in the postcolonial period as labor came increasingly to be seen as a source of commodities or money. It was often replaced by gifts or cash. A second reason had to do with a peculiarly male perspective on cultural etiquette that held women in contempt if they were too eager to enter into a conjugal relationship.[50] However, initial refusal of payments did not mean that the woman's household did not intend to accept them eventually, just as acceptance of payments did not mean that the union was assured. A woman's household was often in a position to withdraw her from a union in the early years if it was dissatisfied with the behavior of the husband toward their daughter or themselves. A woman herself could, as women often did, terminate one union if not content by entering into another of her own accord. Only very rarely did men reject wives.

Uncertainty over the acceptance of payments was also manifest in those subsequent to the first cowry payment. In areas of dual descent, the medium of secondary payments was cattle. In areas of unilineal descent, further payments were made in cowries and other livestock, usually goats and sheep. A woman's household normally withdrew their daughter from a union in order to ensure that later payments would be presented. This was a powerful and highly effective sanction that made the use of physical force or political authority unnecessary.[51] Labouret confirms that among the Dagari and Oulé in the 1920s, this was the most frequent strategy employed for securing deferred payments. Following the withdrawal of the woman, "laborious negotiations" began:

> The husband claims his wife and child; his in-laws answer that the dowry he paid is not enough and must be supplemented by paying three bulls. ... The husband

> protests that he has given his prize possessions, that his household is ruined ... the father-in-law remains unmoved. A first offer of a heifer is made and rejected indignantly. The husband searches around and comes up with two calves and this is discussed. The wife's family makes clear that they would not give up their daughter for such a meager payment. ... The ensuing discussion is confusing, it is laborious, and it generally ends in agreement. ... It is easy to imagine the inevitable complications that lead to these compromises.[52]

What is most striking about this passage is that these were not formalities or rituals, but real events that occasioned a renegotiation of relationships. Just as the amount of cowries was not negotiated, neither was the number of cattle constituting the second substantial transfer of wealth between households. But the age, size, and quality of those cattle was often at issue; so was whether they had all to be presented at once.

These often intense and complicated negotiations fly in the face of written claims that payments were orderly and systematic. The administrative desire for regularity and simplicity and the jural perspective that had become enshrined in anthropological studies by the middle of the century were what gave these written representations their coherence and integrity.[53] Goody, even though he noted that among the LoWiili six separate payments were made during the full history of a conjugal union, wrote of "bridewealth" as if all payments belonged to a single generic category. At no point did a union become unequivocally established. Nor were the payments referred to by a single, categorical term. As John Comaroff has noted, jural conceptualization of conjugal payments see marriage "as structurally prior, and prestations largely as its institutionalized mode of facilitation." He added that this "typically depends upon treating 'marriage' as a single and undifferentiated category of relationship; it assumes *a priori* that all conjugal unions are of a kind and have broadly the same structural significance."[54] In short, it smacks of teleology. The persistent ambiguity and negotiability of LoDagaa conjugal unions do not allow us to treat conjugal practices and payments as part of a single, categorical relationship. Regularity was the product of negotiations; often conflicting normative expectations were maintained only by being negotiated through a process of assertion, contestation, and resolution.

In contrast to anthropological paradigms that interpret conjugal payments in African societies as regulated stages in a clearly defined marital process, among the LoDagaa these payments created ambiguity. At the time of each payment the internal stability of the union was brought into question. At the point of the cattle payment or second cowry installment, the withdrawal of the woman by her household in order to ensure payment effectively suspended the union. It might continue, or it might not; this depended on the outcome of negotiations. However, the status of a conjugal union did not change after successive negotiations: it simply resumed or was terminated. LoDagaa conjugal relations were far from being a cumulative process. To the contrary, they were characterized by a noncumulative cycle of negotiations. Negotiations obscured any process and perpetuated considerable uncertainty. Unions dissolved frequently either because negotiations failed or because one union was displaced by the formation of another.

Sexual Anxieties and the Status of Women

Read's comment that LoDagaa women did not make good wives, made in the immediate aftermath of the Victorian period, reveals a cultural perspective shaped by a decidedly patriarchal intellectual milieu full of sexual apprehension. In middle-class male society in Britain of this time, marriage and family were euphemisms for sex, and sex was the medium for discussing male anxieties about gender relations (i.e., control over women).[55] Since these debates most often talked about "other" rather than British women as a way of disguising their domestic worries,[56] Read and his immediate successors had little difficulty extending metropolitan concerns into the West African savanna.

Colonial rule offered colonial administrators very broad latitude to apply their own cultural and gender assumptions when deciding court cases. Early decisions by district commissioners were consistent with the patriarchal expectations of Muslim husbands in Lawra District, and colonially appointed chiefs were soon enough offering the same types of decisions to Muslim litigants. District commissioners were also eager to provide coercive sanctions to protect conjugal unions against the interference of rivals, so as to protect the interests of migrant laborers. And it was not only in court cases involving Muslim traders and migrant laborers that district commissioners transformed male interests into practical rights over women. As a result of administrators and chiefs protecting the conjugal unions of migrant laborers, all such relationships were being redefined, with the result that women were now being denied the choice to leave unions if their former husbands objected in court to them doing so. What was being lost was the highly contextual language of conjugal unions – language that had accommodated and reflected the latitude that women had been able to exercise in a relatively unimpeded fashion at the beginning of the colonial period. For example, in Loab *vs.* Chiapuun, heard in 1909, Loab explained that his wife, Battyelle, had "asked leave" to go to her father's compound at Lissa a fortnight before, but had not returned because another man, Chiapuun, had "caught" her from her parents. The district commissioner then questioned Battyelle: "Q: Why did you go to Defendant when you were married to Plaintiff? A: I told my husband that if I went to my father I would not come back. Q: Did you tell Chiapuun that you had another husband? A: Yes I told him."

In terms of indigenous social practice, Battyelle's actions were a common strategy for women wishing either to renegotiate their conjugal unions or to leave their husbands.[57] However, in the court's view, they constituted a violation of the conjugal union. Chiapuun admitted knowing that the woman was already another man's wife, but explained that it mattered little to him as the woman had been willing to go with him. He was fined 10s., and Battyelle was returned to Loab despite her evident desire to leave him.[58] Such decisions demonstrate more than a very weak understanding of LoDagaa society. Both the elopement of wives and ensuing retaliatory action were being discouraged, and such decisions were intended to further the project of asserting colonial control.

Chiefs also enjoyed much latitude in deciding cases. The first sanctioned Native Tribunals were established in 1917 under ten of the chiefs, and a "method of procedure" was introduced. Only cases brought before a tribunal of all paramount chiefs were directly supervised; the courts of individual chiefs were more or less autonomous.[59] No attempt was made to define the jurisdiction of individual Native Tribunals, even though officers had made repeated inquiries with regard to the judicial powers of the chiefs before 1917. For example, when a man who had been found guilty by a chief's unsanctioned court and been beaten for not accepting its decision appealed the case to the district commissioner, the latter queried his superiors about the chiefs' jurisdiction:

> I understand we recognise their judgements and if appealed to will enforce them if not inconsistent with our idea of justice. In these cases should we approve and enforce payment of (a) a court fee to the chief and (b) damages for seduction? I shall be obliged if you can give me definite information on these points. It seems to me they cannot well be left to tact, discretion, common sense or any other personal qualities but there should be some definition laid down.[60]

The provincial commissioner responded obliquely that "the powers of the chiefs are only restricted where they are incompatible with our idea of justice," and referred his subordinate to the ordinances.[61] The district commissioner, not satisfied with this response, requested further guidance, only to be told: "If in your discretion however the punishment fitted the crime I think you should overlook it, personally I would."[62] No concern was expressed as to whether the decision of the chief's court was in accordance with indigenous practices. The same tacit approval prevailed in attitudes toward the semi-autonomous courts established after 1917. "Definition" was purposely avoided during the period of direct rule owing to the fundamental lack of intelligence as to which practices were applicable in the courts, let alone legitimate in an indigenous context.

In Lawra District between 1917 and 1935, officers were officially responsible for supervising the operation of the chiefs' courts, where social disputes were largely heard. However, this surveillance was erratic, usually allowing chiefs to act independently unless complaints were brought before the district commissioner. As the 1951 Commission on Native Courts noted of the period before indirect rule, "a haphazard, ineffective control over the activities of the courts [was] maintained," leaving any appeal against a wrong to the "aggrieved party alone."[63] In Lawra District during this period, administrators expressed satisfaction with the chiefs' courts so long as they mimicked the procedures of the district commissioner's own court and provided that their decisions did not give rise to complaints. Commenting on the absence of complaints in 1918, the district commissioner reported: "I notice that all the cases in the native tribunals are conducted in a most orderly manner and the procedure is modelled on that in my court."[64] There was no consideration of the substantive decisions of the courts, which were simply presumed to be applying "customary law." The proper operation of the courts was seen more as a ritual of colonial power than as an exercise of indigenous knowledge.[65]

In 1928 the Commissioner of the Northern Province instructed district commissioners not to hear cases, "matrimonial affairs, land or heritage disputes," except on appeal.[66] This was an attempt both to give more authority to the chiefs' tribunals and to alleviate pressure on officers' time. By 1929 the infrequency of civil litigation in Lawra District was explained by the fact that nearly all cases were either heard as complaints or, more commonly, dealt with by chiefs in courts of first instance. Regrettably, we do not know the exact substance of their decisions or the specific nature of the cases brought before them; this is partly because of the condescending attitude that most officers held toward such disputes. During the first decade of colonial rule, when a large number of such cases had come before officers, they had been seen as unimportant. Read had already recommended in 1911 "that District Commissioners should tend to ignore or relegate to native courts disputes arising out of what we understand as 'mammy palavers.'"[67] Cases of this type that did come before the district commissioner eighteen years later, in 1929, were still regarded as mere "quarrels and squabbles" rather than as serious causes of litigation.[68]

Officers talked to and wrote about African men almost exclusively; African women were treated largely as "silent icons of the primitive – the ultimate 'others.'"[69] Officers expressed little or no interest in the welfare or rights of women during the early years of direct rule, and when attention was focused on the subject in later years it was only in response to metropolitan concerns. A decade after Read's negative comments on the freedom of women, another officer referred to absconding and recalcitrant wives as "shrews," and went so far as to lament: "It is a pity that the ducking stool and bridle ... have gone out of fashion."[70] Contrary to the tone of sentimental nostalgia, these were particularly harsh instruments that had once been used against English women. Significantly, these two instruments of public shaming had been used with greater frequency in the late sixteenth and early seventeenth centuries, a time when, as David Underwood has argued, "masculine worries about sexually aggressive women" and "preoccupation with women who are a visible threat to the patriarchal system" were especially high.[71]

The colonial environment of West Africa was, as Barbara Bush has recently noted, an "ultra-masculine world," where the absence of white female companionship created terrific ambivalence in the attitudes of colonial administrators toward African women. In the Northern Territories in 1931 the non-African population was very small, numbering eighty-nine males and eighteen females. Of the males, twenty-six were married, one was widowed, and the remaining sixty-two were single. Of the twenty-six married men, only twelve had their wives with them. This left only six single women and increased the number of men living without wives to seventy-seven.[72] The absence of "white" women exacerbated loneliness and created a dependence on "the 'dark rapture' of native women." But desire and possible solace created fear: "Colonial officers stressed the 'debilitating' effect, mental and spiritual, of too close contact with the primitive, the unnerving 'ju-ju worship and sensuality' of the African bush and the 'psychological curse' of black women's nakedness, 'flaunted' in a 'lustful and animal-like' fashion. This 'horrible desirability' of black women resulted in a dangerous sexual frustration."[73] In the "male texts" of colonial memoirs, Bush has detected a genuine fear of "powerful female sexuality" that reached beyond personal psychology and touched administrative policies. African women were perceived as threats to colonial order that had to be controlled. This mixture of desire and fear resulted in attitudes toward African women that were decidedly more negative than attitudes toward "white" women. However, this was not the only image of African women. It co-existed with an image of African women as oppressed beings – an image that served as a justification for colonialism. Although Bush contends that it was British colonial women who propagated the image of women as "beasts of burden," this same image had its male advocates in the Northern Territories. So long as African women could be seen as oppressed, colonial rule could be seen as liberating. The two images combined produced "a 'fabulous fiction' of black women's identities, a confused composite of passive drudge, 'she-devil' and sexual temptress."[74] As a result of the notion that African women were at the same time too free (i.e., morally lax) and not free (i.e., exploited), the attitudes of colonial men toward LoDagaa women were often very contradictory.

British men had not expected that African women in the Northern Territories would have so much freedom. After it became apparent that they did, officers were very ambivalent about its advantages. When the chief commissioner issued warnings over the issue of child betrothal in 1911, the Acting Secretary for Native Affairs pointed out that officers should not be unduly concerned. It was "not always possible and often disastrous to judge the institutions of primitive people by the standards of the twentieth century," he asserted. Officers were told they could ignore the warnings without harming the "moral or social welfare" of their "colonial subjects."[75] Such relativism was not unusual, but it was not always predicated on administrative convenience and ethnocentric paternalism. In some cases it was born of a genuine understanding that differences existed between colonial categories and indigenous practices.

In the first published account of the peoples of the Northern Territories, Cardinall wrote in 1920 that although he referred to the practices surrounding the formation and dissolution of conjugal unions among the Kassena, Builsa, Nankanni, and Tallensi as marriage, the term was "misleading. A woman is looked upon primarily as a begetter of children, and secondly as a preparer of food. ... The essential thing is the children, and they, no matter who their father, belong to the owner of their mother. Every woman has, besides her husband, one or two favourite lovers to whom her husband has no objection."[76]

Despite observations such as these, conjugal unions were persistently described as marriage, because such a categorization was extremely convenient for administrators. If native practices did not fulfill the "ideological valuations" of marriage as defined by observers, the administration could not countenance the application of judicial authority in such disputes under some other heading (e.g., purchase). Nor could it approve of the freedom that women enjoyed outside the courts and at the same time maintain the illusion that marriage was an indigenous institution; the former had to be seen as a deviation from the latter. Although the characteristics seen by administrators to be appropriate to marriage – especially the stability of unions – may not have existed, this did not obviate the concern that they should have existed. When heard by colonial courts, disputes concerning conjugal unions had to be treated as matrimonial issues even if they were really just disputes between men.

A variety of social disputes had been conveniently subsumed under the title of marriage, and thereby minimized in both complexity and importance. This meant they were easier to relegate to the jurisdiction of the chiefs. The volume of "matrimonial" litigation was a source of aggravation to district commissioners and a direct challenge to their amateurish grasp of the indigenous issues. Writing in 1920, Cardinall commented that the negotiability and ambiguity of conjugal unions caused innumerable disputes, as did the "growing practice" of women choosing their own husbands:

> This last is progress, but unfortunately it leads to a maze of entanglements. ... Many of these women, having tasted emancipation, are not satisfied until they have tried as many as ten husbands. It is not the white man who has brought this about. Such has been the practice for long past. It led to murder and war and raids; today it leads to disputes and complaints beyond number, and incidentally at times to a half-crazy Commissioner.[77]

These comments highlighted the dilemma that the related phenomena of conjugal instability and autonomy of women presented to officers throughout the colonial period. The rate of conjugal dissolution was often seen as a sign of moral deficiency, or at least as an inconvenient social fact and a source of administrative annoyance, but the only immediate means of restricting such elasticity would have been to impair the freedom of women. Attitudes toward women's autonomy were very ambivalent. Evidently mindful of the growing rights of women in Britain, Cardinall wrote that the freedom available to women, even though it had led in the past to "prevalent immorality," must now be considered "progress."[78] The Catholic missionaries of the early 1930s were far less sympathetic; they complained of "vagabond morals" of women, who sometimes began their conjugal careers at the age of nine or ten and then proceeded to change husbands regularly. Many of those asking to be instructed in Christian marriage had already had anywhere from three to six husbands, all of which made the work of understanding whether a woman was married or not seem like solving a "Chinese puzzle."[79]

The most common image of LoDagaa women was essentially one of immorality and sexuality. Rattray included a photograph of a "Lobi woman" among the plates in his 1932 ethnography of the peoples of the Northern Territories (Figure 16). The image is striking for its informality. The woman is reclined in a three-quarter pose to the camera. Her body is supported with her left arm, her left leg extended. The right shoulder is slightly dropped and the right leg bent back. Overall, her posture seems both seductive and coy. No attempt was made to show anything else in the image, any action or background. Her eyes stare directly into the camera. It is not possible to determine whether it was the model or the photographer who arranged the pose, or what their intentions were. However, the impression that she is a sexual seductress or moral vagabond would have been unavoidable, given how such unmediated "nudity" would

Figure 18. "A Lobi woman." From R.S. Rattray, *The Tribes of the Ashanti Hinterland* (1932), Fig. 119.

have been understood by readers who had no experience of or sensitivity toward African cultures. Of course she was not naked: her body was intricately adorned. However, these decorations would have been relatively invisible to most readers. The photograph seems much more erotic than ethnographic, a "rather precarious alibi for voyeurism."[80] She is not standing, walking, or working, but only sitting there in an open space on the ground, for no other purpose except to be photographed. The background is out of focus, which further decontextualizes this woman, whose personal name has been obscured by the need for ethnic semiosis. It is no coincidence that this photograph accords closely with several administrative attitudes toward LoDagaa women.

Where convenient, administrative attitudes toward women exhibited a certain degree of cultural relativism vis-à-vis acceptable male attitudes toward British women in the metropole. However, this relativism was not evident when it came to other aspects of indigenous life. When in 1930 the Colonial Secretary in Accra requested information on the subject of female circumcision, the same indifference informed the responses. The District Commissioner of Wa reported that the practice was prevalent among all groups in the northwest, and that the same reasons were given for the practice everywhere: "'It [the clitoris] is dirty.' 'It makes women less promiscuous.' 'Our grandfathers did it.'"[81] Another officer noted: "This raises a very large question as to what is detrimental to the health and well being of the people. I suggest many African customs would be detrimental to a European but are apparently not so to an African."[82] Similarly, the assistant medical officer for the protectorate concluded at the end of his report: "It will thus be seen that the only objections to the operation of clitoridectomy are its brutality and its uselessness. It must be remembered that the operation has been judged from the European point of view. The African would not consider this operation as brutal and its suppression by law would probably appear to him to be in the nature of religious persecution."[83] The identification of "the African" as male is revealing, but not surprising, and speaks for itself.

In 1936 the question of "forced marriages" became an issue following another questionnaire, which the Secretary of State for the Colonies issued after the Liberal MP Eleanor Rathbone raised questions about colonial policy in the British Parliament.[84] In his reply, the chief commissioner concluded that women in the Northern Territories enjoyed "only slightly less freedom of choice with regard to their husbands than that to which their sisters in more civilized countries are entitled." With reference to the issue of arranged unions, he correctly noted that "if they prove unsatisfactory to [women] there are means available for their annulment to which girls are not slow to resort. ... If a woman seeks to have her marriage dissolved, it is almost certain that she is contemplating another. In that event the new husband would be called to compensate the former husband, which he is generally given ample time to do." However, these remarks pertained to the private sphere of social life, not to what occurred in the public sphere of the colonial courts, where disputes were exclusively between men. For officers, returning women to their husbands might have seemed only appropriate because of the husband's conjugal payments; but, by frustrating a rival's attempt to take another man's wife in this way, courts were preventing women from leaving unions. The only means of "annulment" available to women was the successful formation of another union. The chief commissioner admitted to a preference toward husbands in the courts: "In the opinion of some officers the native law on divorce is too lax and operates to the advantage of the woman rather than that of the man."[85] Native law was still a presumed entity at this stage, its invention on paper not yet having begun, and divorce was not a category of indigenous representation. This bias toward husbands continued for some time, although different officers deviated from the government line that women enjoyed excessive freedom. In the 1938 annual report for Lawra District, for example, it was observed that women were only "regarded as vehicles for the production of children, or as mere domestic drudges, privileged to give sexual relief to their husbands."[86]

In 1937 the chiefs in Lawra District began complaining to the district commissioner that the missions were offering refuge to the wives of non-Christians. This prompted the chiefs to claim that "the mission is liable for the dowry!" The district commissioner was led to believe that "normally she [a woman] would run to her father who would be liable."[87] Accordingly, he intervened to obtain an undertaking from the missionaries that they would stop affording protection to their women followers after they left their non-Christian husbands. However, no investigation was made into why women were now seeking refuge at the mission rather than returning to their households. One reason was that the chiefs, both officially through their courts and informally through political pressure, were obstructing rivals from taking other men's wives, and in doing so interfering with women's freedom to dissolve one union by entering into another.[88] Another reason was that the chiefs were attempting to make women's households responsible for the return of conjugal payments, whereas formerly such transactions would have taken place only through them. For women, then, conversion offered unprecedented opportunities for autonomy at the same time as their previous strategies for freedom were being restricted by the exclusively male political structures of colonial rule.

At the beginning of 1938, several months after the issue had first been raised and the missionaries had undertaken to stop providing refuge to deserting wives,[89] the district commissioner confronted the Fathers with the case of a man whose wives had left him, allegedly after they had been told by the missionaries "to stop marrying him." Both his wives had received baptism and deserted him and their seven children. "Went up to the Father's place and discussed the morals of a woman saving her soul at the expense of her children. Their reply was that so long as the woman's motive was good 'the Lord would provide' for the children."[90] A month later the missionaries presented a complaint about a wife who had deserted one of their converts. The woman, the daughter of the chief of Gengenkpe (who like all the chiefs of this period was a "pagan"), was reprimanded by the district commissioner and told that she would not be allowed to enter into another union. The chief was informed that the return of conjugal payments would not dissolve the union and permit his daughter to enter into another union.[91] However, her father adamantly refused to force his daughter to return to her former husband, and also refused to keep her in his house as a spinster – a state enjoyed only by women who were either incapacitated or elderly widows. When he announced to the district commissioner his intention of giving her to another man as a wife, he was threatened with "destoolment."[92]

By the end of the period of direct rule, blatant action by district commissioners to protect conjugal relationships from the prevalent competition over women, which effectively extended legal status to conjugal unions as marriages, had become rare. However, at the same time that cases before the District Commissioner's Court were decreasing in number, those being heard by the chiefs' tribunals were increasing. Unfortunately, there are no records of these latter decisions. Even so, as we will see in the discussion of adultery that follows, it is clear that even if the chiefs were not laying down direct sanctions to protect conjugal relationships, both chiefs and litigants were using seduction charges to achieve the same end. Although district commissioners became less involved in matrimonial litigation during indirect rule, the sanctions that they had provided to control wives were sought elsewhere by litigants, who either took their disputes to the Native Authority Courts, or adopted Catholicism in order to avail themselves of the conjugal sanctions offered by the missionaries. This latter strategy seems to have been especially popular among migrant laborers, who were not as severely affected by the concomitant prohibition against polygyny. In some cases, such as the following one from 1942, the two were combined – that is, Catholic marriage and prosecution for seduction before Native Courts:

> Apropos a Native Court case I suggested that if a man went to the Mines for a year or more leaving a newly married wife on her beam ends at home he had only himself to blame if she sought solace elsewhere and it is unfair to convict for seduction. The practice is that a youth who wants to see the bright lights marries in the Mission Church before going, so that the Roman Catholic rules of divorce shall keep the girl on ice for him. By native custom she could free herself on account of desertion.[93]

Officers had been generally negative in their descriptions of indigenous unions; but after 1938 many officers, although not without criticisms, began insisting that indigenous practices were as legitimate as Catholic ones.

Christian marriages raised a series of issues concerning the public recognition and legal legitimacy of indigenous unions. In 1938 the chief commissioner instructed the district commissioner to explain to both converts and pagans that Christian unions were legally protected by sanctions that superseded "native law," and that a father or guardian could not "legally take his daughter or ward away from her husband on any grounds such as non-fulfilment of a duty imposed by native custom and give her in marriage to another man."[94] This policy did not recognize that conjugal payments were deferred over a considerable period of time, and that if the threat that a household could withdraw the woman was removed, later payments would be rendered unclaimable. In the end a compromise was reached between the chiefs and the missionaries whereby all conjugal payments were telescoped into a single payment.[95] However, this too undermined indigenous practices by eliminating further negotiations, which were often used by a woman's natal household to ensure her well-being and fair treatment.

The underlying issue in both types of cases – a woman leaving her pagan husband through (or because of) conversion, or deserting a Christian marriage for a pagan union – was the autonomy of women in LoDagaa society. Until this time the issue had articulated itself only in terms of whether a rival was permitted to take another man's wife or whether a woman's household had to compensate the former husband – questions that both officers and, later, the chiefs (following the former's decisions) answered in the negative and affirmative respectively. Formerly it would have been self-defeating for a husband to attempt to frustrate a rival from making conjugal payments, because even if he had succeeded, the woman could have remained with her household, who were not liable for the return of conjugal payments. A conference of chiefs convened in 1944 to discuss the issue of women seeking refuge at the missions reported that there was a popular sense of grievance among the men present because "the people suspect that unfaithful wives use conversion as a means of changing husbands."[96] As a result of related investigations made after this conference, it was discovered that despite earlier representations by the chiefs to the contrary, there was no indigenous sanction restricting women from leaving unions of their own accord.[97] Yet this had not restrained the courts from making decisions as if there had been such a normative sanction.

Administrative Investigations and Colonial Knowledge

In the early 1930s, as progress was being made toward a system of indirect rule, the need grew for information about LoDagaa customary law, under the presumption that such a body of knowledge existed. From the perspective of the new administrative officers who were responsible for implementing indirect rule, the state of confusion over administrative policy in the Northern Territories during district rule had been appalling. The officer considered most culpable for this state of affairs was Major A.C.H. Walker-Leigh, he of the ducking stool and bridle. He had served as District Commissioner of Lawra on four brief tours of service before becoming Chief Commissioner of the Northern Territories in the 1920s, during which time he actively defended direct rule.[98] A reading of the District Complaint Book during the period that Walker-Leigh was District Commissioner of Lawra gives substance to the criticisms leveled at him. His defective understanding of the LoDagaa can be attributed in no small part to his military (as opposed to administrative) mindset, which seems to have bred in him a cynical, ignorant complacency. An army officer by training, he never made a successful transition to the role of civilian administrator. He had written to the Acting Colonial Secretary in Accra in 1928 that he did not "see how indirect rule could be given at the present time to the more pagan tribes and at the same time our idea of justice maintained, the peace of the country, the right and freedom of the smaller or poorer people upheld."[99] The reference to the maintenance of justice was significant: Other than a rhetorical justification for colonial rule, what was the meaning of this justice?

To better understand just what kind of justice he was referring to in practice, it is worthwhile to examine Walker-Leigh's record on the ground as a district commissioner. An entry in the Lawra District Complaint Book serves well as an illustration. Kurnali of Karni came to Walker-Leigh in 1912 to demand the return of conjugal payments (cowry equivalent of £2.13s. in addition to one sheep and two fowls) that he had made for Kuona of Karni's daughter. The woman, Iyelizu, had left Kurnali three to four years earlier and returned to her household. The following decision was recorded: "Told [Kurnali] has had use of the woman for four years for £2.10.0 and now wants to be paid back, meaning that he has had use of the woman for four years for nothing – No, certainly will not be given a summons. Father told on no account to pay anything back also to come in and report if the son-in-law flogs him. Remark: Ought to belong to the tribe of Judah."[100]

Eight years earlier, in his sketchy compilation of LoDagaa "civil law," Read had correctly observed that when unions dissolved, conjugal payments were returned.[101] Walker-Leigh, unacquainted with and unconcerned about the social context of his decision, misunderstood these payments as compensatory rather than circulatory. The indignant surprise reflected in his appended remark indicates that he was barely familiar with LoDagaa social practices. The role of district commissioners in these matters was largely discretionary. They were empowered to ignore native "law and custom" where it was "repugnant to natural justice and morality."

The establishment of Native Authorities with semiautonomous courts under informal colonial supervision was first seriously considered for the Northern Territories in the late 1920s, but little progress was made until after Walker-Leigh retired in 1929. Legislative provision was made for Native Authorities (including tribunals) in 1932, but it was not until 1935 that Native Authority Courts were established in Lawra District.[102] It has been argued that the effects of indirect rule were marginal in the Northern Territories.[103] Even so, its introduction represented a significant formalization in the process of imposing political and judicial structures on LoDagaa society. The prevailing perception by administrators had been that the LoDagaa had no laws – or, to express this positively, that before colonial rule disputes had been settled by actions (strategies) rather than words (rules). During the period of direct rule these strategic methods of dispute resolution had been significantly displaced; yet the new words that were to replace actions had not been defined.

By the late 1920s several officers had come to realize that the political structures that had been created in areas like Lawra District (i.e., previously decentralized societies of the Northern Territories) were unsatisfactory solutions to the administrative problem of direct rule, as well as inadequate preparation for the judicial structures that were fundamental to indirect rule. Cardinall, who had had extensive experience with administration among decentralized societies, had been discouraging in his assessment of "native administration" in 1928. Writing of the level and quality of judicial organization, he stated: "The extent of jurisdiction of these courts is trivial. It covers matrimonial suits and all those little matters to which the maxim *de minimis lex non curat* would apply."[104] This assessment revealed several implicit administrative attitudes and misunderstandings.

That "matrimonial" disputes were regarded as trivial might well have had something to do with the fact that most officers were unmarried. More to the point, the social and economic contexts of conjugal relations were almost wholly ignored. Conjugal unions represented the means of household reproduction as well as the primary medium of interhousehold relations.[105] Therefore, even if the issues behind cases seemed trivial, their implications were extremely significant, as they involved matters relating to the survival and perpetuation of households. Unfortunately, bachelor officers regarded conjugal unions from an exclusively sexual and moral perspective. With the shift to indirect rule, however, officers could no longer be so dismissive and ignorant of indigenous social practices. A search began for marriage laws as the basis of a written judicial order; this paralleled the search for chiefs, which had already resulted in a written political order.

Among the practical and logistical arguments advanced against indirect rule by officers such as Walker-Leigh, the most prominent was that conditions in the Northern Territories were not the same as those in northern Nigeria and Tanganyika, where indirect rule had been successfully established. They claimed this even though they had never actually done the research necessary to say exactly what the conditions in the Northern Territories were. The new generation of officers, who had taken over the administration with the object of introducing indirect rule, evaded the difficulties posed by their predecessors' lack of ethnographic knowledge by proposing a new beginning. That came when Rattray completed his survey in 1930. After examining the "human records," Rattray concluded that there was "splendid human material" out of which to fashion a Native Administration.[106] This statement alone gave the new generation of administrators the confidence to argue that conditions in the Northern Territories could not be so very different from those among "tribes" in countries where indirect rule had been successfully established.[107] In 1931 the Chief Commissioner of the Northern Territories endorsed Rattray's view that it was preferable to create a policy in response to local conditions rather than a "scissors and paste policy" based on policies already applied elsewhere, even though this "may produce quite satisfactory results – on paper."[108]

Yet the lack of adequate ethnographic intelligence impeded any change in administrative policy. Rattray's thorough study of the "hinterland" should have gone some way to redress this ignorance, but his work was too academic in nature to apply easily to day-to-day administration. Rattray did not see his work as an administrative guide, and in fact had qualified his own observations, quoted so approvingly by the chief commissioner, with the following: "What is required here, however, in view of the present scanty state of our knowledge, is for us to examine those human records which alone can provide us with the information which we require."[109] *The Tribes of the Ashanti Hinterland*, although comprehensive and learned, did not provide "definitions" of indigenous practices – only the information necessary to understand them. Given the level of administrative ignorance, this information was actually more important, even if administrative requirements were much narrower and more specific. Some district commissioners resented Rattray's work, seeing it as an implicit criticism of their own efforts to understand the LoDagaa. Others felt slighted at not having their own amateur ethnographies cited.[110]

Rattray's conclusions were useful in supporting arguments for the implementation of Native Authorities, with officially defined courts and treasuries; but his work did not ultimately remove the practical difficulties. A new chief commissioner wrote to the colonial secretary at the end of 1934 raising many of Cardinall's earlier objections, which had been conveniently ignored in the intervening period. His criticisms of the former regime of direct rule went back to the drafting of the first administrative ordinance, which he argued ignored the "history," "constitution," and "customary laws" of the societies affected. Later administrators had done nothing to remedy the situation due to their preoccupation with establishing colonial order.[111] It was not until 1936 that a record of LoDagaa social practices was drafted, and then only in response to a circular by the chief commissioner requesting such information, following a recommendation by the Colonial Office on the advisability of such groundwork. In instructing his district commissioners, the chief commissioner explained: "When seeking the required information, it would be advisable to assure the Chiefs that we will not regard their laws and customs as now recorded to be immutable. They must be and will be changed with changing circumstances."[112]

The views and opinions of the colonial chiefs were surveyed and then translated into the official categories of the colonial world on paper. The result was a codification of LoDagaa marriage and divorce laws prepared by H.A. Blair.[113] No attention was paid to whether the chiefs were the legitimate interpreters of LoDagaa social practices, let alone whether these could be translated into judicial instruments as "laws and customs." As Rattray had observed of his own informants:

> Were the anthropologist to confine his researches to the doings and sayings of those Natives whom he finds vested with minor authority under local Government, real anthropological history would never be written. In my dealings with the plain folk, from whom most of the anthropologist's really valuable information is ultimately derived, facts were soon disclosed which were irreconcilable with the commonly accepted and current accounts hitherto credited by us and substantiated by the Chiefs or their agents.[114]

Blair had no prior familiarity with the district, having just arrived when the project began.[115] His report gave the impression that LoDagaa social practices were both definite and formalized. This was not surprising, as his informants were chiefs, all of whom were familiar with the expectations of the world on paper through their experience of colonial courts and their own sanctioned and unsanctioned tribunals. It is not surprising, then, that the White Fathers would complain in 1938 that they had incontestable evidence that "the District Commissioners do not have a true understanding of Indigenous Customs, and the Chiefs or interpreters, in whom they confide, tell them only what suits their interests and satisfies their greed."[116]

Furthermore, Blair's report was constrained by the questionnaire the chief commissioner had issued. The questions followed a legal structure, under the assumption that indigenous practices addressed the same concerns. The significance of such paradigms for the organization and categorization of knowledge about African societies is, as Vansina has noted, very important but sometimes overlooked:

> Such questionnaires were utilized by all colonial powers and the ethnographic descriptions of the day betray such a relation by their organization, the divisions and phraseology retained, and their successive development. ... The works thus produced are neither "wrong" nor useless; their data are often valuable and their

> specific interpretations often interesting. But they also often convey prejudice, set purpose, and specific objectives; the underlying intellectual paradigms are often predetermined.[117]

It is necessary to consider the context in which such knowledge was produced and why it was produced. With regard to LoDagaa "laws and customs," such inquiries were conducted within a framework which presumed that marriage was a category of indigenous practice and social representation. Significantly, such knowledge was not designed to reflect reality so much it was intended to help in "acquiring habits of action for coping with reality"[118] – part of a wider program that included maps, diagrams, and record books."

The government questionnaire requested the following details under the heading of "divorce": "1. On what grounds is it obtainable? 2. What repayments, if any, have to be made by the family of the woman? 3. What is the actual ceremony of the divorce (in the Colony the women are marked with white chalk)? 4. What is the position of the woman with regard to marriage after divorce?"[119] Responses were furnished on each of these points, but the questionnaire ignored the more fundamental question: Was there any indigenous equivalent to the jural concept of divorce, let alone marriage as its inverse?

In response to the same questionnaire, Meyer Fortes compiled an infinitely more thorough and subtle account of social practices among the Tallensi. Under the heading of "divorce, adultery and 'seduction'" he commented: "Tallensi ideas about the 'sanctity of marriage' are so different from our own that their attitudes to divorce and adultery cannot be measured by ours." The suggestion that the European categorization of these practices was incommensurable with that of the Tallensi had practical relevance to the disputes that were brought before the native courts: "It should be noted, to begin with, that the term *divorce* is not applicable in the context of Tallensi marriage in the sense it bears for us. There are no legal 'grounds for divorce'; and there is no legal procedure for obtaining a divorce from a spouse. In fact, legal action arises as a result of ruptured marriage, not as a means to dissolve it."[120]

In forwarding Fortes's report to the Secretary for Native Affairs, the chief commissioner noted: "The Attorney-General may possibly like to read the memorandum as it provides proof that even the comparatively primitive Furfura [Frafra] possess a logical and not unjust code of laws on what to them is a most important question."[121] However, Fortes had prefaced his report with substantial qualifications, with the purpose of ensuring that just such a literal reading of Tallensi social practices would not be made:

> For the practical purpose of administering the law it seems necessary to distinguish the more strictly legal customs from the less strictly legal customs. In

> Tallensi Marriage Law such a distinction can be made, with the reservation, however, that even the most innocuous and ostensibly non-legal customs sometimes have great legal importance. ... Indeed the more definitely legal aspects of Tallensi marriage are inconceivable without the background of "non-legal" customs.[122]

He added that "Tallensi Marriage Law" had "changed a good deal since the coming of the white man, and is still in process of change and development." Elsewhere, Fortes stated that the "political and legal behaviour" of the Tallensi had already been "as strongly conditioned by the ever-felt influence of the District Commissioner as by their own customs."[123] Implicit in Fortes's qualifications was the fact that the questions of law and marriage had only arisen as a result of colonial rule. That these qualifications were overlooked can be explained in no small part by the desire of administrators to discover clear, convenient, and unambiguous rules.

Blair mentioned none of the qualifications and distinctions Fortes had raised. Fortes had noted that even though there were formal means and contexts for dissolving unions, these were exceptional. In normal circumstances, unions dissolved without any marked ceremony or procedure. Blair, on the other hand, wrote that certain symbolic acts, which he omitted to note were exceptional, terminated unions, and added that these were the only means of dissolving unions. On the third of the questionnaire's points, Blair furnished the following details: "When a woman seeks divorce, she will hang dawa-dawa leaves on her girdle. ... At Birufo, she will also paint herself with red clay." He stated that divorce was effected by the father-in-law, following the return of his daughter by her husband. He admitted that the father-in-law could not refuse to grant a divorce, but complained that "there is no other competent authority."[124]

In 1944, only six years later, another officer, H.W. Amherst, questioned the validity of this codification of laws relating to divorce: "The procedure for local divorce recorded at a Native Authority conference in 1938 by Blair is a bit ambiguous, and I have some doubts if it is correct. The Nandom Naa [one of the signatories to the drafted 'laws'] says it is not, but I have told him it must be adhered to unless amended at a meeting of the full Native Authority."[125]

When a conference of the chiefs was convened two months later, the district commissioner discovered that the difficulty did not rest with the language of the draft laws; it arose from a more fundamental problem: "It transpires that there is no definite 'divorce,' the only thing anyone is interested in being the repayment of dowry [conjugal payments]."[126] It was argued that the father-in-law was "not a competent authority to pronounce or grant divorce," being merely a witness to the dissolution of a union and "the channel through which the bride price is paid by any new husband to the old husband." Following this last point, the report stressed: "In the event of a wife effecting divorce, the dowry can be reclaimed by the husband only from a subsequent husband." In the amended version of the "laws" drawn up at the same conference, it was stated: "No act, rite, or form of words ... is necessary to effect a divorce between two persons married according to Native Customary Law."[127] The original assumption that some ceremony must necessarily surround the dissolution of a union had proceeded from its corollary: that such unions were distinguished by a similar ceremony at their inception. Because marriage was such a significant category for administrative understanding of LoDagaa society, it was assumed that some ascertainable ceremony or ritual must mark its dissolution. In other words, the LoDagaa were thought to practice "marriage," even though they placed no emphasis on ceremonies surrounding the formation of conjugal unions.

Only in two very exceptional cases was divorce ever an issue before the colonial and postcolonial courts. A Local Authority Court comprised of chiefs heard the first in 1956, and a government-appointed magistrate heard the second in 1974. Their attitudes to divorce were very similar and illustrate clearly its irrelevance to LoDagaa practices as well as to litigation. The chiefs argued that "the couple did not wed in court, and so their divorce will not be accepted by this court. ... The court has no hands in this divorce, they got married outside and should divorce outside and not in this court."[128] Nevertheless, this same court was using the question of whether couples were married to decide other matters, such as seduction, conjugal payments, and child custody. The same attitude was later reflected in the decisions of the District Court, where in 1974 the magistrate argued: "Whether there has been or not any divorce between [the couple] is not the issue for the court to decide." The issue for this court was not the status of the union, but "in whose name and title was [the woman] living" – that is, whose wife she was.[129] Both these cases were exceptional, but they serve to demonstrate that categories such as divorce were extraneous to the logic of indigenous practices. Unfortunately, although the courts were able to appreciate that divorce was an irrelevant category, they were not able to dispense with the idea of marriage. The category of marriage remained central to the framework through which colonial knowledge was constructed and deployed by the courts.

Adultery as Seduction and Litigation as Retaliation

If the Native Authority courts and their successors did not create marriages or preside over their dissolution, then what did they do? The major substantive issue that occupied the Native Authority courts after 1935, the Local Authority Courts in the 1950s, and the District Magistrate's Court into the 1970s, was that of seduction. There was no precedent in LoDagaa practices for the charge of seduction, which was first applied by a District Commissioner of Lawra in 1908.[130] There was an apparently indigenous model on which to justify prosecuting adultery cases, but LoDagaa concepts of adultery were very different from the jural concept that was applied by the courts in their various guises. In his response to a 1931 administrative questionnaire on "customary law," Eyre-Smith replied that "adultery such as we understand the meaning of the word did not exist."[131] The emphasis at this date was already on the past tense; by then litigation before the chiefs' tribunals for the prosecution of jural adultery was already prevalent. Writing at the same time, Labouret noted of *Lobi* perceptions of adultery: "It is essentially a religious crime, and its true character was not taken into consideration by the tribunals."[132]

There were indigenous sanctions against certain heterosexual relations, but they were of a different order from any jural concept of punishment, compensation, or social transgression entailed in the idea of seduction. In its indigenous context, among both the *Lobi* and the LoDagaa, adultery was not a transgression of sanctions protecting conjugal unions (i.e., the concept did not arise from the need to prevent competition and consequent conflict). Instead, sanctions against adultery were a means of warding off potential afflictions that might befall a husband (through his ancestors), or his wife (who though not of the same household, became subject to the influence of its ancestors by residing with them), or their children. Eyre-Smith categorized these sanctions as "religious laws," but noted: "There was no penalty in the sense that we understand the word in relation to laws."[133] Important cultural differences prevented these indigenous beliefs and practices from being translated into laws. In the chiefs' courts adultery was redefined, rather than translated, and imbued with totally different characteristics – namely, punishment of rivals, compensation for husbands, and control over wives. As Labouret observed, also employing the notion of religious beliefs to characterize indigenous practices that did not accord with a jural concept of causality: "This infraction [adultery] has effects that are quite different from the ones we associate with adultery; it is a serious offense against the Earth, goddess of fertility, and against the tutelary gods of the family."[134]

LoDagaa beliefs and practices surrounding heterosexual offenses were incompatible with rule-bound notions of adultery, let alone the legal concept of seduction. The reasons why had to do with a lack of indigenous classificatory specificity. Writing three decades after Labouret and Eyre-Smith, Goody noted that the concept of adultery was perhaps inappropriate for the purpose of cross-cultural analysis.[135] Although he was referring specifically to Fortes's work among the Tallensi, he noted that the same observations applied to the LoDagaa. The Tallensi categorized both adultery and incest with the same term, *pogamboon*, "matters concerning women," whereas the term among the LoDagaa was *paa bume*, "things of the vagina." Distinctions emerged not in words but in how the Tallensi dealt with sexual offenses involving different degrees of social relations. Those with the woman of the same household were regarded as "disreputable," whereas those with the wife of a clan member were regarded with "horror."[136] Similarly, categorizations of sexual offenses among the LoDagaa did not accord with Western patterns. For the LoDagaa, Goody identified "three main types of heterosexual offense: sleeping with a clanswoman, sleeping with the wife of a clansman, and sleeping with other married women."[137] The first type, "incest," required no payment and was not treated as a serious matter. Of the other two, sleeping with the wife of a clansman "not only requires but demands a sacrifice." The requirement for sacrificial expiation for the third type of offense, straightforward adultery with an unrelated man's wife, depended on the degree of physical proximity and ritual cooperation between the households of the husband and his rival.[138] This offense – the one most susceptible to public scrutiny – was more ambiguous and was defined by contingent variables. These variables were themselves based on social and political networks, which had already changed and were still changing when these observations were made. To indigenous areas of social and ritual intercourse must be added the political jurisdictions of the chiefs, which as noted above corresponded with neither social nor ritual networks. With the suppression of retaliatory action, which in the past had been a means to remedy those offenses that did not invite the threat of affliction, offenses were redefined in terms of colonial political and social relations. The resulting expansion in communication through colonial structures extended the potential range for the definition of offenses.

Among the LoDagaa, adultery only occurred where social relations were effective, within areas of ritual jurisdiction, delimited territorially by different *tengaan*. Adultery was a form of deviance, not against a set of rules, but against the reality of ritual interdependence. Outside this effective range of social relations, illicit sexual relations of an adulterine nature did not give rise to the threat of affliction. Instead, they were perceived as direct threats to the control of women by their husbands. During the early colonial period, adultery was inextricably linked with how indigenous conflicts were defined and resolved in LoDagaa society. Sanctions, insofar as they existed, did not prevent conflict; they simply provided the means for limiting it and setting it in a context of ritual observances. This process addressed not the problem of social conflict itself, but the problems that social conflict in its turn gave rise to. In cases where the parties lived in close proximity, it acommodated transgression by redefining relationships after the fact. Rattray provided the following description of the form of resolution:

> The unfaithful wife would prepare beer and the male adulterer be called to come and drink with the husband [after the offense was confessed by the woman and admitted to by the man and the necessary sacrificial items supplied] and an agreement entered into, either to terminate the illicit relations between the parties concerned, or to recognize and, as it were, to legalize it, by the husband agreeing to allow his wife to have her lover.[139]

It should be noted that there were specific, anticipatory as opposed to retrospective, social arrangements that permitted sexual access to a wife by another man. So long as the ancestors were propitiated before the relationship began, the threat of affliction was removed. Situations where these arrangements arose were relatively infrequent, but they serve to illustrate that control over a woman's sexuality was not perceived from the perspective of a husband's coital rights, but in the wider terms of his household's (including his ancestors') interests in a woman's reproductive powers.

Far from clarifying the status of conjugal unions, LoDagaa definitions of sexual offenses only complicated matters. The apparently irregular union between a man's wife and her lover, distinct from "taking a wife," was called *sen kpe dia* or "lover enters the house."[140] In these instances a sexual relationship was authorized between a "married" woman – that is, another man's wife – and her lover through the presentation by the lover of sacrificial items to the husband's household (not to the woman's household or even through them), and through the further provision of farming services.[141] Goody argued, contrary to Labouret's interpretation, that this did not constitute polyandry, even though the liaison had been socially approved, because all children still belonged to the husband's household.[142] Although the two types of unions had different consequences, the LoDagaa did not classify a union with a lover as irregular, or that with a husband as regular. The affiliation of children was the product not of the union *per se*, but of the presentation of a large cowry payment.

Among the Tallensi, the adulterer achieved reconciliation by providing the items required for sacrifice to the husband's household's ancestor shrines. "No material compensation is made to the husband," noted Fortes, "and, in the absence of a judicial system, there is no one who can inflict a penalty on the adulterer."[143] The same can be said for the LoDagaa. Goody reported that following the sacrifice of the surrendered animals, the husband did not participate in the consumption of the meat with the rest of his household: "To eat the flesh of an animal killed for a sin committed by one's wife might be taken as condoning the offense, and even profiting from it." Otherwise, any penalty or punishment outside prescribed areas was effected only through the use of force instead of the threat of the ancestors.[144] It seems that immediately prior to and during the early years of colonial rule, if a wife's lover was too distant, either socially or physically, to satisfy the demands for the necessary sacrificial items, retaliatory action was resorted to. However, these perceptions had changed well before Goody's time.

It is important to note that indigenous understanding of heterosexual offenses persisted simultaneously with prosecutions for seduction in the courts. Litigation did not displace indigenous understanding; it was undertaken for different reasons – to punish a rival, for the sake of material gain, to seek the restitution of a wife, or to obtain legal recognition of a union. The main difficulty that arose in the hearing of these cases related to the shifting and overlapping social and political networks of the colonial period. Cases heard by a chief's court might have included parties who fell outside indigenously defined areas of ritual interdependence, but who now fell under the same political jurisdiction.

In examining indigenous concepts of sexual offenses among the LoDagaa and other politically decentralized cultures of the middle Volta basin, we need to avoid outsiders' religious and jural conceptualizations of these beliefs. Any transgression of sexual prohibitions was expressed in terms of physical affliction, and therefore did not rely on any moral or political sanction. "It may bring sickness or death on the woman's husband or children or even on herself," Fortes explained, "for it is a serious affront to her husband's ancestors."[145] As Eugene Mendonsa has argued, an ethnomedical perspective is more felicitous to indigenous thinking.[146] Adultery threatened the lives of those involved, and therefore required remedy. Remedy was available through sacrificial expiation. In sum, the sanction did not eliminate offenses; rather, it defined them in such threatening terms that other concerns were suppressed in the search for a way of escaping affliction.

According to indigenous perceptions, adultery was not an institutional violation, but an offense against the interests of the husband's household and, more importantly, its ancestors. It could only occur where conjugal unions remained intact, as it was only then that the threat of affliction became operative. This gave rise to a paradoxical situation: the gravity of the offense and fear of the possible repercussions sometimes actually led to the dissolution of conjugal relations, by encouraging the woman to leave one husband and to live with her lover as a wife. In a case heard by the District Commissioner of Lawra in 1913, the plaintiff sought the return of his wife, Woontu, from the defendant. She explained that her refusal to return to her husband had been due to her fear of being afflicted by the ancestors of his household. She had therefore remained with her lover. The district commissioner restored her to her husband and ordered that the matter be settled by "fetish custom."[147] Ignorant of the subtleties of indigenous practices, and dismissive of Woontu's expressed fears, the district commissioner thought that the offense was clearly defined. However, as Fortes noted of the Tallensi, living with a lover made him a husband and not a lover; accordingly, the nature of the transgression changed: "One curious result is that a woman who while away from home, yields to temptation and commits adultery without wishing to leave her husband, often runs off to marry the adulterer in order to avert the consequences of her lapse. She is only too glad to return to her husband when he comes to claim her; but she returns to him as a runaway wife not as an adulteress."[148]

The distinction the LoDagaa made between adultery and taking another man's wife was easily obscured in the context of the District Commissioner's Court. Inside the court, husbands who succeeded in obtaining the return of their former wives often insisted that the conjugal payments their rivals presented were only sacrificial items necessary for what they attempted to reinterpret as adultery; outside the court, "marrying another man's wife" would have been perceived only as rivalry and competition.[149] These practices illustrate some of the ambiguity of conjugal unions, particularly the proximity of "wife-stealing" (i.e., elopement) to adultery. In terms of social action, adultery was not a precisely defined offense but a highly contextual and interpretative category.

The decisions of the District Commissioner's Court during the period of direct rule were supported by the application of seduction as a criminal offense according to the *Laws of the Gold Coast*. There are no records of the decisions of the native tribunals of that period, nor even any administrative observations on the types of decisions applied. Nevertheless, it is evident from a tabulation of "seduction fees" recorded in the District Record Book in 1917 that the chiefs' courts were applying material penalties for offenses that internal social practices did not demand, let alone approve.[150] In 1932, when indirect rule was introduced, seduction was omitted from the new ordinances that were to regulate the Native Authority Courts. In 1935, following complaints by the chiefs, it was restored by the colonial administration as a criminal offense when these courts began to hear cases officially. However, there were two strong dissenting voices. The first was A.F. Kerr, the Assistant District Commissioner of Zuarungu – the district in which Fortes, the second voice, was doing fieldwork. He argued against its reimplementation on the grounds that it encouraged forced marriages by restricting the freedom of women, who, by the authority vested in the chiefs' courts, could be restored to their husbands against their will. By the end of the period of direct rule, administrators generally accepted that women were free to "remarry" elsewhere. Once seduction began to be treated as a legal offense, this latitude was restricted, as the chiefs' courts could (and did) order women to return to former husbands. Consequently, far more importance was attached to the exchange of conjugal payments: a husband could now exert greater control over his wife by taking a rival to court, so long as he had already made these payments and his rival had still not managed to return them. Previously, conjugal payments had been less significant, alienating specific interests from one household to another but not control over women. Kerr expressed serious reservations about the effect of seduction laws on women:

> I do, however, fear that if the Courts are able to force a woman to return as a wife to a man whom she does not want it will mean that the marriage of Frafra girls will become nothing less than a sale by auction. ... It is obvious that the more vocal element among the people – the Chiefs, headmen and old men – wish for the enforcement of restoration orders and support the criminality of seduction because they are the wealthier classes and most able to take advantage of a marriage by auction.[151]

It was only possible to apply seduction charges if the right of women to leave husbands by simply entering into a subsequent union was ignored.

Fortes, who at this time was conducting fieldwork among the Tallensi, took up the point in his report on marriage customs, which he wrote for the colonial administration. He noted that what the Tallensi referred to as "marrying another man's wife" was clearly differentiated from adultery:

> The difference is, essentially, that a woman commits adultery when she, as the wife of A., has sexual relations with B., and returns to live with A. ... But if she goes to B's house as a wife, even if it is only for one night, this is not adultery. She has by this act abandoned her first husband and taken a new husband. The customs and beliefs pertaining to adultery do not apply. ... In Tallensi custom it is and has always been a perfectly legitimate thing to marry another man's wife, provided this does not interfere with kinship and political relationships between the clans and families of the two husbands.[152]

In terms of indigenous social practice, the distinction between adultery and legitimate rivalry over women was clear, being defined by the intentions of women, by the social distance between rivals, and by the different ways in which these conflicts were expressed – either requiring sacrificial expiation or permitting retaliatory action.

No matter how outsiders defined LoDagaa conjugal relations, these arrangements remained strongly ambiguous unless they were brought under the scrutiny of the courts. When chiefs heard cases for seduction and provided restitution of wives to former husbands, the effect of their decisions was to remove this ambiguity by awarding to husbands a jural authority over wives – a form of control that previously had not existed. In the 1930s Fortes similarly observed of the Tallensi: "The prevailing conventions in native custom in regard to marrying another man's wife are at present in a state of flux."[153] The chiefs' courts made possible strategies that sought to suppress the ambiguous character of conjugal relations in favor of relationships redefined in terms of authority supplied by the courts. When the Tallensi brought cases to the court for the restitution of wives, they did so "in the name of the whiteman's law."[154] Neither Tallensi nor LoDagaa chiefs were able to redefine social practices outside their courts so as to remove the inherent ambiguity of conjugal unions.

It was not the application of a specific, foreign category of offense that litigants sought; rather, they wanted to establish the general principle that men had authority over women, and to strengthen the advantage of husbands over rivals. The surviving record books of the Native Authority Courts from Lawra District start in 1940, five years after they began operation.[155] They are littered with seemingly inconsequential litigation. Disappointingly, the records consist mainly of cursory summaries of the charges made and the fines levied. In the two surviving Criminal Record Books from Lawra and Jirapa, beginning in 1940, almost all the cases were brought by the two Native Authorities against local residents for a litany of petty offenses: disturbing the peace, burning grass, allowing water to stand, failing to remove rubbish, creating a "public nuisance" (defecating in an open space), cultivating land reserved by the Native Authorities, and even riding bicycles in town without lights after dark. Besides these colonial public health and safety offenses, which were enshrined as Native Authority rules under the direction of district commissioners, there were several cases of minor assault. Similarly, in the Civil Record Books there were a variety of debt cases involving for the most part petty traders, although disputes over inheritance were sometimes heard. The largest category of civil cases with any possible connection to indigenous practices was claims of compensation for seduction.

Adultery cases and charges for seduction, taken together, represent the only official evidence of the Native Courts' intervening in matters pertaining to indigenous social relations and practices and, therefore, the only area of recorded litigation where social practices could be translated into "customary law." The near wholesale absence of any evidence of the application of substantive "customary law" either went unnoticed by administrators or was ignored. In the Annual Report of 1950–51 it was observed that the Native Courts "leave much to be desired in form and record" even though it was claimed that "standards of justice administered is high":

> There is a tendency for chiefs still to try a man for such offences as "Refusing to take a message for the chief," but the very fact that such offences are recorded is

> a most healthy sign, and while conviction for such offences can in no circumstances be upheld it is understandable that a chief may not be quite clear as to what extent his authority is backed up by the laws of the Gold Coast, and how much he must rely on the willingness of the culprit to abide by Native Custom.[156]

"Native Custom" in this instance was nothing more than colonial political authority. The frequency of adultery and seduction cases in the records is therefore significant, as it serves to underline that these offenses proceeded not from "customary law," but from the courts' understanding of categories of offenses supported by colonial authority.

Nevertheless, the jural concept of adultery, as either a civil offense or a criminal charge (i.e., for seduction), was a significant innovation in terms of the repertoire of indigenous social practices. Through its application by the Native Authority Courts, it affected conjugal strategies and also caused indigenous perceptions of conjugal relations to assume jural characteristics appropriate to an institutional conceptualization of conjugal unions. Understanding how adultery emerged as a novel cause of litigation is crucial to our appreciation of changes in the social and political contexts of conjugal unions. Under colonialism, adultery cases illuminated the differences between conjugal unions as a social practice and marriage as a jural institution. These cases also raise the question of the relationship between internal social practices and colonial political relations.

Husbands, Rivals, and Lovers

By the 1940s charges for seduction and adultery were not used directly to obtain the restitution of wives but to punish rivals. One reason for the absence of cases for restitution in the Native Authority Court records was that the district commissioners from the late 1930s had been alerted to the dangers of the chiefs returning women to their former husbands and so had warned them against such abuses. In response to this curtailment of their jurisdiction, the Native Authority Courts added charges of "abduction" and "detention" for situations where a new husband eloped with the wife of another man without having yet made the necessary conjugal payments. They also applied charges of seduction when a woman had sex with her new husband before he had made the necessary conjugal payments. Seduction charges were only successful if the former husband summoned his rival to court before conjugal payments had been presented, or if he could delay the acceptance of those payments by the woman's household. In either instance, this created a period of ambiguity between the dissolution of one union and the formation of another. One of the earliest recorded cases of charges for detention before a Native Authority Court, from 1942, was a criminal case. Delire, the defendant, had taken the wife of Yarra and refused to return her when the woman's father asked him to do so. The court returned the woman to Yarra, but as she denied having been seduced, the court fined Delire £1 "for keeping the woman for a week as your wife."[157] Although it was not stated, it appears that the defendant's attempt to present conjugal payments for Yarra's wife had been frustrated by the woman's parents, who supported the old husband.

The clearest development documented in these partial records was the inflation of claims from expiatory to compensatory and penal proportions. These ranged from £1, seven fowls, and one sheep in 1943 to £9.9s. in 1952 in the Jirapa Native Court; and from £2.6d. in 1948 to £5, one goat, one sheep, one dog, and ten hens in 1953 in the Lawra Native Court. The grounds for decisions were equally inconsistent, from having "sexual relations" with another man's wife to "marrying" her. In the case of Kyirguu *vs.* Debdaa, the nonspecificity of the indigenous terms *de pog* and *kul sir* (which accounts for the apparent contradictions in translation of the proceedings) was revealed in the plaintiff's claim: "I got to know that my wife got married to the above Debdaa, that is why I have come to issue summons against him to get my wife." The court ordered that the woman be returned to her former husband, and awarded the plaintiff eight animals, ten hens, and ten thousand cowries "in order to sustain the woman's life."[158] When Kyirguu, like so many other former husbands, stated in the records that Debdaa had "married" his wife, he was not conceding the validity of that union. All he was saying was that Debdaa had taken the woman as his wife and that the woman now regarded Debdaa as her husband. Like the directional terms *Lo* and *Dagaa*, the terms translated by the clerks as indicating marriage were merely situational, not institutional or legal.

In a criminal case before the Lawra Native Court in 1950, Kunyelle Dagarti was charged with committing adultery with Nuori, wife of Tangkpele Eremon. The defendant explained that he had not taken the woman from her husband, but that the woman had come to him on three occasions and each time he had reported the matter to the chief of Nandom and returned the woman to her parents following their refusal to accept conjugal payments. Finally, when the woman returned to him yet again, he reported the matter to the assistant district commissioner, who directed him to the Native Court. Although he strenuously denied having had sex with the woman, and even though Nuori adamantly refused to return to her former husband, the court awarded the former husband £2.2s., one goat, one sheep, one dog, and seven fowls.[159] (On appeal to the district commissioner, a rare occurrence, the decision was overruled.) The basis of the Native Court's ruling had simply been that the woman had been residing with the defendant without his having successfully presented conjugal payments to the woman's household. This in itself was defined as an abrogation of the former union. The fact that the woman had herself run away was ignored.

Similarly in the case of Der of Jirapa Tampie *vs.* Kuunohra of Dogo, the plaintiff sought the return of his wife through the Jirapa Native Court. In the recorded claim it was stated that the defendant had "married" the plaintiff's wife even though the plaintiff had not "divorced" her. "I have therefore brought this to court," Der stated, so "that the defendant may explain to me why he has unlawfully married my wife. I want my wife." The defendant explained to the court that he loved the woman and she loved him. The court discovered that the woman did not wish to return to her former husband and so instructed the defendant to return the plaintiff's conjugal payments through the woman's household. However, it noted that the woman had already been residing with the defendant for three months and so instituted criminal proceedings for "adultery" and fined him £2.[160]

In these cases husbands did not use the court as the medium for the return of their wives, but instead employed a more oblique strategy. They brought their rivals to court to pre-empt the presentation of conjugal payments and in doing so, to assert their claim over the woman in question as their wife. They also availed themselves of the court to have their interests in the woman publicly acknowledged by their rivals, who were then forced to satisfy demands for "traditional" adultery fees and to provide compensation. As we will see in the next chapter, this recognition had important implications with regard to child custody cases. If recourse to the courts had not been available, the former husband's only strategic options would have been to refuse the return of conjugal payments from the in-laws, which could have acted only as a delaying tactic, or retaliatory action, which by this time might have invited colonial punishment.

In their efforts to defend the interests of former husbands, the courts created an institutional and legal reality for conjugal unions that, although not directly prejudicial to women, curtailed their freedom by making it more difficult and dangerous for other men to take them as wives. This institutional reading of selected practices ignored the situational (and hence ambiguous) nature of indigenous verbs used, in the absence of any nouns, to define conjugal unions. This terminological ambiguity is well illustrated in the clerk's translation of the case of Boi Dagarti *vs.* Siekpe Tingani, heard in 1952 before the Jirapa Native Court: "Complainant states that my wife went to her father's house, while I was aware of it, and later on my in-laws came and told me that Siekpe Tingani has stolen away your wife for about three months. I do not know whether he has married her or he is simply loving her. That is why I have issued summons against him to tell the court the reason he did so."[161] From this the court recorded a plea of guilty by the defendant and fined him either £3 or one and a half months in hard labor. As was most often the case with these Native Authority Court records, no other details were recorded. The plaintiff's own confusion over whether his rival had "married" or was "simply loving" his former wife was due not to the poor quality of translation, but to the absence of any indigenous equivalents to the social categories on which these offenses were predicated – that is, the lack of an indigenous term for marriage.

Seduction cases before the courts represented an assertion of male control over women, judicial rather than retaliatory punishment of rivals, and an institutional and public recognition of conjugal unions. In its survey of Native Authority Courts, a colonial government commission noted in 1951 that although the courts had been empowered to exercise customary law, the only ostensible native offense that had received statutory recognition was "sexual connection with another man's wife." Because "customary law" had remained largely uninvestigated and unwritten, the chiefs had been able to innovate "rules ... at variance with customary law as it was conceived of two to three generations ago," and regardless of "the local people's idea of marriage."[162]

Despite the sanctions that the Native Courts afforded husbands against their rivals, it would be misleading to assume that competition over women had been suppressed. A complaint brought by Kuber Tugu against Derviin Tugu in 1952 before the Jirapa Native Court suggests how intense feelings could become in these disputes between men. According to the plaintiff, he was drinking *pito* in Babile market with a woman when the defendant approached and called the woman over to him. "I told him that we had not finished the drink yet, and why should he call her in this manner. I asked him whether the woman was his and he replied that I was quoting law to him."[163] Another case that came before the Jirapa Native Court in the same year again illustrates the persistence of male conflict over wives as well as the courts' attempts to suppress such rivalry and, in so doing, to limit the freedom of women. The plaintiff, Sin-nubra, stated that his son had eloped with another man's wife and had been in the process of going down south with her when they were caught and returned. Having failed to take the woman by indirect means, he then attempted to negotiate the acceptance of conjugal payments with the woman's household. At this point Sin-nubra learned that another man, Suuranye, the defendant, had taken the woman. When the plaintiff confronted his son's rival, the defendant was reported to have responded: "It [a wife] is something we are all seeking and so he also caught her, that his house is not a shrub and therefore he would not return her, and secondly he added that they [the defendant's household] are also human beings and not castrated beings." Although awkwardly translated, the case illustrates something of the type and degree of frustration that often led to disputes. The chiefs sitting on this case ordered that the woman be returned to her parents, and issued both litigants with the following warning: "This [elopement] has been a practice which continues to entangle people, for the fact that the Def. used provocative terms which could cause the Compl. and his family to cause a civil harm. This is a warning to all. The courting should be done according to customary law."[164] Sin-nubra had refrained from retaliatory action against Suuranye's household. Instead, he managed to have the defendant fined £3 by coming to court. Although armed conflict had been eliminated,[165] retaliatory action, pre-empted here by legal action, remained current outside the courts.

"Customary law," like the idea of marriage, was little more than a thinly disguised representation of the interests of older and more powerful men. Fortes had noted in his monograph on Tallensi practices that informants often reported that arranged or negotiated forms of conjugal unions were the sole legal means of acquiring a wife: "Chiefs and older men – speaking both as fathers and as prospective husbands of young women whom they would be quite unlikely to get to wife in any other way – usually represent this as the principal and perhaps only legal mode of taking a bride."[166] In the numerous examples of husbands summoning rivals to court found in the record books of both the Local and District Courts, the chiefs were often involved in such litigation, usually as plaintiffs. By marked contrast, in all other types of cases they were normally involved only as witnesses to one of the parties, or when called upon by the court to give expert testimony.

In 1954, just after the Native Authority Courts had been replaced by the Local Courts, W.M. Dakurah, the Tizza Naa, brought a rival to a court whose members were his fellow chiefs, and at which he himself periodically sat as an assessor. He stated:

> My wife went to her mothers at Jirapa, where she stayed for some time and was getting ready to come to me, when the defendant coached her and she refused me. ... In view of the fact that the defendant and his friend did not in anyway realise that I am a chief, and they boldly came to my house to find out [whether the woman was likely to return to the plaintiff] and eloped the girl away, I want the court to get my wife for me and if she will come back I will claim damages from the man, on the other hand if she declines then I want my dowry.[167]

The court decided it could not oblige the plaintiff, as it was apparent that the woman did not wish to return to him. The Tizza Naa maintained that his wife had been "coached" (i.e., seduced); he testified that she was not divorced (i.e., her husband had not rejected her and she had not left her husband), and that she had only consented to elope with the defendant because he went on "persisting." His argument was intended to place responsibility on his rival and thereby encourage the woman to return to him. But after the judgment, he admitted: "Although I have not divorced her and she is divorcing me, she is at liberty to follow her new husband."[168]

Unable to exercise direct control over their wives, husbands attempted to frustrate rivals by summoning them to court.[169] When successful, this affected the capacity of women to leave unions. In a case similar to the previous one, the Zimuopare Naa brought his rival to court claiming defamation of character:

> I married my wife and we stayed together for quite a long time without any troubles. A time came that the Defendant began courting my wife, and as a result of that he played tricks whereby he had spoilt my wife's head by convincing her not to stay with me. I do not know what happened, but the Defendant took away my wife's sandals and her handkerchief, and thereby deceiving her away to his house. I followed the Defendant for the sandals and handkerchief and the Defendant refused to send them, and went away saying that I married his wife because I am a chief.[170]

The element of rivalry is very apparent in this record. Although the plaintiff's recorded claim was for defamation of character, in his testimony he stated that he was also demanding compensation from the defendant for having "spoilt my wife's head."[171] The chief's motive in following this action was no doubt to have the court reprimand the defendant.

In the case of Noyuo Zambo *vs.* Dugo Tampie, the plaintiff brought his rival to court to complain about similar practices and have him punished. He explained that after "marrying" his wife, she had returned to her father's house, where the defendant was "courting" her:

> The defendant gave some medicine to my wife in order to charm her to marry him. The defendant again put a tail under a mat and my wife sat on it. All these charms failed to work on the woman and she came back to me and after staying just for three days, she fell sick. I went and contacted a fortune teller [diviner] who told me that the defendant gave medicine to my wife which was the cause of her sickness. My wife later admitted that the defendant gave her the medicine which she drank and also sat on the tail. But before then, my wife could not speak until such time that I gave her some medicine I had from the fortune teller.[172]

Dugo admitted that he had administered the medicine in an effort to charm the woman, but strenuously denied that it was toxic, saying that the chief of Zambo had himself tested it and shown it to be harmless. The court stated that "it is a bad thing to use medicine in charming women" and fined the defendant £6, a substantial sum, so that it might "serve as a lesson to all young men who have the habit of using medicine in charming women."[173]

These cases from the Local Courts during the 1950s illustrate the attitudes of husbands and, especially, chiefs to the practice of elopement. In all these cases the plaintiffs portrayed their rivals' efforts to abduct their wives as illicit, if not illegal. There was obviously a tension here between the attitudes of men as husbands and as potential rivals. Although age and authority (not to mention wealth) may have determined attitudes, a husband in one situation might be a rival in another.[174] One case that well documents these tensions is Bari Guo Naa *vs.* Machael Naaleryel Kulcha, which came to court in 1966. The plaintiff, again a chief, was suing the defendant for the "detention and seduction" of his wife: "Defendant spoilt my wife's character and as a result married her. While the woman in question was with the Defendant she later returned to me. According to our customs if someone marries your wife and failed to dowry and the woman happens to return to you, the seduction fees must be accordingly collected in line with customs."[175] The defendant had refused Bari's demand for the "necessary" items to carry out "local performances" when he was eventually forced to return the woman. "I have never seen such performances. I know once the woman is not dowried and bears a child [the woman was discovered to be pregnant when she returned]," he told the plaintiff, "the child belongs to you."[176] Machael was referring here to the indigenous notion of adultery. He explained that he had taken the woman as a wife from her parents after she had been residing there for a year. The preferred residence of the woman was highly significant,[177] but the court chose to ignore this and instead saw conjugal payments as the determining factor.

Here the court ruled: "The marriage never received the approval of the woman's parents hence there was no marriage contract according to Lobi Dagarti customs."[178] Therefore the defendant was found liable for seduction, although the plaintiff was refused compensation for the detention of his wife. Yet by their very nature, abduction and elopement did not require consent. These were actually means of circumventing such requirements, although some form of posterior consent, or what was often translated in the records as an "apology," would eventually have been required in order for the new husband, and not the former husband, to be entitled to the custody of the children of the union. Machael's strategy failed and was abandoned because, as he told the court: "I later learnt that the parents said I would never marry their daughter."[179]

Abduction and elopement lacked any formal features that could have been reified into laws. They were practical strategies whose success depended on physical, social, or (after colonial invasion) political distance. Spatially, such distance was created by boundaries: between relatively distant settlements, between particular ritual areas, or between regions (i.e., with the couple eloping by migrating south for a period). Social distance was usually wrought, despite physical proximity, by preceding disputes and rivalries. However, in the political contexts created by the courts, these distancing devices became compressed. Political distance had once been the product of the absence of authority structures and the atomistic nature of social formations; recourse to the courts and related agencies of authority, such as the police, brought husbands and rivals into proximity that otherwise would not have been possible.

Just how these forms of distance had changed during the colonial period is demonstrated in a case that came before the District Court in 1969. Pone Lobi, former wife of "Ex-Sergeant" Kaakah Lobi of Dikpe, had been betrothed to Kaakah sometime during the Second World War. She left her husband after he accused her of moral impropriety, namely, keeping company with a man called Dang – a charge she strenuously denied. She stayed at her parents' house for two-and-a-half months. Kaakah then suspected that she had taken up residence with Dang. He reported the matter to the police in Lawra, presenting as evidence the clothes of his wife, which he had found in Dang's room. The police advised him to take civil action to retrieve his wife, as Dang refused to return the woman, having told Kaakah that he intended to "dowry" her. When Dang eloped with the woman, he had informed the village chief. After the plaintiff tried to demand the return of his wife, Dang presented the conjugal payments to the woman's parents, but they were refused. Two weeks later the dispute was heard in court, with Kaakah claiming damages for seduction from Dang, as well as compensation for "keeping her [Pone] as a concubine."[180]

The case reveals the arbitrary distinction between orthodox and unorthodox means of acquiring wives that was inscribed in court attitudes during the colonial period. The plaintiff, who had the support of the woman's parents, informed the defendant that the woman had told her father that she was leaving the latter's house to attend a funeral, and had not told him that she was going to marry elsewhere. To this the defendant replied: "Women normally do not inform their fathers when going for elopement."[181] This statement highlights the predicament of a social practice that, although possessing equally "traditional" (indigenous) antecedents, was designed to circumvent the more formal aspects of those practices that were translated into orthodox "customs." Although equally valid from an indigenous perspective, this practice was excluded from the orthodox ideology of LoDagaa "marriage" and therefore did not receive legal recognition as a legitimate procedure for conjugal formation. From a jural perspective, it threatened the coherence of the laws that had been distilled from other practices. If the practice of elopement had been recognized it would have brought into question the existence of all marriage laws and marital rights.

Kaakah insisted on one set of procedures that had already been recognized and imbued with an external legality by the courts as social rules, whereas Dang argued in terms of internal social practices whose validity could only be measured by their effectiveness and currency. For example, the plaintiff asked in his cross-examination of the defendant: "Before you marry someone's daughter don't you need to inform him?" Dang's response reflected the reality of social practices as opposed to the status of social rules: "I do not need to inform one whose daughter I am going to elope." Knowing that the defendant's attempt to have conjugal payments (in this case the "apology") accepted by the woman's parents had recently failed, Kaakah argued that Dang could not have "married" her: "I put it to you that you have not married the woman in question. A: The woman is now in my house. Q: If a woman is with you does that mean that she is your wife? A: The woman divorced [left] her husband and came to me, so she is my wife."[182]

Kaakah was eventually defeated in his argument with Dang and relented, saying that if Dang had actually "married" the woman, he would abandon Pone to him and demand the return of conjugal payments. But the court asserted that there had been no "divorce" (i.e., no formal or jural dissolution of the union) between Kaakah and Pone before the woman eloped with Dang, and insisted on the parties complying with "customary laws" relating to "divorce." These ostensible laws were gathered from witnesses in court during the hearing. In many respects they were similar to the formal procedures for dissolving a union that had been reported by Goody almost twenty years earlier.[183] Because none of these formal procedures had been followed, the court concluded that the union had not been dissolved, even though the present residence of the woman and her own statement to the court could have left no doubt that the union had been terminated.

What we see in the exchange between Kaakah and Dang quoted above are the inconsistencies that emerged when social practices were subject to a foreign logic. The apparent contradiction between the orthodox procedures for acquiring wives and their unorthodox counterparts was the result of the translation of one set of practices into "customary law" within the courts, and the marginalization of another set of practices to an area beyond the courts. Because unorthodox practices threatened orthodox ones, the coherence of "customary law" was itself threatened. In the process of creating coherence, the courts were ignoring the logic of the world of experience in favor of the logic of the world on paper. As Bourdieu noted: "One thus has to acknowledge that practice has a logic which is not that of logic, if one is to avoid asking of it more logic than it can give, thereby condemning oneself either to wring incoherences out of it or thrust upon it a forced coherence."[184] The peculiar administrative, chiefly, and patriarchal demands of the courts highlighted ambiguities and contradictions within the indigenous repertoire of social practices for taking a wife. At the same time, the courts attempted to erase these contradictions by imposing coherence and definition.

Despite references to indigenous etiology made in many claims, the exorbitant amounts demanded for both expiation and compensation reinforce the argument that most of these decisions had no basis in indigenous practice. Consider, for example, the case of Sata Dagarti *vs.* Lasi Dagarti, heard before the Lawra Local Court in 1959. The plaintiff explained that the defendant, having taken his wife, had been unable to present the necessary conjugal payments to the woman's household: "My wife had to return to me due to the disappointment from the Defendant. ... I cannot accept her without the necessary native customs being performed." However, the claim for £32 was totally incommensurate with any "customs" – a point that the defendant tried to illustrate to the court: "If I pay this amount I will own the woman [i.e., the claim was in excess of conjugal payments]."[185] In this case the court ruled that £3.6d. was the maximum amount awardable in these circumstances. However, in the District Court, which had powers to award greater amounts for damages, claims of £26.16s. and £50 were satisfied in the early 1960s, and a claim of ¢406 as late as 1972.[186] After 1972 the disposition of successive magistrates altered dramatically, and the number of cases dropped suddenly – due no doubt to a 1973 decision that challenged both the relevance of indigenous "customs" and the authenticity of litigants' claims. On the first matter the magistrate observed: "With my own experience, certain Dagare customs that have been outmoded, their use and contention are fast dying out, and this act described involving the Defendant is one of them. We must not forget that laws are made for the living by the living, and what law that was practiced by a generation is discarded by the succeeding generation whose time it is to believe in what they do."[187]

In the case that had given rise to this decision, the plaintiff had claimed items with which to "purify" his wife, alleging that the defendant had defiled her by making sexual advances toward her. Both parties were government employees – a fact that seems to have allowed the magistrate to overrule ostensibly indigenous perceptions. Although the touching of a woman's breasts and buttocks was perceived among the LoDagaa as interfering with a woman's reproductive powers, the circumstances in which this took place in the case at hand – in the offices of the District Administration, where the woman was also employed – were totally removed from any indigenous context. Indeed, the plaintiff was concerned exclusively with exerting control over his wife and punishing his rival. With respect to the plaintiff's claim of ten goats, seven sheep, one dog, one cat, twenty fowls, and fifty thousand cowries, the magistrate commented:

> On my experience of Dagare customs and customary law, I know as well as the Plaintiff and everybody knows, that in a case of this nature, it only needs about a two to three week old chicken and perhaps twenty cowries to purify the woman if the act of the Defendant was a breach of customs. The claim put forward by the Plaintiff is fantastic, fictitious and fully backed by no customary law, besides the motive of capitalism well hidden behind it.[188]

Although such claims ceased almost entirely after 1974, other strategies designed to assert control over women and punish rivals persisted – namely, the use of the courts to interfere with the dissolution of one union and the formation of another. Two decades earlier, any notion of "customary law" had depended on the Local Courts entertaining just such "fantastic" and "fictitious" ideas from the world on paper.

Chapter Eight

Postcolonial Litigation of Personal Identities

We must not forget that laws are made for the living by the living, and what law that was practiced by a generation is discarded by the succeeding generation whose time it is to believe in what they do.

A.Z. Kpemaal, District Magistrate, 1973

During the colonial period, women demonstrated their autonomy outside the courts regardless of how conjugal unions were represented by colonial administrators, chiefs, and litigants. Women's autonomy, male competition for wives, and the resulting instability of conjugal unions among the LoDagaa threatened the idea that marriage was an indigenous institution; but administrative convenience, chiefly connivance, and patriarchal interests maintained the pretense. During the postcolonial period, the courts began to search for the existence of marriage in precise social practices rather than the "fantastic" and "fictitious" improvisations that had been wrought during the colonial period, in order to restrict the freedom of women and, later, to punish husbands' rivals. The postcolonial courts interrogated the meaning of conjugal payments in their search for clear jural definitions and legal rules. These efforts paralleled similar inquiries by the local Catholic elite, who were eager to defend some indigenous social practices while reforming others. In both court judgments and the elite's writings we find strong echoes of midcentury British anthropological thought.

Inherent in these projects of jural interpretation was a tension between the idea of women as property and the idea of women as autonomous social actors. On the one hand, the direction of conjugal payments seemed to determine their meaning, with rights in women traveling in the opposite direction of payments. However, the ability of women to change their residence made a mockery of the notion that conjugal payments affected the residence of women; in fact, the payments were the *result* of women changing residences (and therefore husbands). In adultery cases where former husbands summoned their rivals to court before their conjugal payments had been returned, the courts attempted to give far greater weight to payments than residence. In doing so they inverted the causal and temporal relationship between payments and residence and treated women as property. But at the same time, the courts were far less sanguine about treating children as property, so by the 1970s we see the courts imposing a literal, biological perspective on the source of personal identity. This second development directly contradicted the first: conjugal payments, not blood, determined descent, yet, the courts often preferred to award custody of children because of blood rather than because of conjugal payments. The last major theme to emerge from litigation before the courts in the postcolonial era is that of how the status of wife was used to determine the nature of the union between a woman and a man. This development owed nothing to the courts, but was based on the arguments launched by litigants themselves. Some litigants were eager to avoid the sterile logic of commercial transactions and jural interpretations, and used the issue of a woman's uxorial status to determine the status of unions. In the end, we learn that not only were unions ambiguous and equivocal, but so too was the status of most women. It was this ambiguity – this equivocal nature of women's identities – that women exploited as a refuge from the world on paper.

The question of the validity of conjugal arrangements brings us back to the divergence between jural extrapolations and the untidy dynamics of the world of experience. The conjugal instability and disputes over the custody of children that Read had observed at the beginning of the twentieth century remained central to the social history of the LoDagaa. In both the colonial and postcolonial periods, they were the major sources of litigation before the courts. In this chapter, court cases from the postcolonial period are examined in detail. What emerges from this are three major themes: changing meanings of conjugal payments; biological sources of personal identity; and, finally, attempts to determine the identity of women as wives. Each of these themes is related to the question of marriage – its constitution and meaning, its consequences, and its diagnostic features. We have already seen that the idea of marriage was not compatible with LoDagaa practices, but its existence had to be imagined or presumed for various reasons by a variety of people during the colonial period, not least by husbands and chiefs eager to constrain the freedom of women and, more directly, to foil the efforts of their wives' suitors, lovers, and potential husbands.

Court Records and the Normalization of Marriage

The jural analysis of conjugal unions among the LoDagaa by colonial administrators, anthropologists, clerks, chiefs, clerics, government magistrates, and Catholic intellectuals, as well as by some litigants themselves, led to the erroneous idea that there was an indigenous institutional reality commensurate with the foreign idea of marriage. However, in 1984 Bishop Kpiebaya broke ranks. He stated in the diocesan newspaper, and later in a pamphlet titled *Dagaaba Traditional Marriage and Family Life*, that most unions among the people of the Nandom area were the result of elopement.[1] The bishop's statement not only caused controversy but also broke the reticence that is found in most written representations of LoDagaa social practices about what Fortes called "marrying another man's wife." Even Goody, who elaborated on the orthodox conjugal practices (betrothal and negotiations) described by Rattray, treated elopement only insofar as it concerned first marriages, and then only as a manifestation of "institutionalized reluctance."[2]

Father Bekye objected to the bishop's statement and pointed out several other forms of conjugal formation. He claimed that although the elopement of unmarried women was still quite prevalent, the elopement of already married women was rare among the LoDagaa.[3] In 1987, Dery went further and argued that elopement was "not normal," and "cannot therefore be taken to be the ordinary way of courting."[4] This was a highly normative statement, relying on the presumed hegemony of the world on paper rather than any evidence from the world of experience. Read had contended that elopement had caused considerable fighting at the beginning of the twentieth century. Twenty-five years before Dery's statement, the Jirapa Native Authority Court had unintentionally highlighted the dissonance between the world on paper (customary law) and the world of experience (practice) when it warned that "courting should be done according to customary law," even while conceding that elopement was "a practice which continues to entangle people."[5]

Dery was attempting regularize the method of conjugal formation in real life by making representations on paper. Discounting elopement as a frequent or legitimate method of forming conjugal unions allowed him to ignore questions about the stability and recognition of unions, which were threatened by the practice of elopement. For Dery the practice of elopement was associated with the idea of marriage by capture – a notion that had featured so prominently in McLennan's theory of primitive marriage and in subsequent Victorian thought.[6] He defined elopement as "the taking of a girl as wife by force," said that it was exceptional, and identified four reasons for it happening: a woman already had a husband; she disliked a prospective husband; she had too many suitors; or she lacked knowledge of correct courting procedures.[7] Thus the disassociation of LoDagaa practice from Victorian ideas was paradoxical, in that all four conditions indicated that elopement was not the result of capture but rather the result of the woman's actions; even when she was not the instigator, her dissatisfaction and cooperation were necessary. To see elopement among the LoDagaa as a form of capture required not only reading external ideas into local practices, but also viewing women as passive and devoid of agency. According to Father Bekye, one reason that a "young girl" would allow herself to be eloped was that she had "no sense or notion of courting methods."[8] Similarly, Dery argued that "a young innocent girl who has little knowledge about courting" was vulnerable to this practice.[9] In order to distance the apparently irregular practice of elopement from orthodox and recognized practices, both Bekye and Dery represented "courting" as the dominant form of conjugal formation. The court records demonstrate that although husbands certainly sympathized with this representation, their rivals did not respect it, nor did women, young or old, oblige it. Nevertheless, Dery's representations were consistent with the increasing formalization of "customary law" in the courts from 1954 onward, and with greater claims of normative hegemony.

As we have already seen, the postcolonial period brought many changes to ideas of ethnic identity, to how local politics was represented, and to how indigenous religious thought and practice was interpreted. It also brought changes in how disputes were articulated and heard in the courts. There were three main changes: the quality of the court records improved (this was accompanied by an increasingly inquisitorial character to proceedings); the role of chiefs became less official and more ceremonial; and the state began intervening more directly, through its magistrates.

In 1954, Local Courts replaced Native Authority Courts in preparation for independence. The chiefs retained their control of the decision-making process, but the quality of court records in Lawra District increased appreciably. Either because the quality of the clerks improved or because issues were contested more heatedly, the transcription of proceedings became more complete, allowing the first clear view of litigants' rhetoric. Also, the law demanded better records. Although the law to be applied by Local Courts remained undefined, the Court Ordinance of 1951 specified the need for litigants and assessors to articulate the basis of claims and decisions: "In all cases in which the party pleading relies upon native law or custom, the native law or custom relied upon shall be stated in the pleading with sufficient particulars to show the nature and effect of the native law or custom in question and the geographical area and the tribe or tribes to which it relates."[10] Even though this often amounted to little more than the formulaic appeal to "Lobi-Dagarti customary marriage law," it did mean that decisions now often indicated what, ostensibly, the relevant laws were. Sometimes the chiefs called on witnesses to ascertain what the law was, other times they just stated what it was as if it were given.

Creating "customary law" involved selecting certain social practices and translating them from the context of experience into that of spoken or written representations. In these circumstances the role of the court clerks became more important. All but a few chiefs were illiterate,[11] and all without exception lacked formal training in official procedures. Even after 1960, when trained magistrates took over from the chiefs, the clerks continued to affect litigation through their framing of litigants' claims. As Moore observed in Tanzania in the 1980s: "In recent decades the court clerks who translate factual descriptions of grievances into conventional legal categories have profoundly affected local ideas about the acceptable words that make wrongs actionable."[12] This reliance on the appropriate words (somewhat like the written charms of Muslim scribes discussed in Chapter 5) reminds us of the tyranny of the world on paper over the world of experience in the courts. Words, not experiences, made "wrongs actionable."

Even though it confirmed the use of jural categories and formal causes of litigation, the substitution of Local for Native Courts was essentially a change in name only in terms of the courts' status. Changes in composition came in 1960 with the creation of District Courts. The most significant difference between Local and District Courts was in the judicial officers themselves: the government-appointed lay magistrates. Once the chiefs were displaced from the courts, they were left with largely a ceremonial role. The official status of chieftaincy would oscillate under the regimes that followed, but would never return to its former heights. However, chiefs continued to hear disputes in an unofficial capacity. Magistrates tolerated them as arbitrators and ignored the fact that they heard the vast majority of disputes as agencies of first instance.[13] Writing of the authority of the neighboring Sisala chiefs in the 1970s, Mendonsa observed:

> Today the power of the chief is limited. He functions mainly as a figurehead and spokesman for the government. Judicial cases are brought before the chiefs, but they have no sanctions except referral to the district court in Tumu. Wise chiefs, however, use persuasion and prestige of office to settle cases before they reach this point. Villagers may bypass the chief and carry a case directly to the police and court in Tumu.[14]

In Lawra District during this period a similar situation existed. Chiefs continued to hear cases, both informally and formally (despite the absence of recognition and often to the annoyance of the magistrates), but always unofficially.[15]

The chiefs' loss of control over the courts in 1960 also represented the direct intervention by the state into the courts as assessors rather than just sponsors. Government-appointed magistrates came to resemble the district commissioners of direct rule of two generations before, whose decisions had been based on a rather vague set of colonial criteria rather than on indigenous norms. Similarly, interventions by magistrates attempting to alter social practices can be seen as assertions of the ideologies of the postcolonial state, particularly in the 1970s and 1980s when successive magistrates appeared intent on changing indigenous practices so that they accorded with the external norms of life in "modern" settings.

The relationship between the District Courts and the unofficial courts of the chiefs after 1960 was complicated. On certain issues, the attitudes of the magistrates and those of the chiefs (as representatives of "tradition") steadily diverged over the years. However, in some other respects their views coincided, especially with regard to men's desire to control women. Just as magistrates were constrained from departing too much from indigenous practices, the chiefs were forced to respond to the direction of the latter's decisions in order to prevent a breakdown in their tenuous and ambiguous roles as self-appointed arbitrators. Had litigants felt that they could readily obtain decisions in the District Court not offered by the chiefs, they would have by-passed the chiefs as agencies of first instance. But this did not happen. Chiefs had to address what the magistrates decided in the District Court when deciding cases of their own; for their part, magistrates often relied on chiefs as sources of what indigenous practices were.

It was not until literate and trained magistrates were appointed in 1960 that any significant clarification of customary laws appeared in the court records. This was the result not of clerical influences but of the relationship of the magistrates to indigenous society. As the chiefs had been thought of as the repositories of customary law, there had obviously been no need on their part to discover what "customary laws" were. As Anthony Allott observed of the substitution of magistrates for chiefs across Ghana, when the courts had been the province of the chiefs, "if the judges could not think of an appropriate rule to cover a case, they would formulate one themselves."[16] The magistrates did not possess this (albeit contrived) legitimacy, and were forced to solicit evidence from witnesses as to the relevant indigenous practices. "Still," Allott continued, "even with the change of the system of courts, the customary law remains. One must ask oneself what will happen to that customary law, now that it is being passed into new hands?"[17] In the absence of any codification or formal procedures for ascertaining what was "customary," chiefs often preserved an authority in such matters through the reliance of the magistrates on them as court witnesses.

In these improved records, the most substantive issues behind litigation concerning conjugal unions, the majority of all litigation, were these: the timing and meaning of conjugal payments; the public definition of unions in the courts (versus their private formation outside the courts); the social implications of unions (namely the custody of children); and the cultural means of defining the social status of women. In dealing with these issues, the courts sought to extend recognition to those indigenous interests and practices that it supported while discouraging those it regarded as socially undesirable. An important theme in these records was the contrast between the public context of the courts and the private reality of LoDagaa social life, where legal distinctions did not exist. By selectively recognizing some practices and interests over others, the courts were not only translating practices from one realm to another, but also asserting certain ideologies of the postcolonial state: the rule of law, the hegemony of political over "traditional" authority, and the secular, national morality of the new republics and intervening regimes.

Although the LoDagaa came to accept marriage as a category for the purposes of litigation in the courts, it was primarily a rhetorical device meant to legitimate claims, and did not alter indigenous practices outside the courts. All the same, it did affect how the LoDagaa negotiated relations between the world of experience, where people deployed strategic practices, and the world on paper, where litigants constructed rhetorical representations. Throughout the recorded proceedings of the courts, marriage was interpreted, defined, disputed, reinterpreted, and redefined; yet as a social category commensurate with LoDagaa practices, it was never successfully defined, except from the standpoint of individual litigants who succeeded in arguing the legitimacy of particular unions and, therefore, the legitimacy of their interests.

Changing Meanings of Conjugal Payments

Charges for adultery in the District Court had virtually ceased by 1974,[18] but a decade later another such case did come before the court. It is a significant case because the plaintiff, a secondary school teacher, gave a very clear statement in English of his idea of marriage and his expectations of how a wife should behave. His wife had left him for the defendant, only to return five months later. Although the woman had initially "denied all knowledge of affairs with any man," when later confronted with a letter from the defendant she apparently admitted that the defendant had been her lover. The plaintiff explained the concept of a "legally married wife" this way: "I have the right to have sex with her from time to time. She has to cook for me to eat as a wife. When I am sick she has to attend to me. Now, the Dagaare custom stipulates that when a legally married wife commits adultery you as the husband have no right to have sex play with her, eat from her or allow her to tender to you while you are in ill health."[19] When asked by the defendant whether the union had been "performed in the Christian or the traditional way," the plaintiff refused to answer, just as he refused to disclose the amount of the "dowry" already presented, saying that this was his household's responsibility, not his own. Unable to ascertain on what grounds the plaintiff was claiming the woman as his "legally married wife," the defendant nevertheless admitted liability. He did challenge the amount of the claim, suggesting that the elders were the best judges of such matters, but the court satisfied the plaintiff's demands, and the defendant was ordered to pay one male goat, four sheep or goats of either sex, ten fowls, thirty-five hundred cowries, ¢5,000 in special damages, and ¢1,000 in costs.[20]

Many features of this case were exceptional,[21] but perhaps most exceptional was how reasonable the plaintiff's claim sounded. Read in the context of other cases of this time, and in isolation from the world of experience, it would appear that there had always been such a thing as marriage among the LoDagaa, and indeed "legal marriage." We can discount the influence of Christianity in this case, even though the plaintiff had a Christian name and the defendant raised it as an issue, because the claim rested on "Dagaare custom." Furthermore, according to the Catholic Church, the attitudes of Christians toward conjugal unions had changed little, as indicated by Bishop Kpiebaya's decidedly negative appraisal in 1979 of the degree to which Christianity had been integrated into the conjugal lives of converts in the region.[22] He suggested that the best way to measure the degree of religious change among Christians was in "their attitude towards women," arguing that in "traditional Dagaare society" women were considered minors without rights and that they were treated as property; symptoms of these attitudes were found in "bride-price," conjugal infidelity by husbands, polygyny, and the treatment of women as laborers. He elaborated with the following observations, or rather interpretations:

> A woman is considered to be only a grown up child. She doesn't have equal rights with the man in many respects. This mentality has given rise to all sorts of adverse customs and practices against women. For instance, in marriage the woman is considered to be the property of the husband and his clan but the man is by no means her property. ... This attitude of treating women as property and as a hired

> hand is strengthened by the payment of the bride-price for a wife. ... The inferior position of the wife also legitimises the practice of the man taking multiple wives or indulging in conjugal infidelity. A man has exclusive sexual rights over his wife, but not the wife over the husband.[23]

For the bishop, "traditional Dagaare society" was a timeless realm of immobility. The position of women in LoDagaa society, as he explained it, may have reflected male attitudes at the turn of the last century, but it was only after colonial rule was imposed that these attitudes prevailed, and even here the bishop's comments exaggerated reality. It was not the society of the past, but contemporary LoDagaa culture, that the bishop was actually describing. He did not understand that the expectations of most LoDagaa men, Christians and non-Christians, had changed considerably during the colonial period; traditional attitudes were actually colonial attitudes. Women were litigated over in the District Court – an institution that remained exclusively male – just as they had been in the District Commissioner's Court, the Native Courts, and the Local Courts. In the courts, male words came to be privileged over female actions. Outside the courts, it was another matter.

Read contended at the beginning of the twentieth century that the "head money system is very similar to purchase" and that "ideas of property as existing among pagan races consist of cattle and livestock, wives, children, clothes and ornaments."[24] Although we do not know whether Read's views reflected LoDagaa men's idealized notions of patriarchy at that time, by the 1960s commercial language had entered into male interpretations of conjugal payments found in the court records. In justifying his claim to the custody of the child of his former wife, a husband used the following metaphor to describe the effect of his conjugal payments, which still resided with her household: "If I buy a female animal I need it to multiply."[25] Such statements must be understood for what they were, as bold ideological claims with little relation to experience. Whatever interests or rights a husband may have thought he had in a wife, there was no way men could actually compel women to comply with these expectations;[26] and as Read also noted, they very often did not.

In an account of women in LoBirifor society during the 1970s, Hagaman reported that "marriage is primarily an economic affair," that attitudes toward it were "enormously practical," and that "economic motivation was the prime mover in most affairs." However, she also noted: "There is no way that a man can force his wife to remain with him or perform the duties he expects from her."[27] Whatever rights *in* and *over* women were established through the presentation of conjugal payments, husbands had no indigenous means of exercising these "rights." As Phil Evans, another observer of the LoBirifor, wrote in the early 1980s:

> According to the theory of LoBirifor marriage exchange, control over the distribution of, and access to, women is exercised by men, who play the predominant role in the arrangement of marriages, and the negotiation and transfer of bridewealth payments. The competition for women which accompanies such processes, however, creates a space in which women can, and do, secure for themselves a degree of autonomy. ... Male control over the distribution of women is in many respects no more than an illusion. As jural minors, women are placed in a position where they are effectively able to select their own marriage partners, and leave men to sort out the consequences. ... The weakness of LoBirifor men in this respect is that there is no legitimate form of sanction available within their practice by which they can compel a woman to remain with the partner they have chosen for them.[28]

LoDagaa women had the capacity to engage in independent action and to dispose of their productive and reproductive labor in directions of their own choosing. The court records clearly document this autonomy, and indicate that in the world of experience conjugal payments were not about rights either in or over women, but about men attempting to deal with the consequences of women's actions.

By mid-century, anthropologists were working hard to obfuscate the economic implications of conjugal arrangements in Africa. Referring to colonial judicial attitudes that equated conjugal payments with purchase, Radcliffe-Brown attributed such views to "ignorance, which may once have been excusable but is so no longer," and to "blind prejudice, which is never excusable in those responsible for governing an African people." He himself contended that bridewealth payments were "symbolic" rather than economic. Nevertheless, the jural analysis that Radcliffe-Brown advocated was predicated on a language of exchange; it equated women with property, albeit unintentionally. Despite his fierce criticism of colonial attitudes, Radcliffe-Brown was forced to accept that within his own analytical framework, "a person may be treated as a thing."[29] As Ann Singer later observed: "The male-centered view, combined with the language of a commercial culture, frequently [led] anthropologists, despite their disclaimers, to describe marriage in terms which sound like the purchase of women."[30] The bishop's interpretation of LoDagaa conjugal payments, like Read's, was based on a similar error in interpretation.

In addressing the question of whether women were property, Goody admitted that rights were "like property," but added that a LoDagaa woman was not property because her "natal kin retain some legal or jural interest in her even after she is married" and "she herself is and never ceases to be right- and duty-bearing persona."[31] However, the first type of rights still treated women as things in which different households held rights. The second type of rights (*jus in personam* as opposed to *jus in rem*), namely the capacity to evade male control, could be exercised only in contradiction of the rights the jural analysis attributed to marriage. The notion of a set of jural rights exchanged through marriage was obviated by a corresponding set of actions that women were free to engage in and that repudiated what Evans described as the "illusion" of patriarchal control. As already noted, women acted and left "men to sort out the consequences."[32] What kept women from being property was men's lack of physical control over them as well as women's capacity for autonomous action. Wives were not property among the LoDagaa if for no other reason than their refusal to act as such and the inability of men to control women. Furthermore, even if men made ideological statements to the contrary, the LoDagaa made a clear distinction between wives and humans who were treated as property: conjugal payments were much more substantial than the cost of slaves, and slaves were not given a proper burial.[33]

The relationship between women and conjugal payments was problematic for administrators, anthropologists, and magistrates alike. The economics of these payments could not be denied, but what meaning did these exchanges have? Had these observers looked at when and why payments were presented in the untidy dynamics of the histories of individual unions, they would have understood that these payments were not made for women. Rather, they were made in reaction to the actions of women. From a careful reading of the cases in the court records, we can see that payments were exchanges between men that, while made with respect to women, did not control women. They were made in order to deal with the shifting interests that households had in women. These interests kept changing, and payments kept circulating, as a consequence of women changing residence. However, this perspective did not fit well with the jural analysis favored by the world on paper; here, in the world of rhetoric, men acted and women reacted.

Among the LoDagaa, conjugal payments were very costly in terms of available wealth, involving substantial outlays of cowries and/or large numbers of cattle. Yet postcolonial observers repeatedly tried to deny the economic value of these payments. The Catholic Church, to which most literate LoDagaa belonged, began to argue for the diminution of such prestations in the 1970s. It based its arguments on the notion that the first elements in the set of prestations were symbolic and separate from later payments. Some indigenous observers even argued, despite considerable historical evidence to the contrary, that the high level of conjugal payments was a recent development, the result of colonial rulings and cowry inflation.[34] Complaining that the high cost of conjugal payments led Christians into "free unions," Bishop Kpiebaya claimed that "the symbolic dowry really constitutes the essential dowry. Once it is given and accepted the marriage is considered to be contracted. The reason for this double dowry ["symbolic" and "exorbitant"] is to make it possible for extremely poor people to marry."[35] The contradiction here, between the actual amounts of wealth presented and the symbolic interpretation of payments, was ultimately one between the world of experience and attempts by observers to rewrite the meaning of payments on paper. The bishop's parishioners obviously did not understand this symbolic reality; otherwise they would not have incurred the further expense of the later, "extortionate" payments.

This formalistic rather than substantive interpretation of conjugal payments was not new. Rattray had stated that among the Lobi, the initial payment made "the marriage binding even at this stage."[36] Just how it was binding was not specified. Writing in the 1970s, Goody noted that among the LoWiili "there is a small payment of 350 cowries which is said to be all that is required to 'legalize' the union."[37] In 1974 the district magistrate, A.Z. Kpemaal, who had a strong antipathy toward the size of conjugal payments among the LoDagaa, observed in a decision: "If the greetings are accepted, the marriage is declared legal and lawful, and without even paying the dowry, the children born by the girl are for the husband."[38] (See payment "A" in Tables 10, 11, and 12.)

Indigenous scholars other than the bishop also attempted to represent conjugal payments as symbolic rather than economic. Father Victor Hien, a priest from the other side of the Black Volta, noted in 1970: "Strictly speaking, the dowry consists of this first ceremony and its accompanying rites, which visibly embody the sacred and religious accord of marriage and bestow on the couple the sacred right to cohabit and procreate."[39] Another priest, Father Kpoda, claimed: "The [initial] dowry both symbolizes and seals the union. In fact, the amount of the dowry, three hundred and sixty cowries and a fowl, is strictly religious."[40] Writing of the LoDagaa of northern Ghana, Kuukure, paraphrasing Radcliffe-Brown, wrote that the "marriage gift" was "the objective instrument by which a 'legal' marriage is established."[41] Echoing Radcliffe-Brown's refutation of connotations of purchase, he argued that "bride-price" among the LoDagaa was symbolic: "The African, here the Dagao, buys a cow, but makes gifts of money and animals for his wife."[42] Father Tengan claimed that the initial payment "establishes the fact that the woman is your legal wife."[43] Francis Korbieh, a local politician and lawyer, asserted that the initial conjugal payment alone "signifies the validation of the marriage which thereby vests the husband with all rights and responsibilities over the woman and her children," even though a later and more substantial payment "really validates the union."[44] These interpretations are difficult to sustain. Court cases from the postcolonial period reveal the practical limitations of using this isolated moment to determine or define the status of conjugal unions. These representations become problematic once read back into the world of experience. If the "symbolic dowry" was legal, what was the meaning of the later payments?

Nevertheless, these narrow jural interpretations of practices made sense in the world on paper: they removed ambiguity from unions and explained conjugal payments in terms of marriage. For Rattray and Goody this was useful because it extended a language of comparison in which the word marriage was an important concept. For members of the Catholic elite, it was useful because it furthered a reformist message. By 1990 some priests were calling for "the law" to intervene in order "to put some sanity and rationale behind the payment of the brideprice." They argued that the high cost of payments led to women being "valued as a commodity in the market," and they advocated set fees and a schedule of payments.[45] The effect of such suggestions, however, was to make both husbands and wives "more exacting and even avaricious." The impression among most Catholics was that such unions would be "cheap and worthless."[46] One commentator argued that although conjugal payments were founded on the un-Christian principles of *lex talonis* and *do ut des*, they did stabilize and legitimize unions, as well as give status to children. He argued that abolishing payments, given their social functions, would "destabilise" society. Instead, the symbolic elements of payments should be retained and their economic value renounced.[47] According to the informants of Father Tengan, women would have felt insulted by a diminution of payments. As one woman explained to the court in 1966: "My father said your husband has not dowried you and this does not give you a worth as his wife and as a housewife." The district magistrate, D.J. Charles, repeated this sentiment in his decision: "In accordance with the Lobi-Dagarti customary way of marriage, it is by dowrying and this dowry gives the woman her full worth as a housewife. But where you fail to dowry the woman becomes a lover and not a wife."[48]

In order to make the jural analysis more coherent and less controversial, observers denied the economics of these exchanges. But this was only because they insisted on seeing women as part of a system of exchange, and not as autonomous agents in their own right. Conjugal relations among the various LoDagaa congeries were punctuated by a series of payments by the man's household to the woman's household. In the courts, these acts were removed from their social context. The direction of payments became more important than the circulatory pattern of the indigenous economy, public intentions were often attributed retrospectively to private actions, and foreign meanings were applied in order to satisfy the jural perspective of the courts. These developments were not merely the result of judicial interventions into the social life of the LoDagaa, although these institutions provided the impetus and structures for such distortions. They were also exacerbated by the fact that the courts were almost exclusively male arenas. Women were almost entirely marginalized.

In the court records, clerks often omitted a woman's name, referring to her instead as merely "the woman in question." The phrase eventually became almost as ubiquitous in the records as "defendant," "plaintiff," and "witness." Although it disguised the personal identities of women and reduced them to a generic status, the phrase is apposite, given that women seldom participated in the courts as litigants even though most disputes were about matters that most directly affected their lives.[49] When women appeared, they did so almost always as witnesses – as interested bystanders without recognized rights. If one were to take the testimony and arguments of most male litigants at face value, women were passive beings and devoid of agency. Yet the actions of women were the fundamental issues behind most litigation: women were, in a sense, litigated. Thus, women may have been conspicuous by their almost complete absence as litigants, but they were by no means peripheral to the courts. Women spoke as witnesses to disputes about their own lives, and because it was often the evidence most relevant to disputes, men told stories about women. The amount of time men spent in the court records reporting and sorting out the consequences of women's actions demonstrates clearly that women were not passive outside the courts.

Because women were denied a voice in the courts but not outside the courts, it is difficult to reconcile the male-centered perspective of litigants with the reality of women's lives. This difficulty is compounded by the gender-specific explanations of conjugal payments offered by anthropologists.[50] While often disclaiming economic connotations, anthropological analyses were often based on implicit notions of purchase in that they emphasized the concepts of market exchange and rights.[51] Their jural language merely obscured the consideration of women as property; as the objects of these rights, women were necessarily if unintentionally interpreted as a form of property.[52] As Singer noted, these analytical perspectives implied:

> powerlessness and lack of initiative, will, or feelings on the part of women. This is not to say that in some cultures men may not talk about buying women. But when the men use phrases like this, they are not necessarily implying women are deprived of intelligence and will, or that they have no choice in marriage. And even in cases where the terms are used with commercial connotations, they do not necessarily describe what happens to the women.[53]

In other words, the powerlessness of LoDagaa women in the world on paper contrasted markedly with the weakness of LoDagaa men in the world of experience. The adherence to a rigid directional perspective, which required equating payments presented with imagined rights, ignored the ethnographic complexities of actual practices.[54] The characteristics of analytical interpretations – simple, straight roads as opposed to complex, meandering footpaths – were echoed in the views of both administrators and male litigants.

The emphasis accorded to the direction of payments in litigation before the courts, combined with the fact that the views most often heard were those of men, placed women in peripheral and passive roles. Several magistrates voiced moral and cultural objections to conjugal payments, but not for this reason; they expressed concern for male rather than female rights. In 1980, for example, Y.B. Siddique objected to the explicit economic considerations entailed in conjugal payments in a decision that contrasted markedly with the court's earlier ruling that "dowry gives the woman her full worth as a housewife. But where you fail to dowry the woman becomes a lover and not a wife." In the case at hand, the former husband claimed a child from the woman's subsequent partner on the grounds that the present husband had not returned his conjugal payments. Siddique ruled: "This idea of having a cow and the cow going out and bringing a calf which automatically belongs to the cow owner must stop. A human being cannot be mistaken for a cow. ... Our women folk even though they are dowried with cattle cannot be regarded as cattle and driven into the woods to flirt and to bring children back home. This cannot be countenanced in these modern times."[55] At first glance this decision seems to have been about the appropriate way to treat women, but what was actually at stake was a claim to the custody of a child that the woman had with a man other than her husband. As we will see later in this chapter, the magistrate sided with the biological father, Andrew Maanyugr, using the treatment of women as a way of doing so.

The use of the analogy of cattle for women was particularly apposite in terms of the male culture of the LoDagaa.[56] Although the connection between women and cattle occasionally found expression in the court records in the form of men's metaphors for describing their own economic interests, the most frequent form of expression of male interests was in a jural language of male rights grounded in the foreign concept of marriage (as a device for exercising control over women). The courts were only too ready to recognize particular interests when they were phrased in terms of marriage as the ideological locus of male rights, even when the arguments made were motivated equally by economic considerations. However, it was difficult to define a legal relationship such as marriage when it had no indigenous precedent.

By denying that conjugal payments had an economic basis, Radcliffe-Brown, like the magistrate in the case just described, isolated payments from the world of experience.[57] Once payments were isolated in this way, new meanings could be attributed to them: "In Africa the marriage payment, whether it be small or large, is the objective instrument by which a 'legal' marriage is established."[58] The problem with applying this statement to LoDagaa practices is that there was no single conjugal payment, and none of the payments referred to marriage.

The possibility that conjugal payments among the LoDagaa were equivalent to contractual obligations, which in turn established marriage, was entertained by colonial administrators and ethnographers during the colonial period and by district magistrates and the indigenous literate elite in the postcolonial period. However, conjugal payments could not be reduced to contractual moments because they were interdependent and often deferred. Jural interpretations of conjugal payments used comparison and translation to generate typologies that subsumed the temporal dimensions of payments.[59] In his description of conjugal unions among the Dagaba, Rattray provided such an interpretative gloss. He identified the first payment as the most significant, even though it amounted to only one to two thousand cowries and was far less than subsequent payments. Although he did not supply the indigenous term for this payment, he described it as "preliminary courting expenses."[60] Among the Lobi he identified three payments. The first payment of one to five hundred cowries was known as *berefo*: "The *berefo* makes the marriage binding even at this stage."[61] But in no sense did this first payment make unions stable. To begin with, a woman could have left such a union of her own accord. From a close reading of Rattray's description of payments, it is clear that each had quite separate implications.[62] The status of unions did not have social implications, so the question of whether a union was legitimate was irrelevant, and was not resolved by conjugal payments. The rights and duties that observers thought to be specific to marriage were not determined by the status of the conjugal union, but by specific and separate payments.[63] Just as there was no lexical equivalent to the concept of marriage among the LoDagaa, neither was there any term that referred to all these payments as a generic set.

Similarly, as we have already seen, Goody reported some forty years after Rattray that among the LoWiili 350 cowries was all that was needed to "legalize" a union.[64] This statement, with its reference to the legality of unions, seems to have recognized the impact of the courts on indigenous representations of social practices. In the years between Blair's compilation of "marriage laws," which did not mention any jural instrument for establishing the legality of a union, and Goody's fieldwork, judicial structures had permeated LoDagaa society to a much greater degree. This initial payment, known as *libie tuo* or "bitter money," was presented with a placation gift of fowls; it was essentially the same as the payment of *berefo* reported by Rattray among the Lobi. The records of the Local Courts do not mention the use of this payment to determine the legality of unions; however, after 1960 the District Court placed increasing emphasis on this payment not only as a *sine qua non* to marriage, but also, under one magistrate at least, as the only social practice capable of determining the legality of a union.

In a relatively unexceptional case in 1974 it was ruled that the "greetings" (also referred to in the Court Record Books as "apology" when made retrospectively, without prior negotiations) was all that was required for a legal union:

> The preliminary and most essential part of the Dagaaba custom of marriage is the greeting which takes precedence immediately a girl has been eloped or detained for marriage by an intendant. This greetings is the fowl, and a guinea fowl [as well as the small cowry payments presented simultaneously] which must be despatched respectfully to the girl's parents within a day or two with an information that the girl has been eloped for marriage. If the greetings are accepted, the marriage is declared legal and lawful, and without even paying the dowry, the children born by the girl are for the husband.[65]

Here the plaintiff claimed custody of his daughter's child from the defendant with whom she had lived, even though no conjugal payments had been made. This ostensible "custom," really an invented law, was only applied negatively here; the real issue was that no payments whatsoever had been presented. Nevertheless, it is an interesting decision that anticipated later thinking by the District Court. When removed from the jural context of the court, and returned to the social context in which such practices operated, rulings like this seem very peculiar.[66] In a dispute that was brought to court shortly before this ruling (and that appears to have influenced this ruling), the same magistrate, Kpemaal, sought to apply this interpretation positively. To do so, he was forced during his cross-examination of witnesses to solicit evidence that would support his aversion to recognizing claims based solely on particular conjugal payments and not proceeding from marriage as a legal category determinant of rights pertaining to, and emanating from, conjugal unions.[67]

The case in question, Brown Topuo Vuu *vs.* Michael Beyuo, concerned the plaintiff's claim for the custody of a child.[68] The plaintiff had "eloped" the defendant's daughter four years earlier, in 1970. Michael refused to recognize the union, primarily on religious grounds. He did so by rejecting the "greetings." He argued that, as a Christian, he could not countenance his daughter entering into a polygynous union. Brown circumvented the defendant's refusal by appealing to the senior members of the woman's household. They accepted the "greetings," even though Michael had told them not to, and agreed to accept the outstanding payments so long as these were all made at once. The defendant's senior brothers had insisted that all conjugal payments be presented immediately because they knew that Michael would otherwise have been able to disrupt the union. However, the conjugal payments were not immediately accepted because of complicated negotiations over the counting of the cowries and the cash equivalent of the cows. The third time the outstanding payments were presented they were again refused, not because of the amount, but because by then it had been noticed that the woman was already pregnant. The mediator was informed by Michael's brothers that the woman should be allowed to give birth before the final payments were accepted.[69]

The delay between the presentation and acceptance of the conjugal payments provided Michael with the opportunity to dissolve the union, by giving his daughter to another man, despite his brothers' attempts to block him by demanding the full presentation of all payments. As Brown said to Michael during cross-examination: "I put it to you that I have done all that warrants a man and his wife to be known and called husband and wife but that you disrupted our marriage and created impediments in our way." The fact remained that Brown had failed in his attempt to have the conjugal payments accepted before the birth of the child.

The strength of the plaintiff's case rested on the earlier support of the defendant's brothers. They had facilitated the union by accepting the "greetings" over Michael's objections. Later, they had attempted to negotiate a settlement between Brown and Michael until the latter removed the possibility of such a settlement by "marrying" his daughter to another man. Although he had withdrawn from their efforts to mediate the matter, Michael called his three brothers as witnesses to establish that the conjugal payments had never actually been accepted. In his cross-examination of the first brother, Brown inquired: "When the fowl was sent to you announcing my marriage did you accept the fowl or not? A: I learnt from Kuupore my brother that the fowl was received by him. Q: Do you remember you once swore an oath before me on top of your own roof that the child is mine and that even if you are hanged for telling the truth you will do so and be hanged? A: I did swear and say so."[70] So far Brown had based his claim for the child on the shortfall in the number of cowries actually returned to him by the defendant's brothers. "To publicly establish the paternity of a newborn child," Goody explained, "the husband presents his wife with a gift of guinea-corn (*pogh tshi*)."[71] Where a man wished to establish paternity over the child of a woman he considered as his wife, but who was not living with him, this payment was made to the household of the rival or new husband through the woman's household.

However, at this point in the hearings the court intervened to discover what precise meaning the acceptance of the "greetings" had in terms of indigenous social practices, cross-examining the first of the brothers to testify for Michael in order to do so:

> According to the Dagaare custom when a woman is eloped and a fowl sent to the parents as the most important part of the preliminary custom and the fowl is accepted what does that depict? A: It confirms that the marriage is accepted. Q: But if the fowl known as the greetings has been rejected what happens? A: The marriage is not binding and accepted. Q: If the fowl is accepted and the couple later have issues without the full payment of the dowry, who owns the child? A: It is the husband.[72]

It is not clear whether by "full payment" the magistrate meant the cattle payment as well as the cowries, nor whether this is what the witness assumed in his response. It is possible that the first brother was referring to a situation where the initial cowry payment had been made but the cattle payment was outstanding. However, when the second of the defendant's brothers was asked by the court what the acceptance of the fowl indicated, he distinguished between the validity of a union regardless of outstanding payments, and the issue of the custody of any children: "If someone elopes your daughter in marriage and sends the greeting of a fowl to you and you accept it, is the marriage valid or not? A: It is valid. Q: If without paying the dowry the couple have issues [children] who is for the issues? A: The issues will be for me although the marriage is valid."[73] Finally the court asked Kuupore Saame, the person who had actually accepted the "greetings": "Having accepted the fowl what does that indicate? A: My accepting it means that the marriage is accepted now leaving the dowry. Q: Is it the dowry that is most important or the greetings in the validity of the marriage? A: It is the greetings that come first and renders the marriage valid *before the debt is paid*."[74]

Kuupore's analysis mirrors Fortes's analysis of Tallensi practices to a remarkable degree. Forty-three years earlier, Fortes had described a similar payment among the Tallensi, *lu sendaan* ("placation"), as "a precise legal technique for entering into and sealing the marriage contract." However, he added that it was "only an earnest of the binding contract, still to be entered into. A marriage can readily be dissolved in spite of it."[75] Even though he described it as a "legal technique ... for sealing the marriage contract," Fortes noted that *lu sendaan* did not legalize a union: "The marriage has first to be sanctioned and the contract, with all the reciprocal obligations, duties and privileges inherent in it, accepted by both parties, *and then fulfilled*."[76]

Based on these inquiries, the court made its judgment, first by interpreting the "greetings" as the *sine qua non* to a valid union and the establishment of an affinal relationship during which successive payments were required:

> When the parents of the girl or those responsible for the marriage accept the fowl accompanied with any other thing – a guinea fowl or cowries or even the fowl alone – the marriage is confirmed and valid. Then the dowry follows. On the other hand, if the fowl known as the "greetings" is rejected, then the marriage is null and void and until and unless the "greetings" are accepted there is no contract of marriage according to the Dagaare custom and no dowry can be sent or accepted.[77]

Then, from the principle of what was deemed necessary for a union to be legitimately established (so that further payments that determined the custody of children could be accepted), the court went on to make this requirement determinant of a legal union. The preliminary payment was thus held to determine not only the status of the union but also the custody of any children of that union, irrespective of successive payments or "steps": "On the evidence as a whole, I am satisfied that the marriage was customarily and lawfully contracted when Kuupore accepted the fowl known as the "greetings" as the first and most important step in contracting marriage according to the customs of the Dagaaba, and as such the plaintiff's marriage was fully constituted under the customary marriage laws."[78]

Accordingly, Brown, the plaintiff, was judged to be entitled to the custody of the child "customarily and lawfully." This argument, constructed and deployed by the magistrate, effectively denied any meaning to the substantial payments that followed according to indigenous practice. In particular it denied the most emphatic and least ambiguous of LoDagaa statements on any aspect of the implications of such payments – namely, that the children belonged to the man who presented the first substantial payment of cowries.[79]

This case has been quoted at length as an example of how magistrates discovered what the pertinent social practices were, and to illustrate the type of jural extrapolations that the courts imposed on social practices. In arriving at this decision the court ignored the temporal dimensions of these payments, which were constitutive of their meaning in the private sphere of social life. This substitution of law for practice may initially seem to have been nothing more than a simple semantic operation, but on closer examination it is clear that it represented a radical reinterpretation of the social practices involved in the formation of conjugal unions.[80] The presentation and acceptance of the "greetings" was significant because it created a relationship of indebtedness and because, in its social context, it was made in anticipation of further payments, and accepted in expectation of them.

To interpret the "greetings" as an explicitly jural instrument was to give it implications that the LoDagaa gave only to successive payments. In other words, this jural reconstruction of meaning was inherently teleological.[81] Despite the court's decision, it is apparent that even from the plaintiff's perspective his entitlement to custody of the child rested not on the "greetings" but on the fact that the cowry payment had been accepted, if only for a time. Had this payment not been made, and witnessed by the brothers of the defendant, it is unlikely that Brown would have received the support of Michael's senior brothers in trying to negotiate the question of custody, and that he would have perceived his position as sound enough to take to court. The magistrate's decision omitted two of the most important features of the testimony. The second brother's version showed that the validity of the union and the custody of children were separate issues. For the LoDagaa, recognition of a union did not confer custody of children. Kupoore's statement to the court, that the "greetings" came first and so rendered the union valid only "before the debt is paid," highlighted the most significant feature of the deferral of conjugal payments. The "greetings" effectively created the debt that was the basis of the affinal relationship. In turn, the establishment and maintenance of the affinal relationship was crucial to the maintenance of the social recognition of the union.[82]

There were two reasons why no single payment could unequivocally establish a conjugal union. First, the LoDagaa did not classify or publicly define unions: unions did not occur within any indigenously defined public arena, and recognition of unions was essentially a private matter between households. So long as the union survived, its status was purely a matter between the two households. Second, whether or not a union was recognized by households was a separate issue from that of whether it had social implications. Conjugal payments did not establish public recognition. They were made in order that a union might continue and so that the children of that union would be attached to the husband's household. Uncertainty over the status of unions, where a union was interrupted by the intervention of a husband's rival, had been an indigenous (albeit male) concern even before the colonial period. Yet it was impossible for husbands to use affinal or private recognition of a union as a means of frustrating a socially distant rival outside the courts. However, in the courts husbands did use private recognition of unions in their attempts to frustrate such rivals.

"Fifty Pesewa Has No Child"

If, as administrators, anthropologists, and the courts assumed, marriage existed among the LoDagaa, a fundamental question must be asked: What did they think marriage did? If marriage existed, it must have determined something. It could not have existed merely as an abstract and nongenerative category of social representation; it must have been more than just an idea; it must have been an actual basis from which social actions proceeded and decisions were made. In this section I examine jural interpretations of conjugal payments among the LoDagaa against the social meanings of those payments. After this, I examine litigation before the courts in the postcolonial period to demonstrate that from the perspective of litigants, these implications were not determined by the status of unions, but rather by specific conjugal payments that, although not defining the status of unions, determined the descent or custody of children. (For the purpose of the arguments presented in this section, Table 11 is useful for comparing the arguments of those litigants whose logic was derived from social practices, with anthropological interpretations found in Rattray, Goody, and later autoethnographic representations, and with the court rulings that reinvented social practices after 1973 so as to make custody congruent with biology.)

In the middle of the last century, a universal definition of marriage was an important project for many anthropologists. Especially influential was Radcliffe-Brown's definition of marriage as "a social arrangement by which a child is given a legitimate position in the society, determined by parenthood in the social sense."[83] This appeared in a book that defined the study of both marriage and kinship in sub-Saharan Africa for over a generation; indeed, this definition of marriage is still very much alive in the autoethnographic writings of the LoDagaa. However, for all its apparent hegemony in the world on paper, it was directly contradicted by the social practices that were operative outside the courts and by the rhetoric of many litigants before the courts. The operative principle governing the custody of children among the LoDagaa was, as Goody reported in the 1956, "the child belongs to the man who paid the bridewealth."[84] In other words, conjugal payments did not define marriage, and marriage did not determine the custody of children; but conjugal payments did determine the custody of children (Table 11).

That custody was not the direct result of marriage had been noted indirectly by Read at the very beginning of the last century. Borrowing from Homer, he stated that "'it is a wise child that knows his father.'" This observation was only applicable to the LoDagaa insofar as paternity was not the direct result of a physiological process, much less the status of conjugal unions, and was therefore often contested. However, the sentiment that informed the observation came from the *Odyssey* via Edwardian Britain; it was not an indigenous perception.[85] Children born to a woman who still lived under the authority of her household's ancestors were attached to that household as her father's children. Writing in the 1950s of the indigenous designation *yirbie*, "housechild," among the LoWiili, Goody referred to such children as "illegitimate" even

Table 11
Arguments over Custody of Children

<table>
<tr><th></th><th>Social practices</th><th>Anthropological perspective</th><th>Court rulings after 1973</th></tr>
<tr><td>1)</td><td>Conjugal payments (A–F)*
| Marriage</td><td>Conjugal payment (A)**
= Marriage</td><td>Conjugal payment A***
= Marriage</td></tr>
<tr><td>2)</td><td>Marriage | Custody</td><td>Marriage = Custody</td><td>Marriage = Custody</td></tr>
<tr><td>3)</td><td>Conjugal payments B +
C, D, and E = Custody</td><td>Conjugal payments B +
C, D, and E = Custody</td><td>Conjugal payments
| Custody****</td></tr>
<tr><td>4)</td><td>Biology | Custody</td><td>Biology | Custody</td><td>Biology = Custody</td></tr>
</table>

*See Table 10 for key to letters.
** Or, alternatively, payment F.
*** Sometimes including later payments.
**** Except when conjugal payments coincided with physiological paternity.

though he also noted that they encountered no disabilities, possessing "the rights and duties of a full [household] member in nearly all respects."[86] The same could have been said of adulterine children. According to Goody, there was a recognized distinction between physiological and social paternity, and where the two did not coincide it was the latter that was socially determinant, and without prejudice. In fact, as has already been noted, when descent and filiation did not coincide it was said of such children "they know their father," with father referring to *genitor* rather than *pater*.[87]

The divergence between a universal definition of marriage and LoDagaa experience raises the question of why, then, the question of legitimacy figured so prominently in Radcliffe-Brown's definition.[88] There was no concept of illegitimacy among the LoDagaa, so this definition of marriage was in no way applicable. When Rattray traveled through the Northern Territories in the late 1920s, he noted that among the LoDagaa and other societies of the region, filiation was far less important than considerations of descent: "I am becoming more and more convinced that here (in the Northern Territories) a man acquires his clan, not because of a physiological process, that is, not because he is the son of his father, or because he is the son of his mother, but by a purely artificial process of adoption into a particular clan by his participation after birth in clan sacrifices and by 'eating clan medicine.'"[89]

In 1938, three decades after Read's complaint about the number of custody disputes, it was observed that the "allotment of children" was still a persistent source of disputes.[90] Yet what was being disputed in these cases was not who the biological father was but rather the timing of conjugal payments – that is, when the conjugal payments had been presented or returned in terms of when the women became pregnant.

As indicated by Read and evident in court records ever since, the ultimate importance of conjugal payments rested almost exclusively on the custody of children (Table 11). The primacy of children was reflected in the indigenous meanings attached to conjugal payments, and so had important implications for the nature of conjugal relations. In his discussion of Tallensi "marriage," Fortes stressed that children were the "raison d'être" of conjugal payments, which would have been incomprehensible without such a purpose.[91] However, disputes over custody found expression indirectly, in the competition for women, rather than directly, over children. As Fortes wrote of conditions in "Taleland" in 1934:

> More than 90 per cent of all cases brought to the chiefs' courts nowadays are concerned with wives ... with two men competing for the woman or her offspring. The reason for this competitive attitude about wives in a society almost devoid of durable goods of great productive or prestige value and possessing few prestige-conferring offices is not difficult to see. ... Wives are the sole means of attaining the supreme end of life for the natives, the perpetuation of a man's lineage.[92]

The desire to ensure the survival of the household through children explains competition over women and disputes in the courts; it also explains the importance and meaning of conjugal payments. Goody observed that the LoDagaa placed little emphasis on "marriage ceremonies," but he added: "On the other hand, ceremonies centering on the conception and birth of children are more elaborate."[93] Paternity or custody was not a result of marriage. Instead it depended on the presentation or refusal of the first substantial conjugal payment, which in this context has been more appropriately categorized by Esther Goody as "childwealth." Writing of indigenous implications of conjugal payments in the wider Voltaic region, she noted: "The out-going funds are not only – nor even perhaps primarily – for sexual (i.e. coital), domestic, or economic services, but relate to the proven procreative powers of the woman. For the payments are not made in a lump sum but by installments, as the children are produced. ... Bridewealth is largely childwealth."[94] Among the LoDagaa, large conjugal payments were made after a woman had "proven her fertility." This was usually after a woman had given birth to three children. Among the LoWiili specifically, the last animal presented to a wife's household was called the "bull of child-bearing."[95]

In the 1950s, the emphasis on conjugal payments in determining the custody of children among the LoDagaa was even more pronounced than among the Tallensi in the 1930s.[96] By this time disputes over child custody had become prominent in the courts and by the 1970s custody cases had become more numerous than adultery cases. It was also in the 1950s that the first assault on the meaning of conjugal payments began. Goody noted that in situations where a woman had been unreservedly and unilaterally rejected by her husband, children of such a union would have normally accompanied the woman to her home as *yirbie* of her agnatic household: "By the formula of rejection, the husband abdicates his position as *pater* or legal father of the children."[97] However, a decision by the District Commissioner of Lawra around the time of Goody's fieldwork in the early 1950s had altered this situation: "He [the district commissioner] maintained that in this case the begetter of the child should be its legal father and this is now generally accepted by the LoWiili in the Gold Coast."[98] This only pertained to disputes between the households of a man and a woman; it was only later that interventions were made in disputes between the households of rival men to extend this principle of rights over children by virtue of physiological parentage.

There was no evidence that the ruling Goody referred to had had any effect on the decisions of the chiefs in the Local Courts. In a case where the plaintiff claimed a child from his former wife's father, the court ruled in 1954: "Since the father has paid and the woman delivered he [the plaintiff] cannot get the child back."[99] The dispute centered on whether the plaintiff had rejected the defendant's daughter or whether she had left him of her own accord. Because the plaintiff had demanded that conjugal payments be returned to him before the woman entered into another union, the court decided that the woman had been rejected. On the other hand, another Local Court awarded custody to the father of a man's former wife not only because the father had returned the former husband's conjugal payments, but also because at the time of the conception the woman was not his wife and he was not the biological father of the child. This case, Kuuluo Panyanti *vs.* Timbiile Dazuuri, was heard in 1959, just at the end of the period of the Local Courts, when the official role of chiefs in hearing disputes was coming to an end. It is interesting not because it explicitly contradicted earlier decisions, but because it anticipated later ones, both in its emphasis on physiological paternity and in its attention to the uxorial status of the woman. The court supported Timbiile's custody of his daughter's child even though Kuuluo's former wife had delivered the child before the plaintiff's conjugal payments had been returned and he had remitted five hundred cowries when the conjugal payments were returned to him for the maintenance of the child until it was weaned. This presentation, usually made with a basket of guinea corn, was made "to publicly establish the paternity of a newborn child." Timbiile refused to accept the remittance; if he had it would have amounted to an acknowledgment of Kuuluo's claim of paternity. Here the court took into consideration the plaintiff's admission "that the girl had not conceived when she left to the father's house," as well as the woman's statement "that if she died the father would be responsible." Because Timbiile had made up a shortfall in the cowries returned to Kuuluo due to the inability of the new husband to raise the whole amount, Timbiile, and not the new husband, was awarded the child.[100] Here the court used the idea of physiological paternity negatively, as a justification for not awarding custody; after all, Timbiile was no more the *genitor* of the child than Kuuluo. With the exception of two cases in the early 1960s, where magistrates invoked "natural law" to deny indigenous descent principles, it was not until 1973 that a consistent change set in.

As late as 1970 the court, under District Magistrate Akalifa, had ruled: "The Dagarti marriage custom allows that no person has any entitlement to any children such person may have with a woman whose dowry has not been paid."[101] But only a few years later two successive magistrates began to attack the divergence between physiological and social paternity. In so doing, they were attempting to define marriage independently of conjugal payments. This is not surprising, given that conjugal payments did not define unions and the courts wanted to override indigenous notions of decent, which were determined by conjugal payments. This was also a strategy used by the courts to try to suppress the practice of large conjugal payments and to compress them into a single moment that could act as "a precise legal technique for entering into and sealing the marriage contract." The magistrate who made this ruling, Kpemaal, ruled in other cases that the presentation of the "greetings" alone, regardless of subsequent payments, was sufficient to establish marriage and, therefore, warranted awarding custody to the genitor of a woman's children rather than to the man who paid the "childwealth." In this case Kpemaal was reinventing "customary law" for the clear purpose of asserting physiological over social paternity. Similarly, in other cases he argued that the remittance of foodstuffs, rather than the presentation of conjugal payments, was the social practice that should determine the custody of children.[102]

We saw how the court imposed a distorted and selective readings of social practices in the case of Topuo Vuu *vs.* Michael Beyuo. In the earlier case of Ben Bonkan Isang *vs.* Dennis Puozuu, which came before the District Court in 1973, we see similar trends. The defendant, a mineworker at Tarkwa, had "eloped" Mary, the plaintiff's elder brother's wife, three years after her former husband's death from her father's house. The woman had returned to her parents after her husband's death, but the defendant did not make conjugal payments until after the birth of two children. The first child had already been claimed by the plaintiff from the woman's household, but the defendant had refused to hand over the second child, which was still living with him, because even though it had been conceived before the conjugal payments had been returned, it was born after they had been returned to the plaintiff. During the hearing the defendant made much of the fact that the plaintiff's household had not presented millet and guinea corn to him after the birth of either child. Following the argument presented by the defendant, the court ignored the fact that the defendant had failed to make the expected conjugal payments, preferring to focus instead on the plaintiff's household's omission of foodstuffs. The court perceived this failure to be a "miserably pitiful negligence which the law cannot side with." It asked the plaintiff: "As a pure Dagaa do you know that you are duty bound by the Dagare customary marriage laws to send a basket of millet and a guinea fowl to your rival and to return an amount of not less than three hundred and not more than five hundred [cowries] out of the dowry to him if you wish to be qualified for any claim in the form of a child?" In fact the plaintiff's household were not in a position to present the foodstuffs for the maintenance of the first child because it was born while the woman was in the south with the defendant. The court was particularly annoyed that in earlier, "highly irresponsible" decisions made by the village and paramount chiefs, the defendant had been denied custody of the second child, thereby "allowing the Defendant to be the loser while the Plaintiff was given the right of the defendant without justification whatsoever. This sort of judgement is a very poor way of administering justice and must be deplored if customary laws are to be applied and upheld in esteem."[103] The strong, upbraiding language of this decision disguised Kpemaal's own predilection, witnessed in subsequent decisions, for overruling the indigenous principle of descent.

With the same magistrate presiding, and following his earlier success over the custody of the second child, Dennis Puozuu then attempted to claim the first child. Although sympathetic to his claim, the magistrate was unable to apply the ruling of the earlier case because the woman's household had itself given the child over to the former husband's household: "The Defendant's failure to send a basket of millet and five hundred cowries to the Plaintiff at Mary's delivery should have been viewed as a contravention to the customary laws, but for the fact that Mary got conception in her father's house renders this part of the custom uncalled for."[104] This should have vitiated the earlier judgment concerning the second child, which had been born in the household of her deceased husband, where Mary had retired following the decision of the village chief that as the conjugal payments had still not been presented by her intended husband, she still remained a wife of the defendant's household. It was only some months later, when the plaintiff returned from the south and presented the necessary payments, that Mary returned to him, sometime around 1969. The magistrate ruled that as far as the first child was concerned, it had been born before Dennis and Mary's union had been "confirmed by proof of dowry," even though this should have applied to the second child also.[105]

After 1977, the succeeding magistrate, Siddique, attempted to affect similar alterations of social practices. However, his interventions were not as circumspect and did not require the same interpretative fictions. This was possible because in that year the government of Ghana issued a decree allowing the courts to overlook "customary law" in cases of child custody where the child's welfare would be adversely affected.[106] Here the adverse effects were based on cultural rather than social or economic considerations.[107] For example, in Saaluah Kpinibo *vs.* Motogo Peter Mwinpuo, the court intervened to award custody to the genitor rather than to the child's social father. In doing so it was forced to ignore the very "Dagare customary marriage laws" that had been invoked four years earlier in order to award Dennis Puozuu custody of the second of his biological children. In this later case, the defendant had taken one of the plaintiff's household's wives as a wife, and the couple produced a child before the defendant presented the necessary conjugal payments to the woman's household to be returned to the plaintiff. When the conjugal payments were eventually returned to the plaintiff, in cash, the plaintiff had subtracted fifty pesewa (100 pesewa = 1¢), which were to be returned to the defendant in lieu of foodstuffs to establish his paternity. What is especially revealing in the record of this case is that the plaintiff did not base his claim on the status of the union, but on the fact that he had been responsible for the conjugal payments, which had not been returned until after the child was born. This was apparent in the defendant's cross-examination of the plaintiff:

> Can you remember you told me if during the delivery of the woman she happens to die you would come for your dowries? A: I said so. Q: If therefore she had died would you have come for the dead child or the dowries? A: I would have demanded the dowries. Q: Now that she has safely given birth why are you demanding the child instead? A: Because you could not pay the return dowry and the woman gave birth. Q: I put it to you that the child is mine and not yours. A: I don't agree with you because according to the custom you did not return the dowries before the woman gave birth. Q: I put it to you that the fifty pesewa you paid cannot cater for a child. ... A: Your parents accepted the fifty pesewa according to custom. Q: I impregnated the woman and she gave birth. Fifty pesewa has no child. A: The child belongs to me because I paid the dowries.[108]

The defendant was attempting to discredit the plaintiff's claim for custody by arguing that the woman was actually his wife, in a social sense determined by the question of funeral performances rather than conjugal payments, and that he was the *genitor* of the child. Both of these arguments had currency in the world on paper, of which the court was part. The plaintiff did not object to either of these assertions, having based his claim instead on the fact that, regardless of these considerations, his conjugal payments conferred custody to his household over any children the woman had until conjugal payments were returned to them. The questions about the custody of the child and the status of a union, while separate in indigenous terms, were conflated in court.

The court ruled that the defendant was the "legitimate" father of the child in dispute, and that "the Plaintiff has no earthly right to claim the child." Although the recorded evidence did not suggest such a decision, an intervention during the proceedings revealed the reasoning behind the ruling. The magistrate asked the plaintiff: "Do you think it is wise to take someone's blood child into your family and call that person what?" There was no recorded response to this admonishment, but it is clear that the perception of the divergence between physiological and social legitimacy proceeded from the magistrate's own cultural sense of propriety. Although in a strict sense this decision contradicted the one offered by his predecessor in the case cited earlier,[109] because of the circumstantial nature of these rulings, a common underlying judicial intention is apparent despite the shifting substantive points between cases:

> To think in modern times that the return of fifty pesewa can claim a child you do not have any connection with biologically is but a dream. ... Indeed this custom whereby fifty pesewa and millet or grains are returned for someone's biologically born child should be frowned at with all indignation. It needs to be changed as it is outmoded. ... The idea of waiting to collect illegal children into one's family must cease.[110]

Here the court supported the defendant's argument that the woman was his wife in spite of his failure to provide for the return of the plaintiff's conjugal payments. The magistrate's undisguised antipathy to conjugal payments was also evident in his later ruling (quoted above) in which he rejected the claim of the former husband on the grounds that social practices treated women like cattle.[111] That dispute had been decided by "traditional assessors" in the defendant's favor by virtue of who had made conjugal payments to the woman's parents. In neither of these cases was there any suggestion that the decisions were consistent with "custom."

In Saturnino Loko *vs.* Amporeh Guyereh, which came before the same magistrate in 1983, judicial intolerance of LoDagaa principles of descent was enunciated in particularly dramatic terms. Saturnino demanded the release of two children he had with Amporeh, who had since deserted him and returned to her parents. Saturnino maintained that it was Amporeh who had persuaded him to defer conjugal payments, only to leave him later in "revolt" after assurances that her household would nevertheless recognize his claim to custody of the children. Whether or not this was true is impossible to assess, because in the middle of the case the magistrate abruptly intervened after Amporeh attempted to illustrate the principle that the children of any union belonged to the household that had made the relevant conjugal payments. Commenting on Saturnino's witness, Augustine Mwankurinaa, Amporeh had explained to the court: "We have earlier mentioned that one cannot be robbed of a child for another. But in this instance the Plaintiff's witness himself was born by one Zuobogu. But in view of the custom and the dowries not paid the present father's name Mwankurinaa had to be attached to the witness. Why is it so?" The magistrate responded: "This is exactly what the court is attempting to abolish. In this instance [case] the children should belong to the Plaintiff as their natural father so that your insult to the Plaintiff's witness is not in any way transferred to the two children in the near future."[112]

Before the 1950s, marriage, or the status of unions, had never determined the custody of a child. By the 1970s the District Court was conflating issues of custody with those of the status of unions. It did this so as to be able to award custody to biological fathers rather than to the households that had paid the "childwealth." Increasingly the court ignored conjugal payments when defining the status of unions. Sensing this shift in the court's disposition, litigants began paying more attention in their rhetoric to the uxorial status of women, so as to define conjugal unions as legal marriages that the court would recognize. Where conjugal payments did not coincide with biological paternity or the residence of a woman, they were often ignored. This change might seem at first to have been more felicitous with the logic of social practices than the literal reading of conjugal payments, which had been enshrined in court decisions since the 1950s; but it was merely transposing another literal reading – that of biology – for the economic model that was implicit in administrative and anthropological interpretations and often explicit in the representations of some litigants. (See Table 11.)

The changing attitudes of the courts were also reflected in the representations of the local Catholic elite. In his 1987 revision of anthropological descriptions of inheritance and marriage by external observers, Dery was concerned not only with refuting allegations of matriliny among the LoDagaa, but also with correcting alleged misrepresentations of conjugal practices. He refuted the notion that "housechildren" were claimed by the woman's household when they resulted from a "marriage in the making," that is, where birth had occurred before the presentation of the first substantial conjugal payment, or where the woman was a "spinster." This assertion seems to have been necessary because Dery derived his definition of marriage from anthropological discourse. He argued that such children did not have social fathers, only *genitors*: "Social Fatherhood is only attained by the children who are offsprings of properly constituted marriages."[113] This interpretation was quite different from Goody's observations, not to mention Rattray's earlier impressions. By the 1980s, biological as opposed to social paternity was gaining legitimacy not only in the courts, but also in the written accounts by the local elites. Dery argued that when such children were claimed it was "never imagined that these children can be fixed in their descent line. These children cannot trace their descent to a common ancestor in that clan."[114] Thirty years earlier, Goody had explained in some detail just how such children were integrated into their mother's household, being placed under the protection of the ancestors of the mother's lineage and taking their place in its affairs.

Death and the Resolution of Ambiguity

So far the social autonomy of women has been mentioned in relation to male competition for wives and the resulting male ideologies of control. Patriarchal statements by men in court expressed the real concerns of older, more powerful, and wealthy males, but they were illusory at the level of experience. The social status or *persona* of women depended on physical context, namely residence, rather than on conjugal payments. Conjugal payments did not transfer the rights that have been attributed to marriage; these were transferred mainly by women's choice of residence. Litigation over the consequences of unions and the implications of conjugal payments often involved questions about the identity of the woman when rhetorical, as opposed to practical, control over women was at issue. Disputes in the District Court between husbands often involved diverging arguments over the status of the woman during the highly ambiguous period between the presentation of payments by a rival and their return to a former husband. In many cases these arguments can be reduced to two propositions. First, that the presentation and acceptance of conjugal payments determined the uxorial status of a woman (an argument usually employed by the former husband). Second, that the status of the woman as wife to a particular husband (either former or new) was the result of her preferred residence (commonly a rival's argument). Often what appear to have been arguments over the definition of marriage were, implicitly, disputes over the status of women.[115] The question that arose in male disputes over the identity of women was this:

Whose wives were they?[116] However, this proprietorial question asked by men had an equivalent female counterpart. Women, in deciding their preference of partners, had been effectively asking their own question, albeit through actions rather than words and in life rather than in the courts. Which man did they prefer? (This question was situational rather than proprietorial.) But in the context of the courts it was men who disputed the social identity of women. Men attempted to define and redefine women in the courts as their wives after women had chosen husbands outside the courts.

In the preceding two sections I discussed the difficulties encountered in defining conjugal unions in terms of the meaning of conjugal payments and the custody of children. We saw how, during the first generation of formalized courts with reliable record keeping, a distorted emphasis on conjugal payments came to be replaced by attempts to deny these payments any significance. We also saw how judgments in child custody cases came to focus increasingly on biological rather than economic considerations. These two trends were obviously linked: efforts to deny that conjugal payments had meaning were necessary in order to override indigenous forms of descent. But because all of this took place within a discourse about "traditional marriage laws," the courts, as well as the litigants who appeared before them, still needed to show that decisions had some basis in indigenous practices and beliefs. Thus, pressure developed to define marriage independently of conjugal payments, but still within the context of other indigenous practices. One way of doing this was to focus on the status of the wife and to use her uxorial standing to determine the status of the conjugal union. In the 1970s this trend became especially pronounced. However, it was not new: litigants had been using the status of women as a means to define the status of unions well before, but only now were the courts listening to them.

In 1966, when Charles, the district magistrate, ruled that "dowry gives the woman her full worth as a housewife,"[117] he was reflecting male ideologies, not indigenous practices. In an earlier case, where a woman's father claimed the remaining conjugal payments from her husband for his deceased daughter, he argued "the case not to be in lines with custom," adding that he had "never heard nor come across a dead woman being dowried by her husband."[118] However, what the magistrate had heard in the court was quite different from what the LoDagaa did outside it. Funerals were important events for establishing the character of conjugal relations. If at the time of a woman's death her husband had not completed the conjugal payments, her household was entitled to bury her.[119] According to Rattray, the timing of the demand in relation to the burial depended on the quality of the affinal relationship: "In the event of the death of a man's wife, if the father-in-law is a 'bad man' he will claim the *doe* even before she is buried. He will send the son-in-law a rope, as a hint to lead the cows back. If, however, he is a 'good man' and if his daughter has borne a female child, he may wait until the husband has received the cows of this daughter, with which, when he does so, he will pay the former debt."[120]

Goody pointed out that the threat to bury a daughter, instead of allowing her husband to do so, was relatively uncommon, unless it was being used to air some other dispute besides the affinal debt. Although it may only have been a threat, it did have a further significance: "There is a recognized connection of jural status with place of burial, which even if it operates mainly in anticipation, has nonetheless a considerable influence over peoples' actions."[121]

These points were clearly articulated in the case of Zebrikuu Guo of Zambo *vs.* Vutaar Dabuo of Eremon Tottoh. In this dispute from 1978 we see the importance of death, and of the performance of funerals in particular, in defining (albeit after the fact) the nature of conjugal relationships. Incidentally, we also see how the logic of social practices was in tension with the logic of jural representations of those practices. Whereas the plaintiff saw conjugal unions as defined by specific payments, the defendant presented a much more subtle picture of how unions were socially recognized and of how their legitimacy was contested outside the courts. The plaintiff was claiming the final payment for the deceased daughter of his senior brother, whom the defendant had "married" thirty years earlier. The defendant maintained that there was no debt between the households because his father had incurred expenses procuring "local treatment" for the woman when, as a small girl, she had been sent to him to be cured by an indigenous herbalist.[122] In his cross-examination of the plaintiff's brother, he tried to establish that there was, therefore, no remaining payment to be presented:

> When my wife died did the Plaintiff attend the funeral? A: I don't know. Q: What customary rites did Sannyara [the plaintiff's senior brother] perform when my wife died as you allege I did not finish paying the dowries? A: I don't know. Q: When someone marries another's daughter according to the Dagaare custom and happens to pay the first part of the dowries and the woman dies, has the father of the girl some performances to make or not? A: I don't know. Q: Do you know that when one marries a woman and pays the first part of the dowries and if the woman dies the father of the woman normally sends a rope asking the bereaved husband to tie the cow with it and to surrender [the] same to him? A: I am not aware. Q: When the deceased [Sannyara] died and I went to the funeral what did you do according to the custom? A: The Plaintiff asked you for the cow for the deceased's funeral performance.[123]

There are two immediate points of interest here. First, the defendant does not seem to have tried to represent the sending of the rope or any other practice as part of "customary marriage laws"; his claim was merely normative. Second, this brief exchange illustrates very well the autoethnographic information found in the court records, albeit in small fragments such as this, and how well it matches what is found in ethnographic sources such as Rattray.

The defendant used the funerals of his wife and father-in-law in an attempt to establish that there was no outstanding debt. According to the defendant's argument, if there had been any debt this would have been established at the time of the death of his wife; or, if not then, at the death of Sannyara himself, when the members of the household settled his estate. In LoDagaa culture, such matters were settled during funerals. What is more, funerals determined, through the participation of others, the identity of the deceased for the rest of the society.[124]

The second substantial conjugal payment was often called for before a man could bury his wife. However, there was a further payment that was required before a man could finally resolve the identity of a wife. There was no institutional recognition of completed or final unions in the realm of LoDagaa practices – at least not until death, and even then, ambiguity lingered: "The series of funeral performances sums up the social personality of the deceased; a woman is buried among her husband's lineage ... but at the final ceremony a stick cut in her name is carried ceremonially to her father's house where it joins the ancestor shrines."[125] During the ceremony in which the stick representing the deceased woman was carried back to her natal home, a final payment of twenty cowries was made, (Payment "F" in Tables 9, 10, and 11) which according to Goody "explicitly represents a further and final instalment of the bridewealth."[126] Only then could a man say that a woman was unequivocally his wife.

There were two main reasons for the protracted ambiguity surrounding the social identity of wives: first, their effective autonomy to take new husbands, and, second, the deferred nature of conjugal payments. The freedom that women had to choose husbands meant that conjugal payments had to be made over the history of a relationship; since there was no assurance the relationship would last, there was no sense in presenting all payments at once. Conversely, it was crucial, if the woman was to be socially recognized as a wife, to ensure that conjugal payments were made even after her death; it follows that earlier payments could not define her status in anything but a momentary and situational fashion until that time. That conjugal unions were not reducible to a clearly defined legal state (i.e., marriage) is apparent in the fact that the element necessary to remove the ambiguity was a *post mortem* act of validation. Yet this act took place too late for such a resolution of the identity of a woman and the status of a conjugal union to have social consequences; it did not satisfy the need for conjugal unions to be defined at an earlier date in order to be useful as a factor in settling disputes. Elucidated in this manner, marriage was little more than an analytical denouement.

This indigenous perspective on the uxorial status of women was evident in litigation before the courts in the second half of the twentieth century. In the 1950s, litigants took this line in their attempts – most often in vain – to avoid charges of adultery, the argument being that they slept with the woman as a husband and not as a lover.[127] After 1960, however, litigants tried to use the status of the woman as a means of defining marriage (before unions had been socially completed), in order to satisfy the magistrates, who were imposing a more rigorous jural logic on social practices at the same time as they were attempting to modify these practices in terms of their own cultural biases. Throughout the period of the magistrates, especially during the 1970s, there was increasing reluctance to satisfy particular demands based merely on the fact that specific conjugal payments had been presented. In other words, interests could only be legitimated in terms of the definition of conjugal unions as marriages, because rights had to be conceptualized by litigants as emanating from the status of unions rather than from conjugal payments.[128] Litigants who argued merely in terms of their economic interests were often disappointed by the courts, which insisted on deciding cases in terms of rights inherent in the status of unions. Yet court decisions based on the status of unions had no currency outside the courts.

The difficulties that both the courts and litigants had in defining the status of unions should not be surprising, given that the LoDagaa did not define the status of unions outside the courts. In addition, not only was the status of unions undefined, but efforts to define unions took place in an arena isolated from the world of experience. Though the LoDagaa made use of the courts, those courts were not part of their society. Litigants adapted to them, but legal institutions were not integrated into their social life, nor did they become an important part of their culture. Attempts by both litigants and the courts to define marriage, and to reduce conjugal unions to a specific and definite status, were the product of the peculiar demands of this form of dispute settlement. Marriage was only relevant for the purpose of representing or acknowledging litigants' interest in the courts. Social practices were not altered by these rhetorical exercises, and continued to be irreducible to a precise definition.

It should not surprise us that LoDagaa men used death, as both a real and a hypothetical event, to define the status of wives in the courts: mortuary performances and rituals were the most important aspect of LoDagaa culture. In 1918 a district commissioner remarked, following a request from his interpreter for leave to attend a funeral: "The funeral custom seems to be what the market is to the Hausa, the court to the Ashanti and a football match to the British workman."[129] In his detailed description and analysis of the mortuary institutions of the LoDagaa, Goody agreed that "funeral ceremonies are the most elaborate of the ceremonial occasions of the LoDagaa, whether this is measured in terms of the numbers attending, the time taken, or emotion generated."[130] In LoDagaa cultural and social life, funerals were more important than either courts or markets. They were the ceremonies during which social identities were articulated. They represented moments of crisis when debts had to be accounted for, and reciprocal acts and obligations had to be fulfilled, and, finally and most importantly, when relationships were redefined and social roles changed.

It was litigants, and not the courts, who used both the hypothesis and the reality of death to attempt to construct a wider definition of conjugal unions beyond the narrow jural perspective of the courts. During the 1950s and 1960s those most likely to resort to such rhetorical strategies were usually younger or less powerful men.[131] In cases before the District Court in the 1970s, the significance of funerals became an increasingly important social index for deciding between rival interests. The case discussed below was heard in 1978, by which time the courts also were seeking alternative ways to define conjugal unions, not to support men whom the courts had once marginalized, but in order to deny meaning to conjugal payments and to assert biological over social paternity. By this time, arguments based on death had become well rehearsed by litigants and familiar to magistrates.

In Saaluah Kpinibo *vs.* Motogo Peter Mwinpuo, which has already been mentioned in another connection, the use of the hypothesis of death arose as a rhetorical device to determine the social identity of the woman in question. The plaintiff "married" a woman for his junior brother, who was in the south at the time of the hearing. The couple had two children before the woman returned home to attend some funerals. She stayed with the plaintiff (her husband's brother), whence she visited her parents only to run back to the south to enter into a union with the defendant, by whom she then had another child. The plaintiff claimed that the last child was that of his brother, as the birth took place before the defendant had returned the plaintiff's payments to him through the in-laws. During cross-examination, the defendant attempted to establish that even the plaintiff had regarded the woman as his wife: "Can you remember you told me if during the delivery of the woman she happens to die you would come for the dowries. A: I said so. Q: If therefore she had died would you have come for the dead child or the dowries? A: I would have demanded the dowries."[132] As the woman did not die, the plaintiff in this case was in a position to claim the child without injuring his position with regard to the return of payments. The defendant apparently had difficulty raising the necessary funds, so the plaintiff's household's payments were not returned until after the woman had given birth. The plaintiff's claim was based on the outstanding debt at the time of the birth.

The defendant's hypothesis, based it seems on an earlier exchange outside the court between the two litigants, was ingenious. Had the plaintiff demanded the return of payments if the woman died, he would have been accepting as an established social fact that the defendant had "married" the woman – that is, taken her as a wife. The defendant would presumably have been entitled to bury the woman and present the payments later. The hypothesis indicated that the plaintiff had abandoned any claim over the woman as a wife. The defendant tried to establish that the plaintiff had abandoned the woman, insofar as he would have been unwilling to perform her funeral in the event of her death. The plaintiff attempted, in turn, to avoid this interpretation by saying that behind his strategy there was always the hope that the woman would return to him. Here the question of death operated as an informal statute of limitations in a society without contractual obligations. It narrowed the range of possible interpretations of actions, which – as in the formation, development, or dissolution of conjugal unions – lacked precise temporal demarcations as in rule-oriented or determined practices. It also resolved questions of identity that would otherwise have remained open.

One final example serves to emphasize the importance of funerals for resolving the ambiguity that arose because of expectations that had been created by the use of the status of unions to determine the distribution of innovatory rights. When litigants came before the postcolonial courts, they sought to construct public definitions of unions, even though there had formerly been no such recognition accorded to unions. They argued specifically in terms of an external category, "marriage," instead of basing their claims on interests established through the presentation of conjugal payments.

In Andrew Maanyugr *vs.* Beatrice Yuornyine and Gilbert Seg-ib, which came before the District Court in 1980, the plaintiff sought the custody of a child of which he was the *genitor* but not the effective *pater*. Beatrice had left Gilbert and taken up with Andrew on the understanding that if she became pregnant she would marry him. She claimed that her infertility had been the cause of the dissolution of her union with Gilbert. But after the child was born she returned to Gilbert before Andrew had been able to present conjugal payments. The case was much more complicated than this rough outline indicates, but this summary is sufficient to understand the following exchange in Gilbert's cross-examination of Andrew:

> Do you maintain that she is not your legally married wife? A: The woman withdrew her support for me when we came home to perform the customary

> dowries. ... Q: When she told you she had no husband did you know she had relatives? A: Yes. Q: Do you take possession of a property before asking the owner for it? A: I did not beg her but she begged me and we arrived at a compromise. Q: If the woman died during the treatment [for infertility by a herbalist] would you have buried her or given her to the parents? A: I had earlier sent word to the parents that she was with me and if she had died I would have brought the corpse home to my family house. Q: This would have meant that you had taken full control of her. A: Yes, as the father of the woman had consented to our being together. Q: Is that how our custom goes? A: Yes. The parents of the girl can demand full dowries before burial takes place or they may choose to bury the corpse themselves or another compromise reached. Q: If you pay full dowries before the burial does it mean that the woman was not your own before the death occurred? A: ... It simply means that while she was alive she was my wife and at death she was my wife. Q: Do you mean that as you did not dowry her she was not your wife? A: She was my wife and we were to follow the custom which was later not supported by the woman.[133]

Gilbert presented an orthodox, jural interpretation of marriage, based on the economic interests that the presentation of conjugal payments established, but Andrew offered an anticipatory argument based on how the matter would have been resolved during the funeral of Beatrice had she died.

Although the case was decided against him, Gilbert had challenged this posterior construction of a socially grounded union by his rival, demonstrating that it did not satisfy his perspective, which saw interests as rights validated by the transfer of conjugal payments and not relying on any wider social recognition. His argument failed because he could not separate the status of the woman from the custody of the child – the two were linked only because the courts thought that marriage, and not conjugal payments, should determine paternity. Given earlier decisions by the District Court, it also did not help that one of Gilbert's witnesses explained the case to Andrew during cross-examination in the following terms: "If one possesses a she-goat and it goes out and comes back with a kid, the he-goat [i.e., Andrew, the plaintiff] cannot claim ownership of the kid."[134]

The cases discussed here represent growing efforts by litigants to move away from a jural interpretation of marriage based on economic interests, and to construct a social definition of marriage from other indigenous practices. In the courts, the use of death as a rhetorical device and as an event that conferred social recognition was an innovation that came from litigants. In the 1950s it was largely ineffectual, but by the 1970s it had been endorsed by the courts. At first glance the willingness of the courts to hear such arguments might seem more congruent with indigenous social practices. However, it was actually a distortion of those practices because of the social category that was being defined (i.e., marriage). In addition, unlike the first litigants to use this argument in the 1950s, Andrew was not a marginalized man. As an employee of the Ministry of Agriculture, he was a salaried man who had the benefits of a school education and was very familiar with the world on paper. Soon after the birth of his child, he had obtained a birth certificate for the child in which he was named as the father. He presented this as an exhibit, along with other written documentation, including a medical certificate, hospital bills, and an antenatal record card. With the exception of an earlier use of a photograph, this was the first recorded instance where such evidence had been used in a civil case in the District Court.

In the context of the courts, especially the District Court, social practices were subject to a variety of definitions when it came to deciding between conflicting interests. These attempts to define conjugal unions in terms of an external category were particularly inappropriate, especially given that definitions of unions in terms of any category was alien to indigenous practice. Nonjural methods of resolving conflicts of interest were displaced by the application of an external category, marriage, to which the courts in their various guises attached different rights. If we must speak of LoDagaa marriage, then we must emphasize that as a social arrangement it was characterized by a high degree of ambiguity. Formerly this ambiguity was not significant; the resolution of conflicts did not require that conjugal unions be defined.

In their study of Tswana marriage litigation, where similar difficulties were encountered in defining conjugal unions, John Comaroff and Simon Roberts observed that outside the courts there was no indigenous, spontaneous effort to define the status of unions:

> When unions endure and their status is not called into question, little spontaneous effort is made indigenously to classify them, a tendency that the non-specificity of everyday terms ... would appear to facilitate. Indeed, the absence of formal bridewealth negotiations, *rites de passage*, and other expressive manifestations of status transformation together underlie the avoidance of definition and perpetuation of ambiguity.[135]

The same observation could also be made of LoDagaa practices. No attempt was made to resolve a conjugal relationship until the death of the wife; leviratic succession precluded the death of a male spouse from having the same effect. In terms of LoDagaa social practices, this formalization did not take place in order to define the status of unions, but rather as a means of resolving personal identities and household (as opposed to conjugal) relationships.

Again, the history of the relationship between LoDagaa social practices and colonial and postcolonial institutions is analogous to the experience of the Tswana: "Ironically, then, it is then in the 'legal' context that the irreducibility of marriage-type relations to simple jural formulations becomes most obvious."[136] Social practices defined neither the status of a union nor that of a woman in any definite, unequivocal sense. These practices only possessed definite meanings in terms of their potential social implications, which proceeded not from any generative category or status (as the execution of rights) but from the successful negotiation of interests. Moreover, the range of potential meanings attached to social practices actually created disputes because of the absence of any indigenous institution through which normative hegemony might have been exercised. In the previous section, I discussed these issues in terms of the custody of children – the analytical *differentia* of anthropological definitions of marriage. Here too the court records reveal a strong divergence between the administrative and anthropological definition of marriage found in the world on paper and the logic of indigenous practices evident in the world of experience. The courts did not have the power to influence social practices, but they did have the power to create new expectations based on a logic foreign to those practices, by denying economic considerations and by introducing biological anxieties.

Generative Knowledge and *Post Facto* Categories

During a three-day seminar in 1990 attended by priests and lay leaders in the Catholic community, the following question was asked of one of the discussion groups: "What constitutes marriage among the Dagaaba?"[137] The question seems deceptively simple, but much depended on who was asking it and why. Radcliffe-Brown had asserted forty years earlier that "Africans distinguish, as we do, between a 'legal' marriage and an irregular union." Given the absence of political authority in matrimonial affairs in many African societies, he went on to ask: "How, then, are *we* to distinguish a legal marriage?"[138] The shift here from an indigenous, African distinction to the perspective of the anthropologist and his readers was significant. Equally significant was the profound influence of Radcliffe-Brown's analysis of marriage on representations of LoDagaa social practices. Western anthropologists, Ghanaian legal scholars,[139] and the LoDagaa Catholic elite often subscribed to it and echoed its words like a formula. Writing of the LoDagaa in the mid-1980s, Kuukure borrowed directly from Radcliffe-Brown, and indirectly from Maine, when he stated that in the formation of conjugal unions "the guardianship of the bride is transferred to the clan of the groom. The transfer of rights over the woman is accompanied by a transfer of property ('bride wealth'), which is the core of the necessary formalities required for a valid marriage." Bishop Kpiebaya wrote that conjugal payments made "the marriage agreement legal thus giving uxorial and genetic rights to the husband and his household over the girl." Similarly, Dery, a university graduate with a degree in social anthropology, wrote that marriage was "an arrangement between man and woman that gives man exclusive sexual claims to the woman and legitimizes his claim to paternity of her children." Father Tengan, in an essay first delivered before the seminar mentioned above to discuss possible marriage reforms among the LoDagaa, began by outlining "marriage from an anthropological perspective." Thinly paraphrasing Radcliffe-Brown, he wrote: "Marriage is a union between man and woman such that the children born to the woman are legitimate and recognised as the offspring of both parties. Marriage thus confers a social status on the children."[140] Little effort was made to define marriage in terms of any indigenous criteria; instead, external authority was resorted to so as to establish the relevance of the paradigm to LoDagaa practices.

That an even more fundamental question than Radcliffe-Brown's was being asked forty years later in at least one part of Africa indicates that it was still very much in doubt what practices constituted marriage, let alone "legal" marriage. As we have seen, the question was first posed at the beginning of the twentieth century, when British administrators began imposing this foreign category of representation on LoDagaa practices. Anthropologist, chiefs, litigants, courts, and, finally, clerics all attempted to answer the question at different times, in different places, and from different perspectives without ever asking whether the question itself was appropriate. That the question could still be asked after almost ninety years of colonial and postcolonial rule indicates that none of their answers ever really worked: there was always an enormous amount of dissonance between written representations of LoDagaa marriage in the world on paper and social practices in the world of experience; between rival and often contradictory rhetorical representations by litigants in the courts; and in the changing criteria the courts used to decide cases. Social practices among the LoDagaa surrounding the formation, maintenance, and dissolution of conjugal unions remained irreducible to definition precisely because such definition was absent from the practices themselves.

By the early 1990s, despite the Catholic Church's claim that it was extending pastoral care to almost half of all LoDagaa souls, perhaps only one-quarter of these Christians were entitled to receive the sacraments, because of conjugal irregularities.[141] Half the litigants before the courts might also be said to be living in states of conjugal irregularity as defined by their adversaries; however, the latter were guilty not of religious noncompliance but of ideological deviation from jural norms. During the 1990 seminar the following plea was made: "We must desist from thinking of the Dagaare idea of marriage in terms of essences as the European does. Dagaaba marriage is a process with various elements each of which is significant for the marriage to be what it ought to be."[142] This statement is reminiscent of the criticisms of the Native Courts made four decades earlier by a colonial government commission, which had argued that what had been construed as "customary law" took no cognizance of "the local people's idea of marriage."[143] This modest assertion of "Dagaaba" or local differences had important implications in terms of the question of inculturation.

In 1991 a Catholic priest asked in the pages of the local diocesan newspaper a series of questions that parishioners had posed: "Can't the church accept traditional marriage as valid? Can't the canonical marriage be tailored to local conditions? Why should traditional marriage be regarded as sinful concubinage if it is not 'blessed'?"[144] In response to these "explosive questions," an editorial insisted that the Christian concept of marriage "cannot be 'watered down' or 'divested of its foreign jacket' so that it would be more appealing to the African cultural sensibility."[145] What was lost in this debate, as in earlier anthropological exchanges on the commensurability of Western and African conjugal practices, was that practices were matters of sensibility, and not a matter of rights and duties or canon law. In his study of British anthropology, Goody noted of Radcliffe-Brown's approach that it "centred on rights and duties rather than 'sentiments,'" so the resulting "kinship studies tended to stress the jural domain, especially in the sphere of marriage and divorce."[146] The absence of any discussion of sentiments, or sensibility, effectively undermined the representations of LoDagaa marriage that I have discussed in this and the previous chapter. This jural discourse was also blind to the autonomy of women.

The classification of the various social practices under the rubric of marriage involved a particular form of literate objectification.[147] Despite the success of ethnographic and autoethnographic writing in simplifying and objectifying social practices on paper, attempts by the world on paper to colonize, define, and control social practices in the world of experience had serious limitations. These limitations include the inability of the world on paper to suppress the complexities of practices to make them match literate simplifications, and the irrelevance of objectified knowledge in the world of experience, where practical knowledge governed. As I have discussed at several junctures already, practical knowledge was implicit. Such knowledge was articulated only rarely in LoDagaa culture, and when it was, was concerned almost entirely with the noumenal world. The articulation of marriage as a representation of LoDagaa social practices took place in the world on paper, not in the world of LoDagaa experience.

In the absence of any indigenous manifestation of a similar ideology, the classification of certain social practices as marital distorted the world of experience; it also denied the logic that informed the social practices the LoDagaa continued to employ outside the courts. The French anthropologist Maurice Godelier, writing about the relationship between "the mental and the material," offered the following observation in a discussion of the role of thought or cultural knowledge in the creation of social relations:

> One cannot imagine individuals marrying each other without knowing what marriage is, or whilst being unaware of the kind of marriage rules operative in their society, or without being aware of the consequences that their marriage will have for their descendants, in other words, without being acquainted with the rules of descent. One can therefore see that the mental part of every kinship relation is first of all the set of marriage and descent rules which individuals and groups must act upon in order to produce this order of relations between them.[148]

But say that we are dealing with a culture that was different in the following respects: descent did not proceed from marriage; the status of women was more significant than that of unions; one procedure of conjugal formation jeopardized another; and there was no unequivocal act by which a union could be said to have been established. We would be dealing with a society in which marriage was neither a social institution nor a category of representation. As the history of litigation by the LoDagaa before various courts illustrates, the intended results of social practices in the world of experience were by no means rule oriented. The negotiation of unions, the recruitment and retention of a wife, the selection of a husband, the establishment and perpetuation of social relations between households, and the maintenance of unions against outside intervention were all uncertain social projects that relied on strategic manipulations and social negotiations; neither the execution nor the invocation of rules was involved. For that reason it is misleading to describe as rights those normative expectations that informed and motivated litigants' interpretations of social practices. Doing so disguised and severely minimized the negotiability and uncertainty of social practices, as well as the nature of the relationships they brought into being.

Although Dery claimed, as has already been noted, that "marriage as a social institution is universal," Kuukure conceded that the term marriage is an "abstraction" in terms of local, *Dagaare* terminology.[149] Keeping in mind Comaroff's comment on Radcliffe-Brown's methodology, "the logic of generating explanation from taxonomic procedures," we must remember that what we call things is significant.[150] In the early 1990s, as he looked back over his career and state of his profession, Goody highlighted the tensions between "local knowledge" and "the framework of a scholarly tradition."[151] At one point, writing of his own research among the LoDagaa, he noted that in his study of funerals he had been particularly interested in the "meaning to the actors of the acts, verbal and gestural, in which they engaged, as a counterpoise to the interpretations of the anthropologist." He found it necessary to avoid anthropological concepts except as "signpost" because they did not "reflect indigenous categories, which were much more complex and shaded than they allowed."[152] But commenting on the emphasis on the "actor's point of view" and "local knowledge" in recent anthropology, he was concerned that it had become the "beginning rather than the end" of academic research, thereby becoming a substitute for "the analysis of research materials."[153] What Goody did not address, and what this book has attempted to highlight, is how such analysis in the world on paper can affect the world of experience – how the local and the written intersect. The two worlds cannot be treated as separate spheres.

Conclusion to Part 4

We have seen in a series of attempts to classify particular social practices in terms of marriage that such descriptions have not accurately represented the ambiguities, uncertainties, and contradictions apparent in social life. These qualifications to the jural analyses of ethnographers and administrators were not merely irregularities, inconsistencies, or variations. Those observers who presumed that marriage was a universal category of social representation distorted the relationship between language (words) and reality (things). They assumed not only that marriage accurately described social practices, but also that it generated them. "An individual cannot base his behaviour on something the existence of which does not belong to his knowledge," Holy and Stuchlik noted, "he cannot react to it, he cannot orient his actions towards something he is unaware of."[154] Marriage was not a generative category of LoDagaa social practices. However, it obviously entered into the consciousness of LoDagaa litigants, many of whom enlisted it in their arguments where it operated as a *post facto* device for reinterpreting intentions and meanings in order to realize new expectations. Plaintiffs appealed to the courts specifically because they offered solutions otherwise unavailable.

The question of marriage in relation to LoDagaa practices was inapplicable, yet – as the history of litigation before the courts illustrates – it was continually posed. Through the imposition of judicial structures, a situation was created similar to that of anthropological inquiry. The courts created structures through which litigants articulated indigenous perceptions as well as new forms of knowledge. But the relationship between the courts and experience was never congruent. What was said in public very often did not accord with what was done in private. New knowledge was produced through judicial procedures, but the fundamental questions asked of LoDagaa culture by literate observers (administrators, anthropologists, magistrates, some litigants, and local intellectuals) remained unanswered because LoDagaa experience, knowledge, and practice remained irreducible to the conceptual expectations and language of the world on paper.

Conclusion: Writing, Blood, and the Politics of Legitimacy

Buried below floor level in a bag that crumbled to nothing as soon as it was touched I also found a cache of wooden slips on which are painted characters in a script I have not seen the like of. ... I have no idea what they stand for. Does each stand for a single thing, a circle for the sun, a triangle for a woman, a wave for a lake; or does a circle merely stand for "circle," a triangle for "triangle," a wave for "wave"?

Coetzee, *Waiting for the Barbarians*

Such are the doubts that afflicted the Magistrate in Coetzee's enigmatic allegory of colonial rule. Pressed by the Colonel, his superior, into an interpretation, he concluded that the script could be read in different ways depending on the reader's orientation. Similarly, there are many different ways of reading the documents that this book has analyzed: as relics of a time when the production of knowledge was one of the fundamental by-products of conquest as well as a necessary condition for its perpetuation; as a means of inventing and appropriating colonial subjects; as discourses that either denied historicity or invented history as a weak substitute; as counter discourses that denied the LoDagaa sovereignty by robbing them of the initiative to make history; as communicative acts designed to obliterate privacy and compress different spaces into a homogenous realm of surveillance and intelligence; as forms of rhetorical deference that disguised unrecognized interests and practices; or, finally, as strategies meant to circumscribe the ambiguity of social relations and impose a literal, fixed reading upon them.

The differences between the lives of the LoDagaa and the representations of their lives in the world on paper are both stark and numerous. Words did not stand in direct relationship to experiences. Writing represented power; indeed, it was a power in itself insofar as it was a means of appropriating reality, imposing a foreign epistemology as well as alien ontology, and constructing or manufacturing legitimacy. The resulting representations, from administrative reports and missionary articles to records of litigants' testimony and the discourses of the local literate elite, are very much like the wooden slips that Coetzee's Magistrate attempted to interpret. The demands that colonial politics and the world on paper imposed on the writers (and speakers) of these documents – their historical as well as presentational contexts – are missing. In her study of Chagga social practices, Moore noted that context was what gave knowledge meaning. Abstract statements of fact were incomplete forms of knowledge, "remnants of a living society, not unlike the material remnants, the broken pieces of pottery and ruins of walls from which archaeologists try to reconstruct civilizations."[1] This is how I have treated written documents throughout this book – as incomplete refractions of reality that must be situated in context if we are to understand what they mean rather than just what they say. That could only be achieved by "connecting what was written to what was said and to what was done."[2] I have sought to restore the world on paper to our understanding of colonialism and its legacies by looking at writing as an intrinsic part of that phenomenon, and not just as an incidental or innocent by-product of it.

The various forms of dissonance evident in the documents I examined had different sources, but they shared the same cognitive bias. In the 1920s the Russian psychologist A.R. Luria noted that the nonliterate inhabitants of the villages he surveyed in Uzbekistan did not read geometric shapes as abstract symbols, but as real things. For example, "they would call a circle a plate, sieve, bucket, watch, or moon."[3] Students from the same villages who had completed just a few years of formal schooling read the shapes as geometric symbols, as things abstracted from the world of experience. Because the words (conceptual language) used to represent the LoDagaa on paper were not generative of their practices and experiences, the use of writing as a medium of representation has resulted in a series of misrepresentations. The foreign words used to describe the LoDagaa were often only very rough approximations that, even if functionally equivalent, did not have any direct relevance to their culture. Nevertheless these words, and everything they implied, created an ontological tyranny that was first enshrined in the discourse of external observers. Observers attempted to match these words with LoDagaa experiences and practices, either to legitimate foreign authority or to manipulate it. Through acts of dissimulation, these words came to be part of the lives of the LoDagaa, even though they remained abstract symbols imported from a foreign cultural geometry of representations. Culture became ethnicity, paths became roads, memory became history, scarification patterns became clothes, Earth priests became chiefs, god became God, noumenal knowledge became political power, arrows became summonses, cowries became coins, speech became writing, actions became words, practices became rules, conjugal payments became blood, and women became wives only.

Before conquest, practices and experiences among the LoDagaa were not generated or governed by writing. Cultural identities had been defined in terms of relationships rather than names. Politics and religion had been about noumenal powers, not phenomenal institutions. Social order had been maintained not by rules and rulers but by beliefs and practices. Conjugal unions had been negotiable and ambiguous rather than contractual. The identity of women had not been defined in terms of the interests of men; rather, it was constantly redefined by the actions of women. Descent had been determined not by blood but by exchange and ritual. In the twentieth century this world, the world of autonomous experience among the LoDagaa, was increasingly constrained by writing. Writing became a source not only of power but also of legitimacy, whether ethnic, political, religious, economic, social, or personal. Accordingly, the LoDagaa adopted things from the world on paper in order to acquire legitimacy – things such as clothes, chiefs, God, and cash. Similarly, they have gone to court to determine social legitimacy, whether as husbands, wives, or children, in a literate ritual of classification and definition.

In the early 1980s, anthropologists such as Clifford and Fabian became aware of the representational limitations that writing, and the concomitant visualism of Western culture, imposed on their discipline. In a survey of approaches to the anthropology of the senses written in the early 1990s, and published in the same series in which this book now appears, David Howes suggested that it is "only by developing a rigorous awareness of the visual and textual biases of Western episteme that we can hope to make sense of how life is lived in other cultural settings."[4] As true as this statement is, it is also true that experiences in "other cultural settings" have already come under the sovereignty of writing to one degree or another as a result of colonization. Writing affects not only how outsiders represent cultures, but also how insiders represent their own cultures.

In various chapters I have scrutinized the distortions involved in particular written descriptions of LoDagaa experience. But much more than examining the construction of different discourses, either written by outsiders for themselves or written and spoken by insiders for external consumption, I have sought to examine the legacy of these discourses – namely, their direct effects on the experiences of the LoDagaa. The representations I have described as misrepresentations are important not only for understanding how the LoDagaa were cognitively appropriated by foreign powers. Much more importantly, they help us appreciate how that conquest continues to affect the reality these documents attempted to represent.

Although writing has yet to complete its colonization of the LoDagaa, its categories of knowledge (ontology) and ways of understanding (epistemology) have spread from the world on paper into the lives of the LoDagaa like an alien calculus, and are gradually reshaping experiences. Ideally, the representations that the LoDagaa make of themselves should be reoriented inwards, in terms of their own sense of what is relevant, what is legitimate, and what is appropriate. Only then can sovereignty be regained, identities (both cultural and personal) liberated, authority legitimated, and fluidity and negotiability preserved in social practices. (This project is implicitly political, but necessary if wider goals of plurality, autonomy, democracy, and gender equality are to be achieved in this corner of the state of Ghana.)

Another purpose of this book has been to call attention to the underlining imbalances that arose at the interface of writing and experience – imbalances that are evident in the resulting documents. As I argued at the outset, the role of writing in colonial and postcolonial African history has been too much in the background. This neglect is especially surprising, given the role that writing has played in attenuating political disputes in the past century. In northern Ghana, where this is particularly evident, the role of writing has perhaps been more fully acknowledged than elsewhere by historians of politics. These conflicts can be traced to differences between the historical consciousness of observers from the world on paper and the sense of the past enshrined in the cultures of the people they wrote about. " 'Happy is the country that has no history,' " wrote the Provincial Commissioner of Wa in 1920 in exasperation at the political intrigues of the Wala kingdom. His superior, Duncan-Johnstone, who was later to become a colonial expert on the constitutional politics of the Dagomba kingdom, wrote in the margins: "Has it any character?"[5] Administrators showed a strong preference for societies that to them had a readily apprehensible history, even though, as the provincial commissioner knew, it meant that political intrigues were complicated and exhausting for administrators.

In Wa, Dagbon, Mamprugu, and Gonja, as well as among the Nanumba and Konkomba, attempts to historicize colonial political engineering more than indirectly contributed to forms of political violence that have claimed many lives in the postcolonial period. The colonial construction of written history, of words inelastic to changing circumstances and incapable of being read in different directions, has bequeathed a terrible legacy to politics in northern Ghana as elsewhere in Africa.[6] Staniland noted that through a "proliferation of government measures defining, regulating, and protecting chieftaincy" among the Dagomba, the British managed to turn indigenous political authority into an empty constitutional shell. This attempt to remove politics from "chieftaincy matters" produced only "confusion, ambiguity, and inconsistency."[7] Officers such as Duncan-Johnstone sought to define Dagomba "tradition," but it was elusive, lacking "permanence, clarity, and immutability" – features not easily rendered in writing.[8] Instead there was "a certain fossilisation of 'traditional' politics ... a mummification of the body politic in a wrapping of ethnography."[9] Among the Wala, as among the Dagomba, history was full of contradictions that cannot be resolved by writing. In his study of twentieth-century Wala politics, Wilks noted that chaos was always part of a political process ungoverned by "rules and norms," so colonial and postcolonial attempts to reduce this situation to one of "harmony" only exacerbated the tensions inherent in the pursuit and contestation of power. Any felicitous description of Wala society must contend with "ambiguities and contradictions" that "reflect equally valid but nonetheless incompatible views of the nature of Wala society."[10]

As this book demonstrates, the LoDagaa did have a history – that is, a sense of historical consciousness – but it was invisible to all but the most unusual of officers and was conceived of spatially rather than temporally. Because of its invisibility, not to mention differences in how the past was perceived and enshrined, the LoDagaa were spared the most negative political aspects of colonial historicism. LoDagaa politics did not suffer from the constitutional straightjacketing described by Staniland and Wilks; however, the world on paper did affect the LoDagaa in other, less dramatic but equally serious ways.

The world on paper has not only denied the LoDagaa the right to describe their culture and society in their own terms, but has also in turn created unresolved cultural, political, religious, and social tensions that continue to affect their capacity to regain lost sovereignty. These tensions, which manifested themselves in different contexts, affected different groups of people differently, whether they were migrant workers in the south, political entrepreneurs in the north, practitioners of a syncretic faith, young men attempting to acquire wives, or women attempting to control their own labor and sexuality. Yet the source of the tensions was the same: the world on paper.

In some respects the LoDagaa were exceptional in terms of their lack of a single, fixed ethnonym, their degree of decentralization, their appropriation of a foreign religion, the intensity of colonial rule, and the ambiguity of conjugal relations; but all these were features of many other societies in northern Ghana. The problems they encountered in their interaction with the world on paper might have been far less violent and seemingly more mundane than those in neighboring states, but their effects were much more representative of what most commoners in northern Ghana have experienced in this century.[11]

The constitutionalism that afflicted administrative attitudes toward politics in the large states of northern Ghana was reflected in administrative attitudes toward LoDagaa conjugal unions. Perhaps it is more than coincidence that it was Blair, co-author (along with Duncan-Johnstone) of the colonial pamphlet *Enquiry into the Constitution and Organisation of the Dagbon Kingdom*, who compiled the first set of marriage laws among the LoDagaa.[12] Just as writing could not encapsulate and order the chaos of Dagomba or Wala politics, neither could it represent the ambiguity and complexity of LoDagaa conjugal unions. In both cases the processes were intrinsically unwieldy and chaotic. When fighting broke out in northern Ghana in early 1994 between, on one side, politically dissatisfied Konkomba and, on the other, their political overlords in surrounding areas – the Dagomba, Nanumba, and Gonja – one of the things the former destroyed were "the traditional regalia and written histories of particular Dagomba chieftaincies."[13] It is not difficult to imagine that some unsuccessful litigants in Lawra District might have been inclined to destroy the magistrate's desk and the Court Record Books, as both were potent symbols and effective instruments of an alien authority, that is, the world on paper.

The world on paper has impacted most emphatically on LoDagaa ideas of social paternity. The form of this intrusion offers an especially apt metaphor for the themes addressed in this book. The idea that custody of children should proceed from notions of blood and filiation rather than socialization and descent is in one sense merely cultural. But in the metaphor of blood there is also something intrinsic about the way the world on paper thinks. Custody among the LoDagaa was contested and complicated; courts sought to eliminate these characteristics by insisting on a form of social literalism. It is perhaps no accident that in literate cultures, biology is more likely to be an important determinant of the custody of children.[14] David Schneider has argued that the Western equation of paternity with biology did not proceed from "scientific fact" but from the "ethnoepistemology of European culture," where blood is valorized as more important, or "thicker," than water.[15]

If blood is an apt metaphor for writing, insofar as it is seen in literate cultures as fact, as incontestable matter, and as being uniquely true, then water is an appropriate metaphor for the world of experience, a world of flux, contestation, and a plurality of perspectives. Jacques Derrida challenged Claude Lévi-Strauss's contention in *Tristes Tropiques* that the Nambikwara of Brazil did not understand writing when it was first presented to them; the anthropologist had noted in his thesis that they had quickly realized its significance, making "diagrams describing, explaining, writing, a genealogy and a social structure." According to Derrida, this accords with "unquestionable and abundant information" demonstrating that "the birth of writing (in the colloquial sense) was nearly everywhere and most often linked to genealogical anxiety."[16] The "genealogical anxiety" that the courts introduced into LoDagaa society in the postcolonial era was just a more explicit form of similar worries that the world on paper created in many other areas, such as ethnic identity, politics, and religion about what it deemed legitimate.

Writing attempted to appropriate, monitor, control, and understand the LoDagaa "in the jagged time of rise and fall, of beginning and end," and not in "the smooth recurrent spinning time of the cycle of the seasons." In some respects the LoDagaa outwitted writing in the same way that other societies in northern Ghana have outwitted the state.[17] The LoDagaa succeeded in maintaining elasticity in their social practices, but they were forced to abandon the nuances and uncertainties of everyday life when they came before the courts. But, insofar as they have had to address writing as the locus of power and a source of legitimacy, they have lost a large degree of autonomy and freedom. Formerly, power resided in the noumenal world accessible through ritual, not the world on paper accessible through writing. Increasingly, power came to reside in writing. Unable to escape ethnic classification, denied the ability to invent a new political order, refused permission to syncretize religious ideas, compelled to accept a foreign currency, required to settle disputes in terms of an alien etiology, and forced to accept a jural interpretation of conjugal practices, the LoDagaa live under the jurisdiction of writing as they once did under the power of the *tengaan* or Earth shrine.

Writing was the enemy of the ambiguity and autonomy of unmediated experience, or what Bourdieu refers to as "the logic of practice."[18] It inverted the generative relationship between life and words among the LoDagaa, and imposed a mimetic tyranny on representations of their experiences. The logic of writing replaced social practices with rules, belonging with blood, and the paths of the ancestors worn into the land with words written on paper.

Notes

Abbreviations

CCNT	Chief Commissioner, Northern Territories
CFA	Communité Finançière Africaine
CNP	Commissioner, Northern Province
CPP	Convention People's Party
CRB	Court Record Book, Civil Proceedings
CRO	Chief Regional Officer
CSP	Commissioner, Southern Province
DC	District Commissioner
DMC	District Magistrate's Court, Lawra
GC	Gold Coast
NA	Native Affairs
NAG	National Archives of Ghana, Accra
NLC	National Liberation Council
NP	Northern Province
NPP	Northern People's Party
NT	Northern Territories
NWP	North-Western Province
PC	Provincial Commissioner
PNDC	Provisional National Defence Council
RA	*Rapports Annuels*, The Society of Missionaries of Africa, Montreal, Quebec (Canada)
RAT	Regional Archives, Tamale
UGCC	United Gold Coast Convention Party

Introduction: Colonialism as an Encounter between "The World on Paper" and the World of Experience

1 I wrote this sentence before reading the following in an introduction to a study of postcolonial literature: "Imperial relations may have been established initially by guns, guile and disease, but they were maintained in their interpellative phase largely by textuality, both institutionally ... and informally." Tiffin and Lawson 1994, 3.

2 Westermann and Bryan 1952, 66. See also Bodomo 1997.

3 Manoukian 1951, 11–12. This figure includes both Dagarti and Lobi. According to Murdock, the total figure was 225,000. Murdock 1959, 78–9. For clarification on these designations see Chapter 1.

4 Westermann and Bryan 1952, 66.

5 Yelpaala 1992, 431–2; Angsotinge 1986, 25.

6 Bodomo 1997, 1. This is an interesting case of inverted linguistic imperialism, subsuming the Wala, citizens of the precolonial state of Wa and speakers of Waale (or Walii), under their decentralized neighbors.

7 Lawra District has existed for most of this century as a distinct geopolitical entity. It emerged in 1907 from the larger Black Volta District, and for several years during the colonial period was combined with Tumu District to the east to form Lawra–Tumu District. Since 1987 it has been divided in two, with the eastern half of the district now being known as Jirapa–Lambussie District. For the sake of clarity, I refer to both of these contemporary districts as Lawra District.

8 See Prussin 1969, chapter 6.

9 Ghana 1989, xx.

10 Piot 1999, 154.

11 Piot 1999, 23. Although Piot was writing of the Kabre of northern Togo, this observation applies equally here.

12 Goody 1972, White *Bagre* 1–10. Afflictions and their avoidance were central to the *Bagre*. After naming the various noumenal agencies that might intervene, the recitation then listed possible causes that might make someone seek out a diviner who, using "the leather bottles," would have determined whether they needed to be initiated within the *Bagre* in order to find protection from disease. Goody noted that the process of consultation and divination leading to initiation was also described as being "caught." Some illnesses such as guinea worm were very closely associated with having been seized by the god of the *Bagre* (*Bagr ngmin*). Goody 1972, 39.

13 ADM 61/5/6, Informal Diary Lawra District, 18 January 1919, 25 February 1919.

14 Waddy 1980, 159, 164. Up until this time the colonial administration had had a very limited effect on the health of the LoDagaa or any of the other societies of

the Northern Territories. There seems to have been very little awareness of the level of privation that was experienced in the district toward the end of the dry season. In the 1930s the first nutritional survey of the region revealed that nutritional intake during this point in the year could often fall as low as five hundred to one thousand calories a day! Patterson 1981, 99.

15 Olson 1994, 19. The phrase "the world on paper," which comes from the title of Olson's book, is used in the subtitle to this book as well as at innumerable junctures throughout. I have omitted the quotation marks from this point onward, but this is not meant to obscure its origins. Although Olson himself borrowed the term (195), I draw on his particular elaboration of it throughout this book.

16 Fabian 2000, 199.

17 Pratt 1992, 204. See also Mitchell (1988, 178) on the importance of exhibitions to colonial power: "The kind of political order epitomised in the world exhibition addresses, and demands, a political subject who must learn that reality is simply that which is capable of representation."

18 Street 1984, 1–11; 1993, 1–10.

19 Goody 1986, 113, 115–16. See also Dauber 1995, 75–6, 82–3.

20 Olson repeatedly stresses that literates are seduced into "living in a world on paper" where writing does not deal with the world, but with "the world as depicted or described." Olson 1994, 19, 195. Street, citing Derrida, makes a similar point about "'literising' experience" (Street 1984, 101).

21 Greenblatt 1991, 12.

22 I do not see any contradiction here in my use of both Olson and Street. Although the latter has criticized the former for subscribing to an "autonomous model," most of the effects that Olson attributes to literacy seem to me to accord well with the particular manifestation dealt with here. In part this may have much to do with the fact that I have used Olson's latest work – one that appeared after Street's most recent criticisms. Furthermore, Street has noted that his "ideological model" does not deny the cognitive features of literacy; it just insists on situating them within their generative cultural structures. Street 1993, 5, 10.

23 NAG ADM 61/5/8, Informal Diary Lawra District, 19, 21 March 1917.

24 Bowman and Woolf 1994, 1, 9.

25 Clanchy 1993, 6, 25, 32, 35; Street 1984, 112.

26 NAG ADM 61/5/8, Informal Diary Lawra District, 10 January 1921. This episode is very similar to that made famous by Claude Lévi-Strauss in his account of writing among the Nambikwara of Brazil. Jacques Derrida has criticized the anthropologist for not recognizing that the Nambikwara could write, that is, make signs. This definition of writing is wider than the one I have used here, but it is important to acknowledge so as not to interpret the signs inscribed on the leaf as meaningless, or as purely mimetic gestures. Derrida 109–10, 120–1;

Mignolo 1995, 78. The signs can be seen as similar to strategies for "oralising" colonial writing in the Transvaal (Hofmeyr 1993, 50–1, 63–5). Or they can be read simply as the assertion of the values of an oral culture similar to those discussed by Clanchy (1993, esp. 34–43).

27 Smith 1998, 540.

28 Jewsiewicki 1991, 146. Lévi-Strauss, reflecting on the implications of the absence of literacy among the Nambikwara, noted that far from writing being a sign of civilization, its primary role in history had been "to facilitate slavery," that is, the exploitation of other humans through large-scale political organization (Lévi-Strauss 1997, 361). For similar analyses see Clastres 1989, 24, 188, 190; Clanchy 1993, 11. For a critique of Lévi-Strauss's argument, see Derrida 1976, 128, 131. The association of government with writing is obvious. As McCaskie has pointed out, the word bureaucracy, the most obvious of literate institutions, comes from the word *bureau*, which originally referred to the covering on the surface of a desk where writing was executed. McCaskie 1995, 14–15. The desk was also the medium across which administrators, and sometimes ethnographers, communicated with their subjects for administrative and ethnographic purposes.

29 Auslander 1993, 184–5.

30 Hutchinson 1996, 283–4.

31 Ewald 1988, 224.

32 Ewald 1988, 212, 215, 222–3.

33 In this encounter the LoDagaa largely controlled their own experiences insofar as they mediated changes that occurred under colonialism; but the British and their successors largely controlled written discourse and monopolized external sources of power.

34 Mitchell 1988; Thornton 1983; Hofmeyr 1993.

35 See Probst 1989; Comaroff and Comaroff 1991; Landau 1995.

36 Notable exceptions to this have been historians critical of the overvaluation of oral testimony in the methodology of African history. See Henige 1974, 1980; Cohen 1989; Law 1991; Wright 1991.

37 Staniland 1975, viii–ix. With regard to an imaginative treatment, many of the conceptual problems discussed in this introduction, especially the meaning of court records and the dilemma of writing the history of an oral culture, are explored indirectly in Coetzee's brilliant novel *Waiting for the Barbarians.*

38 Mitchell 1988, 33.

39 Hofmeyr 1993, 51.

40 Hutchinson 1996, 27.

41 For example, see Headrick 1981; Goody 1986, 113–16; Finnegan 1988, 148–9, 160. Headrick hardly mentioned writing. Goody, in a brief passage, pointed to a less instrumental role for literacy in colonial rule. However, he did not consider

the historical forces that shaped writing in any particular situation, preferring to see it as an autonomous force (1986, xi). A number of critics have taken him to task for this, most notably Street (1984). For a useful summary of these issues see also Street and Besnier (1994). Finnegan has been critical of deterministic studies that see literacy as the *sine qua non* for administration, suggesting, quite rightly, that administration was possible without writing. The argument here is not that European administration would have been impossible without writing, but that the appropriation of colonial subjects, the theft of their historical sovereignty, and the regulation of their lives depended on writing as an expression of power and as an instrument of control.

42 See Niezen 1991; Probst 1989.

43 Axtell 1995, 685. He counted the "perdurable tools of literacy" among the eleven most important themes to emerge around the time of the Columbus Quincentenary. See also Classen 1991.

44 Thornton 1983, 505–6, 509.

45 Mignolo 1992b 311; 1994a, 261.

46 Classen 1991, 410, 412.

47 Mignolo 1992b, 310.

48 Pagden 1993, 118.

49 Pagden 1993, 134–6; Mignolo 1992.

50 See Iliffe 1979, 338–41; Fabian 1986, 70–5, 78–81; Manning 1988, 59–62, 93, 100, 167–71.

51 Ngugi 1981; Fabian 1986.

52 Fortes 1936, 26. "Culture contact is a dynamic process and not a mechanical pitchforking of elements of culture, like bundles of hay, from one culture to another. It is a process of the same order as other processes of social interaction both in literate societies of Europe, America and Asia, and in preliterate societies of other parts of the world." Two of the main problems with this paradigm were that it was conceived of as unilateral and its perspective ignored politics. Ranajit Guha's notion of "dominance without hegemony" might be a more accurate formulation of the modalities of these encounters, as in colonial situations it was generally a one-sided exchange in terms of the distribution of coercive power, but not in terms of the distribution of cultural power (Guha 1997). Nevertheless, although colonized cultures were selective in their assimilation of the concepts of colonizing societies, when the latter possessed writing and former did not, inequalities of cultural power occurred. As Talal Asad noted, "because the languages of Third World societies – including, of course, the societies that social anthropologists have traditionally studied – are 'weaker' in relation to Western languages (and today, especially to English) they are more likely to submit to forcible transformation in the translation process than the other way around." This

wider phenomenon of the relative weakness of indigenous languages, in part the function of the physical and economic powers that are inscribed within Western languages, was exacerbated in those situations where colonized societies were unable either to create their own writing systems or to successfully subvert those deployed against them. Asad 1986, 157–8.

53 Quite rightly, Malinowski's model (as opposed to Fostes's use of it) deserves criticism for ignoring the political and economic realities of colonialism. See Cooper 1996, 372–3. However, the history of European colonialism in Africa is no longer afflicted by such gross, or even deliberate, naivety. The political and economic aspects of colonialism are now well understood; indeed, one could argue that until recently the overwhelming attention paid to these dimensions by historians has impoverished our understanding of the cultural experiences of colonialism. The point is that balance is required between material and cultural prospectives.

54 A comprehensive list of works is not possible here, but see Axtell (1995) for a review of some of this literature.

55 See Cooper (1994) for a critical overview of the historiography of colonialism in Africa.

56 Cooper and Stoler 1989, 620. In answer to the question Cooper and Stoler pose as to whether there ever was "a language of domination, crossing distinct metropolitan polities and linguistic barriers of French, English, Spanish, German, and Dutch, and common models of how to constitute an empire" (611), I would suggest that there was – writing. Common ideological elements were obviously necessary to justify these regimes, most notably racism, but writing provided a structure through which to appropriate, order, and rule the conquered. Writing gave consistency to colonialism as a phenomenon across national boundaries.

57 Comaroff and Comaroff 1997, 18–19.

58 Comaroff and Comaroff 1997, 15.

59 This was the subtitle to the influential collection of essays edited by Clifford and Marcus (1986).

60 Clifford 1986, 2.

61 Fabian 1983, passim. He did suggest the possibility that "because prose narrative is the literary genre of most anthropological writing, devices of temporal sequencing and distancing are simply inevitable aspects of literary expression"; but he rejected this type of purely discursive explanation in favor of a more complex argument that also considered ideological motivations (72). Although he did not highlight writing specifically, Fabian noted that these processes had their roots in the distance between "thing and image, reality and representation," whereby image and representation became more real than experiences (160).

62 Fabian 2000, 241.

63 Bourdieu 1982, 26–7, 96; 1990, 11, 37–40.

64 Olson 1994, 29–33, 62–3, 167–8, 197, 241–3, 250. McCaskie has defined representations in very similar ways in his study of Asante, arguing that representations are "objectifications rather than objects, arguments rather than statements" and that although representations reflect reality, are also part of it: "They reflect political action and embody social practice, but they are covalent with neither, being themselves active constituents of historical reality" (McCaskie 1995, 20). Whereas McCaskie (1995) and Feierman (1990) have both been concerned with the problematic relationship between ideology and economy as surveyed by Gramsci, I have chosen to address the relationship between writing and power.

65 Fortes 1945, vii; also quoted in Von Laue 1975, 401–2. As Fabian noted, "the presumption of fact holds that there *is* a text to be *rewritten*. This is ultimately an ontological statement, one that anchors the taxonomic enterprise in a real world of texts and writers" (1983, 97).

66 The latter studies, although using his earlier fieldwork experiences to illustrate much broader arguments, were largely theoretical rather than empirical. The focus was also much more on the cognitive implications of literacy as opposed to its specific historical effects (Goody and Watt 1968; Goody 1977; 1986; and 1987). Although his theories have been much criticized, there is no denying that they were instrumental in bringing far greater attention to the importance of literacy. Anything approaching even a representative list would be too long to produce here, but see for example Clanchy 1993.

67 Bourdieu 1977; Fabian 1983.

68 MacGaffey 1970; Henige 1974; Dorward 1974; Staniland 1975; Iliffe 1979; Prins 1980; Ranger 1983; Chanock 1985; Moore 1986; Vail 1989; Mann and Roberts 1991; Jewsiewicki and Mudimbe 1993.

69 Ranger 1983, 212.

70 Henige 1974, 7, 104–5; Dorward 1974, 463, 369; Staniland 1975, 14, 189; Iliffe 1979, 323, 337; Prins 1980, 28–9; Bayart 1993, 11.

71 Bayart 1993, 2–10. Colonialism was about denying the historicity of indigenous experiences and attempting to impose a conceptual and ideological framework derived from Western historical experience.

72 Feierman 1990, 27–39; Heehs 1994, 1–5.

73 Bayart 1993, 3, 5.

74 Jewsiewicki and Mudimbe 1993, 5–6.

75 Gabriel Spiegel quoted in Cohen 1994, xxiii.

76 Naameh 1986, 124.

77 Hofmeyr 1993, 4.

78 Jewsiewicki and Mudimbe 1993.

79 *Oxford English Dictionary*, 2nd ed., s. v. "historicism."

80 Henige 1980.
81 Feierman 1990, 44.
82 Stock 1990, 164–6.
83 Clifford 1986, 19.
84 Vogel 1991, 30.
85 Moore 1986, 320–9; Mudimbe 1988, 5; Feierman 1990, 5. Although many of these spatial paradigms for understanding the present were often biased, they are more realistic than temporal terms for understanding the growth of historical consciousness.
86 Feierman 1990, 3; Vansina 1990, 258; Stock 1990, 160–3; Mudimbe 1988, 189.
87 Bourdieu 1977, 78, 95.
88 Bayart 1993, 11; Fabian 1983, 29.
89 Fabian 1983, 155.
90 Clifford Geertz quoted in Moore 1986, 325.
91 Mudimbe 1988, 22.
92 Clanchy 1993, 299.
93 *Brigadoon.* 1954. Hollywood: MGM. A film starring Gene Kelley and Cid Charisse, directed by Vincente Minelli, with story and lyrics by Alan Jay Lerner and music by Frederick Loewe. According to reviews, the film was a disappointing reprise of a popular 1947 Broadway production.
94 Gill 1980, 156.
95 Brog 1954, 6. This is the dilemma of all foreigners. In a study of the dynamics of fieldwork in northern Ghana, Lance noted that one elder explained to him: "Even though you live in our kind of house, you will never be one of us because you can always go away" (Lance 1990, 337). The inability of most people that anthropologists and historians study in Africa to leave the context of their own lives puts them in a position similar to the inhabitants of Brigadoon. Similarly, the power to leave makes the researcher little more than an interested, academic tourist.
96 Lees 1991, 47, 232.
97 Gill 1986, 114.
98 Jewsiewicki 1991, 151.
99 Feierman 1990, 38.
100 Bayart 1993, 21; Bayart 1986, 113.
101 Mudimbe 1988, 5. This location is more ideological than physical: "It [the intermediary space] reveals a strong tension between modernity that is often an illusion of development, and a tradition that sometimes reflects a poor image of a mythical past." Geographical isolation, cultural marginalization, deteriorating economic conditions of the recent past, and encroaching ecological crises have

placed the LoDagaa in an ambiguous relationship with the wider world. The ideology of development, propounded by both the colonial administration in the aftermath of the Second World War and by different postcolonial governments since, has proved unattainable. While working as an anthropologist in the neighboring district of Tumu at several points during the 1970s, Mendonsa reported that conditions deteriorated dramatically: "It [the mid 1960s] was a time of hope and naiveté. Since that time Ghana has slowly lost power in the world economic arena, and the dreams of yesterday have become tempered by the harsh economic realities that persist in many Third World countries today. In Sisala-land, the educational system has been sharply reduced, mechanized farming has been a dismal failure, planned roads and communication systems have failed to materialize, health care remains extremely primitive, and periodic starvation is not unknown." Mendonsa 1982, 172–4.

102 Goody and Gandah 1980, 390, 392.

103 Pratt 1992, 7.

104 I find Rorty's position not only attractive and compelling, but useful in outlining my own purpose in presenting such a study of written representations. The purpose of this study is not to revise representations of the LoDagaa, because, as Rorty notes, we cannot possibly formulate "an independent test of accuracy of representation" (1991, 1, 6).

105 Greenblatt 1991, 7.

106 Mafeje 1976, 318.

107 Piot 1999, 24, 39. Dauber (1995) has made a similar argument, but with far less subtlety.

108 See RAT ADM 430, "Essay on the People of North West Province," PC NWP, 1907. Captain, later Major, Read was also known as Moutray-Read. The report was compiled in March 1907 but not submitted until November 1908.

109 Discussing the "cultural embeddedness" of anthropological discourse, MacGaffey noted: "It is useful to distinguish between moral or judgmental ethnocentrism, which varies from individual to individual, and epistemological ethnocentrism, the problem of translating cultural realities from one set of categories to another." MacGaffey 1981, 263. See also Bohannan 1957, 4–5; Mudimbe 1988, 18–20.

110 Dickerman 1984, 69–70; Roberts 1990, 448–9: Mann and Roberts 1991, 5–9.

111 Hall 1938, 412.

112 Roberts 1985, 380–2.

113 The District Commissioner's Court Record Books and the District Complaint Record Books constitute the largest source of documentation of colonial rule. Over two-and-a-half thousand pages of complaints, evidence, hearings, and

judgments were recorded, often with extreme brevity, but occasionally with satisfying detail. No Native Authority Court Record Books survive from the period 1932–40, and I was only able to locate four Court Record Books covering the period 1940–54. There is, therefore, a noticeable gap in documentation during that period. However, other colonial archival materials, such as diaries, reports, and correspondence, help bridge this gap. Not only because of the incomplete nature of these records, but also because of their disappointing quality, ethnographic and anthropological sources have been used extensively. Finally, although colonial documents cease in 1953, the Record Books of the Local Authority Courts (1954–60) and the District Magistrate's Court (1960–91) provide excellent source material for the postcolonial period. There are sixteen volumes of these court records, each with five to six hundred pages of transcribed proceedings. With the one qualification that they are – as are all the records – translations of proceedings, these volumes are of a reasonably high clerical standard. In 1991 the District Courts became Community Tribunals. From 1985 to 1991 the Ghanaian government attempted a series of reforms of "customary law." Most relevant of these was PNDC Law 112, Customary Marriage and Divorce (Registration) Act of 1985. These attempts were largely unsuccessful, and PNDC Law 163, Customary Marriage and Divorce (Registration) (Amendment) of 1991, superseded PNDCL 112. See Korbieh 1990, 50–2; Wanitzek 1998, 125, 160. This book does not deal with the District Court during the period 1985–91.

114 RAT ADM 153, "Memorandum on Native Authority in the Northern Territories," Ag. CCNT, 18 March 1931.

115 RAT ADM 342–3, Informal Diary Lawra District, September 1942.

116 Moore 1977, 159: "One way to do this is to treat proceedings of dispute settlement as ceremonies of situational transformation. Looked at this way, the hearing of a case can be seen to have many layers of meaning beyond those most immediately evident."

117 Holy and Stuchlik 1983, 58: "The making of a given statement will, on the one hand, derive from the actor's definition of that situation and from his purpose in participating in it, and, on the other hand, will constitute his attempt to manipulate the situation so he can achieve this purpose." Later, they added: "In fact, quite often they are [a norm's] only manifestation because the norm is part of that vast amount of intersubjectively shared background expectancies, which are taken for granted by the actors and therefore hardly ever made explicit." Finally, they noted in another connection: "It is again possible to expect that the generative influence of the interactional processes on their accompanying representations will be brought into focus in situations in which it can be assumed that the

changes in the actors' representational models are occurring at an accelerated rate. This is specifically the case in newly emerging or expanding states, where members of hitherto relatively isolated groups, instead of containing their interactions predominantly within the boundaries of their group, have to interact with members of a state-wide administrative system. ... Continually, these people will have to construct a model of the wider society which they did not have before, or at least with not such clarity." (68, 100) This book is about just such a change in representations.

118 Bourdieu 1977, 106. See also Ong 1982, 43–6: "Writing fosters abstractions that disentangle knowledge from the arena where human beings struggle with one another. It separates the knower from the known. By keeping knowledge embedded in the human lifeworld, orality situates knowledge within a context of struggle. ... For an oral culture learning or knowing means achieving close, empathetic, communal identification with the known. ... Writing separates the knower from the known and thus sets up conditions for 'objectivity,' in the sense of personal disengagement or distancing."

119 For example, disputes within households, as well as disputes between households, were made public when they came before the courts. Private knowledge of the relationship between man and wife, father and son, uncle and nephew, affines, and neighbors was heard in a space far more expansive than any network for village or market gossip. Furthermore, this information was not only heard in public, it was also written down.

120 Lance 1990, 338.

121 Chanock 1985, 145–6.

122 The term "social practice" has two meanings directly relevant to this discussion. In the first sense it can be read as a replacement for the stolid and unhelpful notion of "custom," once so prevalent in the discussion of preliterate societies. See Moore 1986, 330. Having noted that in "nonstate" societies law can only be identified by "functional analogy," she added that descriptions of such cultures often attempted to avoid the problem of identifying law by using the term "custom" – "internalized rules for which no enforcement is necessary, and of unchanging, immutable practices." This brings us to the second way in which the term "social practice" can be read. As Bourdieu has amply demonstrated, even where the same actions are repeated in a society over several generations, such reproduction is not the result of passive forces acting on individuals; rather, it flows out of the active role of individuals in reenacting those actions. Replication is not automatic, but regenerative. Bourdieu 1977, chapter 1.

123 In historical terms, law must not be seen as simply a concomitant of literacy. Instead, both must be viewed as products of particular socio-economic and

political structures. Clastres 1987, 177; Newman 1983. That the LoDagaa had a subsistence economy and a highly dispersed political structure makes them an extreme example of an oral culture, but also serves to emphasize the differences between oral and literate methods of resolving disputes.

124 Scholars know the LoDagaa almost exclusively through the works of Jack Goody. See the Bibliography for a list of his key works on the LoDagaa. Besides Goody's work, that of earlier anthropologists in this region, namely Labouret, Rattray, and Fortes, is equally renowned.

125 Clifford 1986, 11. See Goody 1977, but also the earlier, pioneering work of the Russian psychologist, A.R. Luria, which dealt with the emergence of categorical thought among recent literates. Luira 1976, esp. chapter 3. For an assessment of his conclusions and further discussion of the effects of literacy see Ong 1980, chapters 3 and 4.

126 The seemingly objective methodology of anthropology actually caused the suppression of any mention of historical themes. Commenting on his own and other anthropologists' (including Fortes's) omission of any reference to the colonial context in which they worked, and to which the societies they studied were subject, Goody remarked: "Anthropology is the child of European colonisation, and has failed to transcend the limitations of its ancestry" (1967, v). Only by recognizing its context, Goody was suggesting, could anthropology overcome its particular historical situation. The connections between colonialism and anthropology, ironically made more conspicuous by the absence of any explicit reference to the former by the latter, has been the source of some controversy and ideological scrutiny. It is somewhat unreasonable to expect any discipline to transcend its historical contexts. Similarly, it is somewhat unreasonable for historians to expect another discipline to have abandoned its synchronicity in favor of their diachronic perspective. Anthropologists never denied the existence of history, just its relevance.

127 Goody 1968, 215–16.

128 Chanock 1985, 4.

129 Chanock 1982, 54–5. This of course was once thought of societies without writing.

130 Vansina 1965, 116–17: "Kuba law is thus very different from any European legal system, and to try to define it in terms of European legal concepts is like trying to fit Bantu grammar into a Latin model of grammatical categories, something actually done until descriptive linguistics taught us better."

131 Moore 1978, 9–10: "In simpler societies, without writing or full-time jurists, there seems to be less reason to try to construct an apparently consistent and coherent order out of an aggregation of legal norms. ... Where there is no legal profession, and/or central political authority which legitimates itself through a

synthesized ideology of legal principles and rules, there seems little technical capacity or reason to rationalize a supposed connection among all enforceable norms with any degree of elaboration."

132 Chanock 1982, 66.

133 Chanock 1982, 66. See also Moore 1986, 330 (note 1); Humphreys 1985, 252.

134 Chanock 1985, 145.

135 Comaroff 1980a, 17; Comaroff and Roberts 1981, 132.

136 Comaroff 1980a, 36; 1980b, 192.

137 Radcliffe-Brown 1950, 47–53; Phillips 1953, 4.

138 The need was shared by both anthropologists and administrators, as "many peoples lacked a criterion that could be unambiguously translated into colonial legal criteria for differentiating marriage from transactions involving slaves and debt pawns, both of which transferred rights in people against other items of value." Guyer 1994, 234–5. See also the very important work done by Rodney Needham (1971) in rethinking the study of marriage.

139 Stocking 1987, 197.

140 Stocking 1987, 201. See also Jeater (1993) for the most developed analysis of the inconsistencies between British colonial morality in Africa and metropolitain practices.

141 Stocking 1987, 201–2.

142 Radcliffe-Brown 1950, 5, 46. Radcliffe-Brown's relationship to McLennan is curious. He was deeply critical of McLennan's methodology and ideas, but he never managed to move beyond the deeper assumptions of late nineteenth-century thought about the importance of blood, and hence of legitimacy. See Hawkins, forthcoming.

143 Oyewùmí 1997, 121–8.

144 Staniland 1975, 50. He noted that "the north had the characteristics of a bachelor society" but did not explore the implications of this for the type of colonial regime that these single men created.

145 Chanock 1985, 173. Commenting on the flood of marriage cases before the European Bomas in Northern Rhodesia, Chanock noted that "officials were conscientious in their support of 'custom' ... but their own views of marriage, the relative positions of men and women, and sexual morality, inclined them towards a particular definition of customary law. Furthermore, in most cases, as one colonial commentator was later to put it, they were not exactly experts in this field – 'we were wholly ignorant about connubial life among Africans (for that matter any connubial life, being bachelors).'"

146 Tambiah 1989, 424–5.

147 Guyer 1989, 429.

148 For a fuller discussion of these issues, see Hawkins, forthcoming.

1: Maps and Narratives

1 Kambou-Ferrand 1993a, 83; 1993b, 541.

2 Père 1993, 286.

3 Lentz 1996, 17.

4 See Figure 1.

5 NAG ADM 56/1/50, Reports on Tours of Inspection North West Province, PC NWP, March–May 1905. It was noted in 1903 that although the Dagarti were more "friendly" than the Lobi, where the former lived in proximity to the latter they "seem invariably to be hostile." Awareness of social mixing was later replaced by the notion of physical contamination through intermarriage. See Lentz 1993, 185.

6 NAG ADM 56/51/1, Lawra District Record Book, 6.

7 Labouret 1931, chapter 2.

8 Rattray 1932, 425. Loberu (Lober or Lobri according to other sources) was an indigenous term for a dialect of *Dagaare*. Its similarity with the word *Lobi* (a distinct language) was a source of much confusion.

9 Goody 1954, 26–31.

10 Goody 1956a, 19–24. See also Map 6.

11 Timbume was the anthropologist's collaborator and cook. See his criticisms of Goody's designations, which the latter scrupulously included in his own discussion. Goody 1956a, 22–3. These are discussed in Chapter 2.

12 Censuses of 1911 1921 1931, 1948, and 1960 all used these two terms as the basis for their "tribal" enumerations. See Chapter 2 for relevant references.

13 Leach 1961, 3

14 Angsotinge 1986, 26–7. He admitted that terms similar to Goody's directional names were occasionally used, but added that these were employed only to talk about differences, not similarities. He argued that "there is much more cultural homogenity among the group than meets the eye of an outside observer." Hébert (1976, 21) noted: "On this matter we think no purpose is served by complicating the terminology in the way J. Goody has." Similarly, Yelpaala (1983, 351–2) argued that "too much attention has been focused on these internal differentiating terminologies rather than the fundamental elements of ethnic identity such as a common cultural identity. There is little doubt among the Dagaaba that they form an identifiable unit distinguishable from others." In addition, Bekye (1991, 96) argued that Goody's survey only further complicated the actual situation and that his divisions were "arbitrary" insofar as they had only linguistic, but not ethnic, validity.

15 Unlike the term LoDagaa, neither of these other terms appear to be neologisms,

but where exactly they came from and what they originally meant is unclear. The etymology of the term Dagara has been discussed by several authors and is summarized usefully by Lentz (1994a, 482). Less attention has been paid to the term Dagaaba. To confound matters further, if that is possible, Armitage (1924, 13) used the term "Dagarba (miscalled Dagarti)." Given that this term does not appear in any other source, it would seem that is was a conflation of the terms Dagara and Dagaaba.

16 Lentz 1994a, 490–1; 1994c, 72.

17 Bemile 2000, 212–21; Lentz 2000.

18 Bourdieu 1977, 2.

19 Binger 1892, vol. 1, 1–2. It would therefore be wrong to attribute the origins of negative stereotypes solely to the colonial powers. Lentz has noted that some of the derogatory colonial views of the LoDagaa were passed on to the British by neighboring cultures. Lentz 1993, 189; 1994c, 76.

20 See *Heart of Darkness*.

21 Ryan 1994, 116, 127.

22 Binger 1892, vol. 2, 34–5

23 Binger 1892, vol. 2, 35. Forty years later, Rattray reported that the meaning of the Dagbane name Gurinse (also Gurensi or Grunshi) was "the foolish ones," "bush men," etc. He noted with some surprise that many of the so-designated people not only did not resent the unflattering derivation of the name but also used it in preference to other names. Rattray 1932, 398. Sobriquets such as this are very common within this area not just because of lack of communications, but also because the acephalous cultures that inhabited this area did not possess self-classificatory identities. Besides Gurensi, another common sobriquet that has been applied to many of the same constitutive peoples was "Frafra." See Hart 1971. In the absence of any self-designations, they were often referred to by external names, which in the course of time they accepted.

24 Binger 1892, vol. 2, 36.

25 Arhin 1974, chapter 7.

26 NAG ADM 56/1/50, Reports on Tours of Inspection North Western Province, DC Black Volta District, March–May 1905.

27 NAG ADM 56/1/50, Reports on Tours of Inspection North Western Province, DC Black Volta District, April–May 1906.

28 NAG ADM 61/5/8, Informal Diary Lawra District, 9 January 1919.

29 See NAG ADM 61/5/8, Informal Diary Lawra District, 17 April 1918, 6 November 1918.

30 Lentz 1994c, 75–6.

31 NAG ADM 61/5/8, Informal Diary Lawra District, 6 January 1919.

32 NAG ADM 61/5/8, Informal Diary Lawra District, 6 January 1919.
33 NAG ADM 56/1/50, Reports on Tours of Inspection North Western Province, DC Black Volta District, March–May 1905.
34 NAG ADM 56/1/50, Reports on Tours of Inspection North Western Province, DC Black Volta District, June 1907.
35 Goody 1956a, 17.
36 Labouret 1931, 56. Emphasis mine. The *Lobi* had been "very mobile" in the pre-colonial period, which resulted in highly dispersed settlements. Labouret argued that this incremental pattern of migrations had created extreme localism: "In these circumstances, the source of springs, the course of streams and rivers, and exact location of distant hill-tops, even of nearby villages, remained unknown to these sedentary natives who were bound through fear to their farms" (10–12).
37 Staniland 1975, 50.
38 These issues are discussed in Chapter 3.
39 Yelpaala 1983, 352–7; Skalnik 1987, 301–4; Somé 1989, 138–40.
40 It is important to note that this does not mean that LoDagaa society fit the typology of a "segmentary lineage system," devised by Fortes and Evans-Pritchard: "It [the LoDagaba 'system'] is 'segmentary' in the sense that the constituent units [households] are politically equal. It is not, however, 'segmentary' in the sense that it has a developed lineage system." Goody 1957, 101. For an extremely useful discussion of the issues arising from these political classifications, see Horton 1985, 98–100.
41 Fiéloux 1980, 18–24; Goody 1993a, 55.
42 Vansina came to this valuable conclusion after trying to resolve the complicated and seemingly contradictory origins of the Kuba. Vansina 1978, 43.
43 Naameh 1986, 97–8.
44 Delafosse, the French colonial ethnographer, was the first to make this linguistic identification, in a survey of the French territory of Haut-Sénégal-Niger. See Delafosse 1912, vol. 1, 115, 305–13. These observations were confirmed by Rattray, chief anthropological officer of the Gold Coast Government, twenty years later. Rattray 1932, xii. The notion of the Voltaic region as a discrete area of cultural and historical experience received wider confirmation with Murdock's survey of Africa. Murdock 1959, 77–88. Although the nature of these distant events has not been amended significantly, Delafosse's chronology has been superseded by subsequent historical investigations. For a review of the latter see Wilks 1985, 466–76.
45 Westermann and Bryan 1952, 61–6. According to linguistic classification, both Mole-Dagbane and Grusi belonged to a wider language group designated as Gur by these authors (or Voltaic according to other designations), which also included *Lobi* (a dialect cluster of the Lobi-Dogon language group), which was spoken to

the west of the LoDagaa. The distribution of Gur languages and dialects coincided with the Voltaic zone, extending throughout most of the area south of the Niger Bend and north of the Guinea forests.

46 Wilks 1985, 467–9: "The invaders came to adopt a language of the last cluster [Mole-Dagbane]. Kusal, spoken in the district of which Pusiga is part, is virtually identical with Dagbane and Mamprule, prompting two speculations: first, that it was at the time of Na Gbewa's [founding] settlement at Pusiga that the invaders adopted the language of the autochthones, and second, that the invaders arrived without their own womenfolk."

47 It is said that when Na Gbewa's grandson, Nyagsi, conquered the western portion of what became Dagbon, the Mossi calvary killed or removed many of the *tengdana* (custodians of indigenous territorial shrines). During this time, according to Wilks, "some displacement of the autochthonous peoples occurred." Wilks 1985, 470–1. Goody categorically rejected Tauxier's suggestion (as well as Baumann and Westermann's hypothesis) that *Dagaare*-speaking people migrated west of the White Volta following the expansion of Mamprugu. He was, however, more favorably disposed toward the hypothesis that the Mole-Dagbane speakers dispersed to the west in the wake of the invasion of western Dagomba: "The early movement of Dagari speaking peoples into Wa and Lawra districts ... is more likely to be related to the invasion of that area [Dagomba] by the present ruling lineages coming from Mamprusi. This appears to have been accompanied by a considerable degree of violence towards the indigenous population." Goody 1954, 16, 32.

48 Levtzion 1968, 139–40. This version, recorded by Tait in the 1950s, left Na Zokuli's actual fate somewhat impenetrable, stating that when his followers discovered him he had been transformed into a crocodile.

49 See Levtzion 1968, 141 (note 3). Goody noted that archaeological evidence supported Wala traditions, which maintained that there had been two migrations from the east. "Over large parts of the Wa and Lawra districts it is possible to collect from the surface fragments of rouletted pottery of quite a different type from that made by the present inhabitants; it is variously ascribed by them to the Dyan or to the LoWilisi. These peoples who speak languages of the Lobi-Dogon group themselves claim to have formerly dwelt east of the Black Volta. The present distribution of the western group of Mossi [Mole-Dagbane] speakers appears to be the result of migrations from the Dagomba area. In Wa however there is a structural dichotomy between the chiefly lineages of the later invasion and the commoner clans who had come first and expelled and absorbed the *Lobi* speaking peoples. The names Wala and Dagaba conceptualize this cleavage from the actor's point of view." Goody 1954, 14–16. See also Labouret 1958, 25–6.

50 See Levtzion (1968, 201–3) for an analysis of the chronology of Wa.

51 Wilks, Levtzion and Haight 1986, 160–1, 167.

52 Wilks 1985, 496–8; Staniland 1975, 6–7.

53 Labouret 1931, 26. Eyre-Smith, who was carrying out similar research among the LoDagaa at the same time, reported having uncovered evidence to suggest that the exodus of the Dyan (predecessors to the *Lobi*) from the area north of Wa and east of the Black Volta had been precipitated by an attack from both Gonja and Dagomba marauders, acting as "Ashanti levies," in the latter half of the seventeenth century. Eyre-Smith 1933, 12. As the Asante had not yet even begun to make incursions in their northern hinterland by this time, it is difficult to know (if in fact these events took place) who participated in the "tremendous invasion of the north-west" or what their intentions were. The Asante themselves did not reach Daboya until 1751–52, a century later. See Wilks 1985, 497; Wilks, Levtzion, and Haight 1986, 106, 142–3.

54 The only other acephalous society within the Voltaic region that seems to have had an equal preponderance of cowries was that of the Samo. In their case it has been possible to work out how cowries entered the economy of an apparently nontrading society – it was through slavery. Héritier 1975, 492–3. Although internal slavery, or more exactly pledging, was not unknown among the LoDagaa in the precolonial period, there is no evidence that they traded slaves with outsiders, nor would such trading have been extensive enough to account alone for such large cowry reserves.

55 Héretier 1975; Piot 1996.

56 For some indication of how prevalent, indeed ubiquitous, its cultural uses were, see Goody 1962.

57 Johnson 1970a, 33.

58 Johnson 1970a, 34: "Southward from the Niger, cowries appear to have spread along well-defined trade routes. ... There were areas between main routes, however, where cowries did not permeate." These trade routes were on the periphery of any territory inhabited by the LoDagaa over the several centuries of this diffusion. Therefore one would have expected the LoDagaa to have been excluded from the cowry trade merely by virtue of their situation, not to mention the absence of any suitable trade items other than enslaved people.

59 Johnson 1970a, 36.

60 NAG ADM 61/4/1, Lawra District Civil Record Book, 4 December 1908.

61 Johnson 1970a, 20–1, 28–9; 1970b, 353; Hill 1970, 139–40; Evans 1985. Additionally, southern cowries were strung, whereas northern cowries were kept loose. The latter had also been the practice among the LoDagaa.

62 Person 1975, 1,701. This was the effective death blow to Bouna, well before Samori seized the town.

63 RAT ADM 32, Commutation of Tribute 1935–1937, CCNT to Col. Sec. Accra, 5 November 1934. See also Person 1975, 1706: "Toward the north, [Wa] had not managed to subjugate all the Dagaba, whose political structures remained segmented beyond the Cheripon-Busie line."

64 Person 1975, 1,706: "The state of Wa was never a great power. Frequently subordinate to Gonja, it was fortunate not to suffer such a significant demographic collapse as the Kulango of Bouna. Nonetheless, along the banks of the Volta, toward Cheripon, pressure from the ... Dagga-Wiili made itself felt."

65 It is known that the Gonja attacked Wa on several occasions, just after the first Asante incursions into Gonja territory itself (1738–9), and again in the first half of the nineteenth century. Wilks, Levtzion, and Haight 1986, 100, 129; Ferguson and Wilks 1970, 330. Whether these forays resulted in the capture of any LoDagaa is not known; however, it probably did. In the latter part of the century, Wa sought the assistance of several other parties, including the Asante, Dagomba, Zabarima, and Sofa, to ward off the Gonja threat and revive the diminished integrity of the state. See Holden 1965, 66, 73; Person 1975, 1,706.

66 Labouret 1931, 28–9. According to Labouret, a second migration may already have been under way before the *Lobi* crossed the Volta; it involved the LoWiili and DagaaWiili, who moved north to Ulo and then to Babile. The next migration was apparently that of the LoBirifor from the vicinity of Tyar, some twenty miles west of Wa, at the beginning of the nineteenth century; they settled originally in Batié Nord, which had already been abandoned by the *Lobi* after only one generation. Owing to the poor quality of the land, and the difficulty of moving farther west because of the concentration of *Lobi* settlements, some of the LoBirifor moved southwest; a small faction followed a route ultimately leading to the vicinity of Diébougou; and another moved north into an area beyond Wala control – the area that became Lawra District. See also Labouret 1958, 33.

67 RAT ADM 423, "Interim Report on the Peoples of the Nandom and Lambussie Divisions of the Lawra District," DC Lawra, 1932, 6–7. However, Eyre-Smith presented a different picture of migrations into Lawra District. He argued that the immigrants were "refugees" from external raids, particularly from the Zabarima and the Sofa in the second half of the nineteenth century. RAT ADM 424, "Comments on 'Interim Report on the Peoples of the Nandom and Lambussie Divisions of the Lawra District,'" DC Mampong-Akwapim, 1933, 5, 7, 17–18.

68 Goody 1956a, 16. See also Evans 1983, 86.

69 With regard to administrative inquiries, see for example RAT ADM 423, "Interim Report on the Peoples of the Nandom and Lambussie Divisions of the Lawra District," DC Lawra, 1932, 7: "The word incomplete is used advisedly, for it has to be admitted that most of the stories are badly beheaded if it be held that the

Dagarti people originally came from Dagomba and Mamprussi. Only the Lambussie, and the Dikpielle section at Nandom can remember as far back as Wa: the rest go no further in memory than villages near the north border of the present Wa district." Similarly, Goody noted that among both the LoWiili and LoDagaba household reckoning was extremely limited. Goody 1956a, 15, 71; Goody 1957, 89–90, 101. See also Angsotinge 1986, 32. He also noted that genealogical depth was very shallow, from three to four generations, and that it was "usually enough to know the name of one's father's clan."

70 Writing of the Wala to the south, Wilks has made much the same observation. He noted that although the past was manifest in their construction of reality, it was not preserved in a specific cultural form or formal narrative. Wilks 1989, 29–30.

71 Goody 1987, 149–50. See also Angsotinge 1986, 71–4; Lentz 1994a, 464.

72 Angsotinge 1986, 71, 73, 325. As with the *lasiri* of the Wala, these were thematic rather than narrative. See Wilks 1989, 31.

73 There were in fact very formalized acts whereby cultural information was imparted, i.e., the ceremonies of initiation into the cult of the *Bagre*. But as Goody has pointed out, nothing new (in a substantive as opposed to experiential sense) was acquired by the neophytes during these performances. Goody 1987, 151. See also Goody 1972; 1980.

74 RAT ADM 423, "Interim Report on the Peoples of the Nandom and Lambussie Divisions of the Lawra District," DC Lawra, 1932, 1. See also Goody 1987, 150: "In an oral society, one can neglect the words of the elders only to one's detriment, not simply because of a general idea of respect but also because those words constitute the major source of information. The only way of finding out about the past, about interpretations of the world, is from them."

75 Naameh 1986, 124.

76 Dabiré 1983, 24, 299–311.

77 RAT ADM 424, "Comments on 'Interim Report on the Peoples of the Nandom and Lambussie Divisions of the Lawra District,'" DC Mampong-Akwapim, 1933, 5.

78 Mignolo makes a similiar point about the Spanish material prejudice against Amerindian semiotics that used media such as clay, stone, animal skins, tree bark, and string. They had also rejected Amerindian signs in the belief that since they did not directly represent speech, they must be unreliable, susceptible to falsehood, and prone to heterodoxy (1994a, 227, 235; 1994b, 300).

79 Dabiré 1983, 41. The sense of journey was not merely topographical, but also cosmological. According to Dabiré, for the LoDagaa the world or universe had two levels of existence, the visible (phenomenal) and invisible (noumenal). Dabiré argued that the most important form of travel was "an incessant journey between the visible and invisible."

80 DMC CRB vol. 12, N2/74, Albanu Ziem *vs.* Irinio Mansanyir.

81 See Rattray 1932, 429–32; RAT ADM 455, "The Lobi Tingani," DC Lawra, 1946; and Goody 1962, 335–9.

82 Goody 1956a, 91.

83 See Rattray 1932, 429–32; RAT ADM 455, "The Lobi Tingani," DC Lawra 1946; and Goody 1962, 335–9.

84 Goody 1957.

85 DMC CRB vol. 13, N7/76, Marcel Gyie *vs.* Batholomew Banfu; DMC CRB vol. 14, L7/78, Tangbor Nuukpeng of Zambo *vs.* Aabetereh Yongh of Kalsare. In the former case, the court had to abandon its inspection of the land in question when the Tokuu Naa, allegedly the plaintiff's co-conspirator, warned the magistrate that "if [the court] attempted to inspect the disputed land there would be deaths on the land and that he would not be responsible. When I asked him if he meant what he was saying, he repeated that there would be chaos, confusion and deaths would occur. Upon his words, I instructed the Police Officer to cause his arrest. ... The Tokuu Naa was very rude and boisterous. His attitude is a sure sign that there is a plot being made to disturb the peace when we are there."

86 In several cases it appears that the defendants were using the death of the relevant elders to usurp the rightful holders. See for example DMC CRB vol. 13, L8/76b, Gieru Bozie of Zambo *vs.* Dieoberi Tiokar.

87 In a case heard in 1970, the parties were unable to trace the history of a piece of land back more than forty years, to "the time the locusts were last out in the territory," (1931 according to the court's calculations), even though both lineages had settled there long before that. See DMC CRB vol. 10, N18/70, Kakraba Nataal of Yagtuori *vs.* Naabang Mwintuur of Yagtuori.

88 The first instance of this occurred in DMC CRB vol. 14, L7/78, Tangbor Nuukpeng of Zambo *vs.* Aabetereh Yongh of Kalsare. The defendant maintained that the area in which the disputed land was situated (Napilagn) had originally belonged to the people of Kalsare, but when "refugees" came from Zambo (a mile or so to the north) before the turn of the century, his father's father had loaned land to the man from whom the plaintiff's father acquired a parcel. Ruling in the plaintiff's favor, the magistrate stated: "The people of Napilagn are not Kalsagris but Zambolas. To say that Napilagn people are refugees and must return to Zambo in these modern times is like flogging a dead horse. It is not in line with natural justice, equity and good conscience. The defendant will himself appreciate that Napilagn alias Baakunwor [translated as "no dog should bark there"] has come to stay and has survived through times." Again, in a case heard in 1981, the court acknowledged that even though the ultimate title to the land rested with the defendant, the plaintiff had claim to the land by virtue of having farmed on it for twenty years before the defendant attempted to reclaim it. Here the title to the

land, which descended from the first settler to the defendant, was ruled to have expired, "not withstanding that this prescription is unknown to native law." DMC CRB vol. 15, N8/81, Gabriel Naayuor *vs.* Pio Babaare Kuunifaa.

89 DMC CRB vol. 15, N20/82, Oscar Tenibe of Ko *vs.* Martillo Vuorre of Ko. It was actually one of the defendant's witnesses who was able to trace the history of the disputed farm back farthest in time. He explained to the court that it belonged to neither the plaintiff nor the defendant: "It was one Gbang who put up the building. During the Babatu wars the said Gbang was taken captive and the building stood vacant without occupants. It then belonged to the landowners [*tengaandem*]." The *tengaansob* who then reallocated the land was the present incumbent's father's father. See also DMC CRB vol. 14, L7/78. The *tengaansob* of Napilagn *tengaanble* appeared as a court witness in this case, but was unable to answer the defendant's questions over the original settlement of the area, explaining that during his father's lifetime he had not had the right to inquire about who had borrowed land from whom, and that he had not been told by his father of these events, which occurred when his father's father had been *tengaansob.* As the defendant was attempting to establish that the shrine at Napilagn was subordinate to the *tengaan* of Kalsare, the witness's profession of ignorance might well have only been a strategy to deflect these questions.

90 Great Britain 1908, 8; Yelpaala 1983, 384 (note 52); Angsotinge 1986, 105; Lentz 1993, 186. Lentz suggests (199) that the growing land shortage in the 1990s might enhance the position of the *tengaandem.* But this ignores the reality that after three generations of relatively little emigration or immigration, land once given by the *tengaandem* has been fragmented and borrowed so many times that their original role in the allocation of lands was largely forgotten. Nsiah-Gyabaah noted in his survey of land tenure in the Upper West in the late 1980s that "less than one percent of respondents had acquired land from the *Tendaana*" (1994, 89). Furthermore, commercial agriculture, coupled with land shortages, has changed notions about private property. Yelpaala 1992, 463.

91 See Fiéloux 1980.

92 Père 1988, 372.

2: Labor, Bodies, and Names

1 Père 1988, 375

2 Ferguson and Wilks 1970, 330. See also Holden 1965, 73–4; Hébert 1975, 49–50; Person 1975, 1,706, 1,725 (note 131); Levtzion 1968, 155.

3 Labouret 1931, 37–8: "The Lobis and Birifor took everything from their houses, which in reality was very little, and sought refuge with their herds in places

thought to be inaccessible." See also Goody 1956a, 13; Person 1975, 1,706; Hébert 1975, 51–3.

4 Goody (1956, 13) suggested that "slave-raiding left little trace of any permanent effect on the institutions of the Lobi and Dagari-speaking peoples." However, in the short term its psychological effects on the people themselves must have been significant.

5 Cleveland 1991, 231.

6 Staniland 1975, 39.

7 Thomas 1973, 81.

8 NAG ADM 56/1/50, Reports on Tours of Inspection North West Province, DC Black Volta District, October–November 1906. Recruiting at Dazulu, outside Lambussie, the district commissioner noted that all the old men were against the "labour scheme": "These old obstructionists, fetishists of course, were taunting the King [colonial chief] saying that he had lost his sons [from an epidemic during the last harmattan], he now wished them to lose theirs."

9 Ibid. Given the considerable insecurity that preceded the arrival of the British, such reticence was nothing more than a wise precaution. At the same time that officers were "preaching the labour crusade" they were also noting in their reports (April–May 1906) meeting survivors of the Zabarima raids who had been captured and sold as slaves and had just recently managed to return to their own country.

10 In 1909 a party of 481 Wala, "Dagarti," Sisala, and Kassena, all from the northwest and including twenty men who had been on previous visits, were sent to Tarkwa. This was followed by another contingent of 382 men from the northwest, who left Wa in December 1909. Thomas 1973, 84.

11 For some indication of conditions, see Crisp 1984, chapter 3; Thomas 1973, 100–2.

12 In November 1913 the District Commissioner of Lawra noted that many of the young men who had left the district at the end of the farming season the previous August had returned half-starved owing to insufficient funds with which to support themselves on the long journey to Kumase. NAG ADM 61/5/3, Lawra District Complaint Book, 25 November 1913.

13 In 1909 the District Commissioner of Lawra received a complaint that the Nandom Naa and a man named Iddrisu had come to the complainant's compound to search for his son, who had been nominated as a recruit. Para, the complainant, said that when he told them his son was not there the chief and his alleged accomplice demanded that he pay them several cows in lieu of his son. Although the case was dismissed, Iddrisu was issued with a strong warning as this was the third time that such a complaint had been brought against him. The district

commissioner explained to the chief that there was no compulsion involved in the supply of labour. NAG ADM 61/4/1, Lawra District Civil Record Book, 2 June 1909.

14 Crisp 1984, 36, 41–2.

15 Plange 1979, 666.

16 NAG ADM 61/5/4, Lawra District Complaint Book, 8 October 1918.

17 NAG ADM 61/4/2, Lawra District Civil Record Book, 8 June 1915.

18 NAG ADM 61/5/8, Informal Diary Lawra District, 12 July 1917. Observing that it was difficult to meet the "bush" people except at markets, and recognizing that they were always reluctant to give evidence against headmen and chiefs, the district commissioner admitted that all he could do was address the people at Babile and Lawra markets in the hope of dispelling the rumor before payments started. This incident demonstrates the limited power of writing over speech or rules over rumors.

19 NAG ADM 61/5/8, Informal Diary Lawra District, 25 June 1918.

20 NAG ADM 61/5/8, Informal Diary Lawra District, 26 February 1918, and 17 April 1918; Lovejoy 1983, 155. Gonja and Dagbon sent only five hundred slaves each to Asante in the 1820s.

21 NAG ADM 61/5/8, Informal Diary Lawra District, 4–7 February 1917. No attention was paid to potential demographic variations or the extent of informal migration. For example, in 1918 the district commissioner complained that if Samoa with a population of 1,838 could supply fifty-two recruits, Birifu with 2,001 inhabitants should be able to provide more than the sixteen the chief had already nominated: "It's not a question of depopulating the country, but of what is more important, to get on with the war, and I suppose that is why so many recruits are required" (24 April 1918). What officers also tried to ignore was that such labor losses were not absorbed by divisions as a whole, but were suffered by individual households. The loss of just one young man from a household could have had adverse effects. Human surpluses were not necessarily distributed evenly.

22 NAG ADM 61/5/8, Informal Diary Lawra District, 14 August 1918.

23 NAG ADM 61/5/8, Informal Diary Lawra District, 30 September 1918.

24 Thomas 1973, 98.

25 NAG ADM 61/5/8, Informal Diary Lawra District, 11 November 1917.

26 NAG ADM 61/5/8, Informal Diary Lawra District, 18 April 1918. A particularly perverse irony given that the administration justified such impositions on the north as "a repayment for the maintenance of the *Pax Britannica*." Thomas 1973, 103.

27 Thomas 1973, 99.

28 NAG ADM 61/5/4, Lawra District Complaint Book, 18 October 1918.

29 NAG ADM 61/5/8, Informal Diary Lawra District, 12 February 1919.

30 Thomas 1975b, 58–60.
31 NAG ADM 61/5/8, Informal Diary Lawra District, 11 October 1919.
32 Thomas 1973, 96.
33 NAG ADM 61/5/8, Informal Diary Lawra District, 3 July 1920.
34 NAG ADM 61/5/8, Informal Diary Lawra District, 4 July 1920.
35 NAG ADM 61/5/8, Informal Diary Lawra District, 29 August 1920.
36 Thomas 1973, 98–100.
37 RAT ADM 495, Annual Report Wa District 1938–1939.
38 Gold Coast 1950, table 23.
39 Goody 1954, 9: "The type of long distance migration which resulted differs from the gradual encroachment arising from the practice of shifting cultivation, but, owing to the motor road, contact with the parent villages could be maintained."
40 During the Second World War, when military recruitment was voluntary, many young men enlisted, grateful for opportunities such as better wages, higher status, and adequate provision for their dependants.
41 RAT 342-343, Informal Diary Lawra District, September 1943.
42 Hill 1986, 126.
43 Hill 1970, 42–3. Six percent of all migrants were working in urban areas in the south; most of them were probably skilled workers – clerks, traders, or tailors (28). Regrettably, the 1970 census did not provide any means of ascertaining the number of migrant laborers in the south a decade later. However, there is little reason to suppose that the figures would have declined over this period. Indeed, it is more likely that the rate rose until the late 1970s, when the allure of the south was somewhat diminished by deteriorating economic conditions there.
44 Goody 1956a, 10.
45 Lentz and Erlmann 1989, 87–94; Lentz 1994b, 158–9. Although there has been no systematic study made of the effect of labor migration among the LoDagaa, examinations of the same phenomenon among the "Frafra," Sisala, and Kusasi apply equally to the LoDagaa. Hart 1971, 34; Grindal 1972, 66–73; Cleveland 1991.
46 See for example DMC CRB vol. 13, N7/76, Marcel Gyie of Tokuu *vs.* Batholomew Banfu.
47 See Chapter 6 for a discussion of the effects of the cash economy on migrant laborers.
48 Lentz 1994c, 63; Nsiah-Gyabbah 1994, 165.
49 Cleveland 1991, 225, 238.
50 Plange 1979, 671; Cleveland 1991, 237.
51 Cleveland 1991, 235–8.
52 Cleveland 1991, 239.
53 Nsiah-Gyabaah 1994, 87, 150, 165.

54 Cleveland 1991, 230.

55 Père 1988, 369.

56 The "Burifon" had been classified by Ruelle 1904, 667–8. He wrote that the following formed the basis of his ethnological classification: "habitat, organization of society, customs, language." As early as 1896, Ferguson had suggested to the Gold Coast Government that to apprehend the "tribes" of the then "hinterland," it would be necessary to conduct an extensive survey of dialects, customs, manners, history, migrations, and wars. Arhin 1974, 116. And yet this was not carried out until the late 1920s when Rattray's investigations were commissioned. Besides the major study cited above, Labouret published fourteen articles on the *Lobi* between 1916 and 1929. The first comparable treatment of the people within Lawra District did not occur until Goody's detailed study of 1954 for the Colonial Office.

57 Goody 1956a, 17.

58 NAG ADM 61/5/8, Informal Diary Lawra District, 18 May 1918. See also 15 April 1918: "Yagha: I was informed also that all the Lobi Wilo villages brewed their peto [millet beer] much stronger than any of the other with the exception of the Dagartis of Sabule. That when the Wilos had imbibed enough of their strong peto, they cared for no man."

59 Fabian 2000, 201–2.

60 NAG ADM 61/5/11, Lawra District Record Book, 253–4.

61 Ibid., 255. The remarks on the Dagarti concluded with a quotation from a particularly execrable poem by Adams, "A Passive Resister":

> When a native starts palavering and wont do his
> kindergarten then sooner of later things will reach such
> a state that any man might dishearten.
> Of course its alright
> If he means to alight
> You can easily burst his bubble.
> But if he sits tight,
> Then its Hell's delight
> He can give a whole world of trouble.

62 Rattray 1932, 446 (caption to figures 115–16).

63 The different ways the Lobi and Dagaaba look in Rattray's photographs are not signs of ethnicity but of different styles of fashion. Armitage noted that among the "Dagarba," hair was "dressed according to individual taste," and that among the Lobi, fashion was dictated by "fancy." Among the Lobi (also referred to in the report as "Wiilies") hair was both shaved and braided, the latter giving the appearance of "shaggy head-dresses." Again under the heading of Lobi, he stated that the wearing of a "goat- or sheep-skin hung down the back from the shoulder"

indicated that they as youths had passed through certain rites that permitted them to attend funerals and make their own farms. Armitage 1924, 15, 17.

64 CCNT [Major Read] to DCs NT, September 1912, quoted in Armitage 1924, iii–iv. The works that Armitage referred to in his letter were Mockler-Ferryman's *British Nigeria* and Merrick's *Hausa Proverbs*. The former had claimed that scarification enabled recognition of a person's tribe "at a glance." The latter was more qualified and indicated that although these marks were "the armorial bearings of a tribe," their meaning was as yet unclear.

65 See Pratt's discussion of European uses of landscapes and "bodyscapes" (1992, 64–5).

66 Major Read quoted in Armitage 1924, 13.

67 Armitage 1924, 15.

68 See Figure 14.

69 NAG ADM 61/5/1, Lawra District Record Book, 8–29. These sketches, evidently by different hands from sometime after 1912, lacked the consistency or exactitude that one finds in Armitage's published version of this same information. Instead of the depersonalized template, one finds awkwardly wrought renditions of people, very reminiscent of the Tallensi schoolchildren's drawings analyzed by Fortes (1981). Fortes discussed how the language of graphic representation was learned, just like literacy. When one examines the few images, maps, and human figures that appeared in the District Record Books, one is struck at how poorly acquainted with drawing officers were.

70 Coombes (1994, 138–9) mentions the connection between the development of ethnographic photography and criminology, which is clearly discernible in the "mug-shot" style of much of ethnographic photography. I am arguing here that these caricatures in the District Record Book, although crudely drawn, were used for purposes of surveillance and objectification, which are quite similar to the uses made of criminal photographs. This is even clearer in Figures 16a and 16b.

71 Nederveen Pieterse 1992, 94.

72 NAG ADM 61/5/11, Lawra District Record Book, 249.

73 RAT ADM 423, "Interim Report On the Peoples of the Nandom and Lambussie Divisions of the Lawra District," DC Lawra, 1932, 28.

74 See Cohen 1994, 141–3.

75 Comaroff and Comaroff 1997, 228.

76 Comaroff and Comaroff 1997, 226.

77 Arhin 1974, 100.

78 From a report written by Captain Berthon during a tour of the area at the end of 1903. Quoted in Lentz 1993, 185.

79 Goody 1962, 70–2.

80 NAG ADM 61/5/8, Informal Diary Lawra Distirct, 13 November 1917.
81 Tuurey 1982, 20.
82 Cardinall noted that such "drawers" were already common in the northeast after little more than a decade of colonial rule. Cardinall 1920, 103.
83 Goody 1962, 71–2.
84 RAT 495, Annual Report Wa District 1938–1939.
85 NAG ADM 61/5/8, Informal Diary Lawra District, 13 September 1920.
86 RAT ADM 342–3, Informal Diary Lawra District, April 1944.
87 Der 1983, 316–7.
88 Der 1983, 311.
89 Der 1983, 265–6.
90 Lentz and Erlmann 1989, 88.
91 Père 1988, 317; Lentz and Erlmann 1989, 89.
92 Dery 1987, 52.
93 Père 1988, 371.
94 Lentz, 1994c, 66–7. The interview was conducted in Germany during a meeting of expatriate LoDagaa in 1989.
95 Lentz 1994c, 84.
96 See Lentz 1995.
97 Lentz 1995, 407–16.
98 Lentz 1995, 418–9.
99 Member of the Nandom Youth and Development Association, quoted in Lentz 1995, 419. The project of cultural reform was a shared project of the youth associations and the Catholic Church. See Lentz 1995, 420; 1994b, 160.
100 Tuurey 1982; Yelpaala 1983; Kuukure 1985; Der 1989; Somda 1989; Bekye 1991.
101 Lentz 1994c, 69, 72; 1994a, 458.
102 Tauxier 1912; Labouret 1931; Eyre-Smith 1933; Hébert 1975.
103 Lentz 1994a, 472–80.
104 Lentz 1994a, 480. See also Lentz 1994c, 72.
105 Although only related conceptually, Mignolo noted an explicit equation in the Spanish writer Bernardo de Alderte's thought between language, particularly written or "civilized" language, and clothing. (1995, 33–5)
106 Lentz 1994a, 458, 483; 1994c, 69–71.
107 RAT ADM 143, Political Prisoners, DC Lawra to CNP, 3 September 1927. The first reference to the people of Nandom division inheriting matrilineally that I came across was in NAG ADM 56/1/163, Selected Papers, 8 January 1920. Tibe of Nandom attempted to inherit from his father by complaining to the provincial commissioner at Wa. However, the court interpreter told the district commis-

sioner that this was not the practice in that area. "He is so certain of the custom that he can give the exact boundaries of where the method of inheritance prevails." See also NAG ADM 61/5/8, Informal Diary Lawra District, 8 January 1920. Tibe had originally taken his case to Wa, not Lawra. The district commissioner discovered that it was the nephew and not the son who inherited in the Nandom area. The CCNT noted in his gloss: "Yes, through the female line."

108 Rattray 1932, 433.

109 Murdock 1959, 81–5. He placed the Voltaic societies along a matrilineal/partilineal continuum, consisting of five identifiable stages that could be used to "shed considerable light on the probable evolution of social organization." The history of these societies was reduced to "a shift from avunculocal to patrilocal residence as a norm." The irony was that although he placed the Birifor and *Lobi* in the first stage of this transition, the former had in all probability been a patrilineal society prior to their migration toward the Black Volta some time after the seventeenth century.

110 Marks and Rathbone argued that such transitions were not even inevitable under recent economic conditions of migrant labor, cash crops, and urbanization, let alone the invisible pressures of "evolution." Marks and Rathbone 1983, 152–3.

111 RAT 514, Annual Report Lawra–Tumu District, 1937–38.

112 See Evans 1983, chapter 4; Goody 1956a, 4, 16.

113 NAG ADM 61/5/8, Informal Diary Lawra District, 20 December 1918.

114 See Goody 1961.

115 See Kopytoff 1987.

116 Goody 1970, 440–1. However, this obviously did not apply to unions of an inverted variety.

117 Goody 1962, 309–10, 349–54. Although not as conspicuous, he suggested that the counterpart in agnatic groups to *inter vivo* transmission was "the transfer of property from a mother's brother to a sister's son by 'ritual stealing' and by other means such as the gift of a Cow of the Byre" (168–72, 353).

118 Goody 1954, i.

119 Goody 1956a, 24.

120 Goody 1956a, 19–24.

121 Goody 1956a, 22–3.

122 Fabian 1983, 117. "It patrols, so to speak, the frontiers of Western culture."

123 Goody 1956a, 24.

124 Fabian 1983, 106–7. Slightly later he elaborated on this theme: "As images, places, and spaces turn from mnemotechnic aids into topoi they become that which a discourse is about. When modern anthropology began to construct its Other in terms of topoi implying distance, difference, and opposition, its intent

was above all, but at least also, to construct ordered space and Time – a cosmos – for Western society [consciousness] to inhabit, rather than 'understanding other cultures,' its ostensible vocation" (111–12).

125 See also Lentz 1994b.

126 See Kuukure 1985, 26. He noted, as had both colonial administrators and Goody, that migrants in the mid-1980s still used the term Dagarti (but also Dagara and Dagaare), "but back home among his own he is Dagao/Degabe or Loba or Wiile; or still further, he may refer to himself by the name of his settlement (village) or even clan, depending on the situation." Interestingly, moving from an indigenous to a discursive perspective, Kuurkure added: "Is there not here a clear indication of the underlying consciousness of their unity as a 'tribe' despite the accepted diversity within? Of course, a lopsided interest in the dissimilarities can easily lead one to lose sight of unity." The point that needs to be made in response to Kuukure's question is that if this consciousness existed, then the differences between the various congeries would have been less important and begun to erode. But there was no such homogenization. At the level of practical consciousness, differences remained more important than similarities in terms of defining identities within Lawra District, as well as throughout the wider LoDagaa cultural area.

127 Tuurey 1982, 4.

128 Tuurey 1982, 48.

129 Tuurey 1982, 5. This was the first autoethnographic account of the LoDagaa published in English – that is, if one excludes the works of Goody that included collaborative material, especially from Kumboona Gandah. However, by this time numerous works had been published in French by LoDagaa living across the Black Volta. Given Tuurey's definition of Dagaba ethnicity, these writers would not have qualified on account of their dual descent.

130 Tuurey 1982, 35. The term Dagao has been used as a singular of both Dagaaba and Dagara.

131 Tuurey 1982, 42–3. There are strongly opposed accounts of the Mossi presence among the LoDagaa. See Dougah 1966, 56–63; Hébert 1976, 23–6, 164–5. Tauxier had argued that the initial Mole-Dagbane immigrants into the region of the Black Volta were Mossi. Although both Dougah and Hébert agreed that this initial wave came from Dagbon, the former reported an oral tradition of descent from Mossi ancestors in the village of Kaleo running to nineteen names. Hébert, on the other hand, argued that the Mossi of Kaleo only arrived at the beginning of the nineteenth century, well after the cultural and political features of the LoDagaa had been determined. In either case there were few immigrants from Mossi.

132 Tuurey 1982, 48.

133 Tuurey 1982, 19, 22.
134 Tuurey 1982, 19.
135 Tuurey 1982, 22. This description is so reminiscent of early accounts by colonial administrators that one must wonder whether Tuurey read these in the archives. Whether these views were the result of prejudices that antedated colonial rule is unclear.
136 Rattray 1932, 425.
137 Tuurey 1982, 22, 33.
138 Tuurey 1982, 33.
139 Tuurey 1982, 36.
140 Rattray 1932, 404.
141 Tuurey 1982, 36.
142 Tuurey 1982, 36.
143 NAG ADM 61/5/11, Lawra District Record Book, 287.
144 Tuurey 1982, 51–3.
145 On the ubiquity of the same patriclans see Goody 1956a, 78.
146 Bodomo 1997, 4.
147 Bodomo 1997, 5.
148 Yelpaala 1983, 351.
149 Dery 1987, xv.
150 Here Dery relied very much on the work of Goody, using it to override Tuurey's matrilineal classification.
151 Dery 1987, 20.
152 Dery 1987, 18. Although Dery did not indicate the origin of this tradition, it was probably from around Nandom. In a recording of an oral recitation associated with the cult of the *Bagre*, matrilineal inheritance was also attributed to the resolution of generational tensions between fathers and sons in addition to protecting the aged against neglect. Goody 1972, 7. See also Lentz (1994a, 70–1) for a discussion of the story of Kontol, a similar tradition from around Lawra.
153 Der 1989, 7, 14.
154 Tuurey 1982, 5. See also Lentz 1994a, 485.
155 Hébert 1976.
156 Lentz 1994a, 482.
157 Lentz 1994a, 483.
158 Der 1989, 7–10.
159 Lentz 1994a, 491; 1994c, 72.
160 Tuurey did not mention these Yarse, and although Der acknowledged them he did not provide details. For further information, see Hébert 1976, 150–61.
161 Der 1989, 15, 18–19.

162 Der 1989, 18–19.

163 The relationship between Dagaba or Dagaaba and Dagara is unclear. Kuukure indicated that the origins of the latter were unknown, although different legends did attest to a possible etymology (1985, 25). Five years later, Bekye employed the term Dagaaba, claiming that it referred to people speaking *Dagaare*, whereas those speaking the dialect known as Lobri called themselves Dagara (1991, 94). Lentz and Erlmann (1989, 101) pointed out that the migrant laborers in the southern mining community of Tarkwa began to divide along similar lines after a political dispute in the late 1970s.

164 Der 1989, 21.

165 See Anon. 1989, i. It was noted that at an "all-Dagara Conference" convened at Wa in 1988, "most of the participants" agreed that Dagara should be the generic term. However, as Kuukure's and Bekye's books demonstrate, the most common practice in Ghana was to use the term Dagaba (or Dagaaba). See also Lentz 2000.

166 One possibility is the exclamation "*N ye ya*" or "*Eyaala*," based on the distinctive sound *ya* or *eyaa* that is found in all *Dagaare* dialects. Tuurey (1982, 14) said the equivalent English expression would be "I say!" According to its advocates, this common trait demonstrated affiliation to the Mole-Dagbane language group. The Archbishop of Tamale, Peter R. Dery, proposed it as an actual term of designation for all *Dagaare*-speaking people on 6 November 1984. Angsotinge 1986, 25–6. Kuukure (1985, 25) also stated, without providing any source, that all *Dagaare* speakers, no matter their dialects, were "Eyaale." As yet this term has not become current, but it has the decided advantage of overcoming the Lobi/Dagarti divide of colonial discourse and the Lobi/Dagaba or Dagara/Dagaba divides of contemporary discourses. In addition, it is actually meaningful to speakers of the various *Dagaare* dialects.

167 Naameh (1986, 312) claimed that Christianity had "opened the way to break down the little divisions which existed among the Dagara themselves, and helped in the development of a Dagara consciousness." See also Lentz 1994b, 152; 1994c, 64.

168 Tuurey 1982, 68.

3: Rewriting the Past

1 Sahlins 1995, 119.

2 Binger 1892, vol. 2, 34–5.

3 Arhin 1974, 100, 116.

4 NAG ADM 56/1/50, Reports on Tours of Inspection North West Province, DC

Black Volta District, March–May 1905. At the same time Read also identified other ostensible "tribes," the Dagarti and Lobi-Dagarti, along with the Lobi. Of the latter he reported: "They are uncivilised and turbulent in the extreme on the west, but an improvement is made towards the centre and the east where there are many Mahomedan settlements." However, in 1919 it was reported that Sabuli and Nandaw, which were to the east, were the "Bolshevist" elements of the district. RAT ADM 61/5/8, Informal Diary Lawra District, 6 January 1919.

5 Contemporary accounts of selection do not survive. From subsequent disputes over colonial offices, however, it is apparent that this was often the basis of selection. See for example NAG ADM 61/5/8, Informal Diary Lawra District, 12 December 1917. The chief of Gengenkpe informed the district commissioner that when an officer from Wa passed through the area, all the people had run away except his grandfather. The latter received the "whiteman" and was promised authority over surrounding settlements by the officer. This unfulfilled promise was the source of some frustration to the grandson, who still entertained such aspirations. See also Yelpaala 1983, 384 (note 52).

6 Yelpaala has suggested that anthropologists used the category of "stateless" societies in order to justify "colonialist subjugation and exploitation of the savage." That such concepts were used to justify colonial rule among the LoDagaa is very true, but this had much more to do with the prejudices of the colonizers than the categories of the anthropologists. Yelpaala 1983, 349.

7 RAT ADM 7, Native Administration 1918–1928, Ag. CSP to CCNT, 20 July 1928.

8 RAT ADM 423, "Interim Report on the Peoples of the Nandom and Lambussie Divisions of the Lawra District," DC Lawra, 1932, 28.

9 NAG ADM 61/5/11, Lawra District Record Book, 234.

10 For example, although Ko appeared on a list of villages with headmen under the chief of Nandom as early as 1911, it was not until 1917 that the settlement was actually visited. See NAG ADM 61/5/8, Informal Diary Lawra District, 10 December 1917. "There must be at least thirty compounds. The people were very friendly and said they had never seen a Commissioner there before."

11 NAG ADM 61/5/8, Informal Diary Lawra District, 8 January 1919; RAT ADM 217, Annual General Report, Northern Territories, "Lawra-Tumu Census Report 1931." The populations of each of these divisions were 15,670, 9,807, and 12,767 respectively, yielding individual ratios of 1:435, 1:251, and 1:319.

12 Yelpaala 1983, 378.

13 NAG ADM 61/4/1, Lawra District Civil Record Book, *Rex vs.* Maipuri of Tizza, 18 May 1908.

14 RAT ADM 61/5/8, Informal Diary Lawra District, 5 January 1920.

15 Kayani had come to the attention of officers through a series of "malicious" complaints against Bayo, headman of Kolora, from 1915 to 1927. RAT ADM 144, Tugu Affairs, DC Lawra to CNP, 23 August 1927. These had begun after Bayo complained that Kayani and the chief of Jirapa had usurped him when his sons were unable to work on the chief of Jirapa's farm owing to illness. In 1917, when Bayo was accused of failing to assist in military recruitment, he explained that the chief of Jirapa, with the connivance of Kayani, had seized £28 from his village. The district commissioner regarded this as "plainly a lie."

16 NAG ADM 61/5/8, Informal Diary Lawra District, 25 April 1918. In a list of the divisions of Lawra District from *c.* 1918, Tugu appears as a separate division. Kayani received a 3-inch medallion, but Jirapa already possessed a 4-inch medallion. Seven of the ten divisional chiefs had been awarded medals, the exceptions being the chiefs of Sabuli, Nandaw, and Samoa, which had populations of only 1,830, 2,160 and 1,730 respectively. NAG ADM 61/5/11, Lawra District Record Book, 234.

17 NAG ADM 61/5/8, Informal Diary Lawra District, 21 December 1918.

18 NAG ADM 61/5/6, Informal Diary Lawra District, 23 February 1919.

19 RAT ADM 144, Tugu Affairs, DC Lawra to CNP, 23 August 1927.

20 Ibid., DC Lawra to CNP, 3 September 1927.

21 Ibid., DC Lawra to CNP, 23 August 1927.

22 NAG ADM 61/5/8, Informal Diary Lawra District, 3 January 1921. On 12 December 1917, the same diary stated that the subchief of Gengenkpe had eighteen wives and the finest house of any chief in all of the Northern Territories.

23 RAT 144, Tugu Affairs, CNP to DC Lawra, 12 October 1927.

24 RAT 143, Political Prisoners, DC Lawra to CNP, 17 November 1927.

25 Staniland 1975, 79–82.

26 NAG ADM 56/1/50, Reports on Tours of Inspection North West Province, Ag. DC NWP, 28 April 1920. Such disappointment with the efficacy of British rule was not limited to this period alone. For a later, similar criticism, see RAT ADM 342–3, Informal Diary Lawra District, January 1940: "Reading old diaries I was depressed at the number of good ideas which apparently came to nothing."

27 NAG ADM 61/5/11, Lawra District Record Book, 210.

28 RAT ADM 143, Political Prisoners, CNP to CCNT, 16 September 1927. In fact the official policy of administration through Native Tribunals was not begun in the Northern Province until 1928. See NAG ADM 145–6, Native Administration, CNP to DCs NP, 15 August 1928.

29 RAT ADM 144, Tugu Affairs, CCNT to CNP, 24 September 1927.

30 RAT ADM 144, Tugu Affairs, Ag. DC Lawra to CNP, 15 April 1930. Kayani was restored on a probationary basis soon after. See CNP to Ag. DC Lawra, 8 May 1930. Yet this was only the penultimate irony. The last came in 1935, when

Kayani was "destooled" by the recently created Native Authority Tribunal (i.e., his fellow chiefs) for embezzling Native Authority funds. RAT ADM 247, Informal Diary Lawra, December 1935. See also RAT ADM 301, Informal Diary Lawra, May 1938: "One of the earliest deposed Chiefs [of the Native Authority period], Kayani, remains a sort of assistant Chief, and does his best to usurp the powers of the present Chief, appointed by Armstrong: as he is a close friend of Jirapa-Na, he is in a fair way to doing it."

31 Goody 1956a, 65–105; Somé 1969, 16–17, 22.

32 Goody 1956a, 71–3.

33 Rattray 1932, 426; Goody 1956a, 78.

34 Goody 1957, 88–9; Saighoe 1988, 162.

35 Goody 1957, 81.

36 Labouret 1931, 215.

37 Somé 1989, 147.

38 RAT ADM 145–6, Native Administration, DC Lawra to CNP, 26 November 1928.

39 RAT ADM 424, "Comments on 'Interim Report on the Peoples of the Nandom and Lambussie Divisions of the Lawra District," DC Mampong-Akwapim, 1933, 22.

40 Ibid., 26: "The fact that the outside power of the 'White Man' has set up a Chief irrespective of the existing organisation, has already in some cases set him also beyond the religious sanction or laws of his own community."

41 Ibid., 25.

42 RAT ADM 155, Native Administration, CCNT to CNP, 20 January 1931. Taxation was implemented in 1936, eight years after he and a select number of progressive officers had pointed out the urgent need for such a provision. However, it was implemented for reasons that had less to do with concern over rapacious chiefs than with the fact that the administration itself was no longer allowed to rely on forced labor supplied by the chiefs.

43 RAT ADM 32, Commutation of Tribute, CCNT to Col. Sec. Accra, 5 November 1934.

44 Distinctions between the two methods of administration, as Afigbo argued for elsewhere, are largely misleading and superficial. Afigbo 1972, 3–6. See also Staniland 1975, 103–4; Ladouceur 1979, chapter 3. Both authors described indirect rule in the Northern Territories as a failure.

45 Officially there were four paramount chiefs. The fourth, Lambussie, was created to include all Sisala inhabitants under their own chief, but it never functioned as a separate division.

46 For example, when Gandaa, the chief of Birifu, died in 1950, he left thirty-five widows. Karbo, the chief of Lawra, was said to have had sixty-five wives. See Goody 1975, 97: "I knew no-one in the long-established state of Gonja with

holdings in either women or cattle of anything like the same extent. The largest 'harem' I knew of was that of the Chief of Busunu, a man of comparable age to Gandaa and one who had fought Samori in 1897; it consisted of 13 wives. Compared with the compound of this important sub-divisional chief of an ancient kingdom, the dwellings of Kayaani, Gandaa and Karbo were vast palaces, though being of mud they would fall down with their founder. And their investments in cattle were immensely greater than those of their counterparts in Gonja."

47 RAT ADM 272, Informal Diary Lawra-Tumu District, November 1937; RAT ADM 301, Informal Diary Lawra, January 1938.

48 Yelpaala 1983, 378. In interviews conducted in Ducie, a Chakali settlement in the southeast of Wa District, Daannaa (1994, 80) was told by his informants in the early 1980s that it had been difficult to distinguish between an order from the district commissioner and one from a chief.

49 See for example RAT ADM 342–3, Informal Diary Lawra District, October 1943: "Very successful Nandom N.A. meeting in the morning discussing the vexed question of labour on the chiefs' farms which has been simmering for three years, and which has, in the past, I think, given an easy handle to any malcontents." The identification of any complainants against a chief as "malcontents" was indicative of officers' attitudes during this period. Complainants were regarded as inconvenient trouble-makers, intent not on seeking redress, but simply on making nuisances of themselves.

50 Cooper 1996, 11, 28; Iliffe 1979, 319–21, 326.

51 NAG ADM 56/1/91, Laws and Customs of the Northern Territories, "Report on Dagarti Civil Law," PC NWP, 22 November 1908.

52 RAT ADM 7, Native Administration, "Report on the Native Authorities in the Northern Territories," Ag. CSP to CCNT, 20 July 1928.

53 Ibid. He argued that the Northern Territories Administrative Ordinance no. 1 of 1902, which had provided for the establishment of indigenous tribunals where none previously had existed, as well as recognition for those which predated colonial intervention, had effectively been in abeyance since its inception due to a total ignorance of what the "customary laws" actually were. Section 15 of the ordinance empowered recognized chiefs "to exercise the jurisdiction heretofore exercised by them in the same manner as such jurisdiction has heretofore been exercised." Where such jurisdiction had never existed, as among the LoDagaa and many other politically decentralized societies of the region, this directive was meaningless. It had been written in such tautological language in an effort to disguise the lack of even rudimentary knowledge of the subject societies at the beginning of the century.

54 RAT ADM 7, Native Administration, Ag. CSP to CCNT, 20 July 1928.

55 Rattray 1932.

56 He had issued two preliminary reports. The second contained specific findings and recommendations. See Gold Coast 1930.

57 RAT ADM 153, "Memorandum on Native Authority in the Northern Territories," Ag. CCNT, 18 March 1931.

58 Johnson 1986, 68; 1981, 514. Among the LoDagaa, the slave raiding of Samori and Babatu provided a convenient excuse for rewriting the past to make it compatible with rule through colonial chiefs. The defeat of these slave raiders by colonial forces and the removal of the threat of slavery to the people of the Northern Territories was a theme exploited by the administration in the propaganda that preceded the introduction of taxation. See RAT ADM 229, Native Administration (General) Taxation Assessment 1931–32, PC NP to DCs NP, 6 January 1932.

59 Iliffe 1979, 322–3.

60 RAT ADM 65, Native Authorities, GC Gov. to Sec. of State for the Colonies, copy n.d. [1932].

61 Gold Coast 1930, 8–10, 11.

62 Kuklick 1991, 184, 189–90, 194, 204, 217–18, 228.

63 Kuklick 1991, 225.

64 See RAT ADM 206, Political Conferences, "Minutes of Political Conference 2–3 December 1933." When it was suggested by one DC that "customary laws" for the different courts be recorded, "it was generally agreed that some broad rules might well be laid down, but the fewer the better."

65 RAT ADM 153, "Memorandum on Native Authority in the Northern Territories," Ag. CCNT, 18 March 1931.

66 RAT ADM 169, Native Administration, DC Lawra to CCNT, 31 March 1931.

67 NAG ADM 56/1/292, Handing Over Reports Lawra District, DC Lawra, 25 May 1928. In the same year the CNP advised DCs not to hear "native" cases, except as complaints or on appeal, and therefore this recommendation was never acted upon.

68 See Chapter 7.

69 RAT ADM 145–6, Native Administration, DC Lawra to CNP, 26 November 1928.

70 RAT ADM 868, Native Courts, Ag. Chief Justice to Per. Sec. Ministry of Local Gov., 5 September 1952.

71 Ibid., CRO Tamale to Per. Sec. Ministry of Local Gov., 16 October 1952.

72 As Olson observed, the point of law is to limit interpretations. That is why laws are written – in order to control "what was said" and to create a degree of consensus over possible interpretations. Without writing there is "interpretational anarchy." See Olson 1994, 116, 176.

73 RAT ADM 868, Native Courts, DC Lawra to DC Wa, 19 September 1947.

74 RAT ADM 7, Native Administration, "Report on the Native Authorities in the Northern Territories," Ag. CSP to CCNT, 20 July 1928.
75 Yelpaala 1983, 378.
76 Yelpaala 1983, 377.
77 NAG ADM 56/1/50, Reports on Tour of Inspection North West Province, DC Black Volta District, April–May 1906.
78 NAG ADM 61/5/11, Lawra District Record Book, 209.
79 NAG ADM 61/5/11, Lawra District Record Book, 230–1. What was ignored was that although they were native, they were no longer commoners.
80 For example see NAG ADM 61/5/8, Informal Diary Lawra District, 11 October 1917.
81 Few officers were stationed long enough at Lawra to learn *Dagaare*. Therefore, they conducted almost all communications through "'pakha' Hausa," "not the bastard lingo which serves as a lingua franca up here." NAG ADM 61/5/8, Informal Diary Lawra District, 22 January 1918.
82 NAG ADM 61/5/11, Lawra District Record Book, 231.
83 Thomas 1975, 431.
84 Thomas 1975, 441–2.
85 NAG ADM 61/5/8, Informal Diary Lawra District, 6 September 1920; 20 December 1920; 31 January 1921.
86 RAT ADM 206, Political Conferences 1931–33, "Minutes of Political Conference," 2/3 December 1933.
87 RAT ADM 514, Annual Report Lawra–Tumu District 1937–38.
88 RAT ADM 503, Annual Report Wa District 1947–48.
89 RAT ADM 212, Political Conference 1944–45, DC Lawra to CCNT, 2 January 1945. Aware of possible criticisms of such a program of indoctrination in light of recent history, he added: "Such a course might be analogous to the Labour Camps operated in Germany before the War, but need not be similar to them, and, in this respect, I think we might learn something from our enemies." See also RAT ADM 342–3, Informal Diary Lawra, December 1943. With regard to the desire expressed by Tamale schoolboys at home on holiday to travel south, another officer was more sympathetic: "I regard this as a normal healthy sign (vide the annual exodus to the Mines etc., for the same reason). In the N. T. there may be bread (a modicum) but there is a dismal lack of circuses. So what do we do about that?"
90 Ladouceur 1979, 57–61.
91 Hailey 1951, part III, 265.
92 The former, J.A. Karbo, was a member of an important colonial government commission on constitutional reform, and the latter, S.D. Dombo, Duori Naa, was a special northern representative to the Gold Coast Legislative Council.
93 Ladouceur 1979, 175–6.

94 Ladouceur 1979, 73, 83–96.

95 RAT ADM 72, Native Authority Lawra, Birifu Naa to DC Wa, 4 November 1951; and DC Wa to CCNT, 28 November 1951; Ladouceur 1979, 74, 81, 120–1.

96 Goody 1975, 96–8. Given that one of the requirements for expiation was the destruction of illicitly gained property, the chiefs' anxieties would appear to have been justified. However, there is no evidence that they heeded this injunction.

97 S.D. Dombo, Duori Naa, was elected as member for Jirapa-Lambussie in 1954, 1956, and 1960. His colleague, A. Karbo, son of the Lawra Naa, was equally successful in the Lawra-Nandom constituency over the same period. Both were members of the Northern People's Party.

98 Ladouceur 1979, 175–6; Staniland 1975, 107.

99 Lentz 1993, 210.

100 Lentz 1994b, 164–5.

101 J.A. Braimah expressed their fears in his rallying call for northern solidarity against southern neocolonialism in 1955: "Down with Black Imperialism in the North." For a history of politics in northern Ghana during this period see Ladouceur 1979, 99–211.

102 A prime example of this was the tension that developed between Birifu and Lawra. In 1949 the chief of Birifu's son, B. Gandaa, joined the southern-based UGCC following the Lawra Naa's membership on the Coussey Commission, where he had developed links with other northern chiefs. Following the death of the Birifu Naa that year, his sons began to agitate for their own Local Council (in 1952 these replaced Native Authorities), separate from Lawra.

103 For example, the Nandom Naa, Imoru Puobey, who had been a founding member of the NPP, withdrew his support from the party in the 1954 election when he learned that they had chosen A. Karbo, the Lawra Naa's son, as their candidate. A relative of the Nandom Naa, Polkuu Konkuu Chiri, stood as an independent. Although unsuccessful electorally, he succeeded Imoru in 1958 as Nandom Naa. Because of Karbo's leading role in the opposition, the CPP granted favors to Polkuu and maintained his position as chief in the face of local opposition. Ladouceur 1979, 121, 183.

104 The relevant legislative provisions were established by the Local Courts Act of 1958 and the Local Courts Act (Establishment) Instrument of 1960. Appointment of Local Court Magistrates became the responsibility of the Minister for Local Government. However, the CPP made more direct attacks on the role of chiefs during this period, beginning with the Chiefs (Recognition) Act of 1959, which gave the government the power to appoint or dismiss any chief, and followed by the Local Government (Amendment) Act of 1959, which abolished the representation of "traditional" members on Local Councils. Under the new

constitution of the First Republic, the Chieftaincy Act of 1961 made all chiefs' powers dependent on government recognition. Goldschmidt 1981, 168–75. For a very good synopsis of the changing status of chiefs under different postcolonial governments, see Ray 1996.

105 The first magistrate in Lawra District was B. Gandaa, a member of the chief of Birifu's household, which had supported the CPP in order to pursue their rivalry against the Lawra Naa, a stalwart of the NPP. Gandaa had joined the UGCC in 1949 (before the establishment of the CPP later that year) following a tour of the north by J.B. Danquah. By this time the Gandaas had begun agitating for local autonomy for Birifu, which was then a subdivision of Lawra. The Lawra Naa, J.A. Karbo, had entered politics a year earlier when appointed a member of the Coussey Commission. As Ladouceur noted, the only significant difference in the profiles of CPP and NPP supporters was that the latter tended to have somewhat higher "traditional" status. Ladouceur 1979, 88. In the case of the Gandaa household, the anticolonial line of the CPP would have been appealing, given their struggle against the local administration. In turn, Karbo had little cause for resentment, having done well under colonial rule.

106 Gandaa served as magistrate for only fifteen months (from August 1960 to November 1961), before being replaced by D.A.Q. Dakurah, a member of the ruling lineage in Tizza. Just as the chiefs of Birifu and Lawra were rivals and party-political opponents, the Tizza Naa, W.M. Dakurah, had been a CPP supporter in opposition to S.D. Dombo, Duori Naa. Dakurah served as magistrate for only three months (December 1961 to February 1962), before being succeeded by D.J. Charles, who served until just after the overthrow of Nkrumah (from March 1962 to August 1966). According to the record books, there was some delay before a successor was appointed. In October 1966, A. Braimah (a relative of the Gonja politician J.A. Braimah, who along with S.D. Dombo and A. Karbo had been appointed to the NLC's Political Committee) took up the post (Ladouceur 1979, 215). Like other political appointees, his tenure was short-lived, and he was succeeded five months later, in March 1968, by S. Akalifa, who remained in Lawra until September 1971. From then until July 1976 the office was held by A.Z. Kpemaal. Finally, he was succeeded by Y.B. Siddique, who was still in office at the end of 1984. With the exception of the first two magistrates, all others were outsiders, but Charles was the only southerner.

107 Yelpaala 1983, 372.

108 Somé 1969, 21. Daannaa (1994, 80) noted that residents of Ducie, a Chakali settement in the southeast corner of Wa District, had similar memories in the early 1980s.

109 Skalnik (1989, 152) noted the same thing among the Konkomba.

110 Writing of the authority of the neighboring Sisala chiefs during the 1970s,

Mendonsa observed that "the power of the chief is limited. He functions mainly as a figurehead and spokesman of the government. Judicial cases are brought before chiefs, but they have no sanctions except referral to the district court in Tumu. Wise chiefs, however, use persuasion and prestige of office to settle cases before they reach this point. Villagers may bypass the chief and carry a case directly to the police and court in Tumu" (1982, 49). For a discussion of this phenomenon among the Builsa, see Schott 1985, 162–8. He noted that under the Second Republic (1969–72) the prerogatives of the chiefs were restricted even more, to the point that "the chiefs had been divested of even this restricted jurisdiction in private matters and had been expressly forbidden to intercede even as arbitrators in marital disputes and other disputes." However, this situation improved again under the Third Republic. Goldschmidt 1981, 184–5.

111 Again, Skalnik (1987, 146–7) noted the same thing among the Konkomba.

112 The postcolonial state, even though it seems to have preferred to "relegate" chieftaincy to the past, could not afford to do away with chiefs. Refusing to deal with chieftaincy would have also meant that the state was relinquishing a form of sovereignty, the power to appoint or dismiss office holders – an important power it inherited from the colonial state. It might have also lead to political violence, which, in turn, would have meant the loss of another form of state sovereignty, the monopoly over the use of violence. At times the state also found it necessary to co-opt chieftaincy as a "legtimizing instrument." Skalnik 1989, 165; Ray 1996, 188–91, 193–4. See also the Conclusion for a brief discussion of political violence in northern Ghana.

113 Lentz 1993, 179.

114 It was difficult, and indeed ill-advised, to make too many inquiries into these disputes in the 1980s. Subsequent political tragedies over succession in northern Ghana would probably make such work even less possible, although violence has never erupted in Lawra District. Lentz hoped that her own research would not "increase tensions and embitterment," but noted that a village chief had been removed from office in 1989 for remarks he made to a researcher from the Free University of Berlin (1993, 211 (note 97)).

115 Goody 1962, 81, 109: "Whereas formerly it meant a rich man or a man of influence, the LoDagaa now use the word to refer to a Government-appointed chief."

116 Tuureh 1977, 45. Several years later, Lentz's informants used a similar phrase, speaking of "the time when politics came" to refer to the intersection of national party politics and local chieftaincy politics in the 1950s and 1960s. Lentz 1993, 204.

117 In 1966 one of the first acts of the NLC was to institute the Chieftaincy (Amendment) Decree (NLCD 122), which made provision for redressing any changes

affecting traditional offices made by the previous government. See Mensah-Brown 1969, 57–63.

118 Tuureh 1977, 19.

119 Tuureh 1977, 59.

120 Following the recommendations of the Mensah Commission (1978), the constitution of the Third Republic withdrew the right of the government to interfere with the recognition of "traditional" offices. But as Goldschmidt noted: "It must be emphasized, however, that no constitutional provision withdrawing government recognition of chiefs can erase the fact that the whole chieftaincy system has been influenced by the tradition of government recognition dating from colonial times" (1981, 185). The state remained deeply implicated in chieftaincy matters in areas such as Lawra, where there were no genuinely traditional criteria for succession.

121 Lentz 1993, 178.

122 Lentz 1993, 180, 191, 198.

123 Lentz 1993, 210.

124 Lentz 1993, 211.

125 Wilson and Wilson 1945, 97, 163.

126 Tuurey 1982, 36, 49.

127 Lentz 1994a, 483; 1994c, 71–2. Lentz includes Tuurey among the authors who have been part of the "revalorization" of LoDagaa statelessness, but even though he was a proponent of the Dagomba thesis of origins, his negative attitudes toward Dagaaba statelessness were very clear.

128 Tuurey 1982, 37, 40–3.

129 Tuurey 1982, 17, 36.

130 Yelpaala 1983, 352–7.

131 Yelpaala 1983, 349. For a similar critique of the application of the concept of the state to decentralized societies of northern Ghana, see Skalnik 1987, 301–3. He argued that the concept was "largely inapplicable" to non-Western societies.

132 Daannaa 1994, 72.

133 Somé 1989, 138.

134 Somé 1989, 147; Yelpaala 1983, 355.

135 Yelpaala 1983, 352–7, 363.

136 Yelpaala 1983, 356. Emphasis mine.

137 Yelpaala 1983, 361. Emphasis mine.

138 Yelpaala 1983, 362. Emphasis mine.

139 There is more ethnographic evidence to support the antiquity of the institution of Earth priest than perhaps any other institution in the Voltaic region. On the institution among the LoDagaa, see Rattray 1932; Goody 1956a, 1957, and 1962.

140 Rattray 1932, 429.
141 Yelpaala 1983, 363.
142 Yelpaala 1983, 358.
143 Somé 1989, 140, 150.
144 Skalnik 1987, 315.

4: Reimagining God

1 For the purposes of clarity, god (with the lower case "g") is used to refer to the LoDagaa concept of a supreme being, whereas God (with the upper case "G") is used to refer to the Christian concept. The distinction is necessary for reasons of clarity, but does not imply any sense of hierarchy.
2 Ranger (1993a, 81) argues that although colonial authority often invented traditions, Africans most often imagined and reimagined rather than invented their own traditions.
3 Shorter 1988, 185, 188. This is very similar to the language of the 1936 Native Courts (Northern Territories) Ordinance, which repeated the standard colonial repugnancy test. The ordinance stated that the courts would recognize "the native law and custom prevailing in the area of jurisdiction of such Court, so far as it is not repugnant to natural justice or morality or inconsistent with any other ordinance." In both instances the emphasis was upon custom.
4 Naameh 1986, 284–6, 289–90.
5 Kpiebaya 1976, 493–8; Naameh 1986, 291.
6 Kuukure 1985, 14.
7 McCoy 1988, 64, 76.
8 Naameh 1986, 290.
9 Quoted in Shorter 1988, 211.
10 Naameh 1986, 272–80.
11 Naameh 1986, 243; Bekye 1991, 276.
12 Der 1980; 1983; Kuukure 1985; Bekye 1991.
13 Der 1980, 172; Kuukure 1985, 106; Bekye 1991, 226, 314. For a critique of Der's argument see Hawkins 1998.
14 McCoy 1988, 19; Naameh 1986, 5; Hébert 1976, 246; Der 1974, 52. See also Somé (1998, 34) for other examples.
15 Bekye 1991, 270.
16 Der 1974, 43, 49–51.
17 *RA* 1930–31, 204.
18 Accounts of this incident vary. There are two accounts written by missionaries themselves (Paternot, 1953; McCoy, 1988). One pertains primarily to the history

of the church in the adjoining French colony, whereas the other was written more than a half a century after the event. McCoy was assisted in the research by his cousin, who consulted the original diaries, as well as by a priest who assisted in the writing. I have also relied on Der 1974; 1983. Der based his account on the original diaries of the missionaries as well as interviews. Despite several attempts, I failed to gain access to the original diaries, which are kept in the mission house in Jirapa. These accounts were written from a strong religious conviction that the conversion process was the result of divine intervention, and the narratives of events are colored accordingly.

19 RAT ADM 502, Annual Report Wa District 1946–47.

20 It is necessary to treat these figures with a degree of skepticism, not because of any necessary inaccuracy in the numbers themselves, but because of what was said to constitute conversion. It might be more apt to refer to most of these people as Christian followers. This is not to deny that among them there were a number of devout adherents, but only to say that conversion had political, cultural, and medical as well as religious connotations. In addition, not all converts were baptized, many had been baptized as children of converts, and many more were baptized *in periculo mortis*. Finally, at any one time many of those baptized were no longer eligible to receive the sacraments, most often because of conjugal irregularities. Conversion did not happen in one direction only. Converts could "lapse" back into non-Christian practices, or abandon the new beliefs entirely. Nevertheless, converts had a unique identity that came from their sense of belonging to a community of fellow followers.

21 Bekye 1991, 273; McCoy 1988, 229.

22 McCoy 1988, 18, 312; Dery 1984, 3; Naameh 1986, 184.

23 Recent studies have confirmed this version of the nature of god among the LoDagaa. See particularly Goody 1972, 22–3; Somda 1977, 17; Dabiré 1983, 227–8, 236–7; Bekye 1991, 139.

24 *RA* 1931–32, 147.

25 McCoy 1988, 113–14.

26 McCoy 1988, 129; Bekye 1991, 294.

27 Girault 1959, 332–3; Goody 1972, 22; Dabiré 1983, 236; Bekye 1991, 202.

28 Bekye 1991, 207–11; Kuukure 1985, 45.

29 Goody 1975, 30.

30 Somé 1991.

31 Bekye 1991, 276–8; Kuukure 1985, 121–9.

32 Hien and Hébert 1968–9, 566; Kusiele 1973, 43; Bekye 1991, 154.

33 Bekye 1991, 136–7.

34 Hien and Hébert 1968–9, 566; Kuukure 1985, 45; Naameh 1986, 116; Bekye 1991, 153.

35 Kuukure 1985, 45.
36 Hien and Hébert 1968/9, 566.
37 Naameh 1986, 116.
38 Bekye 1991, 153.
39 Hien and Hébert 1968–9; Somda 1977.
40 Der 1980, 175; Kuukure 1985, 45; Bekye 1991, 216.
41 On the possibility of such change see Chapter 6. Only one missionary source supports the theocentric arguments of Der, Kuukure, and Bekye. Father Girault (1959, 356) wrote of the LoDagaa living around the mission at Diébougou as "monotheistic animists" and their religion as "primitive monotheism." It is significant that this account was written over a quarter of a century after the rain incident at Jirapa and in an area where Christianity was well known and well established.
42 Der 1980, 178
43 Cardinall 1920, 22, 26.
44 Rattray 1932, 308.
45 Fortes 1949, 21.
46 Goody 1972, 22–3 (note 2).
47 Goody 1962, 209. Reiterating what Fortes had said of Tallensi attitudes toward *Naawun*, Goody said that *Naangmin* "means little to the LoDagaa except as a final cause by which to explain the otherwise inexplicable."
48 Goody 1972, 28–33.
49 Goody 1972, 22.
50 Goody 1972, White *Bagre* 2396–9, 6075–9; Black *Bagre* 3755–6, 5175–8. Goody translated *Naangmin* as God here despite his suggestion that the terms were not really analogous.
51 Goody and Gandah 1980, Black *Bagre* 1054–8, 1984–5, 2474–6, 3262–5.
52 See this chapter's epigraph (Dabiré 1983, 227–9). The proverb is also found in Somda 1977, 17; Bekye 1991, 139.
53 Bekye 1991, 283; Kuukure 1985, 163–4.
54 Bekye 1991, 282–3; Naameh 1986, 215–16.
55 Kuukure 1985, 163–4.
56 Goody 1972, 211.
57 Kuukure 1985.
58 Goody 1972, Black *Bagre* 3978–4218.
59 Bekye 282–3.
60 Somé 1991, 40.
61 Somé 1991, 40.
62 Naameh 1986, 255: "The practice of Christian life must not necessarily be taken to imply a corresponding change to a Christian mentality."

63 Naameh 1986, 196–7.

64 Naameh 1986, 179, 190–1.

65 Germain 1937, 84; Naameh 1986, 245.

66 Somé 1998, 32. He noted that "several of the faithful turned back to traditional religion, while many others practiced both."

67 Bongvlaa 1979, 68; Somé 1998, 53.

68 Kusiele 1973, 1.

69 Naameh 1986, 199, 202.

70 Naameh 1986, 199–204, 279.

71 Paternot 1953, 133.

72 Goody 1975, 103.

73 Goody 1975, 103–5; 1972, 15, 32.

74 Ukpong 1983, 198.

75 Goody 1972, 15 (note 1).

76 Goody 1975, 102–5.

77 Although Goody was correct in rejecting the notion that historical change was impossible among the LoDagaa without external stimuli, this does not mean that change necessarily had to have occurred. Surely if a concept as important as *Naangmin* apparently was had oscillated so fundamentally, there would have been some evidence of this in residual practices. Given the individual and local nature of religious experiences, as well as the lack of evidence of anything but consensus on the nature of *Naangmin*, how would all LoDagaa be at the same stage of the cycle at the same time?

78 Horton 1971, 101–4. This model is quite distinct from Goody's internal cycle of religious speculation and change, for here there are clear reasons why change was necessary.

79 Germain 1937, 84.

80 *RA* 1931–32, 147.

81 Germain 1937, 85.

82 Kuukure 1985, 164.

83 Goody 1956a, iv. This adherence to a synchronic perspective was amended in the second edition (Goody 1967), although the work itself was not modified.

84 Marcus and Fischer 1986, 95.

85 Bekye 1991, xxix; Kuukure 1985, 18.

86 Der 1980, 178, 182–3 (note 49).

87 For a discussion of Der's use of this evidence see Hawkins 1998, 41–7.

88 Obeyesekere 1992, xiv. This observation was made in his debate with Sahlins over whether Hawaiians perceived Captain Cook as a god.

89 Der 1983, 232–3; Girault 1959.

90 Bekye 1991, 209–10.

91 Kuukure 1985, 70. Girault maintained that this was not likely as he had not done his interviewing in areas of direct Christian influence (1959, 330). However, he did admit that half of the total population was Catholic, thereby making it unlikely that there was any area free from some Christian influence.

92 Dabiré 1983, 236; Kuukure 1985, 73.

93 Der 1980, 180.

94 Somé 1991, 40.

95 See Peel (1994, 163) for a discussion of these issues in the historiography of Yoruba religion.

96 Kirby 1994, 61.

97 Kuukure (1985, 18) said that it would be "naive" to assume that conversion meant the abandonment of fundamental beliefs. Indeed, he argued that "the world outlook may be virtually untouched." Similarly, Bekye (1991, 17), also claimed it would be "delusive" to assume that conversion was necessarily more than "an overlay on the traditional culture" or "a superficial modification." It is significant that neither author referred to the LoDagaa by name, but spoke instead in abstract terms. The circumspection is revealing. To admit to the incompleteness of conversion in theory is one thing, but to refer to an actual example is quite another. It would be equally naive to believe that just as the beliefs of Christians might not have been totally, or even fundamentally, transformed by conversion, the beliefs of non-Christians might not have been susceptible to influence from Christian sources.

98 Yangyuoro 1984, 210–11, 219. See Hawkins 1998, 56–7 (note 7).

99 Horton 1993, chapter 6; Westerlund 1985, chapter 3.

100 Horton 1993, 174–5.

101 Mudimbe 1988, 195.

102 Westerlund 1985, 45.

103 Girault 1959, 331.

104 Kuukure 1985, 91.

105 Ubah 1982, 92.

106 Bekye 1991, 44, 221–2.

107 Bekye 1991, 221.

108 Bekye 1991, 221. Emphasis mine.

109 Ukpong 1983, 196.

110 Bekye 1991, 283.

111 Somé 1992, 40.

112 Bekye 1991, xxix.

113 See Hawkins 1998.

114 Vansina 1990, 258.
115 Ranger 1993a, 81.
116 Vansina 1990, 259.
117 Ranger 1993a, 75–80.
118 Vansina 1990, 258.
119 Peel 1994, 163.
120 Fisher 1985, 158, 165. Fisher has pointed out that it is useful to delineate different stages of conversion, and that in the initial stage the idea of God may well be far less important, despite the rhetoric of missionaries, than the effect of agents themselves. Most recently, Ranger has attacked conceptualizations of African religions as local. His criticisms were not directed at Horton – and indeed, Ranger's argument does not necessarily contradict that of Horton – but it does help modify the thrust of Horton's analysis. Ranger 1993b.
121 Ranger 1993b.
122 Kuukure 1985, 45.
123 Staniland 1975, 76, 132, 174; Davis 1987.
124 Steiner 1994, 102–4: "For the Westerner, authentic African art only existed in the past, *before* European contact. For the trader, authentic African art only exists in the present, *after* European contact, when the objects were taken out of Africa and declared by the Western authorities to be authentic. The trader's formulation of authenticity thus depends upon contact with Europe to discover the inherent value of an African object."
125 Henige 1974, 6–7.
126 Schoebrun 1993, 38, 56.
127 By appealing to the past, societies such as the Dagomba, the Lozi, and the Shambaa have sought a new locus (the past) for lost sovereignty, which had been appropriated by foreigners and therefore resided outside their societies. Staniland, 1975: 14, 189; Prins, 1980: 28–9; Feierman, 1990: 141–5, 210. The unprecedented nature of chieftaincy among the LoDagaa has made similar efforts both less convincing and less successful. For the LoDagaa, the lack of an appropriate past out of which chiefly traditions could be fashioned resulted in the inability to regain, albeit in a different form, lost sovereignty. In the absence of such a history, real or imaginable, power resided with external agencies that acted as the arbiters of "traditional" legitimacy, that is, local authority.
128 Vansina 1990, 247.
129 Marx 1975, 423.

5: Suppressing Knowledge

1 RAT ADM 430, "Essay on the People of North West Province," PC NWP, 1907.

Labouret highlighted this predicament with more subtlety in his account of the *Lobi*: "The society under study here is held together by very loose bonds, such that one might be tempted to believe that complete anarchy reigned in this land without chiefs and even villages. Closer scrutiny dispels this impression and soon reveals that individualism in the proper sense of the term does not exist among the Lobi" (1931, 215). For Labouret, colonialism created the possibility for individualism through the creation of free markets and the deterioration of communal authority. As one critic has summarized Labouret's perspective, "closed communities" were "opened like a flower" through colonial peace and security. Van Hoven has pointed out that this analysis was based on an evolutionary analysis that saw the *Lobi* moving from a caste society, "état du droit," to a class society, "état du fait." This was similar to Maine's status to contract theory. Van Hoven 1990, 188, 193.

2 See Southall 1970, especially 45. He noted that the use of the term "tribal" depended on "definition by illusion" and the "false application of the concept to artificial or misconceived entities," through "ignorance, illusion, or inattention." Many of the term's defects can be attributed to the dispositions that writing creates.

3 The absence of clearly articulated indigenous terms of social representation was an obstacle to external understanding and description of LoDagaa society; it also highlighted the differences between the assumptions of observers and the oral culture of the LoDagaa. The use of external terms of social representation to describe the LoDagaa meant that what was actually observable and present was often ignored or marginalized. In particular, no mention was made in this report, nor was any specific attention later paid, to the fact that LoDagaa culture and social relations were predicated on oral means of communication, whereas the perspective of administrators was deeply conditioned by the world on paper. In fact, the difficulties of representing or describing social phenomena of oral cultures (which have not been the object of indigenous classification and definition) has been a subject of some considerable difficulty even for professional ethnographers. It is no coincidence that in attempting to arrive at more exacting terms of reference, Southall remarked: "The distinction of tribal societies in their lack of writing and records ... holds fairly well empirically." Southall 1970, 46.

4 NAG ADM 56/1/50, Reports on Tours of Inspection North West Province, DC Black Volta District, March–May 1905.

5 Goody 1956, 94. See also Somé 1998, 35–6.

6 Goody 1956a, chapters 4–5; Somé 1969.

7 RAT ADM 430, "Essay on the Peoples of North West Province," PC NWP, 1907.

8 NAG ADM 56/1/91, Laws and Customs of the Northern Territories, "Report on Dagarti Civil Law," PC NWP, 1908.

9 See Chapter 7 as well as below.

10 Much of the ethnographic detail in this section is derived from Goody (1957). He proposed a similar problematic: "The central problem in analysing any such community is to discover how social control is maintained. To show the order existing within an apparently orderless society" (75).

11 RAT ADM 430, "Essay on the Peoples of North West Province," 1907.

12 Ibid.

13 Ibid. The only description provided of these practices was from among the Wala, where chiefs were said to have conducted the proceedings, although it was the *tengaansob* who administered oaths. It was reported that among the Lobi and Dagarti, for whom there was no "assessor" beyond the household elder (*yirsob*), no offense besides theft was recognized; when this occurred between settlements, it was said to have been settled through a show of force.

14 Ibid.

15 Goody 1957, 85. Read had stated: "Causes were considered proved by the swearing of an oath. Criminal causes by swearing on the fetish and taking fetish medicine which was supposed to poison any person who swore falsely." RAT ADM 430, "Essay on the Peoples of North West Province," 1907.

16 Rattray 1932, 430.

17 RAT ADM 168, Annual Report Lawra District 1928–29.

18 Instances involving resistance by a *tengaansob* as the principal party were rare. In 1926, following a series of complaints against the chief of Tizza involving extortion, the incumbent was removed from office and the elders asked to elect a replacement. But they refused to nominate a candidate satisfactory to the district commissioner, "as they produced young puppets without authority." Their spokesman, Debur, explained that they had all "taken fetish" not to follow Jirapa any longer because of the abuses of their former chief, who had been supported by the Jirapa Naa, the paramount chief of the division. At this time Eyre-Smith was still unaware of the extent of chiefly abuses of power, so he made the *tengaansob* agree to assist the chief-elect and to cancel the oath "on the Tingnana" not to follow Jirapa. He ended by reporting that Debur "was informed he would reside in Tamale or elsewhere for one year if this procedure was not carried out." NAG ADM 61/5/4, Lawra District Complaint Book, 23 May 1927, 2 June 1927.

19 RAT ADM 430, "Essay on the Peoples of North West Province," 1907.

20 NAG ADM 61/5/5, Lawra District Complaint Book, 9 December 1917. Unfortunately only the nature of the complaints, extortion and oppression, were recorded. We have only the district commissioner's observations on the probable cause of disaffection; these were themselves based on the earlier warnings by the subchief intended to discredit possible complaints.

21 Ibid.

22 Nor does the district commissioner seem to have regarded as significant the fact that the elders of the community, as well as the headmen, had been unanimous in their condemnation of Taiboo. No admission of a conspiracy against Taiboo was ever extracted from any of the witnesses.

23 Goody 1957, 86. Expiatory offerings were not made in anticipation of noumenal intervention. "Fulfilment of this obligation would normally occur only as a result of subsequent misfortune attributed by a diviner to this antecedent sin."

24 This approach to indigenous concerns is derived from Mendonsa's study of the neighboring Sisala. See Mendonsa 1982, 85: "Sisala etiology is similar to that described for their neighbours the LoDagaa and the Tallensi. As among them, divination is the mechanism used to discern the causes of misfortune. As this is done, a deviant is labelled as the specific descent group member responsible for the problem." Following the observations of Needham and Pouillon it would be patently misleading to refer to these forms of social knowledge merely as beliefs. The point is that whether or not this knowledge was "true," it was the basis of social practices and actions. See Pouillon 1982, 1–8; Needham 1972.

25 NAG ADM 61/5/4, Lawra District Complaint Book, "Enquiry into the death of one Bassalla," 1 May 1922, 19 June 1922.

26 Goody 1962, 208.

27 LoDagaa concepts of sexual transgression are discussed in Chapter 7.

28 Goody 1962, 211: "Even expiation for the breaking of a taboo, when the person knows he has invited supernatural punishment, is not usually made unless a diviner links some later trouble with the original offense."

29 RAT ADM 169, Native Administration, DC Lawra to CCNT, 31 March 1931. Eyre-Smith postulated that in precolonial times the elders of the settlements had constituted informal tribunals for the purpose of deciding what actions should be taken to propitiate an offended deity, in the case of a known transgression, or, in the case of unexplained misfortune, to divine its cause and make remedy. However, these were not decision-making bodies: "On a person ... being arraigned before the tribunal and accused of neglecting to observe a particular sanction the swearing of his denial on the local Earth fetish was sufficient to exonerate him." They were, instead, ad hoc committees for managing crises.

30 Mendonsa (1982, 149–210) has demonstrated the importance attached by the neighbouring Sisala to discovering the cause of illness and misfortune from the perspective of authority structures. The Sisala, like the LoDagaa, saw illness as stemming from an impairment of social relations, and therefore the search for the causes of, and remedies for, illness took place within a social context. There, as among the LoDagaa, such knowledge was discovered through divinatory processes. Mendonsa held the underlining purpose of divination to be the identification

of deviance and the assertion of a set of social ideologies, but he conceded that the enforcement of norms or rules through these processes was contradictory and dialectical: "The very processes thought to resolve conflict are partly responsible for it" (209).

31 The epigraph for this chapter comes from the traveling diary of the district commissioner. He explained that he carried out this "experiment" to illustrate how "utterly ignorant" and "stupid" the people of the district were. NAG ADM 56/1/50, Reports on Tours of Inspection North West Province, DC Black Volta District, October–November 1906. This is somewhat similar to how the White Fathers used medicine (see the following chapter).

32 Gold Coast 1954, Northern Territories Ordinances, no. 5, 1908.

33 NAG ADM 61/5/8, Informal Diary Lawra District, 4 May 1919. These attitudes were also evident during the later years of colonial rule, by which time Islamic beliefs were more an irritation than a concern. In 1938 the district commissioner recorded the following incident in his diary: "Told Lawra-Na last night to pray for rain in his own fashion, and not to waste money on Moslem sacrifices. A heavy storm last night. I hope it will convince Lawra-Na of the futility of Moslem pretensions. I do not mind good Moslems, but when they begin using their texts and prayers as a sort of magic, and advertising themselves as specially qualified middlemen between earth and heaven, with supernatural powers, I do object." RAT ADM 301, Informal Diary Lawra-Tumu District, July 1938. I assume that this was an indirect criticism of the White Fathers, who just six years earlier had done just this and managed to create a mass movement overnight.

34 An example of the discrete and apparently indistinguishable nature of these shrines is the LoBirifor market shrine at Kalba, not far from Bole. "In Kalba, the market shrine (*datii*) consists of nothing more than a slim, oblong piece of iron, no more than two inches wide and a few inches long, hammered into the exposed root of a large shade tree which dominates the southwestern side of the square. Its inconspicuousness, hidden away as it is among the drinking shelters which are clustered around it, belies the great power which it represents." Evans 1983, 205.

35 Piot 1999, 143. See also Comaroff and Comaroff (1997, 42–50) for a discussion of the "interpretation of less articulate forms of consciousness, forms that leave few textual traces."

36 Goody 1968, 227.

37 NAG ADM 61/5/8, Informal Diary Lawra District, 2 May 1919.

38 NAG ADM 61/5/4, Lawra District Complaint Book, 4 May 1919. He had also provided written charms for Jattogo of Samoa in order to provide him immunity from prosecution before the Native Tribunal, where he was facing charges. But the tribunal found Jattogo guilty, and he reported Ali to a constable. Ali was

found guilty by the district commissioner on the rather spurious charges of "dealing in fetish and charms he pretends have power to protect criminals," "cruelty to animals," and "unlawful possession of a Government Gazetteer" – all of which were pre-existing written colonial offenses. He was sent on to Wa for sentencing and eventually incarcerated in Kumase.

39 RAT ADM 424, "Comments on 'Interim Report' on the peoples of the Nandom and Lambassie Divisions of the Lawra District," DC Mampong-Akwapim, 1933, 28–9. Similarly, Somé has argued that many LoDagaa had lost confidence in their own spirits by the time the missionaries arrived. When people began visiting the White Fathers to ask for rain in 1932, it was because belief in indigenous remedies had been undermined by colonial rule (1998, 42).

40 One case that was thought to merit a hearing was a complaint by the chief of Kunyukuo, Kumbio, that one of the village's elders, Sheay, had used a particular medicine, "Tanga-Tanga fetish," against the chief's brother, and that it had killed him. The chief's brother, Kalu, had been sent to order Sheay to carry loads of grass to Lawra at the district commissioner's request. Shortly before his death, Kalu had told Kumbio that Sheay had put a medicine on him and told him he would die if he continued to delegate Sheay to take grass to Lawra. Although Sheay denied these allegations, his wife admitted that in order to prevent any further dispute between her husband and Kalu over the loads, she had used medicine to incapacitate Kalu's knees so that he could not bring any more loads for dispatch. Despite his denial of Kumbio's allegations and his maintenance that he was ignorant of his wife's action, the district commissioner sentenced Sheay to three months' hard labor for political offenses. NAG ADM 61/4/1, Lawra District Civil Record Book, 7 October 1909.

41 NAG ADM 61/5/4, Lawra District Complaint Book, 28–31 January 1922.

42 NAG ADM 61/5/8, Informal Diary Lawra District, 1 July 1920. For years the inhabitants of Yagha and Punya had resisted the jurisdiction of the chief of Tugu, who was for administrative purposes their subdivisional chief. The resistance of these villages, and of a number of other settlements, had been for the most part passive, involving periodic migrations into Wa District in order to avoid government work allocated by the chief of Tugu, although in both 1914 and 1923 fighting did erupt. NAG ADM 56/1/163, Native Affairs, DC Lawra to PC NWP (Wa), 11 March 1914; and NAG ADM 56/1/301, Native Affairs, PC NP to CCNT, 26 April 1923.

43 NAG ADM 56/1/307, Native Affairs, DC Lawra to PC NP, 15 March 1923.

44 NAG ADM 61/4/1, Lawra District Civil Record Book, *Rex vs.* Madugu, 11 July 1910. The complaint was later heard as a criminal matter, contrary to Sec. 388 GC 1892.

45 NAG ADM 61/5/3, Lawra District Complaint Book, 17 May 1915.
46 NAG ADM 61/5/4, Lawra District Complaint Book, 6 October 1919.
47 NAG ADM 61/5/11, Lawra District Record Book, 235.
48 Hutchinson 1996, 285.
49 NAG ADM 61/4/1, Lawra District Civil Record Book, Dagga *vs.* Iddrisu, 5 June 1909.
50 Tengan 2000, 65.
51 NAG ADM 61/5/8, Informal Diary Lawra District, 2 August 1918.
52 Ibid., 26 September 1918.
53 RAT ADM 145–6, Native Administration, DC Lawra to CNP, 26 November 1928: "Among the Dagati speaking people each clan has its own big oath and it has been their custom to swear on this oath, both parties doing so and the elders administering the oath taking the amount paid by both to swear the oath, a sacrifice is then made."
54 RAT ADM 4, Fetish and Witchcraft Practices and Native Customs, DC Lawra to CCNT, 31 January 1938. These observations were based as much on the officer's experience of the Dagomba as the LoDagaa. Noting that LoDagaa chiefs, unlike their counterparts in Dagbon, did occasionally resort to such methods, he added: "But they would not dare to make profit on the transaction. ... A guarantee of this (in Dagomba at least) is the wholesome awe in which *tindanas* are held by Chiefs." The different origins of chieftaincy in the relative areas made assumptions about Dagbon inapplicable to the LoDagaa.
55 Between 1935 and 1938 the Native Authority Courts raised £879, and £1,747 between 1945 and 1951. See RAT ADM 514, Annual Report Lawra-Tumu District 1937–38; RAT ADM 868, Native Courts 1947–54; RAT ADM 554, Annual Report North West Province 1951–52.
56 RAT ADM 342–3, Informal Diary Lawra District, July 1942.
57 NAG ADM 56/1/301, Native Affairs, Ag. DC Lawra to CCNT, 18 April 1935.
58 RAT ADM 455, "The Lobi Tingani," DC Lawra, August 1946. See also Der 1974, 53.
59 Evans 1983, 205.
60 RAT ADM 430, "Essay on the Peoples of North West Province," 1907.
61 Goody (1956, 102) noted: "The three main causes of armed conflict are said [to have been] women (*pobo*), the theft of pots left in the bush for the white ants (*kpo laar*) and the stealing of livestock (*dun zuune*)." Similarly, Bonnafé et al. identified the theft of women and cattle as the primary cause of armed conflict among the adjacent *Lobi* (Bonnafé, Fiéloux, and Kambou 1982). Finally, Evans noted that among the LoBirifor most disputes (no longer conducted through violent reprisals and counterreprisals) concerned male competition over women. As he observed: "Disputes among the LoBirifor appear to most frequently arise as a

consequence of intense competition between men to secure wives. Although the system of arranged marriage is well defined, marriage by capture or elopement persists" (1983, 42–3). See Chapter 7 for further discussion these issues.

62 Just how prevalent violence was in precolonial times is a subject of conjecture. Early observers commented incessantly upon it, but they did not report specific instances or causes. It is possible that the bearing of arms, which was undoubtedly prevalent, was what prompted observers to such conclusions. Given the considerable insecurity that both preceded and accompanied colonial conquest, the visibility of arms might more often than not have been merely a show for deterrent effect. We do know, from both Ferguson's and Delafosse's reports, that both the Wala and the Koulango deliberately exaggerated the rebelliousness of the LoDagaa and *Lobi* respectively in order to substantiate their claims of nominal sovereignty over them. See Arhin 1974, 136–7; Delafosse 1908, 139. Colonial ethnographers often dealt only with a hypothetical reality and resorted to their own historical reconstructions when addressing these issues. For an interesting case in point see Johnson's (1981) discussion of Evans-Pritchard's work among the Nuer.

63 The jural approach to social theory in the West has both suppressed and obscured violence. Conflict is endemic to all societies. Differences of a cultural order arise in how conflicts are defined and settled. Violence is merely one form through which conflict may manifest itself. As Bohannan noted: "Society is impossible without regulated sexuality: the degree of regulation differs among societies. But total repression leads to extinction; total lack of repression also leads to extinction. Total repression of [violent] conflict leads to anarchy just as surely as does total conflict" (1967a, xi).

64 Instead of seeing the lack of authority as the cause of violence, it is perhaps more appropriate to invert this perspective and argue that the social use of violence precluded the existence of authority structures. Or, as the authors of a detailed examination of the nature and uses of violence among the *Lobi* have argued: "Armed conflict is the political manifestation of the general contradiction between the strong socialization of the fundamental economic units and their clear independence at all levels. The principal direction of Lobi social relations stresses this contradiction" (Bonnafé, Fiéloux, and Kambou 1982, 157).

65 Their campaign was even more ruthless, but it was less successful. This was partly because the attempt at suppression coincided with the imposition of unpopular policies of taxation and military conscription. Another reason for failure was the difference in terrain. It was considerably more difficult to carry out military operations in the densely treed and hilly topography west of the Black Volta than in the relatively open country of Lawra District to the east. Both armed conflict and open resistance to colonialism continued among the *Lobi* until the 1940s.

66 NAG ADM 61/5/8, Informal Diary Lawra District, 10 January 1921.
67 Ibid., 8 August 1920. The conflict involved disputes between Yagha/Malba, Malba/Lemka, Pelu/Dusa, Nako/Gwazin, and Sinkpa/Nako.
68 Ibid., 9 August 1920.
69 Ibid, 28 November 1917. Goody (1956, 103) reported that there had once been a "perpetual state of enmity which still lingers in the thoughts of old men" between Birifu (LoWiili), Malba (LoBirifor), and Tugu (DagaaWiili).
70 Ibid., 26 July 1919.
71 Ibid., 26 November 1917.
72 Goody 1956a, 102–3.
73 Labouret 1931, 375: "At first sight, agreements do not appear to play an important role in this society. However ... the very existence of these populations depends on contracts that, while not containing the same terms or consequences as European contracts, play no less critical a role. Their rules are not rigid, being always flexible enough to adapt to circumstances. ... Obligation flows from neither adherence to law nor obedience to a vague and mysterious 'collective will' ... but from economic needs."
74 Bonnafé, Fiéloux, and Kambou 1982, 93.
75 NAG ADM 56/1/50, Reports on Tours of Inspection North West Province, DC Black Volta District, April–May 1906.
76 Ibid., March 1907. This observation was made following hearings the officer had conducted again at Ulo. He stated that this was "perilously close to slave-dealing" and warned that in future anyone found involved would be dealt with severely.
77 These negotiations are discussed in detail in Chapter 7.
78 NAG ADM 61/5/3, Lawra District Complaint Book, 5, 7 February 1916.
79 DMC CRB vol. 4, J10/5/54 Mwintuo Kunkyeni *vs*. Buntariba.
80 Evans 1983, 119–20.
81 NAG ADM 61/4/1, Lawra District Civil Record Book, Kompailah *vs*. Naiver, 5 August 1908.
82 NAG ADM 61/4/1, Lawra District Civil Record Book, Depang *vs*. Quiniari, 5 August 1908.
83 NAG ADM 56/1/50, Reports on Tours of Inspection North West Province, DC Black Volta District, April–May 1906.
84 NAG ADM 61/5/8, Informal Diary Lawra District, 18 October 1918, 6 February 1919.
85 NAG ADM 61/5/4, Lawra District Complaint Book, 1 December 1923.
86 Precolonial gatherings such as funerals and markets had been relatively public occasions, but they were both relaxed and full of expression. See Goody 1962.
87 Cardinall 1920, 50–2.
88 RAT ADM 4, Fetish and Witchcraft Practices and Native Customs 1937–46, DC Lawra to CCNT, 31 January 1938.

89 Goody reported that in the 1950s the practice was no longer observed among the LoDagaa. Rattray came across it in the late 1920s, although he only made passing reference to in among the Lobi and was told that only those Dagaba who had come under Lobi influence practiced it (Goody 1962, 213; Rattray 1932, 422). However, Der noted that one of the major areas of conflict between Christians and pagans at Jirapa, a Dagaba area of settlement, was "mat-carrying." He described the practice in the following way: "A garment of the deceased was wrapped around a piece of ebony wood and placed in a mat. The mat was tied up, prayers said over it, and persons appointed to carry it round the funeral pyre. If the deceased were killed by another person, the mat, it is claimed, would force its way to the murderer and start battering him or her. ... Abuses appear to have crept into the custom. Innocent people appear to have been victim of the custom." He said that besides prohibiting Christians from engaging in such practices, the missionaries had also tried to eradicate the practice totally (1974, 53). Savonnet (1965) gave a description of the ceremony north of Lawra, in a settlement at Pora. Two decades later, Dabiré (1983, 258) stated that "the interrogation of the dead" was practiced only very sporadically on the other side of the Black Volta in the 1980s.

90 According to Goody, the LoDagaba thought that the *tengaan* protected all members of the same area against external curses or medicines, but within the same ritual area members could invite the malevolent intervention of a variety of noumenal agencies against members of the same matriclan through curses and medicines (1957, 85).

91 Goody 1962, 214.

92 Labouret 1931, 319; Goody 1962, 214.

93 Savonnet 1965, 119–24.

94 Goody 1962, 214–16.

95 For an interesting comparison of the differences between Builsa culture and colonial judicial procedures see Schott 1985, 50–1.

6: Missionary Medicine and Colonial Money

1 Naameh 1986, 328.

2 McCoy 1988, 129; Bekye 1991, 294.

3 Naameh 1986, 171; McCoy 1988, 91.

4 NAG ADM 56/1/301, Native Affairs, DC Lawra to CCNT, 8 September 1932. In his report to the chief commissioner, the district commissioner alleged that these gangs had also broken into stores of cowries secreted in buried pots, which were held up until then by all LoDagaa to be protected by the ancestors of their custodians. If this did occur, and was not merely incriminating propaganda, its motives may have been iconoclastic rather than criminal.

5 Ibid.

6 Dery 1979, 6–7. For similar observations, see Der 1983, 57; McCoy 1988, 45–6; Somé 1998, 48.

7 Der 1974, 54–5.

8 RAT ADM 424, "Comments on 'Interim Report' on the Peoples of the Nandom and Lambassie Divisions of the Lawra District," DC Mampong-Akwapim, 2 March 1933, 28–9. Somé (1998, 37–8) makes very much the same argument as Eyre-Smith does.

9 Der 1974, 54–5.

10 RAT ADM 247, Informal Diary Lawra District, August 1932.

11 McCoy 1988, 134.

12 McCoy 1988, 229.

13 *RA* 1934–35, 262.

14 Naameh 1986, 196.

15 *RA* 1934–35, 262.

16 When the number and enthusiasm of postulants waned after the rain incident, the missionaries attributed this to the work of the devil operating through elders, witches, polygamists, and chiefs. It was described as open warfare against the mission and its followers. *RA* 1933–34: 364; 1935–36: 232; 1936–37: 273; 1938–39: 151. The sense of persecution was totally out of proportion with any substantive evidence of menace, bother, and even vexation on the part of the alleged opposition.

17 Der 1983, 131–2

18 Der 1983, 58–60; Somé 1998, 46.

19 Der 1983, 135.

20 Somé 1998, 50.

21 *RA* 1932–33, 164.

22 *RA* 1933–34, 361; Somé 1998, 50, 52–3.

23 Naameh 1986, 179, 190–1, 196–7.

24 Bekye 1990, 281; Naameh 1986, 204.

25 Naameh 1986, 213.

26 Naameh 1986, 199, 205, 223, 245, 255.

27 See Table 7.

28 See Chapter 3.

29 *RA* 1939–45, 3.

30 *RA* 1951–52, 226.

31 *RA* 1953–54, 282–3.

32 These features were brought out even more clearly in a description of duties from the annual report of the Diocese of Bobo Dioulasso. In 1955 a list of the purposes of these groups concluded: "But the best part of this action is the 'policing of morality,' if one can put it that way." Quoted in Naameh 1986, 400.

33 Dery 1984, 3.

34 See this chapter's epigraph. The Catholic version of Poreku's travails admits to his zeal, but then claims that his intentions were purely religious. Even so, both McCoy and Archbishop Dery admitted that his actions were interpreted as political by the colonial administration. But if the political implications, even if wholly unintended, were so obvious to these political authorities, surely they must have been as apparent to the LoDagaa. Dery 1979, 7–10; McCoy 1988, 75–83.

35 *RA* 1929–30, 182; 1930–31, 204.

36 *RA* 1931–32, 147.

37 Ranger 1981, 265.

38 Ranger 1981, 271–5. "Adaptation" came much more slowly to the medical missions of Tanganyika, and there it caused some controversy between African personnel and foreign missionaries.

39 Goody 1972, 39.

40 See Comaroff and Comaroff 1997; Landau 1995; Vaughan 1991; Ranger 1981.

41 Dawson 1987, 85; Good 1991, 2.

42 Patterson 1981, 99.

43 Waddy 1957, 180; Patterson 1981, 4.

44 The advent of colonial administration had coincided with the arrival of cerebrospinal meningitis. Due to upheavals associated with colonial rule in northern Nigeria, where the disease had been endemic, the first known African epidemic erupted, spreading across the savanna until it reached the Black Volta, and especially Lawra District, in 1906. Colonial rule also facilitated the spread of influenza from the coast to the interior through its transportation network. Regarding trypanosomiasis and onchocerciasis, an ignorant, poorly equipped, and indifferent administration was certainly responsible for allowing these diseases to spread unchecked. Patterson 1984, 14–15; 1983, 501; 1981, 47; 1978, 109.

45 Patterson 1981, 6; Dummett 1993, 226.

46 Patterson 1981, 25.

47 McCoy 1988, 58.

48 McCoy 1988, 55–8; 1979, 31.

49 Germain 1937, 83; Goody 1975, 102; McCoy 1988, 56–9.

50 McCoy 1988, 56–7.

51 Goody 1975, 102.

52 McCoy 1988, 59.

53 Naameh 1986, 119.

54 Goody 1972, 39.

55 Goody 1972, 97–9.

56 Goody 1972, White *Bagre* 4198–200, Black *Bagre* 5286–97.

57 Der 1983, 288.

58 McCoy 1988, 87–8, 113, 118, 122–4; Somé 1998, 41.
59 NAG ADM 61/5/8, Informal Diary Lawra District, 30 May 1918.
60 Goody 1962.
61 Gray 1990, 67.
62 McCoy 1988, 95, 139.
63 See Naameh 1986, 195.
64 Kusiele 1973, 23, 31.
65 Somé 1998, 41. He noted that they worked "to save bodies before souls."
66 Dery 1979, 8.
67 Such as brandy, emetine, and caffeine. See above.
68 McCoy 1988, 98.
69 Germain 1937, 86–7.
70 RAT 301, Informal Diary Lawra-Tumu District, July 1939.
71 RAT 514, Annual Report Lawra-Tumu District 1937–38.
72 Der 1983, 127.
73 McCoy 1988, 137.
74 Der 1983, 245.
75 Dabiré 1983, 263.
76 Somé 1998, 51–2.
77 Kuukure 1985, 160.
78 Goody 1962, 400.
79 Kusiele 1973, 49.
80 Kuukure 1985, 163; Der 1983, 255.
81 Somé 1998, 53.
82 Der 1983, 62–4, 65; Somé 1998, 33, 52.
83 Bongvlaa 1979, 68. See also Somé 1998, 33.
84 Somé 1998, 51.
85 See RAT ADM 455, "The Lobi Tingani," DC Lawra, 1946; Goody 1956a, 104; 1957, 88; Evans 1983, 200–4.
86 NAG ADM 61/5/1, Lawra District Record Book, 429.
87 Binger, 1892, vol. 1, 372; Goody 1956a, 11.
88 Writing about conditions in Burkina Faso up until independence, Boutillier also noted two spheres of exchange, with cowries used for local products and rituals, and colonial money used for imported products and taxes (1993, 251).
89 NAG ADM 61/5/8, Informal Diary Lawra District, 17 May 1917.
90 Ibid., 8 May 1917.
91 Ibid., 2 April 1918, 6 August 1918.
92 NAG ADM 61/5/6, Informal Diary Lawra District, 23 August 1918. In an informal census of foreign traders at Kunyukuo, 449 were counted in 54 compounds; of these, 200 were Hausa, 131 Bambara and Dioula, 43 Zabarima, 41 Mossi, and the rest unclassified.

93 NAG ADM 61/5/8, Informal Diary Lawra District, 6 August 1918.
94 Ibid., 7 November 1919–1 January 1920.
95 Ibid., 7 November 1919.
96 Boutillier 1993, 254–5, 258.
97 RAT ADM 514, Annual Report Lawra-Tumu District 1937–38, Appendices.
98 Hinds 1947, 1,429–31.
99 RAT ADM 272, Informal Diary Lawra-Tumu District, August 1937.
100 Hinds 1947.
101 NAG ADM 61/5/8, Informal Diary Lawra District, 15 June 1918.
102 RAT ADM 168, Annual Report Lawra District 1928–29.
103 Somda 1993, 242.
104 RAT ADM 502, Annual Report Wa District 1946–47.
105 Hill 1970b, 139 (note 4).
106 RAT ADM 502, Annual Report Wa District 1946–47.
107 Gregory 1996, 197, 214.
108 Gregory 1996, 203, 208–11. See also Comaroff and Comaroff (1997, 179) on the importance of the aesthetic values of money.
109 Hinds 1947, 1,430. The Zambo Naa recounted to me the following illustration of the economic complexities that had preserved the cowry for so long into the last century. In 1940: £1 = 20,000 cowries; 1 cow = £1; but, 20,000 cowries = 4 cows.
110 Comaroff and Comaroff 1997, 174, 194.
111 Piot 1999, 62.
112 The LoDagaa did not embrace the colonial economy in the same way as they did colonial courts simply because the former offered them nothing they needed and much that they rightly feared, such as inflation, the breakdown of social boundaries, and the diminution of generational authority within households.
113 RAT ADM 342–3, Informal Diary Lawra District, April 1942.
114 Ibid., December 1942.
115 NAG ADM 61/5/4, Lawra District Complaint Book, 22 November 1922.
116 Evans 1983, 226.
117 Rattray 1932, 439.
118 Goody 1956a, 49, 51; 1969, 55.
119 Hagaman 1977, 101.
120 Rattray 1932, 414; RAT ADM 292–3, Record of Native Law and Custom, "Marriage Laws of the Dagarti Tribes Resident in the Lawra Federation Native Authority Area," DC Lawra, 1938.
121 Goody, 1956, 28.
122 For a description of iron smelting, mainly from a technical perspective, see Pole 1974.
123 Goody 1962, 204–5.

124 Goody 1962, 301–3.

125 Household wealth, which was invested in storable forms of wealth such as cows and cowries, was only partly the result of surplus production. Surplus production was insufficient to meet conjugal payments on its own. "The difference, of course, is made up by the circulation of goods through other bridewealth transactions; the cattle brought in when a young girl marries are sent out again for her brother's bride." Goody 1962, 302.

126 Rattray 1932, 415.

127 Goody 1956a, 50.

128 Goody 1962, 302. Here he would have had to wait until he inherited from the corporate group in order to obtain further wives, or else, informally solicit the support of his mother's brother.

129 Goody 1962, 222.

130 In many respects this resembled the situation of authority through control over the means of reproduction analyzed by Meillassoux. However, this dependence was also reciprocal – elders depended on the labor of younger members. Meillassoux 1972. Although admitting to the applicability of Meillassoux's analysis to the Sisala, Mendonsa argued that this perspective overemphasized control over conjugal payments at the expense of other sources of authority managed by elders, especially access to noumenal agencies (1982, 169, 202–7). However, conjugal payments among the Sisala were relatively small compared to those among the LoDagaa. The exclusive nature of cows and cowries to the internal LoDagaa economy meant that younger men were less dependent on elders than on the system of circulation. This system was perpetuated directly not by a man's elders but rather by his wife's lineage, as it was the recipients of payments who preferred cowries.

131 Their role as a social currency was extended by their use in secondary conjugal payments, even among the Dagaba. Although cattle did not constitute a direct medium of payment, the Dagaba often used them to acquire the cowries necessary for these payments. Hill 1970b, 139–40.

132 NAG ADM 61/5/8, Informal Diary Lawra District, 9 April 1918.

133 Ibid., 8 January 1919.

134 Goody 1956a, 29.

135 Boutillier 1993, 255–6.

136 Hill 1970b, 83–7.

137 Goody 1956, 29; Hill 1970, 135 (table 5.23).

138 Père 1988, 375.

139 For a discussion of these issues, see Benoit, Levi, and Pilon 1986, 43.

140 Goody 1962, 110, 210, 238, 385, 411; 1956, 76.

141 Goody 1962, 408.

142 Lentz 1994b, 155–6, 158–60.

143 Hutchinson 1996, 98.

144 Evans 1983, 227–8. It is possible that the LoBirifor of Kalba, relatively recent immigrants to that area and more isolated than other LoDagaa congeries farther north, never had the same reserves as in the less isolated, longer-standing, less migratory settlements of Lawra District. (As always, the difficulty in studying the cowry phenomenon is that there is no clear indication as to how they entered economies in the first place.) Although the frequency of cowry payments cannot be ascertained, the answer to the question is not particularly important given that payments were "demand insensitive" (Goody 1969, 55). Cowries stabilized payments against inflation even when not used, by acting as the unit of account. It is clear that cash had not displaced the cowry by the mid-1980s, and was still used merely as a substitute. The social significance of cowries was largely unscathed by the increasing use of cash, remaining the preferred medium of payment demanded by recipients.

145 Kpiebaya 1990c, 17; Tengan 1990c, 75.

146 Deri 1980, 12.

147 See discussion in Chapter 8.

148 DMC CRB vol. 14, N8/79 Bewaa Kuufam *vs.* Zamaduor Kpibagr.

149 Ibid.

150 Kofi and Hansen 1983, 12; Crisp 1984, 174.

151 DMC CRB vol. 15, L11/81 Nua Dagarti *vs.* Jaatoe Dagarti. See also Chapter 8.

152 Lentz (1994c, 80) suggested that in the 1930s elders increased the value of conjugal payments, but a close reading of the Court Record Books shows no such increase, and several LoDagaa authors have argued that payments did not increase. However, she is correct in arguing that the high cost of payments was a means by which elders exercised authority over young men.

153 Père 1988, 374. The devaluation of the CFA franc in 1994 perhaps made these informants question this trajectory, for reasons that would have been well understood by their Ghanaian neighbors for several decades due to the rapid decline in the value of the cedi.

154 If a household that received one set of payments in cash immediately realized the value of the payments by acquiring a wife, there were few problems. But to delay in the use of cash payments for any period of time could have easily resulted in substantial losses under inflationary conditions. Similarly, receiving cowries for a daughter and subsequently using the same payments to acquire a wife was potentially dangerous if the first union was dissolved and the woman's former husband demanded repayment in cowries – as was Nua's misfortune. For example, in 1982 Buafiruire demanded the return of conjugal payments from his former father-in-law, Kyongooro, now that the woman had entered into another

union. But Buafiruire demanded repayment in the same medium as he had used. Kyongooro explained to the court, to no avail, that he was unable to find a man to take his daughter as a wife who could also pay in cowries. DMC CRB vol. 15, L2/82 Buafiriure Kyemuo *vs.* Kyongooro Bayuo. A year later, a lorry driver working in Techiman informed the court that he had had to leave work for three months in order to go around exchanging cash for cowries until he was able to acquire the 20,000 cowries needed. DMC CRB vol. 16, L20/83 Isaac Baba Dervuu *vs.* Bokurah Chunnoh and Essie Delle.

155 See Evans 1985, 35–8.

156 Guha 1997, 194. The term "dead labour" comes from Marx: "Capital is dead labour which, vampire-like, lives only by sucking living labour, and lives the more labour it sucks."

157 Ewald 1988, 216.

158 On the varied and complex relationship between evangelism and writing elsewhere in Africa see, for example, Probst 1989; Comaroff and Comaroff 1991; Landau 1995.

7: Women, Marriage, and Adultery

1 Fortes 1937, 19.

2 The terms adultery and seduction were used rather indiscriminately in the court records. Which term was used depended on the framing of claims by clerks as well as which record book, civil or criminal, was in use at the time. The term adultery has been used here to refer to the indigenous idea of transgressing the ancestors. The term seduction has been used to refer to the idea of violating the interests of husbands. The former infraction resulted in sacrificial expiation, the latter in judicial compensation.

3 Several legal anthropologists interested in the rights of women have made similar observations. See Baerends 1990, 36–8; Armstrong et al. 1993, 324–7, 361–3; Wanitzek 1998, 121–5. For a more general discussion of the privileging of narrative over practice, see Comaroff and Comaroff 1997, 48–50.

4 Gold Coast 1908, 9.

5 RAT ADM 430, "Essay on the Peoples of the North West Province," PC NWP, 1907; Homer, *Odyssey*, 1, 216.

6 See Hawkins, forthcoming.

7 Goody 1962, 94, 108. Among the LoDagaa conjugal payments, and not conjugal status, determined the descent of a child.

8 Gold Coast 1908, 9.

9 RAT ADM 514, Annual Report Lawra District 1937–38.

10 NAG ADM 61/4/2, Lawra District Civil Record Book, quoted in PC NWP to DC Lawra, 12 October 1911.

11 Labouret 1920; Rattray 1932; NAG ADM 292–3, Record of Native Law and Custom, "Marriage Laws of the Lobi/Dagarti Natives Resident in the Lawra Native Area," 1938; NAG ADM 61/5/11, Lawra District Record Book, 14 July 1944; Goody 1956a, 1962, 1969; Somé 1968; Kpoda 1977; Hagaman 1977; Deri 1980; Evans 1983; Dabiré 1983, Kuukure 1985; Dery 1987; Tengan 1990d; Kpiebaya 1990.

12 See Hawkins, forthcoming.

13 In order to impose coherence on their material, they exhibited a pronounced methodological adherence to the principle of jural analysis – the reduction of social practices to sets of rules. See references to the work of Bourdieu and Comaroff in the Introduction.

14 Labouret 1931, 256. Emphasis mine.

15 Fortes 1937, 1. Three generations later, Wanitzek made much the same comment independently about Builsa (another of the radically decentralized societies of northern Ghana) conjugal practices: "It is not possible to identify any one of these steps as the decisive event in the formation of marriage. Any of them may be missing, and the union can still be considered a marriage. On the other hand, most or even all of them may have been performed, and yet it can be denied that there is a marriage" (1998, 135).

16 Fortes 1949, 84–7. Comaroff made a very similar point in his discussion of this passage (1980a, 20). Schneider noted the same problem in Evans-Pritchard's analysis of Nuer marital instability: "Confusion arises first because nowhere is it made clear that there is at times an implicit distinction between conjugal relations and certain of the jural relations which arise out of legal marriage [conjugal payments]. That is, the physical separation of the legally wedded couple does not in itself constitute a termination of the legal bonds between them or the legal bonds which follow from their union, particularly with respect to the offspring of the woman. Indeed ... conjugal relations are not nearly so stable as the jural relations of marriage. There is a clear difference here, so that the term 'stable marriage' cannot be held to describe jural bonds and conjugal bonds equally" (1953, 55). Much of the confusion seems to have arisen out of the use of the term marriage to describe those rights, especially the custody of children, which can survive conjugal dissolution. To attribute those rights to "legal marriage" in the face of *de facto* conjugal dissolution seems to rest on what Comaroff referred to as "an analytical artifice" constructed out of the concepts of Western jurisprudence (1980a, 31).

17 There are two minor but very important exceptions to this picture. The first was the virtual disappearance of labor provided by a man for his prospective wife's household. With the increasing demands imposed on the labor supply during the colonial period and the gradual infiltration of cash as a form of disembodied labor, these obligations were gradually ignored or commuted into other forms of

payment. The second important change was the disappearance of arms as an important part of the repertoire of strategies that were once an integral part of the protection of household interests in conjugal unions.

18 For the first two decades of the century I have relied on evidence gleaned from various colonial reports and records. From the 1920s to the 1990s we have a series of accounts by different observers expressly about marriage. See note 11 above.

19 The soundness of this argument is clearly supported by the analysis of court documents presented in this and the next chapter. This evidence is so thoroughly dispersed and fragmentary that to write directly from these sources would be an unnecessary exercise in archival archaeology, especially when congruent ethnographic accounts already exist. Where this archival evidence is relevant to the descriptions discussed here is in influencing the re-presentation of these accounts that I have made in this and the following chapter.

20 NAG ADM 51/1/301, Native Affairs, "Report on Dagarti Civil Law," PC NWP, 1908; Goody 1962, 196. See also Rouville 1987, 203.

21 These were not the only terms, but they were the most generic. Rattray 1932, 54, 91; Goody 1956a, 55; Somé 1968, 11; Dabiré 1983; Kuukure 1985, 30; Tengan 1990d, 10–12; Kpiebaya 1990, 5–10.

22 Dery 1987, 51–2; Kpiebaya 1990, 10; Bekye 1985, 5–6; Tengan 1990d, 10–12. On the significance of the variety of conjugal unions in the face of homogenous categorization, see Guyer 1994, 234; Pilon 1994, 131–47.

23 Dery 1987, 28; Kuukure 1985, 30. According to Kuukure, the equivalent term for women, *kul sir*, meant "to marry," but Dabiré (1983, 156) translated it literally as "goes to a man." It is significant that like the Kpelle, the LoDagaa made no distinction between words for woman and wife. Bledsoe 1980, 7.

24 Rattray 1932, 414–16, 439–40; Goody, 1957, 48–56.

25 Fortes 1937, 18.

26 The terms abduction and elopment occur in the court records interchangeably. They are translations of various indigenous terms from *de pog*, to take a woman/wife, to *pog nyogra*, to seize or capture a woman/wife.

27 Fiéloux, 1980, 104–6.

28 Hagaman 1977, 222.

29 Fortes 1937, 19.

30 Fiéloux 1980, 106.

31 Fiéloux 1980, 105. Among the LoBirifor of Ghana, Hagaman wrote in the 1970s that "there is much competition between villages for 'stealing wives,' and just recently a 'tradition' as begun of erecting tall poles in the village for each successful theft." Hagaman 1977, 230. Writing of the "Lobi Dagara," a designation

which included both LoDagaa and *Lobi* congeries, Benoit found that "abduction is an increasingly common type of marriage." Here, as among the LoBirifor, the former threat of retaliatory action had been removed by the imposition of colonial rule. Benoit added at the end of his discussion of marriage by abduction that "it is worth bearing in mind these remarks when using and understanding the term marriage." Benoit et al. 1986, 52–61. Both Père and Rouville also noted that abduction of a wife had become easier among the neighboring *Lobi* as a result of conditions established during colonial rule. Père 1988, 290; Rouville 1987, 210.

32 NAG ADM 61/4/1, Lawra District Civil Record Book, *Rex vs.* Zanya 18 July 1913.

33 Barbara Cooper also used the term marital career to refer to the lives of Hausa women in Niger. She also noted that because of persistent dislocations, their histories resembled "geosocial maps." Cooper 1997, 62–9.

34 Goody 1956a, 53.

35 Hagaman 1977, 137, 214–15.

36 Goody 1956a, 52–3.

37 Goody 1962, 252.

38 Goody 1962, 54. He continued: "But from the standpoint of the husband and his group, this second transfer of property demanded by the bride's kin is conceptualised as an acquisition of further rights. That these rights are of little practical importance is beside the point ... but to the husband's household they appear as a material extension of interest." This apparent anomaly appears to me to be the product of a jurally bound language of description that translates indigenous interests, expectations, and motivations as rights, even though these are more appropriately rendered as "interests." Goody resorted to this less specific term at this point in his analysis because, having already attributed jural implications to earlier payments, there remained no more rights to be transferred *in* or *over* a woman. This payment is only adequately understood as the fulfillment of an aspect of the affinal debt. Its satisfaction at this point served to resolve that relationship and, thereby, potentially strengthen the conjugal union by removing the threat of affinal disruption.

39 Compare Goody 1956a, 52–3 with Goody 1962, 168–72, 309–11, 349–54. This was not because household affairs were less rulelike than interhousehold relations – indeed, if anything, they were more so.

40 Goody 1962, 168–72, 309–11, 349–54.

41 Moore 1986, 39–41.

42 Rattray 1932, 414; Deri 1980, 6.

43 NAG ADM 61/5/4, Lawra District Complaint Book, Nabayi Dagarti *vs.* Bonye and Andibare Dagarti, 24 July 1930.

44 See Tables 9 and 10.
45 Goody 1969, 54.
46 The first substantial payment was a large number of cowries "equal to that given for the girl's mother" (Goody 1956a, 49; Somé 1969, 22–3). This formula was not merely normative, but took concrete form in amounts presented or at least reported as having been eventually received. Goody 1969, 54–61. Whatever slight variations might have existed, they do not appear to have been disputed in the early years of colonialism or at any time since. This is evident from a reading of Court Record Books from 1954–1984.
47 Labouret 1920, 270.
48 Goody 1969, 54–61.
49 These services were performed only in the case of a woman's first union and only until the woman's residence with the man had become established – a point at which her household might have had some difficulty in withdrawing her from the union. Goody 1956a, 51.
50 Goody 1956a, 48: "If the girl elopes without loud protest, she will be called a bitch. Her sexuality will not have been alienated to outsiders in the particular manner which the social structure demands; she has given herself freely to the first comer, like an animal on heat."
51 Goody 1956a, 102.
52 Labouret 1920, 274.
53 See Radcliffe-Brown 1950, 46, 53.
54 Comaroff 1980a, 35–6.
55 Stocking 1987, 197–208; Barkan 1995, 62–3.
56 Barkan 1995, 85–6.
57 See Goody 1956a, 53.
58 NAG ADM 61/4/1, Lawra District Court Record Book, 24 May 1909.
59 NAG ADM 61/5/11, Lawra District Record Book, 235–7. "This tribunal has been exceedingly well conducted, it has been of great assistance, and there have been very few appeals from it. The etiquette is modelled on that of the District Commissioner's court." The powers of individual tribunals were not defined, but the district tribunal was permitted to impose fines of up to £5 and, in the case of "political offenders," sentences of four months.
60 NAG ADM 56/1/163, Lawra Native Affairs 1914–17, DC Lawra to Ag. PC NWP 15 October 1915.
61 Ibid., PC NWP to DC Lawra 19 October 1915.
62 Ibid., DC Lawra to PC NWP, 23 October 1915; PC NWP to DC Lawra, 25 October 1915.
63 Gold Coast 1951, 14.
64 NAG ADM 61/5/8, Informal Diary Lawra District, 26 September 1918.

65 Although officers were only involved with a small proportion of conjugal disputes after 1917, when the bulk of litigation began to be heard by the chiefs' tribunals, their influence continued to be felt by example. During the period of indirect rule, that influence waned as officers were content to leave the Native Authority Courts in charge of regulating "native" matters. But officers continued to be responsible for supervising these courts, and, therefore, even though they rarely intervened, their tacit approval of the decisions applied by the chiefs was an implicit encouragement. This conclusion is substantiated by the controversy that developed between the chiefs and the missionaries over the issue of the autonomy of women in LoDagaa society that is discussed below.

66 RAT ADM 145–6, Native Administration 1928–31, CNP to DC's NP, 15 August 1928.

67 NAG ADM 61/4/2, Lawra District Civil Record Book, quoted in PC NWP to DC Lawra, 12 October 1911.

68 RAT ADM 168, Annual Report Lawra District 1928–29.

69 Bush 1999, 92.

70 NAG ADM 61/5/8, Informal Diary Lawra District, 18 October 1918.

71 Underwood 1985, 119.

72 Bush 1999, 51, 81–2.

73 Bush 1999, 88.

74 Bush 1999, 89–92.

75 NAG ADM 61/4/2, Lawra District Civil Record Book, Ag. Sec. NA to Ag. CCNT, quoted in PC NP to DC Lawra, 12 October 1911.

76 Cardinall 1920, 79.

77 Cardinall 1920, 76–7.

78 Cardinall 1920, 79–80.

79 *RA* 1930–31, 195.

80 Coombes 1994, 13.

81 RAT ADM 3, Female Excision (Circumcision) 1930–33, quoted in CNP to CCNT, 10 June 1930. It is revealing that these comments all refer to male attitudes. However, in no way was it a male practice. As Hagaman discovered: "For the LoBirifor, men have nothing to do with excision; the decision for having the operation is made by the girl's grandmother, the mother of her father, and the operation is always performed by a woman practitioner." Hagaman 1977, 134.

82 Ibid., DC Kusasi quoted in CNP to CCNT, 10 June 1930.

83 Ibid., Ast. Med. Dir. to CCNT, 2 June 1931. Just how transparent this apparent toleration was can be seen in the distasteful and outlandish prejudices that informed such attitudes. This same officer argued that Jewish practices were equally "dirty": "The Rabbi even seizes the foreskin between his teeth."

84 RAT ADM 259, Rules Made under Section 17 of Native Authority Ordinance,

Sec. of State for the Colonies to Gov. GC, 17 August 1936. The matter had arisen following a question in the House of Commons by the Liberal MP Eleanor Rathbone on 22 July 1936. The Secretary of State appears to have been less than completely earnest about the whole question, stating that "the extent and evil of the pressure which may be exercised on African girls to marry against their will are capable of exaggeration." The questionnaire asked whether physical coercion was involved and, if it was, whether women were free to bring cases to the notice of officers, what actions officers took, and whether such steps were sufficient to prevent serious abuses or whether further measures were necessary. See also Great Britain 1938.

85 Ibid., CCNT to Col. Sec., 21 October 1936.

86 RAT ADM 514, Annual Report Lawra-Tumu District 1937–38.

87 RAT ADM 247, Informal Diary Lawra-Tumu District, March 1937.

88 See below for a fuller discussion of these developments.

89 RAT ADM 247, Informal Diary Lawra-Tumu District, April 1937.

90 RAT ADM 301, Informal Diary Lawra-Tumu District, January 1938. Further inquiry revealed that it was only the second of the two wives whom the missionaries had instructed to leave the husband, and that the husband had driven away his first wife in annoyance as the two were sisters. When the missionaries argued that the first wife was not obliged to return to her husband, the district commissioner replied that in that case she could not enter into another union with a Christian husband. "We both quoted 1 Corinthians, ch. 7, which they interpret quite differently from me." As far as the missionaries were concerned, a pagan union did not constitute marriage.

91 Ibid., February 1938. "Called the girl, and explained that as she herself had chosen the Christian religion, unforced, she had no right to throw it over for a love affair. Told the Chief that the return of dowry, usual in such cases, would not settle the matter in this case as the unfortunate, legitimate husband was debarred from marrying again. Told the girl to return to her father's house as she refused to return to her husband. Probably she will live a spinster's life."

92 Ibid., May 1938.

93 RAT ADM 342–3, Informal Diary Lawra District, November 1942.

94 RAT ADM 292–3, Record of Native Law and Custom, CCNT to DC Lawra, 29 March 1938.

95 RAT ADM 514, Annual Report Lawra District 1937–38, "Appendix B: Lawra Federation Conference," March 1938.

96 RAT ADM 342–3, Informal Diary Lawra District, April 1944.

97 Ibid., July 1944. That is to say there was no procedure for "divorce."

98 From August 1907 to May 1908; an unspecified period between June 1908 to June 1909; February 1911 to June 1911; and finally August 1913 to May 1914. All a decade before becoming chief commissioner in 1924.

99 RAT ADM 7, Native Administration 1918–28, CCNT to Col. Sec. Accra, 21 July 1928. See also Wilks 1989, 166.

100 NAG ADM 61/5/3, Lawra District Complaint Book, 11 November 1912. Most officers during the period of direct rule had tended to assume, incorrectly, that the woman's household was liable for the return of conjugal payments. Although they were not responsible for returning payments to a former husband, the latter was entitled to recompense if the woman entered a subsequent union, but from her new husband *via* the woman's household.

101 NAG ADM 56/1/91, Laws and Customs of the Northern Territories, "Report on Dagarti Civil Law," PC NWP, 1908.

102 Gold Coast 1954, Native Authorities Ordinance 1 (Northern Territories) 1932; Native Courts Ordinance 31 (Northern Territories) 1935. The Lawra Confederacy Court "A" was made up of all three divisional chiefs, plus the chief of Lambussie (Sisala) and the Liman of Lawra, with each paramount chief alternating on a six month cycle as president. It had powers to impose fines of up to £50 in civil actions as well as "unlimited powers in cases relating to land and matrimonial causes." Hailey 1951, 270. The same limit applied to fines in criminal matters. Sentences for adults were limited to a period of six months, and twelve strokes of a whip for males under sixteen years of age. In each of the three divisions, "C" grade courts were gazetted, with power to impose fines of £10 and £5 in civil and criminal cases respectively, and sentences of one month or twelve strokes. Although chiefs were paid separate salaries for their judicial work, members of the three separate Native Authorities in Lawra, Jirapa, and Nandom received emoluments varying from £84 to £6 for chiefs and their councilors, while subchiefs received anywhere from £30 to £6. Hailey 1951, 266.

103 Staniland 1975, 103–4; Ladouceur 1979, chapter 3.

104 RAT ADM 7, Native Administration, "Report on the Native Authorities in the Northern Territories," Ag. CSP to CCNT, 20 July 1928.

105 In Lawra District district commissioners saw conjugal unions primarily as sexual relationships between men and women, not as interhousehold affairs. Officers were often baffled to discover that the party to a dispute they had presumed was a woman's husband was in fact only a household representative, often a brother. In terms of *Dagaare* kinship terminology, all members of the same household and generation referred to each other's wives as *i pog*, the same term by which her actual husband referred to her. See Somé 1968, 11–13: "Among the Dagari the standard term a man uses for this wife is *i pog*, 'my wife,' *pog* meaning woman as opposed to man, the possessive *i* being used to denote property. ... The term used by all brothers and sisters, both immediate and classificatory, to identify the wife of one of them is *i pog*."

106 Gold Coast 1930, 12; Rattray 1932, xxii; also quoted in RAT ADM 153,

"Memorandum on Native Authority in the Northern Territories," Ag. CCNT, 18 March 1931.

107 RAT ADM 153, "Memorandum on Native Authority in the Northern Territories," Ag. CCNT, 18 March 1931.

108 Gold Coast 1930, 12; RAT ADM 153, "Memorandum on Native Authority in the Northern Territories," Ag. CCNT, 18, March 1931.

109 Rattray 1932, xxii.

110 Staniland 1975, 194 (note 89).

111 RAT ADM 32, Commutation of Tribute, CCNT to Col. Sec. Accra, 5 November 1934. See section 15 of the Administrative Ordinance of 1902.

112 RAT ADM 292–3, Record of Native Law and Custom, CCNT to DCs NT, 17 June 1936.

113 RAT ADM 514, Annual Report Lawra-Tumu District 1937–38, Appendix "H."

114 Rattray 1932, xii.

115 He had, however, been extensively acquainted with Dagomba social practices, having compiled and drafted a political constitution of Dagbon with Duncan-Johnstone (Duncan-Johnstone and Blair 1932). Perhaps because of this experience of a historically hierarchical society, he omitted to consider the much different social organization of the LoDagaa.

116 *RA* 1937–38, 185.

117 Vansina 1986, 31.

118 Rorty 1991, 1.

119 RAT ADM 292–3, Record of Native Law and Custom, CCNT to DCs NT, 17 June 1936. In many ways it was also the nature of the questionnaire, and not just its incongruence with indigenous concerns, that created distortion – that is, because of the difficulty of conceptual translation. See Barnard and Good 1984, 119. The authors of this guide to anthropological research provided the following suggestions under the heading "divorce": "Logically, only those who are married can undergo divorce. As 'marriage' cannot be defined with precision, it follows that divorce, too, cannot be unequivocally defined. Further problems arise when marital alliances are contracted in stages, with both parties having a degree of choice at each stage, over whether to proceed further or back out. In such cases you will have to decide whether to reserve the term 'divorce' for the regularized fission of an hitherto fully-established union, or extend its meaning to cover breakdown at some or all of these intermediate stages. Whatever your decision, you will need to ascertain the circumstances under which divorce is permitted, whether it involves prescribed ceremonial, and if so, what form this takes and who participates in it."

120 Fortes 1937, 13–14.

121 RAT ADM 292–3, Record of Native Law and Custom Records, CCNT to Sec. Native Affairs Accra, 1 March 1937.

122 Fortes 1937, 1. The observations were described by their author as having been the product of a "practical *desideratum*"; they were not incorporated into his later published monograph, *The Web of Kinship among the Tallensi* (Fortes 1949), which was addressed to professional anthropologists, and not intended for administrative consumption. Labouret, who had combined the roles of administrator and ethnographer, qualified his observations of *Lobi* customary law similarly: "It is clear that this information does not cover all the cases that could reasonably be presented. It deals with the most common situations; moreover, it is not certain that fixed rules are observed in the identified populations. ... The rules that have been explained seem to be the result of developments triggered by European occupation; under the influence of administrative tribunals all local customs tend to be standardized and thus compromised, such that they no longer reflect indigenous institutions [practices]." Labouret 1931, 256.

123 Fortes 1936, 63. "And always," he added, "the District Commissioner, whether actually present or not, was one of the principal sanctions determining the outcome of events."

124 RAT ADM 514, Annual Report Lawra-Tumu District 1937–38, Appendix "H." Widows, not "divorcees," were covered in clay following the funeral of a husband. See Goody 1962, 186–90. Elsewhere, Goody referred to dissolution by such means as "divorce through death." Goody 1956a, 53–4.

125 RAT ADM 342–3, Informal Diary Lawra District, May 1944.

126 Ibid., July 1944. This observation had been made by an officer a generation before, not as a statement of practice, but as a moral criticism. See NAG ADM 61/5/3, Lawra District Complaint Book, 13 and 15 July 1916. When it appeared that his daughter's husband (a colonial employee) intended to take her south, the chief of Gengenkpe attempted to return the conjugal payments himself. The district commissioner refused to return the children to the chief, but allowed the woman to be withdrawn from the union. However, he was reticent about having done so and commented: "These people seem to think that they can have it both ways and get everything by returning the bridewealth."

127 NAG ADM 61/5/11, Lawra District Record Book, 14 July 1944, 394.

128 DMC CRB vol. 1, L31/12/56, Aamu Kwaku Dodoja *vs.* Aybaghi.

129 DMC CRB vol. 12, N1/74, Firimino Debzie *vs.* Vincent Baaluyel.

130 NAG ADM 61/4/1, Lawra District Civil Record Book, *Rex vs.* Bowo, 27 April 1908.

131 RAT ADM 169, Native Administration, DC Lawra to CCNT, 31 March 1931.

132 Labouret 1931, 378.

133 RAT ADM 169, Native Administration, DC Lawra to CCNT, 31 March 1931.

134 Labouret 1931, 286.

135 Goody 1956b, 286.

136 Goody 1956b, 292–3; 1962, 104–5.

137 Goody 1962, 391–2.

138 Goody 1962, 391–2.

139 Rattray 1932, 416.

140 Rattray 1932, 416. See also Goody 1962, 139; Labouret 1920, 280–3.

141 The existence of this relationship among the Oulé and Dagari led Labouret to remark: "The question that demands to be answered is whether this is a matter of tolerated concubinage with a married woman, or whether we are in the presence of a genuine union, in which case this would be an African form of polyandry" (1920, 281–2).

142 Goody 1962, 139.

143 Fortes 1949, 116.

144 Goody 1962, 392.

145 Fortes 1949, 117.

146 Mendonsa 1982, 89. Although both diagnosis and treatment had judicial and religious characteristics, the similarities were more apparent than real. Sisala problem solving was more medical than judicial, and more social than religious. Procedural similarities were often belied by the different solutions reached. The validity of such interpretations, religious or jural, is often based on analogy rather than correspondence. See Moore 1978, 17: "The conventional category 'law' (meaning rules enforceable by government) is a category of our own culture. When it is applied by anthropologists to societies that are very different in structure, what is being sought are analogous phenomena. Where there is no government, obviously the conventional procedural criterion used to identify law in our society does not exist." See also Janzen 1978, chapter 9. Using a similar approach to "problem solving" among the BaKongo, Janzen noted that, despite analogous features in both therapy and litigation, there were also features unique to each that made them distinct spheres of action.

147 NAG ADM 61/4/2, Lawra District Civil Record Book, Kock *vs.* Aukwaru, 4 June 1913.

148 Fortes 1937, 18.

149 See for example NAG ADM 61/4/2, Lawra District Civil Record Lawra, Wor *vs.* Keyli, 17 July 1912. Wor had taken Keyli's wife and sent the conjugal payments to her household to be returned to Keyli. The woman, Deybuo, remained with Wor for a year before returning to Keyli, after which he refused to return Wor's

conjugal payments, claiming that these represented "juju money because he had slept with my wife." Deybuo explained that she had only remained with Wor because her husband had not come to retrieve her, but eventually returned of her own volition. According to Deybuo, Keyli's 30s. (or thirty thousand cowries) did represent conjugal payments. The DC ordered that Keyli return only 10s. to Wor, the rest presumably being retained by the former as compensation. See also NAG ADM 61/5/3, Lawra District Complaint Book, 22 February 1916, 10 June 1916; NAG ADM 61/5/4, Lawra District Complaint Book, 20 February 1929. This latter complaint was against Kayani, the infamous Tugu Naa.

150 NAG ADM 61/5/1, Lawra District Record Book, "Satisfaction and Adultery Fees Customary in the Chiefs' Courts," 445. This table, although incomplete, not only recorded amounts totally incommensurate with indigenous norms, but also included political categories of persons: paramount chief, heir, subchief, headman, and young man. The correspondence between political status and fees – e.g., Nandom: from £2, two sheep, and six fowls for an offense against a chief to 3s., one sheep, and four fowls for a commoner – indicates that these amounts were compensatory and personal rather than sacrificial and household based.

151 RAT ADM 259, Rules Made under Section 17 of the Native Authority Ordinance 1934–51, Ag. DC Zuarungu to CCNT, 20 August 1936.

152 Fortes 1937, 18. See DMC CRB, vol. 15, N18/82, Beyuo Kunuware *vs.* Kpimeviel Auzore. The plaintiff's first witness argued that the woman had left the plaintiff without "permission" and stayed away for two years, which "had amounted to getting married." When challenged, he conceded that he did not know of any other man and admitted that "dowry" was not returnable until there was a new husband with whom the woman was living.

153 Fortes 1937, 19.

154 Fortes 1937, 20.

155 Jirapa Native Authority Court, Civil Record Book 1940–53; Criminal Record Book 1940–49. Lawra Native Authority Court, Civil Record Book 1947–53; Criminal Record Book 1946–53. These records, found in a disused Local Council office in Lawra, have been deposited in the District Court office in Lawra.

156 RAT ADM 554, Annual Report North West District 1950–51.

157 Jirapa Native Authority Court, Criminal Court Record Book, 10 February 1942.

158 Lawra Native Authority Court, Civil Record Book, 4 September 1953.

159 Lawra Native Authority Court, Criminal Record Book, 3 April 1950.

160 Jirapa Native Authority Court, Civil Record Book, 18 January 1951.

161 Jirapa Native Authority Court, Civil Record Book, 25 March 1952.

162 Gold Coast 1951, 16–18.

163 Jirapa Native Authority Court, Civil Record Book, 10 March 1952.

164 Jirapa Native Authority Court, Civil Record Book, 5 December 1952. It appears that the woman had left her previous husband and was residing with her own household when these events took place.

165 Violence, however, was often very near the surface in disputes between men over wives. See DMC CRB, vol. 6, J13/6/62, Yille Tampie *vs.* Naamwari Zambo. The defendant was fined £15 for adultery even though he denied the accusation. The woman, Kpiera, testified that the defendant had "seduced" her and added: "He denied that he ever seduced me and that if they [her husband's household] should joke with him there will be bloodshed before the case is settled."

166 Fortes 1937, 3.

167 DMC CRB, vol. 4, Jirapa Local Authority Court, W.M. Dakurah – Tizza Naa *vs.* Jirilanya Gbari, 8 December 1954.

168 Ibid.

169 Strategies for exercising male control over women within LoDagaa society operated obliquely, because of male attitudes toward women as minors. "Perceived by men as jural minors for much of their lives, women are not seen as being responsible for their actions to the same degree as men are. Thus, they are not held to be accountable within the processes of dispute into which men enter in their struggle to keep and maintain wives." Evans 1983, 118. Despite this male ideology of control over women, and especially wives, at the effective level of social practices, strategies were only deployed against rivals.

170 DMC CRB, vol. 2, Nandom Local Authority Court, Derkpal Zimuopare Naa *vs.* Yienibe Ko, 8 December 1955.

171 Ibid. Goody (1962, 104) reported that a woman who had committed adultery that remained unexpiated was referred to as *pogh sangna*, "spoiled woman."

172 DMC CRB, vol. 1, Lawra Local Authority Court, Noyuo Zambo *vs.* Dugo Tampie, 8 October 1958.

173 Ibid.

174 The roles were not separate in a polygynous society, so tensions did not just occur between men according to their social positions, but between the different roles a man assumed in different contexts. The conflict between men as rivals, and the contradictory attitude of the same men as husbands, produced ambivalent attitudes. See Hagaman 1977, 215: "For a man, it is a much greater disadvantage to lose an already resident wife than it is an advantage to add a new one. A man can have as many wives as will stay with him, and which his matrilineage can find brideprice for. He is extremely reluctant to lose any of them." However, these calculations were not in themselves sufficient to dissuade even a husband from acquiring more wives by such means and, therefore, becoming another

man's rival. The point is that the roles were interchangeable. Those who tended to construct male ideologies of control were also those most threatened by the possible abduction of their wives.

175 DMC CRB, vol. 7, L29/4/66, Bari Guo Naa *vs.* Machael Naaleryel Kulcha. As demonstrated above, "seduction" was not an indigenous offense, but an innovatory delict derived from colonial law. Yet its adoption by later courts gave it the status of a "customary law." Nor was the £50 fee that the plaintiff was claiming in any way commensurate with the cost of the sacrificial items necessary for the satisfaction of the indigenous offense upon which the concept of seduction was predicated.

176 Ibid.

177 As Goody observed: "The question of how often and for how long a woman should visit her parents is a difficult one; frequent visits indicate dissatisfaction and a long visit may easily widen into a permanent separation, for which the husband's only remedy is to demand the return of bridewealth. Essentially, marriage is virilocal" (1956a, 53). However, these limitations to the husband's strategic options were tied to two considerations. The first was his wealth; he may have been able to acquire another wife without demanding the return of conjugal payments during the period that the other union was effectively suspended. The second was the lack of any wider social agency, besides the affinal relationship, through which to demand the return of his wife. In this case, and at this time, the plaintiff was constrained by neither consideration. As a chief he commanded the resources necessary to resist the need to reclaim the conjugal payments, and he had recourse to the courts to remedy the situation.

When a woman returned to her household, she did so not as another man's wife, but as a daughter of that household. The statement that "marriage" was virilocal referred to the contextual (uxorial) status of a woman, which shifted with the place of her residence. From Machael's perspective his actions had not been adulterous according to the indigenous notion of such action, as he had taken the woman as a wife, and so had not merely had sexual relations with her. Fortes explained that despite the adoption of seduction as an offense, the Tallensi in the 1930s still differentiated between adultery and the practice of "marrying another man's wife" (1937, 18). The defendant in this case was insisting on the same differentiation, although he acknowledged that the plaintiff was entitled to the custody of the child by virtue of his presentation of conjugal payments. The defendant had tried to return these himself, but had been frustrated by the woman's parents' refusal to accept them: "I tried to dowry her through the parents but there was no way out for me. I went with farmers and all that was rejected."

178 DMC CRB vol. 7, L29/4/66, Bari Guo Naa *vs.* Machael Naaleryel Kulcha.

179 Ibid.

180 DMC CRB, vol. 10, L49/69, Kaakah Lobi *vs.* Dang Lobi. According to different accounts, the betrothal took place in either 1939 or 1945. Given the dates, it is not unlikely that Kaakah had betrothed the young girl as a means of acquiring a separation allowance while he was in the army.

181 Ibid.

182 Ibid.

183 Ibid. The following points were recorded in the magistrate's decision concerning "lawful Lobi marriage," derived from the court's cross-examination of witnesses: "1. Upon a man wishing to divorce his wife, the man has to kill a guinea fowl, get some grains and give [them] to his wife [if she is pregnant or still nursing a child]. The man gets his betweener to go with the woman to her parents to announce the divorce. ... 2. Upon a woman wishing to divorce her husband, she only goes to inform her parents and thereby stays with her parents until she gets married when the parents will claim the dowry and refund to the former husband. 3. Upon the failure of both the husband and wife to comply with these customary laws a divorce is not recognised." See also Goody 1956a, 55. Note the absence of such jural or legal formalism in the following official statement by the Lawra Confederacy Traditional Council regarding the dissolution of unions: "There is however no special ceremony which finally tells the world that the man and wife are divorced. The only sign is when the woman is re-married and the dowries refunded to the former husband." Deri 1980, 11.

184 Bourdieu 1977, 109.

185 DMC CRB, vol. 4, L19/2/59, Sata Dagarti *vs.* Lasi Lagos. The plaintiff had left his wife in Zambo while he was working in the Tarkwa gold mines. It was during his absence that Lasi had taken the woman and attempted to raise the necessary funds.

186 See DMC CRB, vol. 6, N15/5/61, Gyangban Nandom *vs.* Francis Nandom; J13/9/61, W.B. Yelpoe, Jirapa Naa *vs.* Buasi Dagarti; and DMC CRB, vol. 11, L5/72, W.M. Dakurah, Tizza Naa *vs.* Guoduri Dagarti. The latter award was the monetary equivalent of fifty thousand cowries, one black goat, one donkey, two pieces of gold, one dog, one ram, twenty-one fowls, and ¢100 compensation for the detention of the plaintiff's wife.

187 DMC CRB, vol. 12, L6/73, Nigre Lawra *vs.* Albert Napeni.

188 Ibid. Regarding the claim for a dog among the other items, the court noted that "it has never been known or heard of in Dagare customs that dogs and cats are claimed for purifying a woman. Dogs are only used on occasions when formerly a man was believed to have killed with affrontry as a deed of daringness in war or in a battle but not in a case of seduction."

8: Postcolonial Litigation of Personal Identities

1 Kpiebaya 1984, 4. In a later version of this article he defined "courtship" as "normal" but argued that it was still not the preferred strategy for forming conjugal unions in the Nandom area (1990, 5–10).
2 Goody 1956a, 48–9.
3 Bekye 1985, 5–6.
4 Dery 1987, 36–7.
5 Jirapa Native Authority Court, Civil Record Book, 5 December 1952.
6 It was from this debate that the idea of capture had emerged in anthropological thinking about conjugal unions. McLennan had theorized, by what Stocking has called the "doctrine of survivals," that "symbolic forms in the present [e.g., ritual resistance] represent corresponding realities in the past." McLennan argued that ritual resistance was evidence of a marriage-by-capture, which had replaced polyandry – a state that had been created by the even earlier practice of female infanticide! Stocking 1987, 166–7, 316; Service 1985, 7–8. Whether Dery was conscious of these associations is not clear from his text, but Radcliffe-Brown, with whom he was familiar, had argued that ritual resistance such as "the pretence of taking the bride by force (the so-called 'capture' of the bride)" could only be explained in symbolic terms as the recognition of "family solidarity" that required the bride or her family to feign reluctance. Radcliffe-Brown 1950, 49. See also Goody 1956a, 49. If Dery was not familiar with McLennan's outlandish theories, he must have been aware of some other very negative connotations associated with elopement in order to have gone so far as to deny that it was a regular practice among the LoDagaa.
7 Dery 1987, 36–7.
8 Bekye 1985 [2], 5.
9 Dery 1987, 37.
10 Gold Coast 1954, Court Ordinance, 1951 (Revision), s. 107 cap. 4.
11 From a list I compiled of eighty paramount chiefs, subdivisional chiefs, and subchiefs in the 1980s, only eleven were literate. This list did not include less prominent subchiefs and headmen, of which there were well over another hundred, only one of whom was reported to be literate. For the most part these literate chiefs were former schoolteachers from the first generation of literate LoDagaa who had succeeded to "traditional" office over the previous thirty years. I had the impression that the new generation of illiterate chiefs resented the idea of literate chiefs because the administration tended to overlook the former in favor of dealings with the latter. The intermediary role assumed by literate chiefs distanced them from their illiterate colleagues.
12 Moore 1986, 170. She added: "When 'customary law' is treated as a set of

mandatory substantive rules enforced by a court rather than as a set of guideline norms ... a major re-interpretation is involved." See also Chanock 1985, 119. He made a similar observation concerning the operation of formal courts under colonial rule in southern Africa during the 1930s and 40s: "It should also be stressed that the kind of record-keeping required of the new courts itself contributed to the development of a rule/judgement system. ... Court clerks were told over and over again that their methods of keeping court books with the facts and judgement alone were defective and they must write down the facts of each case *plus the rule of customary law relied upon* plus the decision of the court. Thus the rules had to be made explicit, simplified, and made applicable."

13 Schott 1985, 162–8. He noted that under the Second Republic (1969–72) the prerogatives of the chiefs were restricted even more, to the point that "the chiefs had been divested of even this restricted jurisdiction in private matters and had been expressly forbidden to intercede even as arbitrators in marital disputes and other disputes." However, this situation improved again under the Third Republic. See Goldschmidt 1981, 184–5.

14 Mendonsa 1982, 49.

15 These formal occasions were gatherings where the chiefs, along with household elders, dressed in their robes and the relevant parties and bystanders assembled to listen to public airings of disputes. Solutions were arrived at after private discussion between chiefs and elders, during which pots of *pito* (millet beer) were usually drunk. My acquaintance with these meetings left the impression that they were forums for political rather than judicial discussions. Decisions often appeared to have been worked out before the dispute was heard in public. Compared to informal arbitration, these meetings were relatively infrequent. Almost all disputes were first heard by chiefs privately, and most never went any further. The purpose of these private consultations was often only for advice or notification.

16 Allott 1960, 96.

17 Allott 1960, 115.

18 Following the decision in DMC CRB, vol. 12, L63/73, Nigre Dagarti *vs.* Albert Napeni.

19 DMC CRB, vol. 16, L6/84, David Gaaru *vs.* Kori Ermileh.

20 Six thousand cedis was roughly half the annual salary of a schoolteacher at this time.

21 Not least of which was the fact that the plaintiff was a literate and nominal Christian, and gave his testimony in English.

22 Kpiebaya 1979, 17–19. He formulated the question in the following terms: "Today there are whole families, clans and villages that have become catholic. Is

there any significant change in the society as a whole which we can say is the result of christianity? Is there any newness in the Dagaare people? What is the degree of christian integration among the people of the North-West?" He answered his own question by saying that after only fifty years it was still too early to tell.

23 Kpiebaya 1979, 22–3.

24 RAT ADM 430, "Essay on the Peoples of the North West Province," PC NWP, 1907.

25 DMC CRB, vol. 7, L13/7/1966, Eribari Zambo *vs.* Tangan Zambo.

26 Evans 1983, 118–9.

27 Hagaman 1977, 101–2, 214.

28 Evans 1983, 118–9.

29 Radcliffe-Brown 1950, 12, 47.

30 Singer 1973, 80.

31 Goody 1962, 275–6.

32 Evans 1983, 119.

33 Tengan 1990d, 26–8.

34 Kpoda 1977, 41; Dery 1987, 41.

35 Kpiebaya 1990, 13. The term "exorbitant dowries" appeared in one of a series of articles that formed the basis of this pamphlet. See Kpiebaya 1985, 80. Here he wrote of "the ever increasing free unions in our society which are the result of exorbitant dowries these days."

36 Rattray 1932, 439.

37 Goody 1973, 3.

38 DMC CRB, vol. 12, N7/74, Victor Duuyeng *vs.* Aatuore Bombie.

39 Victor Hien, "Le mariage coutumier chez les Dagaris affronté au catholicisme et à la vie moderne," I.S.C.R., Abidjan (1969–70), 10; quoted in Kpoda 1977, 41. Note the shift from a legal to a religious reading here.

40 Kpoda 1977, 104.

41 Kuukure 1985, 30.

42 Kuukure 1985, 31. Dery, following the arguments of Radcliffe-Brown, insisted that "bridewealth" had never been considered as a form of purchase among the LoDagaa. Dery 1987, 44. Kpiebaya stated that "the bride-price is never seen traditionally as payments for the girl, but as an indemnity to her family" (1990, 11). The language, not to mention the ideas, are remarkably similar to Radcliffe-Brown's. See especially Radcliffe-Brown 1950, 50–3.

43 Tengan 1990d, 24. It should be noted that Tengan specified that the next payment conferred legal ownership of children, while yet another payment established "full rights of the husband over the wife."

44 Korbieh 1990, 48–9.

45 Tengan 1990c, 75.

46 Kuukure 1985, 175 (note 34). See also Kpiebaya 1990, 15: "The bridewealth gives value and worth to the girl and makes her a legally constituted wife and not just a girlfriend of the man, living an immoral life with him. It gives self respect to the woman." Earlier (Kpiebaya 1985, 8), the phrase "some cheap girl-friend" was used instead of "just a girlfriend."

47 Tengan 1990b, 64–5.

48 DMC CRB, vol. 7, L24/8/66, Taphang Kuunaa Ketuo *vs.* Urumaanu Zowuoh Bu.

49 Whitehead noted the same exclusion of women from litigation among the neighboring Kusasi, where "women are barely represented in 'woman' cases." These cases constituted the majority of litigation before the courts among the LoDagaa, just as they did among the Kusasi. Whitehead 1984, 187–8.

50 Payments are seen to be made *for* wives, and as representing the transfer of rights *in* or *over* women. In order to apply a jural analysis to conjugal payments Radcliffe-Brown claimed that "in certain circumstances a person may be treated as a thing," even though he later objected to the use of such a paradigm in economic interpretations. Radcliffe-Brown 1950, 12, 47. Goody used a similarly proprietorial language (rights *in uxorem* and *in genetricem*) in order to analyze the jural implications of payments among the LoWiili, even though he denied that these had connotations of purchase. Only because anthropologists posit the existence of rights are exchange equations possible. If rights were not elucidated, payments could not be explained in terms of their direction because they would lack an inverse.

51 Radcliffe-Brown attempted to refute any connotation of purchase by arguing that transfer of rights in consideration of payments was not complete or final as payments sometimes had to be returned if the union dissolved. Besides suggesting that these payments were symbolic (it was not specified whether this was in reference to content or meaning), he also offered "indemnity or compensation" as complementary interpretations. Radcliffe-Brown 1950, 50–2. Similarly, Goody remarked, with specific reference to the LoDagaa, that despite the common features of rights in things and rights in persons, "as in the case of many property transactions in non-European societies, the complete alienation implied by our concept of 'gift' or 'sale' is rarely involved." Goody 1962, 275–6. Mair (1969, 5) argued that "the payment does not make the wife her husband's property, or place her in a relationship of slave to him. ... A payment is not necessarily a price, and can be made in many transactions which are not commercial." These attempts to distance the idea of transfer of rights *in* and *over* women from any commercial sense are essentially only differences of degree, not of kind, and do not obviate

the inherently linear perspective of this language and its implicit suggestion of exchange.

52 As with value, rights exist not in abstraction but in relation to things. It is not only marriage that is "a bundle of rights" according to the jural approach, but also women as the objects of those rights. Questions regarding the value of payments, and the transfer of rights are inextricably linked. The emphasis on the direction of payments, and the attempt to make it an explanation for them, resulted in the retention of analytical concepts applicable to commercial cultures from which the jural language of rights emanated. In the case of the LoDagaa, payments were clearly economic in nature. However, in a circulatory and closed economy such as this, value was not a particularly useful analytical device. The value of payments received for a daughter existed in terms of their potential redeployment for acquiring a wife, not in terms of the purchase of "things." But it would be shortsighted to suggest that payments were merely symbolic. As Goody noted: "Whatever 'symbolic' aspects mark these transfers, they also have economic functions, not primarily as intermediaries in a purchase, but as ways of redistributing property." Goody 1973, 1. Yet the jural perspective Goody applied to the analysis of conjugal payments created connotations of exchange (the purchase of rights) rather than of circulation.

53 Singer 1973, 80–1.

54 The classificatory emphasis placed on the direction of conjugal payments (as their defining feature) in anthropological theory has greatly obscured attendant features grounded in particular ethnographic contexts. Comaroff, criticizing this "unquestioning analytical priority," suggested that other features might be equally significant: "Why not, therefore, allow that the contrast between 'undirectional' and 'complementary' alienations of wealth, or for that matter the immediacy or deferral of payment, may be equally fundamental for comparative purposes? After all, the labels 'bridewealth' and 'dowry' select, as analytical significata, only the source and destination of transfers, leaving as residual the dimensions of content, context and meaning" (1980a, 10). The adherence to a directional perspective was directly related to the jural analysis of conjugal payments. The coincidence of payments in one direction and the change of residence of a woman in the other direction was given explanatory weight, and substituted for meaning. For example, in Goody's account of "marriage" among the LoWiili, no less than six sets of "rights" were elucidated from a wider amalgam of relevant social practices. See Table 10. Although each of these was constitutive of marriage (as defined analytically), none of these "rights" was actually established by marriage. Perhaps the most significant criticism of such jural distillations arises when they are resituated within their social context. How can rights be attributed

to an ascribed relationship when in fact there were no jural institutions among the LoWiili (or any of the other LoDagaa congeries) through which such rights could have been exercised?

55 DMC CRB, vol. 15, N4/80, Andrew Maanyugr *vs.* Beatrice Yuornyine and Gilbert Seg-iib.

56 The equation of women with cattle was a distinct part of male perceptions, but also proceeded from cultural associations. "The LoBirifor mode of reproduction creates an intimate link between women and cattle, as the latter are the main means by which the former are acquired. The theft of cattle is thus the formal equivalent of the abduction of women, and, by extension, of possible offspring." Evans 1983, 118.

57 Comaroff 1980a, 14–15; 1980b, 196–7.

58 Radcliffe-Brown 1950, 53.

59 Comaroff warned that the "orthodox 'jural approach'" operates at the expense of ethnographic fact by trading context for comparison in order to sustain the coherence of marriage as an analytical device and descriptive paradigm. Comaroff 1980b, 192.

60 Rattray 1932, 414.

61 Rattray 1932, 439 (note 1). This interpretation, although in some sense satisfying the requirement for a legal definition of unions based on a specific moment, threatened the categorization of successive payments as also pertaining to marriage. If an initial payment actually made a union binding, that would have either effectively removed the necessity of subsequent payments or imparted to them a purpose and meaning quite separate from that relating to the status of the union.

62 Rattray 1932, 414–16, 439–40.

63 The immediate theoretical criticism of reducing these social practices to jural postulates is, again, that they were categorized *a priori* in terms of marriage: "Marriage is seen [within all major paradigms] as structurally prior, and prestations largely as its institutionalized mode of facilitation." Comaroff 1980a, 35–6. However, it was the payments that had consequences, not the status of unions. Similarly, the courts ignored the temporal dimensions of payments, which were constitutive of their meaning, by interpreting their purpose as the definition of the status of unions. In the context of both the Local and District Courts, legal recognition of litigants' interests was conferred in terms of the courts' interpretations of conjugal payments as facilitating the establishment of legitimate unions. When litigants argued that their interests were determined separately, in terms of specific payments alone, and not in terms of the status of unions, they were often disappointed, especially in the 1970s and 80s.

64 Goody 1973, 3.

65 DMC CRB, vol. 12, N7/74, Victor Duuyeng *vs.* Aatuore Bombie.

66 For this magistrate, Kpemaal, as well as his successor Siddique, the issue was the size of conjugal payments. From other decisions (1974–84), both magistrates demonstrated a marked antipathy to the substantial conjugal payments of the LoDagaa. In part this may have been due to their cultural backgrounds. Both came from Wa where (among the Wala) conjugal payments were nominal, as they are elsewhere among the other conquest states – Gonja, Dagbon, and Mamprugu.

67 The fact that the magistrate had to resort to cross-examination of witnesses in order to elicit information that would support such a perspective reflects the relationship of the District Court to the social practices it was charged with applying. Magistrates, who had no indigenous legitimacy or powers to pronounce what these social practices were, were usually obliged to call upon witnesses in order to educe "customary law" from pertinent social practices. Litigants or expert witnesses (usually chiefs whom the magistrates were prone to regard as the most definitive authorities on "customary law") were the magistrates' only source of knowledge of indigenous practices. However, it was the court that decided between conflicting versions and reinterpreted these practices. This power was considerable.

68 DMC CRB, vol. 12, L2/74, Brown Topuo Vuu *vs.* Micheal Beyuo.

69 To have accepted payments at this juncture was thought to be potentially injurious to the gestation of the child as well as its delivery.

70 DMC CRB, vol. 12, L2/74, Brown Topuo Vuu *vs.* Michael Beyuo.

71 Goody 1962, 105.

72 DMC CRB, vol. 12, L2/74, Brown Topuo Vuu *vs.* Michael Beyuo.

73 Ibid.

74 Ibid. Emphasis mine.

75 Fortes 1937, 6–7.

76 Fortes 1937, 5. Emphasis mine.

77 DMC CRB, vol. 12, L2/74, Brown Topuo Vuu *vs.* Michael Beyuo.

78 Ibid.

79 See Goody 1956a, 55, 64.

80 See Bourdieu 1977, 8–9: "It is therefore practice, in its most specific aspect, which is annihilated when the scheme [or strategy] is identified with the model [or rule]: retrospective necessity becomes prospective necessity, the product a project; and things which have happened, and can no longer not happen, become the irresistible future of the acts which made them happen."

81 Bourdieu 1977, 8: "To restore to practice its practical truth, we must therefore reintroduce time into the theoretical representation of a practice which, being temporally structured, is intrinsically defined by its *tempo*."

82 LoDagaa practices are not alone in this respect. For example, Bohannan reported that among the Tiv, the affinal debt, *kem*, gave affinal relations their cumulative and continuous nature: "The *kem* relationship of debt between a man and his wife's guardian is never broken, because *kem* is perpetual, the debt can never be fully paid." Bohannan 1957, 73. The notion of debt was not as pronounced among the LoDagaa, but the continuance of payments beyond the life of a wife, as in the post mortem presentation of *poo tshera libie*, illustrates the importance of the deferral of payments in perpetuating the affinal relationship. In other cases, besides that discussed above, the issue of this debt, its determination of affinal relations, and the distinction between the status of a union and the filiation of children emerged as significant issues between litigants. It has been argued above that the notion of expense, rather than "purchase," "value," or "symbol," is a more appropriate perspective from which to consider conjugal payments. This argument is supported by the notion of debt used by litigants in the courts to refer to the meaning of deferred payments. The deferral of conjugal payments, particularly the cattle or the second cowry payment, raises the question whether these payments can actually be construed as having existed for the purpose of legitimating, let alone legalizing, conjugal unions. Comaroff and Roberts raised a similar question in their analysis of *bogadi* among the Tswana, where "the conditions of transfer appear to allow, rather than eliminate, such ambiguities" – that is, with regard to the status of unions (1981, 139).

83 Radcliffe-Brown 1950, 5. The functional premise of Radcliffe-Brown's definition of marriage was that in all cultures, through the recognition or nonrecognition of conjugal unions, distinctions were made between the legitimate and illegitimate status of children. In other words, wherever jural distinctions were made between different statuses of children, these were the result of the jural implications of unions. The difficulty of applying this analytical paradigm to most African societies was that it ignored the role of descent.

84 Goody 1956a, 64.

85 RAT ADM 430, "Essay on the Peoples of the North West Province," PC NWP, 1907.

86 Goody 1956a, 62–4. Poda, who argued that "the primary objective of the practice of 'bride price' is the legitimation of filiation," claimed that children born to a woman without a husband or before conjugal payments had been presented were illegitimate. Although Poda's sense of the ritual liabilities incurred by such children was greater than Goody's, it is significant to observe that he did not see conjugal payments defining the status of unions. Poda's sense of illegitimacy, in contrast to that of Radcliffe-Brown, had nothing to do with marriage or biology (1993, 73–4).

87 Goody 1962, 94.
88 See Hawkins, forthcoming.
89 Rattary 1932, 411.
90 RAT ADM 514, Annual Report Lawra-Tumu District 1937–38.
91 Fortes 1949, 97. See also Radcliffe-Brown 1950, 51: "An African marries because he wants children." The gendered nature of this observation is hardly surprising, but it is, nevertheless, revealing.
92 Fortes 1949, 83.
93 Goody 1962, 196. Custody was neither exclusively nor even primarily a matter of consanguinity. Fortes observed of the Tallensi that although genealogical relations emanated from consanguinity, "what matters most is the social relations entailed by consanguinity" (1949, 16). Physiological paternity was not a prerequisite of custody. Among both the Tallensi and the LoDagaa children were begotten by an approved lover if a woman's husband was sterile. "Tale sentiment takes no cognizance of physical paternity in this situation" (24). The same type of relationship, more formally instituted, existed among the LoDagaa between a sterile man's wife and an institutionalized lover, where "the woman's husband remains the *pater* of her offspring, whoever the biological father may be." Goody 1962, 139. Although the phenomenon of *yirbie* or "house children" was not widely prevalent, it was also not uncommon. See Goody 1956a, 62–4.
94 Goody 1982, 101.
95 Goody 1956a, 51; Kpiebaya 1990, 13.
96 Relying on these accounts, a slight difference between the LoDagaa and the Tallensi emerges. It seems that despite the fact that the respective reports were written at different times, the Tallensi had a stronger sense of the importance of physiological paternity and its concomitant social implications. When a woman left her husband and "married" another man with whom she had a child only to return to her former spouse, the second husband was able to redeem the child from the woman's husband even if he had not fulfilled "the formalities of marriage" by paying or returning the relevant conjugal payments: "His right rests upon the fact of his acknowledged paternity. Tallensi attach so much importance to having children that they generally make every effort to assert this right." Fortes 1949, 27. In analogous circumstances the LoDagaa appeared to have ignored or suppressed the physiological dimension: "Formerly, if a wife ran away, remarried and then returned to her first husband, the young children by the second husband would be attached to the clan of the first, although the payment of bridewealth at the appropriate times might appear to give the second husband the right to his children." Goody 1956a, 56.
97 Goody 1956a, 55. However, this change in the descent of the children could not

occur, according to one informant, unless the conjugal payments were returned to the ex-husband, either directly by the father-in-law or through the woman "remarrying."

98 Goody 1956a, 55. In this instance social and physiological paternity were closely related, separated by the rejection of the woman and, thereby, the abdication of the former role. The meaning of substitution of physiological for social paternity by administrative injunction in this situation is not perfectly clear. There is a sense in which it was merely an entrenchment of a form of social paternity, despite the circumstances of the dissolution of a union. This perhaps made it more culturally acceptable to the LoWiili. But later, definite developments toward the legal assertion of physiological paternity, where there was no necessary coincidence with a similar social role, whether abdicated or in abeyance, demonstrated an even greater departure from indigenous practice. I found no record of such a decision in the extant records, but in a case that was heard by an officer a decade earlier a similar decision was reached. Here the children of a deceased's man's former wife were claimed by his brother, the Jirapa Naa. The district commissioner noted: "The point at issue was whether conception of the children had taken place after the woman had left the husband's compound. In Dagarti custom, if conception takes place before, even if after the divorce, and the true father is known, the children are for the husband's family; if after, they are illegitimate and belong to the mother's family. I gave judgment in favour of the mother's family, in the case of the younger child on Dagarti custom, and in that of the elder for the benefit of the child." RAT ADM 342–3, Informal Diary Lawra District, 24 December 1942. This decision was reported to the CCNT in a letter dated 2 February 1943, a copy of which was inserted in the same file.

99 DMC CRB, vol. 1, J9/8/54, Kpare Guri *vs.* Tobie Han. Here, as in other decisions by the Local Courts throughout this period, the principle of descent was upheld.

100 DMC CRB, vol. 1, L18/3/59, Kuuluo Panyanti *vs.* Timbiile Dazuuri.

101 DMC CRB, vol. 10, L22/70, Sorita Dakpala *vs.* Darigor Tuor. The details of this case have already been discussed above in relation to other issues.

102 See DMC CRB, vol. 12, L2/74, Brown Topuo Vuu *vs.* Michael Beyuo. It was apparent that the magistrate's intervention and investigation of the meaning of "the greetings" (discussed above) were intended to justify awarding the child to its *genitor* by being able to claim that the plaintiff had "married" the defendant's daughter.

103 DMC CRB, vol. 12, N4/73, Ben Bonkan Isang *vs.* Dennis Puozuu.

104 DMC CRB, vol. 12, N9/74, Dennis Puozuu *vs.* Ben Bonkan Isang.

105 During the second of these cases the plaintiff, Dennis, attempted to establish that the woman, Mary, was his wife by raising the hypothesis of death in order to

mitigate his failure to present the necessary conjugal payments: "I complained to the sub–chiefs and the Nandom Naa to settle the matter and get the child for me. It was there that the Nandom Naa told me that once the child was collected he could do nothing about it. I also told the chief of Nandom that once I have married the woman it is known that even if she dies in my hands I have still to pay the dowries." This tactic was pursued in his cross-examination of the defendant: "If you marry a man's wife without dowrying her and she chances to die while with you, will you pay the dowry or not?" Here the social recognition of a union and the legitimacy of paternity diverged. The plaintiff could have buried the woman if a *post facto* payment had been accepted by the defendant's household. Yet this would not have altered the question of the custody of the children, only that of the woman's recognized husband. In this case the court's difficulty in accepting that conjugal payments in themselves determined paternity stemmed from the fact that not only was the defendant's household not the *genitor* of the children in question in both cases, but the woman's former husband was actually dead. It was either unaware or chose to ignore that in terms of indigenous perception any new children of a deceased man's wife continued to be attached to his household in his name. Goody 1962, 198.

106 Korbieh 1990, 50–1.

107 This magistrate, Siddique, often abandoned "customary marriage laws" in preference for arguments grounded in "modernity" rather than "custom" or even natural justice. There was also a definite element of ethnic bias here, based less on the ideology of a judicial or national morality than on another set of cultural perceptions. Siddique, a Wala, found LoDagaa practices repugnant and backward because they did not coincide with his own understanding of social propriety. Among the Wala, physiological paternity was ascendant.

108 DMC CRB, vol. 14, L23/78, Saaluah Kpinibo *vs.* Motogo Peter Mwinpuo.

109 See DMC CRB, vol. 12, N4/73, Ben Bonkan Isang *vs.* Dennis Puozuu.

110 DMC CRB, vol. 14, L23/78, Saaluah Kpinibo *vs.* Motogo Peter Mwinpuo.

111 See DMC CRB, vol. 15, N4/80, Andrew Maanyugr *vs.* Beatrice Yuoryine and Gilbert Seg-ib.

112 DMC CRB, vol. 16, N7/83, Saturnina Loko vs. Amporeh.

113 Dery 1987, 2.

114 Dery 1987, 45.

115 Fortes acknowledged the theoretical corollary of this in his introduction to *Marriage in Tribal Societies*, where, writing of the general phenomenon of marriage, he stated: "The issue of status is central. To adopt (without disrespect to its most distinguished author) the most hackneyed of all sociological aphorisms, marriage could be briefly defined as the sanctioned movement from the filial status of son or daughter to the conjugal status of husband or wife" (1962,

7–8). The difficulty with this perspective was that it imputed a degree of definitiveness to these statuses, especially those of women, which in the case of the LoDagaa was not evident. Given the incidence of the dissolution of conjugal unions among the LoDagaa, and the phenomenon of "experimental marriages" among the Tallensi, this transition in social identity could not be reduced to a clear, unambiguous jural status. Once a woman left her father's house she entered upon a marital career, often with a series of husbands, so it was difficult to distinguish (in the period of transition between one union and another) to which of them her status of wife pertained. The status of wife was contextual – that is, residential, not exclusive or proprietorial – and when a woman returned to her household she did so as a daughter of that household, not as the wife of another household. It is clear, therefore, that marriage among the LoDagaa did not constitute an irreversible shift in social identity, only an added dimension. There was certainly an uxorial status among the LoDagaa, but it was more contingent than definite. "Although a woman is drawn closer to her husband's lineage in a process marked by successive payments of bridewealth," Goody observed, "she can never become a member of that lineage, nor cease to belong to her own." Despite admitting to this limitation, Goody still conceptualized conjugal payments as fulfilling this purpose: "The successive payments of bridewealth mark stages in the integration of a woman into her husband's domestic group" (1956a, 52–3).

116 In a study of court records from the 1930s and 1960s in Akwapim, an area just outside Accra, Dorothy Vellanga noted that the issue of "who is a wife" was always in question. Among the LoDagaa, once a woman left her natal household and lived with a man in his household she became a wife. However, the issue of whose wife she was mirrored the question of who is a wife in Akwapim. Vellenga 1983.

117 DMC CRB, vol. 7, L24/8/66, T.K. Daniel Keluo *vs.* Urumaanu Zowuoh Bu.

118 DMC CRB, vol. 7, L29/4/66, Ziepag Kog Zambo *vs.* Dukurah Kyilaa.

119 Goody 1956a, 51–2.

120 Rattray 1932, 440. See also Goody 1962, 54.

121 Goody 1962, 53.

122 See Deri 1980, 2. He reported that "betrothal through herbal treatment" was a recognized means of conjugal formation, and that a wife acquired by such means was known as *teepogo* or "medicine wife." See also Tengan 1990d, 12.

123 DMC CRB, vol. 14, L21/78, Zebriku Guo *vs.* Vutaar Dabuo.

124 On these points see Goody 1962, 204–7, 331–5.

125 Goody 1956a, 53.

126 Goody 1962, 251–2.

127 For example, in the case of Nokpog of Eremon *vs.* Kunyelle of Tom, which

came before the Local Court in 1955, the defendant mentioned the question of death as an indication of his intentions and motivations. Kunyelle had taken the plaintiff's father's wife as his wife, and according to the plaintiff: "Since then he [Kunyelle] tried all he could to please the woman's father and to perform the customary rules, before he could own the woman as a lawful wife." The defendant explained to the court that his efforts to have the conjugal payments accepted had been rejected on seven occasions: "For the fact that the woman's fathers refused the dowries for seven continuous times, I therefore thought within myself that since every person is liable to death and may die at any time, I could not keep the woman as a wife without first dowrying her." He had then taken the matter to the Lawra Naa in order to have the payments accepted. The question of death was used by Kunyelle, not as the basis of a claim, but in explanation and mitigation of his own actions. Here the need to have conjugal payments accepted was not to legitimate the union, but to resolve the identity of the woman as his wife in the case of her death. DMC CRB, vol. 2, N8/12/55, Nokpog of Eremon *vs.* Kunyelle of Tom.

128 Outside the courts, death was used continually as an indicator of the "status of a married woman in respect of her husband's and her natal kin." Goody 1962, 53–4. In this context it was reported to have been used as a formula for the hearing of another dispute, or as a retaliatory procedure for claiming a separate conjugal debt, although in the District Court it was used as a device for determining whether the status of a particular conjugal relationship had jural effects or implications imputed to "marriage."

129 NAG ADM, 61/5/8, Informal Diary Lawra District, 30 May 1918: "On arriving Binney asked for leave to attend a funeral custom. He seems to make a hobby of it."

130 Goody 1962, 11. The source of some of the difficulty of arriving at a definition of marriage among the LoDagaa was that this task has been almost exclusively the preoccupation of the courts – institutions foreign to LoDagaa culture. Indigenous reactions were elicited in the context of institutions that they did not control and were not free to develop, and that were created in opposition to their own ways of defining and settling disputes.

131 See for example DMC CRB, vol. 1, L18/3/59, Kuuluo Panyanti *vs.* Timbiile Dazuuri.

132 DMC CRB, vol. 14, L23/78, Saaluah Kpinibo *vs.* Motogo Peter Mwinpuo.

133 DMC CRB, vol. 15, N4/80, Andrew Maanyugr *vs.* Beatrice Yuornyine and Gilbert Seg-ib.

134 Ibid.

135 Comaroff and Roberts 1981, 151.

136 Comaroff and Roberts 1981, 133.

137 Tengan 1990c, 73.

138 Radcliffe-Brown 1950, 46. Emphasis mine.

139 See for example Opuku 1976.

140 Kuukure 1985, 30; Kpiebaya 1990, 10; Dery 1987, 28; Tengan 1990a, 1. Father Kpoda, a Catholic priest from the other side of the Black Volta, fol-lowed Radcliffe-Brown even more closely in representing conjugal payments among the LoDagaa congeries of Burkina Faso in the 1970s: "Through the payment of dowry, marriage is an act of legal transmission of jurisdictional power and authority from one family to another. ... Marriage with dowry confers on the husband and his family rights over his wife and the children of the union: one could describe this as 'jus in rem,' 'jus in peronam' of the husband and in-laws over the wife." Kpoda 1977, 43.

141 Personal communication with Bishop Kpiebaya.

142 Tengan 1990c, 73.

143 Gold Coast 1951, 18.

144 Koya 1991, 5.

145 Anon. 1992, 1.

146 Goody 1995, 94.

147 Here I mean its disposition toward objectification discussed in the Introduction. See references therein to the comments of Clifford, Fabian, and Holy and Stuchlik. Writing of the distortion of social practices through their objectification, Bourdieu observed: "By cumulating information which is not and cannot always be mastered by any single informant ... the analyst wins the *privilege of totalization* (thanks to the power to *perpetuate* that writing and all the various techniques for recording give him, and also to the abundant time he has for analysis). He thus secures the means of apprehending the logic of the system which a partial or discrete view would miss; but by the same token, there is every likelihood that he will overlook the change in status to which he is subjecting practice and its products, and consequently that he will insist on trying to answer questions which are not and cannot be questions for practice, instead of asking himself whether the essential characteristic of practice is not the fact that it excludes such questions." Bourdieu 1977, 106. The mastering of LoDagaa social facts and their collation by observers in the world on paper gave rise to the possibility of classificatory operations not possible to the practitioners of those practices.

148 Godelier 1986, 169.

149 Dery 1987, 28; Kuukure 1985, 30.

150 Comaroff 1980a, 10.

151 Goody 1995, 138, 142.

152 Goody 1995, 125–6.

153 Goody 1995, 138, 142.

154 Holy and Stuchlik 1983, 42. As Bourdieu noted in his attempt to restore practices to their generative reality: "Practice always implies a cognitive operation, a practical operation of construction which sets out to work, by reference to practical functions, systems of classification (taxonomies) which organize perception and structure practice. ... Practical taxonomies, instruments of cognition and communication which are the precondition for the establishment of meaning and consensus on meaning, exert their *structuring* efficacy only to the extent that they are themselves *structured*" (1977, 97). With reference to the LoDagaa, the court records (which manifest the absence of such a consensus of meaning) indicate that the cognitive operations structuring these practices were not based on an indigenous taxonomy in any way analogous to marriage. It was only in the context of the courts that such a representation was operative; practices were only reinterpreted in an attempt to appeal to such a perspective. However, because the category of marriage was not itself part of the cognitive order that generated practices argued over in court, these attempts to redefine their intention and meaning were entirely *post facto*. If marriage had been the generative cognitive premise of these practices, then litigation over marriage would not have been so equivocal and inconclusive.

Conclusion: Writing, Blood, and the Politics of Legitimacy

1 Moore 1986, 41.

2 Cooper and Stoler 1989, 620.

3 Luria 1976, 33–4.

4 Howes 1991, 1.

5 NAG ADM 61/5/8, Informal Diary Lawra District, 21 December 1920. The more accurate question was what kind of history it had, rather than whether it had history.

6 Staniland 1975, 162–6; Evans 1983, 235–44, 299–320; Skalnik 1986; Drucker-Brown 1989; Wilks 1989, 200–1; Ray 1996, 193–8.

7 Staniland 1975, 132.

8 Staniland 1975, 174.

9 Staniland 1975, 13.

10 Wilks 1989, 4, 196. Writing was similarly ineffective in Nanum. Skalnik 1996, 117.

11 On the potential for violence and how community leaders among the different LoDagaa congeries have avoided it, see Lentz 2000.

12 Duncan-Johnstone and Blair 1932; NAG ADM 292–3, Record of Native Law and Custom, "Marriage Laws of the Lobi/Dagarti Natives Resident in the Lawra Native Authority Area," 1938.

13 Ray 1996, 196.

14 This is merely a point of speculation and not central to my argument. However, I do think that it helps explain the separation of rights *in uxorem* and those *in genetricem*, which Tambiah has noted is often a feature of African cultures but which is absent in North India. Tambiah 1989, 429.

15 Schneider 1984, 174–5, 195.

16 Derrida 1976, 124.

17 Skalnik 1989.

18 Bourdieu 1990, 11.

Bibliography

Afigbo, A.E. 1972. *The Warrant Chiefs: Indirect Rule in Southern Nigeria, 1891–1919*. London: Longman.

Allott, Anthony N. 1960. *Essays in African Law: With Special Reference to the Law of Ghana*. London: Butterworth.

Angsotinge, Tuobataabaaro Gervase. 1986. Wisdom of the Ancestors: An Analysis of Oral Narratives of the Dagaaba of Northern Ghana. PhD diss., University of California, Los Angeles.

Anon. 1989. Editor's Notes. *Papers in Dagara Studies – Cahiers d'études Dagara – Dagara Yele Sebe* 1, i–ii.

– 1992. Editorial. *The Diocese, Wa* 100, 1.

Arhin, Kwame, ed. 1974. *The Papers of George Ekem Ferguson: A Fanti Official of the Government of the Gold Coast, 1890–1897*. Leiden and Cambridge: African Studies Centre.

Armitage, Captain C.H. 1924. *The Tribal Adornments of the Natives of the Northern Territories of the Gold Coast Colony*. London: Royal Anthropological Institute of Great Britain and Ireland.

Armstrong, Alice, et al. 1993. Uncovering Reality: Excavating Women's Rights in African Family Law. *International Journal of Law and the Family* 7, 314–69.

Asad, Talal, ed. 1973. *Anthropology and The Colonial Encounter*. New York: Humanities Press.

– 1986. The Concept of Cultural Translation in British Social Anthropology. In *Writing Culture: The Poetics and Politics of Ethnography*, ed. James Clifford and George E. Marcus. Berkeley: University of California Press.

Auslander, Mark. 1993. "Open Wombs!": The Symbolic Politics of Modern Ngoni Witchfinding. In *Modernity and Its Malcontents: Ritual and Power in Postcolonial Africa*, ed. Jean Comaroff and John Comaroff. Chicago: University of Chicago Press.

Axtell, James. 1995. Columbian Encounters: 1492–1995. *William and Mary Quarterly* 52, 685–90.

Baerends, Els A. 1990. Woman Is King, Man Is Mere Child: Some Notes on the Socio-legal Position of Women among the Anufom in Northern Togo. *Journal of Legal Pluralism and Unofficial Law* 30–1, 33–75.

Barkan, Elazar. 1995. Victorian Promiscuity: Greek Ethics and Primitive Exemplars. In *Prehistories of the Future: The Primitivist Project and the Culture of Modernism*, ed. Elazar Barkan and Ronald Bush. Stanford: Stanford University Press.

Barnard, Alan, and Anthony Good. 1984. *Research Practices in the Study of Kinship*. Association of Social Anthropologists, Research Methods in Social Anthropology, 2. London: Academic Press.

Bayart, Jean-François. 1986. Civil Society in Africa. In *Political Domination in Africa: Reflections on the Limits of Power*, ed. Patrick Chabal. Cambridge: Cambridge University Press.

– 1993. *The State in Africa: The Politics of the Belly*. London: Longman.

Bekye, Paul K. 1985. Dagaaba identity – rejoinder [1]. *The Diocese, Wa* 35, 5–6; Dagaaba identity – rejoinder [2]. *The Diocese, Wa* 39, 4–6.

– 1991. *Divine Revelation and Traditional Religions: With Particular Reference to the Dagaaba of West Africa*. Rome: Leberit Press.

Bemile, Sebastian K. 1983. *The Wisdom Which Surpasses That of the King: Dagara Stories*. Brazzaville and Heidelberg: Editions Bantoues.

– 2000. Promotion of Ghanaian Languages and Its Impact on National Unity: The Dagara Language Case. In *Ethnicity in Ghana: The Limits of Invention*, ed. Carola Lentz and Paul Nugent. New York: St Martin's Press.

Benoit, D., P. Levi, and M. Pilon. 1986. *Caractéristiques des migrations et de la nuptialité en pays Lobi Dagara (Haute Volta – 1976)*. Paris: Éditions de l'ORSTOM.

Binger, Le Capitaine [Louis Gustave]. 1892. *Du Niger au Golfe de Guinée*. 2 vols. Paris: Hachette.

Bledsoe, Caroline H. 1980. *Women and Marriage in Kpelle Society*. Stanford: Stanford University Press.

Bodomo, Adams. 1997. *The Structure of Dagaare*. Stanford: Center for the Study of Language and Information.

Bohannan, Paul. 1957. *Justice and Judgment among the Tiv*. London: Oxford University Press.

– 1967a. Preface. In *Law and Warfare*, ed. Paul Bohannan. Garden City, NY: American Museum of Natural History.

– 1967b. The Differing Realms of the Law. In *Law and Warfare*, ed. Paul Bohannan. Garden City, NY: American Museum of Natural History.

– 1969. Ethnography and Comparison in Legal Anthropology. In *Law in Culture and Society*, ed. Laura Nader. Chicago: University of Chicago Press.

Bongvlaa, R. 1979. Interview [by Father A. Bayo] with Robert Bongvlaa (catechist). In *That They May Have Light: An Account of the Activities of the Church in North-West Ghana, 1929–79*, ed. Father V. Gregoire. Wa: Catholic Press.

Bonnafé, Pierre, and Michèle Fiéloux. 1993. La guerre et l'organisation sociale. In *Images d'Afrique et Sciences sociales: Les pays lobi, birifor et dagara*, ed. Michèle Fiéloux, Jacques Lombard, and Jeanne-Marie Kambou-Ferrand. Paris: Editions Karthala et ORSTOM.

Bonnafé, Pierre, Michèle Fiéloux, and J.M. Kambou. 1982. Un vent de folie? Le conflit armé dans une population sans Etat: les Lobis de Haute-Volta. In *Guerres de lignages et guerres d'Etats en Afrique*, ed. Jean Bazin and Emmanuel Terray. Paris: Editions des Archives Contemporaines.

Bourdieu, Pierre. 1977. *Outline of a Theory of Practice*. Cambridge: Cambridge University Press.

– 1990. *The Logic of Practice*. Stanford: Stanford University Press.

Boutillier, Jean-Louis. 1993. Les cauris en tant que monnaie dans le sud-ouest du Burkina-Faso au XXe siècle. In *Images d'Afrique et Sciences sociales: Les pays lobi, birifor et dagara*, ed. Michèle Fiéloux, Jacques Lombard, and Jeanne-Marie Kambou-Ferrand. Paris: Editions Karthala et ORSTOM.

Bowman, Allan K., and Greg Woolf. 1994. Literacy and Power in the Ancient World. In *Literacy and Power in the Ancient World*, ed. Allan K. Bowman and Greg Woolf. Cambridge: Cambridge University Press.

Brog. 1954. Brigadoon. *Variety* 11 August, 6.

Bush, Barbara. 1999. *Imperialism, Race and Resistance: Africa and Britain, 1919–1945*. New York: Routledge.

Cardinall, A.W. [Allan Wolsey] 1920. *The Natives of the Northern Territories of the Gold Coast: Their Customs, Religion and Folklore*. London: George Routledge and Sons.

Champagne, Gabriel. 1941. A Jirapa: principaux faits de l'année. *Les Missions de l'Afrique, Québec* 37, 77–80.

Chanock, Martin. 1982. Making Customary Law: Men, Women and Courts in Colonial Northern Rhodesia. In *African Women and the Law*, ed. Margaret Jean Hay and Marcia Wright. Boston: Boston University.

– 1985. *Law, Custom and Social Order: The Colonial Experience in Malawi and Zambia*. Cambridge: Cambridge University Press.

Clanchy, M.T. 1993. *From Memory to Written Record: England 1066–1307*. 2nd ed. Cambridge: Harvard University Press.

Classen, Constance. 1991. Literacy as Anti-Culture: The Andean Experience of the Written Word. *History of Religion* 30, 404–21.

Clastres, Pierre. 1989. *Society against the State: Essays in Political Anthropology*. New York: Zone Books.

Cleveland, David A. 1991. Migration in West African: A Savanna Village Perspective. *Africa* 61, 222–46.

Clifford, James. 1986. Introduction: Partial Truths. In *Writing Culture: The Poetics and Politics of Ethnography*, ed. James Clifford and George E. Marcus. Berkeley: University of California Press.

Clifford, James, and George E. Marcus, eds. 1986. *Writing Culture: The Poetics and Politics of Ethnography*. Berkeley: University of California Press.

Coetzee, J.M. 1980. *Waiting for the Barbarians*. London: Martin Secker and Warburg.

Cohen, David William. 1989. The Undefining of Oral Tradition. *Ethnohistory* 36, 9–18.

– 1994. *The Combing of History*. Chicago: University of Chicago Press.

Comaroff, John L. 1980a. Introduction. In *The Meaning of Marriage Payments*, ed. John L. Comaroff. London: Academic Press.

– 1980b. Bridewealth and the Control of Ambiguity in a Tswana Chiefdom. In *The Meaning of Marriage Payments*, ed. John L. Comaroff. New York and London: Academic Press.

Comaroff, John L., and Jean Comaroff. 1991. *Of Revelation and Revolution: Christianity, Colonialism, and Consciousness in South Africa*. Chicago: University of Chicago Press.

– 1997. *Of Revelation and Revolution: The Dialectics of Modernity on a South African Frontier*. Chicago: University of Chicago Press.

Comaroff, John L., and Simon Roberts. 1981. *Rules and Processes: The Cultural Logic of Dispute in an African Context*. Chicago: University of Chicago Press.

Coombes, Annie E. 1994. *Reinventing Africa: Museums, Material Culture and Popular Imagination in Late Victorian and Edwardian England*. New Haven: Yale University Press.

Cooper, Barbara. 1997. *Marriage in Maradi: Gender and Culture in a Hausa Society in Niger, 1900–1989*. Portsmouth, NH: Heinemann.

Cooper, Frederick. 1994. Conflict and Connection: Rethinking Colonial African History. *American Historical Review* 99, 1516–45.

– 1996. *Decolonization and African Society: The Labor Question in French and British Africa*. Cambridge: Cambridge University Press.

Cooper, Frederick, and Ann Stoler. 1989. Tensions of Empire: Colonial Control and Visions of Rule. *American Ethnologist* 16, 609–21.

Crisp, Jeff. 1984. *The Story of an African Working Class: Ghanaian Miners' Struggles, 1870–1980*. London: Zed Press.

Daannaa, Henry Seidu. 1994. The Acephalous Society and the Indirect Rule System in Africa. *Journal of Legal Pluralism* 34, 61–85.

Dabiré, Constantin Gbaane. 1983. L'Homme comme relation. PhD dissertation. Université Laval, Quebec.

Daniels, W.C. Ekow. 1977. The Effect of Marriage on the Status of Children in Ghana. In *Law and the Family in Africa*, ed. Simon Roberts. The Hague: Mouton.

– 1988. "Recent Reforms in Ghana's Family Law," *Journal of African Law* 32, 93–106.

Dauber, Kenneth. 1995. Bureaucratizing the Ethnographer's Magic. *Current Anthropology* 36, 75–95.

Davis, David C. 1987. "Then the White Man Came with His Whitish Ideas ...": The British and the Evolution of Traditional Government in Mampurugu. *International Journal of African Historical Studies* 20, 627–46.

Dawson, Marc H. 1987. The Social History of Africa in the Future: Medical Related Issues. *African Studies Review* 30, 83–91.

Delafosse, Maurice. 1908. *Les Frontières de la Côte d'Ivoire, de la Côte d'Or et du Soudan*. Paris: Masson.

– 1912. *Haut-Sénégal-Niger*. Paris: Emile Larose.

Der, Benedict. 1974. Church-State Relations in Northern Ghana, 1906–1940. *Transactions of the Historical Society of Ghana* 15, 41–61.

– 1980. God and Sacrifice in the Traditional Religions of the Kasena and Dagaba of Northern Ghana. *Journal of Religion in Africa* 11, 172–87.

– 1983. Mission Enterprise in Northern Ghana, 1906–1975: A Study in Impact. PhD dissertation, University of Ghana, Legon.

– 1989. The origins of the Dagara-Dagaba. *Papers in Dagara Studies – Cahiers d'études Dagara – Dagara Yele Sebe* 1, 1–25.

Deri, A.T. 1980. Customary Marriage Procedure. Mimeograph. Lawra: Lawra Confederacy Traditional Council.

Derrida, Jacques. 1976. *Of Grammatology*. Baltimore: Johns Hopkins University Press.

Dery, Archbishop Peter P. 1979. The Coming of the Christian Faith to the Upper West. In *That They May Have Light: An Account of the Activities of the Church in North-West Ghana 1929–1979*, ed. Father V. Gregoire. Wa: Catholic Press.

– 1984. Archbishop Speaks (3). *The Diocese, Wa* 24, 3–4.

Dery, Gaspard. 1987. *Inheritance and Marriage among the Dagaaba of Northern Ghana: Second Opinions to Existing Theories*. Accra: Ghana Publishing.

Dickerman, Carol. 1984. The Use of Court Records as Sources for African History: Some Examples from Bujumbura, Burundi. *History in Africa* 10, 69–81.

Dorward, D.C. 1974. Ethnography and Administration: A Study of Anglo-Tiv "Working Misunderstanding." *Journal of African History* 15, 457–77.

Dougah, J.C. 1966. *Wa and Its People*. Legon: Institute of African Studies.

Drucker-Brown, Susan. 1989. Local Wars in Northern Ghana. *Cambridge Anthropology* 13, 86–106.

Dummett, Raymond. 1993. Disease and Mortality among the Gold Miners of Ghana: Colonial Government and Mining Company Attitudes and Policies, 1900–1938. *Social Science and Medicine* 37, 213–32.

Duncan-Johnstone, A.C., and H.A. Blair. 1932. *Enquiry into the Constitution and Organisation of the Dagbon Kingdom*. Accra: Government Printer.

Ekeh, Peter. 1975. Colonialism and the Two Publics in Africa: A Theoretical Statement. *Comparative Studies in Society and History* 17, 91–112.

– 1990. Social Anthropology and Two Contrasting Uses of Tribalism in Africa. *Comparative Studies in Society and History* 22, 660–700.

Evans, Philip A. 1983. The LoBirifor/Gonja Dispute in Northern Ghana: A Study in Inter-Ethnic Political Conflict in a Post-Colonial State. PhD dissertation, University of Cambridge.

– 1985. The Cowrie Economy and the Maintenance of Social Boundaries in Northern Ghana. *Cambridge Anthropology* 10, 29–40.

Ewald, Janet. 1988. Speaking, Writing, and Authority: Explorations in and from the Kingdom of Taqali. *Comparative Studies in Society and History* 30, 199–224.

Eyre-Smith, St J. 1933. *A Brief Review of the History and Social Organisation of the Peoples of the Northern Territories of the Gold Coast*. Accra: Government Printer.

Fabian, Johannes. 1983. *Time and the Other: How Anthropology Makes Its Object*. New York: Columbia University Press.

– 1986. *Language and Colonial Power: The Appropriation of Swahili in the Former Belgian Congo, 1880–1938*. Cambridge: Cambridge University Press.

– 2000. *Out of Our Minds: Reason and Madness in the Exploration of Africa*. Berkeley: University of California Press.

Feierman, Steven. 1990. *Peasant Intellectuals: Anthropology and History in Tanzania*. Madison: University of Wisconsin Press.

Ferguson, Phyllis, and Ivor Wilks. 1970. Chieftaincy, Constitutions and the British in Northern Ghana. In *West African Chiefs: Their Changing Status Under Colonial Rule and Independence*, ed. Michael Crowder and Obaro Ikime. New York: Africana Publishing.

Fields, Karen. 1985. *Revival and Rebellion in Colonial Central Africa*. Princeton: Princeton University Press.

Fiéloux, Michèle. 1980. *Les sentiers de la nuit: les migrations rurales lobi de la Haute-Volta vers la Côte d'Ivoire*. Paris: ORSTOM.

Fiéloux, Michèle, and Jacques Lombard. 1993. Introduction. In *Images d'Afrique et Sciences sociales: Les pays lobi, birifor et dagara*, ed. Michèle Fiéloux, Jacques Lombard, and Jeanne-Marie Kambou-Ferrand. Paris: Editions Karthala et ORSTOM.

Finnegan, Ruth. 1988. *Literacy and Orality: Studies in the Technology of Communication*. Oxford: Blackwell.

Fisher, Humphrey J. 1985. The Juggernaut's Apologia: Conversion to Islam in Black Africa. *Africa* 55, 153–73.

Fortes, Meyer. 1936. Culture Contact as a Dynamic Process: An Investigation of the Northern Territories of the Gold Coast. *Africa* 9, 60–91.

– 1937. *Marriage Law among the Tallensi.* Accra: Government Printing Department.

– 1945. *The Dynamics of Clanship among the Tallensi: Being the First Part of an Analysis of the Social Structure of a Trans-Volta Tribe.* London: Oxford University Press.

– 1949. *The Web of Kinship among the Tallensi: The Second Part of an Analysis of the Social Structure of a Trans-Volta Tribe.* Oxford: Clarendon Press.

– 1959. Descent, Filiation and Affinity: A Rejoinder to Dr Leach. *Man* 59, 193–7, 206–12.

– 1962. Introduction. In *Marriage in Tribal Societies*, ed. Meyer Fortes. Cambridge: Cambridge University Press.

– 1971. Some Aspects of Migration and Mobility in Ghana. *Journal of Asian and African Studies* 6, 1–20.

– 1981. Tallensi Children's Drawing. In *Universals of Human Thought*, ed. Barbara Lloyd and John Gay. Cambridge: Cambridge University Press.

Fortes, Meyer, and E.E. Evans-Pritchard, eds. 1940. *African Political Systems.* London: International African Institute.

Geertz, Clifford. 1983. *Local Knowledge: Further Essays in Interpretive Anthropology.* New York: Harper Row.

Germain, R. 1937. Impressions d'un nouveau-venu. *Les Missions d'Afrique, Québec* 33, 80–9.

Ghana. 1962. *1960 Population Census of Ghana.* Accra: Census Office.

– 1964. *1960 Population Census of Ghana. Special Report.* Accra: Census Office.

– 1972. *1970 Population Census of Ghana.* Accra: Census Office.

– 1987. *1984 Population Census of Ghana. Demographic and Economic Characteristics.* Accra: Statistical Service.

– 1989. *1984 Population Census of Ghana. The Gazetteer.* Accra: Statistical Service.

Gill, Brendan. 1980. The Theatre: Outwitting Witches. *The New Yorker*, 27 October, 156.

– 1986. The Theatre: Scottish Mist. *The New Yorker*, 10 March, 114.

Girault, Louis. 1959. Essai sur le religion dagara. *Bulletin de l'Institut français d'Afrique noire* 21, 329–56.

Godelier, Maurice. 1986. *The Mental and the Material: Thought, Economy and Society.* London: Verso.

Gold Coast. 1901–18. *Annual Report on the Northern Territories of the Gold Coast.* London: HMSO.

– 1930. *Report By the Special Commissioner for Anthropology for the Year 1929–30.* Accra: Government Printing Office.

– 1950. *Census of Population 1948. Report and Tables.* London: Crown Agents for the Colonies.

– 1951. *Report of the Commission on Native Courts.* Accra: Government Printing Department.

– 1954. *The Laws of the Gold Coast.* Accra: Government Printer.

Goldschmidt, Jennifer E. 1981. National and Indigenous Constitutional Law in Ghana: Their Development and their Relation to Each Other. PhD dissertation, University of Leiden.

Good, Charles. 1991. Pioneer Medical Missions in Colonial Africa. *Social Science and Medicine* 32, 1–10.

Goody, Esther [with Jack Goody]. 1982. The Circulation of Women and Children in Northern Ghana. In *Parenthood and Social Reproduction.* Cambridge: Cambridge University Press.

Goody, Jack. 1954. *The Ethnography of the Northern Territories of the Gold Coast, West of the White Volta.* London: Colonial Office.

– 1956a. *The Social Organisation of the LoWiili.* 1st ed. London: HMSO.

– 1956b. A Comparative Approach to Incest and Adultery. *British Journal of Sociology* 7, 286–305.

– 1957. Fields of Social Control among the LoDagaba. *Journal of the Royal Anthropological Institute* 87, 75–104.

– 1961. The Classification of Double Descent Systems. *Current Anthropology* 2, 3–25.

– 1962. *Death Property and the Ancestors: A Study of the Mortuary Customs of the LoDagaa of West Africa.* Stanford: Stanford University Press.

– 1967. Preface to second edition. In *The Social Organisation of the LoWiili.* 2nd ed. London: Oxford University Press.

– 1968. Restricted Literacy in Northern Ghana. In *Literacy in Traditional Societies*, ed. Jack Goody and Ian Watt. Cambridge: Cambridge University Press.

– 1969. "Normative," "Recollected" and "Actual" Marriage Payments among the LoWiili of Northern Ghana, 1951–1966. *Africa* 39, 54–61.

– 1970. Inheritance, Social Change and the Boundary Problem. In *Echanges et communications: mélanges offerts à Claude Lévi-Strauss à l'occasion de son 60ième anniversaire*, ed. Jean Pouillon and Pierre Maranda. The Hague: Mouton.

– 1972. *The Myth of the Bagre.* Oxford: Clarendon Press.

– 1973. Bridewealth and Dowry in Africa and Eurasia. In *Bridewealth and Dowry*, ed. Jack Goody and Stanley J. Tambiah. Cambridge: Cambridge University Press.

– 1975. Religion, Social Change and the Sociology of Conversion. In *Changing Social Structure in Ghana: Essays in the Comparative Sociology of a New State and Old Tradition*, ed. Jack Goody. London: International African Institute.

– 1977. *The Domestication of the Savage Mind.* Cambridge: Cambridge University Press.

– 1986. *The Logic of Writing and the Organization of Society.* Cambridge: Cambridge University Press.

– 1987. *The Interface Between the Written and the Oral.* Cambridge: Cambridge University Press.
– 1993a. Peuplement: études comparatives Nord-Ghana et Burkina Faso. In *Images d'Afrique et Sciences sociales: Les pays lobi, birifor et dagara*, ed. Michèle Fiéloux, Jacques Lombard, and Jeanne-Marie Kambou-Ferrand. Paris: Editions Karthala et ORSTOM.
– 1993b. The bagre considered. In *Images d'Afrique et Sciences sociales: Les pays lobi, birifor et dagara*, ed. Michèle Fiéloux, Jacques Lombard, and Jeanne-Marie Kambou-Ferrand. Paris: Editions Karthala et ORSTOM.
– 1995. *The Expansive Moment: Anthropology in Britain and Africa 1918–1970.* Cambridge: Cambridge University Press.
Goody, Jack, and Ian Watt. 1968. The Consequences of Literacy. In *Literacy in Traditional Societies*, ed. Jack Goody and Ian Watt. Cambridge: Cambridge University Press.
Goody, Jack, and S.W.D.K. Gandah. 1980. *Une Récitation du Bagré.* Paris: Armand Colin.
Gray, Richard. 1990. *Black Christians and White Missionaries.* New Haven: Yale University Press.
Great Britain. 1908. *Northern Territories of the Gold Coast. Report for 1907.* London: HMSO.
– 1938. *Correspondence Relating to the Welfare of Women in Tropical Africa 1935–37.* London: HMSO.
Greenblatt, Stephen. 1991. *Marvelous Possessions: The Wonder of the New World.* Chicago: Chicago University Press.
Gregory, C.A. 1996. Cowries and Conquest: Towards a Subalternate Quality Theory of Money. *Comparative Studies in Society and History* 38, 195–217.
Grindal, Bruce. 1972. *Growing Up in Two Worlds: Education and Transition among the Sissala of Northern Ghana.* New York: Rinehart and Winston.
– 1983. Into the Heart of Sisala Experience: Witnessing Death Divination. *Journal of Anthropological Research* 39, 29–43.
Guha, Ranajit. 1997. *Dominance without Hegemony: History and Power in Colonial India.* Cambridge: Harvard University Press.
Gulliver, P.H. 1963. *Social Control in an African Society: A Study of the Arusha.* London: Routledge & Kegan Paul.
Guyer, Jane. 1989. "Comment." *Current Anthropology* 30, 428–9.
– 1994. Lineal Identities and Lateral Networks: The Logic of Polyandrous Motherhood. In *Nuptiality in Sub-Saharan Africa: Contemporary Anthropological and Demographic Perspectives*, ed. Caroline Bledsoe and Gilles Pison. Oxford: Clarendon Press.
Hagaman, Barbara L. 1977. Beer and Matriliny: The Power of Women in a West African Society. PhD dissertation, Northeastern University.

Hailey, Lord. 1951. *Native Administration in British African Territories*. 3 parts. London: HMSO.

Hall, R. de Z. 1938. The Study of Native Court Records as a Method of Ethnological Inquiry. *Africa* 11, 412–26.

Hart, Keith. 1971. Migration and Tribal Identity among the Frafras of Ghana. *Journal of Asian and African Studies* 6, 21–36.

Hawkins, Sean. 1996. Disguising Chiefs and God as History: Questions on the Acephalousness of LoDagaa Politics and Religion. *Africa* 66, 202–47.

– 1997. To Pray or Not to Pray: Politics, Medicine, and Conversion among the LoDagaa of Northern Ghana, 1929–39. *Canadian Journal of African Studies* 31, 50–85.

– 1998. The Interpretation of *Naangmin*: Missionary Ethnography, African Theology, and History among the LoDagaa. *Journal of Religion in Africa* 28, 32–61.

– Forthcoming. The Ghosts of Maine and McLennan: Defining Marriage From Victorian Britain to Postcolonial Africa.

Headrick, Daniel R. 1981. *The Tools of Empire: Technology of European Imperialism in the Nineteenth Century*. New York: Oxford University Press.

Hébert, Père Jean, et al. 1976. *Esquisse d'une Monographie Historique du Pays Dagara*. Mimeograph. Diébougou: Diocèse de Diébougou.

Heehs, Peter. 1994. Myth, History, and Theory. *History and Theory* 33, 1–19.

Henige, David. 1974. *The Chronology of Oral Tradition: Quest for a Chimera*. Oxford: Clarendon Press.

– 1980. "The Disease of Writing": Ganda and Nyoro Kinglists in a Newly Literate World. In *The African Past Speaks: Essays on Oral Tradition and History*, ed. Joseph Miller. Folkestone: Harvester Press.

Héritier, Françoise. 1975. Des Cauris et des hommes: production d'esclaves et accumulation de cauris chez les Samo (Haute-Volta). In *L'Esclavage en Afrique précoloniale*, ed. Claude Meillassoux. Paris: François Maspero.

Hien, V.M., and J. Hébert. 1968/69. Prénoms théophores en pays Dagara. *Anthropos* 63/64, 566–71.

Hill, Polly. 1970a. *The Occupation of Migrants in Ghana*. Anthropological Papers, 42. Ann Arbor: Museum of Anthropology, University of Michigan.

– 1970b. *Studies in Rural Capitalism in West Africa*. Cambridge: Cambridge University Press.

– 1986. *Development Economics on Trial: The Anthropological Case for the Prosecution*. Cambridge: Cambridge University Press.

Hinds, J.H. 1947. A Currency Problem in the Lawra District: Picturesque Money Customs of the Lobi and Dagarti people of the Gold Coast. *West African Review* December, 1428–30.

Hobsbawm, Eric. 1983. Introduction: Inventing Tradition. In *The Invention of Tradi-*

tion, ed. Eric Hobsbawm and Terence Ranger. Cambridge: Cambridge University Press.

Hofmeyr, Isabel. 1993. *"We Spend Our Years as a Tale Told": Oral Historical Narrative in a South African Kingdom.* Portsmouth, NH: Heinemann.

Holden, J.J. 1965. The Zabarima Conquest of North-West Ghana. *Transactions of the Historical Society of Ghana* 8, 60–86.

Holy, Ladislav, and Milan Stuchlik. 1983. *Actions, Norms and Representations: Foundations of Anthropological Inquiry.* Cambridge: Cambridge University Press.

Horton, Robin. 1971. African Conversion. *Africa* 41, 85–108.

– 1975. On the Rationality of Conversion. *Africa* 45, 219–35.

– 1985. Stateless Societies in the History of West Africa. In *History of West Africa*, ed. J.F.A. Ajayi and Michael Crowder. Vol. 1, 3rd ed. London: Longman.

– 1993. *Patterns of Thought in Africa and the West: Essays on Magic, Religion and Science*. Cambridge: Cambridge University Press.

Howes, David. 1991. Introduction: To Summon the Sense. In *The Variety of Sensory Experience: A Sourcebook in the Anthropology of the Senses*, ed. David Howes. Toronto: University of Toronto Press.

Humphreys, Sally. 1985. Law as Discourse. *History and Anthropology* 1, 241–64.

Hutchinson, Sharon E. 1996. *Nuer Dilemmas: Coping with Money, War, and the State*. Berkeley: University of California Press.

Iliffe, John. 1979. *A Modern History of Tanganyika*. Cambridge: Cambridge University Press.

Janzen, John. 1978. *The Quest for Therapy: Medical Pluralism in Lower Zaire*. Berkeley: University of California Press.

Jeater, Diana. 1993. *Marriage, Perversion, and Power: The Construction of Moral Discourse in Southern Rhodesia, 1894–1930.* Oxford: Clarendon Press.

Jewsiewicki, Bogumil. 1991. Painting in Zaire: From the Invention of the West to the Representation of the Social Self. In *Africa Explores: 20th Century African Art*, ed. Susan Vogel. New York: The Museum for African Art.

Jewsiewicki, Bogumil, and V.Y. Mudimbe. 1993. Africans' Memories and Contemporary African History. *History and Theory* 32, 1–11.

Johnson, Douglas. 1981. The Fighting Nuer: Primary Sources and the Origins of a Stereotype. *Africa* 51, 508–27.

– 1986. Judicial Regulation and Administrative Control: Customary Law and the Nuer, 1898–1954. *Journal of African History* 27, 59–78.

Johnson, Marion. 1970a. The Cowrie Currencies of West Africa: Part I. *Journal of African History* 11, 17–49.

– 1970b. The Cowrie Currencies of West Africa: Part II. *Journal of African History* 11, 331–53.

Kambou-Ferrand, Jeanne-Marie. 1993a. Guerre et résistance sous la période coloniale en pays lobi/birifor (Burkina Faso) au travers de photos d'époque. In *Images d'Afrique et Sciences sociales: Les pays lobi, birifor et dagara*, ed. Michèle Fiéloux, Jacques Lombard, and Jeanne-Marie Kambou-Ferrand. Paris: Editions Karthala et ORSTOM.

– 1993b. Être lobi, ça mérite. In *Images d'Afrique et Sciences sociales: Les pays lobi, birifor et dagara*, ed. Michèle Fiéloux, Jacques Lombard, and Jeanne-Marie Kambou-Ferrand. Paris: Editions Karthala et ORSTOM.

Kirby, Jon. 1994. Cultural Change and Religious Conversion in West Africa. In *Religion in Africa: Experience and Expression*, ed. Thomas Blakely, Walter van Beek, and Dennis Thomson. Portsmouth: Heinemann.

Kofi, T.A., and E. Hansen. 1983. Ghana: A History of an Endless Recession. In *Recession in Africa: Background Papers to the Seminar Africa – Which Way Out of the Recession?* ed. Jerker Carlsson. Uppsala: Scandinavian Institute of African Studies.

Kopytoff, Igor. 1987. The Internal African Frontier: The Making of African Political Culture. In *The African Frontier: The Reproduction of Traditional African Societies*, ed. Igor Kopytoff. Bloomington: Indiana University Press.

Korbieh, Francis G. 1990. Traditional Marriage among the Dagaaba and/or Sisala in Light of Ghanaian Law. In *Dagara and Sisala Traditional Marriages in the Light of Christianity*, ed. Edward Tengan. Wa: Catholic Press.

Koya, Stephen. 1991. Some questions on Christian marriage. *The Diocese, Wa* 97, 5.

Kpiebaya, Bishop Gregory E. 1976. L'Africanisation de l'Eglise: qu'est-ce a dire? *Petit Echo* 9, 493–8.

– 1979. Living the Christian Faith Today. In *That They May Have Light: An Account of the Activities of the Church in North-West Ghana 1929–1979*, ed. Father V. Gregoire. Wa: Catholic Press.

– 1984. Dagaaba Identiy, Courtship (4). *The Diocese, Wa* 32, 4–5.

– 1985. Dagaaba Identiy: Conclusion. *The Diocese, Wa* 42, 8.

– 1990. *Dagaaba Traditional Marriage and Family Life.* Wa: Catholic Press.

Kpoda, Novat Puryiile. 1977. *Traditions en traduction de l'Esprit: Vers une nouvelle lecture chrétienne de l'alliance matrimoniale chez les Dagara.* Mémoire, Institut Catholique de Paris.

Kuklick, Henrika. 1991. *The Savage Within: The Social History of British Anthropology, 1885–1945.* Cambridge: Cambridge University Press.

Kuper, Adam. 1970. The Kgalagari and the Jural Consequences of Marriage. *Man* 5, 466–82.

– 1988. *The Invention of Primitive Society: Transformations of an Illusion.* London: Routledge.

Kusiele, S.R.B. 1973. Système de la divination et conceptions religieuses chez les Dagara. *Savanes et Forêts* 10/11, 1–58.

Kuukure, Edward. 1985. *The Destiny of Man: Dagaare Beliefs in Dialogue with Christian Eschatology*. Frankfurt am Main: Peter Lang.

Labouret, Henri. 1920. Mariage et polyandrie parmi les Dagarti et les Oulé. *Revue d'Ethnologie* 4, 267–83.

– 1931. *Les Tribus du Rameau Lobi.* Paris: Institut d'ethnologie.

– 1958. *Nouvelles Notes sur les tribus du Rameau Lobi: Leurs Migrations, Leur Evolution, Leurs Parlers et Ceux de Leurs Voisins.* Dakar: Institut Français d'Afrique Noire.

Ladouceur, Paul. 1979. *Chiefs and Politicians: The Politics of Regionalism in Northern Ghana.* London: Longman.

Lance, James. 1990. What the Stranger Brings: The Social Dynamics of Fieldwork. *History in Africa* 17, 335–9.

Landau, Paul Stuart. 1995. *The Realm of the Word: Language, Gender, and Christianity in a Southern African Kingdom.* Portsmouth, NH: Heinemann.

Law, Robin. 1991. *The Slave Coast of West Africa, 1550–1750: The Impact of the Atlantic Slave Trade on an African Society*. Oxford: Clarendon Press.

Leach, Edmund. 1961. *Rethinking Anthropology*. London: Athlone Press.

Lees, Gene. 1990. *Inventing Champagne: The Worlds of Lerner and Loewe.* New York: St Martin's Press.

Lentz, Carola. 1993. Histories and Political Conflict: A Case Study of Chieftaincy in Nandom, Northwestern Ghana. *Paideuma* 39, 177–215.

– 1994a. A Dagara Rebellion against Dagomba Rule? Contested Stories of Origin in North-Western Ghana. *Journal of African History* 35, 457–92.

– 1994b. Home, Death, and Leadership: Discourses of an Educated Elite from North-Western Ghana. *Social Anthropology* 2, 149–69.

– 1994c. "They Must Be Dagaba First and Any Other Thing Second ...": The Colonial and Post-Colonial Creation of Ethnic Identities in North-Western Ghana. *African Studies* 53, 57–91.

– 1995. "Unity For Development": Youth Associations in North-Western Ghana. *Africa* 63, 395–429.

– 1997. Creating Ethnic Identities in Northwestern Ghana. In *The Politics of Ethnic Consciousness*, ed. Cora Govers and Hans Vermeulen. New York: St Martin's Press.

– 2000. Contested Identities: The History of Ethnicity in Northwestern Ghana. In *Ethnicity in Ghana: The Limits of Invention*, ed. Carola Lentz and Paul Nugent. New York: St Martins Press.

Lentz, Carola, and Veit Erlmann. 1989. A Working Class Formation? Economic Crisis and Strategies of Survival among Dagara Mine Workers in Ghana. *Cahiers d'Études africaines* 29, 69–111.

Lévi-Strauss, Claude. 1997 [1955]. *Tristes Tropiques.* New York: Modern Library.

Levtzion, Nehemia. 1968. *Muslims and Chiefs in West Africa: A Study of Islam in the Middle Volta Basin in the Pre-Colonial Period.* Oxford: Clarendon Press.

Luria, A.R. 1976. *Cognitive Development: Its Cultural and Social Foundations.* Cambridge: Harvard University Press.

MacGaffey, Wyatt. 1970. *Custom and Government in the Lower Congo.* Berkeley: University of California Press.

– 1981. African Ideology and Belief: A Survey. *African Studies Review* 2–3, 227–74.

– 1983. Lineage Structure, Marriage and Family amongst the Central Bantu. *Journal of African History* 24, 173–87.

Mafeje, A. 1976. The Problem of Anthropology in Historical Perspective: An Inquiry into the Growth of the Social Sciences. *Canadian Journal of African Studies* 2, 307–33.

Maine, Henry Sumner. 1861. *Ancient Law: Its Connection with the Early History of Society and Its Relation to Modern Ideas.* London: John Murray.

Mair, Lucy. 1969. *African Marriage and Social Change.* 2nd ed. London: Frank Cass.

Malinowski, Bronislaw. 1927. *Sex and Repression in Savage Society.* London: Routledge & Kegan Paul.

Mann, Kristin, and Roberts, Richard Roberts. 1991. Law in Colonial Africa. In *Law In Colonial Africa*, ed. Kristin Mann and Richard Roberts. Portsmouth, NH: Heinemann.

Manning, Patrick. 1988. *Francophone Sub-Saharan Africa 1880–1985.* Cambridge: Cambridge University Press.

Manoukian, M. 1951. *Tribes of the Northern Territories of the Gold Coast.* London: International African Institute.

Marcus, George, and Michael M.J. Fischer. 1986. *Anthropology as Cultural Critique: An Experimental Moment in the Human Sciences.* Chicago: University of Chicago Press.

Marks, Shula, and Richard Rathbone. 1983. The History of the Family in Africa: Introduction. *Journal of African History* 24, 145–61.

Marx, Karl. 1975 [1845]. Theses on Feuerbach. In *Early Writings*, trans. Rodney Livingstone and Gregor Benton. Harmondsworth: Penguin.

McCall, Daniel F. 1974. Who Owns the Child? Descent Systems and the Social Position of Women in Gur Myth and Society. *Journal of African Studies* 1, 252–84.

McCaskie, T.C. 1995. *State and Society in Pre-Colonial Asante.* Cambridge: Cambridge University Press.

McCoy, Remigius F. 1979. Foundation and First Years of the Jirapa Mission. In *That They May Have Light: An Account of the Activities of the Church in North-West Ghana, 1929–79*, ed. Father V. Gregoire. Wa: Catholic Press.

– 1988. *Great Things Happen: A Personal Memoir of the First Christian Missionary among the Dagaabas and Sissalas of Northwest Ghana*. Montreal: Society of the Missionaries of Africa.

Meillassoux, Claude. 1972. From Reproduction to Production: A Marxist Approach to Economic Anthropology. *Economy and Society* 1, 93–105.

Mendonsa, Eugene. 1982. *The Politics of Divination: A Processual View of Illness and Deviance among the Sisala of Northern Ghana*. Berkeley: University of California Press.

Mensah, A.K. 1981. A Descriptive List of the Records of the Chief Commissioner in the Tamale Regional Archives. Diploma dissertation, University of Ghana, Legon.

Mensah-Brown, A.K. 1969. Chiefs and the Law in Ghana. *Journal of African Law* 13, 57–63.

Mignolo, Walter D. 1992a. When Speaking Was Not Good Enough: Illiterates, Barbarians, Savages, and Cannibals. In *Amerindian Images and the Legacy of Columbus*, ed. René Jara and Nicholas Spadaccini. Minneapolis: University of Minnesota Press.

– 1992b. On the Colonization of Amerindian Languages and Memories: Renaissance Theories of Writing and the Discontinuity of the Classical Tradition. *Comparative Studies in Society and History* 34, 301–30.

– 1994a. Signs and Their Transmission: The Question of the Book in the New World. In *Writing without Words: Alternative Literacies in Mesoamerica and the Andes*, ed. Elizabeth Hill Boone and Walter D. Mignolo. Durham: Duke University Press.

– 1994b. Afterword: Writing and Recorded Knowledge in Colonial and Postcolonial Situations. In *Writing without Words: Alternative Literacies in Mesoamerica and the Andes*, ed. Elizabeth Hill Boone and Walter D. Mignolo. Durham: Duke University Press.

– 1995. *The Darker Side of the Renaissance: Literacy, Territoriality, and Colonization*. Ann Arbor: University of Michigan Press.

Mitchell, Timothy. 1988. *Colonising Egypt*. Cambridge: Cambridge University Press.

Moore, Sally Folk. 1977. Individual Interests and Organizational Structures: Dispute Settlements as "Events of Articulation." In *Social Anthropology and Law*, ed. Ian Hamnett. London: Academic Press.

– 1978. *Law as Process: An Anthropological Approach*. London: Routledge & Kegan Paul.

– 1986. *Social Facts and Fabrications: "Customary" Law on Kilimanjaro, 1880–1980*. Cambridge: Cambridge University Press.

Mudimbe, V.Y. 1988. *The Invention of Africa: Gnosis, Philosophy, and the Order of Knowledge*. Bloomington: Indiana University Press.

Murdock, George. 1959. *Africa: Its Peoples and Their Culture History*. New York: McGraw-Hill.

Naameh, Peter. 1986. The Christianization of the Dagara within the Horizon of the West European Experience. PhD dissertation, Westfäliache Wilhelms-Universität, Münster.

Nederveen Pieterse, Jan. 1992. *White on Black: Images of Africa and Blacks in Western Popular Culture.* New Haven: Yale University Press.

Needham, Rodney. 1971. Remarks on the Analysis of Kinship and Marriage. In *Rethinking Kinship and Marriage*, ed. Rodney Needham. London: Tavistock Publications.

– 1972. *Belief, Language and Experience.* Oxford: Basil Blackwell.

Newman, Katherine S. 1983. *Law and Economic Organization: A Comparative Study of Preindustrial Societies.* Cambridge: Cambridge University Press.

Ngugi wa Thiong'o. 1981. *Decolonising the Mind: The Politics of Language in African Literature.* Nairobi: Heinemann Kenya.

Niezen, R.W. 1991. Hot Literacy in Cold Societies: A Comparative Study of the Sacred Value of Writing. *Comparative Studies in Society and History* 23, 225–54.

Northcott, Lieut-Col. H.P. 1899. *Report on the Northern Territories of the Gold Coast.* London: HMSO.

Nsiah-Gyabaah, Kwasi. 1994. *Environmental Degradation and Desertification in Ghana: A Study of the Upper West Region.* Aldershot: Avebury Studies in Green Research.

Obeyesekere, Gananath. 1992. *The Apotheosis of Captain Cook: European Mythmaking in the Pacific.* Princeton: Princeton University Press.

Olson, David R. 1994. *The World on Paper: The Conceptual and Cognitive Implications of Writing and Reading.* Cambridge: Cambridge University Press.

Ong, Walter J. 1982. *Orality and Literacy: The Technologizing of the Word.* London: Methuen.

Opoku, Kwame. 1976. *The Law of Marriage in Ghana: A Study in Legal Pluralism.* Frankfurt am Main: Alfred Metzner.

Oyewùmí, Oyèrónké. 1977. *The Invention of Women: Making an African Sense of Western Gender Discourses.* Minneapolis: University of Minnesota Press.

Pagden, Anthony. 1993. *European Encounters with the New World.* New Haven: Yale University Press.

Paternot, M. 1953. *Lumière sur la Volta, chez les Dagara.* Paris: Association des Missionaires d'Afrique.

Patterson, David K. 1981. *Health in Colonial Ghana: Disease, Medicine, and Socio-Economic Change, 1900–1955.* Waltham, MA: Crossroads Press.

– 1983. The Influenza Epidemic of 1918–19 in the Gold Coast. *Journal of African History* 24, 485–502.

– 1984. Cerebrospinal Meningitis in West Africa. In *Cerebrospinal Meningitis in West Africa and Sudan in the Twentieth Century*, ed. David Patterson and Gerald W. Hartwig. Los Angeles: Crossroads Press.

Peel, J.D.Y. 1994. Historicity and Pluralism in Some Recent Studies of Yoruba Religion. *Africa* 64, 150–66.

Pellow, Deborah, and Naomi Chazan. 1986. *Ghana: Coping with Uncertainty*. Boulder, CO: Westview Press.

Père, Madeleine. 1988. *Les Lobis: Traditions et Changement*. 2 vols. Paris: Siloë.

– La société lobi actuelle et ses problèmes. In *Images d'Afrique et Sciences sociales: Les pays lobi, birifor et dagara*, ed. Michèle Fiéloux, Jacques Lombard, and Jeanne-Marie Kambou-Ferrand. Paris: Editions Karthala et ORSTOM.

Person, Yves. 1975. *Samori: Une Révolution Dyula*. 3 vols. Dakar: Institut Français d'Afrique Noire.

Phillips, Arthur. 1953. An Introductory Essay. 1953. In *Survey of African Marriage and Family Life*, ed. Arthur Phillips. London: International African Institute.

Pilon, Marc. 1994. Types of Marriage and Marital Stability: The Case of the Moba-Gurma of North Togo. In *Nuptiality in Sub-Saharan Africa: Contemporary Anthropological and Demographic Perspectives*, ed. Caroline Bledsoe and Gilles Pison. Oxford: Clarendon Press.

Piot, Charles. 1996. Of Slaves and the Gift: Kabre Sale of Kin During the Era of the Slave Trade. *Journal of African History* 37, 31–49.

– 1999. *Remotely Global: Village Modernity in West Africa*. Chicago: University of Chicago Press.

Plange, Nii-K. 1979. "Opportunity Cost" and Labour Migration: A Misinterpretation of Proletarianisation in Northern Ghana. *Journal of Modern African Studies* 17, 655–76.

Poda, Evariste. 1991. Image du mort, effige de l'ancestre. *Systèmes de Pensée en Afrique Noire* 11, 91–101.

– 1994. Mariage et "prix de la fiancée" chez les Dagara. *Journal des africanistes* 64, 65–75.

Pole, Leonard M. 1974. *Iron Smelting in Northern Ghana*. National Museum of Ghana Occasional Papers 6. Accra: Ghana Museums and Monument Board.

Pouillon, J. 1982. Remarks on the Verb to Believe. In *Between Belief and Transgression: Structuralist Essays in Religion, History and Myth*, ed. Michel Izard and Pierre Smith. Chicago: University of Chicago Press.

Pratt, Mary Louise. 1992. *Imperial Eyes: Travel Writing and Transculturation*. London: Routledge.

Princess Marie Louise. 1926. *Letter from the Gold Coast*. London: Methuen.

Prins, Gwyn. 1980. *The Hidden Hippopotamus. Reappraisal in African History: The Early Colonial Experience in Western Zambia*. Cambridge: Cambridge University Press.

Probst, Peter. 1989. The Letter and the Spirit: Literacy and Religious Authority in the History of the Aladura Movement in Western Nigeria. *Africa* 59, 478–95.

Prouzet, M. 1976. Le statut juridique des chefferies traditionelle au Ghana. *Revue Française d'Etat Politique Africaine* 11, 103–14.

Prussin, L. 1969. *Architecture in Northern Ghana: A Study of Forms and Functions*. Berkeley: University of California Press.

Radcliffe-Brown, A.R. 1950. Introduction. In *African Systems of Kinship and Marriage*, ed. A.R. Radcliffe-Brown and Daryll Forde. London: Oxford University Press.

Rainbow, Paul. 1986. Representations Are Social Facts: Modernity and Post-Modernity in Anthropology. In *Writing Culture: The Poetics and Politics of Ethnography*, ed. James Clifford and George E. Marcus. Berkeley: University of California Press.

Ranger, Terence. 1981. Godly Medicine: The Ambiguities of Medical Mission in Southeast Tanzania, 1900–1954. *Social Science and Medicine* 15b, 261–77.

– 1983. The Invention of Tradition in Colonial Africa. In *The Invention of Tradition*, ed. Eric Hobsbawm and Terence Ranger. Cambridge: Cambridge University Press.

– 1993a. The Invention of Tradition Revisited: The Case of Colonial Africa. In *Legitimacy and the State in Twentieth Century Africa*, ed. Terence Ranger and Olufemi Vaughan. Basingstoke: Macmillan.

– 1993b. The Local and the Global in Southern African Religious History. In *Conversion to Christianity: Historical and Anthropological Perspectives on a Great Transformation*, ed. Robert W. Hefner. Berkeley: University of California Press.

Rattray, Capt. R.S. 1932. *The Tribes of the Ashanti Hinterland.* 2 vols. Oxford: Clarendon Press.

Ray, Donald I. 1987. Evaluation of Traditional Rulers as a Policy Instrument for Managing the Food Crisis: The Case of Northern Ghana. *Genève-Afrique* 25, 7–24.

– 1996. Divided Sovereignty in Ghana. *Journal of Legal Pluralism* 37–8, 181–201.

Richard, Donat. 1946. Affaire serieuse: Coutumes matrimoniales chez les Lobi. *Les Missions d'Afrique, Québec* 42, 177–181.

Roberts, Penelope A. 1985. The Court Records of Sefwi Wiawso, Western Region, Ghana. *History in Africa* 12, 379–83.

– 1987. The State and the Regulation of Marriage: Sefwi Wiawso (Ghana), 1900–40. In *Women, Work, and Ideology in the Third World*, ed. Haleh Afshar. London: Tavistock Publications.

Roberts, Richard. 1990. Text and Testimony in the *Tribunal de Première Instance*, Dakar, during the Early Twentieth Century. *Journal of African History* 31, 447–63.

Rorty, Richard, 1991. *Objectivism, Relativism, and Truth.* Cambridge: Cambridge University Press.

Rouville, Cécile de. 1987. *Organisation sociale des Lobi: Une société bilinéaire du Burkina Faso et de Côte d'Ivoire*. Paris: Editions l'Harmattan.

Ruelle, Dr E. 1904. Notes anthropologiques, ethnographiques et sociologiques: sur quelques populations Noire du 2ième Territoire Militaire de l'Afrique Occidentale Française. *L'Anthropologie* 15, 657–703.

Ryan, Simon. 1994. Inscribing the Emptiness: Cartography, Exploration and the Construction of Australia. In *De-Scribing Empire: Post-Colonialism and Textuality*, ed. Chris Tiffin and Alan Lawson. London: Routledge.

Sabelli, Fabrizio. 1981. Poétique et politique de l'espace dagari (Ghana). In *Symboles et Sociétés en Afrique: Contribution à l'Anthropologie Cognitive de l'Afrique Noire*, ed. Micheline Centilivres-Demont et al. Berne: Société suisse d'ethnologie Commission de rédaction.

Sahlins, Marshall. 1995. *How "Natives" Think about Captain Cook for Example*. Chicago: Chicago University of Chicago Press.

Saighoe, Francis A. Kobina. 1988. The Music Behavior of the Dagaba Immigrants in Tarkwa, Ghana: A Study of Situational Change. PhD dissertation, Columbia University.

Savonnet, George. 1965. Interrogatoire d'une défunte chez les Lobi de Pora. *Bulletin de l'Institut Français d'Afrique Noire.* 108, 119–24.

– 1993. Voyage en zig-zag dans le temps et dans l'espace en pays lobi (1954–1981). In *Images d'Afrique et Sciences sociales: Les pays lobi, birifor et dagara*, ed. Michèle Fiéloux, Jacques Lombard, and Jeanne-Marie Kambou-Ferrand. Paris: Editions Karthala et ORSTOM.

Schoenbrun, David L. 1993. A Past Whose Time Has Come: Historical Context and History in Eastern Africa's Great Lakes. *History and Theory* 32, 32–56.

Schneider, David M. 1953. A Note on Bridewealth and the Stability of Marriage. *Man* 74/5, 55–7.

– 1984. *A Critique of the Study of Kinship*. Ann Arbor: University of Michigan Press.

Schott, Rüdiger. 1980. Justice versus the Law: Traditional and Modern Jurisdiction among the Bulsa of Northern Ghana. *Law and State* 21, 121–33.

– 1985. A Case of Living Law: Traditional and Modern Jurisdiction among the Bulsa of Northern Ghana. *Quaderni Fiorentini* 14, 149–72.

Shorter, Aylward. 1988. *Toward a Theology of Inculturation.* Maryknoll: Orbis Books.

Singer, Alice. 1973. Marriage Payments and the Exchange of People. *Man* 8, 80–92.

Skalnik, Peter. 1986. Nanumba Chieftaincy Facing the Ghanaian State and Konkomba "Tribesmen": An Interpretation of the Nanumba-Konkomba War of 1981. In *State and Local Community in Africa*, ed. W. van Binsbergen et al. Brussels: CEDAF/ASCOC.

– 1987. On the Inadequacy of the Concept of the "Traditional State": Illustrated with Ethnographic Material on Nanum, Ghana. *Journal of Legal Pluralism and Unofficial Law* 25/26, 301–25.

– 1989. Outwitting the State: An Introduction. In *Outwitting the State*, ed. Peter Skalník. New Brunswick, NJ: Transaction Publishers.

– 1996. Authority versus Power: Democracy in Africa Must Include Original African Institutions. *Journal of Legal Pluralism* 37–8, 109–21.

Smith, Fred. 1982. Frafra Dress. *African Arts* 15, 37–42.

Smith, James H. 1998. Njama's Supper: The Consumption and Uses of Literary Potency by Mau Mau Insurgents in Colonial Kenya. *Comparative Studies in Society and History*, 40, 524–48.

Somda, Claude Nurukyor. 1989. Les origines des Dagara. *Papers in Dagara Studies – Cahiers d'études Dagara – Dagara Yele Sebe* 1, 26–45.

– 1993. Les cauris du pays lobi. In *Images d'Afrique et Sciences sociales: Les pays lobi, birifor et dagara*, ed. Michèle Fiéloux, Jacques Lombard, and Jeanne-Marie Kambou-Ferrand. Paris: Editions Karthala et ORSTOM.

Somda, M. J.-B. 1977. *Sagasse Dagara I: anthroponymie Dagara*. Koumi: Grand Séminaire.

Somé, A.-P. 1992. *Significant et société: le cas du dagara du Burkina Faso*. Paris: l'Harmattan.

Somé, Bozi. 1968. La parenté chez les Dagari. *Notes et documents voltaiques* 2, 11–20.

– 1969. Organisation politico-sociale traditionelle des Dagara. *Notes et documents voltaïques* 2, 16–41.

Somé, Magloire. 1998. La christianisation des Dagara du Burkina: flux et reflux des conversions (1932–1952). *Revue française d'histoire d'outre-mer* 85, 33–57.

Somé, Roger. 1989. Les bètibè, art et pouvoir chez les Lobi et les Dagara du sud-ouest du Burkina Faso. In *Anthropologie de l'art: formes et signification*, ed. Louis Perrois and Claude-François Baudez. Paris: ORSTOM.

– 1991. La conception Dagara de dieu en question. *Papers in Dagara Studies – Cahiers d'études Dagara – Dagara Yele Sebe* 1, 30–43.

Southall, Aidan W. 1970. The Illusion of Tribe. In *The Passing of Tribal Man in Africa*, ed. Peter C. Gutkind. Leiden: Brill.

Staniland, Martin. 1975. *The Lions of Dagbon: Political Change in Northern Ghana*. Cambridge: Cambridge University Press.

Steiner, Christopher. 1994. *African Art in Transit*. Cambridge: Cambridge University Press.

Stock, Brian. 1990. *Listening for the Text: On the Uses of the Past*. Baltimore: Johns Hopkins University Press.

Stocking, George W. 1987. *Victorian Anthropology*. New York: Free Press.

Street, Brian V. 1984. *Literacy in Theory and Practice*. Cambridge: Cambridge University Press.

– 1993. Introduction: The New Literacy Studies. In *Cross-Cultural Approaches to Literacy*, ed. Brian Street. Cambridge: Cambridge University Press.

Street, Brian, and Niko Besnier. 1994. Aspects of Literacy. In *Companion Encyclopedia of Anthropology*, ed. Tim Ingold. London: Routledge.

Tambiah, Stanley J. 1973. Dowry, Bridewealth and the Property Rights of Women in South Asia. In *Bridewealth and Dowry*, ed. Jack Goody and Stanley J. Tambiah. Cambridge: Cambridge University Press.

– 1989. Bridewealth and Dowry Revisited: The Position of Women in Sub-Saharan Africa and North India. *Current Anthropology* 30, 413–27.

Tauxier, Louis. 1912. *Le noir du Soudan: pays Mossi et Gourounsi*. Paris: Emile Larose.

Tengan, Alexis. 2000. *Hoe-Farming and Social Relations among the Dagara of Northwestern Ghana and Southwestern Burkina Faso*. Frankfurt am Main: Peter Lang.

Tengan, Edward. 1990a. Marriage from an Anthropological Perspective: An Explanation of Certain Basic Terms Used in Discussing Marriage. In *Dagara and Sisala Traditional Marriages in the Light of Christianity*, ed. Edward Tengan. Wa: Catholic Press.

– 1990b. Concluding Pastoral Reflections. In *Dagara and Sisala Traditional Marriages in the Light of Christianity*, ed. Edward Tengan. Wa: Catholic Press.

– 1990c. Reports on Group Discussions. In *Dagara and Sisala Traditional Marriages in the Light of Christianity*, ed. Edward Tengan. Wa: Catholic Press.

– 1990d. The Institution of Marriage among the Dagaaba. In *Dagara and Sisala Traditional Marriages in the Light of Christianity*, ed. Edward Tengan. Wa: Catholic Press.

Thomas, Roger. 1973. Forced Labour in British West Africa: The Case of the Northern Territories of the Gold Coast, 1906–1927. *Journal of African History* 14, 79–103.

– 1975a. Education in Northern Ghana, 1906–1940. *International Journal of African Historical Studies* 12, 427–67.

– 1975b. Military Recruitment in the Gold Coast during the First World War. *Cahiers d'Etudes Africaines* 57, 57–83.

– 1983. The 1916 Bongo "Riots" and Their Background: Aspects of Colonial Response in Eastern Upper Ghana. *Journal of African History* 24, 57–75.

Thornton, Robert. 1983. Narrative Ethnography in Africa, 1850–1920: The Creation and Capture of an Appropriate Domain for Anthropology. *Man* 18, 502–20.

Tiffin, Chris, and Alan Lawson. 1994. The Textuality of Empire. In *De-Scribing Empire: Post-Colonialism and Textuality*, ed. Chris Tiffin and Alan Lawson. London: Routledge.

Tuureh, A.A. 1977. Re: Appeal Record of Proceedings, Zambo Skin Affairs. Mimeograph. Lawra Traditional Council.

Tuurey, Gabriel. 1982. *An Introduction to the Mole speaking Community*. Wa: Ghana Education Service.

Ubah, C.N. 1982. The Supreme Being, Divinities and Ancestors in Igbo Traditional Religion: Evidence from Otanchara and Otanzu. *Africa* 52 (2), 90–105.

Ukpong, Justin S. 1983. The Problem of God and Sacrifice in African Traditional Religion. *Journal of Religion in Africa* 14, 187–203.

Underwood, David. 1985. The Taming of the Scold: The Enforcement of Partriarchal Authority in early Modern England. In *Order and Disorder in Early Modern England*, ed. Anthony Fletcher and John Stevenson. Cambridge: Cambridge University Press.

Vail, Leroy, ed. 1989. *The Creation of Tribalism in Southern Africa*. London: James Currey.

Van Hoven, Ed. 1990. Representing Social Hierarchy – Administrators/Ethnographers in the French Sudan: Delafosse, Monteil, and Labouret. *Cahiers d'Etudes africaines* 118, 179–98.

Van Rouveroy van Nieuwaal, E. Adriaan B. 1977. To Claim or Not to Claim: Changing Views about the Restitution of Marriage Prestations among the Anufom in Northern Togo. In *Law and the Family in Africa*, ed. Simon Roberts. The Hague: Mouton.

Vansina, Jan. 1965. A Traditional Legal System: The Kuba. In *African Law: Adaptation and Development*, ed. Hilda Kuper and Leo Kuper. Berkeley: University of California Press.

– 1978. *The Children of Woot*. Madison: University of Wisconsin Press.

– 1986. Knowledge and Perceptions of the African Past. In *African Historiographies: What History for Which Africa?* ed. Bogumil Jewsiewicki and David Newbury. Beverly Hills: Sage Publications.

– 1990. *Paths in the Rainforest: Toward a History of Political Tradition in Equatorial Africa*. Madison: University of Wisconsin Press.

– 1994. *Living With Africa*. Madison: University of Wisconsin Press.

Vaughan, Megan. 1991. *Curing Their Ills: Colonial Power and African Illness*. Stanford: Stanford University Press.

Vellenga, Deborah D. 1983. Who Is a Wife? Legal Expressions of Heterosexual Conflicts in Ghana. In *Female and Male in West Africa*, ed. Christine Oppong. London: George Allen and Unwin.

Vogel, Susan. 1991. Introduction: Disgesting the West. In *Africa Explores: 20th Century African Art*, ed. Susan Vogel. New York: Museum for African Art.

Von Laue, Theodore. 1975. Transubstantiation in the Study of African Reality. *African Affairs* 74, 401–19.

– 1976. Anthropology and Power: R.S. Rattray among the Ashanti. *African Affairs* 75, 33–54.

Waddy, B.B. 1980. A District Medical Officer in North-West Ghana. In *Health in*

Tropical Africa during the Colonial Period, ed. E.E. Sabben-Clarke et al. Oxford: Clarendon Press.

Wanitzek, Ulrike. 1998. Bulsa Marriage Law and Practice: Women as Social Actors in a Patriarchal Society. In *Sovereignty, Legitimacy, and Power in West African Societies: Perspectives from Legal Anthropology*, ed. E. Adriaan B. van Rouveroy van Nieuwaal and Werner Zips. Hamburg: LIT.

Westerlund, David. 1985. *African Religion in African Scholarship: A Preliminary Study of the Religious and Political Background*. Stockholm: Almqvist & Wiksell International.

Westermann, Diedrich, and M.A. Bryan. 1952. *Languages of West Africa*. London: Oxford University Press.

Whitehead, Ann. 1984. Women and Men, Kinship and Property: Some General Issues. In *Women and Property – Women as Property*, ed. René Hirschon. New York: St Martin's Press.

Wilks, Ivor. 1985. The Mossi and Akan States, 1400 to 1800. In *History of West Africa*, ed. J.F.A. Ajayi and Micheal Crowder. Vol. 1. 3rd ed. London: Longman.

– 1989. *Wa and the Wala: Islam and Polity in Northwestern Ghana*. Cambridge: Cambridge University Press.

Wilks, Ivor, Nehemia Levtzion, and Bruce M. Haight. 1986. *Chronicles From Gonja: A Tradition of West African Muslim Historiography*. Cambridge: Cambridge University Press.

Wilson, Godfrey, and Monica Wilson. 1945. *The Analysis of Social Change in Africa: Based on Observations in Central Africa*. Cambridge: Cambridge University Press.

Wright, Donald. 1991. Requiem of the Use of Oral Tradition to Reconstruct the Precolonial History of the Lower Gambia. *History in Africa* 18, 399–408.

Yangyuoru, Yvon. 1994. Dagara Traditional Cultic Sacrifice as a Thematization of Ultimate Reality and Meaning. *Ultimate Reality and Meaning* 7, 209–19.

Yelpaala, Kojo. 1983. Circular Arguments and Self-Fulfilling Definitions: "Statelessness" and the Dagaaba. *History in Africa* 10, 349–85.

– 1992. Western Anthropological Concepts in Stateless Societies: A Retrospective and Introspective Look at the Dagaaba. *Dialectical Anthropology* 17, 431–71.

Index

ANTHROPOLOGICAL HORIZONS
Editor: Michael Lambek, University of Toronto

Published to date:

1 **The Varieties of Sensory Experience: A Sourcebook in the Anthropology of the Senses**
Edited by David Howes
2 **Arctic Homeland: Kinship, Community, and Development in Northwest Greenland**
Mark Nuttall
3 **Knowledge and Practice in Mayotte: Local Discourses of Islam, Sorcery, and Spirit Possession**
Michael Lambek
4 **Deathly Waters and Hungry Mountains: Agrarian Ritual and Class Formation in an Andean Town**
Peter Gose
5 **Paradise: Class, Commuters, and Ethnicity in Rural Ontario**
Stanley R. Barrett
6 **The Cultural World in *Beowulf***
John M. Hill
7 **Making It Their Own: Severn Ojibwe Communicative Practices**
Lisa Philips Valentine
8 **Merchants and Shopkeepers: A Historical Anthropology of an Irish Market Town, 1200–1991**
Philip Gulliver and Marilyn Silverman
9 **Tournaments of Value: Sociability and Hierarchy in a Yemeni Town**
Ann Meneley
10 ***Mal'uocchiu*: Ambiguity, Evil Eye, and the Language of Distress**
Sam Migliore
11 **Between History and Histories: The Production of Silences and Commemorations**
Edited by Gerald Sider and Gavin Smith
12 ***Eh, Paesan!* Being Italian in Toronto**
Nicholas DeMaria Harney
13 **Theorizing the Americanist Tradition**
Edited by Lisa Philips Valentine and Regna Darnell
14 **Colonial 'Reformation' in the Highlands of Central Sulawesi, Indonesia, 1892–1995**
Albert Schrauwers
15 **The Rock Where We Stand: An Ethnography of Women's Activism in Newfoundland**
Glynis George
16 **'Being Alive Well': Health and the Politics of Cree Well-Being**
Naomi Adelson
17 **Irish Travellers: Racism and the Politics of Culture**
Jane Helleiner
18 **Writing and Colonialism in Northern Ghana: The Encounter between the LoDagaa and "the World on Paper"**
Sean Hawkins
19 **An Irish Working Class: Explorations in Political Economy and Hegemony, 1800–1950**
Marilyn Silverman
20 **The Double Twist: From Ethnography to Morphodynamics**
Edited by Pierre Maranda

www.ingramcontent.com/pod-product-compliance
Lightning Source LLC
LaVergne TN
LVHW090757070826
844660LV00022B/1014
9781442657687